W9-BCD-815

Reusable Software

The Base Object-Oriented Component Libraries

D. COLEMAN, P. ARNOLD, S. BODOFF,
C. DOLLIN, H. GILCHRIST, F. HAYES
AND P. JEREMAES
Object-Oriented Development: The Fusion Method

D. HENDERSON-SELLERS
A Book of Object-Oriented Knowledge

K. LANO AND H. HAUGHTON
Object-Oriented Specification Case Studies

J. LINDSKOV KNUDSEN, M. LÖFGREN,
O. LEHRMANN MADSEN AND B. MAGNUSSON
Object-Oriented Environments: The Mjølner Approach

M. LORENZ
Object-Oriented Software Development: A Practical Guide

D. MANDRIOLI AND B. MEYER (eds)
Advances in Object-Oriented Software Engineering

B. MEYER
Eiffel: The Language

B. MEYER AND J.-M. NERSON
Object-Oriented Applications

P. J. ROBINSON
Hierarchical Object-Oriented Design

R. SWITZER
Eiffel: An Introduction

Reusable software

The Base object-oriented component libraries

Bertrand Meyer

ISE, Santa Barbara
SOL, Paris

First published 1994 by
Prentice Hall International (UK) Limited
Campus 400, Maylands Avenue
Hemel Hempstead
Hertfordshire, HP2 7EZ
A division of
Simon & Schuster International Group

Printed and bound in Great Britain at
the University Press, Cambridge

Library of Congress Cataloging-in-Publication Data

Available from the publisher

British Library Cataloguing in Publication Data

A catalogue record for this book is available from
the British Library

ISBN 0-13-245499-8

1 2 3 4 5   98 97 96 95 94

Short table

The full table of contents starts on page xiii.

Preface

A Linnaean reconstruction of software fundamentals

Reuse is a required condition of any progress in software. Not by any means a sufficient condition, but one without which the others – better methods, new development tools, faster hardware, more formal approaches, improved management techniques – cannot fulfil their promises. As long as software developers across countries, industries, companies and projects continue to spend their time producing endless individual variants of the same basic program patterns, the state of the software world will not change much, no matter how many millions of dollars government agencies and private consortia pour into grandiose Strategic Initiatives on Information Technology.

Although it has become customary in the software literature to pay some homage to reuse, few useful practical references are available to the software developer, the manager or the student who wants good reusable software and good reusability advice. This book is an attempt to fill this crying need. What it offers to its readers is both *components* and *expertise*. The components are reusable software modules which cover some of the fundamental patterns of software development across application areas; the expertise should help you not just to use these modules properly but also to develop your own libraries and make sure they are successful.

Both the components and the expertise derive from a long-term effort started about ten years ago with two purposes: to understand the fundamental structures and paradigms of software construction; and to provide a set of robust reusable libraries that would take care, once and for all, of the most important among them.

The goal of the project is ambitious. It may be characterized as a *Linnaean reconstruction* of the fundamental software structures. Inspired by the example of Linnaeus, Buffon and their colleagues, the 18-th century naturalists who carried out a thorough intellectual reconstruction of the world of plants and animals according to simple and general structuring principles and thus made botany and zoology possible, we have studied the world of software artefacts – from arrays to queues, from binary search trees to sorted lists – to devise a coherent overall structure, in which every important variant will have a precise place deduced from the application of a small number of classification criteria.

This effort is far from complete; many variants have not yet been assigned a slot, and even the overall organization may have to be revised as we continue to improve our understanding of software structures. But I think this work is now advanced enough to warrant publication, especially since the reconstruction is not just theoretical: in the leaf nodes of the classification graph you will find directly usable components – the classes of the Base libraries – which you can use immediately to build powerful software systems of all kinds.

The Linnaean ambition of the Base project may appear overreaching when compared to the relatively small size of the team that has been conducting it so far. Some readers may think that such an effort should be undertaken on a much grander scale, as a sort of all-encompassing, publicly funded "computer genome" project. Yet the manner in which the work is being conducted also has, besides its obvious drawbacks (in particular the necessity to proceed at a somewhat slow speed), at least two important advantages. The first is that a small group can, better than a big one, ensure design unity and consistency, two qualities that are just as important for a library as they are for a programming language. The second is that an effort such as the one reported here, not having relied on government financing, has had to stand the test of the marketplace. To know if your design is *really* that good, there is nothing like having to sell it to people developing actual systems. The Base libraries have been in use for many years in many different organizations, and served to build many commercial systems. They have been warmly received by their users, who in turn contributed numerous suggestions for improvements and extensions.

Techniques and principles

Both the components and the expertise presented in this book would not have existed without the basis that object-oriented technology provides. Classes, preconditions, postconditions, class invariants, short and flat forms, inheritance in its single, multiple and repeated forms, information hiding, disciplined exception handling – these are some of the techniques that can at last turn reusability, a dream first described by Doug McIlroy in an eloquent article more than twenty-five years ago, into reality.

Chapter 2 reviews these fundamental O-O techniques, which have been used to build the libraries described here and can be applied to others. It is not a complete presentation of the object-oriented method or to the underlying language; instead, it briefly explains how object-orientation makes it possible to build quality components.

Chapter 3 is entitled "Principles of library design" and discusses in detail the methodological rules which have proved to be successful in the construction of the Base libraries. Building reusable software is an exacting task; good reusable modules must first be good (*very* good) modules; and in addition they must be reusable. To compound the difficulty, a collection of good and individually reusable modules does not necessarily make a good library: the library must have a coherent design, in which every module fits well. Another way to express this characteristic of successful reusable software is to note that the whole must be greater than the sum of its parts.

More generally, the task of building reusable libraries makes all software quality factors important, even some which for software of a less demanding nature are often considered marginal; for example, the choice of *names* for elements such as features and classes, which in ordinary software development is not a matter of life or death, becomes a major issue for a library that grows to hundreds or thousands of elements. This is one of the issues that, among many others, chapter 3 explores in depth.

Classes and features

Parts B (chapters 4 to 13) and C (chapters 14 to 23) present the classes of the Base libraries and their features, providing a large number of directly reusable software components in domains that are of interest to most software developers.

The chapters of part B introduce the concepts behind the classes; those of part C, which constitute the reference part of this book, include the precise specifications of all the classes and features discussed. These specifications use the software documentation technique known as flat-short interfaces, discussed in detail in chapters 2 and 3. Flat-short documentation is both abstract, as it hides implementation properties, and precise, as it relies on clear comments and formal assertions.

Also important to the understanding and use of the libraries is the unusually long Index, with close to 4000 entries that include every class and feature presented in the book, pointing directly to the corresponding flat-short interfaces.

Doubts and certainties

If any obvious trait characterizes the literature on software methodology it is its assurance. Books on analysis and design are full of peremptory statements: Prototype! Avoid multiple inheritance! Underline the nouns! Do not use inheritance for implementation! No wonder software developers sometimes feel like soldiers being ordered into battle – and may wonder whether this impression is a harbinger of their eventual fate.

Were it always rooted on sound scientific ground, this aplomb would be good. But much of the advice that you will find in the methodological literature – in particular in its object-oriented subset – is based on opinions, on experience from older techniques whose lessons may not be applicable any more, or on implicit and possibly invalid assumptions. Some of it is moot or just wrong. For example the four precepts just cited, all of which are frequently found in books on O-O topics, are at best highly debatable.

In its methodological part, this book has its share of "Do this!" advice, based on the experience accumulated in developing thousands of classes with tens of thousands of features. Care has been taken to justify such rules by rational arguments, rather than forcing them on the reader as self-evident eternal truths.

In other cases, however, you will encounter that rarest and most dangerous of attitudes: doubt. On such topics as what degree of repeated inheritance is desirable, or just how flat the flat-short form of a class should be, the solutions presented in this book represent the best decisions that our group was able to make, but have some drawbacks as well, which the discussion does not hide. You will read about the cons as well as about the pros and – who knows? – you might be able to find a better solution.

The candid admission of uncertainty about certain matters will, I hope, give more credence to the firm precepts given in other areas where no room was found for any hesitation.

Language independence

The components described in this book have been written in Eiffel. The C package generation facilities of ISE Eiffel 3 make them usable by C programs or, more generally, by programs written in any language that supports an interface to C routines. But of course their most obvious use is from other Eiffel software,

Since this book presents not just the components but the associated expertise some readers may ask whether that expertise may be transposed to other languages, in particular other object-oriented languages and environments. The answer is: partly yes, partly no.

The "yes" comes from the obvious property that the principles described in chapter 3 are methodological principles, not tied to any particular syntax. So readers interested in building other object-oriented libraries will, I believe, benefit greatly from them.

But such an approach also has limitations. This is very difficult to explain since many people in the software industry, especially managers, have been convinced (in part by the proponents of inadequate languages) that language independence is a viable and desirable goal for libraries. But if it were possible to develop perfect language-independent libraries, this would mean that language differences are irrelevant. In such a messianic world, where the lion would graze with the ewe, we should indeed go further and forget about syntactic differences, merging all O-O languages into one. This dream, however, has little connection with reality. Languages *are* different, not just because some use brackets where others use parentheses, but because they rely on different semantic models.

The advice to look for language-independent libraries is all the more remarkable that *even within the same language* such interoperability is often a myth. Much of the push for C++, for example, has been based on the interoperability promise; this goes well with managers and buyers, but once the products have been purchased the software developers who actually have to work with them soon find out that C++ libraries from company M (say) simply will not work with those of company B. This is due to the fast evolution of the language, new and often difficult features being added each year, and to the incompatible library architectures selected by the different vendors.

The Eiffel picture is much more reassuring for managers and others preoccupied with long-term viability. Since its creation the language has undergone only one significant set of changes and in spite of its relative youth it is close to a fully stable form, defined by a precise and detailed reference manual (*Eiffel*: *The Language*, Prentice Hall). Any compiler that faithfully implement this manual will be able to process the Base libraries with the same semantics.

Coming back to technical considerations, it is important to understand that the relation between Eiffel and the libraries described here is not a casual one. Describing Eiffel as the language in which these libraries were implemented captures only part of the truth only. More important is the reverse observation: that Eiffel is, before anything else, *the method and language that were designed to make the libraries possible*. The idea of Base predated Eiffel, and begot Eiffel. What started the entire project was the desire to write modern libraries of reusable software components. When it was found out that existing languages were not up to this need, a notation was devised for that purpose, which became the Eiffel language. In fact the very first document about Eiffel presented an early version of some of the classes discussed in this book, showing how to build them using the notation and the underlying method.

It is not surprising, then, that although the principles of library design discussed in the following pages can be applied elsewhere they require Eiffel to reach their full realization. To take just two examples of language features, unique to Eiffel, that are essential for libraries: good library documentation would be impossible without Eiffel's assertion mechanism (and the associated concept of flat-short form); and the sophisticated inheritance hierarchies used for the multi-criterion classification of container structures in this book require Eiffel's powerful repeated inheritance facility. Without these mechanisms, you can of course imitate Base (sometimes by emulating the missing mechanisms, as has been done in some projects using other object-oriented languages), but you cannot get its full power.

From reuse consumer to reuse producer

This book is meant both for the users of the libraries that it presents and for developers who are interested in building their own libraries. These two categories, which we may call **reuse consumers** and **reuse producers**, are of course not disjoint. It is indeed one of the intended effects of this book that software developers who begin as pure consumers of reusable components will be inspired by the example of these components and, little by little, will move a little closer to the producers' side.

The notions of reuse consumer and producer are developed further in the second edition of the book "Object-Oriented Software Construction", Prentice Hall, 1994.

The libraries described here cover only a small (if fundamental) part of the potential for reusable software. Tremendous challenges await those software developers who take seriously the idea of an industry of software components. If you like the approach to software construction promoted by this book, we hope you will contribute to it. One way is to send us feedback or proposed improvements on the classes described here. Another, more ambitious, is to participate in the **Eiffel Shelf**. The Shelf, which we see as playing a central role in making the software components industry take shape, is a mechanism for finding, verifying and distributing quality software components.

There is room in the Shelf both for general-purpose components such as those of this book, and for domain-specific components, in any application field such as financial data processing, scientific computing and many others. The Shelf is also open both to public-domain components, made available for free or for a nominal charge, and to commercial components which the Shelf will distribute for a fee. What is common to all these categories is the notion of quality: no component will be admitted to the Shelf unless it passes a quality assurance process, based on the principles developed in this book and enabling the Shelf users to expect the appropriate standard of quality. This does not mean that everything must be perfect from the start; around; in fact, we expect that many candidate components will fail the quality assurance checks the first time around, and as a result will undergo a process of improvement so as to make it the second time.

Send comments and proposals to: Eiffel Shelf, Interactive Software Engineering Inc., 270 Storke Road Suite 7, Goleta CA 93117 (USA), phone 805-685-1006, fax 805-685-6869. E-mail is the preferred medium of communication; please use the address <shelf@eiffel.com>.

Acknowledgments

Many people contributed to the libraries described here and to the development of the corresponding method.

Jean-Marc Nerson has been associated with the effort since the beginning. Frédéric Deramat played a key role in the systematic restructuring and classification effort that took place in 1991 as we were moving from the 2.3 version of the Eiffel basic libraries, as they were then known, to the version 3 level of what is now called Eiffel Base. The influence of John Potter from the University of Technology Sydney was also decisive at that stage.

Although many developers participated in the development of the libraries, it is important to note the key contributions of Yves Auger, Philip Hucklesby, Philippe Lahire, Jean-François Macary, Raphaël Manfredi and Philippe Stephan. Complete passes through the whole Base were performed at various stages by Reynald Bouy (who implemented the very first version), Stefan Ludwig and Frédéric Philibert. The decisive last passes were performed by Didier Dupont and finally by David Morgan – who put everything in place and also provided comments on the draft version of this book.

The evolution of the Parse library was helped by the contributions of Per Grape and Kim Waldén from ENEA Data (Stockholm), who gave us the improvements they had made.

Users of the libraries who contributed useful insights or corrections are just too numerous to list here, but I must make an exception for Christine Mingins from Monash University (Melbourne, Australia) and David Hollenberg from the Information Sciences Institute of USC (Marina del Rey, California).

Roxanne Rochat helped prepare an earlier version of the text. To produce the final version I was helped by Annie, Isabelle and Sarah Meyer.

A collective acknowledgment is also due to my colleagues at ISE who developed the ISE Eiffel 3 environment and its predecessors. It is hard to imagine how the libraries could have been finished without the facilities offered by the environment, in a convenient graphical form, for compiling, browsing and testing. In particular, the environment's Melting Ice Technology made it possible to experiment repeatedly with various changes and to see the results right away, while benefiting from all the advantages of strong typing and other language constraints. Typical of the support provided by the environment is the way I came to smile rather than grumble when seeing a compilation error, as I knew the message would usually point to a mistake or oversight which in another approach might have taken days of debugging. "Computer-Aided Design" as applied to software takes its full meaning here; I hope that some day all software developers will have access to such facilities.

About the environment, see the individual acknowledgments in "An Object-Oriented Environment: Principles and Application".

Santa Barbara   B.M.
January 1994

Contents

Part A

Techniques and principles

1

Introduction to the Base libraries

1.1 OVERVIEW

The libraries presented in this book cover a number of areas of interest to most software developers.

The name "Base libraries" covers several hundred reusable classes grouped into clusters, a notion defined more precisely in the next chapter. The clusters are themselves gathered into five main libraries:

- The **Kernel** library covers fundamental concepts close to the language: basic structures such as arrays and strings, general-purpose classes inherited by all others, and execution mechanisms such as memory management.
- The **Data Structure** library, the largest and probably the most important part of Base, covers fundamental data structures and algorithms, organized along a specially devised Linnaean structure as mentioned in the Preface and described in detail in chapter 4.
- The **Iteration** library provides facilities for performing systematic traversals of certain data structures. It may for many practical purposes be treated as a part of the Data Structure library.
- The **Lex** library supports lexical analysis.
- The **Parse** library supports syntactical analysis.

The following sections review the contents of these libraries in more detail, after giving a glimpse of other available libraries described elsewhere.

A note on terminology: ISE Eiffel documentation uses the names "Base libraries" or "EiffelBase" to cover the Kernel and Data Structure libraries only. For this book it was judged desirable to include Lex and Parse in Base too, as the relatively small size of these libraries would not justify a separate book.

1.2 OTHER LIBRARIES

Base is only one component of a more general effort at laying down the basis for an industry of software components. Two other major libraries are Vision, for graphics and user interfaces, and Store, for databases and persistence.

1.2.1 Graphical components: the Vision Library

Vision, which will be documented in a future book, makes it possible to build advanced interactive systems offering advanced Graphical User Interfaces (GUIs) to their users. Vision frees software developers from the need to learn the details of windowing systems such as X or Windows by providing high-level classes that represent the major GUI abstractions: geometrical figures, windows, menus, commands, contexts, applications. Vision also shields developers from variations between individual GUI toolkits: a client application is written entirely in terms of the Vision abstractions, which Vision then maps to the selected toolkit. This makes it possible to port a GUI application to various toolkits without changing it; Vision guarantees source compatibility.

Vision is complemented by an interface and application generator, EiffelBuild, which provides interactive mechanisms for building graphical interfaces and associating commands with the various components of the interface. EiffelBuild itself, as well as the entire ISE Eiffel graphical development environment, are built with Vision.

Internally, the classes of Vision fundamentally rely on those of Base. Although this book does not cover Vision, you will encounter a few references to the more than 500 classes of Vision in the chapter on library design.   *See chapter 3.*

The figure on the next page shows an EiffelBuild screen, illustrating some of the facilities of Vision. The top window is the EiffelBuild control panel, used to display and hide the catalogs and editors of reusable visual components. One of the catalogs, the Context Catalog, shows a subset of its components ("primitives" such as push buttons, toggle buttons and text fields). The bottom-right window shows part of the interface of the application under construction, a small editor with a scrolling area and some buttons. The internal structure appears in the Context Tree at the bottom left. The History Window provides unlimited Undo and Redo facilities. Not shown are the command facilities, which associate commands with the various events (such as mouse clicks) that can occur in each context. Each command is an object, whose associated Eiffel text may be edited to support arbitrary application semantics.

Although not directly related to the topics discussed in the rest of this book, this figure shows mechanisms that are entirely built from reusable components which either belong to Base or fundamentally rely on components from Base.

1.2.2 Persistence and database access components: the Store library

Besides Vision, another library that addresses the needs of many users is Store, a general-purpose persistence mechanism providing interfaces to various database management systems.

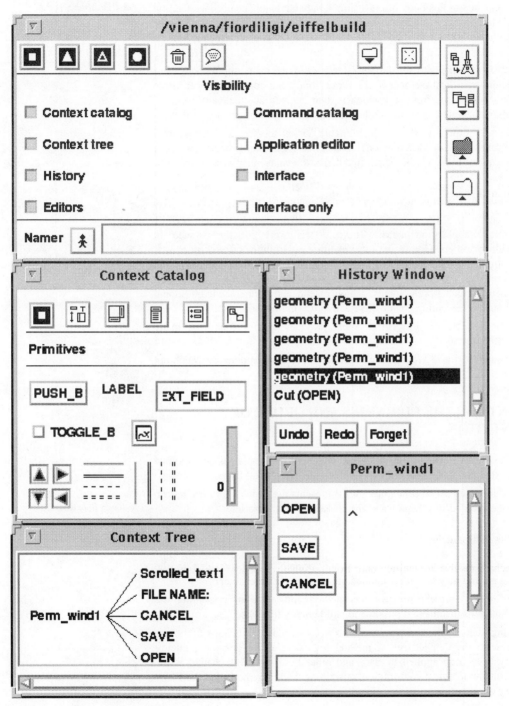

Figure 1.1:
A screen of
EiffelBuild, a
product built
out of the
classes of the
Base and
Vision
libraries

Base as documented in this book offers a simple but convenient persistence facility: the *STORABLE* class, which you can use to store object structures in long-term storage and retrieve them later. You can also use *STORABLE* to transmit object structures over a network.

On STORABLE see 13.6, page 254.

Class *STORABLE* suffices to fill the persistence needs of many applications. For those which require true database access, the Store library provides the answer. Store defines a uniform persistence front-end which is then mapped automatically to many different database management systems, both relational and object-oriented.

Using techniques similar to those which enable Vision to offer a single source-compatible interface to many different GUI platforms, Store can process the same source text into requests to the various supported database management systems.

1.2.3 Application libraries

This book also builds on ISE's and SOL's experience of developing domain-specific libraries in various application areas. These efforts were usually pursued in collaboration with customers. One of the most exciting possibilities offered by object-oriented technology is indeed two have a group of reusable software construction specialists team up with application specialists to produce sound libraries of domain-specific components. Such developments, which extend and complement traditional forms of consulting, are becoming one of ISE's and SOL's major activities.

As noted in the Preface, the Eiffel Shelf provides further room for many components in diverse areas.

The libraries are continually refined and extended with new components; watch out for new versions.

1.3 CONTENTS OF THE LIBRARIES AND ORDER OF PRESENTATION

Here now is an overview of the rest of this book, which will also serve as an overview of the libraries, examined in the order in which they will be described later.

Part A introduces the general principles. Part B presents the various libraries in turn. Part C contains the detailed specifications of the classes in these libraries.

Part A consists of chapters 1 to 3; part B, of chapters 4 to 13; part C, of chapters 14 to 23.

1.3.1 Techniques and principles

The rest of part A describes the techniques and principles that presided to the construction of Base and may be widely applied. It consists of two chapters.

The first of these chapters reviews the method and notation, presenting the techniques and notations that make it possible to build quality libraries.

Chapter 2.

The following chapter, the longest in the book, is entitled "Principles of library design" and presents the detailed set of methodological rules for designing quality libraries, as they have been applied to Base and other libraries. This chapter is the book's principal methodological contribution, describing what may be called the Eiffel method of library construction.

Chapter 3.

1.3.2 Data Structure library

The first few chapters of part B cover the Data Structure library, whose classes are the most commonly used in everyday software development. The library is divided into a number of clusters, each described by a separate chapter. Each cluster contains one or more "deferred" classes, which provide the general high-level abstractions; other classes in the cluster inherit from the deferred ones.

On deferred classes see 2.7.3, page 34.

The first chapter of part B describes general container data structures. It presents the central part of the Linnaean taxonomy announced in the Preface as one of the main results of this book, and introduces the high-level components of that taxonomy, represented by deferred classes of which all container classes in the other clusters are descendants. The highest-level class is *CONTAINER*, with the following heirs:

Chapter 4.

- *COLLECTION*, which describes containers through their access properties (defining how to access a container's items, for example through an index or according to a last-in, first-out policy).

- *TRAVERSABLE*, which considers their traversal properties, such as sequential or hierarchical.

- *BOX*, which describes their storage properties, such as being bounded or unbounded.

The Mathematical cluster contains a few classes describing important mathematical properties: partial and total order relations, ability of an object to be hashed.

Chapter 5.

The Linear cluster contains classes describing sequential and circular structures. Among the most general classes, all deferred, are *LINEAR*, *BILINEAR*, *SEQUENCE* and *CHAIN*, each an heir of the preceding one. Lists are covered by class *LIST*, also deferred, and its non-deferred heirs *LINKED_LIST* and *TWO_WAY_LIST*. Circular structures are described by such classes as *CIRCULAR* (deferred), *LINKED_CIRCULAR* and *TWO_WAY_CIRCULAR*.

Chapter 6.

The classes of the Dispenser cluster describe structures which at any given time, like a very simple vending machine, can produce only one specific item. What this item is determines the kind of dispenser: for queues it is the oldest item inserted but not yet removed, for stacks the youngest, for priority queues the one which has the highest value according to some order relation. The classes include *QUEUE*, *STACK*, *PRIORITY_QUEUE* (deferred) and various implementations such as *ARRAYED_STACK* and *LINKED_QUEUE*.

Chapter 7.

The classes of the Tree cluster, all descendants of the deferred class *TREE*, describe various kinds of trees. Some treat trees as completely recursive structures; they include the representations *ARRAYED_TREE*, *LINKED_TREE* and *TWO_WAY_TREE*, as well as the special cases *BINARY_TREE* and *BINARY_SEARCH_TREE*. Other forms of trees are manipulated through a cursor which may move up, down, left and right; they are described by the descendants of the deferred class *CURSOR_TREE*, such as *LINKED_CURSOR_TREE* and *TWO_WAY_CURSOR_TREE*.

Chapter 8.

The Set cluster includes the deferred class *SET* and implementations such as *LINKED_SET*, as well as the important class *HASH_TABLE* which provides a convenient way to store objects that can be identified by keys. The keys must be "hashable" into an integer, so as to ensure quick insertion and retrieval.

Chapter 9.

1.3.3 Iteration library

The Iteration library classes provide iterators: objects which offer iteration facilities   *Chapter 10.*
over various structures. An iterator encapsulates the basic control structures applicable
to a container, for example loops and conditional traversals.

The general class is *ITERATOR*; descendants include *LINEAR_ITERATOR* and
CURSOR_TREE_ITERATOR.

1.3.4 Lexical analysis and parsing

The Lex and Parse libraries support analysis of texts defined in various languages:
programming languages, specification languages, command languages, or just about any
precisely defined format describing user input or external data.

The Lex library, through such classes as *SCANNING* and *METALEX*, makes it   *Chapter 11.*
possible to build lexical analyzers for arbitrary languages. This library illustrates a
technique which may be applied to many other cases: providing a succession of classes,
from the most general to the most specific, each serving to build the following ones. The
most general classes provide many options; they are very flexible but because of the
wealth of possibilities require their users to fill in many details. The most specific
classes, in contrast, concentrate on the most common cases and provide a ready-made
framework, less versatile but easier to use for ordinary applications.

The Parse library provides classes such as *CONSTRUCT* (the highest-level deferred   *Chapter 12.*
class), *AGGREGATE*, *CHOICE* and *REPETITION*, thanks to which you may produce a
parser for an almost arbitrary context-free language. It is based on an object-oriented
approach to parsing and is particularly useful when you want to apply several sets of
possible semantic actions to the same base language – for example when building
various tools (such as a compiler, a pretty-printer and an automatic documenter) that all
apply to the same language.

1.3.5 Kernel

The final chapter of part B presents the various components of the Kernel library, which   *Chapter 13.*
provides basic mechanisms used by many applications. The classes of the Kernel library
are divided into five clusters:

- Universal classes serving as ancestors to all other classes, in particular class
  GENERAL which defines fundamental operations – copying, cloning, equality
  tests and so on.

- Facilities that are close to the language: basic types such as *INTEGER* and
  REAL; arrays and strings (classes *ARRAY* and *STRING*); basic facilities such as
  PRIMES, *ASCII*, *BASIC_ROUTINES*.

- Input and output: *STD_FILES*, *FILE*, *UNIX_FILE*, *DIRECTORY*.

- Classes for controlling run-time mechanisms and accessing internal structures:
  MEMORY (control over memory management and garbage collection);
  EXCEPTIONS (control over exception handling); *ARGUMENTS* (access to
  command-line arguments); *INTERNAL* (internal object structure).

1.3.6 Class specifications

Part B, as just previewed, talks about the classes of the various clusters but does not present the details of the classes themselves.

Part C contains the class specifications. Its chapters are in one-to-one correspondence with those of part B; for example chapter 18, which gives the specifications of tree classes, corresponds to chapter 8 of part B, which explains the concepts behind these classes.

The class specifications are given as **flat-short forms**, a notion explained in detail in the next chapter. A flat-short form is extracted from the actual class text to guarantee accuracy; but it only retains high-level, abstract properties, excluding implementation properties which, although necessary in the actual class text, should not appear in documentation meant for uses of the class by other ("client") classes.

1.4 TWO NOTES ON THE KERNEL LIBRARY

The library mentioned last, the Kernel, deserves a few more comments.

1.4.1 Order of presentation

As you will have noted, the Kernel library comes at the end of the presentation in parts B and C even though most applications will need to use some of its facilities. There are two reasons for this treatment.

First, some of the more important classes of the Kernel library – those which describe concepts close to the language, such as basic types, arrays, strings and universal classes – are described in detail in *Eiffel: The Language*; readers familiar with that book will prefer to see the new aspects first.

Second, the major contribution of the present book is in the Data Structure, Iteration, Lex and Parse libraries; it was proper, then, to introduce them first in spite of the Kernel's practical usefulness. The Kernel classes are, however, documented in detail through their flat-short forms.

1.4.2 The Kernel self-sufficiency issue

The Kernel library raises a particular problem. Some people would like it not to have any dependency on any other library, so that a user can rely on the Kernel library and not need any other.

Although the argument for self-sufficiency of the Kernel library was given careful consideration, it was felt more important to ensure that the Kernel, like all others libraries, should reflect the most elegant and consistent design possible. Class *ARRAY*, for example, is not just a utility class; it also describes a category of objects that fits at a particular place of the general Linnaean taxonomy devised for this book. It would be quite wrong to treat it as a being from outer space that has no connection to anything else in our class universe.

The form retained for *ARRAY* reflects this analysis for simplicity, consistency and maintainability. *ARRAY* inherits from the various classes describing the applicable abstract properties: *RESIZABLE* (a special case of *FINITE*) for the storage properties and *INDEXABLE* (a special case of *TABLE*) for the access properties.

Storage and access are two of the three fundamental criteria in the data structure taxonomy. See 4.2, page 123.

Although this policy may at first seem to rule out any possibility of delivering a self-sufficient Kernel, in practice the situation is more flexible. It is in fact not difficult to produce compatible but self-sufficient versions of *ARRAY* and other Kernel library classes: versions that have exactly the same interface properties (the same flat-short forms) as the classes described here, and so are equivalent from the client's perspective, but do not rely on any class outside the Kernel library.

Such variants of the Kernel library classes will address the needs of clients that, for any reason, need a self-sufficient Kernel.

2

Building libraries: techniques

2.1 OVERVIEW

The libraries described in this book were made possible by a number of techniques which form the core of the object-oriented method. Before we explore the libraries proper it is important to review these techniques briefly.

The following chapter will complement this presentation by introducing the methodological principles that yield the best libraries. Here we limit ourselves to a descriptive rather than prescriptive discussion, by examining the basic conceptual tools that we will need.

There are many introductions to object-oriented techniques, to which you may refer for a more thorough presentation of the method and language. In particular, the book *Object-Oriented Software Construction* (Prentice Hall) presents the concepts and the methodology in detail; *Eiffel*: *The Language* (Prentice Hall, 1992, second printing) describes the supporting notation. You will also find a general overview in the book *Object-Oriented Applications* (Prentice Hall, 1993), which presents a number of projects having applied these techniques, and includes (in chapter 1) a thirty-page introduction to the method and the notation.

Here our aim is more modest: examining the fundamental mechanisms that make libraries possible. If you are familiar with the basic concepts, please treat this chapter as a quick refresher on both the method and the vocabulary.

2.2 THE MODULAR STRUCTURES

2.2.1 Classes

Object-oriented technology is based on the concept of data abstraction. Here the word **data** indicates that the modular structure is based on object types, rather than on functional decomposition; **abstraction** indicates that these object types are characterized by high-level descriptions rather than by implementation considerations.

The software structure that supports data abstraction is the class, which serves as the basic modular component of object-oriented software construction and of the libraries described in this book.

A class is a module, that is to say a unit of software decomposition; it is also a type, that is to say the description of a set of objects – the **instances** of the class – which may be created, in arbitrary numbers, at execution time. (The class is said to be the **generating class** of these objects.)

A library such as Base is made of a set of classes; each class represents the properties of data structures of a certain type. Typical examples of classes are *LINKED_LIST* and *BINARY_SEARCH_TREE*. An individual linked list, used by some software system during its execution, is an instance of *LINKED_LIST*.

Each class is characterized by a number of features. A feature is an operation applicable to the instances of the class. For example class *LINKED_LIST* has, among many others, the following features:

- *count*, which gives the number of items in a list.
- *put*, which adds an element to a list.

The first feature, *count*, is an example of **query** feature, which returns some information about an object but does not modify it. The other category of feature includes **commands**. When applied to an object, a command does not return a result but may modify the object. Feature *put* is a typical example of command.

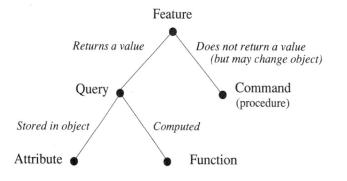

Figure 2.1:
Feature categories

A query such as *count* may be represented in either of two ways:

- We may reserve, in each instance of the class, a field to represent the query's value. For example, we may decide that any object representing a linked list has a field which contains the number of items. In this case, the query is directly represented in memory and is called an **attribute**. Attributes are similar to components of record types in Pascal or structure types in C.
- Alternatively, we may avoid any direct space overhead for the query and instead associate an algorithm with it. For example, an implementation of *LINKED_LIST* may, whenever asked for the value of *count* on a certain object, to perform a traversal of the list and count the items. In such a case the query is said to be a *function*, in the usual programming sense of a routine (subprogram) returning a result.

For a command, only the second choice makes sense: we must use a routine. In this case the routine does not return any result, but it may (and usually will) change the object to which it is applied. Such a routine is called a **procedure**. Functions and procedures are the two kinds of routine.

From an implementation viewpoint we may classify features into attributes (represented by memory) and routines (represented by algorithms), routines being in turn classified as either procedures of functions, as suggested by the figure below. But for the purpose of this book the more convenient classification is the first one, which distinguishes between queries and commands; a command is a procedure, and a query is either a function or an attribute. The reason for preferring this classification is that for the users of a class (called *clients* in the rest of this discussion) there should not be any difference, at least in the absence of formal arguments, between an attribute and a function. For example if you need to use class *LINKED_LIST*, the only relevant information about *count* is that it is a query returning an integer, the number of items; you do not have to worry about which of the two implementations cited above is used internally. This is part of the **information hiding** policy discussed in more detail below.

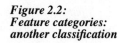

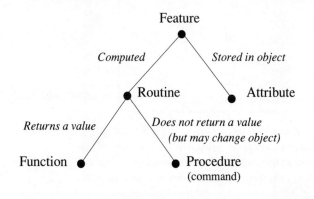

Figure 2.2:
Feature categories:
another classification

2.2.2 An example class

Here is a small class which describes a cell of a linked list, or linkable. Note that a linkable is not a linked list; a linked list is a data structure made of a header object, itself an instance of class *I_LINKED_LIST*, and zero or more linkables, which are instances of *I_LINKABLE*.

The linkable cells will contain integer values (hence the *I_* in the class names). We will see below how to define a notion of linked list and linkable applicable to all possible types of values.

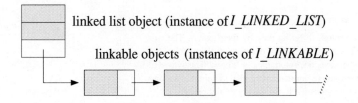

Figure 2.3:
Linked list and linkable

Here is the class:

```
class I_LINKABLE feature
    item: INTEGER;
        -- Value associated with cell

    right: I_LINKABLE;
        -- The cell, if any, to which cell is chained

    put (val: INTEGER) is
            -- Set the item value to val.
        do
            item := val
        end;

    put_right (other: I_LINKABLE) is
            -- Chain cell to other.
        do
            right := other
        end
end
```

This class has four features. Two, *item* and *right*, are queries, implemented as attributes; the other two, *put* and *put_right*, are commands (procedures). The role of each feature is explained by a comment, known as the feature's **header comment**. For a routine, the header comment appears after the keyword *is* and is followed by a sequence of instructions, enclosed in *do ... end*, giving the routine's algorithm. (This applies to functions as well as procedures, although the two routines seen so far are both procedures.)

Because of the way the class has been defined, a client – that is to say, another class using *I_LINKABLE* through its official interface – may perform four operations on a linkable: find out its associated *item* value; replace that value by a new one through *put*; find out, through *right*, the linkable to which it is chained, if any; and chain it to another linkable through *put_right*.

In some cases it is useful to declare two or more features as **synonyms**. For example we could have had two synonym features for *put*:

> *put, set (val: INTEGER) is*   ... The rest as above ...

This is equivalent to writing two feature declarations differing only by their names. The two features remain distinct; in particular, if you redeclare one in a descendant class (using the techniques studied later in this chapter) the other does not automatically follow. The synonym facility gives library designers precious flexibility in implementing the systematic naming policies which, as discussed in the next chapter, are essential to the quality of a library.

2.2.3 Clusters

It is useful in practice to gather classes into groups which may be called **clusters**.

A cluster is a group of classes addressing the same general area, big enough to provide a significant set of functionalities, but small enough to be manageable by one person or a very small team. Although there are no rigid bounds, a typical cluster includes five to twenty classes. Some of the libraries of this book fit in one cluster; others, such as the Data Structure library, use several clusters.

In the language, the class is the highest-level module structure, and there is no direct support for the notion of cluster because none is needed: all modern operating systems, with their hierarchical file structure as illustrated on the figure below, provide a ready-made implementation of clusters; it suffices to identify a cluster of the software with a directory of the operating system. A directory is a set of files, some of which will contain class texts. (Some of the other files in a directory may themselves be directories.) If we associate a cluster with a directory, the classes of the cluster will be those whose texts are contained in the directory's files.

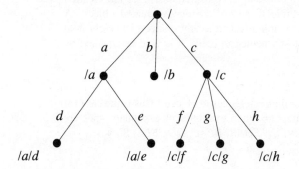

Figure 2.4:
Hierarchical file
structure with
directories

There remains a need to tell language processing tools, in particular compilers, about the directories in which they will find the clusters and their classes. It would clearly be inappropriate to enter this information in the software's source text, since this would make the classes tied to physical locations in the file system.

About Lace see appendix D of "Eiffel: The Language".

The solution in Eiffel relies on Lace (the Language for Assembly of Classes in Eiffel), a small control language which is used to assemble classes into systems and direct the compiler's actions. A Lace specification, called an Ace, contains, along with various compilation options, the list of clusters and their associated directories.

2.3 THE RUN-TIME MODEL

2.3.1 Objects, creation, references, entities

Classes are the software text's way of describing objects that can exist at run time.

For the run-time model we adopt the most flexible solution possible: every object is created during execution as a result of a creation instruction, which in its basic form is written

!! *x*

The name *x* in this instruction, known as an **entity**, must have been declared of some type, based on a class. For example *x* could have been declared as

x: *I_LINKABLE*

The effect of the creation instruction is then to create a new object of type *I_LINKABLE*, also known as a **direct instance** of this class, and to attach *x* to the resulting object. The new object has one field for each of the attributes of the class, meaning here two fields: an integer field for *item* and an *I_LINKABLE* field for *right*.

item   right

Figure 2.5:
A newly created I_
LINKABLE object

In most cases the value of an entity is not an object, but a reference to potential objects. For example the value of *x* in this example is a reference; after the creation instruction, that reference makes it possible to access the newly created object. A reference may be void; this means that it is not attached to any object. (The *right* field on the above figure is void.) You may test whether an entity *y* is void or attached by using the value *Void*, as in

if *y* = *Void* **then** ...

Some entities do denote objects rather than references to objects. This is the case for entities whose type is **expanded**. The most common examples of expanded types are the basic types *BOOLEAN, CHARACTER, INTEGER, REAL, DOUBLE*. So when you declare

n: *INTEGER*

the possible values for *n* are (as appropriate) integers, not references to objects that contain integers.

You can define expanded types other than the basic types by writing class declarations that begin with *expanded class* rather than just *class* as above. The basic types are in fact no exception: like all types they are defined through classes. A typical declaration, found in the Kernel library, begins

expanded class *INTEGER* **feature**

  ...

An entity declared of an expanded type will never be void; it has an associated value, to which (for consistency with the terminology used for reference types) it is said to be attached. For example the integer entity *n* may, at some time during execution, be attached to the value *3*.

2.3.2 Reattachment and initialization

During execution, any entity is either void (for an entity of reference type only) or attached to an object. You may change the attachment through **reattachment**.

The most obvious form of reattachement is the assignment instruction. For example in procedure *put_right*, where *right* and *other* are both declared of type *I_LINKABLE*, the assignment

   right := other

attaches *right* to the same object as *other*, or makes *right* void if *other* is void. Because the entities involved are of reference types, this is a reference reattachment, whose result is to make the two entities refer to the same object.

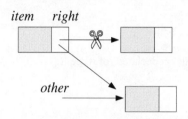

Figure 2.6:
Reference reattachment

For entities of expanded types, the assignment instruction is a copy operation. So in procedure *put*, where *item* and *val* are of type *INTEGER*, the assignment

   item := val

is a normal assignment of integer values, replacing the value of *item* by that of *val*.

The creation instruction, besides allocating a new object, initializes all its fields according to standard default values: 0 for numbers, false for booleans, void references for entities of reference types. For example the above creation instruction, applied to *x* of type *I_LINKABLE*, creates an object whose two fields contain zero for *item* and a void reference for *right*, as shown on figure 2.5.

2.3.3 Memory management

The run-time object structure that results from the mechanisms just described is very dynamic: objects get created only when needed; references may freely be reattached from object to object. This dynamic structure reflects the dynamic nature of the object-oriented method.

As a result individual objects, or entire substructures, may become unreachable. Having to reclaim such objects manually, as in Pascal, C or C++, would be a developer's nightmare. The object-oriented method demands an automatic mechanism to take care of this important task. This mechanism is called the garbage collector.

Garbage collection is not just an implementation issue. Its availability, or lack thereof, conditions the developers' ability to perform true object-oriented analysis and design, concentrating on concepts rather than on petty but tricky memory management tasks.

ISE Eiffel uses an incremental garbage collector whose impact on performance is, for most applications, hardly perceptible. (Some users in fact do not realize that there is such a mechanism.)

For advanced applications that need finer control, a Kernel library class described in this book, *MEMORY*, provides the necessary features, making it possible in particular to turn off garbage collection temporarily, turn it on again, or start a full cycle. Class *MEMORY* also provides a procedure *dispose* which can be redefined to trigger specific actions (typically to free some external resources) whenever the garbage collector reclaims an object.

13.7.3, page 258.

2.3.4 Calls

The basic computational mechanism is **feature call**. With x declared of type *I_ LINKABLE* as above, the following are valid calls:

x.put (3)
x.item

The first is an instruction since *put* is a procedure; the second is an expression since *item* is a query (more precisely an attribute, but there is no difference between attributes and functions here). The feature to the right of the dot, *put* and *item* in the examples, must in all cases be a feature of the class having served to declare x.

In any call such as the above, there is a target, represented by the entity before the dot sign – x in both cases. The call will apply the given feature to the object attached to the target. (It is an error, causing an exception at run-time, to permit any situation in which the target is void at the time of the call.)

The above calls use the most common form, known as dot notation. It is more convenient in certain cases to use the notation of expressions, with prefix or infix operators. For example, you may use an expression of the form

$a < b$

to denote a feature call which in dot notation could have been written *a.less_than (b)*, relying on a comparison feature *less_than*. It is indeed easy to provide such a facility in a library class: instead of an identifier name such as *less_than*, declare the feature with the name

infix *"<"*

More generally, the name of a function with one argument may be of the form **infix** *"§"*, where § is an operator (either a predefined one such as + or <=, or a "free operator" beginning with #, @, | or &). Such a feature is normal in all respects except that the corresponding calls, instead of using dot notation, will be expressions of the form $a \ § \ b$. Similarly, a function with no argument (or an attribute) may be declared as **prefix** *"§"*.

Comparison features such as <, <= and others may be found in the Base class *PART_COMPARABLE*, describing any objects that may be compared with a partial order relation, and shown later in this chapter.

PART_COMPARABLE is shown in 2.7.3, page 34.

2.3.5 Argument passing

Consider a routine (with either an identifier name or an operator name) that has formal arguments; for example, in *I_LINKABLE*:

> *put* (*val*: INTEGER) **is** ...

A call to that routine will provide the corresponding actual arguments; for example:

> *x*.*put* (*3*)

The call temporarily associates the actual argument with the corresponding formal argument. That association is a reattachment operation and has exactly the same semantics as assignment. So for an expanded type as here the value of *val* will be replaced by *3* at the time of the call. For a call that passes a reference, the result is simply to attach the formal to the same object as the corresponding actual, or or to make the formal void if the actual is void.

2.3.6 The current object

The basic form of calls, whether written in dot notation as *x*.*r* (...) or in operator notation as *x* § *y* for some operator §, is relative to a target object *x*.

Assume that the feature (*r* or **infix** *"§"*) is a routine. Within the body of that routine, it may be necessary to refer to the target object itself. The predefined expression *Current* is available for that purpose.

Here is a typical example of the use of *Current*. Assume we want to define linked cells which are chained both ways, not just to the right neighbor but also the left one. Then we will have not just *put_right* as above but also *put_left*. Then the new implementation of *put_right*, in a class that we may call *I_BI_LINKABLE*, may be of the form:

2.7.4, page 36, will explore the notion of bi-linkable element in more detail.

```
put_right (other: I_BI_LINKABLE) is
        -- Chain current cell to other, and conversely:
    do
            -- As before:
        right := other:

            -- Left-chaining too to maintain consistency:
        other.put_left (Current)
    end
```

The last instruction ensures that whenever an element is chained right to another it is also automatically chained left to the first.

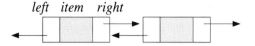

Figure 2.7:
Chaining both ways

One might think that *Current* needs to be used constantly to refer to features of the current object. But a simple convention avoids this: within a class, the name of a feature of the class, appearing with no further qualification, denotes the application of the feature to the current object. For example, assuming a procedure *putint* is available for printing an integer, a routine of *I_LINKABLE* that needs to print the value associated with the current cell may do so simply through

Procedure 'putint' is indeed available in class STD_ FILES, from which it may be obtained through inheritance. See 13.5, page 252.

   putint (*item*)

which has the same meaning as *putint* (*Current*. *item*). The latter form, although valid, is not needed. You only need *Current* for cases such as *put_left* where you must refer to the current object as a whole.

> The preceding example illustrates another property of the notation. It would be incorrect to write an assignment of the form *other*. *left* := *Current*. Syntactically, this is simply because *other*. *left* is an expression, not an entity; you may not assign a value to it, any more than to the expression *a* + *b* (as in *a* + *b* := *some_value*, an obviously illegal assignment). But the real reason is more profound. Letting clients change the value of an attribute of the current object, such as *left*, is a privilege that the author of the class is responsible for granting, or not granting, to authors of client classes. To grant it, he will provide a procedure *put_left* that performs the assignment; in the absence of such a procedure, clients cannot directly change *left*. This is part of the policy of **information hiding**, an important component of the method studied in more detail below.

2.3.7 Creation calls

A class may declare a number of its procedures as **creation procedures**, as in the following example from class *ARRAYED_QUEUE* (queues implemented by arrays) from the Data Structure library:

```
class ARRAYED_QUEUE ... inherit ... creation
    make
feature -- Initialization
    make (n: INTEGER) is
            -- Create queue for at most n items.
        ... Rest of routine omitted ...
        end;
    ... Rest of class omitted ...
end
```

In such a case the basic form given above for the creation instruction (just !! *x*) is not permitted. Instead, a creation instruction, for *aq* declared of a type based on *ARRAYED_QUEUE*, will be of the form

   !! *aq.make* (*some_integer_value*)

which creates the object, initializes its fields as before, and then calls the procedure on the object. This makes it possible to initialize an object, upon creation, to values other than the default ones.

> The technique is also good for safety: because with a **creation** clause the basic form with no call is invalid, you can force your clients to provide the proper values on object creation, thereby avoiding the problems of uninitialized or improperly initialized entities.

ARRAYED_QUEUE has only one creation procedure, but in general a class may have as many as it needs, providing alternative object initialization mechanisms. (The names of the creation procedures must appear in the **creation** clause, separated by commas.) When there is only one creation procedure, the recommended name is *make*.

2.3.8 Systems

Because of the method's emphasis on reusable components, there is no notion of program in the traditional sense. Developers build components – classes – and then assemble them as needed into executable units called **systems**. Systems tend to be of a more transient nature than the classes of which they are composed. A given class may of course be included into more than one system; this is particularly true of the reusable library classes described in this book, which are specifically designed for use by many different systems.

One of the classes of a system is designated as the system's **root**. To execute the system is to create an instance of the root using a designated creation procedure, which will usually fire off a chain of further object creations and feature calls.

2.4 INFORMATION HIDING

To build large systems and perhaps even more importantly to manage their evolution it is essential to ensure that the various components can be developed separately, and to minimize their interdependencies.

In particular, it must be possible for a component *C* (the client) to rely on a component *S* (the supplier) without becoming dependent on *C*'s internal properties. This is important for at least two reasons:

- Avoiding the need for the developer of the client to waste time understanding many possibly irrelevant details in the supplier.
- Minimizing the impact on clients of future changes in the supplier.

One of the mechanisms that achieves this separation between clients and suppliers is information hiding, thanks to which you can keep certain features of a supplier inaccessible to clients. If you keep the features away from all clients, they are said to be **secret**, and will only be usable within the class itself. If you make them accessible to certain designated clients only, they are said to be **selectively exported**.

Class *I_LINKABLE* as studied above is a good example for selective exports. Few client classes will use linkable cells directly; what they normally use is classes describing structures, such as linked lists, made of linkables. Such structures will be described by instances of class *CHAIN* and its descendants (the notion of descendant is defined below). So *I_LINKABLE* should actually be declared as follows:

---

class *I_LINKABLE* **feature**

    ... Declarations of *item* and *put* as before ...

feature {*CELL*, *CHAIN*}

    ... Declarations of *right* and *put_right* as before ...

end

The class now has two **feature** clauses; in general a class may have as many as needed. The second clause has a so-called Clients part, which lists in braces the classes, here *CELL* and *CHAIN*, to which the following features, *put* and *put_right*, are selectively exported. This means that for *ilink* of type *I_LINKABLE* a call of the form

    $x := ilink.right$

is invalid unless it appears in *CELL*, *CHAIN*, or one of their descendants.

To make a feature fully secret, it suffices to write its declaration in a **feature** clause of the form

    feature {*NONE*}
        ... Feature declarations ...

NONE is a special Kernel library class which has neither instances nor descendants other than itself, so this is equivalent to exporting the features to no class at all. You may also use just **feature** { }, with an empty Clients list, but the form with *NONE* makes the intent more visible to readers of the class text.

More on NONE in 2.7.12, page 46.

Information hiding is essential for keeping complexity in check in the development of software systems, especially large ones. It is one of a panoply of techniques that address one of the central problems of software construction: imposing drastic controls on communications between modules.

For the fulfilment of this aim information hiding provides the basic *structural* mechanism. But other mechanisms are needed too, directed at the *semantic* properties of inter-module communication. This is where the next basic component of the method comes in: Design by Contract.

2.5 ASSERTIONS AND DESIGN BY CONTRACT

It is not possible to build a library of reusable components or, more generally, satisfactory object-oriented software, without some way of associating with each software element a precise, implementation-independent description of its effect. Assertions and of the associated principle, Design by Contract, which is the basis of the Eiffel method, address this need.

2.5.1 Assertions

The presence of assertions – elements of formal specification – is perhaps the most immediately visible aspect of the library classes in this book, especially of their specifications as they appear in part C.

An assertion is the expression of some property of objects: for example, if a class has integer attributes a, b and c, an assertion may state that the field corresponding to c is the sum of the other two; or an assertion may express that a certain reference is not void. Assertions appear at specific positions in the software text and serve to characterize the abstract semantic properties of classes and features.

Three language constructs using assertions are particularly relevant to the construction and use of libraries: preconditions, postconditions and invariants.

Here is an example of the first two. The class *FIXED_TREE* describes trees whose nodes each have a fixed number of children. It includes a routine *put_left_sibling*, similar to *put_right* above, which replaces the sibling to the left of a tree node:

FIXED_TREE is discussed in 8.2.3, page 166.

```
put_left_sibling (other: TREE ...) is
        -- Make other the left sibling of current node
    require
        not is_root;
        left_sibling /= Void
    do
        ... Routine implementation ...
    ensure
        left_sibling = other
    end
```

The **require** clause introduces the precondition, which is the condition under which a call to *put_left_sibling* is correct: here the node must not be a root, and must have a previous left sibling. (/= is the "not equal" comparison operator.)

The **ensure** clause introduces the postcondition, which characterizes the situation resulting from a successful execution of the call; here it states that the new left sibling is the node passed as argument to the routine. In some later postcondition examples you will encounter expressions of the form **old** a, denoting the value that an attribute or expression a had on routine entry.

A missing precondition clause is equivalent to **require true**, and a missing postcondition clause to **ensure true**.

The same class includes an example of the third major construct using assertions, an invariant clause:

invariant

> *non_negative_arity*: *arity* >= 0;
> *leaf_definition*: *is_leaf* = (*arity* = 0);
> ... Many other invariant properties ...

Here *arity* is the number of children of a node. The second property states that query *is_leaf* (an attribute or function) must return true if and only if the *arity* is 0.

More generally, the invariant of a class expresses properties which must be ensured on instance creation and maintained by every exported routine.

As illustrated by the class invariant, an assertion may have a label, such as *non_negative_arity*. The label has no direct semantic effect, but provides more information to the software reader and additional debugging help when assertions are monitored at run time, as explained below. All assertions in Base are labeled.

A hardware analogy is useful to understand why assertions are essential to reusable libraries. An electrical engineer who needs an amplifier and is examining possible choices in a catalog of electronic components will need at least three elements of information for each candidate item:

- What range of input voltage is acceptable – the precondition.
- What the corresponding output voltage will be – the postcondition.
- What general conditions, such as the temperature range, will be both expected and maintained – the invariant.

Without such information, there would be no way to use the amplifier except by resorting to internal implementation information such as wiring diagrams.

The same holds in software. It is impossible to achieve large-scale reuse unless the users of a library are able to understand its properties without having to peruse the source code; they must be able to rely on high-level descriptions based on external, abstract properties.

Assertions are not a control structure; in other words, they are not a substitute for conditional instructions such as

if "The node is a root" *then* ...

which test for expected (although possibly not desired) situations. In contrast, the execution of a correct system will never cause an assertion to be violated. A violated assertion is always the manifestation of an error in the construction of the software – a bug.

2.5.2 Run-time assertion monitoring

As a consequence of the previous observation, assertions provide an excellent tool for testing, quality assurance and debugging.

A compilation option makes it possible to monitor assertions at run time at various levels: preconditions; postconditions; invariants. Each of these levels includes the preceding ones, since it makes no sense to monitor postconditions without preconditions or invariants without postconditions. It is also possible to disable assertion monitoring altogether, in which case the assertions have no effect on the execution.

If assertion monitoring is enabled at any level, the effect of an assertion violation at run time will be to trigger an exception.

On exceptions see 2.5.6, page 27 below.

Run-time assertion monitoring provides the basis for a truly object-oriented approach to software quality assurance.

The choice of monitoring level is a tradeoff between three criteria:

• Performance constraints.

• Trust in the correctness in the software.

• Risks of abnormal operations.

In the testing and debugging phase, developers greatly benefit from the full assertion monitoring option. In other circumstances the default compilation option – check preconditions only – is often appropriate, as it provides protection against disaster without implying an undue performance overhead. As will be explained in more detail below, this possibility is particularly precious for library users.

2.5.3 Design by contract

The presence of assertions illustrates the underlying theory of software construction, "Design by Contract", which plays an important role in the design and use of libraries.

Reusing a software component, rather than writing a new component, is similar to contracting for a job, rather than doing the job yourself. In software contracts, as in human ones, both parties are entitled to some benefits and subject to some obligations. Assertions are the contract document, which expressly specifies each party's obligations and benefits. More precisely:

A1 • The precondition is an obligation for the client and a benefit for the supplier.

A2 • The postcondition is a benefit for the client and an obligation for the supplier.

Here is an illustration of the contract for the above *put_left_sibling* example:

	Obligations	Benefits
Client	Provide node which is not a root and has a left sibling.	Make *other* the new left sibling.
Supplier	Get tree updated so that *other* is the current node's left sibling	No need to care about roots, or nodes which have no left sibling.

Figure 2.9: A contract

The bottom-right box is particularly important. It shows the precondition as a protection for the supplier – limiting the set of cases that the supplier must be prepared to handle. Without such limitations, it would be difficult to write useful reusable components; the sheer burden of dealing with all possible cases (those which make sense and those which do not) would make components far too complicated, decreasing the likelihood that they are correct, efficient – or just usable.

This goes against much of the conventional wisdom in software engineering, which favors "defensive programming" – the principle according to which programs elements should be as general as possible.

A system approach to the construction of reliable software leads to the realization that it is impossible to obtain reliability by trying to make every software element responsive to every kind of possible input, a futile pursuit which usually results in elements that are too complex – and hence *less* reliable: in software, complexity breeds bugs. More conducive to the production of reliable systems is an approach which ensures that every element is characterized by a precise indication of its duties as well as its rights.

The developer of a client module does not expect the supplier to perform in every imaginable case; he knows this to be unrealistic. Much more important to him is the precise definition of what constraints must be satisfied by the client, and the knowledge that this performance will be guaranteed if he abides by those constraints.

This assurance that the precondition is *sufficient* to guarantee correct functioning – in other words, that the contract has no hidden clauses – is what makes it possible to write correct client modules. This is a more fruitful approach to software reliability than an endless race for ever more general supplier modules.

Software may have bugs, of course, leading to contract violations. This justifies the presence of a general-purpose mechanism to monitor satisfaction of assertions – observance of contracts. This software equivalent of the "Better Business Bureau" is the run-time assertion checking mechanism.

2.5.4 Contracts and information hiding

The Design by Contract principle yields a rule on preconditions. For contracts to be useful, clients must be able to ascertain the conditions imposed on them. This would be impossible if a precondition included a call to a feature not available to these clients. Hence the rule: if a feature of a class S is available to a certain client class C – that is to say, either exported to all classes or selectively exported to a set of classes that includes S – then any feature used in its precondition must also be available to S.

There is no need for such a rule in the case of postconditions: you can state that a feature will ensure a number of properties at the end of its execution; that some of these properties are not directly available to certain clients will prevent these clients from relying explicitly on them, but will not cause any harm.

2.5.5 Using library preconditions for application development

Coupled with the central role of libraries in object-oriented software construction, Design by Contract and the possibility of monitoring assertions at run time have an important practical implication for developers who need help in ensuring the correctness of their applications.

It was noted earlier that an assertion violation is always the manifestation of a bug. This observation can be made more precise:

V1 • A precondition violation denotes a bug in the client (the calling routine): the call did not observe the required conditions – the client's side of the contract.

V2 • A postcondition violation denotes a bug in the supplier (the called routine): the routine cannot do its job – fulfil the supplier's side of the contract.

Case V1 is particularly interesting for developers of application software if they rely on a library such as Base which makes extensive use of assertions: they can use the library's preconditions to find bugs on their own side of the software.

Assume for example an application system that relies on *FIXED_TREE* and includes a call of the form

> *my_node.put_left_sibling* (*my_other_node*)

An error in the client software might cause *my_node* to be a reference to a root. This violates the first precondition clause of the tree class, and so will be detected by precondition monitoring.

Another example, elementary but common for applications using Base, is the case of an array operation with an out-of-bounds index, which will violate the following routine precondition in class *ARRAY*:

> **require**
>> *lower* $<=$ *i*; *i* $<=$ *upper*

Such cases are particularly interesting because they show that the development of application software can benefit from assertions even if these assertions are not in the applications themselves. The mere decision to rely on good libraries (where "good" implies in particular the presence of assertions) can help find bugs in the application.

These observations explain in part why precondition monitoring is the default compilation option. They also suggest that during application development it is usually wise to use a version of the libraries compiled in the mode that monitors preconditions only. If, as may be expected, the libraries are correct, it would be useless to monitor postconditions; as noted above, this would only serve to detect bugs in the libraries themselves. But keeping precondition monitoring will help find bugs in the clients – that is to say, in the application software. As for the newly developed application classes, the choice of compilation option will depend on circumstances; it will often be useful to subject them to a higher level of assertion checking, such as postcondition or invariant monitoring.

In all cases, the effect of an assertion violation will be to trigger an exception.

2.5.6 Exception handling

Assertion violations are just one of the causes of possible exceptions. More generally, an exception occurs when the execution of a system encounters a condition which makes it possible to continue the computation as planned. The most important examples are:

E1 • An assertion violation, under one of the assertion monitoring options.

E2 • An attempt to execute a call of the form $x.f$ (...) where the value of x is a void reference.

E3 • An attempt to execute a creation instruction !! x ... when there is not enough memory available.

E4 • An abnormal condition such as arithmetic overflow, detected by the hardware or operating system.

The Kernel library also provides a mechanism to raise an exception explicitly.

Procedure 'raise'; see 13.7.1, page 256.

The theory of Design by Contract provides the proper perspective to understand the nature of all such cases: they result from the inability of some party to fulfil its obligations. For example in case E1 there is a bug in the client (for a precondition violation) or in the supplier (for a postcondition violation). In the case of arithmetic overflow (E4), the arithmetic operation was unable to perform its job.

In all cases the exception will interrupt the execution of a certain routine, called the **recipient** of the exception. Then only three responses are possible: failure, retrying and false alarm.

Failure is the most common case: the recipient is unable to continue its execution and fulfil its contract. All it can do is pass on the exception to its caller, after restoring the invariant of the affected objects if possible. The caller becomes the new recipient, and will itself have to react with one of the same three responses.

Retrying is the case in which the author of the recipient routine has planned for the possibility of an exception, and has provided an alternative strategy to ensure the contract anyway.

The false alarm case is rare; it occurs when the exception was in fact not justified. A typical example is an operating system signal, such as "user resized window", which was passed to the software as an exception but has no adverse effect.

Eiffel's Rescue-Retry mechanism supports this systematic handling of exceptional situations.

2.6 INTERFACE DOCUMENTATION

If software construction is based on contracts, these contracts should be clearly documented. Answering this requirement will help us address the more general problem of how best to document software.

2.6.1 Software and its documentation

The documentation problem affects all software and all software developers, but it is more acute for library software than for any other kind. Fortunately, assertions and information hiding provide elements of a solution.

The basic idea, which is developed in more detail in the next chapter, is that we should avoid treating software and its documentation as separate products. Instead, all the information will appear in the software text (the classes); then we may consider the various forms of documentation as various **views** of the software, which can be extracted from the software text by appropriate automatic tools.

On techniques for library documentation see 3.5, page 72.

What makes this approach realistic is the structure of the language and in particular the presence of assertions: the documentation of a class is, essentially, the specification of the various contracts is provides, freed of implementation details.

2.6.2 The short form

The short form of a class, also called its abstract form, shows the interface properties which are relevant to client programmers – but no implementation detail. This excludes any information on non-exported features and, for an exported feature, includes only the signature declaration (number and types of arguments and result), the assertions and the header comment.

For example, the routine *put_left_sibling* given above appears in the short form of its class as

 put_left_sibling (*other*: *TREE* [*T*])
    -- Make *other* the left sibling of current node
  require
   not *is_root*;
   left_sibling /= *Void*
  ensure
   left_sibling = *other*

Part C of this book consists almost entirely of short forms, as this is the primary form of documentation used to describe the libraries.

Note that in practice the form used for documentation will usually not be the plain short form but a variant known as the flat-short form, which involves inheritance and will be discussed below. The main difference between the short and flat-short forms is the selection of features to be taken into consideration for the documentation of each class.

The flat-short form is described in 2.7.15, page 50 below.

The use of the short form as the primary form of class documentation is an application of a general principle of software documentation:

Internal documentation principle.

Information about software should reside in the software itself rather than in separate documents.

This principle follows from two basic observations:

- Keeping everything in one place helps the software and its documentation remain consistent during software evolution, avoiding the very dangerous prospect of divergence.

- Making the documentation part of the software text makes it possible to build tools that will extract the information as needed.

2.6.3 Tools

The short and flat-short forms of a class are entirely deducible from the class text; so they can be produced by software tools.

In the ISE Eiffel environment, Short and Flat-short are two of the **formats** under which users can display a class text. The default format used by Class Tools – the windows which display information about a class – is the Text format, which simply shows the class text as is:

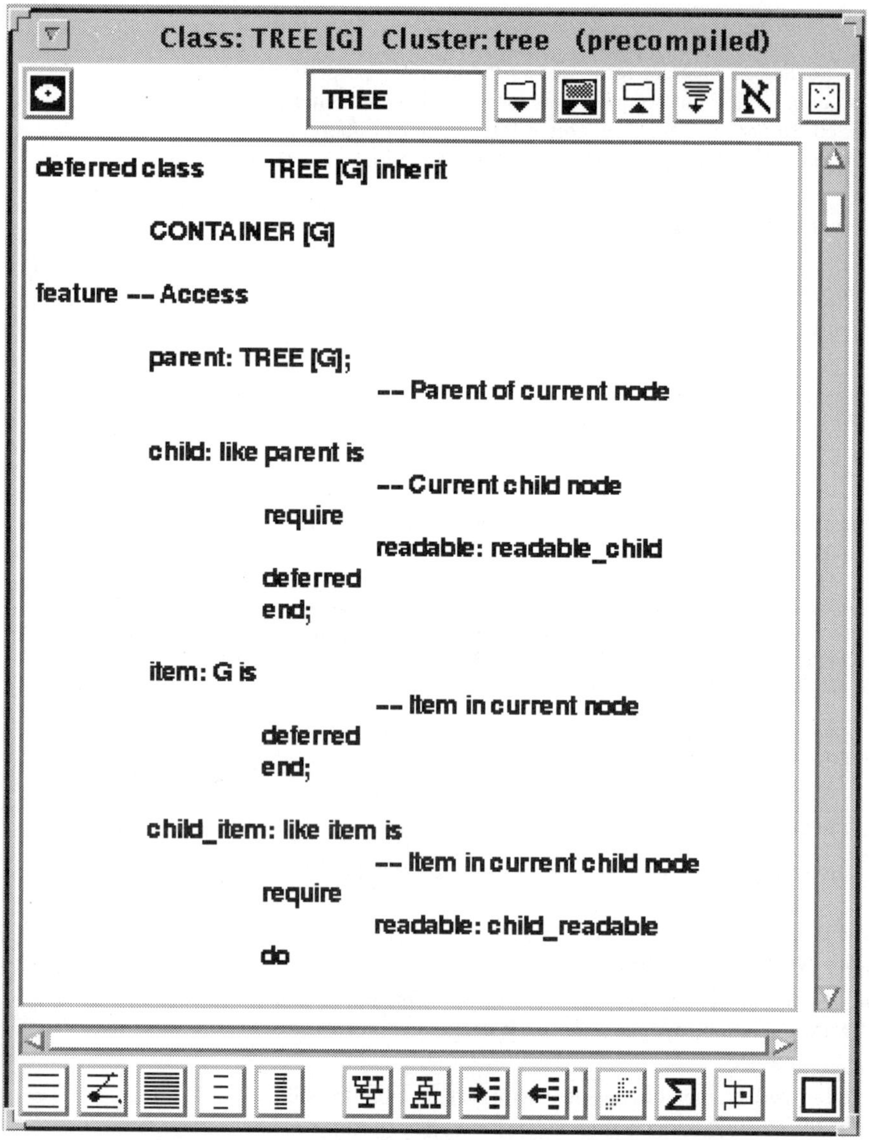

Figure 2.10:
Class Tool in Text
format

The icons in the bottom row make it possible to select different formats. Examples include the Routine format, which will show the list of routines, the Attributes format, the Ancestors format which will show the inheritance hierarchy, the Descendants formats and several others. The fourth icon from the left is for the Short format. If you click on that icon, the content of the window will be replaced by the short form of the class.

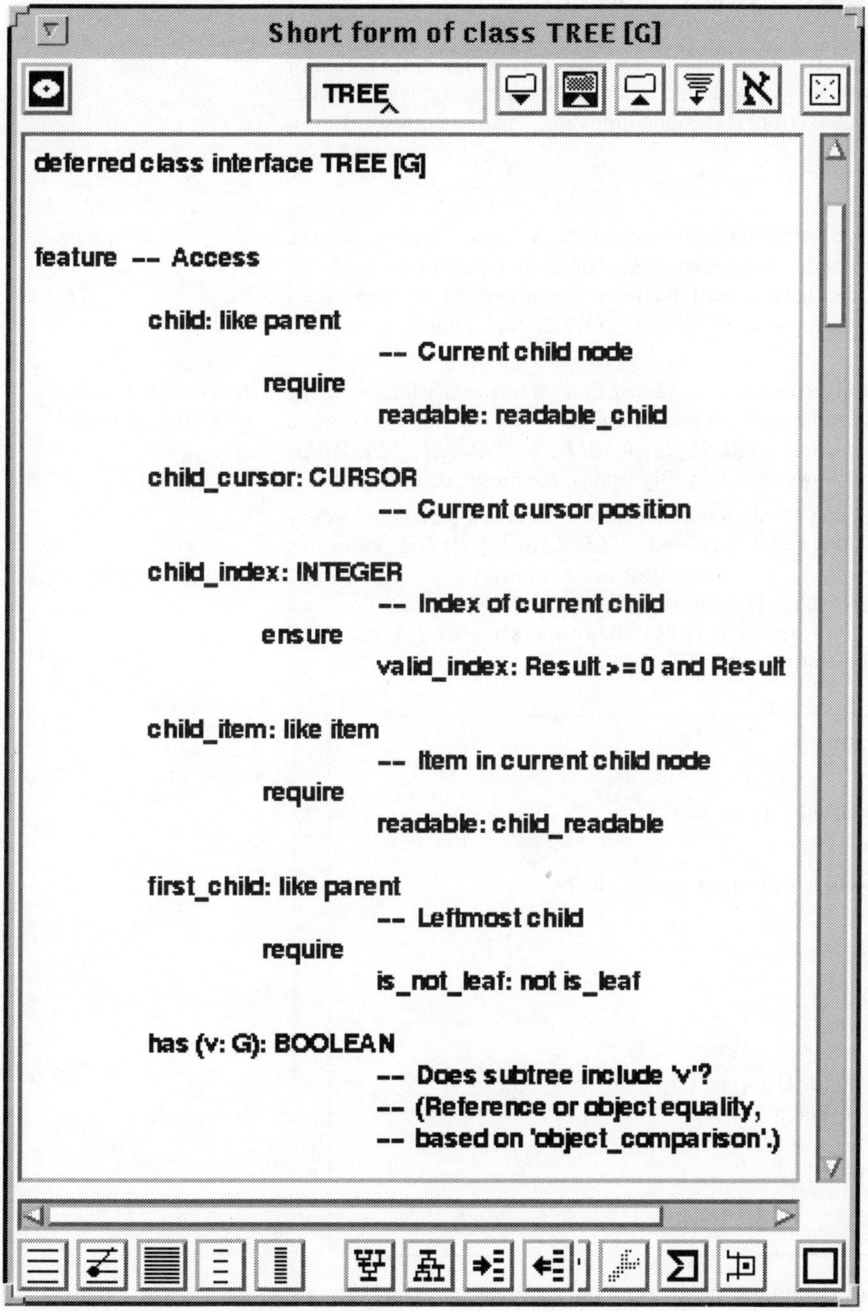
Short form of class TREE [G]
TREE
deferred class interface TREE [G]
feature -- Access
child: like parent
-- Current child node
require
readable: readable_child
child_cursor: CURSOR
-- Current cursor position
child_index: INTEGER
-- Index of current child
ensure
valid_index: Result >= 0 and Result
child_item: like item
-- Item in current child node
require
readable: child_readable
first_child: like parent
-- Leftmost child
require
is_not_leaf: not is_leaf
has (v: G): BOOLEAN
-- Does subtree include 'v'?
-- (Reference or object equality,
-- based on 'object_comparison'.)

Figure 2.11: Class Tool in short format

2.7 GENERICITY, INHERITANCE AND TYPING

Two extension mechanisms, genericity and inheritance, complement the basic notion of class described above. Together, they provide the basis for strong typing, which makes it possible to detect many potential errors at compile time rather than run time.

2.7.1 Genericity

Many classes of Base describe **container** structures such as arrays, lists or queues. These structures must have the ability to contain objects of many types; for example we may need lists of integers and lists of real numbers but also lists of employees, containing instances of an appropriate class *EMPLOYEE* (or references to such instances).

The first example class of this chapter, *I_LINKABLE*, does not satisfy this need: the lists elements it describes are usable only for lists of integers. The solution of writing a new class for each type of list element (*REAL_LINKABLE*, *EMPLOYEE_LINKABLE* and so on) is rather unattractive; it would go directly against the reuse goal.

The initial declaration of I_ LINKABLE is on page 13.

Genericity solves the problem by allowing us to declare classes parameterized by types. For example Base includes a class declared as *LINKABLE* [*G*]; *G* is known as the formal generic parameter of the class, and represents an arbitrary type, used for the elements contained in linkable cells. Here is (in slightly simplified form) the class *LINKABLE*; apart from the class header it is essentially the same as *I_LINKABLE* above, but uses *G* wherever the original used *INTEGER*.

```
class LINKABLE [G] feature

    item: G
        -- The value associated with the cell

    right: LINKABLE [G];
        -- The cell, if any, to which current cell is chained

    put (val: G) is
            -- Set the item value to val.
        do
            item := val
        end;

    put_right (other: LINKABLE [G]) is
            -- Chain current cell to other.
        do
            right := other
        end
end
```

To use class *LINKABLE*, you must provide a type, serving as actual generic parameter and corresponding to *G*. For example a client class may declare an entity *emplink* as *emplink*: *LINKABLE* [*EMPLOYEE*]

Almost all classes of the Data Structure library in Base are generic since they describe containers. Some have two generic parameters rather than just one. For example, to use a hash table, you will write a declaration such as

my_table: *HASH_TABLE* [*EMPLOYEE*, *STRING*]

The first generic parameter of *HASH_TABLE* indicates the type of elements in the table (as the single generic parameter did for *LINKABLE*); the second indicates the key type, which serves for hashing, that is to say for finding a quickly retrievable location in the table.

About hash tables see chapter 9.

2.7.2 Inheritance

The second fundamental extension mechanism is inheritance. Inheritance enables a class, called an **heir**, to obtain some of its features from another, called a **parent**. Then the *feature* clauses of the new class will only list new features and features that need to be changed, or, to use the proper terminology, **redeclared**.

For example, class *LINKABLE* is not actually declared in a stand-alone fashion as suggested above. It has as parent a class *CELL* [*G*] which describes a more general notion of cell and introduces the features *put* and *item*. Then *LINKABLE* itself is declared as

```
class LINKABLE [G] inherit

    CELL [G]

feature {CELL, CHAIN}

    right: LINKABLE [G];
            -- The cell, if any, to which current cell is chained

    put_right (other: LINKABLE [G]) is
                -- Chain current cell to other.
        do
                right := other
        end;

    ... Other specific LINKABLE features ...

end
```

It is often convenient to use a graphical representation to show the classes and their relations. The recommended notation represents classes as ellipses and inheritance relation as single arrows. The other fundamental system structuring mechanism of the method, the client relation, is shown by double arrows (on the figure as in Base, *LINKED_LIST* is a client of *LINKABLE*).

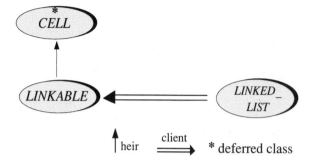

Figure 2.12:
Inheritance and client
relations

Discussions of inheritance use the following terminology. The **ancestors** of a class are the class itself and, recursively, the ancestors of its parents (that is to say the parents, grandparents, grand-grandparents and so on). The reverse notion is **descendants**. To exclude the class itself, use the terms **proper ancestors** and **proper descendants**.

2.7.3 Deferred classes

The classes seen so far provide a full implementation of a certain notion (such as the notion of linkable cell or hash table); they are said to be effective. There is also a need for classes which do not provide a complete implementation. Such a class is said to be deferred. As will *CELL* on the above figure, the graphical representation shows an asterisk above the class name. Instead of just *class*, the declaration of a deferred class must begin with

   deferred class ...

A deferred class has at least one deferred feature. A feature is deferred in a class if has no implementation in that class; in its declaration, the body (the sequence of instructions starting with *do*) is replaced by the single keyword *deferred*. The intent is to preserve abstraction by deferring – hence the name – the full implementation to proper descendants.

As with classes, a non-deferred feature is called effective. An attribute is always effective, since it implies a choice of implementation – by memory rather than computation. A routine is effective if its body begins with *do*, or with one of the two other forms which we have not seen yet, *once* and *external*.

A rule governs the use of a deferred class: you cannot instantiate it. If x is declared of type C and C is deferred, the instruction !! x is invalid. The justification is straightforward: were such an instruction permitted, the resulting run-time object would be deficient, since it would be missing some of its feature implementations, leading to execution failure if clients try to call these features. But it is still perfectly legal to declare x of type C; the corresponding run-time objects will be obtained (through polymorphism, as explained later) by applying creation instructions not to C but to effective proper descendants of C.

Here as a typical example of deferred class is a version of the class *PART_ COMPARABLE* from Base. (The type declarations for arguments will be improved below when we study anchored types.)

On anchored types see 2.7.6, page 39.

The notation **ensure then** *is a variant of* **ensure** *used for the postcondition of a redeclared routine. For details see 2.7.10, page 44 below.*

---

indexing

　description:
　　"Objects that may be compared according to a total order relation";

deferred class COMPARABLE inherit

　PART_COMPARABLE
　　, redefine
　　　infix *"<"*, **infix** *"<="*,
　　　infix *">"*, **infix** *">="*
　　end

feature -- Comparison

　infix *"<"* (*other*: *COMPARABLE*): *BOOLEAN* **is**
　　　-- Is current object less than *other*?
　　deferred
　　ensure then
　　　Result **implies not** (*Current* >= *other*)
　　end;

　infix *"<="* (*other*: *COMPARABLE*): *BOOLEAN* **is**
　　　-- Is current object less than or equal to *other*?
　　do
　　　Result := **not** (*other* < *Current*)
　　ensure then
　　　Result **implies not** (*Current* > *other*)
　　end;

　infix *">"* (*other*: *COMPARABLE*): *BOOLEAN* **is**
　　　-- Is current object greater than *other*?
　　do
　　　Result := *other* < *Current*
　　ensure then
　　　Result **implies not** (*Current* <= *other*)
　　end;

　infix *">="* (*other*: *COMPARABLE*): *BOOLEAN* **is**
　　　-- Is current object greater than or equal to *other*?
　　do
　　　Result := **not** (*Current* < *other*)
　　ensure then
　　　Result **implies not** (*Current* < *other*)
　　end

end

This example shows two important properties of deferred classes:

D1 • Although a deferred feature has no implementation, it has a signature – that is to say, the numbers and types of its arguments and results are declared – and it may be semantically specified through assertions. (Similarly, a deferred class may have an invariant clause, although this is not the case here.)

D2 • Not all the features of a deferred class need to be deferred. In fact here there is only one deferred feature, "<"; the others, "<=", ">" and ">=", are effective since it is possible to define their implementations in term of "<".

Because they provide ways to describe high-level abstractions, deferred classes are essential to the proper structuring of libraries. Many of the non-terminal nodes in the inheritance graph of a library such as Base are deferred classes – particularly, of course, in the upper part of the taxonomy.

A descendant of *COMPARABLE* may provide an effective (non-deferred) declaration of *infix* "<". This process is called **effecting** the feature. The other features, being already effective and defined in terms of "<", do not need to be redeclared.

2.7.4 Redefinition and effecting

The basic property of inheritance is that each class inherits all the features of its parents. But to obtain the flexibility needed for libraries libraries we need to enable class authors to adapt inherit features to the new context. Such an adaptation is called **redeclaration**.

There are two forms of redeclaration:

• The first form has already been seen: if you provide an implementation for an inherited feature which was deferred in the parent, you are **effecting** the feature (making it effective).

• If you inherit an effective feature and change its signature, assertions or implementation (*do* clause), you are **redefining** the feature.

In addition, it is also possible to undefine a feature (change its status from effective to deferred) or to redefine a deferred feature into another deferred feature with slightly different properties, in particular different assertions.

A typical example of redefinition is provided by class *BI_LINKABLE*, which inherits from the class *LINKABLE* discussed above. As noted earlier in this chapter, bi-linkable elements are chained not just to a right neighbor but also to a left neighbor. This implies a redefinition of *put_right*, of the following approximate form:

```
class BI_LINKABLE [G] inherit

    LINKABLE [G]
        redefine
            put_right
        end

feature -- Access
```

```
    put_right (other: BI_LINKABLE [G]) is
            -- Put other to the right of current cell;
            -- make sure that other has current cell to its left.
        do
            right := other;
            other.put_left (Current)
        end;

    ...

end
```

Both forms of redeclaration – effecting and redefinition – are subject to the same rules governing type and assertion changes. The only syntactical difference is the **redefine** subclause, which is required for redefinitions, but has no equivalent for effectings.

Type rules are studied next, assertion rules in 2.7.10, page 44.

2.7.5 Don't call us, we'll call you

The redeclaration mechanism supports one of the most powerful forms of reuse promoted by object-oriented libraries: **reuse of common behaviors**. This is in particular a consequence of the above D2 property: the ability for an effective routine to call deferred ones means that you can use a high-level class to describe common behaviors, that is to say algorithmic schemes which can be defined in that class even though the details of their various algorithmic steps are left to descendants.

As an example, the deferred class *LINEAR*, which describes linearly organized structures such as one-way and two-way linked lists as well as circular chains, has an effective function *has* which describes a common behavior:

```
has (v: G): BOOLEAN is
        -- Does v appear in the structure?
    do
        from
            start
        until
            exhausted or else equal (v, item)
        loop
            forth
        end;
        Result := not exhausted
    ensure
        Result implies equal (v, item)
    end
```

The function is shown here in simplified form. Its actual implementation relies on procedure *search*; here the two routines have been collapsed into one, and the question of object *vs.* reference comparison has been ignored.

Function *has* implements a general searching scheme, common to all variants of the notion of linear structure. The individual algorithmic steps, such as *start* which sets the current position to the first element, *forth* which advances the current position by one step, and *item* which gives the value of the item at the current position, are left to the implementation of each specific variant; but their combination into an algorithm for *has*, which is the same for all the classes describing linear structures, can be factored out at the level of the deferred class *LINEAR*, their common high-level ancestor.

It is also possible to describe the individual steps, in the original class, by effective rather than deferred features. Such features describe default behavior; descendants can redefine them to substitute specific behavior. For example the procedure *semantics* of class *CONSTRUCT* in the Parse library, defining the semantic actions to be applied to each construct of a text being parsed, begins with a call to routine *pre_action* and ends with a call to *post_action*. In many cases there is no need for any pre-action or post-action; so as declared in *CONSTRUCT* these procedures do nothing. A descendant may redefine them, however, to perform specific actions. This technique is useful when defaults exist, since descendants will only need to redefine the steps which differ from the corresponding default. (In contrast, if you are inheriting from a deferred class and want to produce an effective one, you must individually effect every deferred routine even if you do not actually need it.)

Whether it relies on redefinition or on effecting, reuse of common behaviors may be called the "don't call us, we'll call you" form of reuse. A high-level, partially deferred class defines a general scheme where some of the details are either left unfilled (in the form of calls to deferred features) or filled with temporary solutions (calls to features that are meant to be redefined). Descendant classes fill in the details by effecting the deferred features and redefining some of the others. This should be contrasted with the more traditional form of reuse, in which reusable components are available to be called by new applications. Here it is the reverse: the calling routines, such as *has* in *LINEAR* and *semantics* in *CONSTRUCT*, are already defined; they call features such as *start* and *forth* in the first case and *pre_action* in the second, for which each application will provide its specific variants. So the reusable software calls the application software, not the reverse.

In this form of reuse the application class is usually a descendant of the reusable class, not a client as in the traditional approach.

This technique yields some of the most powerful reuse mechanisms of Base. It plays a central role, for example, in the Iteration library, whose classes provide general-purpose mechanisms for traversing certain data structures. Each traversal will apply a test and an action, represented by routines *test* and *action*, to every data structure item that it encounters. Descendants of the iteration classes may redeclare *test* and *action* to define specific tests and actions depending on the context of each application.

Chapter 10 covers the Iteration library.

Another example is class *SCANNING* of the Lex library, which provides a general framework for any application that needs to build and use a lexical analyzer. Classes that perform lexical analysis may inherit from *SCANNING* and use its procedure *analyze*. This procedure applies to each input token an action described by procedure *do_a_token*, which any descendant of *SCANNING* can redefine to describe specific processing. (The default version simply prints information about the token.) Like *semantics* in class *CONSTRUCT*, procedure *analyze* also relies on initialization and

See 11.5, page 205 about SCANNING.

termination procedures: *begin_analysis*, which just prints a header, and *end_analysis*, which does nothing. Descendants may redefine these default actions.

The classes of the Parse library also follow the same approach. The general-purpose procedure *process* defines the overall scheme for parsing a document and applying semantic actions. Descendants will take this scheme for granted, redeclaring the appropriate routines to describe application-specific syntactic properties and semantic actions.

Chapter 12.

2.7.6 Type redeclaration rules and anchored declarations

A few validity constraints govern the use of inheritance.

Let us look first at the type rules. The redeclaration of a query (attribute or function) may change the result type; the redeclaration of a routine (procedure or function) may change the type of some arguments. It is not possible, however, to change the number of arguments, or to switch between commands and queries, since such changes would make static type checking impossible.

In the case of type changes, the so-called **rule of covariance** applies: the new type must be a descendant of the old. This is the case above with the redeclaration of *put_right*, where the type of the argument *other* in the original version was *LINKABLE* [*G*].

In this example the redeclaration changes the routine's implementation by providing a new *do* clause. But other redeclarations affect the type only, not the implementation. For example *LINKABLE* has a feature *right* whose declaration was given above as

right: *LINKABLE* [*G*]

In class *BI_LINKABLE* this must be redefined to be of type *BI_LINKABLE* [*G*]: a bi-linkable element should only be chained to other bi-linkable elements, not to arbitrary linkables.

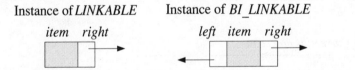

Instance of *LINKABLE*   Instance of *BI_LINKABLE*

item   right   *left   item   right*

Figure 2.13:
Linkable and bi-linkable

A similar situation arises with the arguments of the features of class *COMPARABLE*. The "less than or equal to" function, for example, was declared above as

infix *"<="* (*other*: *COMPARABLE*): *BOOLEAN* **is**
   do
      Result := **not** (*other* < *Current*)
   ...
   end;

This would normally require a redefinition in every proper descendant of *COMPARABLE*, to guarantee that we compare temperatures only with temperatures, ages only with ages and so on. These redefinitions are annoying, however, since they only serve to enforce type rules; the *do* clauses will all be identical, causing unpleasant duplication of software texts.

Such cases are very frequent; were they to require explicit redefinitions, they would clutter and obscure class texts. The notion of type anchoring addresses this problem. You may anchor a feature or an argument to *Current* by declaring it as

x: **like** *Current*

If this declaration appears in a class *C*, it simply means that *x* will be considered in any descendant *D* of *C* to have been declared with the type *D* – without any need for explicit redefinition.

For example the declaration for "<" in *COMPARABLE* actually appears as

infix *"<=" (other:* **like** *Current): BOOLEAN is ...*

Similarly, in class *LINKABLE*, feature *right* is also declared as being of type **like** *Current*. The argument *other* of *put_right* in both *LINKABLE* and *BI_LINKABLE* is also declared as **like** *Current*, although in this case there must still be a redefinition in *BI_LINKABLE* since a new implementation is required.

These declarations all anchor the type of an entity or feature to *Current*. Other anchors are possible. In particular, if *a* is an attribute or function, you may use a declaration of the form

b: **like** *a*

which means that in any descendant of the enclosing class *b* will be considered to have been declared of the same type as *a*. In other words, any redeclaration of the type of *a* in a proper descendant causes the corresponding implicit redefinition of *b*.

It is possible to declare a feature so as to **prevent** redefinition in descendants: just specify the feature as "frozen". An example appears with the routines for copying objects, from the Base class *ANY*:

Every class that you write is a descendant of ANY; *see 2.7.12, page 46 below and 13.3.4, page 246, which also discusses 'copy' and other features for object copying and equality testing.*

---

copy (other: **like** *Current)* **is do ... end**;

frozen *standard_copy (other:* **like** *Current)* **is do ... end**

Descendants may redefine *copy* to account for specific notions of copying, but it is important to keep around the original form of field-by-field copy, hence *standard_copy*.

Frozen features are not very common: using many of them would defeat the remarkable flexibility that object-orientation and inheritance bring to software development. Good uses of this facility usually follow the above scheme: they involve twin features, one redefinable, the other frozen. Proper descendants may redefine the non-frozen version, while the other continues to provide the exact original semantics.

2.7.7 Polymorphism

An important consequence of inheritance is the ability for an entity to become attached at run time to objects of various types.

The mechanism for achieving this is very simple: polymorphic attachments. Assume that *x1* is declared of type *X* and *y1* of type *Y*. In an assignment of the form

$x1 := y1$

or a call of the form

$r (y1)$

where $x1$ is the corresponding formal argument, the types X and Y need not be the same: it suffices that Y be a descendant of X. If these types are indeed different, the attachment (assignment or actual-formal argument association) is said to be polymorphic.

> This assumes that X is a reference type, so that the operations simply involve updating a reference to reattach it to an object of a different type. There is no polymorphism for entities of expanded types.

A consequence of a polymorphic attachment such as the above is to make $x1$ attached to an object whose type is different from the type declared for $x1$, here X. So for example an entity of type *LINKABLE* may become attached to an instance of *BI_ LINKABLE*.

Polymorphism also results from a variant of the creation instruction. The form seen above, for example !! *link.make* (...) where *link* is declared of type *LINKABLE* [T] for some T, creates an object of that type. In some cases, you may want to use a proper descendant type right from the creation; this is achieved by writing the instruction in a form such as

! *BI_LINKABLE* [T] ! *link.make* (...)

with a type appearing between the two exclamation marks. That type must be a descendant of the type declared for the target of the creation, here *link*, and the creation procedure, here *make*, must if present be one of the creation procedures of the corresponding class. The effect is then to create a direct instance of the given type, rather than of the type that appears in the target's declaration.

A consequence of these properties is a clarification of the terms "instance" and "direct instance". A direct instance of a class C is an object created directly from the pattern defined by C. An instance of C, without further qualification, is a direct instance of any descendant of $C - C$ itself or a proper descendant. Polymorphism implies that if x is declared of type C the objects to which x may become attached at run time are instances of C, not just direct instances.

2.7.8 Dynamic binding

The natural complement to polymorphism is dynamic binding: the rule that a feature call of the form $x1.f$ (...), where x is a polymorphic entity, will always call the version of f that is appropriate for the run-time object to which x is attached at the time of the call.

Assume for example that $x1$ is declared as above of type X and, because of the assignment or argument passing, becomes attached to an object of type Y. Assume further that f has a certain version in X but is redefined in Y. Dynamic binding in this case means that in spite of the declaration of $x1$ the call will trigger the version redefined in Y. To do otherwise could result in the wrong semantics – calling a version of a feature which is not adequate for the target object.

Polymorphism and dynamic binding are particularly precious for library users since they enable them to manipulate high-level entities without knowing what exact implementations will be chosen for the corresponding objects in any particular execution. For example the author of a class *LISTUSER* can manipulate a list through an entity declared just as

>   *my_list*: *LIST* [*SOME_TYPE*]

without knowing what exact type of list *my_list* will represent at run time among all the list implementations supported by Base: one-way and two-way linked lists, arrayed lists (fixed or resizable) and others. The author of *LISTUSER* has the guarantee that any call to a feature of class *LIST*, such as

>   *my_list.put* (*some_element*)

will always use the appropriate version of the feature, here *put*, adapted to the type of the currently attached object.

Of course some class of the system must have created that object, and so must have chosen an actual type (which must be effective, whereas *LIST* is deferred). The corresponding creation instruction may for example have been:

>   ! *TWO_WAY_LIST* [*SOME_TYPE*] ! *my_list.make* (...)

But this instruction and its choice of type are irrelevant to the author of class *LISTUSER* that just uses *my_list* and calls features such as *put* on it. For example *my_list* may be a formal argument to a routine of *LISTUSER*:

>   *some_routine* (*my_list*: *LIST* [*SOME_TYPE*]; ...) *is* ...

so that *LISTUSER* obtains the list from other classes, which are responsible for creating the corresponding objects and choosing their actual types. If you are the author of class *LISTUSER*, you only need to know the specification of class *LIST*, as given by the flat-short form in this book. You do not need to read the specification of *TWO_WAY_LIST*, *ARRAYED_LIST* and other effective descendants of *LIST*; in fact, you do not even need to know about the existence of these classes.

The flat-short form of LIST is in 16.4, page 295.

For the library user, then, polymorphism and dynamic binding are abstraction mechanisms: they make it possible to manipulate objects through high-level views, ignoring the detailed implementation choices that may have been made in a particular case, but having the guarantee that all operations on the objects will be consistent with the representation chosen – by someone else – for that object.

2.7.9 Accessing type information

Thanks to the power of dynamic binding, library clients seldom need to ask explicitly the question "what is the type of the object attached to x?", where x is a possibly polymorphic entity. Instead, you just call the appropriate features to apply the operations that you need on x; dynamic binding does the type discrimination for you.

Some cases may, however, require a more explicit approach to type determination. These cases are relatively rare, and if you think you have encountered one of them it is always worthwhile to double-check before adopting one of the techniques suggested below, since with a little more reflection you may find out that dynamic binding is better after all. These cases belong to two categories:

T1 • Low-level system programming, where you need to access the internal properties of objects, usually to interface your system with outside mechanisms such as a database management system.

T2 • Situations in which the software developer expects an object to be of a certain type, but the corresponding entity cannot be declared of that type because the software itself does not have the information statically.

To address T1, classes of the Kernel library provide the required low-level mechanisms. In particular, class *INTERNAL* has a feature *dynamic_type* that can be applied to any object.

See 13.7.5, page 259 about INTERNAL.

T2 generally arises when a system retrieves an object from the outside – from a file, from a database, from a network. This means that the software cannot know for sure the type of the object. The **assignment attempt** instruction, using the ?= symbol, addresses this needs. Assume two entities $x1$ and $y1$ of reference types X and Y. In the instruction

   $x1 \ ?= y1$

there is no need to observe the requirement on declared types, imposed on ordinary assignment :=, that Y be a descendant of X. Instead what will count is the type of the object (if any) to which $y1$ is attached whenever the instruction is executed. If that type is a descendant of X, then all ends well: the instruction will cause a reference reattachment, as ordinary assignment would have done. But if the attached object's type does not conform to X (or if $y1$ is void, in which case there is no attached object) the effect will be to make $x1$ void. So in general an assignment attempt such as the above will be immediately followed by an instruction of the form

   if $x1 = Void$ **then**
      ... We did not get what we expected ...
   else
      ... Call appropriate features on the object attached to $x1$ ...
   end

The thousands of classes of Base, Vision and other fundamental libraries include only a handful of assignment attempt instructions, and clients of these libraries also need this instruction very rarely. But in those few cases it would be impossible to work without it. For example, the *retrieved* feature of class *STORABLE*, which accesses an object previously stored into a file (or sent to another application through a network) is declared with a very general result type. A system that retrieves an object through *retrieved* will use assignment attempt to force the appropriate type.

2.7.10 Assertion redeclaration

Polymorphism and dynamic binding require some discipline in the use of redefinition. Design by Contract provides the best perspective to understand what this discipline should be.

The general rule of client-supplier relations is mutual trust. In particular, a class C which is a client of a class S and includes a call of the form

$x.f(...)$

for x declared of type S, and f an exported feature of S, must have the guarantee that if the precondition of f is satisfied before that call then the call will terminate and yield a state that satisfies the postcondition. In other words there is **no more** obligation on C before the call than the precondition; and the the guarantee provided after the call is **no less** than the postcondition.

In the absence of polymorphism, the name f as used by the author of class C unambiguously denotes the feature called f in S; so the preceding rules simply mean that the implementation of f in S is correct – that it lives up to the advertized contract. But with polymorphism and dynamic binding this is not sufficient any more. If at the time of the call x is attached to an object of some type T which is a descendant of S, and f has been redeclared in T (or in-between S and T), the version called will be the redeclared one, not the original.

This is only acceptable if every redeclared version is bound by the same contract as the original. It could fail to meet this requirement by either strengthening the precondition (thereby assuming more than what the clients have been requested to satisfy before the call) or weakening the postcondition (thereby returning less than advertized). The new assertions should instead:

- Keep or weaken the precondition.
- Keep or strengthen the postcondition.

The language rules automatically enforce these important obligations. In the redeclaration of a routine, it is not permitted to use the forms *require* and *ensure*, as it would be impossible (in the general case) for a compiler to ascertain whether the weakening and strengthening obligations have been met.

Instead you have the choice between two strategies. If you want to keep an assertion (precondition or postcondition) as it was in the inherited version of the routine, do not include any clause for it in the redeclaration. But if you want to change it, use one of the following two forms:

- For a precondition, *require else* newpre, which means that the routine's updated precondition is *original_precondition* *or* newpre, guaranteed to be weaker than or equal to *original_precondition*.
- For a postcondition, *ensure then* newpost, which means that the routine's updated postcondition is *original_postcondition* *and* newpost, guaranteed to be stronger than or equal to *original_postcondition*.

These requirements are rules of honest subcontracting: with polymorphism and dynamic binding we may view a proper descendant such as T, providing a redeclared version of an inherited feature, as being similar to a subcontractor that performs a certain task in lieu of the original contractor. Because of dynamic binding, clients may not be aware that any subcontracting is taking place: in the above example, C uses x as an entity of type S, and the author of C may not even know that T exists. So it is essential that the original contract defined by S for its clients be also binding on any of its proper descendants such as T.

Complementing these rules on precondition and postcondition redeclaration, a rule governs the invariants of descendant classes. The invariant of a class is automatically considered to include the conjunction of all the parents' invariants. So there is no need to repeat consistency properties which were already true of the parents. Full class invariants, as a result, are built in an incremental way; they accumulate down the inheritance hierarchy. This property plays an essential role in producing the rich invariants that characterize many classes of the Base libraries.

2.7.11 Combining inheritance and genericity

Inheritance and genericity provide complementary extension mechanisms. They may be combined in two interesting ways.

The first is the notion of polymorphic data structure, which follows directly from the preceding discussion. In the above declaration of *my_list* as being of type *LIST* [*SOME_TYPE*], the basic inheritance type rule seen above implies that the elements of the list, inserted by procedure *put*, may be of any descendant type of *SOME_TYPE*. This allows the construction of lists which have elements of various types, all conforming to *SOME_TYPE*. Such a list is known as a polymorphic data structure. The combination of genericity and inheritance yields the desired reconciliation of flexibility (with the ability to mix elements of various types in a single structure) and safety (with the guarantee that they will all conform to a chosen common type, which can be chosen as general or as specific as desired).

The other way of combining inheritance and genericity is to use the mechanism known as **constrained genericity**, under which a formal generic parameter represents not an arbitrary type, but one which is required to be a descendant of a particular type known as the constraint. This is important for libraries since it will often be necessary to assume the availability of certain operations on the elements of a generic structure, even though the exact type of these elements is not known.

A typical example is the class describing hash tables in Base. It has two formal generic parameters and is declared as

See 9.2, page 173 about HASH_TABLE; the class specification appears in 19.2, page 381.

> **class** *HASH_TABLE* [*G, H –> HASHABLE*] ...

This shows the syntax for a constrained generic parameter: *–> CONSTRAINT*, where *CONSTRAINT* is the constraining type. Here *HASHABLE* is a deferred class introducing a function *hash_code* that returns an integer. The above declaration means that a generic derivation of the class, as in

> *my_table*: *HASH_TABLE* [*SOME_ITEM_TYPE, SOME_KEY_TYPE*]

is only valid if *SOME_KEY_TYPE* is a descendant of *HASHABLE*. An example of such a descendant is *STRING*, which introduces a version of *hash_code* applicable to strings. The features of *HASH_TABLE* use *hash_code* to compute for each item a position where the item will be stored in the table. For a type that does not conform to *HASHABLE*, it would not be possible to compute the hash value; hence it is not permitted to use such a type as the actual generic parameter corresponding to *H*.

2.7.12 *ANY* and *NONE*

The object-oriented type system is structured by inheritance. Two Kernel Library classes, *ANY* and *NONE*, make it complete by closing the inheritance lattice.

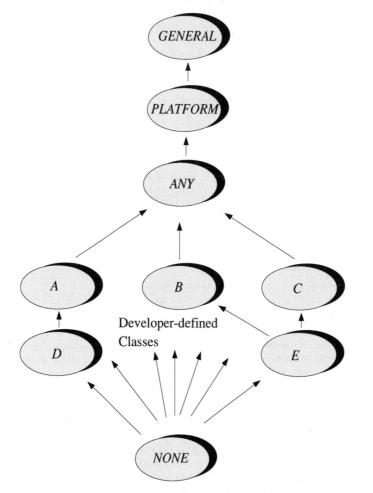

Figure 2.14:
The inheritance
structure

The language rules imply that any developer-defined class is a descendant of *ANY*. More precisely, any class which does not have an explicit **inherit** clause is understood to have one of the form

> **inherit**
>   *ANY*

As a result, it is possible to obtain a completely polymorphic data structure, containing items of arbitrary types, by declaring it for example as

> *full_palette*: *LIST* [*ANY*]

As the figure shows, *ANY* itself has a parent and a grandparent. *GENERAL* includes a number of features which may be applied to all objects: copying, cloning, equality comparison, rudimentary input and output. *PLATFORM* introduces a few constants describing machine and operating system dependencies, such as the number of bits in the representation of an integer. *ANY* itself does not in its standard form introduce any new feature; individual groups or projects can use it to introduce features that will be made available to all classes, without modifying *GENERAL* or *PLATFORM* which should be the same everywhere.

The complete specification of ANY, including features from GENERAL and PLATFORM, is in 23.2, page 425.

NONE is a fictitious class. Were it actually to exist, it would inherit from all developer-defined classes (and, because of the rules explained below, would need huge **rename** clauses). But it serves theoretically to close the type system, and practically to provide a type for the feature *Void*, as declared in *GENERAL*. Also part of *NONE*'s practical role is the recommended technique for making a feature secret, as described earlier: introduce it in a Feature clause beginning with

2.4, page 21, explained the notation **feature** {*NONE*}.

> **feature** {*NONE*}

2.7.13 Multiple inheritance and renaming

Many classes of the Base libraries have more than one parent. For example the data structure taxonomy described in detail in a later chapter defines three inheritance hierarchies – access, storage, traversal – so that classes describing specific kinds of data structure, for example stacks implemented as arrays, are produced by inheriting from the appropriate classes in each of these hierarchies.

Chapter 4.

Multiple inheritance raises the issue of how to distinguish features inherited from separate parents if they have the same name. Such name clashes would lead to ambiguous classes and must be removed through a Rename clause. Here is an example from class *ARRAYED_QUEUE*, which describes queues implemented as arrays and whose **creation** clause was seen above:

```
class ARRAYED_QUEUE [G] inherit
    QUEUE [G]
        ...
    ARRAY [G]
        rename
            count as array_count,
            item as i_th,
            put as put_i_th,
            ...
        redefine
            ...
        end
creation
    ...
```

This class inherits a number of features from *QUEUE*: *count*, the number of elements; *item*, the oldest element not yet removed; *put*, which inserts an item at the other end. But *ARRAY* uses these names for other features: *count* is the number of elements in an array; *item*, a function with an integer argument, returns the value of the array element at the corresponding position; *put* replaces the value at a certain position.

That *QUEUE* and *ARRAY* should have all these feature names in common, although surprising at first, is a result of the systematic naming policy enforced by the Base libraries and explained in the next chapter. But even without such a policy, name clashes would be bound to occur.

On the naming policy see 3.8, page 92.

Unless corrected by a Rename clause, a name clash will make the resulting class invalid. You may use a Rename clause to remove name clashes by giving new local names to inherited features. In *ARRAYED_QUEUE* as shown above, although the features inherited from *QUEUE* keep their names (a desirable property since *QUEUE* and *ARRAYED_QUEUE* offer the same interface to clients), some of the features inherited from *ARRAY* have new names for their use by *ARRAYED_QUEUE*, its descendants and its clients. So for example the feature known as *count* in *ARRAY* will be known as *array_count* in *ARRAYED_QUEUE*. This avoids any confusion between the number of elements in the queue, given by feature *count* inherited from *QUEUE*, and the number of elements in the array used for the representation, given by *array_count*. The class invariant will indicate that the value of *count* is always less than or equal to that of *array_count*.

It is useful to contrast renaming with redefinition. Redefinition changes a feature, but keeps its name. Renaming is exactly the reverse. It may of course be necessary to rename a feature and redefine it too.

Beyond removing name clashes, renaming is useful to enforce any naming policy that you may have defined for a library development project: you can use renaming to enforce a feature terminology adapted to each specific class, independently of the terminology used in its parents.

2.7.14 Repeated inheritance and selection

Multiple inheritance brings the possibility of repeated inheritance – the case in which a class is a proper descendant of another in more than one way. As illustrated by the figure on the next page, repeated inheritance may be direct (a) or indirect (b).

Repeated inheritance raises two issues. First, does a feature *f* from the repeated ancestor, *A* on the figure, yield one or two features in the repeated descendant, *D*? Second, in the case of conflicting redefinitions, which version should be chosen?

The answer to the first question follows directly from the naming policy. If a feature of *A* is inherited from the two paths under the same name, it will give just one feature in *D*; this is known as sharing. If the names are different, conceptual replication occurs: *D* will obtain two features from a single feature of *A*.

The second question arises in the replication case if one of the two variants has been redefined en route. Let *f* be the name of the feature in *A*, *f1* and *f2* the names of the versions in *D* (one of them, but not both, may actually be called *f*). Because of redefinition, *f1* and *f2* are different features. The question is due to dynamic binding: should a call of the form *a.f* (...), where *a* is declared of type *A* but dynamically attached to an instance of *D*, trigger a call to *f1* or to *f2*?

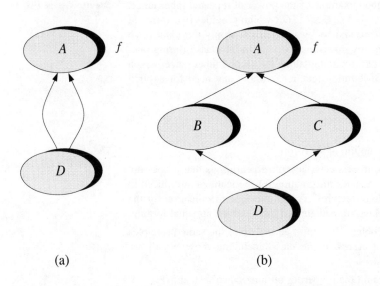

Figure 2.15:
Repeated inheritance

(a)   (b)

Answering this question requires that the author of *D* disambiguate the situation. This is the role of the *select* subclause of the *inherit* clause. Class *ARRAYED_QUEUE*, whose *inherit* clause was given above without the *select* subclause, provides a good example:

```
class ARRAYED_QUEUE [G] inherit
    QUEUE [G]
        ...
        select
            count, empty, put
        end
    ARRAY [G]
        rename
            count as array_count,
            item as i_th,
            put as put_i_th,
            ...
        redefine
            ...
        end
    ...
```

The *select* clause is needed because *ARRAY* and *QUEUE*, as explained in the discussion of the taxonomy, have common ancestors. With the selections shown, a call of the form *a.count*, where the type of *a* is one of these common ancestors and the attached object is of type *ARRAYED_QUEUE*, will cause evaluation of the *QUEUE* version.

The general taxonomy of data structures appears on the figure of page 124.

The Iteration library provides a good example of the power of repeated inheritance, enabling the definition of a class *TWO_WAY_ITERATOR* which provides two forms of iteration over bilinear structures: forward and backward. The class only introduces two new features, and takes care of the rest by inheriting twice from the class offering one-way iteration only, *LINEAR_ITERATOR*; renaming along the second inheritance branch automatically yields the second set of iteration features, without any need for explicit redefinitions.

See 10.5.4, page 193.

2.7.15 The flat-short form

Inheritance introduces a variant of the notion of short form.

The notion of short form was introduced in 2.6.2, page 29.

A problem with the plain short form of a class, as defined earlier, is that it does not take inheritance into account: it only includes information for the features introduced in the class itself, known as the **immediate** features. A full interface specification for the class should treat all features of the class, immediate and inherited, on an equal footing.

The flat-short form solves this problem. It is built according to the same principles as the short form, but includes all features of the class, including those which are inherited from direct or indirect ancestors.

The flat-short form takes into account the properties of inheritance seen above:

- A feature appears in its latest redeclared and renamed form.
- The invariant is the concatenation of all ancestors' invariants.
- The precondition is the *or* of all applicable *require* and *require else* clauses.
- The postcondition is the *and* of all applicable *ensure* and *ensure then* clauses.

The last two properties are essential in light of the above discussion of honest subcontracting. The contracts of inherited features may be different from those of the original versions, and client authors must be able to base the software on the most accurate description of these contracts. The flat-short form provides such a description, based on the actual contracts enforced by each class.

The individual class specifications appearing in part C of this book indeed rely systematically on the flat-short form.

Note that for readability the successive additions to a precondition or postcondition appear separately in the flat-short form, for example:

```
      r is
            -- Header comment
      require
            "Original precondition clause"
      require else
            "Second precondition clause"
      ensure
            "Original postcondition clause"
      ensure then
            "Second postcondition clause"
      ensure then
            "Third postcondition clause"
```

2.8 CONSTANTS AND SHARED INFORMATION

Two related mechanisms, constant attributes and Once routines, of less portentous theoretical significance than what we have seen so far, nevertheless provide mechanisms that are needed to build practical libraries.

2.8.1 Manifest constants and Unique values

All attributes seen so far had variable values. You may also need to define symbolic constants. You will declare them as constant attributes, with a self-explanatory syntax, as in:

> *Carriage_return*: *INTEGER is 11*;
> *Avogadro*: *REAL is 6.02e23*;
> *Street_sign*: *STRING is "NO LEFT TURN"*

Other than their inability to change values, such attributes are similar to other features of a class. Indeed many library classes offer constants among their features; an extreme example is class *ASCII* from Base, in which all features are constants representing the ASCII character codes. The *Carriage_return* example above was extracted from that class.

It is sometimes convenient to define a set of integer constant attributes with the guarantee that their values are all different, without going into the trouble of defining their individual values. The Unique declaration achieves this, illustrated by this example from class *HASH_TABLE* in the data structure library of Base:

> *Inserted_constant*: *INTEGER is **unique***;
>   -- Insertion successful
>
> *Found_constant*: *INTEGER is **unique***;
>   -- Key found
>
> *Changed_constant*: *INTEGER is **unique***;
>   -- Change successful
>
> *Removed_constant*: *INTEGER is **unique***;
>   -- Remove successful
>
> *Conflict_constant*: *INTEGER is **unique***;
>   -- Could not insert an already existing key
>
> *Not_found_constant*: *INTEGER is **unique***;
>   -- Key not found

These declarations introduce a number of constant attributes that describe the various possible results of an attempted insertion, removal or replacement operation. The values are guaranteed to be all positive, and all different. (These attributes are all secret; clients find out about the result of an operation through higher-level queries such as *inserted*, which internally rely on the attributes.)

On the query features of hash tables see 9.2.4, page 177.

When a complex operation has several variants, it is usually not appropriate to use Unique constants to distinguish between them. You will obtain a better structured and more flexible solution by declaring the variants as redeclarations of the same original feature, and relying on polymorphism and dynamic binding as explained above.

2.8.2 Once routines

Closely related to constants is the notion of Once routine. If you use the keyword *once* in lieu of *do* in the declaration of a routine, you obtain a routine whose body will be executed only at the time of the first call. Further calls will not execute any actions; if the routine is a function, they will always return the result computed by the first call.

This provides a technique to obtain shared objects: use a Once function whose result is of a reference type; the first call will compute the needed object, and subsequent calls will return a reference to it.

Once functions are not used very often in libraries because they introduce close coupling between various clients of a common supplier. You will find some examples, however, in the Parse and Kernel libraries.

12.7.4, starting page 227, shows an example use of once functions in Parse.

2.9 LIBRARY MANAGEMENT

Building good libraries, managing their evolution and making them attractive to application developers requires two more mechanisms from the method and the language: a way to mark features and classes as obsolete, and a facility for indexing and retrieving classes through keyword-based queries.

2.9.1 Feature and class obsolescence

Perfect reusable components are seldom obtained at the first shot. Yet in developing component libraries, and in the long run an industry of reusable software components, perfection is what we should eventually strive for.

This raises the question of what you do when you have produced a first version of a reusable class, or even a second and a third, and you realize that you could have done better. In many cases the method and language will help you protect clients from the effect of changes:

- Adding features is usually not a problem.
- Thanks to information hiding, you may change the implementation of a feature (for example the body of a routine) with no visible effect on clients.
- Weakening a precondition or strengthening a postcondition is also fine for clients.

But sometimes you will want to remove a feature or change some of its properties – its name, its signature, its assertions – in ways that affect the class interface and cannot be ignored by clients. What can be done then? The problem is to preserve existing software without stifling the natural process of evolution and perfecting.

Fortunately the language includes a mechanism that directly supports this need: declaring features or classes as obsolete.

An example in the evolution of the Kernel library was the set of changes that occurred for class *ARRAY*. The name of the routine *enter* was changed to *put* for conformance to the standard naming conventions (which were devised after the initial release of *ARRAY*), and the order of arguments was reversed for consistency with routines applicable to other data structures. But the updated class retained a feature *enter*, marked as obsolete:

```
enter (i: V; v: G) is
        obsolete "Use "put (value, index)" "
    do
        put (v, i)
    end
```

A feature declared in this way is normal in every respect but two. It can be used by clients (if it is exported) and by descendants, but such uses will trigger compile-time warnings, listing the message given after the **obsolete** keywords. Furthermore, an obsolete feature does not appear in the short form of the class.

Because they cease to be documented in the official reference, obsolete routines pose no immediate threat to the simplicity of the class as perceived by new users. This is different from what would occur if both old and new features were merely kept as synonyms.

More sophisticated effects could have been devised for obsolete features; for example, one may imagine a mechanism which would on option take care of updating client calls (although this is not so trivial when the new routine has different arguments or, as in the above example, changes the order of arguments). As it is, however, the mechanism has played a key role in allowing library developers to take advantage of afterthoughts without disturbing existing clients too much.

Of course, if you uncover a serious design mistake in the original version of the class you should not leave it around but just rewrite the class. Feature obsolescence is useful in the following cases:

O1 • You can think of a better name for a feature. This usually occurs as you are doing an after-the-fact cleanup of your library and realize that naming conventions could be made more consistent.

O2 • You can think of a better signature or specification. This occurs for example if you realize that a routine has too many arguments and should be split into two or more routines, perhaps on the basis of the operand-option distinction introduced in the next chapter.

On operand and option arguments see 3.7.2, page 89.

O3 • You want to advise programmers to cease using the feature. This may happen when you find out that a routine's action is not needed any more, as with a routine which performed some initialization which you later realize can be carried out automatically on object creation.

Cases O1 and O2 often involve changes small enough that it is tempting to forsake them and leave good enough alone. But in the long term this is dangerous to the quality of the library; and the longer you wait, the harder it will be to perform the needed changes.

Besides features, it is also possible to declare a class as obsolete:

class C **obsolete** *"Message"* ... The rest as usual ...

This possibility is useful in particular when you want to change the name of a class (a case similar to O1) or to replace it by a better abstraction.

2.9.2 Indexing components

An obvious problem in the library-based approach to software development is how to enable client programmers to find out about available components and retrieve them easily.

To a certain extent, the concern over this issue, especially among managers, is exaggerated. When compared to the needs for reusable components, the libraries that now exist are only a small beginning. A manager or programmer who hesitates about reuse for fear of being overwhelmed by the potential number of resulting components is like someone who refuses a pay raise for fear of not knowing what to do with the money.

As the number of components grows, however, systematic techniques for indexing and retrieving them become increasingly necessary.

The key principle for addressing this issue was encountered above in the discussion of software documentation, which led us to the notion of short form: the internal documentation principle, which states that information about software should reside in the software itself rather than in separate documents. Most of the required information is indeed already in the class text: whether the class is generic, what its parents are, its features, their signatures, their preconditions and postconditions, the class invariant and so on. But there may be a need for extra information, which would not otherwise figure in the class because it has no effect on its compilation or execution, but will be precious to potential reusers and can be extracted by automatic tools. Examples of such information include keywords, author names, and more generally elements of **domain analysis** (the study of the library's application domain).

See 2.6.2, page 29.

The Indexing clause addresses the need to include such information in a standardized (and hence automatically processable) way. An Indexing clause appears at the beginning of a class and is a list of entries, each consisting of an index and a number of values:

> **indexing**
>   *index*: *value1*, *value2*, ...
>
>   ...

The *index* is an identifier; the values may be any legal lexical elements of the language, most commonly strings, identifiers and integers. Here for example is the Indexing clause of class *ARRAYED_QUEUE*:

> *indexing*
>> *description:*
>>> *"Unbounded queues, implemented by resizable arrays";*
>>
>> *status*: *"See notice at end of class";*
>> *names*: *dispenser, array;*
>> *representation*: *array;*
>> *access*: *fixed, fifo, membership;*
>> *size*: *fixed;*
>> *contents*: *generic*

This clause uses some of the standard indexing conventions recommended as part of the style guidelines, and explained in more detail in the next chapter.

On indexing guidelines see 3.9.2, page 106. Some recommendations also appear in "Eiffel: The Language", appendix A.

2.10 ENVIRONMENT SUPPORT

As a conclusion to this review of the base technology, here is a brief presentation of the tool support that helps make the preceding ideas applicable in practice. The presentation is based on the ISE Eiffel 3 implementation of Eiffel.

In its most common use, the environment relies on a graphical user interface; a non-graphical version is also available, so that all major operations can be triggered from the command line.

2.10.1 Melting ice technology

The heart of the environment is the **melting ice compiler**. The name "melting ice" denotes a novel compiling technology which solves one of the oldest and most pressing problems of software development: how to obtain a very fast edit-change-execute cycle, in particular in the case of a **small change** to a **large system**, without endangering efficient and safe execution.

The Eiffel method, supported by the libraries described in this book, enables developers to write large and ambitious systems; but then it must be possible to change a few classes and experiment right away with the result of these changes.

Most traditional approaches rely on compilation and linking, implying that the time needed to process changes is proportional to the size of the system. In contrast, the melting ice compilation technology requires time proportional to the logical size of the changes, regardless of the system's overall size. This yields a comfortable development environment which reconciles the benefit of interpreted solutions (quick turnaround, immediate feedback) with those of compiler-based techniques (safety through type checking, efficiency of the generated code).

2.10.2 Cross compilation

The final output of the compiler is ANSI-C code.

C is used here less as a programming language than as a portable assembly language. This technique guarantees the long-term viability of the approach (since C compilers are available on almost every existing hardware platform) and ensures portability. It also supports cross-development: it is possible to produce software on one platform (the host), then C-compile and run it on another (the target).

2.10.3 Precompilation

Most systems rely on one or more libraries: Base in almost all cases, then possibly Vision (for graphical user interfaces), Store (for persistence and database access) and others.

It is possible to compile such libraries as part of the system. This approach, however, means that at the inception of each development you must wait while compiling hundreds, possibly thousands of classes. Even more serious is the resulting disk space penalty: each developer's compiled software will include the code generated for all the necessary libraries. In many cases, this is just prohibitive.

Precompilation solves this problem. It is possible to precompile a library, or a combination of libraries, so that the result may be used by any system. A precompiled library is used by reference rather than by copy: in other words, the systems that rely on it will not duplicate its code. As a consequence, every developer will only use disk space for his own classes; the space for libraries is shared.

The ISE Eiffel 3 delivery comes with Base (the libraries of this book, except Lex and Parse) precompiled. A particularly attractive consequence of this approach is that a new user may almost instantaneously compile and execute any one of a set of fairly large example systems. These examples heavily rely on the precompiled classes of Base, to which they only add a few specific classes; so thanks to the melting ice technology you will be able to compile a significant example system in a matter of seconds.

Any set of classes, however large, may be precompiled together provided it satisfies the completeness requirement: if a class belongs to the precompiled set, any class on which it depends directly or indirectly as client or descendant must also be part of that set.

Precompilation is meant for classes that have reached a stable state. If you want to change a class that is part of a precompiled library, you will need to recompile the entire library, or to start using a non-precompiled version of the library.

2.10.4 Tools

A wide battery of tools supports interactive development. Particularly important in connection with both the use and the design of libraries are the tools for exploring and documenting classes.

The environment is based on a novel set of interface principles, described in detail in a separate book. These principles derive from a systematic application of object-oriented principles to the interaction between developers and the environment. In particular:

See "An Object-Oriented Environment: Principles and Application".

- In accordance with the object-oriented view of the world, each tool is based not on a functional abstraction (as the debuggers and compilers of traditional environments) but on a data abstraction, representing one of the object types that matter to developers, or **developer objects**. Examples include class tools, feature tools, system tools, explanation tools, execution object tools.
- Reflecting the typed nature of the method, the environment is typed: every operation works on some operands (developer objects) which must be of a clearly specified type.

- The basic operation is **typed drag-and-drop**. It consists of dropping a "pebble" representing a certain developer object (class, feature etc.) into a "hole" of a corresponding tool (such as a class tool or a feature tool).

This model turns out to be particularly convenient and practical. The figure below illustrates a typical application among many. The power of polymorphism and dynamic binding often causes library users to ask themselves: "what will this feature be in a different class?". For example you may have the declaration and call

my_tree: *TREE* [*SOME_TYPE*];

...

how_many_children := *my_tree*.*arity*

Assume you have some suspicion that *my_tree* may dynamically be of type *FIXED_TREE* (one of the effective descendants of *TREE*). You may want to see what *arity* (the feature which gives the number of subtrees) is in class *FIXED_TREE*. Here is a simple and intuitive way to do it.

On the figure, the Feature Tool on the left has been "targeted" to feature *arity* of class *TREE*; it shows that in that class the feature is deferred. In the System Tool on the right, the name of class *FIXED_TREE* appears. We catch that class by clicking on its name with the rightmost mouse button and releasing the button immediately; the cursor takes the shape of a class pebble, an ellipse. By moving the mouse we start dragging that pebble towards the class hole of the Feature Tool, identified by its matching shape.

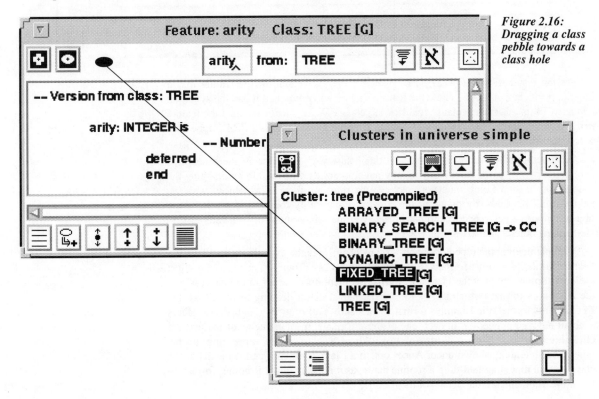

Figure 2.16: Dragging a class pebble towards a class hole

We now drop the pebble into the hole (by clicking and releasing the rightmost mouse button). This retargets the Feature Tool, which now shows procedure *arity* for *FIXED_TREE*, and hence gives us the answer to the original question: "What version of *arity* will be applied for an object whose type is not just *TREE* but, more specifically, *FIXED_TREE*?".

Figure 2.17:
Retargeting a Feature
Tool

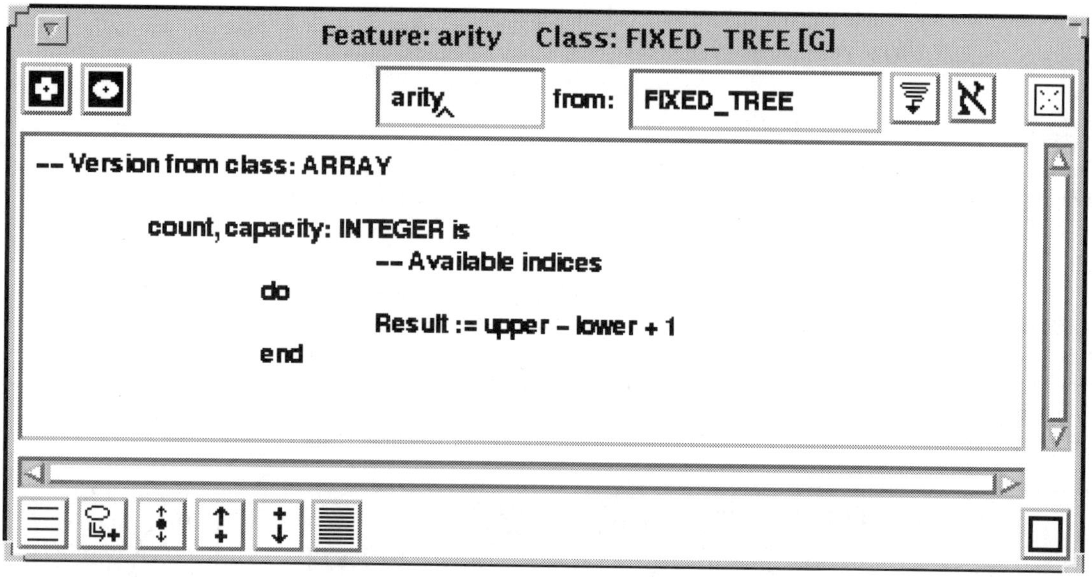

As the result shows, *FIXED_TREE* uses for *arity* a version of the feature that it inherits from class *ARRAY*, where the feature's name was *count* and it had the synonym *capacity*. In its inheritance clause for *ARRAY*, class *FIXED_TREE* renamed the feature *arity*. If you want to know more you can click on the name of class *ARRAY* appearing before the feature's text, and drag it into a Class Tool.

All operations of the environment work in this way. When using the interactive debugging facilities, for example, you may put stop points on a routine by dragging the routine into a Stop Point hole; you may see the run-time form of an object, with the values in all its fields, by dragging the corresponding entity to an Object hole; if the object contains a reference to another object, you may drag-and-drop that reference to see the new object; and so on.

Complementing the typed drag-and-drop mechanism is the availability, in Class and Feature Tools, of various formats. For example in a Class Tool you can select not just the Text format, but also the Flat-short format (as mentioned earlier in this discussion), the Ancestors format (which shows the inheritance structure leading to the class), the Descendants format, the Routines format (which shows all routines), and several others – about a dozen altogether. In each one of these formats, most elements of the text are **clickable**: for example, you may drag-and-drop a class name, appearing in the inheritance hierarchy shown under Ancestors, to a Class Tool, and see the details of the class; or you may drag-and-drop a routine name, as it appears in the Routines format, to a Feature Tool, and see the details of the routine.

The combination of these ideas – tools based on developer objects, typed drag-and-drop, multiple format, universal clickability – provides a powerful and intuitive interaction metaphor, fully consistent with the object-oriented paradigm, with the rest of the Eiffel method, and with the spirit of Base.

2.10.5 Other components

Other elements of the environment include the previously mentioned Vision and Store libraries, the EiffelBuild interface and application generator and the EiffelCase analysis and design workbench.

These various tools are designed to work closely together: for example an application generated by EiffelBuild can be immediately compiled thanks to the combination of precompiled Vision and of the melting ice compilation technology. But they are built and delivered as separate components, so that it is possible to use some without the others.

This set of components fundamentally relies on the Base libraries as described in this book. Conversely, the environment enables developers, through its facilities for compilation, precompilation, browsing, documentation and debugging, to make the best possible use of these libraries.

3

Principles of library design

3.1 OVERVIEW

The libraries described in this book are the result of a long-going search for the best reusability techniques, those most likely to satisfy quality-conscious software developers. This search has yielded a number of principles, whose application is pervasive throughout the libraries and their documentation.

This chapter explains the most important of these principles. It examines the following topics in turn:

- What makes libraries special?
- General library design principles.
- Design by Contract: how to build correct and robust libraries and use them properly.
- How to document a class.
- How big should a library class be? A feature?
- How to name features and classes – a surprisingly important and tricky question.
- Other important conventions, in particular the choice of feature categories and indexing guidelines.
- Designing the proper inheritance structures.
- The human side: who is the ideal library designer?

Like the rest of this book, this chapter is intended both for library users (called reuse consumers in the Preface, and also known as *client authors*) and for library designers (reuse producers, or *supplier authors*), whether they are different people or the same person at different times. If you are a library user or prospective user, the discussion will help you increase the benefits that the libraries bring to the development of your applications. If you plan to design library components yourself – either extensions to the libraries presented here, or independent developments – it will, I hope, provide you with fresh insights into the crucial problem of how to produce industrial-grade reusable software components.

Although meant for both communities, however, the discussion does not hide its bias. Whenever it has to choose between the producer's convenience and the consumer's interests, it favors the consumer. After all, any successful library will have many times more consumers than producers. So it is always legitimate to make the producers work a little harder if the result will help the consumers.

3.2 THE LIBRARY CHALLENGE

What makes library design any different from the design of other software?

The basic requirements are the same, of course: correctness, robustness, efficiency, extendibility and other fundamental software quality factors. But for libraries the stakes are higher. Components meant for large-scale reuse raise new problems:

- They must provide facilities that are useful to many possible applications of widely different nature.

- The form in which these facilities are provided (their interface) must meet the clients' needs and tastes in many different contexts.

- The documentation must be accurate and well-organized, so that a library user may quickly find the relevant information about a specific component.

- Ease of use, always an important factor, takes on a new meaning for libraries containing many components: a client author who decides to use one of these components must be able to understand quickly how to use it, and this usage information must be mnemonic enough that, after a few uses of the component, he will remember it without having to go back to the documentation.

- Since even the best library designers will think up improved techniques over time, the library design must leave a few doors open to allow for its own evolution. This is a particularly delicate problem since it must be possible to improve the library while preserving the viability of existing applications, built with earlier versions.

We will now explore some of the implications of these requirements.

3.3 SOME GENERAL PRINCIPLES

Let us look first at a number of important general design guidelines for building successful libraries.

3.3.1 Consistency

If you remember only one idea from this chapter, it should be the following principle:

The consistency principle:

All the components of a library should proceed from an overall coherent design, and follow a set of systematic, explicit and uniform conventions.

For a library on non-trivial size, having components of high individual quality is obviously necessary, but no longer sufficient; they must also fit into a homogeneous whole. If you start developing serious libraries, you will soon realize that the second requirement consumes more effort than the first.

Throughout this chapter, we will repeatedly come across the consistency issue and study the techniques that help obtain a consistent library design.

3.3.2 Abstraction and objects

The object-oriented approach has proved superior to others for building libraries because of its emphasis on data abstraction. Any good object-oriented library derives from a judicious set of abstractions.

It is not the purpose of this book to provide a theoretical discussion of how to find the proper abstractions. But much of the answer lies in the study of good examples, and I hope that the class abstractions described in the following chapters will provide a powerful guide if and when you have to design your own libraries or just to extend existing libraries.

One idea to keep in mind is that not all classes describe "objects", at least in the sense of physically recognizable objects. The literature on object-oriented analysis (which, in its current state, provides little guidance to the library designer) is largely to be blamed for spreading this naïve view of the method. What we are dealing with is data abstractions; some of these abstractions have direct correspondents in the world of external objects, but many do not. In fact those which do – and to which the object-oriented analysis literature devotes so much attention – are the obvious ones; it would be rather hard to miss in a Graphical User Interfaces library the need for classes *WINDOW* and *MENU*, or in an accounting library the need for classes *ACCOUNT* and *CUSTOMER*. The classes that are more difficult to find are those which result from intelligent design decisions.

The Vision and Store libraries, two Eiffel libraries not described in this book, which respectively cater to graphics and to object persistence (database access), provide a good illustration. Both of these libraries achieve portability and environment independence through a class *HANDLE* which provides an abstract view of the underlying platform (graphics toolkit, database management system). This is a crucial abstraction which does not directly correspond to any type of object in the usual sense of the term.

Great library design, then, results from a far-sighted choice of abstractions. This is true of object-oriented design in general, and advice on this topic may be found in books on the object-oriented method, although the key recommendation is simple: study, reuse and imitate good existing designs.

See the book "Object-Oriented Software Construction".

Here are some practical hints to help spot a class which probably does **not** cover a good abstraction:

- If the natural name for the class is a verb in the imperative form, such as *ANALYZE*, this is usually a sign of inadequate design. (I know of only one case in which such names may be justified: classes that represent command objects in an interactive system.)

The question of class names and how they can signal design flaws is discussed further in 3.8.10, page 101 below.

- Similarly, a name ending with *er*, such as *ANALYZER*, should also be considered as a warning of possible trouble, although in some cases it may be just fine provided the class does not fall into the next pitfall. The question of class naming will be discussed in more detail below.

- A class has no parent and only one exported routine is another indication that something may be amiss. Often such a class is just a functional decomposition module in object-oriented clothing.

- You should also be wary of a class that introduces no new feature, and does not effect any deferred feature inherited from a parent. This is most often the result of an over-zealous effort at classification, introducing a useless node in the inheritance graph. Almost every class should have its own features; otherwise it usually does not deserve to exist. We will study below whether this rule can suffer exceptions.

See 3.10.8, page 115.

3.3.3 Objects as machines

If the word "object", as noted above, is sometimes misleading, a better metaphor is available. In many cases we should think of each object – each instance of a class – as a little machine; the feature names are the buttons on the machine, each one corresponding to one of the operations offered by the machine.

Classes, then, are meta-machines – machines to make machines. A library user has a number of meta-machines – the library's classes – at his disposal; each describes the specification of a potentially infinite number of similar machines, which the client software may create at its will during execution.

3.3.4 The command-query separation principle

When we design the machines, the Eiffel method suggests that we should carefully distinguish between two kinds of "button", that is to say, two kinds of feature. Some of the buttons on a machine cause the machine to change its state. Others make it possible to obtain information about that state; in a non-software machine, they would light up some display, showing the value of that information, for example a temperature or a voltage.

Features of the first kind are the **commands**; they are implemented as procedures (computations which may modify the target object, but do not return a result). Features of the second kind are the **queries**; they may be implemented either as functions (computations which return a result, but do not modify the target object in any externally observable way) or as attributes (data fields, present in each instance of the class). Together, procedures and functions are called routines.

The most important practical consequence of the injunction to distinguish between queries and commands is to prohibit *side-effect-producing functions*, a programming style which has been particularly popularized by C. A side-effect-producing function changes some of the computation's context, for example the state of some objects and the values of some entities, and also returns a result.

The reason for prohibiting side-effect-producing functions is covered in detail elsewhere; it follows from the observation that such functions gravely endanger clarity and reliability, by making expressions evaluate to values that may be quite different from what a simple reading suggests. For example, if f may produce side effects (change some of the values accessible outside of f), then evaluating the expression $f(a)$ + $f(a)$ may produce some unpredictable results. Also, elementary mathematical properties, such as the equivalence of this expression to $2 * f(a)$, cease to be satisfied.

On why functions with side effects should be avoided, see the discussion in the book "Object-Oriented Software Construction".

The command-query separation principle is not enforced by the Eiffel language for two reasons. First, it is a rather radical departure from common practices, so it was felt inappropriate to impose it on people who may not fully appreciate it, or plainly disagree with it, and still want to benefit from the rest of the Eiffel approach. Second, the prohibition only applies to visible side effects; some internal side effects are tolerable (again, please refer for details to the book mentioned above), but the task of distinguishing between "bad" and "acceptable" side effects is not easily performed by a compiler.

Although not imposed by the language, however, the principle is definitely part of the Eiffel method and has prevailed throughout the construction of Base and other Eiffel libraries. This explains some peculiarities which, when first encountered, may surprise the reader accustomed to older approaches. For example, the classes performing sequential input, such as *FILE*, do not have the traditional *get* function to read an element (such as an integer) and return its value. Such a feature would be a side-effect-producing function: it returns a result, the element read, but also changes the state by moving the input cursor irrevocably over that element. Instead, class *FILE* uses feature pairs, each with a command and a query, typically used under the form

my_file.readreal;
some_value := *my_file.lastreal*

where *lastreal* (and similarly for *lastint* etc.) contains the value of the last element read. These queries do not change the state: successive calls to *lastreal* will always return the same value if there is no intervening *readreal*.

Surprising as it may be at first to newcomers, the command-query separation principle has yielded a characteristic design style which, in my opinion, is a central reason for the reliability and ease of use of Base and other Eiffel libraries.

3.4 DESIGN BY CONTRACT

The next set of general design principles comes from the use of assertions, the embodiment of the Design by Contract principle.

3.4.1 Using assertions

A library is made of a number of classes, each characterized by the set of its exported features.

For a well-designed library, each one of these features corresponds to the implementation of a useful piece of functionality on the data abstraction represented by the class. That functionality should be characterized by a specification, as precise as possible – the feature's contract. It is the role of the assertions and the header comment to express the contract. Assertions cover what can be stated formally; the header comment covers the rest.

The presence of assertions, as discussed in the previous chapter, is essential. Without them it would be impossible to characterize properly the effect of features.

3.4.2 Invariants

Aside from preconditions and postconditions, invariants provide a powerful way to characterize the semantics of a class. Whether you are learning to use a library class or building a new class of your own, do not hesitate to spend all the necessary time to explore the relations between the various queries of each class (in particular its attributes) and derive the corresponding invariant clauses. This is time well used. In fact this effort is required if you really want to understand what the class is about.

Here is an example of invariant – for class *LIST* – which shows the many relations that exist between features of a class. Note that except for minor details this is the way in which the invariant appears in the flat-short form given later in this book, but the actual clause appearing in the class itself is shorter; the full invariant reconstructed by the flat-short operation includes all ancestors' invariant clauses.

The flat-short form of LIST, appears in 16.4, page 295. It lists the same clauses in a different order and with assertion tags.

---

not (*after* **and** *before*);
off = (*after* **or** *before*) ;
before = (*index* = *0*); *after* = (*index* = *count* + *1*);
empty = (*count* = *0*);
empty **implies** *off*;
count >= *0*;
offleft = *before* **or** *empty*; *offright* = *after* **or** *empty*;
index >= *0*; *index* <= *count* + *1*;
off = ((*index* = *0*) **or** (*index* = *count* + *1*));
isfirst = (*index* = *1*);
(**not** *off*) **implies** (*item* = *i_th* (*index*));
writable **implies** *readable*;
empty **implies** (**not** *readable* **and not** *writable*);
empty **implies** *off*; *off* **implies** *exhausted*

Here is what the first few clauses of this invariant tell us about the various consistency properties that must hold between the queries of the class:

- Queries *after*, which indicates whether the cursor is after the last element if any, and *before*, which indicates whether it is before the first element if any, cannot both be true. (If you think that this property is obvious, think again: it requires a proper convention for what *after* and *before* mean for an empty list.)

- The list is said to be *off* if and only if it is either *after* or *before* (but not both, which is impossible because of the previous clause).

- The elements are numbered from 1 to *count*, implying relations between *before*, *after*. 1, *count* and *index* (the current integer position of the cursor).

- The empty list is characterized by a zero number of elements.

And so on. Needless to say, such exhaustive clauses also provide a thorough mechanism for quality assurance and debugging, as you will be able to catch many of the potential mistakes simply by enabling assertion monitoring and finding out that an invariant clause is violated.

3.4.3 Explicit restrictiveness, or the tough love principle

How strong should the preconditions be? This is an important question of class design. Two general design policies are possible:

- In a *tolerant* approach, the library routines have weak preconditions, or no preconditions. (Having no precondition is the same as having **true** as precondition.) This means that routines have an effect for most or all possible calls; for calls which correspond to abnormal cases and cannot yield the results expected in normal cases, a routine will either do nothing or produce some special result to notify the client of an abnormal situation.

- A *demanding* approach is the reverse: routines have preconditions which protect them against cases that cannot be handled using the normal algorithm. This means that the responsibility of handling these cases rests not with the supplier but with the client.

A typical example where we have to choose between these two policies is that of a stack class including a feature that removes the top of a stack, and one which accesses the top of a stack. For reasons explained below, these features will be called *remove* and *item* (rather than the more traditional "pop" and "top") in the stack classes of the Data Structure library. Should *remove* and *item*, using a tolerant policy, accept requests applied to an empty stack, and try to do something sensible in this case? Or should they be demanding, in other words have a precondition of the form

   not *empty*

which requires clients to call the features on non-empty stacks only, leaving them with the responsibility of ensuring that property, and not guaranteeing any result if it is not satisfied?

> Often the choice between tolerant and demanding is not as clear-cut; there may be several possible preconditions, some more tolerant, some more demanding.

Given the radical consumer-rights declaration at the beginning of this chapter, you may expect this section to endorse the tolerant approach. In fact it does exactly the reverse. The experience of the Base libraries and many other developments has shown that trying to be all things to all clients is the wrong way of helping them.

The example of *remove* and *item* for stacks is a good way to understand why, when it comes to serving clients, less can be more. At first a *remove* procedure which handles empty stacks may appear helpful. But in most cases it is not. What is the meaning of an attempt to pop an empty stack? It may be a boundary case, in which the *remove* procedure should do nothing; it may be an exceptional but expected case, in which *remove* should record somewhere that is was called on an empty stack; or it may be a software error – a bug in the client code, which should never have called *remove* with an empty stack. But the author of the stack class **has no way to know** which of these three hypotheses is the right one. Who is he to decide for the client what, if anything, *remove* should do for an empty stack? Only the context of the client – a parsing module, a memory management module or any other of the many different kinds of module that may require a stack – can determine what an empty stack means, and what the desired action is.

The case of *item* is even more flagrant. In this case the "do nothing" approach is not possible, since *item* is a query that must return a result (of the same type as the stack elements). How in the world could a stack module determine what result is expected by the client in this case?

This example is representative of hundreds of others that occur throughout the Base libraries. It is a mistake to believe that client authors (the consumers) prefer know-it-all features which try to guess their intentions in all possible cases, including erroneous cases. What they need is a precise specification of what they must do to be entitled to use the routine, and what they will get in return. This is why specifying the contract is so essential, and why it is impossible to build a good library without an assertion mechanism. With the contract specification tools in place, you do not need to bend over backwards trying to handle cases for which the operations make no sense anyway; instead, you define the cases which do make sense, and you publicize both your requirements and your promises.

The policy described here may be called **explicit restrictiveness**: designing features that are as restrictive as may be necessary to provide useful functionality, and making all the restrictions explicit so that client authors know exactly their obligations. Another name for this approach is the "tough love principle": one can be strict and be helpful or, in this case, be strict *so as to* be helpful.

Classically trained readers may prefer to call this the "Qui bene amat bene castigat" principle.

This approach has been applied throughout the Base libraries and shows that it is possible for the same technique to be beneficial to both clients and suppliers (consumers and producers):

- Authors of client modules know that each library class provides a useful implementation of a well-defined contract. They know what to expect from each routine, and also know the set of reasonable requirements that they have to satisfy to obtain it.

- Authors of library classes can devote their entire attention to the meaningful cases, so as to handle them in the best possible manner – correctly and efficiently. They do not need to try to second-guess client authors for cases which are meaningless. They do not risk wasting their efforts and (more importantly) compromising the design quality of their products because of such cases. They avoid the need to use ad-hoc techniques such as setting global error indicators, outputting messages on some medium which may or may not be the right one and may or may not be available, devising special values for impossible results, and so on.

Base is entirely designed in this way. Each feature states in its *require* clause what conditions (if any) it demands in order to do its job properly, and then relies on these conditions in its body (its *do* clause).

The reaction of the user community has consistently confirmed that the "tough love" approach, based on reasonably and explicitly restricted features, yields libraries that are practical and easy to use.

3.4.4 What restrictions are acceptable?

Explicit restrictiveness assumes, of course, that the restrictions are reasonable. Otherwise it would be easy to produce an impressive library: just write classes with hundreds of routines which promise the moon through extravagant postconditions, but all have precondition clauses of the form *require false* followed by an empty body.

Let us explore more precisely what "reasonable" means for preconditions. A restriction is acceptable if the reason behind it can be readily understood and accepted by authors of client modules. This means two categories of conditions:

R1 • Those which are logically necessary for the underlying abstract operation to make sense.

R2 • Those which, if not satisfied, would cause considerable loss of efficiency, for reasons that can easily be explained to client authors (that is to say, reasons that intrinsically follow from the nature of the abstract operation, not from the internal choices made by the library producer for the implementation of the routine).

Conditions which do **not** fall into any of these categories, and are therefore not acceptable, are those which are only a consequence of the implementation technique used by the library producer. The reason in this case is purely internal, and cannot be justified in a way that is acceptable to the clients.

An example of category R1 is the stack case above: the *not empty* requirement for *remove* and *item* follows from the very nature of the underlying abstract operations – popping a stack and accessing its top item. In fact, the mathematical specification of the abstract data type *STACK*, which is implicit in any stack class, includes the corresponding preconditions.

An example of case R2 is the precondition of procedure *put* for class *ARRAY*. The procedure, when called under the form *some_array.put* (*some_value*, *i*), replaces by *some_value* the value of the array element at index *i*. The precondition requires *i* to be between the current array bounds. It turns out that Eiffel arrays are (as arrays should always be) resizable; so in principle *put* could dispense with the precondition, and silently resize the array if *i* is out of bounds. As any user of the library will readily understand, however, resizing is a much more expensive operation than the normal array modification; in fact, resizing must usually re-allocate the array and copy all the elements to the new location. This is the primary reason why *put* has the precondition on the index. Another procedure, *force*, has the same basic semantics as *put* but no precondition; *force* will resize the array if necessary.

We may consider in this example that category R1 also applies since for some arrays the requirement to stay within the bounds may be a logical part of the specification, not just a consequence of the desire to avoid costly resizing. Here is another example which we can justify by either R1 or R2. It comes from one of the stack classes, is *BOUNDED_STACK*, describing stacks of a fixed capacity. In that class the procedure *put*, which pushes an element on top of a stack, has the precondition *not full*. This is a logical consequence of the notion of fixed stack (R1); on the other hand, the very existence of fixed stacks is largely motivated in the first place by a reason of the R2 kind (using an array representation for the efficiency of its access operations). Since all this is easy to explain to library users, such restrictions are acceptable.

The book "Object-Oriented Software Construction" contains a detailed discussion of abstract data types, and the full formal specification of STACK.

It should be noted, however, that the Base libraries contain very few fixed structures; in fact only three (*FIXED_LIST*, *BOUNDED_STACK*, *BOUNDED_QUEUE*) in the current state of the library, out of hundreds of classes. To these one may add *FIXED_TREE*, describing describing trees whose nodes each have a finite number of children, although the nodes themselves are created dynamically with no limit on their number.

In most cases, even when the implementation uses arrays, we recommend relying on automatic resizing. Classes *ARRAYED_LIST*, *ARRAYED_STACK*, *ARRAYED_QUEUE*, and others which indirectly inherit from *BOUNDED* rather than *FINITE*, do not require any **not** *full* precondition on *put* and similar routines.

Classes BOUNDED and FINITE are discussed in 4.5.2, page 132.

3.4.5 Abstract preconditions

A thorough application of the theory of Design by Contract leads to another important technique: abstract preconditions. This technique makes it possible to handle redeclaration correctly even in cases that might at first appear to justify a departure from the rules on assertions and inheritance.

From the discussion of Design by Contract you will remember the basic rule governing the precondition of a redeclared feature: in a redeclaration (redefinition or effecting) you may weaken the precondition, through the **require else** syntax, but you may never strengthen it. Such strengthening would violate the Design by Contract principle since it would mean that a subcontractor – the redeclared feature, which through polymorphism and dynamic binding may be called in lieu of the original one – is imposing a harsher requirement than what is stated in the contract officially advertized to clients. The language syntax, which permits only **require else** but not **require** for a redeclared feature, automatically prohibits strengthening.

Assertion redeclaration was discussed in 2.7.10, page 44.

Some cases, however, may seem to require precondition strengthening. Once again, the stack classes of the Data Structure library provide a good example. Procedure *put* pushes an element on top of a stack; it is called under the form

my_stack.put (*some_element*)

The above discussion mentioned *FIXED_STACK*, an heir of class *STACK* which describes stacks with a finite size. For such stacks *put* is not always applicable: the stack must not be full. This is expressed by the precondition

count <= capacity

where *capacity* is the maximum size and *count* is the number of stack elements. If, however, *put* did not have a precondition in class *STACK*, we cannot add it to *FIXED_STACK*; this would be reinforcing the precondition. As noted, the language does not permit us to do this; any precondition that *put* may have in *FIXED_STACK* must be of the form **require else** *newpre*, where *newpre* will be **or**-ed with the original, making it equal or weaker.

The solution lies in introducing a precondition for *put* at the level of *STACK*. In that class (with formal generic parameter *G*) the routine will appear as

```
put (x: G) is
        -- Push x on top.
    require
        not full
    do
        ...
    ensure
        ...
    end
```

the class now having a new deferred feature *full*:

```
full: BOOLEAN is
        -- Is representation filled to capacity?
    deferred
    end
```

Descendants of *STACK* which do not enforce a size limitation, such as *LINKED_STACK*, effect *full* so that it never returns true:

```
full: BOOLEAN is
        -- Is representation filled to capacity? (Answer: no.)
    do
        Result := false
    end
```

In class *FIXED_STACK*, however, *full* determines whether the representation has been filled to capacity:

```
full: BOOLEAN is
        -- Is representation filled to capacity?
    do
        Result := (count = capacity)
    end
```

It may seem at first that such a change violates the subcontracting rule. Assume that in class *STACK* *full* were not deferred but effective and always true, as it is in *LINKED_STACK*; then the above scheme would still work, even though we have weakened *full* in *FIXED_STACK*. But in reality there is no violation. All that counts is that the precondition **as seen abstractly by the client** should remain the same or weaker. This is satisfied here, since the abstract precondition is still *full*, enabling a client to ensure that a call will always be correct, for example by writing it as

if not *my_stack.full* **then**
    my_stack.put (*some_element*)
end

where *my_stack* is declared of type *STACK* [*SOME_TYPE*] but can become polymorphically attached to an instance of some other descendant of *STACK*, including *FIXED_STACK*. The protected call will work for all possible cases thanks to the test for *full*.

A precondition such as this one, relying on a deferred boolean feature which descendants can effect in various way, is called an **abstract precondition**.

> A potential criticism of the approach described here is that it may force you to go back to an existing class and add abstract preconditions to some of its routines, simply because a descendant is adding a requirement. But this is the inevitable price to pay for using inheritance, the "is-a" relation, in this manner. If we want *C* to be a descendant of *A*, then, because an object known as an *A* may actually be a *C*, an operation of *A* may actually denote an operation of *C*. So if the *C* version of the operation has more restrictions than the default *A* version, there must be some way for clients to comply with these restrictions even if the only supplier they know about is *A*. In particular if the original design of *A* did not include any restrictions at all, we must adapt it to include a restriction, even if only an abstract one.

3.5 DOCUMENTING LIBRARY CLASSES

What is the most effective way of documenting a library class? The answer is of particular importance to the success of a library. Here the method of Design by Contract and the notion of short form contribute the fundamental idea, on which class specifications rely throughout this book.

3.5.1 How to document a class

Following traditional approaches to software documentation, we would document a class either through the class text itself, or through some separate description written by software developers or technical writers (or through some combination of these solutions). Each of these forms of documentation has serious drawbacks:

- The software's source text is not abstract enough. Along with information that is interesting for client authors, it includes all low-level implementation properties. This raises two serious risks: drowning client authors in a mass of mostly irrelevant documentation, which leaves them with the task of sorting out the important from the futile; and encouraging them to take for granted internal implementation choices which the library producers may change with the next release of the library, invalidating the client software even if the interface is still the same.

- Documentation produced separately from the software itself raises the problem of accuracy. How to we know that what the software does is the same thing as what the documentation says it does? Guaranteeing such accuracy is difficult initially, and becomes next to impossible in the long run as both the software and the documentation evolve.

When viewed as a product separate from the software itself, documentation also raises another problem, of a practical rather than conceptual nature: finding people to write it. The problem is particularly acute for a technical product such as a library, meant for software developers rather than for the general public. Technical writers usually do not have the required knowledge, and library developers tend to shy away from writing documentation, a tedious process that requires almost as much attention as actual software development but is generally viewed as less rewarding intellectually.

The advantage of each approach is the other side of its deficiencies:

- The source text is faithful to the actual software being run.

- Separate documentation can choose to concentrate on the abstract properties that are relevant for clients.

The Eiffel approach to class documentation reconciles these advantages while avoiding the drawbacks. It bases the documentation of each class on the **flat-short form** of the class.

As you will recall, the flat-short form is the abstract interface, obtained by flattening and then shortening the class. **Flattening** means producing a version of the class that includes the features inherited from parents as well as the immediate features (those introduced in the class itself). For inherited features, the flattened form must take renaming and redeclaration into account, and reconstruct full preconditions and postconditions by *or*-ing all applicable *require* and *require else* clauses and **and**-ing all applicable *ensure* and *ensure then* clauses. **Shortening** means removing all information that is not relevant to client authors: non-exported features, *do* clauses of routines, and any clue that would enable a client author to distinguish between an attribute and a function without arguments. The short form, however, retains feature headers (which give the signature of each routine: number and types of arguments and result, if any), the header comment (which explains in informal terms the purpose of the feature) and, most importantly, preconditions, postconditions and invariants.

The notion of flat-short form was introduced in 2.7.3, page 34.

The flat-short form of a class is an excellent form of documentation, and the primary one used in part C of this book to describe the individual classes of the Base libraries. Being extracted from the class text itself, it has the advantage of accuracy; but it only includes the interface properties that are of interest to library users.

The use of the flat-short form as primary documentation format is only possible because of the presence of assertions, which make it possible to express precise yet abstract properties of each feature (through preconditions and postconditions) and of a class as a whole (through the class invariant).

This approach to documentation has been extremely successful in the Eiffel community and has enabled many people to learn the Eiffel libraries quickly and use them to great benefit.

3.5.2 Reading the flat-short forms

If you are familiar with the basics of the approach you will have no trouble understanding the flat-short forms of part C. In fact you only need to know a subset of the mechanisms introduced in the preceding chapter, since the flat-short forms do not use any of the operational aspects of the approach: assignments, control structures, procedure calls and other forms of instructions. One may indeed view the notation of flat-short class interfaces as a **specification language**, obtained by removing all operational constructs from a wide-spectrum language – the Eiffel notation – that covers specification and design as well as implementation.

One notational device, which you will frequently encounter in reading the flat-short forms, deserves a comment. In the discussion of Design by Contract we encountered the notion of subcontracting, resulting from inheritance, redefinition, polymorphism and dynamic binding, and yielding the rules on assertion redeclaration: the assertions on a redeclared routine, if present, should be of the forms

This discussion was briefly previewed in 2.7.15, page 50.

> *require else* ...
> *ensure then* ...

The associated semantics is that after one or more redeclarations the successive preconditions (*require* and *require else* clauses) will be or-ed, and the successive (*ensure* and *ensure then* clauses) will be and-ed.

The flat-short form shows the reconstructed assertions. This could have been done by building a boolean expression including all the needed *or* for preconditions and *and* for postconditions – corresponding essentially to what a compiler internally does to implement the semantics of redeclared assertions. But the result would not have been very readable and would have failed to reflect the accumulation process that leads to a complex assertion.

*The operators are in fact **or else** and **and then**; see "Eiffel: The Language" for an explanation of the difference.*

A different convention was chosen. A reconstructed multi-clause assertion will start with *require* or *ensure*, and continue with one or more *require else* or *ensure then* clauses, showing the accumulation of clauses coming from the earlier versions of the feature. Here for example is how procedure *put*, which pushes an item of a stack, appears in the flat-short form of *ARRAYED_STACK*:

The interface of ARRAYED_ STACK is in 17.3, page 335.

---

put (*v*: **like** *item*)
      -- Push v onto top.
  require
    extendible: *extendible*
  ensure
    item_pushed: *item* = *v*
  ensure then
    one_more_occurrence: *occurrences* (*v*) = **old** *occurrences* (*v*) + *1*
  ensure then
    item_inserted: *has* (*v*)

The various subclauses of the postcondition come from the successive ancestors:

- The property labeled *item_pushed* comes from class *STACK*, a parent of *ARRAYED_STACK*. It states the fundamental last-in first-out property of stacks: the last element pushed will be the first one retrieved.

- The property *one_more_occurrence* comes from *BAG*. It is possible to treat a stack as a bag (a collection of elements where multiple occurrences are distinguished); *put* will add one more occurrence of the pushed element.

- The property *item_inserted* comes from *COLLECTION*. If we treat a stack as a collection, the just inserted element will be found to be present by a subsequent call to the search query *has*.

As this example shows, the order of the various subclauses is from the most recent redeclaration to the most distant ancestor. This corresponds to the language semantics and also has the advantage of listing the most specific properties first.

Occasionally the results of such assertion accumulation may appear strange to the untrained eye. For example the flat-short form of *STRING* contains the following feature specification:

23.4, page 430.

---

prune (*c*: *CHARACTER*)
      -- Remove first occurrence of *c*, if any.
  require
     true
  require else
     prunable: *prunable*

To the casual observer this will look silly: **true or** *prunable* is the same thing as **true**, and it is common practice to omit the **require** clause altogether when the precondition is **true**. The picture is clear, however, if you view *STRING* not as an isolated class but as a component of the overall data structure taxonomy. Feature *prune*, when it shows up in *STRING*, does not walk in without warning; it is preceded by a long and distinguished lineage going as far back as *COLLECTION*, one of the highest levels of ancestry possible. At some point along the chain, its original precondition *prunable* was weakened to require just **true**, that is to say, nothing at all. The flat-short form shows some trace of the feature's history; although not immediately useful to a client using *STRING* independently of anything else, this information is precious for polymorphic usage and, more generally, to understand the class and its place in the overall order of things.

> Both of the preceding examples also evidence, through their preconditions, a property of the assertions that appear throughout the Base libraries: every assertion clause is labeled, with results that are sometimes surprising at first. For abstract preconditions such as *extendible* and *prunable* whose names are simple and clear there was not much room for creative labels, so the label simply repeats the assertion. Here too the consistency principle prevailed: better include a few redundant labels, the reasoning went, than depart from the healthy rule that all assertions should be labeled.

3.5.3 Documentation by reference: how flat should flat-short be?

Early versions of this book relied on a fully flat form of the flat-short documentation: the entry for each class listed all the exported features of the class, whether they were introduced in the class, inherited from a parent and redeclared, inherited and renamed, or inherited with no change.

This **full-flat** approach has the advantage of consistency and completeness. When you see the documentation for a class you know that you have everything you need to write a client class, concentrated in a single place.

When applied to a large library, however, the full-flat approach also has a serious drawback: it produces bulky and redundant documents. If a class has many descendants, its features will appear in the documentation of each one of these descendants. This is particularly true in the Base libraries because of its extensive use of inheritance; almost every class documented in this book, for example, includes the half-dozen or so features from *CONTAINER*, some of which, such as *object_comparison*, are useful in certain cases only.

About 'object_comparison' see 4.3.2, page 126.

Had the full-flat method been applied to this book, the total length would have exceeded a thousand pages, for not more information than what it has in its present form. It might actually have been less convenient to use because of the sheer mass of repetitive information. The problem here is the nature of printed documents, which are poorly adapted to the dissemination of redundant information. In an interactive environment such as the browsing facilities of ISE Eiffel 3 (as sketched at the end of the previous chapter), or with hypertext tools, the question would call for different solutions, although in all cases it is essential to provide readers or users with mechanisms enabling them to go directly to the essential information.

> By default the flat-short forms never include the features of the general-purpose classes *GENERAL*, *PLATFORM* and *ANY*. This at least avoids repeating for each class the universal features, such as *equal* and *clone*, which are applicable to all classes.

We might try the opposite extreme of the full-flat method – what may be called the **short-only** form of documentation. In this approach each class specification would only list, in short form, the immediate features of each class (those which are introduced or redeclared locally) and the list of parent classes. But this remedy would be worse than the ill it is supposed to cure: with libraries such as Base, Vision or any other endowed with a rich multiple-inheritance structure (a characteristic of most good libraries), finding information would become a labyrinth walk; one can picture the poor library user trying to find information about a class by constantly flipping pages back and forth. Even with an interactive environment this would be very inconvenient.

The solution, then, lies between these two extremes. Full-flat is too much, short-only is too little. We need someone to make a judgment call, for each class, on which ones of the ancestor features the interface should show.

I made this judgment call for each class of the present book, aided of course by the tools of the environment. For classes which are frequently used by themselves, all features were included, or at least all features from the most important ancestors. For classes which are used less often, or which are mostly used for their own new features, the interface discards features inherited from parents in unchanged form. I based my decisions on our experience of using the classes; I hope they will prove satisfactory.

For each class of part C, the interface is preceded by a brief explanation of the judgment call – which ancestors have their features included, and which ones have theirs present only by reference. Here is an example of such a paragraph, about class *METALEX* from the Lex library:

This example comes from 21.5, page 407.

> This interface shows the features introduced or redeclared in
> *METALEX*'s parent *HIGH_BUILDER*, but not those from for other
> parents, in particular *LEX_BUILDER* which provides the more
> complete set of features. The interface of *LEX_BUILDER* appears
> next.

For consistency, the removal of features from the class interfaces implies the
removal of assertion clauses containing calls to removed queries. This explains why
some of the partially-flat class interfaces of part C show fewer postcondition and
invariant properties than the class actually possesses. Preconditions, however, always
appear in full form, since authors of client modules need to know the full precondition
to guarantee that a call is correct – to observe the contract.

Another simplification of the flat-short documentation principle, complementing the
idea of documentation by reference, is grouped documentation: some classes which
have an identical interface (because they are alternative effectings of the same deferred
ancestor) appear in a single section, the specification of one serving also for the other.
This is the case for example for *LINKED_PRIORITY_QUEUE* and *HEAP_PRIORITY_*
QUEUE, two implementations of *PRIORITY_QUEUE*, in the chapter on dispenser
classes.

*The priority queue classes
appear in 17.10, page 347.*

There is a practical difference between grouped documentation and documentation by
reference: indexing. For grouped documentation, the features appear in the index in the heading
for all the grouped classes, for example feature *put* for both *LINKED_PRIORITY_QUEUE* and
HEAP_PRIORITY_QUEUE. But when the documentation of a class interface refers to the class
interface of an ancestor, the inherited features which are not repeated in the documentation
appear in the index for the ancestor only.

If successful, the documentation style that results from these combined techniques
will work a little like virtual memory or instruction caches for computers, or like the
hash table algorithm implemented in one of the classes of this book: most of the time,
you will find information about a class at the first place where you look; but once in a
while, you will trigger a "class fault", that is to say, you will have to look in one other
place, more rarely in two.

3.5.4 Informal descriptions

Full-flat, short-only or somewhere in-between, the flat-short form of documentation
does not always suffice. It lacks context information that a client author may need to
understand what a class is about and why its features were designed in a certain way.
Such information can only be conveyed through non-formal explanations.

Such explanations appear in the chapters of part B, each one of which corresponds
to one of the chapters of part C. The part C chapter, for example chapter 21, also about
lexical analysis, gives the flat-short class specifications of a set of classes; the
corresponding part B chapter, for example chapter 11, also about lexical analysis,
contains the informal explanations and serves as a preview of the specifications.

This technique improves the clarity of the descriptions, but potentially suffers from
the accuracy problem mentioned above. If you ever run into an apparent contradiction
between the informal text in part B and the corresponding flat-short form in part C, you
should believe the flat-short form.

Somewhere between formal and informal documentation, you will find a few comment-assertions such as this postcondition clause of procedure *append* in class *STRING*, expressing that the characters of *s* have been appended to those of the current string:

This example appears in the interface of STRING, 23.4, page 430.

    -- appended: For every *i* in 1..*s*. *count, item* (**old** *count* + *i*) = *s*. *item* (i)

Properties of this kind must be expressed as comments since the assertion language does not include the quantifiers of first-order logic. such as "For every...". Although for the moment only *STRING* and a few other classes contain such comment-assertions, the libraries's evolution towards increased formality will likely cause them to become more widespread in the future.

3.5.5 Cluster-level documentation

Flat-short specifications also suffer from another obvious limitation: they are appropriate for the documentation of individual classes, but do not remove the need for more general, cluster-level descriptions, showing the overall set of classes and the relations between these classes.

A "cluster" is a group of closely related classes. See 2.2.3, page 15.

Although there will always remain a need for human-language explanations, it is possible to document the overall structure of a cluster or library with the same approach that this book applies, thanks to flat-short forms, to the documentation of individual classes: by extracting the documentation from the software text itself. For cluster-level documentation, the most appropriate way of showing the information is graphical, through cluster diagrams which clearly show the classes of the cluster and their connections. The BON method ("Business Object Notation") achieves this goal. BON provides diagramming standards to present the overall structure of an object-oriented system divided into clusters; the method is particularly good if you have a large or very large system, which BON can describe at various levels of abstraction, keeping in control of the system's complexity. The recently released EiffelCase system, developed as part of ISE Eiffel 3, directly supports BON and makes it possible to produce such manageable, multi-view system diagrams.

On BON see Jean-Marc Nerson and Kim Walden, "Seamless Object-Oriented Software Architectures", Prentice Hall, 1994.

Although EiffelCase came too late to be used for the preparation of the present book, it will will enable future library descriptions to make as systematic a use of BON diagrams as part C of this book does of flat-short forms.

3.6 THE SHOPPING LIST APPROACH: HOW BIG SHOULD A LIBRARY CLASS BE?

It is not always clear, when you are building a class, where you should stop. Should you aim for small or big classes?

Answering this question will lead us to define the "shopping list" approach. But we must first define an acceptable measure of size.

3.6.1 Metrics for library class size

In traditional programming, the conventional measure of size (often criticized but widely used) is the number of lines. This measure and most of the proposed replacements follow *internal* criteria; they are intended as a predictor of the amplitude of the task of writing the software. This is still interesting for object-oriented programming, but only from the perspective of the library producers. Here we are mainly interested in the consumer's perspective, so we will focus on *external* criteria – those which make sense for the clients.

Let us first see what is **not** relevant in measures of size. We are not interested in the size of any particular routine (in number of instructions, number of lines or some other measure). The library user could not be less interested; and even from the producer's viewpoint, code size is not always a good indication of complexity in object-oriented software construction.

What really matters for the present discussion is the functionality offered by the classes of library. A piece of functionality, in the object-oriented method, is a feature. So the most attractive way to measure class size, and the one on which the rest of this discussion is based, is to count the **number of features** of each class.

This choice still leaves two questions open as to which features we should consider:

• Should we count exported features only, or all features?

• Should we only count the features introduced by the class itself, or include those which it inherits from its parents?

First, the question of export status. For the library consumers, all that matters is exported features; they do not care about non-exported features, which are used for implementation purposes only, and which they cannot use directly. (For simplicity, "exported features" will include only those which are exported to all clients; features exported selectively to some clients only will be treated as non-exported.) If we take the producer's viewpoint, however, all features, exported or not, have to be written. So if we are trying to evaluate the functionality of a library from the client's perspective, as will usually be the case, we should consider exported features only; but we should include all features whenever we want to correlate the measure with the effort needed to produce the class.

Next, the question of what to do with features from parents. In Eiffel terminology, the "features of a class" include both the features declared in the class itself, called its **immediate** features, and those which it obtains from its parents, called **inherited** features. Another subset includes both the immediate features and those among the inherited features which are redeclared (redefined or effected) in the class. This gives rise to different notions of size:

Definitions (size of a class):

• The **flat size** of a class is the number of its features.

• The **immediate size** of a class is the number of its immediate features.

• The **incremental size** of a class is the number of its immediate and redeclared features.

If these measures include non-exported features, they are called **internal** (internal flat size etc.); if they only include exported features they are called **external**. In the absence of further qualification, they always denote the external sizes.

The term "flat size" follows from the Eiffel notion of flat form of a class – the reconstructed form which includes the features inherited from parents as well as the immediate features.

Which of the measures should we use? If we consider a class in isolation, as seen from a client, the (external) flat size seems appropriate; indeed what the library users will see in the standard flat-short documentation of classes, as used in this book, is all the exported features, which correspond to the flat size.

In this discussion, however, the question is whether we should put any limits on class size. Were we to adopt flat size as the measure, the only reasonable answer to that question would be "no limits whatsoever", since imposing an upper bound on the total number of features would mean restricting the depth of inheritance graphs and hence the ability to inherit ever increased functionality from ancestors. Any such attempt would put a severe limitation on the power of the object-oriented method.

It is more reasonable, then, when studying possible methodological rules that might put a ceiling on the size of classes, to use the immediate size or the incremental size. Arguments may be found for choosing either of these measures. We will use the incremental size because it is a good indicator of the class's own added value, independently of any functionality inherited "as is" from the parents. (If we took a bit too seriously the analogy suggested by the word "inheritance", this would mean that we tax people only on what they earn or improve as a result of their own work, but not on any capital they may have inherited and left idle.)

> A small practical incentive for using incremental size is that it is somewhat easier to measure than immediate size. With a parser, or just a text processing tool, it suffices to count the number of feature declarations. To count the immediate size, you need a more ambitious apparatus: since you must distinguish between new features and redeclarations of inherited features, you cannot do the measurement on just the text of one class, and you need to have access to a semantic data structure giving the features of each class and the inheritance relations between classes. This does not raise any particular problem if you can perform your measurements by instrumenting an existing compiler, but makes things harder if you do not have access to the internals of a compiler.

For the rest of this discussion, then, "size of a class" means the incremental size – the number of immediate and redeclared features. Following the convention mentioned earlier, we will be looking, unless explicitly specified otherwise, at the **external** incremental size, considering exported features only.

3.6.2 The shopping list approach

Now that we have a suitable definition of class size (or more precisely a few variants of the same basic definition – number of features), we may examine whether to put limits on that size. How far should we allow a class to grow?

Beyond a certain size, a class can becomes complex and unmanageable. It is impossible to say precisely what that pragmatic threshold is; when I asked various developers having played a key role in the Base libraries what they thought was a reasonable average size, I got rather diverse answers – and some non-answers, of the form "the number of features is irrelevant, they just have to be the right features". I do, however, suggest the following rough guidelines, which correspond to what you will find in most Base classes: the vast majority have between 5 and 20 immediate features, with a few particularly important ones reaching the forties, and some going into the fifties or higher. (Some precise measurements will be given below.)

As to the maximum allowable size, a class with more than 80 new features should prompt you to ask whether it is too big and needs to be split (through inheritance). Only to ask: the class may be fine as it is, but you should take a closer look.

Such numbers, however, are not that interesting. The more fundamental question is: how much extra baggage should we allow beyond the absolutely indispensable features of a class?

A group which has been quite vocal, the minimalist school, holds that a library class should only contain the fundamental operations on an abstract data type − what we may call the **atomic** features. Any redundant operation − meaning any feature that can be expressed in terms of the atomic features − should be kept out of the class for the sake of simplicity and small size.

The minimalist view, in my opinion, is highly detrimental to the quality of a library. It favors the producers' convenience − the smaller the classes, the easier they are to write and maintain, there is no doubt about that! − over the consumers' needs. If you use a library, it is because you want it to do things for you. If you need a certain piece of functionality and discover that the producers left it out simply because it is not atomic and so can be programmed using other facilities (in other words, because *you* can program it from those facilities), you are entitled to hold a grudge against these producers. As a library user, little do you care about how small the classes are; you care about the possibilities that they offer to you.

There are limits anyway to how small even the most fanatical minimalist will want classes to be. Here is a good example. Consider a container class representing data structures which can be traversed by moving a "cursor", as will often be the case in the structures studied in subsequent chapters. In such a class a function *has* may be written, which determines whether a certain element *v* occurs in the structure under consideration. Here is a simple implementation of *has*:

> *This example was suggested by Frédéric Deramat. The function 'has' was already encountered, in a slightly different form, in 2.7.5, page 37.*

```
has (v: G): BOOLEAN is
        -- Does v occur in the structure?
    do
        from
            start
        until
            after or else equal (v, item)
        loop
            forth
        end;
        Result := not after
    end
```

> *G is the formal generic parameter of the enclosing class, i.e. the type of the elements in the container.*

Here *start* is the procedure which moves the cursor to the first position, if any; *forth* advances it by one position; *after* is true if and only if the cursor is past the last position (if the structure is empty, *start* will cause *after* to become true, so the loop body will never be executed); and *item* yields the element at cursor position, if any. These features are atomic, since none of them can be expressed in terms of the others; but *has* is non-atomic, and so, from a minimalist perspective, redundant.

Few people, however, would argue that *has* should be left out of the class. (At least one may hope so.) This feature provides important functionality, is frequently needed, and re-writing it from the atomic features requires non-trivial work on the part of the library user.

Such an example, and many other similar ones, make it impossible to sustain the minimalist view in its extreme form. The choice of features will always result from a designer's decision of whether each potential feature is *pragmatically* useful to library users, not just from a yes-or-no determination of whether it is *theoretically* necessary. A sustainable minimalist position, then, is simply one which recommends that in all but the more clear-cut cases the decisions should be conservative: if there is any doubt, do not include the feature in the class.

The opposite view seems more productive. It may be called the **shopping list approach** and holds that in cases of hesitation, you should opt for including the candidate feature if some conditions are satisfied, even if the feature can be expressed in terms of other already present, and even if you are not absolutely sure that it will be useful to any client author. The conditions are the obvious ones:

- The feature must fit nicely in the conceptual framework (the abstract data type) defined by the class.

- It must satisfy class correctness; in particular it must preserve the class invariant. (Remember that we are talking about exported features, which language rules require to preserve the invariant if the class is to be correct.)

- It should provide some potentially useful functionality.

- It should not duplicate the functionality of an existing feature.

- It should obey all the rules of good feature design as defined elsewhere in this chapter – rules regarding the number of arguments, use of assertions to define the contract, carefully thought-out header comment, choice of feature name, choice of feature category.

If these conditions are met, do include the feature without any qualms. One more feature will hurt no one – and may well help someone tremendously.

The shopping list approach sometimes seems scary at first: does it not lead to classes that become so complex as to grow out of control? But such a risk does not exist if we combine the shopping list approach with the rather stringent design rules introduced in the rest of this chapter. In particular:

- Each feature is characterized by a well-defined contract. Features will be accessed through their specifications, not through their implementations.

- The class documentation follows a uniform and helpful format, showing the contract for each feature and ignoring details that are not relevant to library users.

- Feature names follow strict principles, detailed below. In many cases just seeing the name of a feature will immediately tell the library user what the feature is about.

- Features are grouped in precisely defined categories, providing a strong structuring principle in the library documentation.

- The categories are the same for all classes and always appear in the same order; within a category, the features are always listed alphabetically.

Most of the time, people who are concerned that too many features will lead to complex and unusable classes have not been exposed to these rules and, more generally, to the techniques of professional library construction. It is true that without such rules the classes could become a mess, making the whole library dream fade away. But with a systematic approach to library construction there is no such risk.

To illustrate the shopping list approach, a good example is provided by the *STRING* class of the Kernel library. With its 61 exported features, it is definitely not minimalist, and may in fact be close to the upper bound of the reasonable size for a class. (For that reason we use it to test the speed of compilers and other tools of the environment.) It is possible to criticize this class as having numerous features that from a theoretical point of view may not be essential properties of the *STRING* abstract data type, such as *replace_substring*, *fill_blank* and *left_adjust*. But the practitioners' viewpoint is different. I do not recall any library user complaining about the class size; but I do recall requests for even more features.

A class is a machine that the library designer builds for his clients. (As noted at the beginning of this chapter it is actually a machine to create machines, the objects, but we can ignore this distinction here.) As long as the machine's design is elegant, its structure consistent, its operation easy and its facilities useful, it is in no one's interest – neither the supplier's nor the client's – to limit the power of the machine. If you are the client, you will want as much functionality as possible for your money (or, if the software is free, for your efforts in installing it). If you are the supplier, it is your responsibility to give clients all the features they may need. The more the better.

3.6.3 Some statistics

It is interesting to examine the classes of the Base libraries in light of the above discussion. Here is the distribution of the number of features per class.

> The measures cited in this chapter result from an analysis of the Base libraries described in this book, including not just the Kernel, Data Structure and Iteration libraries but also Lex and Parse. In addition, some measures apply to the significantly bigger Vision library, which covers graphical user interfaces. All percentages (except if less than 1) have been rounded to the nearest integer, which explains why in some cases the percentages do not exactly add up to 100.

0 to 5 features	45
6 to 10 features	17
11 to 15 features	11
16 to 20 features	9
21 to 40 features	13
41 to 80 features	4
81 to 142 features	1

Figure 3.1:
Incremental size of
classes in Base
(exported features
only): percentages

These figures are derived from 149 classes totaling 1823 exported features. They suggest some immediate comments:

- Most classes would satisfy a minimalist. Close to two-thirds have ten exported features or less. Only one in twenty classes has more than 40 features.
- Big classes, however, do exist; in practice, they tend to be some of the most important and useful classes, such as *STRING* (61 exported features) and *TREE* (44 exported features), although in a few cases the size is simply due to a need to interface with many external mechanisms (*UNIX_FILE*, 105 exported features) or to provide a set of constants (*ASCII*, 142 features).
- A significant minority (13%) are in the "medium" range: 21 to 40 features.

The pattern evidenced by these figures applies to a more application-oriented libraries such as Vision. In this case the percentages were computed for 546 classes containing 3666 exported features.

0 to 5 features	68
6 to 10 features	12
11 to 15 features	7
16 to 20 features	4
21 to 40 features	6
41 to 78 features	2

Figure 3.2:
Incremental size of classes in Vision (exported features only): percentages

Here there is a larger percentage of small classes, but there remains a need for a few big classes with as many as 78 features.

It is interesting to examine what the statistics become if we take all features into account, including those which are exported selectively to some clients, or not at all. The figures apply to 2317 features for Base and 5293 features for Vision.

	Base	Vision
0 to 5 features	37	55
6 to 10 features	23	18
11 to 15 features	7	7
16 to 20 features	6	5
21 to 40 features	16	10
41 to 80 features	9	4
81 features or more	2	0.4

Figure 3.3:
Incremental size of classes (all features): percentages

The ratio of total feature count to exported feature count is 1.27 for Base and 1.44 for Vision. This seems to be in line with experience from other libraries and indicates that developers write a non-exported feature for every two to four exported features.

3.6.4 Minimalism revisited

The main criticism that may be addressed to the minimalist approach in light of the preceding observations is that it confuses complexity with functionality. Complexity should be minimized, but functionality should be maximized. A library designer should make his classes as easy to learn and use as he can, but he should not lose track of the primary goal of library design, which is to provide as many useful facilities as possible.

Viewed against this goal, the advice to limit class size seems dubious. Assume that the controversy hinges on whether to add a set of non-atomic features to a class C. Assume further that these features are useful to some clients and their functionality not trivially provided by other, already present features; without this assumption there is no controversy, since no methodologist will advocate including the features in any class. Then three attitudes are possible:

M1 • Not including the features anywhere.

M2 • Adding them to C.

M3 • Writing a new class D, a descendant of C, and making them features of D.

M1 is not tenable if the library supplier wants to satisfy his clients. In the choice between M2 and M3, the only criterion that counts is the proper application of object-oriented design principles, which hold that any class should be the implementation of some abstract data type. The relevant question is then: are the features conceptually part of the abstract data type represented by C, or do they represent a significant enough extension or change of viewpoint to justify introducing a new abstract data type?

If there is indeed room for a new abstraction, D should be introduced even if C is a small class. If not, the features should be added to C even if this makes C a big class. In either case, the size of C is almost irrelevant. All that matters is the designer's perception of whether there is a new abstract data type or not.

That this perception is entirely subjective may explain the intuitive attraction of the minimalist approach: it is so tempting, in cases that require design decisions (in other words, cases that require *thinking*), to rely instead on concrete, quantitative, easily enforceable rules such as "no more than 10 immediate or redeclared features per class". But such rules do not solve anything. If our goal really is to minimize complexity, adding a new class to the inheritance graph is often worse, in its effect on the system's structure, than adding a few possibly non-essential features to a class.

These observations are all the more important that a strong minimalist current does run through the Eiffel method. The language, in particular, is the result of a minimalist construction. The book *Eiffel: The Language* names, as the major design rule, the Principle of Uniqueness, which states that

> *The language design should provide one good way to express every operation of interest; it should avoid providing two.*

See "Eiffel: The Language" (Prentice Hall, 1992), appendix B, "On language design and evolution".

It is hard to be more minimalist than that. The book also mentions that one of the principal goals was to maximize the "signal-to-noise" ratio: to include a small number of powerful constructs (the signal) and exclude any construct with marginal value (the noise).

Not only is there no contradiction between minimalism in language design and maximalism (of the kind suggested above) in library design, but each of them is made possible by the other. The language is the obligatory vehicle for anyone who ever uses the method; because every such user will have to learn all of it, it is crucial to rid it of any non-essential element. Every potential addition must be weighed carefully, as if you were embarking on a space mission for which every gram counts: should I take a small toothbrush or a bag of seeds? A pillow or my favorite volume of Proust? But the libraries are different. Precisely because the language is small, enabling its users to master it entirely, they will only need to look at the library classes which they need; and if the library design has observed the strict guidelines of this book on class organization, feature categories and systematic naming, the library users will quickly find the features that they need, learn to use them, and ignore the others. The more potentially useful features you have included, the more clients you will make happy.

When the rocket reaches the space colony and you unpack the seeds, having wisely picked them over the toothbrush and been permitted to take them precisely because they were so light, you may plant them and watch their progeny proliferate to feed the hungry newcomers. No one then may complain that the garden is too rich.

3.7 THE SIZE OF FEATURE INTERFACES

More relevant than class size to the usability of a library is what we may call feature size: the number of arguments of the features in the library's class. The library is used through feature calls; for each call, the client must provide zero, one or more arguments. The need to remember for each feature the number of arguments, their order, and the type of each, may be the biggest technical hurdle involved in using the library.

If there is any area where strict design principles can make the difference between success and failure in reuse, this is it. So we need to take a close look at how to keep the number of arguments to the lowest possible values.

3.7.1 Some statistics from the Base and Vision libraries

It is interesting first to examine the evidence from the libraries presented in this book, to which we may add some data from Vision.

Browsing through the class specifications in this book, you will quickly notice that most features have very few arguments. Here in fact are the actual statistics, computed over the same 149 classes of Base (including Lex and Parse) used for the above measures of class size:

Number of features	1823
Percentage of queries	59
Percentage of commands	41
Average number of arguments to a feature	**0.4**
Maximum number	3
No argument	60%
One argument	37%
Two arguments	3%
Three arguments	0.3%

Figure 3.4:
Arguments to exported features in Base

The average is one-half argument per exported feature; two-fifths of the features have no argument whatsoever; what is perhaps most remarkable is that no feature has more than three arguments, and only a handful have more than one.

Some of the features with no argument are constants, such as the 142 ASCII character codes found in class *ASCII*. But this introduces no significant bias into the above figures; if we count non-constant features only, the average becomes 0.5, with 54% of the features having with no argument, 42% having one and 3% having two.

One of the classes cited earlier as being both large and important, *TREE*, provides a typical example. None of its 44 exported features has more than one argument; 31 of them – more than two thirds – have no argument.

It is also interesting to study what the figures become if we take non-exported features as well. (Non-exported here means either secret or selectively exported to some classes only.) Here is the result:

Number of features	1817
Percentage of queries	60
Percentage of commands	40
Average number of arguments to a feature	**0.5**
Maximum number	6
No argument	57%
One argument	36%
Two arguments	5%
Three arguments	1%
Four arguments	0.6%
Five or six arguments	0.2%

Figure 3.5:
Arguments to all
features in Base

Non-exported features tend to have slightly more arguments, but the difference hardly affects the average number (which grows to 0.5 from 0.4); the main novelty is the presence of a few features with longer lists (close to 2% with three and more, with a maximum of six). There are two reasons, one factual, the other more of conjecture, why non-exported features have a tendency to have a few more arguments on the average:

• A number of non-exported features provide interfaces to mechanisms from the hardware, the operating system or various software packages. They have to abide by the conventions of these mechanisms, which may require more arguments than the results of a pure object-oriented design as represented by the exported features of the Base classes. Examination of the non-exported features with the most arguments confirms that many of them indeed come from classes such as *UNIX_FILE* which provide access to external facilities.

• There may also be a conscious or unconscious tendency on the library writers' part, since they know that non-exported features are made for internal use only and will not appear in the documentation, to mellow a bit in their application of library design principles when it comes to writing such features.

All this, however, causes hardly more than a ripple. Even if we consider *only* non-exported features the statistics do not stray much from the above:

Percentage of queries	62
Percentage of commands	38
Average number of arguments to a feature	**0.9**
No argument	46%
One argument	31%
Two arguments	14%
Three arguments	4%
Four arguments	3%
Five or six arguments	1%

Figure 3.6:
Arguments to non-exported features in Base

Another influence to take into account is the nature of Base: a general-purpose library dealing with well-understood software engineers' abstractions – linked lists, binary trees and the like – rather than the more messy, human-related abstractions of an application library. One might expect an application library to have a somewhat higher number of arguments per feature, reflecting the need to handle many special cases. To investigate this conjecture we may look at Vision. This large graphics library has to take into account the many peculiarities of a window system (currently X) and individual graphical toolkits (Motif, OpenLook). Here are the figures:

Number of classes	546
Number of features	3666
Percentage of queries	39
Percentage of commands	61
Average number of arguments to a feature	**0.7**
Maximum	7
No argument	49%
One argument	32%
Two arguments	15%
Three arguments	3%
Four arguments	0.4%
Five to seven arguments	0.4%

Figure 3.7:
Arguments to exported features in Vision

Contrary to the preceding expectation, then, the average number of arguments again grows only marginally, to 0.7. Almost half of the features still have no argument, and less than a fifth have two or more. There is, however, a small number of "large" features – three to seven arguments. Examination of the library shows most of them to be creation procedures for objects requiring a number of initialization values.

The most obvious novelty of the Vision figures is the dramatic reversal of the division into commands and queries. Two-thirds of the features are now commands, as opposed to two-fifths before.

There are two possible non-exclusive explanations for this phenomenon. One is that a graphics library, by its very nature, is meant to enable its users to *do* things, as made possible by commands. The other is that in Vision, which is younger than Base, the effort of associating all the possible queries with a command (that is to say, of enabling clients, as explained below, to find out about the status of all parameters that can be set by commands) has not been pursued as thoroughly yet.

The various statistics collected above, confirmed by informal studies of good application-specific libraries, shows that it is possible to design a library, in widely different application domains, in such a way that most features have zero or very few arguments. It is reasonable to expect the following values:

- An average of about 0.5 argument per feature.
- 50% to 60% features with no argument.
- 30% to 35% with one argument.
- Less than 10% with two or more arguments, including only a few percent, if any at all, with three or more.

3.7.2 Operands and options

The number of feature arguments in most of the software libraries available today tends to be significantly higher on the average than the above guidelines suggest. In particular, Fortran and C libraries for numerical analysis (the area in which routine libraries have enjoyed the most widespread success) often have routines with many arguments. How can you manage to keep feature size down and reach the kind of figures shown above for Base and Vision?

An examination of "big" features – features with many arguments – in such non-Eiffel libraries suggests an important part of the answer. A long argument list for a feature usually contains arguments of two kinds: **operands**, representing the values on which the feature operates; **options**, representing modes that govern how the feature will operate.

This distinction was introduced in "Principles of Package Design", in Communications of the ACM, *25, 7, July 1982, pages 419-428.*

Although the distinction may appear fairly vague at first, two criteria may in almost all cases help dispel any hesitation regarding a given argument to a given feature:

- If, assuming the argument were removed, the supplier could still pick a reasonable default value to process any particular call, then the argument is an option. The default may be a universal value applicable to all calls by all clients, or it may be deduced from earlier calls to other features, in particular from object initialization values provided at creation time. But if the supplier cannot do a reasonable job of processing a call unless the client specifically includes the argument's value for that call, the argument is an operand.
- During the evolution of a class and its features, the operands should as much as possible remain unchanged, but new options may be added.

A simple example in an input-output library would be a procedure to print a floating-point number. The number itself is an operand; without it, the routine cannot do its job. But properties such as the number of significant digits to print and the printing format (fixed point, with exponent and so on) are options: in the absence of an explicit choice made by the client, the routine may find reasonable defaults.

Note that with an object-oriented library the number to print may not be an argument at all if the routine is called in the "qualified" form *number.print* (...). This indicates that in any qualified call there is always one operand, the call's target (the expression appearing before the period, *number* in the example). Further operands may appear in the argument list.

Here is another example from the Base libraries. Many container data structures such as arrays, lists, stacks or trees will hold not objects but references to objects. Many of the features of the corresponding class need to perform comparisons between an external value and the value in the data structure. Two examples are features called under the form

s.prune (*v*);
    -- Remove from *s* one occurrence of *v*, if any.

p := *s.has* (*v*)
    -- Make *p* true if *v* occurs in *s*, false otherwise.

In some cases the comparisons, and the corresponding notion of "occurrence", pertain to reference equality; in others, to object equality. In other words, the call to *has* may mean "is there a reference to the object that *v* references?", or it may mean "is there a reference to an object that has the same contents as the object that *v* references?". Although the first interpretation is more common, either may be appropriate depending on the client's context.

In this example *v*, the reference to be compared, is an operand for *remove*, *has* and all similar features. The comparison mode (compare references, or compare objects) is an option, since in the absence of an explicit directive from the client we may choose a default – the more common convention, reference comparison.

3.7.3 Setting options

The distinction between operands and options suggests the principal rule for keeping argument lists short: keep the options out.

Argument rule:

The arguments of a feature should only include its operands.

How then can the library producer enable clients to set the options? Each option will be represented by an attribute and an associated procedure which (for an attribute *opt* of type *T*) will be of the form

---

set_opt (*val*: *T*) *is*
        -- Make *val* the value of *opt*
  do
     opt := *val*
  ensure
     opt = *val*
  end

---

so that clients can change the option value through calls of the form *obj. set_opt* (*some_value*). The value will then remain in effect, for the object attached to *obj*, for all subsequent calls to the features that rely on *opt*.

Some minor variants may be useful in practice:

- If *opt* is a boolean attribute it is generally clearer to have two procedures, whose names may be of the form *set_opt* and *unset_opt*.

- Using an attribute means that you can set the option separately for each instance of the class. If such flexibility is not needed, and the same option value will apply to all objects, you can use the Eiffel Once function mechanism to use a single shared value rather than reserve a field in each object.

Once functions are explained in 2.8.2, page 52.

The option-setting technique is used by the Base libraries for the problem of object or reference comparison mentioned above. In class *CONTAINER*, which is an ancestor to all classes describing container structures, you will find the boolean attribute *object_comparison*, which indicates whether search, removal and other features that need to compare values should compare objects or references. By default *object_comparison* is false, so that references will be compared. The class contains two procedures, called under the forms

s. compare_objects
s. compare_references

enabling a client to change the comparison mode for any container structure *s* by changing the value of *s. object_comparison*.

In applying the option-setting technique, you will have to decide how to set the default for each option and each object. This will be done through the creation procedures of the class. Three cases arise:

C1 • If the option has the same default for all objects and can be set globally for all objects, you may, as noted above, avoid adding an attribute; use a shared object through a Once function.

C2 • If the option has the same default for all objects but must be settable separately for each object, the creation procedures must initialize the corresponding attribute to the default value.

C3 • If the option's value must be specified by the client for each object on creation, make it an argument to the appropriate creation procedure.

In case C2, it is often possible to avoid including explicit initialization instructions in the creation procedures: by using suitable conventions you may be able simply to take advantage of Eiffel's default initialization rules. For a boolean option, in particular, always use an attribute that denotes the **negation** of the default value; then you can rely on the rule that booleans are always initialized to false. This is why in class *CONTAINER* as discussed above, where the default is to compare references, the corresponding attribute is called *object_comparison*, and has value ***true*** only if the current policy is the reverse – comparing objects.

3.7.4 The option-setting technique: a discussion

A criticism which comes to mind about the option-setting technique is that it merely moves the complexity from the features to the class. For each argument that it removes, it adds two or more features – an option attribute and at least one option-setting procedure.

This criticism, however, is not justified. In general most client calls will be able to rely on the default values. If you include the option among the arguments, you require every client and every call to cater explicitly for the option, even if only one client in a million needs it. In the long run, this attitude is untenable; so to avoid argument lists that grow forever you end up sacrificing possibly useful options. With the option-setting technique, you may add as many options as you like; clients that do not need it simply do not use it. As noted above, a class whose documentation is well-organized may be big without being difficult to learn; library users simply scan the class documentation once, decide which features they need and which ones they do not, and quickly remove the second category from consideration.

The only valid objection I know to the option-setting technique is one of space efficiency: any time you add an attribute to a class, you add a field to every run-time instance of the class. This criticism is mitigated by two observations:

- If the option can be set globally, rather than individually for each object, the problem disappears since, as noted above (case C1), the value can appear in a single shared object.

- For boolean attributes, which are probably the most common kind of option, the space overhead is negligible – one bit in a good implementation. (There is actually no overhead at all if, as is often the case, the implementation can take advantage of space which was wasted for word alignment.)

The overhead does remain, however, in other cases. Usually it is well worth the simplification of the class interface afforded by the option-setting technique; but occasionally an extra attribute will be considered too high a price to pay.

3.8 NAMING ISSUES

A fascinating issue in the design of libraries is the choice of names for classes and features. This question, although it may appear cosmetic at first, illuminates the problems that library designers and users face when libraries reach industrial size, causing the concern for consistency and regularity to overshadow concerns about the individual properties of each class and feature.

Let us look first at the choice of feature names; the simpler question of class names will be examined next.

3.8.1 Ad hoc naming

The evolution of feature names in the container classes of the Base libraries provides an interesting illustration of the importance of choosing names judiciously.

Initially the Library contained only a few dozen classes. At that level one tends to select names·based on the precise functionality of each feature, and to rely for each variant on the established terminology.

Class	**Example features**		
STACK	*top*	*push*	*pop*
ARRAY	*entry*	*enter*	
QUEUE	*oldest*	*add*	*remove_oldest*
H_TABLE	*value*	*insert*	*delete*

Figure 3.8:
A casual choice of names

For example, the three basic operations for stacks originally used the conventional names: *top*, *push*, *pop*. The operation to push element x on stack s would be written

$s.push\ (x)$

Another fundamental data structure is the array, for which the two basic operations affect an element, or "entry", known through its integer index; the first one returns the value of the entry, and the second replaces it by a new value. In the original version of Base, the names *entry* and *enter* naturally suggested themselves. Typical calls for an array a of entries of type G, an integer i and a value x of type G, were:

$x := a.entry\ (i)$
$a.enter\ (i, x)$

Other structures, such as queues (similar to stacks, but with a first-in-first-out policy) and hash tables, used similarly specific names, as illustrated on the figure above. All these names are familiar to a computer scientist, and indeed used (with some variants) in textbooks on data structures and algorithms. So everything appeared to be in order.

3.8.2 Towards consistency

As both the external usage of the library and its internal size started to grow, we realized that all was not quiet on the naming front. For a large library used by many different people, what matters most is consistency. In particular it becomes critical to enable a library user who is presented with the description of a library class, normally in the form of a flat-short version of the class, to find out very quickly – typically in less than a minute – whether the class fits his needs of the moment, and, if so, to learn how to use it, a process that we may call **learning the class** (in the sense of learning how to use it through its interface, not of learning its internals, which is another matter).

But here the choice of feature names is crucial. For if it is not made with the utmost care, learning a class will become a process similar to learning a new programming language. Even though such programming languages are relatively small, this process quickly becomes unacceptable as the library grows. Who wants to learn dozens of little incompatible languages?

If not properly addressed, this problem is potentially the major practical obstacle to reuse. A good choice of names can go a long way towards solving it.

Here "good" means in particular "consistent". The name set that replaced the above one is based on a small number of standard words, chosen with particular care. For the classes mentioned the names became the following (a more complete list of standardized names will be given below).

Class	Example features		
STACK	*item*	*put*	*remove*
ARRAY	*item*	*put*	
QUEUE	*item*	*put*	*remove*
H_TABLE	*item*	*put*	*remove*

Figure 3.9:
A consistent name set

The change from the previous style is rather extreme. Exactly the same names are now used for all structures, regardless of the semantic differences.

3.8.3 The benefits of systematic naming

At first sight the new policy may seem to introduce much confusion: why use a single name such as *item* for operations which have a quite different practical behavior? But further analysis shows, quite to the contrary, that this is the best possible policy if we take a global look at the library and its usage (rather than a microscopic look at individual classes). The global view shows that for almost all structures there are, among other features:

The notion of obsolete feature was discussed in 2.9.1, page 52.

- A basic mechanism to access elements (corresponding to the first subcolumn in the "Example features" part of the above tables).
- A basic mechanism to change elements (second subcolumn).
- A basic mechanism to remove elements (third subcolumn).

Of course these operations behave differently for each kind of data structure; otherwise we would not have a need for so many different classes. But when we consider the library as a whole it is much more important to emphasize the commonality (the presence of the basic operations) than the differences (the specific properties of these operations in each case).

The reason why we do not create any confusion by using the same name for features with the same general role, such as the versions of *item*, is that the differences are obvious anyway: they are reflected in the different signatures and specifications of the variants, as they will appear in the flat-short documentation. (The signature of a feature is given by the number and types of arguments and result, if any; its specification is given by its precondition and postcondition.) Here are the signature differences for various versions of *item*, *G* being the formal generic parameter:

- The signature for arrays is *item* (*i: INTEGER*): *G*; the feature takes an integer argument chosen by the client and returns the corresponding array element.

- The signature for hash tables is *item* (*key*: *HASHABLE*): *G*; the feature takes a "hashable" argument, such as a string, again chosen by the client, and returns the associated table element if any.

- The signature for stacks and queues is simply *item*: *G*. Here the client has no choice: the structure decides, as it were, what element to return – the oldest one for a queue, the youngest one for a stack. (In Base, because of this behavior, stacks, queues and similar structures are called "dispensers" by analogy with a simple vending machine where pressing the single button yields an element chosen by the machine, not the client.)

The specifications are correspondingly different. In the various classes you will find preconditions and postconditions which express the particular properties of the features. For example the **require** clause of *item* for arrays states that a client calling this feature must make sure that the index passed as argument for *i* is within bounds. For a hash table, the only requirement is that the *key* must be non-void. For a stack or queue, the structure must not be empty. For a stack, *item* immediately applied after *put* will always yield the element just inserted; this is not true for a queue.

To use the class effectively, a library user (that is to say, an author or potential author of client classes) will need to understand the signature and specification, as part of the process of learning the class. He will be able to do so by reading the flat-short form. Different feature names would not mean more functionality but more difficulties – more things to learn.

Contrast these difficulties with the benefit of a consistent naming scheme which enables the library user to approach a new class and feel instantly comfortable as he spots the features which correspond to common operations, of which he has already seen many variants in previous classes. This helps him grasp quickly what each feature is about and removes the need to learn unfamiliar terminology.

3.8.4 The practical perspective

Since the choice of consistent names was arrived at only after a detour through the more class-specific conventions illustrated above, it is interesting to note the reaction of the user community. As so many names were changing we had expected some kind of backlash – the shock of seeing a *STACK* module with no *push* operation and other departures from tradition – but it did not occur. Library users welcomed the change because the consistency and regularity it brought were so clearly beneficial. Eiffel's obsolete mechanism was of course essential in making the change acceptable; most of the old names were still there, with declarations such as (in class *ARRAY*):

```
enter (i: INTEGER; x: G) is
        obsolete "Use "put (element, index) instead""
    do
        put (x, i)
    end
```

Note that for this particular case there was not just a change of name but a change of argument order; keeping the original order would have caused an inconsistency with other structures (for example in a hash table the call is of the form *table.put (value, hash_key)*). Consistency, consistency again.

One exception to the favorable response to the above name changes was caused by the use of *put* for operations which appear to add an element in some cases and merely replace an element in others. This caused some confusion. Further analysis has led to the following finer-grain solution, which takes advantage of Eiffel's ability to have synonyms for feature names:

- A routine which replaces an existing element, associated with a certain key k, by a new value v, uses the name *replace*. This applies for example to arrays and hash tables. The postcondition in this case is of the general form $item (k) = v$.

- A routine which adds a new value v uses the name *extend*. The postcondition in this case must state that the structure now includes one more occurrence of v than before. Examples are lists or dispenser structures (stacks, queues).

If a class has only one of these two variants, or one of them is more commonly used than the other, it can still be used under the name *put*, which is normally a synonym to either *replace* (as in arrays) or *extend* (as in stacks). In such cases *put* is the preferred name since it is immediately recognizable as the basic element change operation. The postcondition of *put (... v)* should always include, in some form or other, the property *has (v)*, which states that v is present in the structure.

Note how the reasoning which led to this solution required (as almost always in such cases) a precise analysis based on assertions.

3.8.5 The standard names

Here is the list of some of the basic names that you will encounter over and again in the Base libraries, each with an indication of its role. Some of the name choices may be surprising at first; they will be explained next.

---

capacity
> The size allocated to the representation of a bounded structure. Normally, *full* has the same value as *count* = *capacity*; this property will appear as class invariant in the affected classes.

count
> The number of elements in a structure.

empty
> Query which determines whether a structure is empty.

extend
> The basic operation to add an element.

Figure 3.10:
The standard set of
feature names

extendible, prunable, readable, writable
> Queries which determine various properties of structures; *extendible* serves as precondition for *extend*, and *prunable* for *prune*.

force
> Has the same effect as *put*, but may work in cases in which the precondition of *put* does not hold. For example, *put* for an array requires the index to be within the array's bounds, but *force* will work for any index, resizing the array if necessary.

from_c, from_external, to_c, to_external
> Functions used to convert certain Eiffel structures, for example arrays and strings, to their closest equivalents in another language. The first and the third correspond to the case in which that language is C.

full
> Query which determines whether a structure fills to capacity the memory space allocated to its representation (if that space is bounded).

has
> The basic membership test: yields a boolean value indicating whether an element occurs in a structure. Normally called in the form *s. has* (*v*) for a structure *s* and an element *v*.

infix "@"
> A synonym for *item* in some cases where *item* takes a single argument. For example, the *i*-th element of an array *a* may be written *a. item* (*i*) or just *a @ i*.

item
> The basic access operation.

make
> The basic initialization mechanism; generally the most commonly used creation procedure.

prune
> The operation which removes one occurrence of a specific element.

put
> The basic element change operation. May be a synonym for *extend* or *replace* (see next).

remove
> The basic element removal operation. May be a synonym for *prune* (see next).

replace
> The basic operation to replace an element.

wipe_out
> The operation which removes all elements.

3.8.6 Some guidelines for choosing names

Apart from the consistency requirement, several important rules should be applied to the choice of names. The standard names discussed above may serve to illustrate these rules; the discussion will also help understand the reason behind some of these names.

The names of exported features should be simple and easy to remember. This usually implies that they should be short. Single words from English (or another natural language known to prospective library users) work best. Most of the names in the above list fit this last requirement. In application libraries it is not always possible to have short one-word names; in case of hesitation, clarity should be favored over brevity.

Library authors should resist the temptation to over-qualify names. In particular, avoid the typical beginner's mistake of including information about the class in a feature name. Assume for example that a class *EVENT*, perhaps in a real-time library, or in a graphics package, has a procedure which handles the current event. Then you should not call it *handle_event* or *event_handle*; this would be over-qualifying. Simply call it *handle*. Remember that one of the key aspects of the object-oriented method is dynamic binding, which could also be called "dynamic overloading" and enables calls of the form

> *ev1*.*handle*

where the type of the object attached to *ev1* (which could be *EVENT*, or a descendant of *EVENT* in which the procedure *handle* has been redefined, or even a class appearing in another part of the inheritance graph, although in that case the target will probably be called something else than *ev1*) determines what procedure *handle* actually denotes. Qualifying the name of the feature by the name of the class would go against this central part of object-orientation.

In one case, however, it is appropriate to use class-qualified names without contradicting the preceding observations. This is when you inherit a feature *feature* from a class *class*, redefine it, but want to keep the old version, usually thanks to inheritance (The old version is often made secret in the new class.) Here is an example from class *ARRAYED_LIST* which uses *ARRAY* to provide an implementation of lists:

```
class ARRAYED_LIST [G] inherit
    ARRAY [G]
        rename
            ...
            make as array_make
        export
            ...
            {ARRAYED_LIST} array_make
        ...
        end;
    DYNAMIC_LIST [G]
        ...
    ... Rest of class omitted ...
end
```

Here the creation procedure *make* of arrays is not appropriate as a creation procedure for lists any more, but it is still needed internally. In such cases, a name of the form *class_feature*, as *array_make* here, may be just what you need since you do want to recall the origin of the feature.

The convention is not universal, however; for example the Rename clause partially shown above also lists

item **as** i_th

This indicates that the *item* feature of arrays, which gives access to an element identified by its index, is still useful for lists, but under a different name. In this case the new name should not recall the feature's array origin since it makes perfect sense in terms lists alone, and is indeed introduced in deferred form as early as *CHAIN*, one of the ancestors of *LIST*. (Since *i_th* is still deferred in *LIST*, the renaming of *item* into *i_th* is a **join** operation that merges the two features: the effective feature inherited from *ARRAY* serves to effect the deferred feature inherited from *CHAIN*.)

When you do need composite names, use underscore characters _, as in *array_make*. The practice of in-word capitalization, as in *ArrayMake*, has become common in some programming languages, but is not part of the recommended style as it makes names hard to read and violates the conventions of normal English usage.

3.8.7 Grammatical categories

To facilitate quick recognition and understanding of the role of each feature, it is desirable to follow uniform rules governing the grammatical categories for feature names.

F1 • For commands (procedures), use verbs in the imperative, as in *put*. The verb can have a noun as complement, as in *compare_objects* (a procedure of class *CONTAINER*), or be qualified by an adverb or adjective, as in *deep_copy* (class *GENERAL*).

F2 • For queries (attributes or functions) returning a result of type other than boolean, use a substantive (a noun), as in *item*. Here too the noun may be qualified by an adjective or another noun, as in *Growth_percentage* (class *RESIZABLE*). In this last example the first letter is in upper case to signal a constant attribute; this is the standard Eiffel convention. In some cases the noun may be implicit, as in *Last_printable* (class *ASCII*), which really stands for *Last_printable_character* (unless we interpret it as a qualified noun resulting from substantiving the adjective *printable*).

F3 • For a boolean query, use either an adjective which suggests a true or false property, such as *full*, or, if no simple and unambiguous adjective exists, a name of the form *is_prop*, where "prop" denotes the property, as in *is_leaf* (class *TREE*).

These rules cannot be fully rigorous when English provides the underlying vocabulary: as human languages go, English is among the least "typed", having many words which play several syntactical roles. For example the word *empty* may be used both as an adjective and as a verb, and the word *count* both as a noun and a verb. (In the first case, if there is any ambiguity, you may use *is_empty* as per rule F3; in the Base libraries, however, *empty* is always used as an djective and *count* as a noun.)

The lack of a perfect division into categories is not all bad, as it gives us some flexibility in the application of the rules. Class *GENERAL* provides an example with two of its deep duplication features:

- The name of feature *deep_copy*, a procedure (that is to say, a command), should be understood as a qualified verb, as in: "Copy the structure for me – deeply, please."

- The name of feature *deep_clone*, a function (that is to say, a query) should be understood as a qualified noun, as in: "The deep clone of the structure".

This choice of names takes advantage of the imprecision of grammatical categories in English to reconcile the above rules with the desire to have consistent names for two closely related operations.

3.8.8 Interpreting names from the target's perspective

Another general guideline is meant to facilitate learning the class and remembering its features.

In the object-oriented style of computation, every call is relative to an object, the **target** of the call. Except for unqualified calls (whose target is the current object), the target appears explicitly, in the basic call syntax

  target.feature (argument, ...)

As a consequence, the name of the *feature* should always make sense from the perspective of the *target*. An illustration was provided above by the name of the basic membership query, *has*, which is normally called under the form

  structure.has (element)

returning a boolean value which is true if and only if at least one occurrence of *element* appears in *structure*. Because this is an operation on the *structure*, whose various versions are declared in the classes describing various forms of container structures, the name was chosen from the perspective of the *structure*.

A more traditional name for such a search operation would be one of

  occurs
  occurs_in
  member
  search

All these names, however, are unsatisfactory for our purposes in light of the above reasoning. A call of the form *structure.occurs (element)* would suggest that the query asks whether the *structure* occurs in the *element*; a call of the form *structure.member (element)*, whether the *structure* is a member of the *element*. In both cases this is the reverse of the intended interpretation. The word *search*, used here as a verb, would be appropriate for a command but not for a query.

Note that some classes of the Base libraries do have *search* commands; for example classes describing cursor structures use this name for the procedure that moves the cursor to the first item containing a certain value. This usage of *search* is perfectly appropriate; in several such classes the implementation of *has* internally relies on *search*.

COMMENT

3.8.9 Grammatical consistency between features

Yet another useful criterion is consistency between related features.

You may have wondered, for example, why the standard name given above for the command that adds an element to a structure is *extend* rather than *add*, which may appear more natural at first. The reason is the presence of an abstract precondition: often, applying *extend* requires that a certain boolean query be satisfied; that query determines whether it is permitted to add elements to the structure. It is desirable to choose related names for the command and the associated query.

With *add* this is difficult; *addable* would be just as inadequate as *occurs* and *search* were in the preceding example, since a call of the form

   structure.addable

would seem to signify "can the structure be added?" (without saying to what it would be added). What we want to suggest is: "Can we add elements to the structure?".

By choosing *extend* as the name of the command, we can use *extendible* for the query; the two names are clearly related, and a call of the form *structure.extendible* suggests exactly the right meaning.

Similarly, the basic operation to take away one occurrence of an item in a structure is called *prune*, with the associated abstract precondition *prunable*.

3.8.10 Naming classes

The naming issue also arises for classes, although it is less delicate there than for features.

Class names should be clear and precise. They should almost always be substantives, possibly qualified, but never verbs in the imperative or infinitive forms (these are the same in English). In other words, avoid calling a class *PARSE* or *SHOOT*.

In Eiffel practice there has been one exception to this rule: classes describing commands. In an interactive system, the notion of command is a relevant data abstraction, especially if the system offers an undoing mechanism; commands may be viewed as objects to which procedures *execute* and *undo* are applicable; other features may include *help* and various attributes that model the context of a command's execution. The technique of treating commands as objects has been widely applied in ISE Eiffel 3 tools and in the Vision library, using a class *COMMAND* of which classes describing individual commands are descendants.

It has become customary to give each one of these classes the name of the corresponding command, a verb; examples are classes called *SAVE*, *OPEN* or *DISPLAY*, which violate the above advice.

It would have been preferable to use names that better suggest the nature of the underlying objects: *SAVER*, *OPENER*, *DISPLAYER*. This will probably be the convention in the future. But even if the current choice of names is questionable, the command classes are legitimate – they correspond to valuable data abstractions.

Excepting the case of command classes, the use of verbs as class names is often the sign of a design that is not very object-oriented. If you detect such class names in a proposed system, you may have a serious design problem. If, however, you feel the design is fine, fix the names to avoid any confusion.

A less clear-cut situation is the presence of a class whose name, often ending in *er* or *or*, as in *CONTROLLER*, suggesting an operational role. (The replacements suggested above for command class names, such as *SAVER*, fall in this category.) Although perfectly legitimate in some cases, *er*-named classes deserve careful scrutiny. Many object-oriented designs will need a class or two of that kind, and the corresponding objects at run time; but their presence could also be a warning of poor object-oriented design. Here are a few danger signals:

- A very large *er* class.
- Many *er* classes.
- An *er* class with just one routine, or one routine which calls all the others directly or indirectly.

If your system has any of these characteristics, it may well be a functional design masquerading as an object-oriented decomposition. Here too name changes will not help you correct the design, but at least the presence of *er* names can alert you to the problem.

One case in which *er* names are legitimate is for classes whose instances, in line with an important observation made at the beginning of this chapter, describe machines, with many different "buttons" – many features. *Er* names are indeed natural for machines (as in "computer", "tractor" and so on); but for object-oriented machines, as suggested by the preceding discussion, we should only consider software machines whose abstract buttons (the features of the underlying classes) enable them to perform several different operations.

See "objects as machines", 3.3.3, page 64.

The command classes mentioned above provide an example. Another is the Iterator library, where you will find classes such as *LINEAR_ITERATOR* and *CURSOR_TREE_ITERATOR*. An instance of *LINEAR_ITERATOR* is an iterating machine: an object which has the ability to iterate an arbitrary action, in various ways, over a linear data structure such as a list. The class has many different iteration features, of which two typical examples are the procedures *until_do* (execute a certain action on all items up to the first one that satisfies a certain test) and *do_all* (execute on all items). The presence of many different features is a good sign that we have a true class, describing multi-button machines, not a disguised functional decomposition unit.

One more comment applies to the choice of class names. You may have to consider a practical problem, mundane but sometimes annoying. It is often desirable for practical reasons to store every class of name *NAME* in a file called *name*.**e**. With some operating systems such as MS-DOS or older versions of Unix you may run into the limits on the length of file names.

3.9 OTHER CONVENTIONS

Two sets of design rules, not yet examined, are essential to the good organization of a library. They address the division of features into categories, and the proper choice of index terms.

3.9.1 Feature categories

As noted in the earlier discussion, classes that provide rich functionality may have a relatively large number of features, especially when we include inherited features. To facilitate class learning (as defined above) we must be careful to organize these features in groups. Once again the crucial factor is consistency.

We will be helped here by the Eiffel convention for Feature clauses. A class may have as many Feature clauses as desired, in the form

---

class C inherit

 ...

creation

 ...

feature -- Category 1

 ... Feature declarations

feature {*A*, *B*} -- Category 2

 ... Feature declarations

 ...

feature {*NONE*} -- Category *n*

 ... Feature declarations

invariant

 ...

end

One of the primary purposes of having more than one clause is to provide various groups of features with different export privileges. Here for example the category 1 features are available to all clients, the category 2 features to classes *A*, *B* and their descendants only, and category *n* features are secret (usable only within the text of *C*). But this facility also has another important application for libraries and in particular for library documentation: you may use it to divide the features of a class, even in the absence of export restrictions, into conceptual categories. Each category corresponds to one feature clause.

The comment that follows the keyword *feature* in each case (such as "-- Category 1" above) is known as the clause header; like the header comment of a routine, a clause header is an expected comment that can be processed by some of the the tools of the environment. In particular, the flat-short version of a class, which serves as the standard documentation, will:

- Merge all Feature clauses with an identical clause header from the class itself and from its ancestors.
- Retain the division into separate Feature clauses when the clause headers are different.
- For each merged Feature clause, retain the clause header.
- Within each merged Feature clause, order features alphabetically.

These rules help make the structure of all classes regular and predictable. They are complemented in Base by a strict convention governing the order of clauses and the permitted headers. Only the headers shown in the table below occur in Base, always in the order given. The rationale behind that order is:

- Start with the initialization features, in particular the creation procedures which are needed for creating instances of the class.
- Continue with the queries – the features which return some information about existing instances.
- Then show the commands having a local effect, modifying modify one property or one element of a structure.
- Continue with the commands having a global effect, in particular structure transformations and conversions.
- End with the obsolete and secret features, which do not appear in the flat-short documentation.

Here is the complete list of categories following this general order.

-- Initialization
    Commands used to set up the contents of objects; usually they are creation procedures.
 	
-- Access
    Queries used to obtain elements in the structure.
 	
-- Measurement
    Queries pertaining to the size of the structure.
 	
-- Comparison
    Features (usually queries) which compare elements according to various order relations.
 	
-- Status report
    Queries used to determine general properties of the structure, including options as defined earlier in this chapter.

Figure 3.11:
Standard feature
categories

-- Status setting

Procedures which change general properties, in particular options
(which can then be queried through features of the preceding category).

-- Cursor movement

For structures which maintain a "current position" marked by a cursor,
procedures which change that position.

-- Element change

Procedures which change elements of the structure, or add elements to
it.

-- Removal

Commands which remove elements from the structure.

-- Resizing

Commands which change the size allocated to the structure.

-- Transformation

Commands which may transform the overall organization of the
structure.

-- Conversion

Features which produce different structures made of some or all of the
same elements.

-- Duplication

Features which produce copies of the structure.

-- Basic operations

Features implementing various standard mechanisms (such as
arithmetic operations).

-- Miscellaneous

Anything that does not fit in the other categories (there is currently no
example of this category in the Base libraries).

-- Obsolete

Features declared obsolete, kept only for compatibility with previous
versions. Such features will not appear in the flat-short form.

-- Inapplicable

Features inherited from ancestors where they were exported to clients,
but made secret or restrictively exported in the current class. Such
features will not appear in the flat-short form.

-- Implementation

Secret or restrictively exported features, used only for the
implementation of the current class. Such features will not appear in
the flat-short form.

3.9.2 Indexing guidelines

The **indexing** clause of Eiffel provides a powerful mechanism for cataloging reusable classes and permitting query-based retrieval of components. Although retrieval tools are still in their infancy, the proper use of indexing clause is crucial to the success of the goal pursued by this book and by the Base libraries: the development of an industry of reusable software components.

Although the choice of indices and values is free (values may be identifiers, integers etc.), it is desirable to follow a standardized style, at least within a given library or installation. Such a style has been defined for and applied to the Eiffel libraries, based on the following guidelines:

- Keep the Indexing clauses short (3 to 8 entries is typical). (This might change in the future as the needs of cataloging and retrieval tools are better understood.)

- Avoid repeating information which is in the rest of the class text. This is an essential requirement: the principle developed throughout this chapter and the Eiffel method (recall in particular the discussion of class documentation) is that as much as possible of the information about a class should be extracted from the class text itself. In the Indexing clause one should only find what is not readily obtainable from the rest of the class.

- Use a set of standardized indices for properties that apply to many structures, such as choice of representation. (Examples of such indices are given below.)

- For values, define a set of standardized possibilities for the common cases.

- Include positive information only. For example, a *representation* index is used to describe the choice of representation (linked, array, ...). A deferred class does not have a representation. For such a class the clause should not contain the entry *representation*: *none* but simply no entry with the index *representation*. A reasonable query language will make it possible to use a query pair of the form *<representation, NONE>*.

The indices that appear in the Base libraries, along with typical values, are the following, listed in the same order in which they should appear in the clause.

The first entry should always be present. Its index is *description* and its value is a string that gives a short overview of the abstraction described by the class. An example was introduced in the previous chapter: the clause for class *ARRAYED_QUEUE*, which reads

> *description:*
>   *"Unbounded queues, implemented by resizable arrays"*

By convention, the *description* entry should be phrased so as to refer (whenever applicable) to the typical **instances** of the class. So the following alternative phrasings would not conform to the standard style:

- "An unbounded queue, implemented as a resizable array": singular rather than plural, thus describing an object rather than the class − a serious mistake.

- "The notion of unbounded queue, ...": describes the class, but not in terms of its instances.

- "This class describes unbounded queues, ...": needlessly verbose.

Although it is desirable to keep the *description* entry short, it may need more than one line. Since it is syntactically a single string, it should then use the syntactical rule for writing a string over more than one line: end each line but the last with a percent character %, and begin each line with the first with a percent character possibly preceded by blanks or (preferably) tabs.

> Earlier practice had each class begin with a header comment similar to the header comment of routines. The *description* entry of the Indexing clause is a more systematic convention and removes the need for class header comments.

An entry of index *status* indicates that a status notice, for example a notice of copyright or other proprietary rights, is present. The notice itself, as well as any other practical information that the class author wishes to include even though it is not directly related to the technical properties of the class, should appear in the form of a comment at the end of the class so as not to bother the library user who routinely edits class texts: since a text editor, when first invoked on a file, will normally show the beginning of that file, it is important not to clutter the beginning of the class text with elements that are not immediately helpful to users. So you may have in the Indexing clause an entry of the form

> *status*: *"See notice at end of class"*

and include at the end of the class a comment, as long as necessary, which lists the desired practical information. In Base such class-end comments list ISE's address and the contact points to be used for customer support.

An entry of index *names* is used to record the names under which the corresponding data structures are known. Although a class has only one official name, the abstraction it implements may be known under other names. For example, a "list" is also known as a "sequence". Also, the official name may need to be of an abbreviated form; in such a case, the *names* entry may give the expanded form of the abbreviation.

An entry of index *representation* indicates a choice of representation. Value *array* indicates representation by contiguous, direct-access memory areas. Value *linked* indicates a linked structure.

An entry of index *access* records the mode of access of the data structures. Standard values, of which the entry can list more than one, include:

- *fixed* (only one element is accessible at any given time, as in a stack or queue).
- *fifo* (first-in-first-out policy).
- *lifo* (last-in-first-out).
- *index* (access by an integer index).
- *key* (access by a non-integer key).
- *cursor* (access through a client-controlled cursor, as with the list classes).
- *membership* (availability of a membership test).
- *min*, *max* (availability of operations to access the minimum or the maximum).

An entry of index *size* indicates a size limitation. Among common values:

- *fixed* means the size of the structure is fixed at creation time and cannot be changed later (there are few such cases in the library).

- *resizable* means that an initial size is chosen but the structure may be resized (possibly at some cost) if it outgrows that size. For extendible structures without size restrictions this entry should not be present.

An entry of index *contents* is appropriate for "container" data structures. It indicates the nature of the contents. Possible values include *generic* (for generic classes), *int, real, bool, char* (for classes representing containers of objects of basic types).

Entries of indices *date* and *revision* have string values and are meant for automatic processing by configuration management tools.

The Indexing clause is an important part of the class documentation, and so appears (with the exception of the *status*, *date* and *revision* entries, which bring no useful information to library users) in the flat-short specifications of this book.

The indexing clause of class *MULTI_ARRAY_LIST* – which describes lists implemented by one or more arrays, chained to each other – reflects the preceding guidelines:

---

indexing

    description:
        "Lists implemented as sequences of arrays, the last of which %
        %may be non-full. No limit on size (a new array is allocated %
        %if list outgrows its initial allocation)."

    status: "See copyright notice at end of class";
    names: list, sequence;
    representation: array, linked;
    access: index, cursor, membership;
    contents: generic;
    date: "$Date: $";
    revision: "$Revision: $"

3.10 USING INHERITANCE

Designing the right inheritance structures is of course one of the most important tasks of the object-oriented software constructor. This is true of all object-oriented development, but particularly of library construction, since the inheritance structure determines the fundamental properties of the library for both supplier and client authors.

The question of using inheritance properly is one of these general object-oriented design problems which, as noted above, are the business of books other than this one. The present discussion will focus on the aspects which are of prime importance in relation with the design and use of libraries.

3.10.1 Heirs and clients

Inheritance is only one of the two structuring relations for object-oriented systems; the other is the client relation. The broader subject of this discussion, then, is when to use inheritance and when to use client.

The general rule is clear:

- Inheritance is the **is** relation. To make class B inherit from class A is to state that every instance of the abstraction described by B is also an instance of the abstraction described by A; in short, that every B is an A.

- Client is the **has** relation. To make C a client of A is to express that every instance of B may need to access an instance of A; in short, that every B has an A.

This simple distinction is the fundamental guideline for using inheritance and client properly. It makes it possible to avoid the most obvious – yet still common – mistakes. Such mistakes often come from thoughtless uses of inheritance in cases where **is** does not apply. When made by an over-enthusiastic beginner who has just discovered inheritance and is eager to apply it, they are understandable; but you find them in more unexpected places, such as the latest revision of a widely used software engineering textbook, whose single example of multiple inheritance is a class *CAR_OWNER* that inherits from *OWNER* and, for good measure, inherits from *CAR* too!

Such examples are of course hard to defend. But unfortunately making the right decision is not always easy. More precisely, of the two possible mistakes, one is easy to spot, the other is more subject to discussion.

The first mistake, illustrated by the *CAR_OWNER* case, is to use inheritance (**is**) when only client (**has**) is appropriate. To have is not to be; a car owner is not a car.

In the reverse case, however, things are not as clear-cut. Often, to be is also to have. A simple non-computer example can serve to illustrate this observation.

Consider the notion of software engineer and let us accept for the sake of the discussion that this is a proper designation (ignoring the raging debate about whether software engineering deserves to be called engineering). Then between the abstractions *SOFTWARE_ENGINEER* and *ENGINEER* there clearly exists an **is** relation; if they were classes, the first would be an heir of the second.

But there is another way to look at the situation. We may consider that every software engineer has some part of himself, however small, which is the engineer component of his personality. With just a little twist of the reasoning, then, to be an engineer is to *have* an engineer in oneself.

This observation applies to most uses of the **is** relation. By using **has**, you lose polymorphic substitution – in our example, the ability to provide a software engineer in response to a classified advertisement asking, without further details, for an engineer. But in the absence of polymorphism inheritance is **never** required; you can use the client relation instead. This is the reason why the question of using inheritance properly is a delicate one. If "to be" and "to have" were entirely disjoint categories the problem would be easy, but in many cases both relations can in principle be used.

In such cases the library designer should use his sense of structure and elegance to decide between inheritance and client. There is fortunately another guideline, frequently applicable. To understand it properly it is preferable to abandon non-computer analogies and come back to software objects. If class C is a client of class A by having an attribute such as

   $a1 : A$

Because $a1$ is declared of type A, every instance of A will have a field containing a value of type A, or more commonly (in the absence of expanded types) a reference to an object of type A. At run time, that value can be changed; for that to happen, it suffices that a routine of C execute the assignment

   $a1 :=$ "Some other value of type A"

The value on the right-hand side does not even have to be of exactly the same type as the original value of $a1$: any type that conforms to A (that is to say, roughly speaking, any descendant of A) will be acceptable.

With inheritance, however, such a change of property can never happen. If class B inherits from class A, instances of B cannot be dynamically reconfigured to contain sub-objects of a type other than A. To come back to the earlier analogy: once an engineer, always an engineer; you cannot suddenly replace that part of you by, say, a component of type *ARTIST*, *POET* or *AUTO_MECHANIC*, even if someone convinces you that one of these is more appropriate to describe the deeper roots of your profession.

This property has important implications for the use of inheritance. Making B inherit from A makes the A part an indestructible component of every instance of B. If there is any possibility that an instance of B might need to replace its A component by something else, then you should use the client relation, not inheritance.

3.10.2 Classification

One case, the most obvious use of inheritance, does not leave much doubt as to which of the two relations is appropriate. Inheritance is clearly the proper technique for organizing software components into categories and sub-categories.

Here inheritance, together with data abstraction, is the vehicle through which we can apply to software engineering one of the central tools of scientific thought: classification. As noted in the Preface, a systematic approach to classification was essential to the emergence of the natural sciences; it is just as essential to the emergence of software science. What we need to classify is human-designed software objects, not natural ones, but this is not such a novelty: in mathematics too classification is essential, and the objects that mathematicians classify – groups, monoids, fields and the like – are just as artificial as those of software science.

Inheritance is the clear and uncontested tool for classification in software. The **is** relation clearly holds here: to classify data structures, we will state that every binary tree is a tree, in exactly the same way that every poplar is a tree, every lizard a reptile, and every group a monoid.

Having this tool is essential for libraries. It is not possible to manage a library, with its potentially large number of components, without a systematic classification scheme for these components. Without inheritance, we could still use such a scheme, but the classification and the components would remain separate. This approach has been attempted, with little success, to libraries written in non-object-oriented languages, notably Ada. The reason for the lack of success is easy to understand, as it follows directly from the arguments made in the above discussion of documentation, which apply even more forcefully here. No classification can be successful unless it is built into the components themselves.

Base as described in this book is the result of a systematic approach to the classification of software components, based on inheritance. The Preface called this effort a Linnaean reconstruction of software fundamentals. Subsequent chapters will discuss in detail the resulting inheritance structures.

3.10.3 Multi-criterion classifications

In the natural sciences, classifications are tree-structured; in object-oriented terms this means that they rely on single inheritance. Every new category is defined by reference to just one existing category. For example whales are classified as mammals; it might seem desirable to use two categories (mammal and sea creature), but we have to choose. If you want to separate land mammals from sea mammals, you will use subcategories of "mammal"; then if the same distinction is needed for reptiles, you will have to duplicate those subcategories in the reptile part of the hierarchy.

The relative simplicity of the hierarchies used in the natural sciences makes single inheritance tolerable. For software artefacts it does not suffice. The ingenious structures devised by software scientists over the years, be they binary search trees, heaps, sorted queues or finite automata, require a multi-criterion classification such as the fundamental classification of container structures described in a later chapter.

On the taxonomy of container structures, see chapter 4, page 123.

3.10.4 Inheriting implementation

Classification is the most widely accepted use of inheritance. But it is not the only legitimate one.

One form of inheritance that you will find frequently used throughout the Base libraries enables a class to inherit from another for its implementation. A typical example is the class *ARRAYED_STACK*, describing an array-based implementation of stacks. This class is a descendant of both *STACK* and *ARRAY*. *STACK*, a deferred class, gives *ARRAYED_STACK* its abstract interface, in particular the specification (through preconditions and postconditions) of the fundamental stack features, such as pushing an element onto the top, accessing the top element, popping the top element. *ARRAY* gives the implementation by providing features to manipulate the array representation of arrayed stacks.

The role of the two parents is definitely not symmetric. *ARRAYED_STACK* exports all the features inherited from *STACK*, but hides the features inherited from *ARRAY*. The *ARRAY* features are, however, essential since they make it possible to implement the *STACK* features. For example the procedure that pushes an element x onto the top of a stack is implemented as

top := top + 1
force (*x, top*)

where *force* (properly renamed) is the feature from *ARRAY* that replaces the value of an array element identified by its index, here *top*. (Procedure *force* will also resize the array if *top* is bigger than the current array size.)

This distribution of roles – one parent providing the specification, another the implementation – is common in the Base libraries. In some cases the separation is less clear-cut: rather than exporting or hiding all the features inherited from a certain parent, a class may export some and hidden some others, indicating that the parent is used partly for specification and partly for implementation.

Although this use of implementation inheritance has been known to raise a few eyebrows, it is one of the most important applications of object-oriented principles, and one may say without exaggeration that the Base libraries would not have been possible without it. It is fully compatible with the presentation of inheritance given earlier, based on the **is** relation: an arrayed stack is a stack, and it is an array as well.

The above analysis of inheritance and its consequences both justifies this technique and provides guidance on how to use it properly. It noted that to make class B an heir of a class A is a more committing decision than to make it a client of A, since it does not leave open the possibility of easily replacing the A component of B instances by a component of some other type. This tells us when implementation inheritance is appropriate: when the choice of implementation is an integral part of the design of the class. *ARRAYED_STACK* is an example: the very notion of arrayed stack, as defined above and confirmed by the name, indicates that the array implementation is an essential part of the class, not a circumstantial choice of implementation. In such cases using the client relation would mean that the class has an attribute, called for example *array_rep*, of type *ARRAY* [G] (where G is the generic parameter), and that all array features would have to be accessed through that attribute. In the implementation sketched above for the push operation, for example, the unqualified call to *force* would be replaced by a qualified call of the form

   array_rep.force (x, *top*)

This implies some performance degradation and, more importantly, a degradation of the simplicity, readability and maintainability of the class. It is interesting to note that a competent object-oriented designer, noting the repeated occurrences of qualified calls of the above form (*array_rep. force*, *array_rep.item* and so on) in the class, would have the natural reaction: adding to the arrayed stack class, for each one of the array features that it uses, a small routine encapsulating the corresponding qualified call, so as to hide the "*array_rep.*" part. But then this amounts to giving arrayed stacks the features of arrays, which is exactly what inheritance is for!

In such situations, then, implementation inheritance is clearly the proper technique, and you should not hesitate to rely on it as boldly as the Base libraries do.

3.10.5 The handle technique

Implementation inheritance does not apply to cases in which an implementation choice for a certain aspect of a class C is circumstantial rather than essential, and you suspect that it may change later. We have seen that inheritance cannot represent a changeable property. Such cases, then, call for the client relation; but using it requires that you can isolate an abstraction common to all implementations, write the corresponding deferred class – say *ABSTRACT_REPRESENTATION* – and perform all implementation-dependent operations through that abstraction.

This means introducing a feature that generalizes the above *array_rep* and may be declared as

handle: *ABSTRACT_REPRESENTATION*

Class *C* will then access the implementation-dependent properties through *handle*, using calls of the form

handle.some_feature ...

similar to the calls using *array_rep* above. For every possible implementation you must write the proper effective descendant of *ABSTRACT_REPRESENTATION*, effecting the features needed by *C*.

This device, the **handle technique**, is one of the best contributions that the Eiffel method has to offer to the principle of information hiding. It is particularly appropriate when you want to allow the choice of implementation to be changed not just during software design but also at run time. Thanks to polymorphic assignment and dynamic binding, it is possible, when an object initially has a handle of some type conforming to *ABSTRACT_REPRESENTATION*, to re-attach it to an object of a different (but still conforming) type.

3.10.6 Facility inheritance

The preceding study has shown that there is more to inheritance than specification inheritance. Another original and fruitful technique which, like implementation inheritance, sharply departs from dogmatic views of the method, is facility inheritance. This term covers the ability for a class to inherit from a general-purpose class which simply provides a set of useful facilities. Here are a few typical example from Base:

- Class *EXCEPTIONS* offers facilities for fine-tuning the exception handling mechanism. An example of feature from this class is the query *exception*, which returns the integer code of the last exception that occurred.

- Class *MEMORY* provides facilities for controlling the garbage collector mechanism. For example procedures *collection_off* and *collection_on* make it possible to stop the garbage collector temporarily and to re-enable it.

- Class *ASCII* simply gives symbolic names, in the form of constant attributes such as *Back_space* or *Last_printable*, for the characters of the ASCII character set.

- Class *BASIC_ROUTINES* provides a number of mathematical operations.

It is possible to use these classes through the client relation, as in

character_properties: *ASCII*;
...
!! *character_properties*;
...
if *last_character_read* > *character_properties.Last_printable* **then**
   ...
end

But this is usually overkill. For all the burden of new features such as *exception_properties*, of creation instructions for the essentially useless associated objects, and of qualified calls on these objects, there does not seem to be any tangible benefit.

Facility inheritance in such cases simply means that classes that need access to the facilities will inherit from the corresponding class, for example *ASCII*. Then they can refer to the needed facilities under their names, for example *Last_printable*, without further ado.

Different as this use of inheritance may be from classification inheritance, it is perfectly valid. At first it may seem hard to reconcile it with the **is** interpretation of inheritance, and more generally with the object-oriented view of the world, based on classes describing abstract data types. But all it takes is an original perspective. We may quite legitimately view a class such *ASCII* an abstract data type describing a set of objects: simply define these to be **any objects that have access to the properties of the ASCII character set**. Similarly, instances of *BASIC_ROUTINES* are objects which have access to the basic mathematical operations provided by this class.

> To say that an object has access to the features of a class is a slight abuse of language, to be viewed as an abbreviated form of the statement that the **features** applicable to the object have access to these features.

To make a class *C* inherit from *ASCII* or *BASIC_ROUTINES*, then, is simply to state that the instances of *C* are also instances of the chosen classes: objects that have access to the corresponding facilities.

Like implementation inheritance, facility inheritance is a remarkable application of the object-oriented method, which makes it possible to avoid burdening the language with many special facilities, such as "include" directives and module import mechanisms. It is another testimony to the power, simplicity and versatility of the concept of inheritance in object-oriented software construction.

3.10.7 The shape of inheritance graphs

In the same way that we asked ourselves earlier about the ideal sizes for a class and for a feature, it is proper to examine a similar question for inheritance structures. How wide and how deep should inheritance graphs be?

Some of the object-oriented literature contains strong advice both against narrow hierarchies and against shallow ones. For the second case, in particular, Johnson and Foote advise against writing a class which has many individual heirs, themselves with few or no descendants.

See "Designing Reusable Classes" by Ralph Johnson and Brian Foote, Journal of Object-Oriented Programming, 1, 2, pages 22-35, June-July 1988.

This advice is not quite matched by the experience of the Eiffel libraries. It simply happens in practice that some notions have many distinct variants, with little further structure. The Vision library provides two immediate examples:

- The deferred class *COMMAND* covers the notion of executable and possibly undoable commands in an interactive system. Many practical systems (think for example of a text editor) have several dozen commands, with little or no commonality between them. It is perfectly legitimate to make all the corresponding classes direct heirs of *COMMAND*.

- To describe the many different "widgets" (menus, buttons and the like) available in a powerful graphical user interface environment as supported by Vision, it is again reasonable to have a class with many heirs but little further structure underneath.

I have not been able to find good arguments against using a wide and shallow inheritance structure in cases such as these two examples, for which this kind of structure is intrinsic.

What about the depth of inheritance structures? Here again there is no universal rule, but it is true that structures that are much more deep than wide should arise suspicion. In particular, it was noted above that there is no good justification for a class that has only one descendant; it is almost always the result of an over-classification frenzy which, if allowed to proceed, will make the library structure needlessly hard to understand, hurting both the producers and the consumers.

3.10.8 Purely taxonomical classes

The last observation provides an opportunity to explore a little further a comment made earlier in this chapter: the advice to avoid classes that do not introduce or redeclare any feature, playing a classification role only. Should we totally prohibit such classes?

See the mention at the end of 3.3.2, page 64.

In most of the cases that I have seen the class was indeed unjustified. Many of these cases belong to the category just seen – a class that has just one heir and makes the inheritance hierarchy unnecessarily deep. Two situations, however, may justify a featureless class.

The first situation arises when an early design of the class hierarchy is incomplete but the designers want to leave room for future additions. So a class might have just one heir and no feature now simply because it is meant as a placeholder for future heirs and features.

This reason may be valid but you should not accept it without question, as it may be simply a lame excuse for a bad design; the promised future classes and features might never materialize. After all the method does offer a convenient mechanism for describing planned software elements in outline form only: declaring them as deferred. If the designer really sees the need for classes and features to be added later, he can take a few minutes to produce the corresponding deferred declarations.

The other possible justification for purely taxonomical classes is an effort to simplify the inheritance hierarchy. In the development of an example class hierarchy dealing with sports games, John Potter and Christine Mingins come up with a structure having the following shape:

The example is taken from "The Eiffel Method", Tutorial notes, TOOLS PACIFIC, Melbourne, December 1993.

Figure 3.12: Inheritance structure with many links

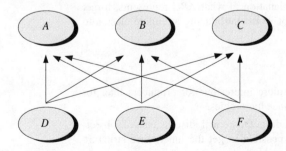

The three bottom classes all inherit from the three top ones. (Arbitrary letters are used here, but in the original example all the classes shown represent legitimate abstractions and the inheritance links all appear appropriate.) The authors suggest introducing a new class, which we may call *ABC*, representing the combination of *A*, *B* and *C*. The visual representation of the resulting structure looks simpler:

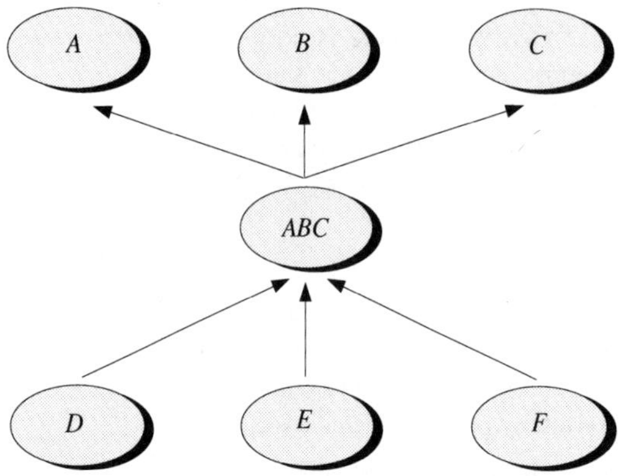

Figure 3.13:
Inheritance structure
with many links

Here too some caution is necessary. Conventional inheritance graphs are only a partial view of a system's complexity; the ability to make these graphs planar (that is to say, to avoid any edge crossing) is one desirable but not absolute criterion, which must be balanced against all others. (With the browsing facilities of ISE Eiffel 3, users routinely manipulate inheritance structures that might appear hopelessly complicated if they were drawn on paper.) In the end what counts more than anything else is the principle that every class should represent a significant data abstraction. If you can see that *ABC* – the combination of the abstractions represented by *A*, *B*, and *C* – denotes a useful abstraction distinct from any one that has been previously captured, then the possibility of simplifying the inheritance graph is one more argument to write a special class for *ABC*.

How do you know what is a meaningful abstraction and what is not? Try the following criterion: you should be able to explain to someone else what *ABC* means, without mentioning the goal of simplifying the inheritance graph, and in fact without referring to *D*, *E* or *F* at all. If that is the case, do write the class; the process of understanding and explaining the abstraction might even suggest a feature or two, removing any doubt that *ABC* is needed.

But if you cannot give a self-standing explanation of what *ABC* represents, forget about it. Simplifying the original picture is not worth introducing a zombie class into your design.

3.10.9 Generalization

One final set of questions, which perhaps is more interesting for producers than for consumers, is how we should construct inheritance hierarchies.

One often has the impression, when reading theoretical discussions of object-oriented techniques, that it should always be possible to get the inheritance structure right from the start. The reality is usually more painful.

Classification tends to be the result of iterative improvement as much as of immediate insight. The improvement process may be called **generalization** and is worth more attention.

On generalization see "The New Culture of Software Development" in the book "Advances in Object-Oriented Software Engineering", Prentice Hall, 1991.

Inheritance hierarchies result from a constant quest for abstraction. Ideally, we should always work from the abstract to the concrete: we should see the general notion first, often yielding a deferred class, and then devise descendants that corresponding to specific effective versions of that notion.

In practice, however, the scheme is not always as smooth and intellectually satisfying. Even professional library producers tend to produce classes which initially are often too specific: particular implementations of a certain abstraction, rather than the abstraction itself. It is hard to blame them: software developers are problem solvers. Nobody will complain if they get the job done first.

If reusable products are part of the goal, however, the process cannot stop there. When you realize that a certain class is less general than it could have been, you should use this discovery as an opportunity to reorganize the inheritance hierarchy. This *a posteriori* introduction of more abstract classes is the generalization process.

Several cases of this phenomenon occurred during the evolution of the Base libraries. To quote two examples:

- The *TREE* class has fulfilled many roles, serving as a basis for the hierarchical windowing system of Vision, for earlier graphical libraries, for the Winpack non-graphical windowing library, for the data structures of the Parse library, and for the abstract syntax trees of ISE's ArchiText structural editor. But it was too specific, describing just one implementation of trees rather than the general concept. Recognition of this situation led to a deferred class, of which the original became an heir.

- The *STRING* and *ARRAY* classes were initially developed almost in a stand-alone fashion, with no relation to other data structures. Later, during the development of the general taxonomy of data structures described in the next chapter, strings and arrays naturally fell into place as special cases of container data structures, corresponding to two clearly identified nodes in the multi-criterion inheritance architecture that underlies Base.

The process of a posteriori generalization is aided in the Eiffel environment by the notion of short form. One variant of the short form of a class is a deferred version, with where exported features have been made deferred and non-exported features have been removed. This is usually a good starting point if you wish to obtain a more abstract class while keeping the original interface for clients.

3.10.10 Extraction of commonalities

Closely related to generalization is an activity which arises from the a posteriori realization that different people, or even the same person at different times, have produced similar classes.

Normally, the ideal mechanism for capturing commonalities between similar component is inheritance. If the similarities had been detected beforehand, the normal approach would have been to write the sister classes as descendants of the same general class. But if the library producers initially missed the commonalities, it is always possible to reconstruct the inheritance structure a posteriori.

As with the previous case, the result will be is to produce more abstract classes, often deferred, of which the original classes will become descendants.

3.10.11 Switching to reverse

What is common to the previous two activities – abstraction, extraction of commonalities – is that they depart from the view of inheritance which is sometimes conveyed (albeit perhaps involuntarily) by the object-oriented literature: the idea that the bright designer will somehow obtain the proper inheritance structure the first time around.

It is always preferable, of course, to get the inheritance right initially. But it serves no useful purpose to pretend that this will always be the case. Better recognize that the process may involve trial and error, as a result of our yearning for concrete, and our frequent failure to detect commonalities early enough. Better be prepared for the inevitable changes of direction – "switching to reverse" – in building the inheritance hierarchy. What counts is that in the end we should get the useful and elegant class structures that are required for successful libraries of reusable components.

The Eiffel method helps make the generalization and extraction effort smooth thanks to information hiding. Clients of a class are only concerned with its interface (the set of exported features with their preconditions and postconditions, and the invariant), not with the inheritance hierarchy that led to the class. Normally the generalization process will not affect the interface, so that you will be able to reorganize hierarchies on the supplier side, adding more abstract classes as needed, without disturbing any of the existing clients. In the ISE Eiffel environment, the automatic (makefile-free) recompilation mechanism will further recognize that an interface has remained untouched, so that the compiled versions of the clients are still valid.

This observation highlights a fundamental, although often misunderstood, aspect of inheritance: except for polymorphic uses, inheritance is primarily and producer's rather than a consumer's technique. Such tools as the flattener and flattener-shortener support this view by providing inheritance-free versions of a class when needed for the benefit of clients.

As a result of the abstraction and extraction activities, a general phenomenon may be observed in organizations that have made a serious effort at producing, using and maintaining libraries: the continuous elevation of the classes' overall level of abstraction. As you start reusing your previous classes, cataloging them, archiving them into libraries, producing their documentation, and encouraging others to use them too, you realize the need for more general versions and, if your management and working environment support the culture of reuse, keep improving the classes through generalization and extraction of commonalities. It would be useless to lament that they were not produced right from the start; what counts is the constant improvement in quality and generality that follows from this constant effort, so obviously in tune with the spirit of the object-oriented method, and so beneficial to an organization that is clairvoyant enough to accept and encourage it.

3.11 THE IDEAL LIBRARY DEVELOPER

To conclude this review of principles it is interesting to turn our attention from the technical issues to the human side. This discussion will be directly applicable if you want to develop libraries, or if you are a project leader and must recruit library developers; even if your relation to libraries is just that of a user, it may provide you with some useful insights.

What kind of qualities are we looking for when selecting a library producer? Here are some; the list follows largely from the technical principles studied earlier in this chapter.

Abstraction-prone
Detail-oriented
Order-maniac
Literate
Top programmer and designer
Egoless

Figure 3.14:
The ideal library
producer

To develop a good library, we will want someone who has excellent abstraction abilities and is able to perceive the structure behind the appearance, the general behind the particular. But at the same time the good library producer must constantly pay extreme attention to detail: in a library, every little property counts. This is very different from more ordinary types of software, where we can usually tolerate some imperfections if the overall result is good enough. In libraries, we seldom can afford to leave "good enough" alone.

We also want an order-maniac: someone who is obsessed with classification, with finding a place for everything and putting everything in its place. Better yet, if he will be involved early in the construction of a library, he should be able to help design the optimal order – the set of classes and their relations, client and inheritance –, not just to adapt to an existing order.

The library designers should be literate. They should have the sense of style and elegance that is usually associated with the humanities more than with engineering. In particular, some of what they will be writing, along with program text in the strict sense of the term, is human-readable prose as needed in the header comments of routines, in the *description* entries of indexing clauses, in "obsolete" messages. Such elements, although formally embodied in software texts in the form of comments or strings, are bits of prose writing, not program writing; English or French, not C or Eiffel.

The requirement that software developers be also able to write is not entirely specific to library development, since non-library software has comments and strings too. The new twist is that for libraries such text elements will not just be seen by fellow writers and maintainers of the software: they will appear in the official library documentation (short or flat-short forms), in error messages, in catalogs of reusable components, in information produced by browsing tools, and in other documents all intended for frequent perusal by users of the library – novices and experts alike.

So the standards for libraries are much higher than for the occasional island of natural language text that appears in ordinary software. Here the natural-language elements must be clear, concise and correct. Not all programmers have the necessary skills (it is indeed always amazing to see otherwise talented software professionals who seem never to have mastered spelling, vocabulary and composition). For ordinary software, we may be willing to tolerate such a deficiency; but not for library components.

Perhaps this combination of requirements sounds a little like the kind of checklist that may be used by a prospective mother-in-law. In practice perfection cannot always be expected; but it helps. More precisely, if the phrase *egoless programming* has any applicability, then it is to library construction. Egoless programming, an idea that had its hour of glory in the nineteen-seventies in connection with some of the work on structured programming, refers to a desire to obtain software that does not reveal the identity of its author. When taken to imply that individual creativity is to be discouraged, egoless programming is not desirable: software is not assembly-line work, and in most cases creativity is good, not bad. But for library design, more than for any other kind of software, we are entitled to require that various developers follow a consistent style, especially when it comes to aspects such as class interfaces, naming conventions and use of inheritance, which, as this chapter has discussed at length, are so important for the usability of the library.

So we do not want to stifle developer's creativity, which will largely determine the range of facilities offered by the library, and how well it provides them; but we want to channel that creativity into the areas were it is productive, such as key decisions of specification and design, construction of the inheritance structure, choice of algorithms and selection of data structures.

3.12 FURTHER READING

In addition to the references mentioned earlier in this chapter the following three article add useful ideas to the preceding discussion:

- *Managing Class Evolution in Object-Oriented Systems* by Eduardo Casais, in *Object Management*, ed. Dennis Tsichritzis, Université de Genève, Centre Universitaire d'Informatique, 1990, studies the evolution of class libraries, using as example the history of early versions of the Eiffel Base libraries. In general, the yearly collections of papers published by the CUI under the editorship of Dennis Tsichritzis since 1988 provide precious material on the question of component libraries, their role, their design and their evolution.

- *Collection and Analysis of Software Metrics from the Eiffel Class Hierarchy* by Christine Mingins, Bohdan Durnota and Glen Smith, in TOOLS 11 (Technology of Object-Oriented Languages and Systems), Prentice Hall, 1993, pages 427-435, analyzes the Lex library to derive a number of measures of class coherence. Other publications by the same group from Monash University in TOOLS 12 & 9 (Prentice Hall, 1993) pursue this work and define a number of tree-based class metrics.

  The Lex library is discussed in chapter 11.

- *The Many Faces of a Class*: *Views and Contracts* by Richard Bielak and James McKim, also in TOOLS 11, pages 153-161, emphasizes the importance of contracts for class design and discusses how to associate several views with a single class.

Part B

Presentation of the libraries

4

Abstract container structures: the taxonomy

4.1 OVERVIEW

In this chapter we will review the basic criteria used to classify container data structures, and explore the corresponding classes.

Three clusters are involved: access, storage and traversal, corresponding to the three fundamental viewpoints that may be used to study container data structures.

> The flat-short interfaces of the classes discussed in this chapter appear in chapter 14.

4.2 THE THREE CRITERIA

A container data structure (or just container in the sequel) is an object which serves to store and access collections of objects, called the *items* of the container. All classes describing containers are descendants of the deferred class *CONTAINER*.

A container can be studied from three viewpoints: access, storage and traversal.

The **access** criterion affects how the clients of a container can access its items. For example, in a stack or queue, only one item is accessible at any given time, and clients do not choose that item; in contrast, clients of an array or hash table must provide an index, or more generally a key, to access an item.

The **storage** criterion affects how the items are put together. For example some containers are finite, others potentially infinite; among finite structures, some are bounded, others unbounded.

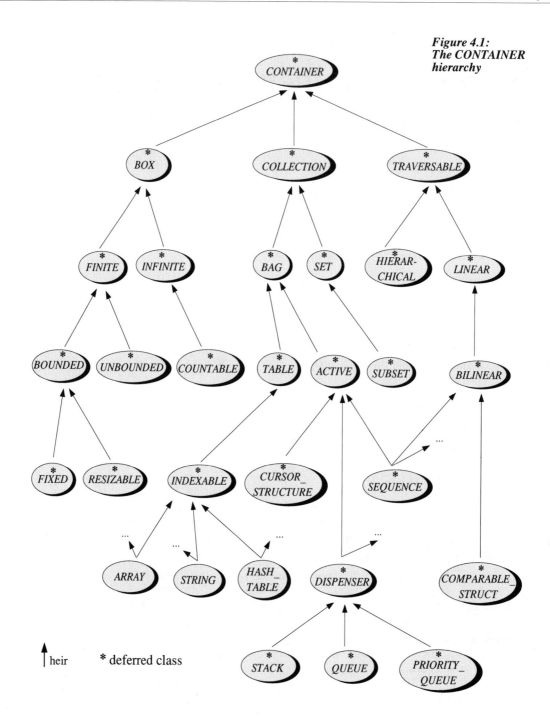

The **traversal** criterion affects how, if in any way, the items of a container can be traversed. A traversal is a mechanism which makes it possible to examine each item of a container once, in a clearly specified order. For example some containers can be traversed sequentially, in one direction or two; tree structures lend themselves to preorder, postorder and breadth-first traversals.

For each one of these criteria the Base libraries offers a single-inheritance hierarchy of deferred classes. The top of the access hierarchy is class *COLLECTION*; the top of the storage hierarchy is class *BOX*; the top of the traversal hierarchy is class *TRAVERSABLE*. These three classes are heirs of the most general class, *CONTAINER*.

The technique for building a class describing a specific form of container is to pick one class from each of the three hierarchies above and to combine these classes through multiple inheritance, yielding a class which is fully characterized by its access, storage and traversal properties. As you will have noted, this process causes many occurrences of repeated inheritance since all such classes will be descendants of *CONTAINER* through several paths.

The figure on the preceding page shows the overall *CONTAINER* hierarchy. You will find it useful to refer to it repeatedly when following the discussion in this chapter.

The diagram shown is, for the most part, a single inheritance hierarchy. Some of the classes appearing at the bottom (*ARRAY, STRING, SEQUENCE, DISPENSER*) have been included in the figure to give concrete examples of the variants of the notion of *COLLECTION*. These classes make full use of multiple inheritance, although the figure does not show all the relations. For example *SEQUENCE* is an heir not just of *ACTIVE* as shown but also of *FINITE*, a class of the storage hierarchy, and *LINEAR*, a class of the traversal hierarchy. The presence of extra parents is indicated by an inheritance arrow pointing to three dots "...". Such multiple inheritance and the resulting repeated inheritance are used in the construction of all effective container classes − those which define directly usable structures − in subsequent chapters.

4.3 CONTAINER OPERATIONS

Only a few features, defined in *CONTAINER*, are applicable to all container objects: membership testing, emptiness testing, and routines to change and query the object comparison mode.

The interface of class CONTAINER appears in 14.15, page 281.

4.3.1 Basic container operations

The boolean queries *has* and *empty* support membership and emptiness testing for any container.

Let *c* be attached to a container − an instance of *CONTAINER* [*T*] for some type *T*. Let *v* be of type *T*. The following basic two operations are available on *c*:

- *c.empty*, a boolean, has value true if and only if no items appear in *c*.
- *c.has* (*v*), also a boolean, has value true if and only if the object attached to *v* appears in the container. The postcondition of *has* indicates that the function's result can only be false if *empty* is true.

In addition, a container often has a standard linear representation, given as *c. linear_ representation*. The result is of type *LINEAR [T]*, using class *LINEAR* from the traversal hierarchy.

4.3.2 Object comparison

A general problem arises for *has* and, in general, for any feature that needs to compare an external item and an item in a container to determine whether they are equal: what does "equal" mean? Besides *has*, the question will for example apply to the procedure *prune_all* which in some classes, as seen below, removes from a container all items equal to a given item.

If, as is often the case, the items actually stored in the container are not objects but references to objects, and the value to be compared is itself a reference, equality between *a* and *b* has two possible interpretations:

- Reference equality, written *a* = *b*, only holds if the two references being compared are attached to the same object.

- Object equality, written *equal (a, b)*, holds if the two references are attached to objects that are equal in the sense of the *equal* function from class *ANY* (which by default determines field-by-field equality, and may be redefined in any class to account for more specific notions of equality).

More about 'equal' in 13.3.4, page 246.

On the figure, properties *equal (a, b), equal (a, c), equal (b, c)* and *a = b* are all true, but *a = c* is false.

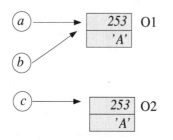

Figure 4.2:
Reference and object equality

These definitions assume that both references are attached to objects. If one of the references is void (not attached to any object) equality holds, in either interpretation, if and only if the other reference is void too.

Reference equality implies object equality, but the reverse is obviously not true: two separate objects, such as the ones marked O1 and O2 on the figure, may be field-by-field identical.

Which of the two interpretations should be used in reference comparisons? There is no universal answer. Assume for example a container that represents a mailing list; it contains references to objects representing individuals on the list. When searching the list you may at different times need to answer two different questions:

- Have I already encountered this entry?

- Is this entry a duplicate of another? (In other words: is this person also listed elsewhere?)

Reference equality is appropriate to answer questions of the first kind; object equality (with a suitable redefinition of *equal* to account for a reasonable notion of duplicate) is appropriate for the second.

It would be possible to have two kinds of search feature, for example *has_reference* and *has_equivalent*. This solution, however, causes container classes to contain a pair of otherwise similar *_reference* and *_equivalent* features not just for *has* but for every other operation, such as *prune_all*, that may need both forms of comparison.

Base uses a different technique – a direct application of the notion of option introduced in the previous chapter. It relies on two option-setting procedures, *compare_references* and *compare_objects*, defined in class *CONTAINER*. Clients of a container may use the calls

Options were discussed in 3.7.2, page 89.

> c.compare_references
> c.compare_objects

to switch between the two modes for the container attached to *c*. The mode selected through one of these calls will remain in effect for all search operations on this container until another call changes the setting. The default, in the absence of any call, is *compare_references*. To find out what mode is in effect on *c*, use the boolean expression

> c.object_comparison

whose value is true if and only if the current search mode for *c* compares objects (default: false).

> To avoid any confusion, be sure to note that the search mode as set by the above procedures only applies to a container which contains references – values whose type is a reference type. There is another kind of type: expanded types, whose values are objects rather than references to objects. The basic types *BOOLEAN*, *CHARACTER*, *INTEGER*, *REAL*, *DOUBLE* are examples of expanded types. The search mode has no effect for such values, which are always compared using object equality. Reference equality is not applicable in this case since no reference is involved.

4.4 THE ACCESS HIERARCHY

The access hierarchy has class *COLLECTION*, a direct heir of *CONTAINER*, as its top. In addition to their general container properties, collections are characterized by their ability to have items added to them and removed from them.

The interface of COLLECTION is in 14.9, page 272.

Collections are further divided, according to their access mechanisms. into various categories such as bags (and their variants, active and cursor structures) and tables.

4.4.1 Collection features

Procedures *put* and *extend* add an item to a collection. At the level of class *COLLECTION* these procedures are synonymous. Procedure *fill* takes an arbitrary container as argument and fills the current collection with the items of the other container.

Procedure *prune* removes an occurrence of a given item from a collection. Procedure *prune_all* removes all occurrences of an item. In both cases, the criterion used to determine what constitutes an occurrence follows from the current setting of *object_comparison*, as affected by the procedures seen above. Procedure *wipe_out* removes all items from a structure.

Addition and removal are not always possible. All the addition procedures have the property *extendible* as part of their precondition; all the removal procedures have *prunable* as part of their precondition. The two queries *extendible* and *prunable* are boolean-valued features of the class.

> The name *prune* may look a bit far-fetched at first but, as explained in the previous chapter, it fits in with *prunable*, in the same way that *extend* goes with *extendible*.

4.4.2 Types of collection

For any collection c of items of type T, and any item v of type T, the question "does v occur in c?" is always meaningful; function *has*, actually introduced in *CONTAINER*, gives the answer. The query $c.has$ (v), known in mathematics as membership, is applicable to all containers.

A related question is: "How many times does x occur in c?". This question does not always make sense. Whether it does is one of the important properties distinguishing the various kinds of collection. A collection will be called a *BAG* if it is indeed characterized not just by what items occur in it but also by how many times each item occurs. It will be called a *SET* if the number of occurrences is not relevant. If $c.has$ (v) is true, the call

The interface of BAG is in 14.10, page 274.

    $c.extend$ (v)

has the effect, if c is a bag, of increasing by 1 the number of occurrences of v in c; but if c is a set this call has no directly observable effect on c.

> Note that it is not forbidden to add an already present item to a set (unless *extendible* has value false), and that this operation may actually change the set's internal representation; but any such change is invisible to any client that uses the structure through its set features only.

If c is a bag, you may find out the number of occurrences of v in c through the query call

    $c.occurrences$ (v)

The notion of occurrence used to determine the result depends on the setting of *object_comparison*: reference equality or object equality.

4.4.3 Sets and subsets

Class *SET* introduces feature *count*, representing the number of items of a finite set. Its heir *SUBSET* introduces features corresponding to set theory's basic operations on subsets of a given set: the queries *is_subset* (subset inclusion), *is_superset* and *disjoint*, and the procedures *intersect* (intersection), *merge* (union), *subtract* and *symdif* (symmetric difference).

The use of procedures in the last four cases means that calls are of the form

s1.merge (s2)

which modifies the subset attached to *s1* by adding all the items from the container attached to *s2*. It is easy to achieve the effect of functions, with no side effects on their targets and arguments; for example, a descendant of *SUBSET* may include the function

> *union (other: SUBSET [G])* **is**
> > -- New subset containing the items of current subset
> > -- and those of *other*
>
> **require**
> > *other_not_void: other /= Void*
>
> **do**
> > *Result := clone (Current);*
> > *Result.merge (other)*
>
> **end**

Function *clone* follows the redefinition of *copy* so as to produce a subset made of the same items as the current subset.

> There is no deep conceptual reason for separating the notions of *SET* and *SUBSET*. The reason is pragmatic: you may want to write a class describing containers that possess the basic set property (multiple occurrences of a given item are indistinguishable) without having to implement the subset operations – *merge*, *intersect* and others – if you do not need them. Such a class will inherit from *SET*; a class implementing the subset operations will inherit from *SUBSET*.

4.4.4 Bags: tables and active structures

Two major kinds of bag are tables and active structures, represented by classes *TABLE* and *ACTIVE*. They differ in the way occurrences of items are added and accessed, as represented in particular by the signatures of the two basic procedures *put* and *item*:

Class interfaces: TABLE, 14.11, page 275; ACTIVE, 14.13, page 278.

- In a table, there is a key associated with each item. As a result the class has two generic parameters: it is declared as *TABLE [G, H]*, where *G* represents the type of items and *H* the type of keys. Examples of tables are arrays (where the keys are integers), hash tables (where the keys are strings or other hashable values), strings (which are conceptually similar to arrays of characters). There is no constraint on *H* in class *TABLE*, but there will be in descendants of *TABLE* such as *INDEXABLE* and *HASH_TABLE*. The basic insertion or replacement operation is of the form *c.put (item, key)*; the basic access operation is *c.item (key)*, which returns an item associated with *key*. This last operation can also be written as *c @ key*, using the function **infix "@"**.

- An active structure, as represented by class *ACTIVE* and its descendants, is characterized by the existence, at each stage of its life, of a "current position" which may have an associated "current item". The basic access and modification operations apply to the current position. Examples of active structures include stacks (where the current position is always the the position of the latest insertion, the stack's "top") and lists (which, as discussed in a later chapter, have an associated cursor that various procedures can move forward and backward, and where the current position is the cursor's position). Here *put* takes just one argument, the item to be inserted or modified at the current position; and *item* takes no argument, since it simply returns the current item when defined.

It is interesting to contrast the various boolean queries applicable to an active structure – some of them defined in *COLLECTION* and hence applicable to collections of all kinds, others introduced in *ACTIVE*:

- *extendible* (from *COLLECTION*) determines whether new items may be added to a container.

- *prunable* (from *COLLECTION*) determines whether new items may be removed from a container.

- *readable* (from *ACTIVE*) determines whether there is a current item that may be read.

- *writable* (from *ACTIVE*) determines whether there is a current item that may be modified; as expressed by the invariant of *ACTIVE*, *writable* may only hold if *readable* does.

4.4.5 Cursor structures

An important special case of active structure is the notion of cursor structure, represented by the class *CURSOR_STRUCTURE*.

A cursor structure is an active structure in which the current position is known through a marker, or cursor. Various operations will make it possible to move the cursor. At the level of *CURSOR_STRUCTURE* there is only *go_to*, but descendants introduce *forth, back* and others for linear structures such as lists, as well as *up* and *down* for hierarchical structures such as trees.

Cursors are in fact already present conceptually in *ACTIVE* structures, since there is a notion of current position, which we may visualize as a fictitious cursor marking a certain item of the structure. The novelty with *CURSOR_STRUCTURE* is that the cursor now becomes an object on its own.

As declared in *CURSOR_STRUCTURE* the cursor is of type *CURSOR*, another deferred class which has various descendants. In simple structures such as *ARRAYED_LIST* (lists implemented by arrays) the cursor may be implemented as an integer, but more elaborate forms of cursor are possible. To preserve simplicity and abstraction, however, all cursors are viewed by clients as being of type *CURSOR*.

The interface of CURSOR_STRUCTURE is in 14.14, page 279. The other important forms of active structures are DISPENSER and SEQUENCE; see next.

4.4.6 Dispensers

Another common case of active structure is the dispenser. This name comes from an analogy with an simple real-life dispenser, such as an unsophisticated vending machine that has just one button and delivers just one product. Similarly, a dispenser is a container in which you may at any given time access, remove or replace, remove at most one item – the current item. You do not choose that item: the "machine" (the dispenser) chooses it for you. So when you insert an item you have no control over where it goes into the container, that is to say, when you will get it back.

The interface of class DISPENSER is in 14.15, page 281.

The two most common kinds of dispenser are the stack, in which the current item is the one inserted most recently, and the queue, in which the current item is the oldest one inserted and not yet removed.

4.4.7 Sequences

The third major variant of the notion of active structure is the sequence. A sequence is a linear structure with a notion of current position. Class *SEQUENCE* serves as ancestor to such classes as *LIST* and *CIRCULAR_CHAIN*.

Chapter 6 discusses sequences, lists, circular chains and other linear structures in detail.

The basic notion of sequence allows for insertion at the end only. Variants such as *DYNAMIC_LIST* and *DYNAMIC_CHAIN* will support insertion at any position.

4.4.8 Kinds of table

Let us come back to the second main variant of bags (the first was active structures): tables. Two interesting special cases are indexable tables and hash tables.

An indexable is simply a table for which the key (corresponding to the second generic parameter, H, of *TABLE* $[G, H]$) is *INTEGER*. In other words, class *INDEXABLE* describes tables in which each item is identified through a unique integer. The two most common example are arrays and strings, represented by classes *ARRAY* (a generic class, declared as *ARRAY* $[G]$ and representing arrays of items of an arbitrary type) and *STRING*, representing character strings.

The interface of INDEXABLE is in 14.12, page 277.

> It may seem advisable to make *STRING* an heir of *ARRAY* [*CHARACTER*]. All the *ARRAY* features indeed apply to strings. This solution, however, might be too constraining for the implementation of strings; it was deemed preferable to leave open the possibility of choosing a string implementation that is not burdened by the choices made for the implementation of arrays. So both *STRING* and *ARRAY* inherit from *INDEXABLE* [*CHARACTER, T*]; for class *ARRAY*, T is the generic parameter G of the class; for class *STRING*, T is *CHARACTER*.

Finally, a hash table is a table in which the keys can be hashed; hashing a key means deriving from it an integer, so that the items can be kept in an array where the hashed key serves as index. The requirement that keys must be hashable is expressed by constrained genericity: the class is declared as

class HASH_TABLE $[G, H \rightarrow HASHABLE]$

meaning that the type used as second actual parameter in any generic derivation must be a descendant of *HASHABLE*. *HASHABLE* is a deferred class with the feature

> *hash_code*: *INTEGER* **is**
>   -- Hash code value
> **deferred**
> **ensure**
>   *Result* >= 0
> **end**;

Descendants must effect *hash_code* to provide a hash function. Examples of such descendants, describing values that can be hashed, include *STRING* – the kind of hash key most commonly used in practice – but also *INTEGER*, making it possible to hash integers.

4.5 THE STORAGE HIERARCHY

The storage hierarchy has class *BOX*, a direct heir of *CONTAINER*, as its top. In addition to their general container properties, boxes are characterized by how many items they may contain and whether this property may be changed.

For the interface of BOX see 14.3, page 266.

BOX has two heirs: *FINITE* and *INFINITE*, describing containers that hold finite and infinite quantities of items.

Class interfaces: FINITE, 14.4, page 267; INFINITE, 14.8, page 271.

4.5.1 Infinite containers

The presence of infinite containers may appear strange at first, since only a finite structure can be directly represented in a computer's memory. But infinite structures are in fact perfectly acceptable as long as no client ever tries to evaluate more than finite parts.

For example we cannot represent the set of prime numbers directly as a memory structure. But we can write a function *prime* such that a call to *prime* (i), for integer i, returns the i-th prime number; such a function provides a representation of the set of prime numbers, an infinite structure.

In practice the only effective descendants of *INFINITE* are descendants of its heir *COUNTABLE*, describing countable structures (those whose items are in one-to-one correspondence with the integers), and more precisely of *COUNTABLE_SEQUENCE* which inherits from *COUNTABLE*, *ACTIVE* and *LINEAR*. The current cases are:

- Class *PRIMES*, describing prime numbers.
- Class *RANDOM*, describing pseudo-random number sequences.

PRIMES and RANDOM are discussed in chapter 13. There is also a class FIBONACCI.

COUNTABLE has a deferred feature *i_th*, such that $c._{th}$ (i) is the i-th item of a countable structure such as the set of primes or a pseudo-random sequence.

4.5.2 Bounded, unbounded, fixed and resizable containers

Of course, most of the structures with which you will deal in practice are finite. Class *FINITE* has heirs *BOUNDED* and *UNBOUNDED*. In a bounded container there is, at any given time, an upper limit to the number of items that can be inserted (through the *put* operation); the limit is represented by feature *capacity*, an integer query, usually implemented as an attribute. An unbounded container has no such limit.

The interface of BOUNDED is in 14.5, page 268.

Class *BOUNDED* itself has two heirs: *FIXED* and *RESIZABLE*. In a fixed container, the *capacity* is hard-wired at creation time (normally it will be an argument of the creation procedure); in a resizable container, procedures are available to change the *capacity* on request. In particular, a call of the form

Class interfaces: FIXED, 14.6, page 269; RESIZABLE, 14.7, page 270.

    $c.grow$ (n)

ensures that, as a result, $c.capacity$ will be at least equal to n.

Be sure not to confuse the notions of infinite, unbounded and resizable container:

- An instance of class *INFINITE* is a structure that is intrinsically infinite. An example is the set of prime integers.

- An instance of class *UNBOUNDED* is a structure that is finite, but with no upper limit on the number of items it may contain. An example is a linked list (a list in chained representation).

- An instance of class *RESIZABLE* is a finite structure that at any time has such an upper limit, but with mechanisms available to change that limit if needed.

Descendants of *RESIZABLE*, such as *ARRAY* and *STRING*, have a procedure *resize* which relies on *grow*. In addition, they have a procedure *force* which complements *put*; assuming for example that *a* is an array, both of the two calls

a.*put* (*x*, *i*)
a.*force* (*x*, *i*)

are intended to put value *x* at position *i* in the array; the difference is that the first call is only correct if *i* is within the bounds of the array, whereas if this condition is not satisfied *force* will automatically call *grow* to resize the array. This difference is reflected in the assertions: the precondition of *put* requires the index to be within the bounds; *force* has no such precondition.

One might ask why we should at all bother with *put*; why not just use *force* which suffers no restriction? Part of the answer has to do with efficiency requirements. Resizing a structure is an expensive operation, particularly for an array: while *put* is a fast operation which works on just one array position, *force* may once in a while (when the index is out of bounds) work on the entire array since it is usually necessary, when resizing, to copy all the old values. Although this property is often desirable since it frees the developers from having to worry about manual resizing, it would be unwise to let them incur its potential cost unless they request it explicitly. In addition, an out-of-bounds access should not always lead to silent resizing; sometimes it is just a plain error, which will be detected by using *put* and precondition monitoring.

4.6 THE TRAVERSAL HIERARCHY

The traversal hierarchy has class *TRAVERSABLE*, a direct heir of *CONTAINER*, as its top. In addition to their general container properties, traversable structures are characterized by one or more traversal mechanisms.

A traversal mechanism defines an ordering of all the items of a container and makes it possible to apply an arbitrary operation to all these items in the order thus defined.

4.6.1 Traversable structures

Class *TRAVERSABLE* introduces only a few features. Procedure *start* starts a traversal; the boolean query *exhausted* indicates whether the latest traversal is complete. Internally, a traversal will use a cursor, so that traversable structures share some properties with instances of *CURSOR_STRUCTURE* seen above; the equivalent features will be merged in common descendants thanks to the sharing facility of repeated inheritance. In particular *off* is false if and only if there is no item at the current cursor position; if *off* is false, *item* gives the item at cursor position.

The interface of TRAVERSABLE is in 14.16, page 283.

Note the difference between *off* and *exhausted*. If *off* is true, there is no item at the cursor position. If *exhausted* is true, there is no more item to be visited in the current traversal if any, but there may be an item at cursor position, for example in a circular structure. So *off* implies *exhausted* but not the reverse.

Together with *start*, you might expect, since a traversable structure defines an ordering of its items, a procedure *forth* which advances the cursor to the next position. The corresponding mechanism indeed exists implicitly for all traversable structures; but it is not always possible (or at least not always easy) to express it algorithmically as a procedure. A typical example is the preorder, postorder or breadth-first traversal of a tree structure: whereas it is trivial to express such a traversal globally as a recursive procedure, the task of writing *forth* – that is to say of devising an algorithm which, given an arbitrary node in a tree, will find out the next node to be visited in the chosen traversal policy – is a difficult programming problem. For other traversable structures the solution might not even be known. Since in practice you will not need *forth* if you can use a global traversal mechanism, there is no *forth* in *TRAVERSABLE*.

4.6.2 Linear and bilinear structures

If the procedure *forth* is indeed present in a traversable container we may say that the container is linear. Class *LINEAR* describes such structures; it introduces *forth* as a deferred procedure. Procedure *finish*, which brings the cursor to the last item if any, is also deferred.

The interface of LINEAR is in 14.18, page 285.

Although still deferred, class *LINEAR* is able to provide an effecting of the general container query *has*, using an algorithm that searches for an item in a linearly traversable container by traversing the container until it either finds the item or runs out of items. Descendants of *LINEAR* may of course, thanks to their specific properties, offer more efficient searching algorithms, in which case they will redefine *has* to override this default.

A bilinear structure is a linear structure which can be traversed in both directions. As a consequence, class *BILINEAR* (an heir of *LINEAR*) provides the deferred procedure *back* along with *forth*. Class *BILINEAR* plays an essential role as ancestor of the sequence, list and chain classes and will be discussed in the chapter devoted to them.

About BILINEAR see 6.3.2, page 142, and the class interface in 16.2, page 293.

4.6.3 Hierarchical structures

Hierarchical containers are structured as trees. Class *HIERARCHICAL* has remarkably few features:

For the class interface see 14.17, page 284.

- $c.back$ will move to c's predecessor (parent).
- $c.forth$ (i) will move to the i-th successor (child) of c. Note the presence of an argument to *forth*.

More elaborate traversal mechanisms such as preorder or postorder may be found in the descendants of class *TREE* and in the classes of the Iteration library.

Tree classes are covered in chapter 8 and the Iteration library in chapter 10.

5

Mathematical properties

5.1 OVERVIEW

To understand the Base classes described in the following chapters, you will need to be familiar with a few classes that describe mathematical properties of objects: ability to be compared according to a partial or total order relation, to be treated as numbers, to be hashed.

The brief discussion which follows introduces these simple but important concepts and the corresponding four classes: *PART_COMPARABLE*, *COMPARABLE*, *NUMERIC* and *HASHABLE*.

> The flat-short interfaces of the classes discussed in this chapter appear in chapter 15.

5.2 CLASS USAGE

The classes described below are most frequently used as constraining types in constrained genericity, to express that the the types to be used as actual generic parameters for a certain class must possess some operations and associated properties.

See 2.7.12 about constrained genericity.

For example the class *BINARY_SEARCH_TREE* described in a later chapter requires the ability to compare the objects stored in nodes. This is expressed by declaring that class with a generic parameter constrained by *COMPARABLE*:

See 9.2, page 173 about HASH_TABLE; the class specification appears in 19.2, page 381.

    class BINARY_SEARCH_TREE [G –> COMPARABLE] ...

so that any actual generic parameter must be a descendant of *COMPARABLE*.

5.3 PARTIAL AND TOTAL ORDER RELATIONS

Class *COMPARABLE* describes elements of any set on which a total order relation is defined. Its parent *PART_COMPARABLE* describes elements on which a partial order relation is defined. Both are deferred.

The interface of COMPARABLE appear in 15.3, page 288, and that of PART_COMPARABLE in 15.2, page 287.

5.3.1 Comparison operations

Instances of either class can be compared pairwise using the standard comparison operations, all defined as infix functions:

infix "<"
infix "<="
infix ">"
infix ">="

This makes it possible to write calls using usual infix notation, as in

this_date <= that_date

assuming that *this_date* and *that_date* are of type *DATE*, and class *DATE* is a descendant of *COMPARABLE*.

5.3.2 Partial orders

PART_COMPARABLE describes partial order relations, that is to say binary relations enjoying the following three properties:

- Irreflexivity: $a < a$ is always false.
- Transitivity: $a < c$ is true whenever $a < b$ and $b < c$ are.
- Asymmetry: $a < b$ and $b < a$ are never both true.

> This definition of partial order is expressed in terms of the "<" relation, which provides a convenient basis for this discussion since the other relations are defined relative to "<" and *equal*. It is also possible to define partial order in terms of "<=" by stating that this relation must be reflexive ($a <= a$ is always true), antisymmetric ($a <= b$ and $b <= a$ are never both true unless *equal* (a, b) is true) and transitive.

COMMENT

Only *infix "<"* is deferred. The other functions are defined relative to it:

Expression	Definition
$a <= b$	$a < b$ **or** *equal* (a, b)
$a > b$	$b < a$
$a >= b$	$b <= a$

The symbol "<=" means "less than or equal", as expected; note, however, that "equal" here means object equality, as expressed by the *equal* function, not reference equality, as expressed by the = sign. Reference equality would be meaningless here, since we need to compare objects. For basic type instances such as integers or reals (as for any other expanded types) the distinction is irrelevant since = and *equal* have the same semantics.

5.3.3 Total orders

Class *COMPARABLE* inherits from *PART_COMPARABLE* but covers total order relations. A total order is a partial order that in addition to the above properties satisfies:

- Completeness: for any *a* and *b*, one of *a* < *b*, *equal* (*a*, *b*) and *b* < *a* is true. (Using the definition in terms of "<=" this would be stated as: one of *a* <= *b* and *b* <= *a* is true.)

As you may have noted, the definition of *a* >= *b* in the last line of the above table could be changed to **not** (*a* < *b*), but only for *COMPARABLE* objects. For a partial order relation, it is possible that neither of *a* < *b* and *a* >= *b* holds.

Class *COMPARABLE* extends the postconditions of the functions inherited from *PART_COMPARABLE*, using **ensure then** clauses. For example, **infix** *"<"* now has the new postcondition clause

>   *Result* **implies not** (*Current* >= *other*)

You will need comparable elements to define data structures that contain components to which comparison applications must be applicable. The corresponding generic classes use *COMPARABLE* as a generic constraint. The example of binary search trees was already noted at the beginning of this chapter. Another example is the class describing sorted lists, whose declaration begins with

>   **deferred class** *SORTED_LIST* [*G* –> *COMPARABLE*] ...

This ensures that only descendants of *COMPARABLE* may be used as actual generic parameters corresponding to *G*.

5.3.4 Basic classes

The classes describing the basic types *CHARACTER*, *INTEGER*, *REAL* and *DOUBLE*, as well as *STRING*, are descendants of *COMPARABLE*, which equips them with the usual order relations (alphabetical order for characters and strings).

This means in particular that you can insert the corresponding values into binary search trees, sorted lists and other structures relying on a notion of order.

The basic classes are discussed in "Eiffel: The Language" and, briefly, in 13.4.1, page 248 of the present book. Their interfaces appear in chapter 23, starting with BOOLEAN on page 470.

5.4 NUMERIC OBJECTS

The deferred class *NUMERIC* describes objects of any set on which the usual arithmetic operations (+, − etc.) are defined.

See 15.4, page 289 for the class interface.

5.4.1 Numeric operations

The arithmetic operations are declared as infix functions and called using standard infix notation, as in

> *this_tensor* + *that_tensor*

assuming that *this_tensor* and *that_tensor* are of a type *TENSOR*, and class *TENSOR* is a descendant of *NUMERIC*.

5.4.2 Basic classes

The classes describing the basic types *INTEGER*, *REAL* and *DOUBLE* are descendants of *NUMERIC* (as well as *COMPARABLE*). This equips them with all the usual arithmetic operations.

5.5 HASHABLE OBJECTS

The deferred class *HASHABLE* describes objects on which a hashing query *hash_code* is available, making it possible to store and retrieve such objects efficiently in hash tables. It consequently serves as the constraint for the generic parameter of class *HASH_TABLE*.

See 15.5, page 290 for the class interface. The discussion of hash tables is in 9.2, page 173.

Function *hash_code* returns an integer value which, as stated by the postcondition, must be non-negative.

Apart from *hash_code*, the class defines a boolean query *is_hashable*, serving as the precondition of *hash_code* and requiring the value to be different from the type's default value. This condition is only meaningful for expanded types, since for reference types the default value is a void reference.

One of the important descendants of *HASHABLE* is *STRING*, which introduces a default string hashing function. Since *STRING* is a reference type any string, including an empty one, may be used as hash key. Another descendant of *HASHABLE* is *INTEGER*: the hash function there simply hashes an integer into its absolute value. The definition of *is_hashable* implies that any integer except 0 (the default value for *INTEGER*) is acceptable as a hash key.

6

Linear structures: sequences, chains, lists, circular chains

6.1 OVERVIEW

Many applications need sequential structures, also called linear structures, in particular lists and circular chains. This chapter introduces the necessary classes.

> The flat-short interfaces of the classes discussed in this chapter appear in chapter 16.

Apart from three classes describing individual list cells, all the classes involved are descendants of class *LINEAR*, one of the deferred classes describing general traversal properties and introduced in the chapter that described the general data structure taxonomy. More precisely, all but one of the classes of interest for the present discussion are descendants, direct or indirect, from a class called *CHAIN* which describes general sequential structures possessing a cursor as well as insertion properties. The exception is class *COUNTABLE_SEQUENCE*, which describes infinite structures; all the others describe finite structures.

CHAIN is an heir of *SEQUENCE*, which describes a more general notion of sequence. *SEQUENCE* is a descendant of *LINEAR*.

There are two main categories of sequential structures: some, called circular chains, are cyclic; others, called lists, are not. Another distinction exists between dynamic structures, which may be extended at will, and fixed ones, which have a bounded capacity.

In all of the structures under review you may insert two or more occurrences of a given item in such a way that the occurrences are distinguishable. In other words, the structures are **bags** rather than just sets, although it is possible to use them to implement sets.

The distinction between bags and sets was introduced in 4.4.2, page 128.

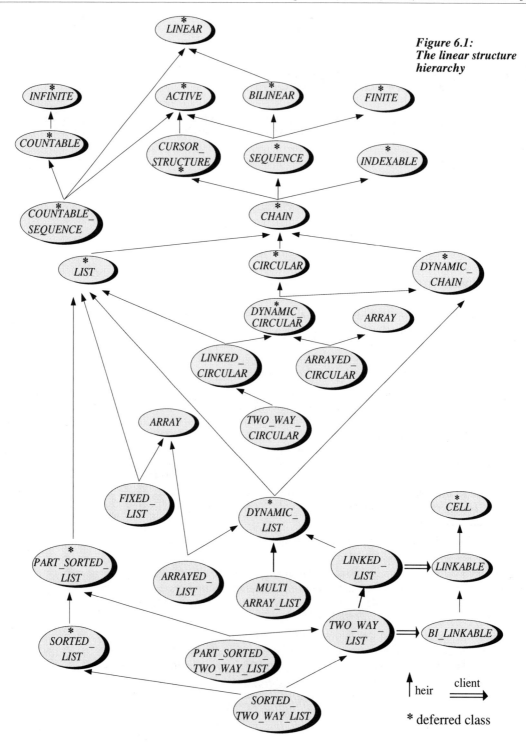

Figure 6.1:
The linear structure
hierarchy

6.2 THE INHERITANCE STRUCTURE

The figure on the preceding page gives the overall inheritance structure of the classes discussed in this chapter. Class *ARRAY*, which does not properly belong to that structure but is used for some implementations, appears in two different places so as not to clutter the diagram.

6.3 HIGHER-LEVEL TRAVERSAL CLASSES

The list and chain classes are characterized, for their traversal properties, as being linear and, more precisely, bilinear. In the traversal hierarchy, the deferred classes relevant for this chapter are *LINEAR* and *BILINEAR*, introduced in the discussion of the general taxonomy.

On the three hierarchies (access, storage, traversal) see 4.2, page 123. The interface of LINEAR appears on pages 285, that of BILINEAR on page 293.

6.3.1 Linear structures

LINEAR describes sequential structures that may be traversed one way. It introduces in particular the following features, illustrated on the figure below:

- *after*, a boolean-valued query which determines whether you have moved past the last position (a more precise specification is given below).
- *off*, a boolean-valued query which is false if and only if there is no item at the current position; for *LINEAR* this is the same as *empty* **and** *not after*.
- *item*, a query which returns the item at the current position – provided of course there is one, as expressed by the precondition: **not** *off*.
- *start*, a command to move to the first position if any (if *empty* is true the command has no effect).
- *forth*, a command to advance by one position; the precondition is **not** *after*.
- *finish*, a command to move to the last position; the precondition is **not** *empty*.

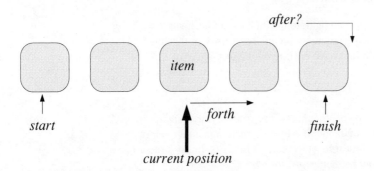

Figure 6.2:
Linear structure

About 'has' see 4.3.1, page 125.

There is also a procedure *search* with one argument, which determines whether the value of that argument appears in the structure at or after the current position, and if not makes *after* become true. This procedure is internally used by the default implementation of the *has* function (the general membership test) for linear structures. Like *has* for all containers, *search* uses object or reference equality depending on the value set for *object_comparison*.

An invariant property of *LINEAR* structures is that the current position may go off one step past the last item if any, but no further. The precondition of *forth* – **not** *after* – helps ensure this. The first item (if any) being at position 1, the maximum allowable position is *count + 1*, where *count* is the number of items.

6.3.2 Bilinear structures

BILINEAR describes linear structures which may be traversed both ways. It inherits from *LINEAR* and extends it with two new features which ensure complete symmetry between the two directions of movement:

The class interface appears in 16.2, page 293.

- *before*, a boolean-valued query which determines whether you have moved to the left of the first position (a more precise specification is given below).

- *back*, a command to move backward by one position; the precondition is **not** *before*.

For bilinear structures the position can range between 0 (not just 1) and *count + 1*. Query *off* is accordingly redefined so as to yield the value of *after* **or** *before*.

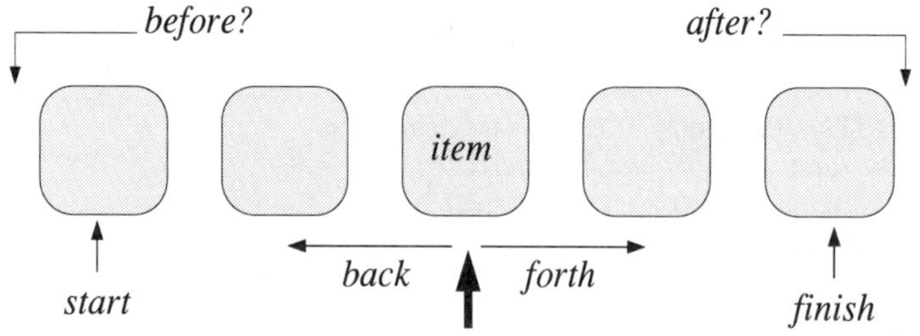

Figure 6.3:
Bilinear structure

6.3.3 Invariant properties for *after*, *before* and *off*

The redefinition of *off* illustrates a general methodological advice about invariants: be careful about not over-constraining the invariant by including properties that may be made more general in descendants. It might have been tempting to include in *LINEAR* an invariant clause of the form

$$off = empty \text{ or } after$$

This property, however, would be too constraining. More precisely, it is always true that the right-hand side implies the left-hand-side: if a linear structure is either *empty* or *after*, then it is *off*. But the converse is not true, since certain kinds of linear structure, for example bilinear ones, may be *off* but neither *empty* nor *after*.

The actual invariant for class *BILINEAR* is obtained in three stages. In class *TRAVERSABLE* the feature *off* is deferred and a basic property of that feature is expressed by the invariant clause

$$empty\_constraint: empty \text{ \textbf{implies} } off$$

In *LINEAR*, feature *off* is effected through an implementation which returns the value of the expression *empty* **or** *after*. The class adds an invariant clause which, however, says less than the implementation to leave some room for variation:

after_constraint: *after* **implies** *off*

Finally *BILINEAR*, an heir of *LINEAR*, redefines *off* to return the value of the expression *before* **or** *after*, and adds the invariant clause

before_constraint: *before* **implies** *off*

The new implementation of *off* – *after* **or** *before* – would not guarantee the invariant clause inherited from *TRAVERSABLE* were it not for another clause introduced in *BILINEAR*:

empty_property: *empty* **implies** (*after* **or** *before*)

which indicates that an empty bilinear structure must always be *after* or *before* – but not both, however, as stated by the last new clause, the reason for which is discussed in detail below:

not_both: **not** (*after* **and** *before*);

The flat-short form of *BILINEAR*, which appears in a later chapter, shows the complete reconstructed invariant:

See 16.2, page 293 for the interface of BILINEAR.

---

not_both: **not** (*after* **and** *before*) ;
empty_property: *empty* **implies** (*after* **or** *before*) ;
before_constraint: *before* **implies** *off*;
after_constraint: *after* **implies** *off*;
empty_constraint: *empty* **implies** *off*

6.3.4 Iteration patterns

With the features shown above, a typical iteration mechanism on a non-empty linear structure *lin* is of the form:

For a more general form of this scheme, applicable to circular chains as well as other linear structures, replace 'off' by 'exhausted'. See 6.5.4, page 151 below.

```
from
    lin. start;
    some_optional_initializing_operation (lin)
until
    lin. off
loop
    lin. some_action (lin. item);
    lin. forth
end
```

The value of *lin. off* is always true for an empty structure, so in this case the loop will, correctly, execute only its initialization actions if present.

You may have wondered when reading about *start* above why this procedure does not have a precondition of the form **not** *empty*, since its informal role of "moving to the first item" assumes that there is such an item. It is preferable, however, to define the specification as "move to the first item if any, otherwise do nothing"; this way the above scheme will work for an empty structure, always a desirable goal.

About iterator classes see chapter 10.

This is a very common pattern, which you will find in the library classes themselves (for example *has* is implemented in this way) and many application clients. The iterator classes corresponding to linear structures (*LINEAR_ITERATOR*, *TWO_WAY_CHAIN_ ITERATOR*) turn this pattern and several related ones into actual reusable routines.

For bilinear structures there is another traversal mechanism going backward rather than forward; it is the same as above except that *finish* replaces *start* and *back* replaces *forth*. The exit condition remains *off* since *before*, like *after*, implies *off*.

6.3.5 A precise view of *after* and *before*

Getting the specification of *after* and *before* right, so that it will handle all cases properly, requires some care.

For every one of the structures under discussion there is a notion of current position, which we may call the cursor position even though for the moment the cursor is a virtual notion only. (Actual cursor objects will come later when we combine *LINEAR*, *BILINEAR* and other classes from the traversal hierarchy with *CURSOR_STRUCTURE* and other classes from the collection hierarchy.) The informal definition is that *after* is true if and only if the cursor – in this informal sense of a fictitious marker signaling the current position – is one position after the last item, if any, and that *before* is true if and only if the cursor is one position before the first item. If, as done throughout this book, we picture linear structures with their items appearing in order from left to right, the view is this:

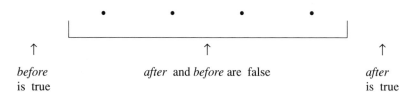

Figure 6.4:
Linear structure with
its items

When the cursor is on any of the items (shown as •), *after* and *before* are false; *after* holds when the cursor is to the right of the last item, and *before* when it is to the left of the first item.

This leaves open the question of what conventions to take for an empty structure. If iteration schemes of the above type are to work, then *after* must be true for an empty structure. For a bilinear structure, however, we should have total symmetry between the two pairs of features

- *start*, *forth*, *after*.
- *finish*, *back*, *before*.

So for an empty list both *before* and *after* should be true. This scheme was used in early version of the Base libraries. It has some disadvantages, however; in particular it is not compatible with the simple, symmetric properties

$$after = (index = count + 1)$$
$$before = (index = 0)$$

For a version of the library that uses the earlier scheme see "Object-Oriented Software Construction", 1988 edition, appendix A, in particular pages 154-155.

which express elementary definitions for *after* and *before* in terms of *index*, the current position, and *count*, the number of items (items being numbered from 1 to *count*). For an empty structure *count* is zero, so if we want *after* and *before* to be both true in this case we have to sacrifice one of the above properties, since the first would imply *index = 1* and the second *index = 0*. But again symmetry reigns supreme: we should either keep both properties or renounce both. The solution was to renounce both and replace them by slightly more complicated ones:

$$after = (empty \textbf{ or } (index = count + 1))$$
$$before = (empty \textbf{ or } (index = 0))$$

When a structure is created, some initializations will have to be made; the default initializations will usually lead to a value of 0 rather than 1 for *index*, although this dissymmetry is not apparent in the assertions.

Although acceptable, this solution leads to small but unpleasant complications, in particular frequent conditional instructions of the form

if *after* **and not** *empty* **then** ...

The solution finally retained for the Base libraries uses a different technique, which has turned out to be preferable. The idea is to replace the above conceptual picture by one in which there are always two fictitious **sentinel** items:

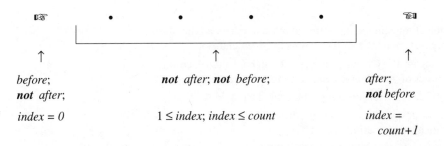

Figure 6.5:
Linear structure with extra sentinel items

The two sentinel items, which appear as ☞ and ☜ on the figure, are only present conceptually. They are of course not taken into account for the computation of *count* and, although it is possible to conceive of an implementation which would actually reserve space for them (for example in an array representation), none of the implementations used in Base for the classes of this chapter and other descendants of *LINEAR* does. The only purpose of the sentinels is to provide two valid theoretical cursor positions, which exist regardless of the number of actual (non-sentinel) items in the structure.

The sentinel items always appear at positions 0 and *count + 1*; this property is true even if the structure is empty of items, in which case *count* is zero. As a result, the following properties are part of the invariant:

0 <= index;
index <= count + 1;
before = (index = 0);
after = (index = count + 1);
not (*after* **and** *before*)

The last property given indicates that a structure can never be both *after* and *before*, since even in an empty structure the two sentinels are still present, with the cursor on one of them:

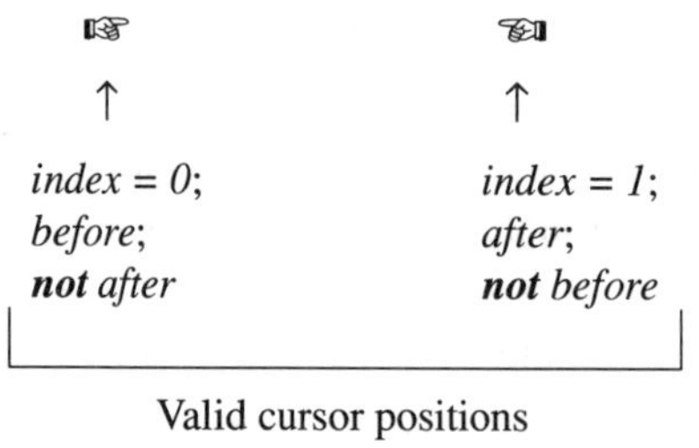

$index = 0$;
before;
not *after*

$index = 1$;
after;
not *before*

Valid cursor positions

Figure 6.6:
Empty structure with
the sentinels

For an empty structure, *index* will be zero by convention, so that *before* will be true and *after* false. But this property is not reflected in any of the invariant clauses.

6.3.6 Some lessons

This discussion illustrates some of the important patterns of reasoning that are involved in serious object-oriented design. Here are two of the lessons to be remembered.

First, consistency is once again the central principle. Throughout the design of a class library, or as here of a cluster of that library, we must constantly ask ourselves:

- "How do I make my next design decision compatible with the previous ones?"
- "How do I take my next design decision so that it will be easy – or at least possible – to make future ones compatible with it?"

The concern for symmetry which guides the discussion for the above example is but a special case of the concern for consistency.

Second, the only way to make delicate design decisions such as the ones considered here is to express the issues clearly through assertions, in particular invariants. To analyze the properties under discussion, and weigh the various alternatives, we need the precision of mathematical logic. Once again we note that without assertions it would be impossible to build a good library; we would have no way to know precisely what we are talking about.

6.4 SEQUENCES AND CHAINS

Still deferred, classes *SEQUENCE* and *CHAIN* provide the basis for all list and chain classes, as well as for many trees and for dispensers.

6.4.1 Sequences

SEQUENCE is the first class we encounter to be constructed with the full extent of the technique described in the discussion of the taxonomy: using multiple inheritance to combine one class each from the access, traversal and storage hierarchy. *SEQUENCE* indeed has three parents:

For the class interface see 16.3, page 294.

- *ACTIVE* gives the access properties. A sequence is an active structure with a notion of current item. Remember that active structures are a special case of bags.
- *BILINEAR*, as studied above, indicates that a sequence may be traversed both ways.
- *FINITE*, from the storage hierarchy, indicates that the class describes finite sequences. (A class *COUNTABLE_SEQUENCE* is also present, as described below.)

To the features of *BILINEAR*, *SEQUENCE* principally adds features for adding, changing and removing items. A few procedures in particular serve to add items at the end:

- *s.put* (*v*) adds *v* at the end of a sequence *s*.
- *extend* and *force*, at the *SEQUENCE* level, do the same as *put*.
- *s.append* (*s1*) adds to the end of *s* the items of *s1* (another sequence), preserving their *s1* order.

Other procedures work on the current position:

- *s.remove* removes the item at current position.
- *s.replace* (*v*) replaces by *v* the item at current position. *SEQUENCE*, however, does not provide a procedure to insert an item at the current position, since not all implementations of sequences support this possibility; you will find it in descendants of *SEQUENCE* seen below.

Yet another group of features are based on the first occurrence of a certain item, or on all occurrences:

- *s.prune* (*v*) removes the first occurrence of *v* in *s*, if any.
- As usual, *s.prune_all* (*v*) removes all occurrences of *v*.

These procedures have various abstract preconditions: *s.extendible* for additions, *s.writable* for replacements, *s.prunable* for removals. Properties *extendible* and *prunable* characterize general categories of container structures rather than individual instances; for example *extendible* is always true for the "dynamic" structures seen below. In contrast, *writable* depends on the current status of each instance. In general *writable* will be true if there is an item at the current position.

6.4.2 Chains

Chains are sequences with a few more properties: items may be accessed through their indices, and it is possible to define cursor objects attached to individual items.

Class *CHAIN* is an heir of *SEQUENCE*. It gets its access properties from *CURSOR_STRUCTURE* (which adds the notion of cursor to the features of *ACTIVE*, already present in *SEQUENCE*) and is also an heir of *INDEXABLE*. This ancestry implies in particular the presence of the following features:

For the class interface, which is the same as for LIST, see 16.4, page 295.

- *cursor*, from *CURSOR_STRUCTURE*, which makes it possible to keep a reference to an item of the structure.

- *i_th* and *put_i_th* from *TABLE*, via *INDEXABLE*, which make it possible to access and replace the value of an item given by its integer index. These features were called *item* and *put* in *TABLE*, but are renamed here to remove the conflict with homonymous features from *SEQUENCE*.

Procedure *put* for chains is the version obtained from *CURSOR_STRUCTURE*, which has the same effect as *replace* – replacing the value of the item at cursor position. The *put* procedure from *SEQUENCE* is renamed *sequence_put*. This feature is not exported by *CHAIN*, however, since its effect (adding an item at the end) may be obtained through the simpler name *extend*.

6.4.3 Dynamic chains

By default, chains can only be extended at the end, through *extend* and *sequence_put*. Of particular interest are those chains where clients can insert and remove items at any position. Such chains are said to be dynamic, and described by *CHAIN*'s heir *DYNAMIC_CHAIN*. The new features are predictable:

- Procedure *put_front* adds an item before the first. (As noted, the procedures to add an item after the last are already available in chains.)

- Procedures *put_left* and *put_right* add an item at the left and right of the cursor position.

- Procedures *remove_left* and *remove_right* remove an item at the left and right or the cursor position.

- Procedures *merge_left* and *merge_right* are similar to *put_left* and *put_right* but insert another dynamic chain rather than a single item. As the word "merge" suggests, the merged structure, passed as argument, does not survive the process; it is emptied of its items. To preserve it, perform a *clone* or *copy* before the merge operation.

The class also provides implementations of *prune*, *prune_all* and *wipe_out* from *COLLECTION*. To make these implementations useful, it defines queries *extendible* and *prunable* so that they return the value true.

6.5 LISTS AND CIRCULAR STRUCTURES

A chain is a finite sequential structure. This property means that items are arranged in a linear order and may be traversed from the first to the last. To do this you may use a loop of the form shown above, based on procedures *start* and *forth*.

See 6.3.4, page 143 above.

This property leaves room for several variants. In particular chains may be **straight** or **circular**.

6.5.1 Lists

A straight chain, which from now on will be called a **list**, has a beginning and an end:

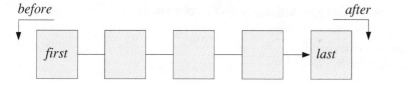

before   *after*

first · · · *last*

Figure 6.7:
List

Such structures are described by class *LIST*.

For the class interface, which is the same as for CHAIN, see 16.4, page 295.

6.5.2 Circular chains

A **circular chain**, as represented by class *CIRCULAR* and its descendants, has a much more flexible notion of first item. It is organized so that every item has a successor, hence the natural pictorial representation, which justifies the name "circular":

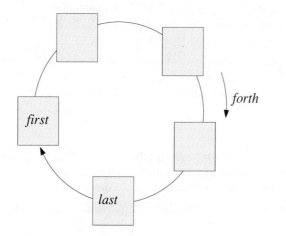

forth

first

last

Figure 6.8:
Chain

This representation is conceptual only; in fact the implementations of circular chains found in the Base libraries are based on lists, implemented in one of the ways described below (in particular linked and arrayed).

The major originality of circular chains is that unless the structure is empty procedure *forth* is always applicable: it will cycle past the last item, coming back to the first. This is suggested by the appearance of *forth* with a curved arrow on the figure. The symmetric property applies to *back*.

The cyclic nature of *forth* and *back* for circular chains is expressed precisely by the assertions. The version of *forth* for class *CHAIN*, which comes from *LINEAR*, has precondition

   not *after*

Similarly, the precondition for *back* is **not** *before*. For lists, *after* becomes true when the cursor moves past the last item. For circular chains, however, *after* and *before* are never true except for an empty structure; this is expressed by the invariant clauses of class *CIRCULAR*:

   not_before_unless_empty: *before* **implies** *empty*;
   not_after_unless_empty: *after* **implies** *empty*;
   not_off_unless_empty: *off* **implies** *empty*

For a non-empty circular chain, then, you can circle forever around the items, using *forth* or *back*.

6.5.3 Choosing the first item

For a list, the first and last items are fixed, and correspond to specific places in the physical representation.

A circular chain also needs a notion of first item, if only to enable a client to initiate a traversal through procedure *start*. Similarly, there is a last item − the one just before the first in a cyclic traversal. (If the chain has just one item, it is both first and last.)

For circular chains, however, there is no reason why the first item should always remain the same. One of the benefits that clients may expect from the use of a circular structure is the ability to choose any item as the logical first. Class *CIRCULAR* offers for that purpose the procedure

For the interface of class CIRCULAR see 16.11, page 318.

   set_start

which designates the current cursor position as the first in the circular chain. Subsequent calls to *start* will move the cursor to this position; calls to *finish* will move the cursor to the cyclically preceding position.

With most implementations, there will then be two notions of first position: the logical first, which clients may freely choose through calls to *set_start*; and the physical first, which results from the implementation. In a representation using an array with indices from 1 to *capacity*, for example, the physical first is position 1, and the logical first may be any index in the permitted range. In a linked representation, there will be a cell *first_element* corresponding to the physical first, but the logical first is any cell in the chain.

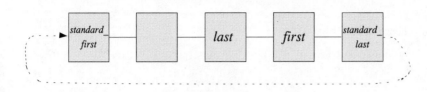

Figure 6.9:
Circular chain
implemented as a list

In such cases the circular chain classes have features called *standard_first*, *standard_last*, *standard_start* and so on, which are not exported (so that you will not see them in the flat-short forms of chapter 16) but serve to implement visible features such as *first*, *last* and *forth*. For example a possible implementation of *forth* for circular chains is

```
forth is
        -- Move cursor to next item, cyclically.
    do
        standard_forth;
        if standard_after then
            standard_start
        end;
        if isfirst then
            exhausted := true
        end
    end
```

6.5.4 Traversing a list or circular chain

The properties of *forth* for circular chains imply that a traversal loop written as

```
from lin.start until lin.off loop
    ...;
    lin.forth
end
```

would not work if *lin* is a non-empty circular structure: *off* would never become true, so that the loop would forever cycle over the structure's items. The same would apply to a loop using *finish* and *back* instead of *start* and *forth*.

This behavior is the natural result of the semantics defined for *off*, *forth* and *back* for circular structures. But it prevents us from using these features to perform a single traversal which will visit every item once.

Using *exhausted* in lieu of *off* solves this problem. In class *CIRCULAR*, *exhausted* is an attribute which is set to **false** by *start* and *finish*, and is set to **true** by *forth* when advancing from the last item to the first and by *back* when backing up from the first item to the last. So you should write the loop as

> *from*
>   *lin.start*;
>   *some_optional_initializing_operation* (*lin*)
> *until*
>   *lin.exhausted*
> *loop*
>   *lin.some_action* (*lin.item*);
>   *lin.forth*
> *end*

This form is applicable to all linear structures, circular or not, since *exhausted* is introduced in class *LINEAR* as a function which returns the same value as *off*. Its redefinition into an attribute, modified by *start*, *finish*, *forth* and *back*, does not occur until class *CIRCULAR*.

Because *exhausted* is more general than *off*, the iteration scheme just given (and its equivalent going backwards) is preferable to the earlier one using *off*, especially if there is any chance that the iteration might one day be applied to a *lin* structure that is circular. Classes of the Iteration library, in particular *LINEAR_ITERATOR*, rely on this scheme for iterating over linear structures.

6.5.5 Dynamic structures

For both lists and circular chains, the most flexible variants, said to be dynamic, allow insertions and deletions at any position.

The corresponding classes are descendants of *DYNAMIC_LIST* and *DYNAMIC_CIRCULAR*, themselves heirs of *DYNAMIC_CHAIN* studied above.

6.5.6 Infinite sequences

Class *COUNTABLE_SEQUENCES*, built by inheritance from *COUNTABLE*, *LINEAR* and *ACTIVE*, is similar to *SEQUENCE* but describes infinite rather than finite sequences.

The class interface is in 16.15, page 327.

6.6 IMPLEMENTATIONS

We have by now seen the concepts underlying the linear structures of the Base libraries, especially lists and circular chains. Let us look at the techniques used to implement them.

6.6.1 Linked and arrayed implementations

Most of the implementations belong to one of four general categories, better described as two categories with two subcategories each:

- Linked implementations, which may be one-way or two-way.
- Arrayed implementations, which may be resizable or fixed.

A linked implementation uses linked cells, each containing an item and a reference to the next cell. One-way structures are described by classes whose names begin with *LINKED_*, for example *LINKED_LIST*. Two-way structures use cell which, in addition to the reference to the next cell, also include a reference to the previous one. Their names begin with *TWO_WAY_*.

An arrayed implementation uses an array to represent a linear structure. If the array is resizable, the corresponding class name begins with *ARRAYED_*, for example *ARRAYED_LIST*; if not, the prefix is *FIXED_*.

6.6.2 Linked structures

A linked structure requires two classes: one, such as *LINKED_LIST*, describes the list proper; the other, such as *LINKABLE*, describes the individual list cells. The figure should help understand the difference; it describes a linked list, but the implementation of linked circular chains is similar.

For the class interface of LINKED_LIST and TWO_WAY_LIST see 16.5, page 299.

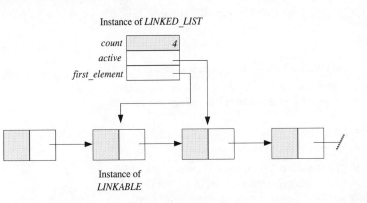

Instance of LINKED_LIST

count   4
active
first_element

Instance of
LINKABLE

Figure 6.10:
Linked list and linked cells

The instance of type *LINKED_LIST* shown at the top contains general information about the list, such as the number of items (*count*) and a reference to the first element (*first_element*). Because lists are active structures with a notion of current position, there is also a reference *active* to the cell at the current position. An entity declared as

   my_list: *LINKED_LIST* [*SOME_TYPE*]

will have as its run-time value (if not void) a reference to such an object, which is really a list header. The actual list content is given by the *LINKABLE* instances, each of which contains a value of type *SOME_TYPE* and a reference to the next item, called *right*. Clearly, a header of type *LINKED_LIST* [*SOME_TYPE*] will be associated with cells of type *LINKABLE* [*SOME_TYPE*] for the same actual generic parameter *SOME_TYPE*.

Features such as *active* and *first_element* are used only for the implementation; they are not exported, and so you will not find them in the flat-short specifications, although the figures show them to illustrate the representation technique.

A similar implementation is used for two-way-linked structures such as two-way lists (pictured below) and two-way circular chains.

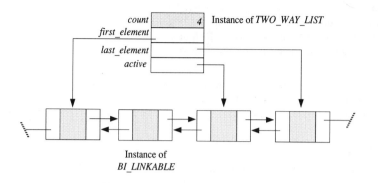

Figure 6.11:
Two-way linked list

6.6.3 Linked cells

The classes describing list cells are descendants of a deferred class called *CELL*, whose features are:

- *item*, the contents of the cell.
- *put* (*v*: **like** *item*), which replaces the contents of the cell by a new value.

Class *LINKABLE* is an effective descendant of *CELL*, used for one-way linked structures. It introduces features *right*, a reference to another cell to which the current cell will be linked.

Two-way linked structures use *BI_LINKABLE*, an heir of *LINKABLE* which to the above features adds *left*, a reference to the preceding cell in the structure.

Do not confuse the *item* feature of *CELL* and its descendants, such as *LINKABLE*, with the *item* feature of the classes describing linear structures, such as *LINKED_LIST*. For a linked list, *item* returns the item at cursor position; it may be implemented as

```
item: G is
        -- Current item
    do
        Result := active.item
    end
```

using the *item* feature of *LINKABLE*, applied to *active*.

6.6.4 One-way and two-way linked chains

If you look at the interfaces of one-way and two-way linked structures, you will notice that they are almost identical. This is because it is possible to implement features such as *back* for one-way structures such as described by *LINKED_LIST* and *LINKED_CIRCULAR*. A simple implementation of *back* stores away a reference to the current *active* item, executes *start*, and then performs *forth* until the item to the right of the cursor position is the previous *active*.

Although correct, such an implementation is of course rather inefficient since it requires a traversal of the list. In terms of algorithmic complexity, it is in O (*count*),

See 16.5, page 299 for the interface of LINKED_LIST and TWO_WAY_LIST, and 16.12, page 322 for that of LINKED_CIRCULAR and TWO_WAY_CIRCULAR.

meaning that its execution time is on the average proportional to the number of items in the structure. In contrast, *forth* is O (1), that is to say, takes an execution time bounded by a constant.

As a consequence, you should not use one-way linked structures if you need to execute more than occasional *back* operations (and other operations requiring access to previous items, such as *remove_left*). Two-way linked structures, such as those described by *TWO_WAY_LIST* and *TWO_WAY_CIRCULAR*, treat the two directions symmetrically, so that *back* will be just as efficient as *forth*. Hence the following important advice:

> If you need to traverse a linked structure both ways, not just left to right, use the *TWO_WAY_* classes, not the *LINKED_* versions.

The *TWO_WAY_* structures will take up more space, since they use *BI_LINKABLE* rather than *LINKABLE* cells, but for most applications this space penalty is justified by the considerable gains in time that will result if right-to-left operations are frequently needed.

It is legitimate to criticize the very presence of *back* and related features in the one-way classes, on the grounds that they openly invite inefficiency. But since these features are conceptually defined for one-way structures, there is no reason to deny them to clients. As long as the features are used only occasionally, it is convenient to have them in the one-way classes, especially if space efficiency is a concern.

6.6.5 Arrayed chains

Arrayed structures as described by *ARRAYED_LIST*, *FIXED_LIST* and *ARRAYED_CIRCULAR* use arrays for their implementations. A list or circular chain of *count* items may be stored in positions 1 to *count* of an array of *capacity* items, where *capacity* ≥ *count*.

See 16.6, page 304 for the interface of ARRAYED_LIST and 16.13, page 324 for ARRAYED_CIRCULAR.

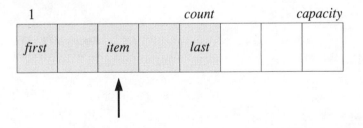

Figure 6.12:
List implemented as an array

An instance of *FIXED_LIST*, as the name suggests, has a fixed number of items. In particular:

For the class interface see 16.8, page 309.

- Query *extendible* has value false for *FIXED_LIST*: you may replace existing items, but not add any, even at the end. A *FIXED_LIST* is created with a certain number of items and retains that number.
- As a result, *FIXED_LIST* joins the deferred feature *count* of *LIST* with the feature *count* of *ARRAY*, which satisfies the property *count = capacity*.

- Query *prunable* has value false too: it is not possible to remove an item from a fixed list.

In contrast, *ARRAYED_LIST* has almost the same interface as *LINKED_LIST*. In particular, it is possible to add items at the end using procedure *extend*; if the call causes the list to grow beyond the current array's *capacity*, it will trigger a resizing. This is achieved by using the procedure *force* of class *ARRAY* to implement *extend*.

ARRAYED_LIST even has the insertion procedures (*put_front*, *put_left*, *put_right*) and removal procedures (*prune*, *remove*, *remove_left*, *remove_right*) that apply to arbitrary positions and appear in the linked implementations. These procedures, however, are rather inefficient, since they usually require moving a whole set of array items, an O (*count*) operation. (Procedure *extend* does not suffer from this problem, since it is easy to add an item to the end of an array, especially if there is still room so that no resizing is necessary.)

The situation of these features in *ARRAYED_LIST* is similar to the situation of *back* in classes describing one-way linked structures: it is convenient to include them because they may be needed once in a while and an implementation exists; but using them more than occasionally may result in serious inefficiencies. If you do need to perform arbitrary insertions and removal, use linked structures, not arrayed ones.

Arrayed structures, however, use up less space than linked representations. So they are appropriate for chains on which, except possibly for insertions at the end, few insertion and removal operations or none at all are expected after creation.

FIXED_LIST offers few advantages over *ARRAYED_LIST*. I tend to use *ARRAYED_LIST* since it is internally almost the same implementation, benefiting from the efficiency of arrays, and does not prevent me from adding items at the end. *FIXED_LIST* may be useful, however, for cases in which the fixed number of items is part of the specification, and any attempt to add more items must be treated as an error.

For circular chains only one variant is available, *ARRAYED_CIRCULAR*, although writing a *FIXED_* version would be a simple exercise.

6.6.6 Multi-arrayed lists

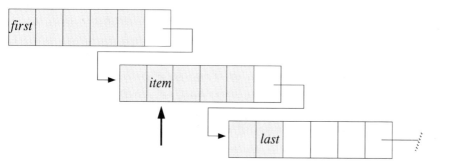

Figure 6.13:
Multi-arrayed list

For lists one more variant is available, combining some of the advantages of arrayed and linked implementations: *MULTI_ARRAY_LIST*. With this implementation a list is divided into a number of blocks. Each block is an array, but the successive arrays are linked.

For the class interface see 16.7, page 307.

6.7 SORTED LINEAR STRUCTURES

The class *COMPARABLE_STRUCT*, an heir of *BILINEAR*, is declared as

For the class interface, given together with that of SORTED_STRUCT, see 16.14, page 326.

> **deferred class** COMPARABLE_STRUCT [G −> COMPARABLE] **inherit**
>
>   *BILINEAR*
>
> **feature**
>
>   ...

As indicated by the constrained generic parameter it describes bilinear structures whose items may be compared by a total order relation.

> Note that the class name, chosen brevity's sake, is slightly misleading: it is not the structures that are comparable but their items.

COMPARABLE_STRUCT introduces the features *min* and *max*, giving access to the minimum and maximum elements of a structure; these are always present for a finite structure with a total order relation.

SORTED_STRUCT, an heir of *COMPARABLE_STRUCT*, describes structures that can be sorted; it introduces the query *sorted* and the command *sort*.

The deferred class *PART_SORTED_LIST* describes lists whose items are kept ordered in a way that is compatible with a partial order relation defined on them. The class is declared as

For the class interface see 16.9, page 311.

> **deferred class** PART_SORTED_LIST [G −> PART_COMPARABLE] ...

An implementation based on two-way linked lists is available through the effective heir *SORTED_TWO_WAY_LIST*.

The deferred class *SORTED_LIST*, which inherits from *PART_SORTED_LIST*, assumes that the order relation on *G* is a total order. As a result, the class is able to introduce features *min, max* and *median*. Here too a a two-way linked list implementation is available, through the effective class *SORTED_TWO_WAY_LIST*.

For the class interface see 16.10, page 312.

7

Dispenser structures: stacks, queues, priority lists

7.1 OVERVIEW

The classes in this chapter describe dispensers: data structures for storing and retrieving objects blindly – that is to say in such a way that each structure's internal policy, not the client, determines the relationship between the order in which the objects are stored and the order in which they are retrieved.

The fundamental operations are *put* (insert an item), *item* (retrieve an item without removing it), *remove* (remove an item) and *empty* (test for empty structure).

The most common dispensers are stacks and queues, corresponding to last-in-first-out and first-in-first-out retrieval techniques. Another category is priority queues, for which Base offers an efficient implementation, heaps.

> The flat-short interfaces of the classes discussed in this chapter appear in chapter 17.

The figure on the next page shows the inheritance hierarchy of the dispenser classes. It must be complemented by the following links: *ARRAYED_STACK* and *ARRAYED_QUEUE* inherit from *ARRAYED_LIST*; *LINKED_STACK* and *LINKED_QUEUE* inherit from *LINKED_LIST*; *LINKED_PRIORITY_QUEUE* inherits from *SORTED_TWO_WAY_LIST*; *HEAP_PRIORITY_QUEUE* inherits from *ARRAY*.

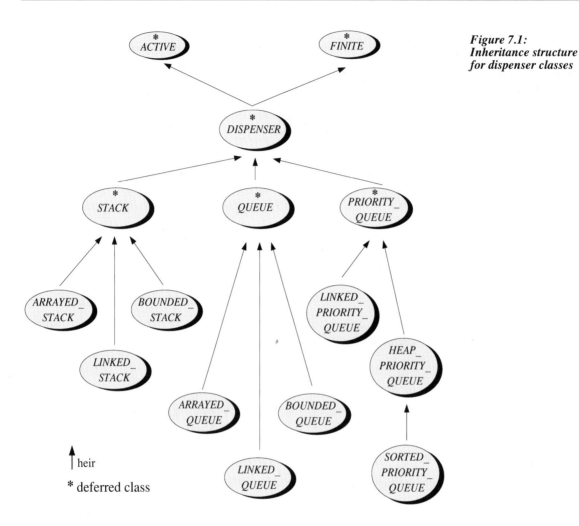

Figure 7.1:
Inheritance structure
for dispenser classes

7.2 THE NOTION OF DISPENSER

A dispenser is called that way because of the image of a vending machine (a dispenser) of a rather primitive nature, in which there is only one button. If you press the button and the dispenser is not empty, you get one of its items in the exit tray at the bottom, but you do not choose that item: the machine does. There is also an input slot at the top, into which you may deposit new items; but you have no control over the order in which successive button press operations will retrieve these items.

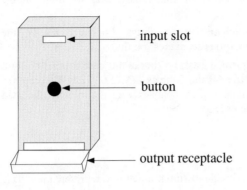

Figure 7.2:
A dispenser

The deferred class *DISPENSER* provides the facilities which will be shared by all specialized classes. In fact, the interface of all dispenser classes is nearly identical, with the exception of a few extra possibilities offered by priority queues.

The class interface of DISPENSER appears with the interfaces of other abstract container classes in 14.15, page 281.

Many kinds of dispenser are possible, each defined by the relation that the machine defines between the order in which items are inserted and the order in which they are returned. The Base libraries support three important categories – stacks, queues, and priority queues:

- A stack is a dispenser with a last-in, first-out (LIFO) internal policy: items come out in the reverse order of their insertion. Each button press returns the last deposited item.

- A queue is a dispenser with a first-in, first-out (FIFO) internal policy: items come out in the order of their insertion. Each button press returns the oldest item deposited and not yet removed.

- In a priority queue, items have an associated notion of order; the element that comes out at any given time is the largest of those which are in the dispenser.

7.3 STACKS

Stacks – dispensers with a LIFO retrieval policy – are a ubiquitous structure in software development. Their most famous application is to parsing (syntactic analysis), but many other types of systems use one or more stacks.

Class *STACK* describes general stacks, without commitment to a representation. This is a deferred class which may not be directly instantiated.

For the class interface see 17.2, page 333.

The fundamental operations are *put* (add an element at end of queue), *item* (retrieve the oldest element, non-destructively), *remove* (remove the oldest element), *empty* (test for empty queue).

Three effective heirs are provided:

- *LINKED_STACK*: stacks implemented as linked lists, with no limit on the number of items (*count*).

Class interface in 17.5, page 339.

- *BOUNDED_STACK*: stacks implemented as arrays. For such stacks, the maximum number of items (*capacity*) is set at creation time.

17.4, page 337.

- *ARRAYED_STACK*: also implemented as arrays, but in this case there is no limit on the number of items; the interface is the same as *LINKED_STACK* except for the creation procedure. If the number of elements exceeds the initially allocated capacity, the array will simply be resized.

17.3, page 335.

7.4 TYPES OF QUEUES

Class *QUEUE* describes general queues, without commitment to a representation. This is a deferred class which may not be directly instantiated.

Class interface in 17.6, page 340.

Three non-deferred heirs are also provided, distinguished by the same properties as their stack counterparts:

- *LINKED_QUEUE.*

17.9, page 346.

- *BOUNDED_QUEUE.*

17.8, page 344.

- *ARRAYED_QUEUE.*

17.7, page 342.

7.5 PRIORITY QUEUES

In a priority queue, each item has an associated priority value, and there is an order relation on these values. The item returned by *item* or removed by *remove* is the element with the highest priority.

The most general class is *PRIORITY_QUEUE*, which is deferred. Two effective variants are provided:

The interfaces for these classes are in 17.10, page 347.

- *LINKED_PRIORITY_QUEUE*, a linked list implementation.

- *HEAP_PRIORITY_QUEUE* which is more efficient and is to be preferred in most cases. A heap is organized like a binary tree, although physically stored in an array; elements with a high priority percolate towards the root.

Because it must be possible to compare priorities, the type of the items must conform to *PART_COMPARABLE*. Constrained genericity ensures this; all the priority queue classes have a formal generic parameter constrained by *PART_COMPARABLE*, for example

PART_COMPARABLE describes values on which an order relation exists. See 5.3.2, page 136.

class *PRIORITY_QUEUE* [G –> *PART_COMPARABLE*] ...

Constrained genericity was discussed in 2.7.11, page 45.

8

Trees

Trees and their immediate generalization, forests, are useful for any system that manipulates hierarchically organized information. The range of applications is broad, from abstract syntax trees in compilers through document structures in text processing systems to company organization charts in business software.

Trees, in particular binary trees and their variants, also provide convenient implementations of container data structures.

This chapter presents the various forms of trees supported by the classes of the Base libraries.

> The flat-short interfaces of the classes discussed in this chapter appear in chapter 18.

The first figure on the following page represents the inheritance structure of the classes discussed in this chapter. It also includes other classes used as parents by various tree classes. The inheritance link between *BI_LINKABLE* and *LINKABLE* has been omitted.

8.1 BASIC TERMINOLOGY

A tree consists of a set of nodes. Each node may have zero or more **children**, other nodes of which it is the **parent**. Each node has at most one parent, although it may have an arbitrary number of children.

The first figure on the next page (the class inheritance graph) provides an example of a graph that is **not** a tree, since certain nodes have more than one parent.

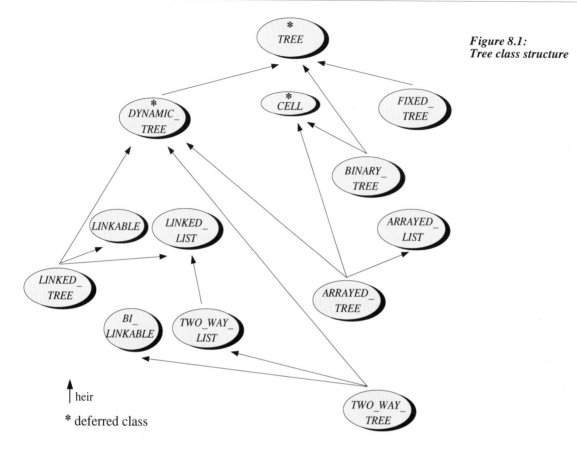

Here in contrast is a tree; by compatibility with other figures of this book, the arrow represents the "parent" relation (it points from every node to its parent if any).

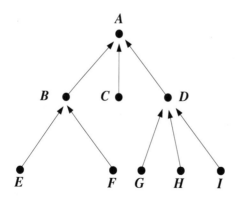

A node with no parent, such as the node marked *A* on the figure, is called a **root**; a node with no children, such as *E, F, G, H* and *I*, is called a **leaf**. The length of a path from the root to a leaf (that is to say, the number of nodes on the path minus one) is the **height** of the tree; the average length of all such paths is the **average height**. On the figure the height is 2 and the average height is 11/6 since of the six paths five have length 2 and one has length 1.

The children of a common node are called **siblings**. For example *G, H* and *I* are siblings on the figure. The siblings of a node are usually considered to be ordered; the order corresponds to the direction from left to right on conventional figures such as this one.

The **descendants** of a node are the node itself and, recursively, the descendants of its children. The **ancestors** of a node are the node itself and, recursively, the ancestors of its parent. For example the descendants of *A* are all the tree's nodes; and the ancestors of *I* are *A, D* and *I*.

To obtain a tree rather than a more general kind of graph, there is an extra requirement: in we start from an arbitrary node, go to the parent, to the parent's parent and so on (for as long as there is a parent), we will never find the starting node again. In more precise terms the condition is that the "parent" relation must not have any cycles. (That relation is in fact a partial function, since every node has zero or one parent.)

> If we consider infinite as well as finite trees the above condition must be restated to express that
> if we start from an arbitrary node and repeatedly go to the parent we will eventually hit a root.
> This discussion, however, will only consider finite trees (those with a finite number of nodes),
> for which the two statements are equivalent.

The definition given so far properly defines **forests** rather than trees. A tree is a forest with at most one root (that is to say, with exactly one root unless it is empty), such as the example on the last figure. The discussion and the library classes will handle trees rather than forest, but this is not a very important difference since by using an obvious device you can treat any forest as a tree: simply add an extra node, and make it the parent of all the forest's roots.

Another important observation is that there is a one-to-one correspondence between trees and nodes. To any node N of a tree T we can associate a tree: take T, remove all nodes that are not descendants of N, and use N as the new root. Conversely, to any tree we can associate a node – its root. This correspondence enables us to treat the two concepts of tree and node as essentially the same.

8.2 RECURSIVE TREES

The closeness of the notions of tree and node yields an elegant definition of trees in terms of lists.

On list cells see 6.6.3, page 154.

8.2.1 A tree is a list and a list cell

The discussion of lists in an earlier chapter used an auxiliary notion: list cell. If we now look at trees or, equivalently, at tree nodes, we can consider each node as being both:

Chapter 6.

- A list: the list of its children.
- A list cell (similar to a *LINKABLE* or *BI_LINKABLE* for one-way and two-way linked lists), paired with the node's siblings.

This yields a simple definition of trees by multiple inheritance from *LIST* and *CELL*.

8.2.2 Dynamic recursive trees

An example of dynamic tree structure is provided by class *TWO_WAY_TREE*, an heir of both *TWO_WAY_LIST* and *BI_LINKABLE*.

The class interface of TWO_WAY_TREE and LINKED_TREE is in 18.3, page 354.

> There is also *LINKED_TREE*, which inherits from *LINKED_LIST* and *LINKABLE*, but *TWO_WAY_TREE* is generally preferable since children of a node often needs to be traversed both ways; the notion of order is usually less significant here than for lists.

Such a form of definition is a particularly effective way of conveying the profoundly recursive nature of trees. The corresponding classes are useful in many different areas such as graphics, text processing and compilation.

To create a one-way or two-way linked tree, use

!! *my_tree.make* (*root_value*)

This will attach *my_tree* to a new one-node tree, with *root_value* at the root node. Here *my_tree* must be declared of type *TWO_WAY_TREE* [*MY_TYPE*] for some type *MY_TYPE*, and *root_value* must be of type *MY_TYPE*.

A class with a similar interface but using arrays rather than lists to represent nodes is also available: *ARRAYED_TREE*. This class is more efficient in both time and space for trees whose nodes have many children that are accessed randomly, if relatively few child insertions occur after node creation. Here the creation procedure indicates the initial number of children:

Class interface in 18.4, page 361.

!! *my_tree make* (*max_estimated_children*, *root_value*)

The integer argument *max_estimated_children* only serves for the initial allocation; the array will be resized if the number of children grows beyond the initial size. As with the previous kinds of tree, the newly created node initially has no children.

8.2.3 Fixed trees

TWO_WAY_TREE is useful for fully dynamic trees, in which a node may get new children at any time. For some applications, the number of children of a tree, although still arbitrary, is set for each node when the node is created, and will not change after that. Of course, some children may be absent; the corresponding entries will be void references. Class *FIXED_TREE* provides the basic mechanism; as you may have guessed, the implementation associates with each node an array of its children, arrays usually being the right structure when a collection of objects is known not to change size after creation.

The class interface of FIXED_TREE is in 18.5, page 363.

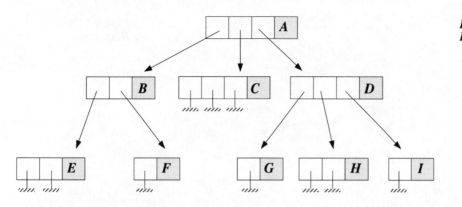

Figure 8.3:
Fixed tree

To create a fixed tree, use

!! *my_fixed_tree.make* (*how_many_children*, *root_value*)

The root will have the associated value *root* value and will have *how_many_children* children, all initially void. Unlike the argument *max_estimated_children* for the creation procedure of *ARRAYED_TREE*, the value of *how_many_children* is the final arity of the newly created node; since it set separately for each node on creation, the various nodes of a tree can have different arities, as illustrated on the above figure.

8.2.4 Properties of recursive trees

Whether fixed or dynamic, recursive trees fully enjoy their dual origin. This means in particular that each node is viewed as a list of its children, and can apply to this list the features inherited from *LIST*, appropriately renamed; for example:

child_put_left
child_forth
child_put

and so on. Feature *count*, inherited from *LIST*, indicates the number of children; it is renamed *arity* to conform to accepted tree terminology. (The word is a substantived form of the "ary" adjective ending, as in "ternary", "quaternary" and so on, which yielded the expression "*n*-ary".)

8.3 BINARY TREES

Binary trees are a special case of fixed trees in which nodes always have two children, although either or both of these children may be void.

8.3.1 Basic binary trees

Class *BINARY_TREE* describes binary trees.

Class interface in 18.6, page 365.

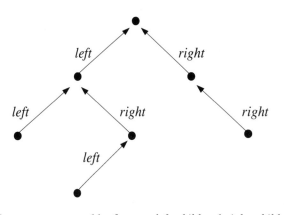

Figure 8.4:
Binary tree

The children are represented by features *left_child* and *right_child*. Queries *has_left* and *has_right* indicate whether any of these is non-void; *arity* is redefined to yield the number of non-void children (0, 1 or 2).

8.3.2 Binary representations of trees

For any ordinary tree, there exists a standard representation as a binary tree, which is useful in some applications. The correspondence is one-to-one, so that the original tree may be reconstructed without ambiguity. It actually applies to forests rather than trees and works as follows, *fr* being the first root in a forest: the binary tree's root corresponds to *fr*; its left subtree is obtained recursively from the forest made by the subtrees of *fr*; and its right subtree is obtained recursively from the original forest deprived of the tree rooted at *fr*. If you start from a tree rather than a forest the binary tree's root will have no right child.

Function *binary_representation*, in *TREE*, creates a binary tree representation (the function's result) obtained from the current tree. Procedure *fill_from_binary*, in *DYNAMIC_TREE*, reconstructs a tree from a binary tree representation passed as argument.

8.3.3 Binary search trees

Class *BINARY_SEARCH_TREE* describes binary search trees, an implementation of bags which is appropriate for comparable items.

Class interface in 18.7, page 368.

Binary search trees rely for insertion on a policy whereby any item less than the root is inserted (recursively) into the left subtree, and any item greater than the root into the right subtree. So if the insertion order is reasonably random the items will distribute evenly among the various branches, This means that the average height of the tree will be not much more than the optimal: $\lfloor \log_2 n \rfloor$ where n is the number of nodes and $\lfloor x \rfloor$, for any x, is the integer part of x.

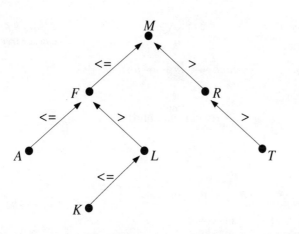

Figure 8.5:
Binary search tree

Since search operations will follow the same principle (search left if smaller than the root, and so on), the time to find an item or ascertain that it is not there is proportional to the average height. In normal cases this means about $\lfloor \log_2 n \rfloor$ basic operations, rather than n with a linear structure such as a list, and hence much better performance for large n.

8.4 CURSOR TREES

Recursive trees, as described so far, are not active data structures: even though each node has its own cursor to traverse the list of its children, there is no global cursor on the tree as a whole. It is not hard to see that the notion of recursive tree is in fact incompatible with the presence of a global cursor.

The notion of active data structure was discussed in 4.4.4, page 129.

In situations where you need such a cursor, enabling you to move freely from a node to its children, siblings and parents, you may use class *CURSOR_TREE* and its descendants.

Class interface in 18.8, page 369.

8.4.1 The conceptual model

With cursor trees the model is different from what we have seen earlier in this chapter: there is a clear distinction between the nodes and the tree itself. The manipulated object is a tree, and the notion of node is merely implicit.

In the various operations presented below and illustrated on the following figure, "up" means towards the root and "down" towards the leaves. This, of course, is the reverse of the properties of trees of the other kind – those which grow towards the sun and serve to print books about software.

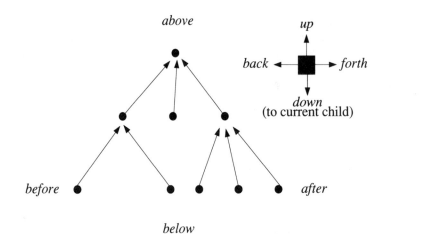

8.4.2 Operations on cursor trees

The cursor supported by instances of *CURSOR_TREE* has a position referring to a node of the tree, which is then considered to be the active node, or is *off* the tree. The different *off* positions are: *above* (above the root), *below* (below a leaf), *before* (before a leftmost sibling), *after* (after a rightmost sibling.) As with linear structures, fictitious sentinel elements are assumed to be present to the left, right, top and bottom.

The notion of sentinel element was introduced in 6.3.5, page 144.

Various procedures are available to move the cursor in all directions:

- *down* (*i*) moves the cursor down to the *i*-th child of the active node. If *i* is equal to 0 the cursor ends up *before*; if *i* is equal to the *arity* of the current parent plus 1, the cursor ends up *after*. Calling *down* (*i*) when the cursor is on a leaf node results in setting *below* and *before* to true if *i* is equal to *0*, or *below* and *after* to true if *i* is equal to *arity+1*.

- *forth* and *back* move the cursor forward and backward between siblings and can cause the cursor to end up *after* or *before*.

- *up* moves the cursor up one level. The call may be made even when the cursor is *after* or *before*. If the cursor is on the root of the tree or *below* in an empty tree, the cursor ends up *above*.

You can move the cursor in any one direction (*up, down, forth, back*), repeatedly until it is *off* (*above, below, after, before* respectively), but once it is *off*, further movement in the same direction is prohibited. For example the precondition of *put_left* requires *before* to be false, and the precondition of *put_right* requires *after* to be false.

It is possible to move down from an *above* position; in an empty tree this brings the cursor *below*. Similarly, it is possible to move up from *below*, left from *after*, right from *before*.

The sentinel element above the tree's root is considered to be the root of a forest containing just one tree. This view justifies the convention for the result of *arity* when the cursor is *above*: 0 if the tree is *empty*, 1 if it has a root (viewed as the child of the fictitious sentinel element).

8.4.3 Manipulating the cursor explicitly

The cursor attached to a cursor tree is not just a conceptual notion but an actual object, of type *CURSOR*.

You may use the query *cursor* to obtain a reference to the current cursor. Procedure *go_to* takes a cursor as argument and brings the tree's cursor to the node identified by the value of that argument.

8.4.4 Traversals

A useful notion associated with trees and particularly applicable to cursor trees is that of traversal.

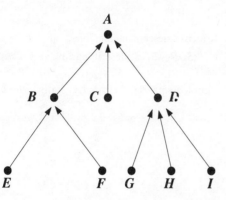

Figure 8.7:
A tree

A traversal is a certain policy for ordering all the nodes in a tree – usually to apply an operation to all these nodes in the resulting order. *CURSOR_TREE* and its descendants support three forms of traversal: preorder, postorder and breadth-first. They correspond to the most commonly used traversal policies on trees, illustrated on the figure (where the children of each node are assumed to be ordered from left to right):

- Preorder is the traversal that visits the root first, then (recursively) traverses each subtree in order. On the figure we will visit node *A* first then, recursively, the subtrees rooted at *B* (which implies visiting *E* and *F*), *C* and *D*. The resulting order is: *A B E F C D G H I*.

- Postorder first traverses (recursively) the subtrees, then visits the root. On the example this gives: *E F B C G H I D A*.

- Breadth-first visits the nodes level by level, starting with the root: first the root, then all its children, then all their children and so on. Here the resulting order is: *A B C D E F G H I*.

These traversal policies are also supported by routines of the Iteration library.

See 10.5.5, page 194.

For each of the traversals, procedures are available to move the cursor accordingly, for example *breadth_start* and *breadth_forth* for breadth-first, and similar names for the others.

8.4.5 The features

Here is a summary of the features of cursor trees:

- General container features: *count*, *empty*, *wipe_out*, *full*.
- General tree features: *depth*, *level*, *breadth*, *arity*, *subtree*, *parent_tree*, *child_tree*.
- Cursor movement commands: *start*, *forth*, *back*, *up*, *down*, *go_to*, *preorder_forth*, *postorder_forth*, *breadth_forth*, *postorder_start*, *start_on_level*.
- Cursor position queries: *position*, *is_valid*, *off*, *after*, *before*, *above*, *below*, *isfirst*, *islast*, *is_root*, *is_leaf*.
- Modification commands: *put*, *put_right*, *put_left*, *remove*, *fill*, *fill_from_active*.

8.4.6 The classes

CURSOR_TREE is the most general deferred class. Effective descendants include:

- *LINKED_CURSOR_TREE* and *TWO_WAY_CURSOR_TREE*, describing linked implementations, one-way and two-way.

  Class interfaces in 18.9, page 372.

- *COMPACT_CURSOR_TREE*, a packed implementation, currently still experimental.

  18.10, page 376.

9

Sets and hash tables

9.1 OVERVIEW

A set is used to keep together a collection of objects. This chapter presents classes describing the abstract notion of set as well as a few implementations.

A related class, widely used for its convenience and efficiency, has also been included: *HASH_TABLE*, describing containers that hold objects identified by keys.

> The flat-short interfaces of the classes discussed in this chapter appear in chapter 19.

The figure on the following page shows the inheritance structure of the classes discussed in this chapter.

9.2 HASH TABLES

Let us begin with hash tables since they are probably the most frequently useful of the structures discussed in this chapter. Hash tables are indeed a convenient mechanism to store and retrieve objects identified by unique keys.

9.2.1 Why use hash tables?

The main advantage of hash tables is the efficiency of the basic operations: store (*put* in the terminology of this book) and retrieve (*item, remove*).

The idea behind hash tables is to try to emulate the data structure that provides the ultimate in efficiency: the array. On an array a, for some integer i whose value lies within the bounds of a, the basic operations are

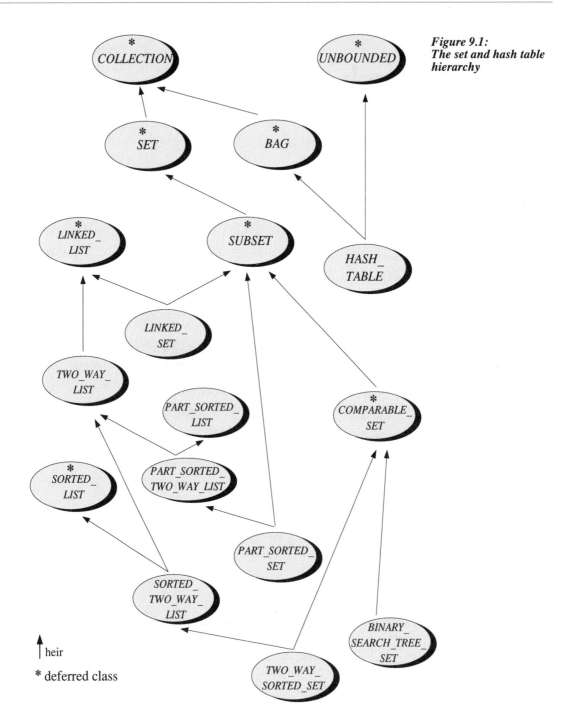

Figure 9.1:
The set and hash table
hierarchy

↑ heir

* deferred class

a.put (*x*, *i*)
x := *a.item* (*i*)
x := *a* @ *i*

The first causes the value of *a* at index *i* to be *x*; the second (and the third, which is simply a syntactical variant) access the value at index *i* and assign it to *x*. With the usual computer architectures, these operations are very fast: because arrays items are stored contiguously in memory, a computer will need just one addition (base address plus index) and one memory access to perform a *put* or *item*.

Not only are the operation times small; they are constant (or more precisely bounded by a constant). This is a great advantage over structures such as lists or trees which you must traverse at least in part to retrieve an item, so that access and modification times grow with the number of items. With an array, disregarding the influence of other factors such as memory paging, the time for a *put* or *item* is for all practical purposes the same whether the array has five items or five hundred thousand.

These properties make arrays excellent data structures for keeping objects. Unfortunately, they are only applicable if the objects satisfy three requirements:

A1 • For each object there must be an associated integer, which for the purpose of this discussion we may call the object's index (since it will serve as index for the object in the array.)

A2 • No two objects may have the same index.

A3 • If we want to avoid wasting huge amount of storage, all the indices must lie in a contiguous or almost contiguous range.

Hash tables may be viewed as a rehabilitation mechanism for objects that do not naturally possess these three properties. If we are unable to find a natural index, we can sometimes devise an artificial one. To do so we must be able to find a **key**. Each key must uniquely identify the corresponding object; this is the same as property A2, making keys similar to indices. But keys are not necessarily integers (violating property A1), although it must be possible to associate an integer with each key. The mechanism that maps keys to integers is called the **hashing function**.

Thanks to the hashing mechanism we will indeed be able to store suitable objects into arrays, approaching the optimal efficiency of this data structure. The efficiency will not be quite as good, however, for two reasons:

• We must pay the price of computing the hash function whenever we store or retrieve an object.

• Different keys may hash into the same integer value, requiring extra processing to find an acceptable index.

With good implementations, however, it is possible to use hash tables with a performance that is not much worse than that of arrays and, most importantly, may be treated as if the time for a *put*, an item or a *remove* were constant. This will mean that you can consider operations such as

h.put (*x*, *k*)
h := *a.item* (*k*)

where *h* is a hash-table and *k* is a key (for example a string) as conceptually equivalent to the array operations mentioned above.

The quality of a hashed implementation will depend both on the data structure that will store the objects, and on the choice of hashing function. Class *HASH_TABLE* in the Data Structure library attempts to address the first concern; for the second, client developers will be responsible for choosing the proper hashing function, although Base provides a few predefined functions, in particular for class *STRING*.

9.2.2 When hash tables are appropriate

You may keep objects in a hash table if for each one of these objects you can find a key that uniquely identifies it. The objects and their keys may be of many possible kinds:

H1 • In a simple example, the objects are integers; each integer serves as its own key. (More precisely we will use its absolute value, since it is convenient to have non-negative keys only.) This case is of more than theoretical interest, since it makes hash tables appropriate for storing a set of integers with widely scattered values, for which simple array storage would be a waste of space (see requirement A3 above).

H2 • Frequently, the objects will be composite, that is to say, instances of a developer-defined class, and one of the attributes of that class, of type *STRING*, can serve as the key. For example if you were writing an Eiffel compiler you would probably need to keep a data structure that includes information about classes of the system. Each class is represented by an object with several fields describing the properties of the class; one of these fields, the class name, corresponding to an attribute of type *STRING*, will serve as key.

H3 • Instead of being the full object (as in case H1) or one of the object's fields (as in case H2), the key may have to be computed through a function of the generating class, which will take into account several attributes of the class (that is to say, for each object, several fields).

What this practically means is that in all cases you will need, in the generating class of the objects to be stored, a query (attribute or function) that gives the key. The type of the key is highly variable but must in all cases be a descendant of *HASHABLE*. This is true of both *INTEGER* (case H1) and *STRING* (case H2). The requirements for being a *HASHABLE* are not harsh: all you need is a function *hash_code* that returns a non-negative integer.

Class HASHABLE was discussed in 5.5, page 138. Its (simple) specification is in 15.5, page 290.

9.2.3 Using hash tables

Class *HASH_TABLE* takes two generic parameters:

class HASH_TABLE [G, H –> HASHABLE] ...

For the class interface see 19.2, page 381.

G represents the type of the objects to be stored in the hash table, *H* the type of their keys.

When viewed as an implementation of containers, *HASH_TABLE*, in a strict sense, represents bags rather than sets: unlike the other classes in this chapter, it allows an object to have two or more distinct occurrences in a single container. But this is only true if we consider a hash table as a repository of objects of type *G*. In reality each item of the table is identified by a pair of values, one from *G* and one from *H*. Because the keys must uniquely identify objects, the hash table viewed as a container of such pairs is indeed a set.

The creation procedure *make* takes an integer argument, as in

!! *my_table.make* (*n*)

The value of *n* indicates how many items the hash table is expected to have to accommodate. This number of items is **not** a hardwired size, just information passed to the class. In particular:

- The actual size of the underlying array representation will be higher than *n* since efficient operation of hash table algorithms require the presence of enough breathing space – unoccupied positions.
- If the number of items in the table grows beyond the initial allocation, the table will automatically be resized.

It is useful, however, to use a reasonable *n* upon creation: not too large to avoid wasting space, but not too small to avoid frequent applications of resizing, an expensive operation.

9.2.4 Main features

To insert an item into a hash table, the basic command is *put*, as in

my_table.put (*my_value*, *my_key*)

This is meant for cases in which there is no element of key *my_key* in the table yet. To replace an existing element, use *replace* instead of *put*; to insert or replace, use *force*. These procedures have the same signature; they differ in how they react to the presence or absence of a previous element with the same key:

Operation	Key in use	Key not in use
put	No effect	Insert
replace	Replace	No effect
force	Replace	Insert
remove	Remove	No effect
replace_key	Change key	No effect

Two other useful commands have been included in this table. Procedure *remove* takes a single argument, a key, and removes the corresponding item. Procedure *replace_key* takes two arguments and replaces the key of a previously inserted element; the first argument is the new key and the second is the old key.

For each of these operations, the client can find out about the exit status through the following boolean-valued queries:

- *inserted* (for *put* and *force*).
- *removed* (for *remove*).
- *replaced* (for *replace* and *replace_key*)

9.2.5 Keys

Let *H* be the type of the keys, corresponding to the second generic parameter of *HASH_TABLE*. *H*, as noted, must be a descendant of *HASHABLE*. There is an extra requirement: you may not use as a key the default value of type *H*. This requirement is expressed by the function

Default values were discussed in 2.3.2, page 17.

> *valid_key* (*k*: *H*): *BOOLEAN*

which serves as abstract precondition for *put, replace, force, replace_key* (for both the old and new keys) and *remove*.

For a reference type, the default value is a void reference, so any non-void value will be acceptable as key. This applies in particular to type *STRING*, which is a reference type: you may use an empty string as key, although you may not use a void string reference.

Integers, as noted in the discussion of class *HASHABLE*, are hashable: each integer hashes into its absolute value. *INTEGER* is an expanded type, for which the default value is 0. The *valid_key* rule means that you may not use 0 as a key in a hash table for which the keys are integers. All other integer values are acceptable.

9.3 SETS

As you will remember from the discussion of abstract structures, sets are containers where successive occurrences of the same item are not distinguished: the same item twice has the same observable effect as inserting it once.

4.4.3, page 128. Structures which distinguish between occurrences are called bags (4.4.4).

9.3.1 Deferred classes

The most general class describing sets is *SET*. As noted in the earlier discussion, the usual operations of set theory such as union and intersection have been relegated to *SUBSET*, an heir of *SET*. This enables a class to inherit from *SET* without having to effect these operations if it satisfies the basic set property but has no convenient implementation of the subset operations.

See 19.3, page 383 for the interface of SET, and 19.4, page 385, for the interface of SUBSET.

9.3.2 Sets without a notion of order

LINKED_SET provides a basic implementation of *SET* by linked lists (*LINKED_SET*).

See 19.5, page 386 for the interface of LINKED_SET.

9.3.3 Sets of comparable elements and sorted sets

The deferred class *COMPARABLE_SET*, declared as

For the class interface see 19.6, page 388.

> **deferred class** *COMPARABLE_SET* [*G* –> *COMPARABLE*] **inherit**
>
>   *SUBSET* [*G*];
>
>   *COMPARABLE_STRUCT* [*G*];
>
>   ...

describes sets whose items may be compared by a total order relation. The class has the features *min* and *max*.

Two implementations of *COMPARABLE_SET* are provided. One, *TWO_WAY_ SORTED_SET*, uses sorted two-way lists. The other, *BINARY_SEARCH_TREE_SET*, uses binary search trees.

See 19.8, page 391 for the interface of these two implementations.

If the items are partially rather than totally ordered, you may use the class *PART_ SORTED_SET* [*G* –> *PART_COMPARABLE*], which uses a two-way sorted list implementation.

For the class interface see 19.7, page 389.

10

Iteration

10.1 OVERVIEW

The classes of the Iteration library encapsulate control structures representing common traversal operations. This chapter describes the principles behind iteration classes and explains how to use them.

> The flat-short interfaces of the classes discussed in this chapter appear in chapter 20.

The figure on the following page shows the inheritance hierarchy of the classes described in this chapter. It also shows some of the client classes from the Data Structure library and part of their own ancestor hierarchy.

10.2 THE NOTION OF ITERATOR

Let us first explore the role of iterators in the architecture of a system.

10.2.1 Iterating over data structures

Client software that uses data structures of a certain type, for example lists or trees, often needs to traverse a data structure of that type in a predetermined order so as to apply a certain action to all the items of the structure, or to all items that satisfy a certain criterion. Such a systematic traversal is called an iteration.

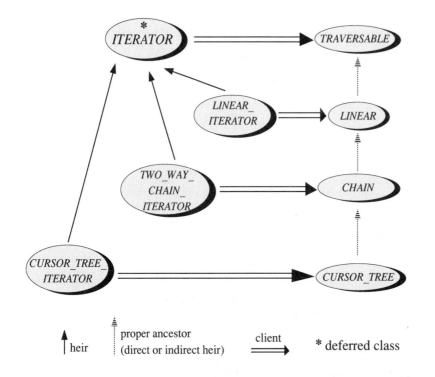

Cases of iteration can be found in almost any system. Here are a few typical examples:

- A text processing system may maintain a list of paragraphs. In response to a user command, such as a request to resize the column width, the system will iterate over the entire list so as to update all paragraphs.

- A business system may maintain a list of customers. If the company decides that a special promotion will target all customers satisfying a certain criterion (for example all customers that have bought at least one product over the past six months), the system will iterate over the list, generating a mailing for every list item that satisfies the criterion.

- An interactive development environment for a programming language may maintain a syntax tree. In response to a program change, the system will traverse the tree to determine what nodes are affected by the change and update them.

These examples illustrate the general properties of iteration. An iteration involves a data structure of a known general type and a particular ordering of the structure's items. For some structures, more than one ordering will be available; for example a tree iteration may use preorder, postorder or breadth-first (as defined below). The iteration involves an operation, say *item_action*, to be applied to the selected items. It may also involve a boolean-valued query, say *item_test*, applicable to candidate items. Finally, it involves a certain policy, usually based on *item_test*, as to which items should be subjected to *item_action*. Typical example policies are:

- Apply *item_action* to all the items in the structure. (In this case *item_test* is not relevant).
- Apply *item_action* to all items that satisfy *item_test*.
- Apply *item_action* to all items up to the first one that satisfies *item_test*.

The Iteration library provides many more, covering in particular all the standard control structures.

10.2.2 Iterations and control structures

You can perform iterations without any special iteration classes. For example if *customers* is declared as

> *customers*: *LIST* [*CUSTOMER*]

then a class *SPECIAL_PROMOTION* of a text processing system may include in one of its routines a loop of the form

```
from
    customers. start
until
    customers. exhausted
loop
    if recent_purchases. has (customers. item) then
        target_list. put (customers. item)
    end;
    customers. forth
end
```

Such schemes are quite common. But it is precisely because they occur frequently that it is useful to rely on library classes to handle them. One of the principal tasks of object-oriented software development is to identify recurring patterns and build reusable classes that encapsulate them, so that future developers will be able to rely on ready-made solutions.

The classes of the Iteration library address this need. Using them offers two benefits:

- You avoid writing loops, in which the definition of sub-components such as exit conditions, variants and invariants is often delicate or error-prone.
- You can more easily adapt the resulting features in descendant classes.

The rest of this chapter shows how to obtain these benefits.

10.3 SIMPLE EXAMPLES

To get a first grasp of how one can work with the Iteration library, let us look at a typical iteration class and a typical iteration client.

10.3.1 An example iterator routine

Here, given with its full implementation, is a typical Iteration library routine: the procedure *do_until* from *LINEAR_ITERATOR*, the class defining iteration mechanisms on linear (sequential) structures.

```
until_do is
        -- Apply action to every item of target,
        -- up to but excluding first one satisfying test.
        -- (Apply to full list if no item satisfies test.)
    require
        traversable_exists: target /= Void
    local
        finished: BOOLEAN
    do
        from
            target.start
        invariant
            invariant_value
        until
            target.exhausted or else test
        loop
            action;
            target.forth
        end
    ensure
        achieved: target.exhausted or else test;
        invariant_satisfied: invariant_value
    end
```

> The precise form of the procedure in the class relies on a call to another procedure, *until_continue*, and on inherited assertions. Here everything has been unfolded for illustration purposes.

This procedure will traverse the linear structure identified by *target* and apply the procedure called *action* on every item up to but excluding the first one satisfying *test*.

The class similarly offers *do_all*, *do_while*, *do_for*, *do_if* and other procedures representing the common control structures. It also includes functions such as *exists* and *forall*, corresponding to the usual quantifiers.

These iteration schemes depend on the procedure *action*, defining the action to be applied to successive elements, and on the function *test*, defining the boolean query to be applied to these elements. These features are declared in class *ITERATOR* (the highest-level deferred class of the Iteration library); here is *test*:

```
test: BOOLEAN is
        -- Test to be applied to item at current position in target
        -- (default: value of item_test on item)
    require
        traversable_exists: target /= Void;
        not_off: not target.off
    do
        Result := item_test (target.item)
    ensure
        not target.off
    end
```

This indicates that the value of the boolean function *test* will be obtained by applying *item_test* to the item at the current position in the target structure. In *ITERATOR*, function *item_test* always return false; descendant classes will redefine it so as to describe the desired test.

Similarly, *action* is declared in class *ITERATOR* as a call to *item_action* (*target.item*). Descendants will redefine *item_action*, which as initially declared in *ITERATOR* is a procedure with a null body.

Going through *item_action* and *item_test* provides an extra degree of flexibility. Normally the action and test performed at each step apply to *target.item*, so that it suffices to redefine the *item_* features. This is the case will all examples studied in this chapter. In a more general setting, however, you might need to redefine *action* and *test* themselves.

10.3.2 An example use of iteration

Here now is an example illustrating the use of these mechanisms. The result will enable us to resize all the paragraphs of a text up to the first one that has been modified – as we might need to do, in a text processing system, to process an interactive user request.

Assume a class *TEXT* that describes lists of paragraphs with certain additional features. The example will also assume a class *PARAGRAPH* with a procedure *resize*, and a boolean-valued attribute *modified* which indicates whether a paragraph has been modified. Class *TEXT* inherits from *LINKED_LIST* and so is a descendant of *LINEAR*:

```
class TEXT inherit

    LINKED_LIST [PARAGRAPH];

    ...
feature

    ...
end
```

In a class *TEXT_PROCESSOR*, you can use an iteration procedure to write a very simple procedure *resize_ paragraphs* that will resize all paragraphs up to but excluding the first one that has been modified:

```
class TEXT_PROCESSOR inherit

    LINEAR_ITERATOR [PARAGRAPH]
        redefine
            item_action, item_test
        end
feature

    resize_paragraphs (t: TEXT) is
            -- Resize all the paragraphs of t up to but excluding
            -- the first one that has been modified.
        do
            set (t);
            until_do
        end;
feature {NONE}

    item_test (p: PARAGRAPH): BOOLEAN is
            -- Has p been modified?
        do
            Result := p.modified
        end;

    item_action (p: PARAGRAPH) is
            -- Resize p.
        do
            p.resize
        end;

        ...

end
```

Thanks to the iteration mechanism, the procedure *resize_paragraphs* simply needs two procedure calls:

- To set its argument *t* as the iteration target, it uses procedure *set*. (This procedure is from class *ITERATOR* which passes it on to all iterator classes.)

- Then it simply calls *until_do* as defined above.

Procedure *item_action* is redefined to describe the operation to be performed on each successive element. Function *item_test* is redefined to describe the exit test.

As presented so far, the mechanism seems to limit every descendant of an iteration class to just one form of iteration. As shown later in this chapter, it is in fact easy to generalize the technique to allow a class to use an arbitrary number of iteration schemes.

What is interesting here is that the redefinitions of *item_test* and *item_action* take care of all the details. There is no need to write any loop or other control structure. We are at the very heart of the object-oriented method, enjoying the ability to encapsulate useful and common software schemes so that client developers will only need to fill in what is specific to their application.

10.4 A DISCUSSION

The previous example gives a good idea of the practical use of iteration classes. But before we explore the remaining details and alternative techniques it is appropriate to reflect briefly on the role of these classes in object-oriented software architectures. This small detour also addresses objections that may have come to your mind when reading this chapter so far.

10.4.1 Do we really need iterator classes?

A natural reaction when first hearing about iteration classes is to wonder why we altogether need special classes. Their purpose, after all, is to support iteration over lists, trees and other structures described by the classes of the Base libraries presented elsewhere in this book; would it not be preferable, then, to include each iteration mechanism in the corresponding data structure class? Under such a scheme the facilities for iterating over lists would be declared in class *LIST*, which would pass them on to all its descendants describing specific list implementations; tree iteration mechanisms would similarly be declared in class *TREE*; and so on.

Although this approach seems at first to follow from object-oriented principles, a little further investigation shows it to be inadequate. The hitch is that iteration is not a property of the data structures: it is a property of the structures' **clients**.

Consider an example such as the one examined earlier, where a routine of a class *TEXT_PROCESSOR* needs to apply the same operation to all paragraphs in a list. This is a typical iteration; but if we treat the ability to iterate over list as a feature of lists, any class element that performs an iteration must be considered to be a list! So class *TEXT_PROCESSOR* must be a descendant of *LIST*, and so must every class of the system that iterates over lists.

Such a use of inheritance would be quite wrong – comparable in fact to the "car-owner" example mentioned in an earlier chapter. Inheritance is the **is** relation; by no twist of reasoning can a text processing system considered to be a list of paragraphs. This is clearly a case in which client, not inheritance, is the appropriate relation.

On CAR_OWNER see 3.10.1, page 109.

Having iterator classes solves the problem. From the viewpoint of abstract data types, iterator classes describe clearly identified abstractions: we may interpret *LINEAR_ITERATOR*, for example, as describing **objects that have the ability to iterate over linear structures**. It is perfectly legitimate, then, for a class such as *TEXT_PROCESSOR* to be a descendant of *LINEAR_ITERATOR*, since the abstraction represented by *TEXT_PROCESSOR* conforms to this description: the corresponding objects must indeed – that was the assumption made above – have the ability to iterate over lists.

Chains include lists as a special case. See chapter 6.

There will actually be two ways for a class to use the iterator classes, for example to apply an action to all elements of a list up to the first one that meets a certain condition (procedure *do_until*).

The first technique, illustrated through *TEXT_PROCESSOR*, is to be a descendant of the desired iterator class. In such a case the iteration actions will be written in the form

set (*my_text*)
do_until

where *my_text* is the structure over which you wish to iterate. The call to *set* defines *my_text* to be the target of future iterations; later calls to *set* may change that target.

The other technique is more flexible when you need the possibility of iterating several different actions. This technique takes to its full conclusion the idea, introduced above, of treating the notion of iterator as a data abstraction – and, consequently, of treating iterators as objects. You will first create such an object, then set its target, then use it to iterate over a structure:

!! *my_iterator*;
my_iterator. *set* (*my_text*);
my_iterator. *do_until*

The following sections will show how to attach actions and tests to an iterator, so as to ensure that an iterating feature such as *do_until* will have the desired effect.

10.4.2 Understanding iterator objects

Iterator objects stand apart from the more obvious objects found in elementary presentations of the object-oriented method.

Both analysis objects and implementation objects lend themselves to intuitive interpretation. An analysis object, such as an instance of class *INVENTORY_ITEM* in an inventory management system or an instance of class *PLANET* in an astronomy system, has a concrete enough counterpart in the external system being modeled. An implementation object such as a linked list or binary search tree is also a quite tangible notion, at least if you are a software developer.

Iterator objects are at first less intuitive, but it is not hard to understand them in light of the previous discussion: you may consider such an object as a set of mechanisms that has the ability to iterate for its clients over data structures of a specified type. For example a chain iterator, as noted, is an object that has the ability to iterate over lists and other chains.

> Although one should always be careful about applying anthropomorphic terminology to software issues, here it is rather tempting to say that such an object "knows" how to iterate over chains.

Iterator objects provide a good example of what may be called **design objects**. Design objects represent high-level architectural choices. Unlike analysis objects, they are not directly connected to objects of the application domain being modeled. They are not implementation objects either, although like implementation objects they belong to the solution rather than to the problem. As pointed out in an earlier chapter, choosing the proper design classes is one of the challenges of object-oriented software construction – much harder than finding the analysis classes.

See 3.3.2, page 63.

10.5 USING THE ITERATION LIBRARY

Let us now explore the classes of the Iteration library and the different ways of using them.

10.5.1 Overview of the classes

There are only four Iteration classes, whose simple inheritance structure appeared at the beginning of this chapter.

See the figure on page 182.

- *ITERATOR*, a deferred class which describes the most general notion.
- *LINEAR_ITERATOR*, for iterating over linear structures and chains.
- *TWO_WAY_CHAIN_ITERATOR*, a repeated heir of *LINEAR_ITERATOR*, for iterating in either direction over a bilinear structure.
- *CURSOR_TREE_ITERATOR*, for iterating over trees.

As you will remember from the presentation of the abstract overall taxonomy, the traversal hierarchy describes how data structures can be traversed; its most general class is *TRAVERSABLE*. Each one of the iterator classes is paired with a traversal class (or two in one case):

The traversal hierarchy was discussed in 4.6, page 133.

ITERATOR [G]	*TRAVERSABLE* [G]
LINEAR_ITERATOR [G]	*LINEAR* [G]
TWO_WAY_CHAIN_ITERATOR [G]	*TWO_WAY_LIST* [G], *TWO_WAY_CIRCULAR* [G]
CURSOR_TREE_ITERATOR [G]	*CURSOR_TREE* [G]

Figure 10.2:
Iterator classes and their matching traversal classes

Each iterator class relies on the corresponding traversal class to provide the features for traversing the corresponding data structures, such as *start*, *forth* and *exhausted* for linear structures.

> Of course the data structure class used in connection with a given iterator class does not need to be the iterator's exact correspondent as given by the above table; it may be any one of its descendants. For example you may use *LINEAR_ITERATOR* to iterate over data structures described not just by *LINEAR* but also by such descendants as *LIST*, *LINKED_LIST*, *ARRAYED_LIST*, or even *TWO_WAY_LIST* if you do not need the backward iteration features (for which you will have to use *TWO_WAY_CHAIN_ITERATOR*).

10.5.2 General iteration facilities

Class *ITERATOR* defines the features that apply to all forms of iterator.

An iterator will always apply to a certain target structure. The target is introduced in *ITERATOR* by the feature

For the class interface see 20.2, page 393.

    target: *TRAVERSABLE* [G]

Both the iterator classes and the traversal classes are generic, with a formal generic parameter *G* as shown on the above table. The actual generic parameters will be matched through the choice of iteration target: for a generic derivation of the form

SOME_ITERATOR [*ACTUAL_TYPE*]

the target can only be of type *SOME_TRAVERSABLE* [*ACTUAL_TYPE*] for the same *ACTUAL_TYPE*, where *SOME_TRAVERSABLE* is the traversal class matching *SOME_ITERATOR* according to the preceding table (*LINEAR* for *LINEAR_ITERATOR* and so on), or one of its proper descendants.

Each of the proper descendants of *ITERATOR* redefines the type of *target* to the matching proper descendant of *TRAVERSABLE*, to cover more specific variants of the iteration target, For example in *LINEAR_ITERATOR* the feature is redefined to be of type *LINEAR* [*G*].

ITERATOR also introduces the procedure for selecting a target:

```
set (s: like target) is
        -- Make s the new target of iterations.
    require
        s /= Void
    do
        target := s
    ensure
        target = s;
        target /= Void
    end
```

Next *ITERATOR* introduces the routines describing the elementary action and test that will be applied to items of the iteration targets:

```
action is
        -- Action to be applied to item at current position in target.
        -- (default: item_action on item at current position.)
        -- Note: for iterators to work properly, redefined versions of
        -- this feature should not change the traversable structure.
    require
        traversable_exists: target /= Void;
        not_off: not target.off;
        invariant_satisfied: invariant_value
    do
        item_action (target.item)
    ensure
        not target.off;
        invariant_satisfied: invariant_value
    end;
```

> *test*: *BOOLEAN* **is**
>   -- Test to be applied to item at current position in *target*
>   -- (default: value of *item_test* on item)
> **require**
>   *traversable_exists*: *target* /= *Void*;
>   *not_off*: **not** *target.off*
> **do**
>   *Result* := *item_test* (*target.item*)
> **ensure**
>   **not** *target.off*
> **end**

These routines rely on two others, *item_action* and *item_test*, which both take an argument of type *G*, the formal generic parameter. The reason, already noted above, is that in a vast majority of cases the iterated *action* and *test* solely depend, at each step of the traversal, on the item (of type *G*) at the current position. To define an iteration process, then, it suffices to redefine *item_action* and *item_test* in a descendant of the appropriate iteration class. Only in complex cases will it be necessary to redefine *action* and *test* themselves.

> If you encounter such a case, note the caveat about *action* changing the target's structure. Understandably enough, an iterator that attempts to change the data structure while traversing it may engage in strange behavior. No such risk exists if you only redefine *item_action*, which may change the contents of items but not the structure itself.

Another feature introduced in *ITERATOR* is the query *invariant_value*, describing invariant properties that must be ensured at the beginning of any iteration and preserved by every iteration step. As declared in *ITERATOR* this query always returns true, but proper descendants can redefine it to describe more interesting invariant properties.

For discussions of the notion of loop invariant see "Object-Oriented Software Construction" and "Eiffel: The Language".

Finally, *ITERATOR* introduces in deferred form the general iteration routines applicable to all iteration variants. They include two queries corresponding to the quantifiers of first-order predicate calculus:

- *forall* will return true if all items of the target structure satisfy *test*.
- *exists* will return true if at least one item satisfies *test*.

The other routines are commands which will traverse the target structure and apply *action* to items selected through *test*:

- *do_all* applies *action* to all items.
- *do_if*, to those items which satisfy *test*.
- *until_do*, to all items up to but excluding the first one that satisfies *test*.
- *do_until*, to all items up to and including the first one that satisfies *test*.
- *while_do* and *do_while*, to all items up to the first one that does not satisfy *test*. (This can also be achieved with *until_do* or *do_until* by choosing the opposite *test*.)

All these features, and most of the other iteration features introduced in proper descendants of *ITERATOR* and described next, have no argument. Information about the target of iteration comes from feature *target*, set by procedure *set*; information about what needs to be done for each item of the target structure comes from *item_action* and *item_test*.

10.5.3 Linear and chain iteration

LINEAR_ITERATOR, an effective class, refines the iteration mechanisms for cases in which the target is a linear structure, such as a list in any implementation or a circular chain.

For the class interface see 20.3, page 396.

The class effects all the deferred features inherited from *ITERATOR*, taking advantage of the linear traversal mechanisms present in the corresponding traversal class, *LINEAR*. Here for example is the effecting of *do_if*:

```
do_if is
        -- Apply action to every item of target satisfying test.
    do
        from
            start
        invariant
            invariant_value
        until
            exhausted
        loop
            if test then action end;
            forth
        end
    end
```

This routine text relies on features *start*, *forth* and *exhausted* which, together with *off*, have for convenience been carried over to *LINEAR_ITERATOR* from their counterparts in *LINEAR*, with feature declarations such as

```
off: BOOLEAN is
        -- Is position of target off?
    require
        traversable_exists: target /= Void
    do
        Result := target.off
    end
```

and similarly for the others.

In addition to effecting the general iteration features from *ITERATOR*, class *LINEAR_ITERATOR* introduces iteration features that apply to the specific case of linear structures:

- *search* (*b*: *BOOLEAN*) moves the iteration to the first position satisfying *test* if *b* is true, or not satisfying *test* if *b* is false. This use of a boolean argument to switch between two opposite semantics is not part of the recommended style, and you will find few if any other examples in the Base libraries. Here, however, it was deemed preferable to the alternative, which would have involved four separate procedures (if together with *search* we consider *continue_search* discussed next).

- With a linear structure we can implement an iteration corresponding to the "for" loop of traditional programming languages, defined by three integers: the starting position, the number of items to be traversed, and the step between consecutive items. This is provided by procedure *do_for* (*starting, number, step*: *INTEGER*).

- Since with a linear target the iterator can advance the cursor step by step, the basic iteration operations are complemented by variants which pick up from the position reached by the last call: *continue_until, until_continue, continue_while, while_continue, continue_search, continue_for*.

10.5.4 Two-way iteration

Class *TWO_WAY_CHAIN_ITERATOR* has all the features of *LINEAR_ITERATOR*, to which it adds features for iterating backward as well as forward.

For the interface of TWO_WAY_CHAIN_ITERATOR see 20.4, page 398.

The class introduces commands *finish* and *back*, applying the corresponding operations to the two-way target. It also has a backward variant for every iteration feature. The name of each such variant is the name of the forward feature followed by *_back*: *do_all_back, until_do_back* and so on.

> An alternative design would have kept just one set of features and added two features: a command *reverse* to reverse the direction of future iteration operations, and a query *backward* to find out the direction currently in force.

Contrary to what one might at first imagine, class *TWO_WAY_CHAIN_ITERATOR* is extremely short and simple; its Feature clause only contains the declarations of two features, *finish* and *back*. The trick is to use repeated inheritance. *TWO_WAY_CHAIN_ITERATOR* inherits twice from *LINEAR_ITERATOR*; the first inheritance branch yields the forward iteration features, the second yields those for backward iteration. There is no need for any explicit declaration or redeclaration of iteration features. Here is the entire class text that yields this result:

On repeated inheritance see 2.7.14, page 48.

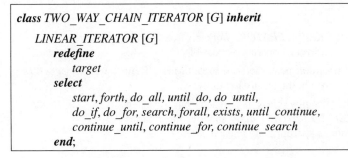

```
class TWO_WAY_CHAIN_ITERATOR [G] inherit
    LINEAR_ITERATOR [G]
        redefine
            target
        select
            start, forth, do_all, until_do, do_until,
            do_if, do_for, search, forall, exists, until_continue,
            continue_until, continue_for, continue_search
        end;
```

```
    LINEAR_ITERATOR [G]
        rename
            start as finish, forth as back, do_all as do_all_back,
            until_do as until_do_back, do_until as do_until_back,
            do_if as do_if_back, do_for as do_for_back,
            search as search_back,
            forall as forall_back, exists as exists_back,
            until_continue as until_continue_back,
            continue_until as continue_until_back,
            continue_for as continue_for_back,
            continue_search as continue_search_back
        redefine
            target
        end
feature -- Status report

    target: BILINEAR [G]
            -- The structure to which iteration features will apply

feature -- Cursor movement

    finish is
            -- Move cursor of target to last position.
        do
            target.finish
        end;

    back is
            -- Move cursor of target backward one position.
        do
            target.back
        end

end
```

This class provides a good example of the economy of expression that the full inheritance mechanism affords through the combination of renaming, redefinition, repeated inheritance rules and selection, without sacrificing clarity and maintainability.

The notion of cursor trees was introduced in 8.4, page 169. For the class interface of CURSOR_TREE_ ITERATOR see 20.5, page 400.

10.5.5 Tree iteration

Tree iterations, provided by class *CURSOR_TREE_ITERATOR*, work on trees of the cursor tree form; only with this form of tree are traversal operations possible.

Three forms of iteration are provided: preorder, postorder and breadth-first. They correspond to the three traversal policies described in the discussion of trees.

See 8.4.4, page 171.

Here too it would seem that a rather lengthy class is needed, but repeated inheritance works wonders. *CURSOR_TREE_ITERATOR* simply inherits three times from *LINEAR_ITERATOR*, renaming the features appropriately in each case:

- *pre_do_all*, *pre_until* and so on.
- *post_do_all*, *post_until* and so on.
- *breadth_do_all*, *breadth_until* and so on.

All it needs to do then is to redefine the type of *target* to be *CURSOR_TREE* [*G*], and to redefine six features: the three renamed *start* (*pre_start* etc.) and the three *forth* (*pre_forth* and so on). These seven redefinitions give us a full-fledged battery of tree iteration mechanisms.

10.6 BUILDING AND USING ITERATORS

To conclude this discussion, let us now put together the various mechanisms studied so far, to see how authors of client software can use the Iteration library to perform possibly complex iterations on various data structures without ever writing a single loop or test. The basic ideas were sketched above but now we have all the elements for the full view.

An application class may use one of the iteration classes in either of two ways: as a descendant (single or repeated) or as a client. The descendant technique is extremely simple but less versatile.

10.6.1 The single descendant technique

Assume an application class *PROCESSOR* that is a proper descendant of one of the effective iteration classes studied in this chapter. Then a routine of *PROCESSOR*, say *iterate*, may iterate a certain action over a data structure, subject to a certain test.

First, class *PROCESSOR* must specify the action by redefining *item_action* and *item_test* (or, in the most general case, *action* and *test*).

Then routine *iterate* must specify the target data structure through a call of the form

  set (*t*)

where *t* represents the selected target data structure. The type of *t* must correspond to the iteration class selected as ancestor of *PROCESSOR*: for *LINEAR_ITERATOR* it must be a descendant of *LINEAR* (such as *LINKED_LIST*, *ARRAYED_LIST*, *LINKED_CIRCULAR* or any other list or circular chain classes); for *TWO_WAY_CHAIN_ITERATOR* it must be a descendant of *BILINEAR* such as *TWO_WAY_LIST* or *TWO_WAY_CIRCULAR*; for *CURSOR_TREE_ITERATOR* it must be a descendant of *CURSOR_TREE*. In all cases the actual generic parameters of the iterator class and of the data structure class must be compatible.

Then the iteration proper is obtained simply by calling the appropriate procedure, without any qualification or arguments, for example:

  do_if

It is hard to imagine a simpler scheme: no loops, no initialization, no arguments.

Feature *item_action* may need to rely on some variable values. Because it does not take any argument, such values will have to be treated as attributes, with the corresponding *set_...* procedures to set and change their values. This also applies to the two schemes set next.

The single descendant technique has one drawback: it provides the iterating class, *PROCESSOR*, with only one set of iteration particulars. This limitation does not affect the number of targets: you may use as many targets as you wish, as long as they are of compatible types, by calling a routine such as *iterate* several times, or calling several such routines, each call being preceded by a call to *set* to define a new target. The limitation also does not affect the iterating scheme: one iteration could use *do_if*, the next *do_all* and so on. But it does require the *action* and *test* to be the same in all cases.

The next two techniques will remove this limitation.

10.6.2 Using repeated inheritance

One way to obtain several iteration schemes is a simple extension to the single descendant technique. You can use repeated inheritance to provide two or more variants. We have in fact already encountered the technique when studying how to derive *TWO_WAY_CHAIN_ITERATOR* and *CURSOR_TREE_ITERATOR* from *LINEAR_ITERATOR*. The general pattern, applied here to just two iteration schemes but easily generalized to more, is straightforward:

```
class DUAL_PROCESSOR inherit
    LINEAR_ITERATOR [SOME_TYPE]
        rename
            item_action as action1,
            item_test as test1,
            do_if as do_if1
        redefine
            action1, test1
        select
            action1, test1
        end;

    LINEAR_ITERATOR [SOME_TYPE]
        rename
            item_action as action2,
            item_test as test2,
            do_if as do_if2
        redefine
            action2, test2
        end;
feature
    action1 is
            -- The action for the first scheme
        do ... end;

    test1: BOOLEAN is
            -- The test for the first scheme
        do ... end;
```

```
    action2 is
            -- The action for the second scheme
        do ... end;

    test2: BOOLEAN is
            -- The test for the second scheme
        do ... end;

    iterate1 is
            -- Execute iteration of first kind.
        do
            set (...); do_if1
        end;

    iterate2 is
            -- Execute iteration of second kind.
        do
            set (...); do_if2
        end;
    ...
```

The repeated inheritance machinery takes care of the rest.

10.6.3 Using explicit iterator objects

To obtain maximum flexibility, classes that need iteration facilities should be clients rather than descendants of the iteration classes. The resulting scheme is completely dynamic: to perform iterations you use iterator objects as discussed earlier in this chapter.

Iterator objects were first discussed in 10.4.2, page 188.

The following example illustrates the technique. Consider a deferred class *FIGURE* describing the notion of graphical figure, with many effective descendants (*POLYGON*, *CIRCLE* and so on). It is useful to define *COMPLEX_FIGURE*, describing figures that are recursively composed of sub-figures. This is a remarkable example of multiple inheritance:

```
class COMPLEX_FIGURE inherit

    FIGURE;

    LINKED_LIST [FIGURE]

feature

    ...

end
```

In the **feature** clause we want to provide the appropriate effectings for the deferred features of class *FIGURE*: *display*, *hide*, *translate* and all other basic figure operations. We can use loops for that purpose, for example

```
display is
        -- Recursively display all components of the complex figure
    do
        from
            start
        until
            exhausted
        loop
            item. display;
            forth
        end
    end
```

Although acceptable and even elegant, this scheme will cause significant duplication: all the *FIGURE* features – not just *display* but also *hide*, *rotate*, *move* and others – will have the same structure, with a loop. We can use iterators to avoid this duplication. The repeated inheritance technique would work, but given the large number of *FIGURE* features the amount of repeated inheritance that would be needed seems unwieldy. It is also not very desirable to have to change the inheritance structure of the system just to add a new feature to *FIGURE*. The more dynamic approach using iterator objects seems preferable.

To implement this approach, define a class for iterating on complex figures:

```
class COMPLEX_FIGURE_ITERATOR creation
    set
inherit
    LINEAR_ITERATOR
        redefine
            target
        end
feature
    target: COMPLEX_FIGURE;
end
```

Then for each operation to be iterated define a small class. For example:

```
class FIGURE_DISPLAYER creation

    set

inherit

    COMPLEX_FIGURE_ITERATOR
        redefine
            item_action
        end

feature

    item_action (f: FIGURE) is
            -- Action to be applied to each figure: display it.
        do
            f.display
        end
end
```

Similarly, you may define *FIGURE_HIDER*, *FIGURE_MOVER* and others. Then
the features of *COMPLEX_FIGURE* are written almost trivially, without any explicit
loops; for example:

```
display is
        -- Recursively display all components of the complex figure
    local
        disp: FIGURE_DISPLAYER
    do
        !! disp.set (Current);
        disp.do_all
    end
```

and similarly for all the others.

Note the use of *set* as creation procedure, which is more convenient than requiring
the clients first to create an iterator object and then to call *set*. This is also safer, since
with *set* as a creation procedure the client cannot forget to initialize the target. (If a class
C has a **creation** clause, the creation instruction !! *x* with no creation call is invalid for *x*
of type *C*.)

On creation procedures see
2.3.7, page 20.

Developers who are unfamiliar with the style illustrated above sometimes feel
uneasy at the sight of many small classes such as *FIGURE_DISPLAYER*. But there is
nothing wrong with such classes. A similar case arises for interactive systems
supporting undoing; the solution suggested by the Eiffel method and used extensively in
the Vision library relies on command classes, of which there may also be quite a few, all
descendants of a common deferred class.

COMMENT

11

Lexical analysis: the Lex library

11.1 OVERVIEW

When analyzing a text by computer, it is usually necessary to split it into individual components or **tokens**. In human languages, the tokens are the words; in programming languages, tokens are the basic constituents of software texts, such as identifiers, constants and special symbols.

The process of recognizing the successive tokens of a text is called lexical analysis. This chapter describes the Lex library, a set of classes which make it possible to build and apply lexical analyzers to many different languages.

> The flat-short interfaces of the classes discussed in this chapter appear in chapter 21.

Besides recognizing the tokens, it is usually necessary to recognize the deeper syntactic structure of the text. This process is called **parsing** or **syntax analysis** and is studied in the next chapter.

The figure at the top of the following page shows the inheritance structure of the classes discussed in this chapter. Class *L_INTERFACE* has also been included although we will only study it in the next chapter; it belongs to the Parse library, where it takes care of the interface between parsing and lexical analysis.

L_INTERFACE is discussed in 12.9.1, page 231.

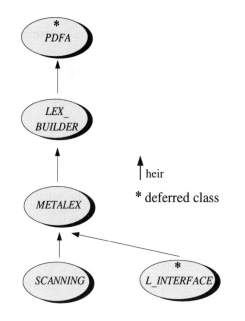

11.2 AIMS AND SCOPE OF THE LEX LIBRARY

To use the Lex library it is necessary to understand the basic concepts and terminology of lexical analysis.

11.2.1 Basic terminology

The set of tokens accepted by a lexical analyzer is called a **lexical grammar**. For example, the basic constructs of Eiffel (identifiers, keywords, constants, special symbols) constitute a lexical grammar. For reasons that will be clear below, a lexical grammar is also known as a **regular grammar**.

A lexical grammar defines a number of **token types**, such as Identifier and Integer for Eiffel. A token that conforms to the structure defined for a certain token type is called a **specimen** of that token type. For example, the token *my_identifier*, which satisfies the rules for Eiffel tokens, is a specimen of the token type Identifier; *201* is a specimen of the token type Integer.

To define a lexical grammar is to specify a number of token types by describing precisely, for each token type, the form of the corresponding specimens. For example a lexical grammar for Eiffel will specify that Identifier is the token type whose specimens are sequences of one or more characters, of which the first must be a letter (lower-case or upper-case) and any subsequent one is a letter, a digit (0 to 9) or an underscore. Actual grammar descriptions use a less verbose and more formal approach, studied below: regular expressions.

A lexical analyzer is an object equipped with operations that enable it to read a text according to a known lexical grammar and to identify the text's successive tokens.

The classes of the Lex library make it possible to define lexical grammars for many different applications, and to produce lexical analyzers for these grammars.

11.2.2 Overview of the classes

For the user of the Lex libraries, the classes of most direct interest are *TOKEN*, *LEXICAL*, *METALEX* and *SCANNING*.

An instance of *TOKEN* describes a token read from an input file being analyzed, with such properties as the token type, the corresponding string and the position in the text (line, column) where it was found.

An instance of *LEXICAL* is a lexical analyzer for a certain lexical grammar. Given a reference to such an instance, say *analyzer*, you may analyze an input text through calls to the features of class *LEXICAL*, for example:

analyzer.get_token

Class *METALEX* defines facilities for building such lexical analyzers. In particular, it provides features for reading the grammar from a file and building the corresponding analyzer. Classes that need to build and use lexical analyzers may be written as descendants of *METALEX* to benefit from its general-purpose facilities.

Class *SCANNING* is one such descendant of *METALEX*. It contains all the facilities needed to build an ordinary lexical analyzer and apply it to the analysis of input texts. Because these facilities are simpler to use and are in most cases sufficient, *SCANNING* will be discussed first; the finer-grain facilities of *METALEX* are described towards the end of this chapter.

These classes internally rely on others, some of which may be useful for more advanced applications. *LEX_BUILDER*, one of the supporting classes, will be introduced after *METALEX*.

11.2.3 Library example

The ISE Eiffel 3 delivery includes (in the ***examples/library/lex*** subdirectory) a simple example using the Lexical Library classes. The example applies Lex library facilities to the analysis of a language which is none other than Eiffel itself.

The root class of that example, *EIFFEL_SCAN*, is only a few lines long; it relies on the general mechanism provided by *SCANNING* (see below). The actual lexical grammar is given by a lexical grammar file (a concept explained below): the file of name *eiffel_regular* in the same directory.

11.2.4 Dealing with finite automata

Lexical analysis relies on the theory of finite automata. The most advanced of the classes discussed in this chapter, *LEX_BUILDER*, relies on classes describing various forms of automata:

- *DFA*: deterministic finite automata.
- *PDFA*: partially deterministic finite automata.
- *NDFA*: non-deterministic finite automata.
- *AUTOMATON*, the most general: finite automata.
- *FIXED_AUTOMATON, LINKED_AUTOMATON*.

These classes may also be useful for systems that need to manipulate finite   *21.6, page 408.*
automata for applications other than lexical analysis. The interface of *LEX_BUILDER*,
which includes the features from *AUTOMATON*, *NDFA* and *PDFA*, will provide the
essential information.

11.3 TOKENS

A lexical analyzer built through any of the techniques described in the rest of this
chapter will return tokens – instances of class *TOKEN*. Here are the most important
features of this class:

- *string_value*: a string giving the token's contents.
- *type*: an integer giving the code of the token's type. The possible token types and
  associated integer codes are specified during the process of building the lexical
  analyzer in one of the ways described below.
- *is_keyword*: a boolean indicating whether the token is a keyword.
- *keyword_code*: an integer, meaningful only if *is_keyword* is true, and identifying
  the keyword by the code that was given to it during the process of building the
  analyzer.
- *line_number, column_number*: two integers indicating where the token appeared
  in the input text.

11.4 BUILDING AND USING LEXICAL ANALYZERS

The general method for performing lexical analysis is the following.

L1 • Create an instance of *LEXICAL*, giving a lexical analyzer for the desired
     grammar.

L2 • Store the analyzer into a file.

L3 • Retrieve the analyzer from the file.

L4 • Use the analyzer to analyze the tokens of one or more input texts by calling the
     various features of class *LEXICAL* on this object.

Steps L2 and L3 are obviously unnecessary if this process is applied as a single
sequence. But in almost all practical cases you will want to use the same grammar to
analyze many different input texts. Then steps L1 and L2 will be performed once and
for all as soon as the lexical grammar is known, yielding an instance of *LEXICAL* that
step L2 stores into a file; then in every case that requires analyzing a text you will
simply retrieve the analyzer and apply it, performing steps L3 and L4 only.

The simplest way to store and retrieve the instance of *LEXICAL* and all related objects is to use the facilities of class *STORABLE*: procedure *store* and one of the retrieval procedures. To facilitate this process, *LEXICAL* inherits from *STORABLE*.

About STORABLE see chapter 13.

The next sections explain how to perform these various steps. In the most common case, the best technique is to inherit from class *SCANNING*, which provides a framework for retrieving an analyzer file if it exists, creating it from a grammar description otherwise, and proceed with the lexical analysis of one or more input texts.

11.5 LEXICAL GRAMMAR FILES AND CLASS *SCANNING*

Class *SCANNING* may be used as an ancestor by classes that need to perform lexical analysis. When using *SCANNING* you will need a **lexical grammar file** that contains the description of the lexical grammar. Since it is easy to edit and adapt a file without modifying the software proper, this technique provides flexibility and supports the incremental development and testing of lexical analyzers.

The class interface is in 21.2, page 403.

11.5.1 The *build* procedure

To obtain a lexical analyzer in a descendant of class *SCANNING*, use the procedure

> *build* (*store_file_name*, *grammar_file_name*: STRING)

If no file of name *store_file_name* exists, then *build* reads the lexical grammar from the file of name *grammar_file_name*, builds the corresponding lexical analyzer, and stores it into *store_file_name*.

If there already exists a file of name *grammar_file_name*, *build* uses it to recreate an analyzer without using the *grammar_file_name*.

11.5.2 Lexical grammar files

A lexical grammar file (to be used as second argument to *build*, corresponding to *grammar_file_name*) should conform to a simple structure, of which the file *eiffel_regular* in the examples directory provides a good illustration.

Here is the general form:

```
Token_type_1 Regular_expression_1
Token_type_2 Regular_expression_2
...
Token_type_m Regular_expression_m

-- Keywords

Keyword_1
Keyword_2
...
Keyword_n
```

In other words: one or more lines, each containing the name of a token type and a **regular expression**; a line beginning with two dashes -- (the word **Keywords** may follow them to signal that this is the beginning of keywords); and one or more lines containing one keyword each.

Each *Token_type_i* is the name of a token type, such as *Identifier* or *Decimal_constant*. Each *Regular_expression_i* is a regular expression, built according to a precisely specified format. That format is defined later in this chapter, but even without having seen that definition it is not hard to understand the following small and typical example of lexical grammar file without keywords:

The notion of regular expression is explained in detail in 11.7, page 209 below.

Decimal	'0'..'9'
Natural	+ ('0'..'9')
Integer	['+'|'−'] '1'..'9' *('0'..'9')

The first expression describes a token type whose specimens are tokens made of a single-letter decimal digit (any character between *0* and *9*). In the second, the + sign denotes repetition (one or more); the specimens of the corresponding token type are all non-empty sequences of decimal digits – in other words, natural numbers, with leading zeroes permitted. In the third, the | symbol denotes alternation, and the asterisk denotes repetition (zero or more); the corresponding tokens are possibly signed integer constants, with no leading zeroes.

As explained below, keywords are regular expressions which are treated separately for convenience and efficiency. If you are using lexical grammar files of the above form, all keywords must be specimens of the last regular expression given (*Regular_expression_m* above). More details below.

See 11.7.8. page 212 about keywords.

11.5.3 Using a lexical analyzer

Once *build* has given you an analyzer, you may use it to analyze input texts through calls to the procedure

analyze (*input_file_name*: STRING)

This will read in and process successive input tokens. Procedure *analyze* will apply to each of these tokens the action of procedure *do_a_token*. As defined in *SCANNING*, this procedure prints out information on the token: its string value, its type, whether it is a keyword and if so its code. You may redefine it in any descendant class so as to perform specific actions on each token.

The initial action *begin_analysis*, which by default prints a header, and the terminal action *end_analysis*, which by default does nothing, may also be redefined.

To build lexical analyzers which provide a higher degree of flexibility, use *METALEX* or *LEX_BUILDER*, as described in the last part of this chapter.

11.6 ANALYZING INPUT

Let us look more precisely at how we can use a lexical analyzer to analyze an input text.

11.6.1 Class *LEXICAL*

Procedure *analyze* takes care of the most common needs of lexical analysis. But if you need more advanced lexical analysis facilities you will need an instance of class *LEXICAL* (a direct instance of *LEXICAL* itself or of one of its proper descendants). If you are using class *SCANNING* as described above, you will have access to such an instance through the attribute *analyzer*.

The class interface is in 21.3, page 405.

   This discussion will indeed assume that you have an entity attached to an instance of *LEXICAL*. The name of that entity is assumed to be *analyzer*, although it does not need to be the attribute from *SCANNING*. You can apply to that *analyzer* the various exported features features of class *LEXICAL*, explained below. All the calls described below should use *analyzer* as their target, as in

   analyzer. set_file ("my_file_name")

11.6.2 Creating, retrieving and storing an analyzer

To create a new analyzer, use

   !! *analyzer.make_new*

   You may also retrieve an analyzer from a previous session. *LEXICAL* is a descendant from *STORABLE*, so you can use feature *retrieved* for that purpose. In a descendant of *STORABLE*, simply write

On STORABLE see 13.6, page 254 and the class interface in 23.17, page 458.

   analyzer ?= retrieved

   If you do not want to make the class a descendant of *STORABLE*, use the creation procedure *make* of *LEXICAL*, not to be confused with *make_new* above:

   !! *analyzer.make*
   analyzer ?= analyzer.retrieved

11.6.3 Choosing a document

To analyze a text, call *set_file* or *set_string* to specify the document to be parsed. With the first call, the analysis will be applied to a file; with the second, to a string.

   If you use procedure *analyze* of *SCANNING*, you do not need any such call, since *analyze* calls *set_file* on the file name passed as argument.

11.6.4 Obtaining the tokens

The basic procedure for analyzing successive tokens in the text is *get_token*, which reads in one token and sets up various attributes of the analyzer to record properties of that token:

- *last_token*, a function of type *TOKEN*, which provides all necessary information on the last token read.
- *token_line_number* and *token_column_number*, to know where the token is in the text. These queries return results of type *INTEGER*.
- *token_type*, giving the regular expression type, identified by its integer number (which is the value *No_token* if no correct token was recognized).
- *other_possible_tokens*, an array giving all the other possible token types of the last token. (If *token_type* is *No_token* the array is empty.)
- *end_of_text*, a boolean attribute used to record whether the end of text has been reached. If so, subsequent calls to *get_token* will have no effect.

Procedure *get_token* recognizes the longest possible token. So if <, = and <= are all regular expressions in the grammar, the analyzer recognizes <= as one token, rather than < followed by =. You can use *other_possible_tokens* to know what shorter tokens were recognized but not retained.

If it fails to recognize a regular expression, *get_token* sets *token_type* to *No_token* and advances the input cursor by one character.

11.6.5 The basic scheme

Here is the most common way of using the preceding facilities:

```
from
    set_file ("text_directory/text_to_be_parsed");
        -- Or: set_string ("string to parse")
    begin_analysis
until
    end_of_text
loop
    analyzer.get_token;
    if analyzer.token_type = No_token then
        go_on
    end;
    do_a_token (lexical.last_token)
end;

end_analysis
```

This scheme is used by procedure *analyze* of class *SCANNING*, so that in standard cases you may simply inherit from that class and redefine procedures *begin_analysis*, *do_a_token* and *end_analysis*. If you are not inheriting from *SCANNING*, these names simply denote procedures that you must provide.

11.7 REGULAR EXPRESSIONS

The Lex library supports a powerful set of construction mechanisms for describing the various types of tokens present in common languages such as programming languages, specification languages or just text formats. These mechanisms are called **regular expressions**; any regular expression describes a set of possible tokens, called the **specimens** of the regular expression.

Let us now study the format of regular expressions. This format is used in particular for the lexical grammar files needed by class *SCANNING* and (as seen below) by procedure *read_grammar* of class *METALEX*. The *eiffel_regular* grammar file in the examples directory provides an extensive example.

Each regular expression denotes a set of tokens. For example, the first regular expression seen above,

   '0' .. '9'

denotes a set of ten tokens, each consisting of a single digit.

11.7.1 Basic expressions

A character expression, written *'character'* where *character* is a single character, describes a set of tokens with just one element: the one-character token *character*. For example, *'0'* describes the set containing the single-digit single token *0*.

Cases in which *character* is not a printable character use the following conventions:

'\ooo'	Character given by its three-digit octal code *ooo*.
'\xx'	Character given by its two-digit hexadecimal code *xx* (Both lower- and upper-case may be used for letters in *xx*.)
'\r'	Carriage return
'\"	Single quote
'\\'	Backslash
'\t'	Tabulation
'\n'	New line
'\b'	Backspace
'\f'	Form feed

11.7.2 Intervals

An interval, written *lower..upper* where *lower* and *upper* are character expressions, describes a set of one-character tokens: all the characters whose ASCII code is between the codes for the characters in *lower* and *upper*. For example, *'0'..'9'* contains all tokens made of a single decimal digit.

11.7.3 Basic operator expressions

A parenthesized expression, written (*exp*) where *exp* is a regular expression, describes the same set of tokens as *exp*. This serves to remove ambiguities in complex regular expressions. For example, the parenthesized expression (*'0'..'9'*) also describes all single-decimal-digit tokens.

A difference, written *interval* − *char*, where *interval* is an interval expression and *char* is a character expression, describes the set of tokens which are in *exp* but not in *char*. For example, the difference *'0'..'9'* − *'4'* describes all single-decimal-digit tokens except those made of the digit *4*.

A difference may only apply to an interval and a single character.

11.7.4 Iterations

An unbounded iteration, written ∗ *exp* or + *exp* where *exp* is a regular expression, describes the set of tokens made of sequences of zero or more specimens of *exp* (in the first form, using the asterisk), or of one or more specimens of *exp* (in the second form, using the plus sign). For example, the iteration + (*'0'..'9'*) describes the set of tokens made of one or more consecutive decimal digits.

A fixed iteration, written *n exp* where *n* is a natural integer constant and *exp* is a regular expression, describes the set of tokens made of sequences of exactly *n* specimens of *exp*. For example, *3* (*'A'..'Z'*) describes the set of all three-letter upper-case tokens.

11.7.5 Other operator expressions

A concatenation, written $exp_1\ exp_2\ ...\ exp_n$, describes the set of tokens made of a specimen of exp_1 followed by a specimen of exp_2 etc. For example, the concatenation *'1'..'9'* ∗ (*'0'..'9'*) describes the set of tokens made of one or more decimal digits, not beginning with a zero − in other words, integer constants in the usual notation.

An optional component, written [*exp*] where exp is a regular expression, describes the set of tokens that includes the empty token and all specimens of *exp*. Optional components usually appear in concatenations.

Concatenations may be inconvenient when the concatenated elements are simply characters, as in *'A'* *' '* *'T'* *'e'* *'x'* *'t'*. In this case you may use a **string** in double quotes, as in

> *"A Text"*

More generally, a string is written $"a_1 a_2\ ...\ a_n"$ for $n \geq 0$, where the a_i are characters, and is an abbreviation for the concatenation $'a_1'\ 'a_2'\ ...\ 'a_n'$, representing a set containing a single token. In a string, the double quote character " is written \" and the backslash character \ is written \\. No other special characters are permitted; if you need special characters, use explicit concatenation. As a special case, "" represents the set containing a single empty token.

A union, written $exp_1\ |\ exp_2\ |\ ...\ |\ exp_n$, describes the set of tokens which are specimens of exp_1, or of exp_2 etc. For example, the union (*'a'..'z'*) | (*'A'..'Z'*) describes the set of single-letter tokens (lower-case or upper-case).

11.7.6 Predefined expressions

A joker, written $*\bullet$, describes the set of all tokens made of exactly one character. A joker is considered to be an interval expression, so that it may be the first operand of a difference operation.

A printable, written P, describes the set of all tokens made of exactly one printable character.

A blank, written B, describes the set of all tokens made of one or more specimens of the characters blank, new-line, carriage-return and tabulation.

The following non-elementary forms are abbreviations for commonly needed regular expressions:

Code	Equivalent expression	Role
L	$'\backslash n'$	New-line character
N	$+('0'..'9')$	Natural integer constants
R	$['+'\|'-'] +('0'..'9') '.' *('0'..'9')$ $['e'\|'E' ['+'\|'-'] +('0'..'9')]$	Floating-point constants
W	$+(\$P - '\ ' - '\backslash t' - '\backslash n' - '\backslash r')$	Words
Z	$['+'\|'-'] +('0'..'9')$	Possibly signed integer constants

Figure 11.2: Abbreviations

A **delimited string**, written $->string$, where *string* is of the form, "$a_1 a_2 ... a_n$", represents the set of tokens made of any number of printable characters and terminated by *string*.

One more form of regular expression, case-sensitive expressions, using the $\sim$ symbol, will be introduced below.

11.7.9, page 213.

11.7.7 Combining expression-building mechanisms

You may freely combine the various construction mechanisms to describe complex regular expressions. Below are a few examples.

$'a'..'z' - 'c' - 'e'$
    Single-lower-case-letter tokens, except *c* and *e*.

$*\bullet - '\backslash 007'$
    Any single-character token except ASCII 007.

$+('a'..'z')$
    One or more lower-case letters.

$['+'|'-']'1'..'9' * ('0'..'9')$
> Integer constants, optional sign, no leading zero.

$->"*/"$
> Any string up to and including an occurrence of $*/$
> (the closing symbol of a PL/I or C comment).

$"\"" -> "\""$
> Eiffel strings.

11.7.8 Dealing with keywords

Many languages to be analyzed have keywords – or, more generally, "reserved words". Eiffel, for example, has reserved words such as **class** and *Result*.

> In Eiffel terminology reserved words include keywords; a keyword is a marker playing a purely syntactical role, such as **class**. Predefined entities and expressions such as *Result* and *Current*, which have an associated value, are considered reserved words but not keywords. The present discussion uses the term "keyword" although it can be applied to all reserved words.

In principle, keywords could be handled just as other token types. In Eiffel, for example, one might treat each reserved words as a token type with only one specimen; these token types would have names such as *Class* or *Then* and would be defined in the lexical grammar file:

Class	$'c'$ $'l'$ $'a'$ $'s'$ $'s'$
Then	$'t'$ $'h'$ $'e'$ $'n'$
...	

This would be inconvenient. To simplify the task of language description, and also to improve the efficiency of the lexical analysis process, it is usually preferable to treat keywords as a separate category.

If you are using class *SCANNING* and hence a lexical grammar file, the list of keywords, if any, must appear at the end of the file, one per line, preceded by a line that simply reads

-- *Keywords*

For example the final part of the example Eiffel lexical grammar file appears as:

```
... Other token type definitions ...
Identifier      ~('a'..'z') * (~('a'..'z') | '_' | ('0'..'9'))
-- Keywords
alias
all
and
as
BIT
BOOLEAN
... Other reserved words ...
```

Every keyword in the keyword section must be a specimen of one of the token types defined for the grammar, and that token type must be the last one defined in the lexical grammar file, just before the **Keywords** line. So in Eiffel where the keywords have the same lexical structure as identifiers, the last line before the keywords must be the definition of the token type *Identifier*, as shown above.

> The rule that all keywords must be specimens of one token type is a matter of convenience and simplicity, and only applies if you are using *SCANNING* and lexical grammar files. There is no such restriction if you rely directly on the more general facilities provided by *METALEX* or *LEX_BUILDER*. Then different keywords may be specimens of different regular expressions; you will have to specify the token type of every keyword, as explained later in this chapter.

11.7.9 Case sensitivity

By default, letter case is not significant for regular expressions and keywords. So if *yes* matches a token type defined by a regular expression, or is a keyword, the input values *Yes*, *yES* and *yES* will all yield the same token or keyword. This also means that $'a'..'z'$ and $'a'..'z'|'A'..'Z'$ describe the same set of tokens.

The regular expression syntax introduced above offers a special notation to specify that a particular expression is case-sensitive: ~ *exp*, where *exp* is a regular expression. For example, ~ (*'A'..'Z'*) only covers single-upper-case-letter tokens. But for all other kinds of expression letter case is not taken into account.

You may change this default behavior through a set of procedures introduced in class *LEX_BUILDER* and hence available in its descendants *METALEX* and *SCANNING*.

To make subsequent regular expressions case-sensitive, call the procedure

ignore_case

To revert to the default mode where case is not significant, call the procedure

distinguish_case

Each of these procedures remains in effect until the other one is called, so that you only need one call to define the desired behavior.

For keywords, the policy is less tolerant. A single rule is applied to the entire grammar: keywords are either all case-sensitive or all case-insensitive. To make all keywords case-sensitive, call

keywords_distinguish_case.

The inverse call, corresponding to the default rule, is

keywords_ignore_case

Either of these calls must be executed before you define any keywords; if you are using *SCANNING*, this means before calling procedure *build*. Once set, the keyword case-sensitivity policy cannot be changed.

11.8 USING *METALEX* TO BUILD A LEXICAL ANALYZER

(You may skip the rest of this chapter if you only need simple lexical facilities.)

Class *SCANNING*, as studied above, relies on a class *METALEX*. In some cases, you may prefer to use the features of *METALEX* directly. Since *SCANNING* inherits from *METALEX*, anything you do with *METALEX* can in fact be done with *SCANNING*, but you may wish to stay with just *METALEX* if you do not need the additional features of *SCANNING*.

The interface of class METALEX is in 21.5, page 407.

11.8.1 Steps in using *METALEX*

METALEX has an attribute *analyzer* which will be attached to a lexical analyzer. This class provides tools for building a lexical analyzer incrementally through explicit feature calls; you can still use a lexical grammar file, but do not have to.

The following extract from a typical descendant of *METALEX* illustrates the process of building a lexical analyzer in this way:

```
Upper_identifier, Lower_identifier, Decimal_constant, Octal_constant, Word:
                     INTEGER is unique;

...

distinguish_case;
keywords_distinguish_case;
put_expression ("+('0'..'7'")", Octal_constant, "Octal");
put_expression ("'a'..'z' * ('a'..'z'|'0'..'9'|'_')",
                    Lower_identifier, "Lower");
put_expression ("'A'..'Z' * ('A'..'Z'|'0'..'9'|'_')",
                    Upper_identifier, "Upper");
dollar_w (Word);

...

put_keyword ("begin", Lower_identifier);
put_keyword ("end", Lower_identifier);
put_keyword ("THROUGH", Upper_identifier);

...

make_analyzer
```

This example follows the general scheme of building a lexical analyzer with the features of *METALEX*, in a class that will normally be a descendant of *METALEX*:

M1 • Set options, such as case sensitivity.

M2 • Record regular expressions.

M3 • Record keywords (this may be interleaved with step M2.)

M4 • "Freeze" the analyzer by a call to *make_analyzer*.

To perform steps M2 to M4 in a single shot and generate a lexical analyzer from a lexical grammar file, as with *SCANNING*, you may use the procedure

read_grammar (*grammar_file_name*: *STRING*)

In this case all the expressions and keywords are taken from the file of name *grammar_file_name* rather than passed explicitly as arguments to the procedures of the class. You do not need to call *make_analyzer*, since *read_grammar* includes such a call.

The rest of this discussion assumes that the four steps are executed individually as shown above, rather than as a whole using *read_grammar*.

11.8.2 Recording token types and regular expressions

As shown by the example, each token type, defined by a regular expression, must be assigned an integer code. Here the developer has chosen to use Unique constant values so as not to worry about selecting values for these codes manually, but you may select any values that are convenient or mnemonic. The values have no effect other than enabling you to keep track of the various lexical categories. Rather than using literal values directly, it is preferable to rely on symbolic constants, Unique or not, which will be more mnemonic.

Unique values and other symbolic constants were introduced in 2.8.1, page 51.

Procedure *put_expression* records a regular expression. The first argument is the expression itself, given as a string built according to the rules seen earlier in this chapter. The second argument is the integer code for the expression. The third argument is a string which gives a name identifying the expression. This is useful mostly for debugging purposes; there is also a procedure *put_nameless_expression* which does not have this argument and is otherwise identical to *put_expression*.

The rules for regular expressions were given in 11.7, page 209.

Procedure *dollar_w* corresponds to the *$W* syntax for regular expressions. Here an equivalent call would have been

put_nameless_expression ("$W", Word)

Procedure *declare_keyword* records a keyword. The first argument is a string containing the keyword; the second argument is the regular expression of which the keyword must be a specimen. The example shows that here – in contrast with the rule enforced by *SCANNING* – not all keywords need be specimens of the same regular expression.

The calls seen so far record a number of regular expressions and keywords, but do not give us a lexical analyzer yet. To obtain a usable lexical analyzer, you must call

make_analyzer

After that call, you may not record any new regular expression or keyword. The analyzer is usable through attribute *analyzer*.

A note for readers knowledgeable in the theory of lexical analysis: one of the most important effects of the call to *make_analyzer* is to transform the non-deterministic finite automaton resulting from calls such as the ones above into a deterministic finite automaton.

Remember that if you use procedure *read_grammar*, you need not worry about *make_analyzer*, as the former procedure calls the latter.

Another important feature of class *METALEX* is procedure *store_analyzer*, which stores the analyzer into a file whose name is passed as argument, for use by later lexical analysis sessions. To retrieve the analyzer, simply use procedure *retrieve_analyzer*, again with a file name as argument.

11.9 BUILDING A LEXICAL ANALYZER WITH *LEX_BUILDER*

To have access to the most general set of lexical analysis mechanisms, you may use class *LEX_BUILDER*, which gives you an even finer grain of control than *METALEX*. This is not necessary in simple applications.

The class interface is in 21.6, page 408.

11.9.1 Building a lexical analyzer

LEX_BUILDER enables you to build a lexical analyzer by describing successive token types and keywords. This is normally done in a descendant of *LEX_BUILDER*. For each token type, you call a procedure that builds an object, or **tool**, representing the associated regular expression.

For the complete list of available procedures, refer to the flat-short form of the class; there is one procedure for every category of regular expression studied earlier in this chapter. Two typical examples of calls are:

```
interval ('a', 'z')
    -- Create an interval tool

union  (Letter, Underlined)
    -- Create a union tool
```

Every such procedure call also assigns an integer index to the tool it creates; this number is available through the attribute *last_created_tool*. You will need to record it into an integer entity, for example *Identifier* or *Letter*.

11.9.2 An example

The following extract from a typical descendant of *LEX_BUILDER* illustrates how to create a tool representing the identifiers of an Eiffel-like language.

```
Identifier, Letter, Digit, Underlined, Suffix, Suffix_list: INTEGER;

build_identifier is
    do
        interval ('a', 'z'); Letter := last_created_tool;
        interval ('0', '9'); Digit := last_created_tool;
        interval ('_', '_'); Underlined := last_created_tool;

        union (Digit, Underlined); Suffix := last_created_tool;

        iteration (Suffix); Suffix_list := last_created_tool;
        append (Letter, Suffix_list); Identifier := last_created_tool
    end
```

Each token type is characterized by a number in the *tool_list*. Each tool has a name, recorded in *tool_names*, which gives a readable form of the corresponding regular expression. You can use it to check that you are building the right tool.

11.9.3 Selecting visible tools

In the preceding example, only some of the tools, such as *Identifier*, are of interest to the clients. Others, such as *Suffix* and *Suffix_list*, only play an auxiliary role.

When you create a tool, it is by default invisible to clients. To make it visible, use procedure *select_tool*. Clients will need a number identifying it; to set this number, use procedure *associate*. For example the above extract may be followed by:

---

select_tool (*Identifier*);
associate (*Identifier*, *34*);

put_keyword (*"class"*, *Identifier*);
put_keyword (*"end"*, *Identifier*);
put_keyword (*"feature"*, *Identifier*)

If the analysis encounters a token that belongs to two or more different selected regular expressions, the one entered last takes over. Others are recorded in the array *other_possible_tokens*.

If you do not explicitly give an integer value to a regular expression, its default value is its rank in *tool_list*.

12

Parsing: The Parse Library

12.1 OVERVIEW

Parsing is the task of analyzing the structure of documents such as programs, specifications or other structured texts.

Many systems need to parse documents. The best-known examples are compilers, interpreters and other software development tools; but as soon as a system provides its users with a command language, or processes input data with a non-trivial structure, it will need parsing facilities.

This chapter describes the Parse library, which you can use to process documents of many different types. It provides a simple and flexible parsing scheme, resulting from the full application of object-oriented principles.

> The flat-short interfaces of the classes discussed in this chapter appear in chapter 22.

Because it concentrates on the higher-level structure, the Parse library requires auxiliary mechanisms for identifying a document's lexical components: words, numbers and other such elementary units. To address this need it is recommended, although not required, to complement Parse with the Lex library studied in the previous chapter.

The figure at the top of the following page shows the inheritance structure of the classes discussed in this chapter.

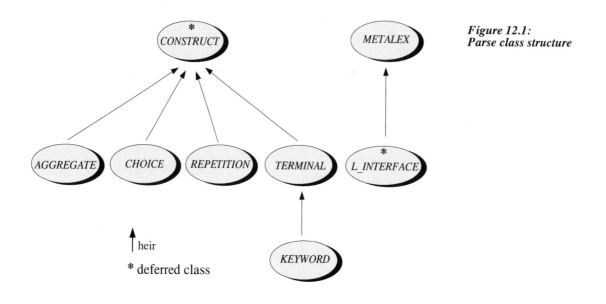

Figure 12.1:
Parse class structure

12.2 WHY USE THE PARSE LIBRARY?

Let us fist look at the circumstances under which you may want − or not want − to use
the Parse library.

12.2.1 The Parse library *vs.* parser generators

Parsing is a heavily researched area of computing science and many tools are available
to generate parsers. In particular, the popular Yacc tool, originally developed for Unix,
is widely used to produce parsers.

In some cases Yacc or similar tools are perfectly adequate. It is also sometimes
desirable to write a special-purpose parser for a language, not relying on any parser
generator. Several circumstances may, however, make the Parse library attractive:

- The need to interface the parsing tasks with the rest of an object-oriented system
  (such as a compiler or more generally a "document processor" as defined below)
  in the simplest and most convenient way.

- The desire to apply object-oriented principles as fully as possible to all aspects of
  a system, including parsing, so as to gain the method's many benefits, in
  particular reliability, reusability and extendibility.

- The need to tackle languages whose structure is not easily reconciled with the
  demands of common parser generator, which usually require the grammar to be
  LALR (1). (The Parse library uses a more tolerant LL scheme, whose only
  significant constraint is absence of left-recursivity; the library provides
  mechanisms to detect this condition, which is easy to correct.)

- The need to define several possible semantic treatments on the same syntactic
  structure.

*On Yacc see: S.C. Johnson,
"Yet Another Compiler-
Compiler", CSTR 32, Bell
Laboratories, Murray Hill
(N.J.), 1975, usually included
(often in revised form) in the
documentation of Unix
platforms.*

*Readers not familiar with the
theory of parsing may ignore
this point.*

The last reason may be the most significant practical argument in favor of using Parse. Particularly relevant is the frequent case of a software development environment in which a variety of tools all work on the same basic syntactic structure. For example an environment supporting a programming language such as Pascal or Eiffel may include a compiler, an interpreter, a pretty-printer, software documentation tools (such as Eiffel's short and flat-short facilities), browsing tools and several other mechanisms that all need to perform semantic actions on software texts that have the same syntactic structure. With common parser generators such as Yacc, the descriptions of syntactic structure and semantic processing are inextricably mixed, so that you normally need one new specification for each tool. This makes design, evolution and reuse of specifications difficult and error-prone.

In contrast, the Parse library promotes a specification style whereby syntax and semantics are kept separate, and uses inheritance to allow many different semantic descriptions to rely on the same syntactic stem. This will make Parse particularly appropriate in such cases.

12.2.2 A word of caution

At the time of publication the Parse library has not reached the same degree of maturity as the other libraries presented in this book. It should thus be used with some care. You will find at the end of this chapter a few comments about the work needed to bring the library to its full realization.

On desirable further work see 12.13, page 241.

12.3 AIMS AND SCOPE OF THE PARSE LIBRARY

To understand the Parse library it is necessary to appreciate the role of parsing and its place in the more general task of processing documents of various kinds.

12.3.1 Basic terminology

First, some elementary conventions. The word **document** will denote the texts to be parsed. The software systems which perform parsing as part of their processing will be called **document processors**.

Typical document processors are compilers, interpreters, program checkers, specification analyzers and documentation tools. For example the ISE Eiffel 3 environment contains a number of document processors, used for compiling, documentation and browsing; the language to which they apply is either Eiffel itself or the Lace control language.

About Lace see appendix D of "Eiffel: The Language".

12.3.2 Parsing, grammars and semantics

Parsing is seldom an end in itself; rather, it serves as an intermediate step for document processors which perform various other actions.

Parsing takes care of one of the basic tasks of a document processor: reconstructing the logical organization of a document, which must conform to a certain **syntax** (or structure), defined by a **grammar**.

The more complete name **syntactic grammar** avoids any confusion with the *lexical* grammars discussed in the previous chapter. By default, "grammar" with no further qualification will always denote a syntactic grammar. A syntactic grammar normally relies on a lexical grammar, which gives the form of the most elementary components – the tokens – appearing in the syntactic structure.

Once parsing has reconstructed the structure of a document, the document processor will perform various operations on the basis of that structure. For example a compiler will generate target code corresponding to the original text; a command language interpreter will execute the operations requested in the commands; and a documentation tool such as the short and flat-short commands for Eiffel will produce some information on the parsed document. Such operations are called **semantic actions**. One of the principal requirements on a good parsing mechanism is that it should make it easy to graft semantics onto syntax, by adding semantic actions of many possible kinds to the grammar.

The Parse library provides predefined classes which handle the parsing aspect automatically and provide the hooks for adding semantic actions in a straightforward way. This enables developers to write full document processors – handling both syntax and semantics – simply and efficiently.

As noted at the beginning of this chapter, it is possible to build a single syntactic base and use it for several processors (such as a compiler and a documentation tool) with semantically different goals, such as compilation and documentation. In the Parse library the semantic hooks take the form of deferred routines, or of routines with default implementations which you may redefine in descendants.

12.4 LIBRARY CLASSES

The Parse library contains a small number of classes which cover common document processing applications. The classes, whose inheritance structure was shown at the beginning of this chapter, are:

See the inheritance graph on page 220.

- *CONSTRUCT*, describing the general notion of syntactical construct.
- *AGGREGATE*, describing constructs of the "aggregate" form.
- *CHOICE*, describing constructs of the "choice" form.
- *REPETITION*, describing constructs of the "repetition" form.
- *TERMINAL*, describing "terminal" constructs with no further structure.
- *KEYWORD*, describing how to handle keywords.
- *L_INTERFACE*, providing a simple interface with the lexical analysis process and the Lex library.
- *INPUT*, describing how to handle the input document.

12.5 EXAMPLES

The ISE Eiffel 3 delivery includes (in the *examples/library/parse* subdirectory) a simple example using the Parse Library classes. The example is a processor for "documents" which describe computations involving polynomials with variables. The corresponding processor is a system which obtains polynomial specifications and variable values from a user, and computes the corresponding polynomials.

This example illustrates the most important mechanisms of the Parsing Library and provides a guide for using the facilities described in this chapter. The components of its grammar appear as illustrations in the next sections.

12.6 CONSTRUCTS AND PRODUCTIONS

A set of documents possessing common properties, such as the set of all valid Eiffel classes or the set of all valid polynomial descriptions, is called a **language**.

In addition to its lexical aspects, the description of a language includes both syntactic and semantic properties. The grammar – the syntactic specification – describes the structure of the language (for example how an Eiffel class is organized into a number of clauses); the semantic specification defines the meaning of documents written in the language (for example the run-time properties of instances of the class, and the effect of feature calls).

To discuss the Parse library, it is simpler to consider "language" as a purely syntactic notion; in other words, a language is simply the set of documents conforming to a certain syntactic grammar (taken here to include the supporting lexical grammar). Any semantic aspect will be considered to belong to the province of a specific document processor for the language, although the technique used for specifying the grammar will make it easy to add the specification of the semantics, or several alternative semantic specifications if desired.

This section explains how you may define the syntactic base – the grammar.

12.6.1 Constructs

A grammar consists of a number of **constructs**, each representing the structure of documents, or document components, called the **specimens** of the construct. For example, a grammar for Eiffel will contain constructs such as Class, Feature_clause and Instruction. A particular class text is a specimen of construct Class.

Each construct will be defined by a **production**, which gives the structure of the construct's specimens. For example, a production for Class in an Eiffel grammar should express that a class (a specimen of the Class construct) is made of an optional Indexing part, a Class_header, an optional Formal_generics part and so on. The production for Indexing will indicate that any specimen of this construct – any Indexing part – consists of the keyword *indexing* followed by zero or more specimens of Index_clause.

Although some notations for syntax descriptions such as BNF allow more than one production per construct, the Parse library relies on the convention that every construct is defined by **at most one** production. Depending on whether there is indeed such a production, the construct is either **non-terminal** or **terminal**:

BNF, or Backus-Naur Form, is a widely used syntax specification formalism originally introduced for the description of Algol 60.

- A non-terminal construct (so called because it is defined in terms of others) is specified by a production, which may be of one of three types: aggregate, choice and repetition. The construct will accordingly be called an aggregate, choice or repetition construct.

- A terminal construct has no defining production. This means that it must be defined outside of the syntactical grammar. Terminals indeed come from the **lexical grammar**. Every terminal construct corresponds to a token type (regular expression or keyword) of the lexical grammar, for which the parsing duty will be delegated to lexical mechanisms, assumed in the rest of this chapter to be provided by the Lex library although others may be substituted if appropriate.

All specimens of terminal constructs are instances of class *TERMINAL*. A special case is that of keyword constructs, which have a single specimen corresponding to a keyword of the language. For example, *if* is a keyword of Eiffel. Keywords are described by class *KEYWORD*, an heir of *TERMINAL*.

The rest of this section concentrates on the parsing-specific part: non-terminal constructs and productions. Terminals will be studied in the discussion of how to interface parsing with lexical analysis.

On the interface with lexical analysis see 12.9, page 231 below.

12.6.2 Varieties of non-terminal constructs and productions

An aggregate production defines a construct whose specimens are obtained by concatenating ("aggregating") specimens of a list of specified constructs, some of which may be optional. For example, the production for construct Conditional in an Eiffel grammar may read:

Conditional $\triangleq$ *if* Then_part_list [Else_part] *end*

This means that a specimen of Conditional (a conditional instruction) is made of the keyword *if*, followed by a specimen of Then_part_list, followed by zero or one specimen of Else_part (the square brackets represent an optional component), followed by the keyword *end*.

This notation for productions uses conventions similar to those of the book *Eiffel: The Language*. Keywords are written in **boldface italics** and stand for themselves. Special symbols, such as the semicolon, are written in double quotes, as in ";". The $\triangleq$ symbol means "is defined as" and is more accurate mathematically than plain =, which, however, is often used for this purpose (see *Introduction to the Theory of Programming Languages*, Prentice Hall, 1991, for a more complete discussion of this issue).

A choice production defines a construct whose specimens are specimens of one among a number of specified constructs. For example, the production for construct Type in an Eiffel grammar may read:

Type $\triangleq$ Class_type | Class_type_expanded | Formal_generic_name
      | Anchored | Bit_type

This means that a specimen of Type is either a specimen of Class_type, or a specimen of Class_type_expanded etc.

Finally, a repetition production defines a construct whose specimens are sequences of zero or more specimens of a given construct (called the **base** of the repetition construct), separated from each other by a **separator**. For example, the production for construct Compound in an Eiffel grammar may read

Compound $\triangleq$ {Instruction ";" ...}

This means that a specimen of Compound is made of zero or more specimens of Instruction, each separated from the next (if any) by a semicolon.

In Eiffel the semicolon between instructions is optional, but recommended.

These three mechanisms – aggregate, choice and repetition – suffice to describe the structure of a wide array of practical languages. Properties which cannot be handled by them should be dealt with through **semantic actions**, as explained below.

12.6.3 An example grammar

The example directory included in the delivery implements a processor for a grammar describing a simple language for expressing polynomials. A typical "document" in this language is the line

$x; y$: $x * (y + 8 - (2 * x))$

The beginning of the line, separated from the rest by a colon, is the list of variables used in the polynomial, separated by semicolons. The rest of the line is the expression defining the polynomial.

Using the conventions defined above, the grammar may be written as:

Line	$\triangleq$ Variables ":" Sum
Variables	$\triangleq$ {Identifier ";" ...}
Sum	$\triangleq$ {Diff "+" ...}
Diff	$\triangleq$ {Product "-" ...}
Product	$\triangleq$ {Term "*" ...}
Term	$\triangleq$ Simple_var	Int_constant	Nested
Nested	$\triangleq$ "(" Sum ")"

This grammar assumes a terminal Identifier, which must be defined as a token type in the lexical grammar. The other terminals are keywords, shown as strings appearing in double quotes, for example "+".

12.7 PARSING CONCEPTS

The Parse library supports a parsing mechanism based on the concepts of object-oriented software construction.

12.7.1 Class *CONSTRUCT*

The deferred class *CONSTRUCT* describes the general notion of construct; instances of this class and its descendants are specimens of the constructs of a grammar.

For the interface of CONSTRUCT see 22.2, page 414.

Deferred though it may be, *CONSTRUCT* defines some useful general patterns; for example, its procedure *process* appears as:

> *parse*;
> *if parsed* **then**
>   *semantics*
> **end**

In the common case when the document processor is a compiler, a descendant of CONSTRUCT may rename 'process' as 'compile'.

where procedures *parse* and *semantics* are expressed in terms of some more specific procedures, which are deferred. This defines a general scheme while leaving the details to descendants of the class.

Such descendants, given in the library, are classes *AGGREGATE*, *CHOICE*, *REPETITION* and *TERMINAL*. They describe the corresponding types of construct, with features providing the operations for parsing their specimens and applying the associated semantic actions.

12.7.2 Building a processor

To build a processor for a given grammar, you write a class, called a **construct class**, for every construct of the grammar, terminal or non-terminal. The class should inherit from *AGGREGATE*, *CHOICE*, *REPETITION* or *TERMINAL* depending on the nature of the construct. It describes the production for the construct and any associated semantic actions.

To complete the processor, you must choose a "top construct" for that particular processor, and write a root class. In accordance with the object-oriented method, which implies that "roots" and "tops" should be chosen last, these steps are explained at the end of this chapter.

The next sections explain how to write construct classes, how to handle semantics, and how to interface parsing with the lexical analysis process. All these tasks rely on a fundamental data abstraction, the notion of **abstract syntax tree**.

12.7.3 Abstract syntax trees

The effect of processing a document with a processor built from a combination of construct classes is to build an abstract syntax tree for that document, and to apply any requested semantic actions to that tree.

The syntax tree is said to be abstract because it only includes important structural information and does not retain the concrete information such as keywords and separators. Such concrete information, sometimes called "syntactic sugar", serves only external purposes but is of no use for semantic processing.

The combination of Eiffel techniques and libraries yields a very simple approach to building and processing abstract syntax trees. Class *CONSTRUCT* is a descendant of the Data Structure Library class *TWO_WAY_TREE*, describing a versatile implementation of trees; so, as a consequence, are *CONSTRUCT*'s own descendants. The effect of parsing any specimen of a construct is therefore to create an instance of the corresponding construct class. This instance is (among other things) a tree node, and is automatically inserted at its right place in the abstract syntax tree.

About TWO_WAY_TREE see 8.2.2, page 166.

As noted in the discussion of trees, class *TWO_WAY_TREE* makes no formal distinction between the notions of tree and tree node. So you may identify the abstract syntax tree with the object (instance of *CONSTRUCT*) representing the topmost construct specimen in the structure of the document being analyzed.

12.7.4 The production function

A construct class describes the syntax of a given construct through a function called *production*, which is a direct representation of the corresponding production. This function is declared in *CONSTRUCT* as

```
production: LINKED_LIST [CONSTRUCT] is
        -- Right-hand side of the production for the construct
    deferred
    end
```

Function *production* remains deferred in classes *AGGREGATE*, *CHOICE* and *REPETITION*. Every effective construct class that you write must provide an effecting of that function. It is important for the efficiency of the parsing process that every effective version of *production* be a Once function. Several examples of such effectings are given below.

The Once function mechanism was explained in 2.8.2, page 52.

Classes *AGGREGATE*, *CHOICE*, *REPETITION* and *TERMINAL* also have a deferred function *construct_name* of type *STRING*, useful for tracing and debugging. This function should be effected in every construct class to return the string name of the construct, such as *"INSTRUCTION"* or *"CLASS"* for construct classes in a grammar of Eiffel. For efficiency reasons, the *construct_name* function should also be a Once function. The form of such a function will always be the same, as illustrated by the following example which may appear in the construct class *INSTRUCTION* in a processor for Eiffel:

```
construct_name: STRING is
        -- Symbolic name of the construct
    once
        Result := "INSTRUCTION"
    end
```

The examples of the next few sections, which explain how to write construct classes, are borrowed from the small "Polynomial" language mentioned above, which may be found in the examples directory in the ISE Eiffel delivery.

12.8 PREPARING GRAMMARS

Having studied the Parse library principles, let us see how to write grammar productions for various kinds of construct. The main task is to write the *production* function for each construct class.

12.8.1 Aggregates

The *production* function for a descendant of *AGGREGATE* will describe how to build a specimen of the corresponding function from a sequence of specimens of each of the constituent constructs. Writing this function from the corresponding production is straightforward.

For the interface of AGGREGATE see 22.3, page 417.

As an example, consider the *production* function of class *LINE* for the Polynomial example language. The corresponding production is is

Line ≙ Variables ":" Sum

where Variables and Sum are other constructs, and the colon ":" is a terminal. This means that every specimen of Line consists of a specimen of Variables, followed by a colon, followed by a specimen of Sum.

Here is the corresponding production function as it appears in class *LINE*:

```
production: LINKED_LIST [CONSTRUCT] is
    local
        var: VARIABLES;
        sum: SUM
    once
        !! Result;

        !! var; put (var);

        keyword (":");

        !! sum; put (sum)
    end
```

As shown by this example, the *production* function for an aggregate construct class should declare a local entity (here *var* and *sum*) for each non-keyword component of the right-hand side, the type of each entity being the corresponding construct class (here *VARIABLES* and *SUM*).

The body of the function should begin with

!! *Result*

to create the object containing the result. Then for each non-keyword component, represented by the local entity *component* (this applies to *var* and *sum* in the example), there should be a sequence of two instructions, of the form

> !! *component*; *put* (*component*)

For any keyword of associated string *symbol*, such as the colon *":"* in the example, there should be a call to

> *keyword* (*symbol*)

The order of the various calls to *put* (for non-keywords) and *keyword* (for keywords) must be the order of the components in the production. Also, every !! *component* instruction must occur before the corresponding call to *put* (*component*).

All components in the above example are required. In the general case an aggregate production may have optional components. To signal that a component *component* of the right-hand side is optional, include a call of the form

> *component*. *set_optional*

This call may appear anywhere after the corresponding !! *component* instruction. The recommended place is just after the call to *put* and on the same line, as in

> !! *component*; *put* (*component*); *component*. *set_optional*

12.8.2 Choices

The *production* function for a descendant of *CHOICE* will describe how to build a specimen of the corresponding function as a specimen of one of the alternative constructs.

For the interface of CHOICE see 22.4, page 418.

As an example, consider the *production* function of class *TERM* for the Polynomial example language. The corresponding production is

> Term ≜ Simple_var | Poly_integer | Nested

where Simple_var, Poly_integer and Nested are other constructs. This means that every specimen of Term consists of one specimen of any one of these three constructs.

Here is the corresponding production function as it appears in class *TERM*:

```
production: LINKED_LIST [CONSTRUCT] is
      local
            id: SIMPLE_VAR;
            val: POLY_INTEGER;
            nest: NESTED
      once
            !! Result;

            !! id; put (id);

            !! val; put (val);

            !! nest; put (nest)
      end
```

As shown by this example, the *production* function for a choice construct class must declare a local entity – here *id*, *val* and *nest* – for each alternative component of the right-hand side. The type of each entity is the corresponding construct class – here *SIMPLE_VAR*, *POLY_INTEGER* and *NESTED*.

The body of the function must begin by

!! *Result*

Then for each alternative component represented by a local entity *component* (in the example this applies to *id*, *val* and *nest*) there should be two instructions of the form

!! *component*; *put* (*component*)

The order of the various calls to *put* is irrelevant in principle. When a document is parsed, however, the choices will be tried in the order given; so if you know that certain choices occur more frequently than others it is preferable to list them first to speed up the parsing process.

12.8.3 Repetitions

The *production* function for a descendant of *REPETITION* will describe how to build a specimen of the corresponding function as a sequence or zero or more (or, depending on the grammar, one or more) specimens of the base construct. The class must also effect a feature *separator* of type *STRING*, usually as a constant attribute. (This feature is introduced as deferred in class *REPETITION*.)

For the interface of REPETITION see 22.5, page 419.

As an example, consider the construct Variables in the Polynomial example language. The right-hand side of the corresponding production is

Variables ≜ {Identifier ";" ...}

where Identifier is another construct, and the semicolon ";" is a terminal. This means that every specimen of Variables consists of zero or more specimens of Identifier, separated from each other (if more than one) by semicolons.

Here are the corresponding production function and separator attribute as they appear in class *VARIABLES*:

```
production: LINKED_LIST [CONSTRUCT] is
      local
          base: IDENTIFIER
      once
          !! Result;
          !! base; put (base);
      end;
separator: STRING is ";";
```

As shown by this example, function *production* is built along the same ideas as for aggregates and choices, except that here only one component, *base*, is required; its type must be the class corresponding to the construct serving as the base of the repetition, *IDENTIFIER* in the example.

12.9 INTERFACE TO LEXICAL ANALYSIS

One more type of construct class remains to be discussed: terminal construct classes. Since terminal constructs serve to elevate lexical tokens (regular expressions and keywords) to the dignity of syntactical construct, we must first take a look at how the Parse library classes collaborate with their counterparts in the Lex library.

About the Lex library see chapter 11.

12.9.1 The notion of lexical interface class

To parse a document, you need to get tokens from a lexical analyzer. This is achieved by making some construct classes, in particular those describing terminals, descendants of one of the lexical classes.

The best technique is usually to write a class covering the lexical needs of the language at hand, from which all construct classes that have some lexical business will inherit. Such a class is called a lexical interface class.

Lexical interface classes usually follow a common pattern. To take advantage of this uniformity, the Parse library includes a deferred class *L_INTERFACE* which describes that pattern. Specific lexical interface classes may be written as descendants of *L_INTERFACE*.

For the interface of L_ INTERFACE see 22.8, page 422.

L_INTERFACE is a simple deferred class, with a deferred procedure *obtain_analyzer*. It is an heir of *METALEX*.

About METALEX see 11.8, page 214, and 21.5, page 407.

12.9.2 Obtaining a lexical analyzer

An effective descendant of *L_INTERFACE* must define procedure *obtain_analyzer* so that it records into the lexical analyzer the regular expressions and keywords of the language at hand. In writing *obtain_analyzer* you may use any one of three different techniques, each of which may be the most convenient depending on the precise context, to obtain the required lexical analyzer:

- You may build the lexical analyzer by defining its regular expressions one by one, using the procedures described in the presentation of *METALEX*, in particular *put_expression* and *put_keyword*.

- You may use use procedure *retrieve_analyzer* from *METALEX* to retrieve an analyzer which a previous session saved into a file.

- Finally, you may write a lexical grammar file (or reuse an existing one) and process it on the spot by using procedure *read_grammar* from *METALEX*.

12.9.3 A lexical interface class

An example of lexical interface class is *POLY_LEX* for the Polynomial example language. Here is the complete text of that class:

```
indexing
    description: "Lexical interface class for the Polynomial language"

class POLY_LEX inherit

    L_INTERFACE

feature

    Special, Simple_identifier, Integer_constant, Blanks:
            INTEGER is unique;

    obtain_analyzer is
            -- Create lexical analyzer for the Polynomial language
        do
            ignore_case; keywords_ignore_case;
            build_expressions;
            build_keywords;
            make_analyzer
        end;

feature {NONE} -- Implementation

    build_expressions
            -- Define regular expressions for the Polynomial language
        do
            put_expression ("", Special, "Special");
            put_expression ("", Simple_identifier, "Simple_identifier");
            put_expression ("", Integer_constant, "Integer_constant");
            put_expression ("", Blanks, "Blanks");
        end;

    build_keywords is
            -- Define keywords (special symbols)
            -- for the Polynomial language
        do
            put_keyword ("+", Special);
            put_keyword ("-", Special);
            put_keyword (";", Special);
            put_keyword (":", Special);
            put_keyword ("(", Special);
            put_keyword (")", Special);
            put_keyword ("*", Special)
        end
end
```

This class illustrates the straightforward scheme for writing lexical interface classes. It introduces constants such as *Special* to represent the regular expressions supported, and effects procedure *obtain_analyzer*. The role of this procedure is to define lexical conventions (here through calls to *ignore_case* and *keywords_ignore_case*), to record the regular expressions (through calls to *put_expression*, packaged in a procedure *build_* *expressions* for clarity), and records the keywords (through calls to *put_keyword*, packaged in *build_keywords*).

All the classes of a document processor that need to interact with the lexical analysis should inherit from a lexical interface class such as *POLY_LEX*. This is true in particular of the root class of a processor, as discussed below.

12.9.4 More on terminal constructs

Terminal construct classes are examples of classes that need to interact with the lexical analysis, and should thus inherit from the lexical interface class.

Class *TERMINAL* includes a deferred function *token_type* of type *INTEGER*. Every effective descendant of *TERMINAL* should effect this feature as a constant attribute, whose value is the code for the associated regular expression, obtained from the lexical interface class. As every other construct class, such a descendant should also effect *construct_name* as a Once function. For example, in the Polynomial language, class *INT_CONSTANT* has the following text:

For the interface of TERMINAL see 22.6, page 420.

```
class INT_CONSTANT inherit
    TERMINAL;
    POLY_LEX
feature
    token_type: INTEGER is
        do
            Result := Integer_constant
        end;
    construct_name: STRING is
        once
            Result := "INT_CONSTANT"
        end
end
```

12.10 SPECIFYING THE SEMANTICS

As mentioned at the beginning of this chapter, parsing is usually done not for itself but as a way to perform some semantic processing. The Parsing Library classes define the general framework for grafting such semantics onto a syntactical stem.

12.10.1 Semantic procedures

The principal procedures for defining semantic actions are *pre_action* and *post_action*. These are features of class *CONSTRUCT*. Procedure *pre_action* describes the actions to be performed before a construct has been recognized; *post_action*, the actions to be performed after a construct has been recognized.

As defined in *CONSTRUCT*, both *pre_action* and *post_action* do nothing by default. Any construct class which is a descendant of *CONSTRUCT* may redefine one or both so that they will perform the semantic actions that the document processor must apply to specimens of the corresponding construct. These procedures are called automatically during processing, before and after the corresponding structures have been parsed.

For *TERMINAL*, only one semantic action makes sense. To avoid any confusion, *post_action* is renamed *action* in that class and *pre_action* is renamed *unused_pre_action* to indicate that it is irrelevant.

Often, the semantic procedures need to compute various elements of information. These may be recorded using appropriate attributes of the corresponding construct classes.

> Readers familiar with the theory of parsing and compiling will see that this scheme, using the attributes of Eiffel classes, provides a direct implementation of the "attribute grammar" mechanism.

12.10.2 Polynomial semantics

As an example let us examine the semantics of the Product construct for the polynomial language. It is a repetition construct, with Term as the base construct; in other words a specimen of Product is a sequence of one or more terms, representing the product $term_1 * term_2...* term_n$. Here is the *post_action* procedure in the corresponding class *PRODUCT*:

```
post_action is
    local
        int_value: INTEGER
    do
        from
            child_start;
            int_value := 1
        until
            child_after
        loop
            child.post_action;
            int_value := int_value * info.child_value;
            child_forth
        end;
        info.set_child_value (int_value)
    end
```

Here each relevant construct class has an attribute *info* used to record the semantic information associated with polynomials and their components, such as *child_value*, an integer. The *post_action* takes care of computing the product of all *child_value*s for the children. First, of course, *post_action* must recursively be applied to each child, to compute its own *child_value*.

Recall that an instance of *CONSTRUCT* is also a node of the abstract syntax tree, so that all the *TWO_WAY_TREE* features such as *child_value*, *child_start*, *child_after* and many others are automatically available to access the syntactical structure.

12.10.3 Keeping syntax and semantics separate

For simple examples such as the Polynomial language, it is convenient to use a single class to describe both the syntax of a construct (through the *production* function and associated features) and its semantics (*action* routines and associated features).

For more ambitious languages and processors, however, it is often preferable to keep the two aspects separate. Such separation of syntax and semantics, and in particular the sharing of the same syntax for different processors with different semantic actions, is hard or impossible to obtain with traditional document processing tools such as Yacc on Unix. Here is how to achieve it with the Parse library:

S1 • First write purely **syntactic classes**, that is to say construct classes which only effect the syntactical part (in particular function *production*). As a consequence, these classes usually remain deferred. The recommended convention for such syntactic classes is to use names beginning with *S_*, for example *S_INSTRUCTION* or *S_LOOP*.

S2 • Then for each construct for which a processor defines a certain semantics, define another class, called a **semantic class**, which inherits from the corresponding syntactic class. The recommended convention for semantic classes is to give them names which directly reflect the corresponding construct name, as in *INSTRUCTION* or *LOOP*.

To build a semantic class in in step S2 it is often convenient to use multiple inheritance from a syntactic class and a "semantics-only" class. For example in a processor for Eiffel class *INSTRUCTION* may inherit from both *IS_INSTRUCTION* and from a semantics-only class *INSTRUCTION_PROPERTIES* which introduces the required semantic features.

One of the advantages of this scheme is that it makes it easy to associate two or more types of processing with a single construct, by keeping the same syntactic class (such as *IS_INSTRUCTION*) but choosing a different pure-semantics class each time.

As noted earlier in this chapter, this is particularly useful in an environment where different processors need to perform differents actions on specimens of the same construct. In an Eiffel environment, for example, processors that manipulate classes and other Eiffel construct specimens may include a compiler, an interpreter, a flattener (producing the flat form), a class abstracter (producing the short or flat-short form), and various browsing tools such as those of ISE Eiffel.

For obvious reasons of convenience and ease of maintenance, it is desirable to let these processors share the same syntactic descriptions. The method just described, relying on multiple inheritance, achieves this goal.

12.11 HOW PARSING WORKS

Classes *AGGREGATE, CHOICE, TERMINAL* and *REPETITION* are written in such a way that you do not need to take care of the parsing process. They make it possible to parse any language built according to the rules given – with one limitation, left recursion, discussed below. You can then concentrate on writing the interesting part – semantic processing.

To derive the maximum benefit from the Parse library, however, it is useful to gain a little more insight into the way parsing works. Let us raise the veil just enough to see any remaining property that is relevant to the building of parsers and document processors.

12.11.1 The parsing technique

The Parse library relies on a general approach known as **recursive descent**, meaning that various choices will be tried in sequence and recursively to recognize a certain specimen.

If a choice is attempted and fails (because it encounters input that does not conform to what is expected), the algorithm will try remaining choices, after having moved the input cursor back to where it was before the choice that failed. This process is called **backtracking**. It is handled by the parsing algorithms in an entirely automatic fashion, without programmer intervention.

12.11.2 Left recursion

Recursive descent implies the danger of infinite looping when parsing is attempted for left-recursive productions of the form

$A \triangleq A \ldots$

or, more generally, cases in which the left recursion is indirect, as in

$A \triangleq B \ldots$
$B \triangleq C \ldots$
$\ldots$
$L \triangleq A \ldots$

Direct left recursion is easy to avoid, but indirect recursion may sneak in in less trivial ways.

To determine whether the production for a construct is directly or indirectly left-recursive, use the query *left_recursion* from class *CONSTRUCT*.

12.11.3 Backtracking and the *commit* procedure

Another potential problem may arise from too much backtracking. In contrast with left recursion, this is a performance issue, not a threat to the correctness of the parsing algorithm. Automatic backtracking is in fact essential to the generality and flexibility of the recursive descent parsing algorithm; but too much of it may degrade the efficiency of the parsing mechanism.

Two techniques are available to minimize backtracking. One, mentioned above, is to organize the *production* functions for choice construct classes so that they list the most frequent cases first. The other is to use the *commit* procedure in the *production* functions for aggregate constructs.

A call to *commit* in an aggregate *A* is a hint to the parser, which means:

> "If you get to this point in trying to recognize a specimen of *A* as one among several possible choices for a choice construct *C*, and you later fail to obtain an *A*, then forget about other choices for *C*: you won't be able to find a *C* here.
>
> You may go back to the next higher-level choice before *C* − or admit failure if there is no such choice left."

Such a hint is useful when you want to let the parser benefit from some higher-level knowledge about the grammar, which is not directly deducible from the way the productions have been written.

Here is an example. The *production* function for *NESTED* in the Polynomial language, which attempts to parse specimens of the form

   (*s*)

where *s* is a specimen of *SUM*, is written as

> *production*: LINKED_LIST [CONSTRUCT] *is*
>   **local**
>   *expression*: SUM
>   **once**
>   !! *Result*;
>   !! *expression*;
>   *keyword* ("(");
>   *commit*;
>   *put* (*expression*);
>   *keyword* (")")
>   **end**

The *commit* after the recognition of the keyword "(" is there to use the following piece of higher-level knowledge:

> No choice production of the grammar that has *NESTED* as one of its alternatives has another alternative construct whose specimens could begin with an opening parenthesis "(".

Because of this property, if the parser goes so far as to recognize an opening parenthesis as part of parsing any construct *C* for which *NESTED* is an alternative, but further tokens do not match the structure of *NESTED* specimens, then we will have failed to recognize not only a *NESTED* but also a *C*.

Some readers will have recognized "commit" as being close to the Prolog "cut" mechanism.

In this example, *NESTED* is used in only one right-hand side production: the choice production for *TERM*, for which the other alternatives are *SIMPLE_VAR* and *POLY_INTEGER*, none of whose specimens can include an opening parenthesis.

The use of *commit* assumes global knowledge about the grammar and its future extensions, which is somewhat at odds with the evolutionary approach suggested by the Eiffel method. Applied improperly, this mechanism could lead to the rejection of valid texts as invalid. Used with care, however, it helps in obtaining high-performance parsing without impairing too much the simplicity of preparing parsers and other document processors.

12.12 BUILDING A DOCUMENT PROCESSOR

We are ready now to put together the various elements required to build a document processor based on the Parse library.

12.12.1 The overall picture

The documents to be processed will be specimens of a certain construct. This construct is called the **top construct** for that particular processing.

> Be sure to note that with the Parse library there is no room for a concept of top construct of a **grammar**: the top construct is only defined with respect to a particular *processor* for that grammar.
>
> Attempting to define the top of a grammar would be contrary to the object-oriented approach, which de-emphasizes any notion of top component of a system.
>
> Different processors for the same grammar may use different top constructs.

A document processor will be a particular system made of construct classes, complemented by semantic classes, and usually by other auxiliary classes. One of the construct classes corresponds to the top construct and is called the **top construct class**.

This notion of top construct class has a natural connection to the notion of root class of a system, as needed to get executable software. The top construct class could indeed be used as root of the processor system. In line with the previous discussion, however, it appears preferable to keep the top construct class (which only depends on the syntax and remains independent of any particular processor) separate from the system's root class. With this approach the root class will often be a descendant of the top construct class.

The notion of root class was introduced in 2.3.8, page 21.

This policy was adopted for the Polynomial language example as it appears in the delivery: the processor defined for this example uses *LINE* as the top construct class; the root of the processor system is a class *PROCESS*, which inherits from *LINE*.

12.12.2 Steps in the execution of a document processor

As any root class of a system, the root of a document processor must have a creation procedure which starts the execution. Here the task of this class is the following:

E1 • Define an object representing the input document to be processed; this will be an instance of class *INPUT*.

E2 • Obtain a lexical analyzer applicable to the language, and connect it with the document.

E3 • Select an input file, containing the actual document to be processed.

E4 • Process the document: in other words, parse it and, if parsing is successful, apply the semantics.

To execute these steps in a simple and convenient fashion, it is useful to declare the root class as a descendant of the lexical interface class. The root class, being an heir to the top construct class, will also be a descendant of *CONSTRUCT*.

See 12.9, page 231, about lexical interface classes.

12.12.3 Connecting with lexical analysis

To achieve the effect of steps E1 and E2, a simple call instruction suffices: just call the procedure *build*, inherited from *L_INTERFACE*, using as argument *document*, a feature of type *INPUT*, obtained from *METALEX* (the lexical analyzer generator class) through *L_INTERFACE*. The call, then, is just:

For the interface of INPUT see 22.9, page 423.

    build (*document*)

Although you may use this line as a recipe with no need for further justification, it is interesting to see what *build* does. Feature *document* describes the input document to be processed; it is introduced as a Once function in class *CONSTRUCT* to ensure that all instances of *CONSTRUCT* share a single document – in other words, that all processing actions apply to the same document. The text of *build* is:

```
build (doc: INPUT) is
        -- Create lexical analyzer and set doc
        -- to be the input document.
require
        document_exists: doc /= Void
do
        obtain_analyzer;
        make_analyzer;
        doc.set_lexical (analyzer)
end;
```

The call to *obtain_analyzer* defines the regular grammar for the language at hand. Recall that *obtain_analyzer* is deferred in *L_INTERFACE*; its definition for the *POLY_LEX* example was given above. The call to *make_analyzer* freezes the regular grammar and produces a usable lexical analyzer, available through the attribute *analyzer* obtained from *METALEX*. Finally, the call to *set_lexical*, a procedure of class *INPUT*, ensures that all lexical analysis operations will use *analyzer* as the lexical analyzer.

12.12.4 Starting the actual processing

The call *build* (*document*) takes care of steps E1 and E2 of the root's creation procedure. Step E3 selects the file containing the input document; this is achieved through the call

    document.set_input_file (*some_file_name*);

where *set_input_file*, from class *INPUT*, has a self-explanatory effect.

Finally, step E4 (processing the document) is simply a call to procedure *process*, obtained from *CONSTRUCT*. Recall that this procedure simply executes

```
parse;
if parsed then
    semantics
end
```

12.12.5 The structure of a full example

The polynomial example provides a simple example of a full document processor, which you may use as a guide for your own processors. The root class of that example is *LINE*. Its creation procedure, *make*, follows the above scheme precisely; here is its general form:

```
make is
    local
        document_name: STRING
    do
        build (document);
        ... Instructions prompting the user for the name of the
            file to be parsed, and assigning it to document_name ...

        document. set_input_file (document_name);

        process
    end
```

Although it covers a small language, this example may serve as a blueprint for most applications of the Parse library.

12.13 FUTURE WORK

It was mentioned at the beginning of this chapter that further work is desirable to make the Parse library reach its full bloom. Here is a glimpse of future improvements.

12.13.1 Expressions

Many languages include an expression construct having the properties of traditional arithmetic expressions:

- An expression is a succession of basic operands and operators.
- The basic operands are lexical elements, such as identifiers and constants.
- Operators are used in prefix mode (as in $-a$) or infix mode (as in $b-a$).

- Each operator has a precedence level; precedence levels determine the abstract syntactic structure of expressions and consequently their semantics. For example the abstract structure of $a + b * c$ shows this expression to be the application of the operator + to a and to the application of the operator $*$ to b and c. That this is the correct interpretation of the instruction follows from the property that $*$ has a higher precedence ("binds more tightly") than +.

- Parentheses pairs, such as ( ) or [ ], can be used to enforce a structure different from what the precedence rules would imply, as in $(a + b) * c$.

- Some infix operators may be applied to more than two arguments; in this case it must be clear whether they are right-associative (in other words, $a \, \hat{} \, b \, \hat{} \, c$ means $a \, \hat{} \, (b \, \hat{} \, c)$, the conventional interpretation if $\hat{}$ denotes the power operator) or left-associative.

It is of course possible to apply the Parse library in its current state to support expressions, as illustrated by this extract from the Polynomial grammar given in full above:

Variables	$\triangleq$	{Identifier ";" ...}
Sum	$\triangleq$	{Diff "+" ...}
Diff	$\triangleq$	{Product "-" ...}
Product	$\triangleq$	{Term "$*$" ...}

The problem then is not expressiveness but efficiency. For such expressions the recursive descent technique, however well adapted to the higher-level structures of a language, takes too much time and generates too many tree nodes. Efficient bottom-up parsing techniques are available for this case.

The solution is straightforward: write a new heir *EXPRESSION* to class *CONSTRUCT*. The preceding discussion of expressions and their properties suggests what kinds of feature this class will offer: define a certain terminal as operator, define a terminal as operand type, set the precedence of an operator, set an operator as left-associative or right-associative and so on. Writing this class based on this discussion is indeed a relatively straightforward task, which can be used as a programming exercise.

Beyond the addition of an *EXPRESSION* class, some changes in the data structures used by Parse may also help improve the efficiency of the parsing process.

12.13.2 Yooc

To describe the syntax of a language, it is convenient to use a textual format such as the one that has served in this chapter to illustrate the various forms of production. The correspondence between such a format and the construct classes is straightforward; for example, as explained above, the production

Line $\triangleq$ Variables ":" Sum

will yield the class

```
class LINE inherit
    AGGREGATE
feature
    production: LINKED_LIST [CONSTRUCT] is
            local
                var: VARIABLES;
                sum: SUM
            once
                !! Result;
                !! var; put (var);
                keyword (":");
                !! sum; put (sum)
            end;
        ...
end
```

This transformation of the textual description of the grammar into its equivalent Eiffel form is simple and unambiguous; but it is somewhat annoying to have to perform it manually.

An tool complementing the Parse library and known as YOOC ("Yes! an Object-Oriented Compiler", a name meant as an homage to the venerable Yacc) has been planned for future releases of Parse. Yooc, a translator, will take a grammar specification as input and transform it into a set of parsing classes, all descendants of CONSTRUCT and built according to the rules defined above. The input format for syntax specification, similar to the conventions used throughout this chapter, is a variant of LDL (Language Description Language), a component of the ArchiText structural document processing system.

LDL is described in detail in: "LDL User's Manual", Report TR-AN-2/UM, Interactive Software Engineering Inc., 1992.

12.13.3 Further reading

The following article describes some advanced uses of the Parse library as well as a Yooc-like translator called PG:

> Per Grape and Kim Walden: *Automating the Development of Syntax Tree Generators for an Evolving Language*, in Proceedings of TOOLS 8 (Technology of Object-Oriented Languages and Systems), Prentice Hall, 1992, pages 185-195.

13

The Kernel Library

13.1 OVERVIEW

The Kernel Library includes essential classes that complement the language and are of direct interest to many applications.

> The flat-short interfaces of the classes discussed in this chapter appear in chapter 23.

13.2 CLUSTERS OF THE KERNEL LIBRARY

In addition to basic concepts close to the language level, the Kernel library covers such common needs as input and output, storage and retrieval of objects on persistent storage, fine control over exception handling and memory management, and access to operating system facilities.

The subsequent sections describe the various categories of classes in the Kernel library, which are divided into five clusters.

The clusters as identified here represent a logical division which does not exactly match the division of the delivery into directories. In an earlier version of the libraries a distinction was made between Kernel and Support libraries. This distinction has been removed for the present discussion but it is still reflected in the directory structure.

The first cluster contains the universal classes defining facilities accessible to all other classes: *ANY*, *PLATFORM* and *GENERAL*. Every developer-defined class is a descendant of these classes.

The second cluster includes classes whose facilities are directly related to language concepts:

- Classes describing the basic types: *BOOLEAN, CHARACTER, INTEGER, REAL* and *DOUBLE*.
- Arrays: class *ARRAY*.
- Strings: class *STRING*.
- Basic facilities: classes *BASIC_ROUTINES* for conversions, *MATH_CONST*, *SINGLE_MATH* and *DOUBLE_MATH* for mathematical values and functions, *PRIMES* for prime numbers, *RANDOM* for pseudo-random sequences, *ASCII* for character codes.

Except for the last category, these classes are explained in detail in *Eiffel: The Language*, so the description in this chapter will be limited to the bare essentials, although the flat-short forms do appear in part C of this book for ease of reference.

The third cluster provides input and output facilities:

- *STD_FILES* offers basic mechanisms, sufficient for simple input and output.
- *FILE* describes the notion of sequential file, viewed as a sequence of characters and fully integrated in the data structure library.
- *UNIX_FILE* provides access to the many specialized facilities of Unix and Unix-like file systems.
- *DIRECTORY* gives properties of directories (files serving as collections of other files).

The next cluster, through class *STORABLE*, makes it possible to store object structures on persistent storage and retrieve them later. This facility can also be used to transmit object structures through pipes or over a network.

The last cluster provides access to internal properties of the compiler and environment, useful for applications that need some fine-tuning of the basic mechanisms:

- Class *EXCEPTIONS* (complemented by *UNIX_SIGNALS* for Unix-type platforms) provides control over the exception handling mechanism, in particular for applications that need to handle different types of exception in different ways.
- Similarly, classes *MEMORY* and *GC_INFO* provide ways to control the garbage collector and tailor it to specific needs.
- Class *ARGUMENTS* gives access to the command-line arguments.
- Class *INTERNAL* provides information about the internal representation and properties of objects.

13.3 UNIVERSAL CLASSES AND THEIR FEATURES

The Eiffel inheritance mechanism is set up in such a way that every class is a descendant of a Kernel Library class called *ANY*.

The features of this class (coming from its ancestor *GENERAL*) provide a number of generally applicable facilities covering such needs as comparison, copying and rudimentary input and output.

These classes are covered in detail in *Eiffel: The Language*. Only the basic properties will be summarized here; the flat-short forms give all the details.

13.3.1 The structure of universal classes

Every class which has no inheritance clause is understood to have an inheritance clause of the form

> **inherit**
> > *ANY*

As a result, every developer-defined class is a descendant of *ANY*. *ANY* itself, as delivered, has no feature of its own; it is an heir of *PLATFORM*, itself an heir of *GENERAL* which has no parent. An earlier figure showed the overall structure.

The global inheritance structure appears on the figure of page 46.

GENERAL introduces the most general features, *PLATFORM* a few platform-dependent properties. The reason for using an empty *ANY* class is to let each installation, if it so desires, define its own general-purpose features which every class in the installation will inherit. Use only *ANY* for this purpose; do not modify *GENERAL* or *PLATFORM*.

The interface of these classes is in 23.2, page 425.

There may of course be several versions of *ANY* in an installation, corresponding for example to different projects, each with its own set of general-purpose features. Each compilation should make sure that the Ace file (the control file used to specify the directories where the various clusters are stored) lists the directory containing the desired version of *ANY*.

Also apparent on the earlier figure is class *NONE*. This fictitious class, whose text would be rather hard to write (think of all the necessary **rename** and **select** clauses), really represents "no class at all". It serves in particular for information hiding (to export a feature to *NONE* only is to export to no client at all), and as type for the feature *Void*, declared in *GENERAL*.

13.3.2 Using the universal classes

If you need to rename or redefine a feature inherited from one of the universal classes, you should include an explicit inheritance clause, as in

```
class C inherit
    ANY
        rename
            out as basic_out
        redefine
            print
        end
    ...
feature
    ...
end
```

The features of *ANY* are usable in both qualified and unqualified form. For example, the argumentless function *out*, which produces a printable representation of any object, may be called under either of the forms

$x := out$
$x := a.out$

The first call yields a printable representation of the current object; the second, which assumes that *a* is not void, yields a printable representation of the object attached to *a*.

13.3.3 Input and output features

Some of the features of *ANY* cover common input and output needs.

Feature *io*, of type *STD_FILES*, gives access to standard input and output facilities. For example, *io.input* is the standard input file and *io.new_line* will print a line feed on the standard output. Feature *io* is declared as a once function which, when first called, returns the value of an instance of *STD_FILES* that provides access to the standard input, the standard output and the error output. As a result, *io* is never void, so that operations such as *io.new_line* are always possible.

Class STD_FILES and more general input-output facilities are covered in 13.5, page 252.

Function *out*, of type *STRING*, is a universal mechanism for obtaining a simple external representation of any object. For non-void *x* of any type, the string *x.out* is a printable representation of *x*. This works for *x* of all types, reference or expanded. For example, if *x* is an integer expression, *x.out* is its string representation, such as *−897*; if *n* is a non-void reference, *x.out* is (recursively) the concatenation of the result of applying *out* to the successive fields of the attached object, each labeled by the name of the corresponding attribute. You may redefine *out* in any class to specify any suitable format for displaying instances of the class. To obtain the default representation regardless of any redefinition of *out*, use *tagged_out*, declared as a frozen synonym of the original *out*.

The call *print* (*x*) will output the value of *x.out* on the default output if *x* is not void, and do nothing otherwise.

13.3.4 Copy and comparison routines

Procedure *copy* copies the fields of an object onto those of another. It is used under the form

    target.copy (*source*)

Here both *target* and *source* must be non-void; this means that *copy* is only good for copying onto an object that already exists. If you need both to allocate a new object and to initialize it as a copy of another, use the function *clone*. For non-void *source*, the assignment

    target := clone (*source*)

starts by creating a new object. If *source* is void, *target* will be made void too.

The boolean function *equal* compares two objects for field-by-field equality. This is different from the equality operators = and /= which, in the case of reference types, compare references, not objects.

The function *deep_clone* produces a duplicate of an entire object structure. The boolean function *deep_equal* determines whether two object structures are recursively identical. These routines are the "deep" counterparts of the shallow copy and equality tests provided by *clone* and *equal*.

A class that needs a specific notion of equality and the corresponding copy semantics may redefine *copy* and *is_equal* (from which *equal* follows, since *equal* (*a*, *b*) is defined as *a*. *is_equal* (*b*) for non-void *a*). You will find such redefinitions in a number of classes of the Base libraries. For example an instance of *STRING* is a string descriptor containing a reference to the actual character sequence, not that sequence itself, so that what the default *equal* compares and the default *copy* copies is the descriptor, not the string. Class *STRING* redefines these routines to yield the semantics normally expected by string clients; the frozen variants *standard_copy* and *standard_ equal*, originally declared as synonyms to *equal* and *copy*, remain available with the default semantics.

The notion of frozen feature was introduced in 2.7.6, page 39.

The function *clone* is defined in terms of *copy*, and so will follow any redefinition of *copy*. This makes it impossible to change the semantics of one but not of the other, which would be a mistake. The variant *standard_clone* is defined in terms of *standard_ copy*.

Two features of *GENERAL*, function *consistent* and procedure *setup*, were not mentioned in *Eiffel: The Language* but have proved necessary for *copy* and *clone*, although they are mainly of interest to implementors of fundamental libraries such as Base. A special object such as a string or an array may be in a state that precludes copying a certain other object onto it. For example the space allocated for the characters of a string may not be big enough to copy those of another. The call *o1*. *consistent* (*o2*) will determine whether the content of *o2* may be copied onto that of *o1*. If not, the call *o1*. *setup* (*o2*) will do to *o1* whatever is necessary to make the copy possible, ensuring *consistent* as its postcondition. The implementation of *clone* in terms of *copy* performs a *setup* after creating an object but before copying the content of another.

For standard objects (instances of the usual developer-defined classes) the problem normally does not arise; so *consistent* as declared in *GENERAL* always returns true, and *setup* does nothing. In Base only *STRING*, *ARRAY* and a few related classes redefine these features.

13.3.5 Type information

The string-valued query *generator*, applied to any object, returns the name of the object's generating class: the class of which it is an instance.

The boolean function *conforms_to* makes it possible to test dynamically whether the type of an object conforms to that of another – that is to say whether the first one's generator is a descendant of the second one's.

These two features enable clients to ascertain the dynamic type of an entity at run time. They are only useful for low-level components; the normal mechanism for type-dependent operations is dynamic binding.

On dynamic binding see 2.7.8, page 41.

13.3.6 Miscellaneous

The query *Void*, of type *NONE*, denotes a reference that is always void – not attached to any object.

Procedure *do_nothing* does what its name implies. Function *default* also has an empty body; its result type is **like Current**, so what it returns is the default value of the current type. This is mostly interesting for expanded types, since for reference types the default value is simply a void reference.

Procedure *die* (*code*: *INTEGER*) causes the application to terminate its execution with the given return code.

13.4 LANGUAGE-RELATED FACILITIES

A number of classes offer facilities which are very close to the language level. Here too the book *Eiffel: The Language* covers the classes in detail, so we can satisfy ourselves with a quick summary; the flat-short forms appear in part C.

13.4.1 Basic types

The basic types *BOOLEAN, CHARACTER, INTEGER, REAL* and *DOUBLE* are defined by classes of the Kernel library.

In reading the class specifications for the numeric types *INTEGER, REAL* and *DOUBLE*, you might think that the type declarations are too restrictive. For example the addition operation in class *REAL* reads

infix *"+"* (*other*: *REAL*): *REAL*

The specifications are in chapter 23, starting with 23.25, page 470, for BOOLEAN.

This may seem to preclude mixed-type arithmetic involving for example entities *r* of type *REAL*, *d* of type *DOUBLE* and *i* of type *INTEGER* in the expression

$a + d + i$

but there is actually no problem here. A language convention applicable to all arithmetic expressions, the **Balancing rule**, states that in any such expression all operands are considered to be converted to the heaviest type, where *DOUBLE* is heavier than *REAL* and *REAL* is heavier than *INTEGER*. So mixed-type arithmetic, consistent with common practice, is possible and indeed frequent.

For details of the Balancing rule see chapter 23 of "Eiffel: The Language".

13.4.2 Arrays

To create and manipulate one-dimensional arrays, use class *ARRAY* of the Kernel Library.

Arrays are not primitive language elements; instead, they are handled through class *ARRAY*. This class is "normal" in the sense that it may be used just as any other class by client and descendant classes. It is also somewhat special, however, in that the Eiffel compiler knows about it and uses this knowledge to generate efficient code for array operations.

For the interface see 23.3, page 428. Two-dimensional arrays are covered by class ARRAY2 of the Data Structure Library, with a very similar specification.

To create an instance of *ARRAY*, use the creation instruction

!! *my_array*.*make* (*l, u*)

where the arguments indicate the lower and upper bounds. These bounds will then be accessible as *my_array*.*lower* and *my_array*.*upper*. The number of items is *my_array*.*count*; feature *capacity* is a synonym for *count*. The class invariant expresses the relation between *count, lower* and *upper*.

To access and change the item at index *i* in array *a*, you may use features *item* and *put*, as in

x := *my_array*.*item* (*i*)
my_array.*put* (*new_value, i*)

Function *item* has an infix synonym, **infix** *"@"*, so that you may also write the first assignment above more concisely as

$x := my\_array @ i$

Features *item*, **infix** *"@"* and *put* have preconditions requiring the index (*i* in the above calls) to be within the bounds of the array. This means that you can detect bounds violations (which correspond to bugs in the client software) by using a version of class *ARRAY* compiled with precondition checking on.

The bounds of an array may be changed dynamically through procedure *resize*. Previously entered elements are retained.

Rather than an explicit *resize*, you may use calls to procedure *force* which has the same signature as *put* but no precondition; if the index is not within the current bounds *force* will perform a *resize* as necessary.

13.4.3 Optimizing array computations

Although *ARRAY* benefits from an efficient implementation, its more advanced facilities such as resizing do not come for free. For extensive computations on large arrays, an optimization may be desirable, bypassing these facilities. The technique yields loops that run at about the same speed as the corresponding loops written in C or Fortran (the usual references for array computations). It is of interest for advanced uses only, so that you may safely skip this section on first reading unless your domain of application is numerical computation or some other area requiring high-performance array manipulations.

The optimization relies on the class *SPECIAL*, used internally by *ARRAY* but of no direct interest to client developers in most common uses. With the declarations

For the interface of class SPECIAL see 23.5, page 434.

my_array: *ARRAY* [*SOME_TYPE*]

direct_access: *SPECIAL* [*SOME_TYPE*]

you may use *direct_access* in lieu of *my_array* within a critical loop, provided none of the operations may resize the array. Typically, the operations should only include *put* and *item*. In such a case you can use the following scheme:

```
direct_access := my_array. area;
    -- The critical loop:
from
    some_initialization;
    index := some_initial_index
until
    index = some_final_index
loop
    ...
    x := direct_access. item (index);
    ...
    direct_access. put (some_value, index)
    ...
end
```

This replaces an original loop where the operations were on *my_array*. Feature *area* of *ARRAY* gives direct access to the special object, an instance of *SPECIAL*, containing the array values. Features *put* and *item* are available in *SPECIAL* as in *ARRAY*, but without the preconditions; in other words, you will not get any bounds checking.

Instances of *SPECIAL* are always indexed from zero, in contrast with arrays, whose lower bound is arbitrary, 1 being the most common value. But rather than performing index translations (that is to say, subtracting *my_array.lower* from *index* throughout the loop) it is preferable to use the following simple technique: if the lower bound *lb* of *my_array* is 1 or another small integer, use 0 as lower bound instead when creating *my_array*, but only use the positions starting at *lb*. You will waste a few memory positions (0 to *lb−1*), but will not have to change anything in your algorithm and will avoid costly subtractions.

It is important to note that this optimization, if at all necessary, should at most affect a few loops in a large system. You should always begin by writing your software using the normal *ARRAY* facilities; then once you have the certainty that the software is correct, if you detect that a large array computation is hampering the efficiency of the system, you may apply the above technique to get the fastest performance out of that computation. The change to the software will be minimal − a few lines − and will be easy to undo if necessary.

13.4.4 Strings

Strings are handled by class *STRING*, similar in many respects to *ARRAY*.

For the interface see 23.4, page 430.

Strings are of arbitrary size. The *make* creation procedure takes an integer argument, as in

> *s, s1, s2, s3: STRING*;
> ...
> !! *s.make* (30)

The argument indicates the number of characters for the initial allocation. This is not an absolute limit: the string will automatically grow or shrink as a result of future operations. You may always request a resizing explicitly by calling procedure *resize*.

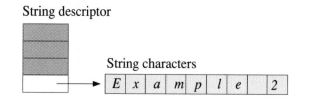

Figure 13.1:
String and string descriptor

The object attached at run-time to an entity such declared of type *STRING*, such as *s* above, is not the actual sequence of characters but a string descriptor, which contains a reference to the actual string contents.

As a result, four assignment or assignment-like operations are possible:

A1	*s1 := s*
A2	*s2. share (s)*
A3	*s3 := clone (s)*
A4	*s4. copy (s)*

As illustrated below, A1 is a reference assignment: *s1* will be attached to the same descriptor as *s*. A2 keeps the descriptors distinct, but make them refer to the same sequence of characters. A3 uses the redefinition of *clone* for class *STRING*: *s3* will be attached to a new string, completely distinct from the string attached to *s1* although made of identical characters. A4 has almost the same effect as A3, but is only applicable if *s4* was not void, and will override the existing descriptor rather than creating a new one.

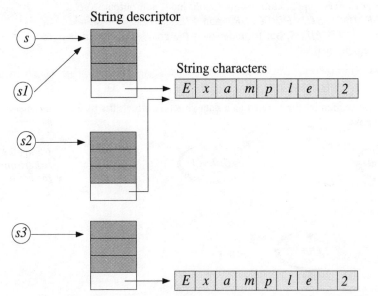

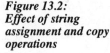

Figure 13.2:
Effect of string
assignment and copy
operations

13.4.5 Conversions, mathematical properties and ASCII characters

A few utility classes complement the previous facilities. *PRIMES*, *RANDOM* and *FIBONACCI* are part of the data structure taxonomy; the others are meant to be used as ancestors by classes needing their features.

   BASIC_ROUTINES provides a number of conversion functions, such as *real_to_integer*.

Class interface in 23.6, page 435.

   Two classes provide basic mathematical functions such as logarithms and trigonometric functions: *SINGLE_MATH* for single precision and *DOUBLE_MATH* for the double-precision variants. *MATH_CONST* contains mathematical constants: π, the square root of two, Euler's constant *e*.

23.7, page 436.

PRIMES, *RANDOM* and *FIBONACCI* are data structure classes – heirs of *COUNTABLE_SEQUENCE*. In all of these classes function *i_th* takes an integer argument *i* and will return the *i*-th element of the sequence under consideration – prime numbers, pseudo-random numbers or Fibonacci numbers. These sequences are active structures, on which *forth* will advance the current position and *item* will return the value at the current position. A few other features are specific to each case: for example *higher_prime* will yield the smallest prime greater than or equal to a certain value, and *set_seed* will define the seed to be used for starting the pseudo-random sequence. These features are readily understood from the class interfaces in part C.

PRIMES: *23.8, page 437*;
RANDOM: *23.9, page 439.*

ASCII is a large collection of constant attributes representing the character codes of the ASCII character set. Typical examples are *First_printable* and *Ctrl_c*.

23.10, page 441.

13.5 FILES, INPUT, OUTPUT

A few classes of the Kernel Library support file manipulation, input and output: *STD_FILES*, *FILE*, *UNIX_FILE*, *UNIX_STD*, *DIRECTORY* and *FILE_INFO*. For simple applications it suffices to use *STD_FILES*, but to understand the concepts better it is preferable to look first at the other two.

13.5.1 General files

FILE describes the notion of sequential file viewed as a data structure which fits in the general taxonomy of this book:

*Class interface in 23.11,
page 444.*

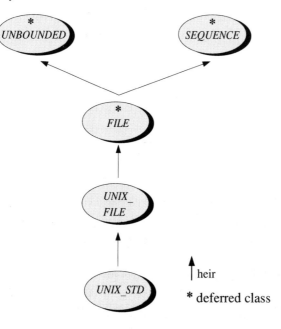

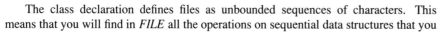

***Figure 13.3:
Inheritance structure
for FILE***

The class declaration defines files as unbounded sequences of characters. This means that you will find in *FILE* all the operations on sequential data structures that you have come to know and love by reading the previous chapters of this book – at least, all that apply. Just as stacks and linked lists, files have *put, extend, has, item* and so on.

More specific to files are the typed input and output operations. For output, you will find *putchar, putint, putreal, putdouble* and *putstring*, as well as *new_line*. For input you will find *readint* and its co-conspirators.

Note the application to input features of the command-query separation principle. The input features such as *readint* do not by themselves return a result; they set the values of queries such as *lastint*. So the normal way to read is through two operations:

> *my_file.readint;*
> *new_value := my_file.lastint*

The command-query separation principle is discussed in 3.3.4, page 64.

Queries are available to determine the status of a file, in particular *exists, is_readable, is_executable, is_writable, is_creatable, is_closed, is_open_read* and so on.

You will notice in the flat-short form that all these queries except the first have *exists* as a precondition. This precondition is good for efficiency since it saves an existence test – a relatively expensive operation – when you know that a certain file exists. But it also means that if you have any doubt about the file's existence you must use the queries in the style

> **if** *my_file.exists* **and then** *my_file.is_readable* **then** ...

13.5.2 Unix-style files and directories

FILE is a deferred class. Various implementations are possible. A quite detailed one is *UNIX_FILE*, which adds many features for accessing internal properties, such as *inode* and *links*. The name does not necessarily mean that the corresponding files are stored on a Unix platform, simply that they have the general properties of Unix files.

The interface of UNIX_FILE is in 23.12, page 448.

UNIX_FILE is the only proper descendant of *FILE* whose flat-short form appears in this book. If using another operating system, you should check your version of the library for other variants.

UNIX_FILE_INFO describes objects that contain internal information, such as protection mode and size, about a file. Its interface has been included because function *file_info* of class *UNIX_FILE* returns a result of type *UNIX_FILE_INFO*.

Class interface in 23.13, page 454.

UNIX_STD extends *STD_FILES* with a few features commonly used by applications using Unix or Unix-like files.

23.14, page 455.

The class *DIRECTORY* describes those files which are directories – nodes in the tree describing the file structure.

23.15, page 456.

13.5.3 Basic input and output

Regardless of the operating system that you use, for simple input and output *STD_FILES* is sufficient. You may inherit from that class to gain direct access to its features; or you may declare an entity of type *STD_FILES*. But remember that a feature of this type is always available: *io*, from class *ANY*. Thanks to this feature you may include simple input and output in any class, with instructions such as

Class interface in 23.16, page 457.

io.putstring (*"My message"*)

STD_FILES defines three default files through features *input*, *output* and *error*. These features are Once functions, so that the first reference to any one of them will automatically create the corresponding file descriptor and open the associated file.

To simplify the writing of common input and output operations, the most frequently used features of class *FILE* – for reading and writing integers, reals and so on, as discussed next – have been repeated in *STD_FILES* so as to apply to the default input and output. Procedure *putstring* in the example at the beginning of this section is typical: it writes its output on the standard output. More generally, *STD_FILES* has all the *putxxx*, *readxxx* and *lastxxx* features of *FILE*.

13.6 PERSISTENCE, STORAGE AND RETRIEVAL

Most object-oriented applications need the ability to store object structures on persistent storage for later retrieval, and to transfer such object structures to other applications.

Class *STORABLE* addresses this need. Here again the book *Eiffel: The Language* provides a detailed description, so we shall look at the essential properties only.

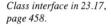
Class interface in 23.17, page 458.

> You may notice a slight discrepancy between the two descriptions regarding the precise names of the storing procedures. The names given below (*basic_store*, *general_store*) are the up-to-date ones.

13.6.1 Persistence completeness

A fundamental requirement on object persistence mechanisms is the Persistence Completeness rule, stated as follows in *Eiffel: The Language*:

> Whenever a routine of class *STORABLE* stores an object into an external file, it stores with it the dependents of that object. Whenever one of the associated retrieval routines retrieves a previously stored object, it also retrieves all its dependents.

Storing an object just by itself would usually result in wrong semantics: most objects contain references to other objects, which must also be stored and retrieved with it. The persistence completeness rule ensures that this is always the case. It also means, of course, that the features of *STORABLE* must do much more than simple input and output; they must perform complete traversals of object structures.

13.6.2 Using the storage and retrieval facilities

Class *STORABLE* is meant to be used as ancestor. You can use its features in any descendant *C*; for example a routine of *C* may contain a call of the form

basic_store (*my_descriptor*)

The effect of this call will be to store the current object and all its dependents into the file denoted by *my_descriptor*.

Although *basic_store* and other procedures of *STORABLE* will in general process objects of many different types, only the generating class of the structure's initial object, *C* in our example, needs to be a descendant of *STORABLE*.

13.6.3 Varieties of store operations

Two variants of the store operation are supported: basic store and general store. Basic store produces more compact structures in the resulting files, and is slightly faster; but the resulting structure is dependent on the system which executes the store operation. ("System" is taken here, as elsewhere in this book, in its Eiffel sense of an executable assembly of classes, compiled together with the help of an Ace specification.) This means that you can use procedure *basic_store* to store an object structure during an execution of a system if you will only retrieve it later in that execution, or in a subsequent execution of the same system.

If you need to store objects from a certain system and then retrieve them from a different system, possibly running on a different computer, use *general_store*.

> The result of *general_store* is still platform-dependent; the representation of numbers, in particular, is determined by the underlying machine architecture. A third variant called *portable_store* will be added in the future to *STORABLE*, using an entirely platform-independent storage format; then a system running on a computer with a certain architecture will be able to retrieve, without any explicit conversion operation, object structures stored by a system running on a machine of a completely different architecture. With *general_store* the storing and retrieving computers must have compatible architectures.

13.6.4 Retrieval

You only need to be aware of the difference between basic and general store at storage time. The stored structure will always be available through feature *retrieved*; this feature will figure out, from the format of the stored structure, whether it was stored by *basic_store* or *general_store*, and will decode it accordingly.

Feature *retrieved* returns a result of type *STORABLE* and is typically used through an assignment attempt of the form

About assignment attempt see 2.7.9, page 42.

  x ?= *retrieved* (*my_descriptor*)

The assignment attempt is necessary because *retrieved* returns a result of type *STORABLE* whereas the type of *x* will be based on a proper descendant of *STORABLE*.

If the structure in the file has been corrupted and *retrieved* is unable to do its job, it will trigger an exception. The code for that exception in class *EXCEPTIONS* (which inherits it from *EXCEP_CONST* and is discussed in the next section, together with the notion of exception code) is *Retrieve_exception*.

> This exception only occurs when *retrieved* is able to start its job but the file content that it finds is not appropriate. The other conditions – existence of a file, read permissions – are expressed as usual by the precondition clauses of *retrieved*.

13.7 ACCESS TO INTERNAL PROPERTIES

In some applications you may need to fine-tune the exception handling and memory management mechanisms. You may also need a simple way to access command-line arguments. In less common cases you may require low-level access to internal properties of objects.

13.7.1 Exception handling

Class *EXCEPTIONS* enables you to control the handling of exceptions. *UNIX_SIGNALS*, discussed next, complements it for the special case of fine-grain signal handling on Unix or Unix-like platforms. Both are meant to be inherited by any class that needs their facilities.

Class interface in 23.18, page 459.

The basic exception mechanism treats all exceptions in the same way. In some cases it may be useful to discriminate in a Rescue clause between the various possible causes. Class *EXCEPTIONS* provides the features to do this. Each kind of exception has an integer code, which you can use through several features:

On exception handling see 2.5.6, page 27.

- The integer-valued query *exception* which gives the code of the latest exception.

- Queries which determine the general nature of the latest exception: *is_signal* which determines whether the exception was an operating system signal; *is_developer_exception* which determines whether it was explicitly caused by a *raise*, as explained next; *assertion_violation*.

- Query *recipient_name* which gives the name of the exception's recipient – the routine that was interrupted by the exception.

The class also provides a set of constant integer-valued attributes which denote the various possible codes, such as *No_more_memory*, *Routine_failure* and *Precondition_violation*. So you can test the value of *exception* against these codes if you need to ascertain the precise nature of an exception. To keep *EXCEPTIONS* simple these constant attributes are declared in a class *EXCEP_CONST*, of which *EXCEPTIONS* is an heir.

Another occasional requirement is for a mechanism to trigger an exception explicitly. Procedure *raise* answers this needs; the argument, a string, is the tag chosen for the exception. The code in this case is *Developer_exception*; the query *is_developer_exception* will return true; and the tag is accessible through feature *tag_name*.

You will notice in the interface specification for *EXCEPTIONS* that for some properties of the latest exception there are two features, one with a name such as *exception* or *recipient_name* as seen above and the other with a name prefixed by *original_*: *original_exception*, *original_recipient_name*.

The reason for the presence of these pairs is that the immediately visible cause of a routine interruption may not be the real one. Assume that routine *r* from class *C*, which has a Rescue clause, calls *s* from *D* with no Rescue clause, and that some call executed by *s* causes a precondition violation. (The figure uses the conventional symbol for routines, a cross-like icon, as it appears in the ISE Eiffel 3 graphical environment.)

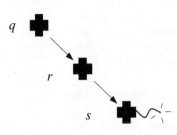

Figure 13.4:
Call chain leading to
an exception

Because *s* has no Rescue clause of its own, *s* will fail. Up the call chain, the first routine that has a Rescue clause – *r* itself, or one of its own direct or indirect callers – may process the exception; but if it examines the exception code through attribute *exception* it will get the value of *Routine_failure*. This may be what you want; but to handle the situation in a finer way you will usually need to examine the code for the original exception, the one that interrupted *s*. This code will be accessible through the attribute *original_exception*, which in this case will have the value of *Precondition*, the exception code for precondition violations. So you have the choice between exploring the properties of the original exception, or those of the resulting routine failures. Just make sure you know what you are looking for.

As you will see from the header comments in the flat-short form of class *EXCEPTIONS*, the queries that return detailed information about an exception, such as *assertion_violation*, all give an answer determined by *original_exception* rather than *exception*, since when the two are different (that is to say, when you handle the exception in a routine other than the original recipient) the value of *exception* is always *Routine_failure* and there is nothing more to say about it.

13.7.2 Signal handling

The features of class *EXCEPTIONS* enable you to determine whether a certain exception is a signal – an operating system event such as may result from a child process that disappears, a window that is resized, a user that hits the Break key and many others. But they do not give you more details because the exact set of possible signals is highly platform-dependent.

Class *UNIX_SIGNALS* complements *EXCEP_CONST* by providing codes for the signals of Unix and similar systems, such as *Sigkill* for the "kill" signal and *Sigbus* for bus error.

Class interface in 23.19,
page 461.

Query *is_defined* (*some_signal*), where *some_signal* is an integer code, will determine whether *some_signal* is supported on the platform.

A class whose routines need to perform specific processing depending on the nature of signals received should inherit from *UNIX_SIGNALS*, or a similar class for another platform.

Because signal codes are platform-dependent, the features of *UNIX_SIGNALS* are implemented as once functions – computed on the first call – rather than constants, although this makes no difference to clients.

13.7.3 Memory management

Class *MEMORY*, like *EXCEPTIONS*, is meant to be used as an ancestor by classes that need its facilities. It offers a number of features for controlling memory management and fine-tuning the garbage collection mechanism, a key component of the ISE Eiffel environment.

Memory management and garbage collection were defined in 2.3.3, page 17. The interface of MEMORY is in 23.20, page 463.

One of the most useful features in this class is *dispose*. This procedure describes actions to be applied to an unreachable object just before the garbage collector reclaims it. By default, as declared in *MEMORY*, the procedure does nothing; but you may redefine it in a proper descendant of *MEMORY* to describe dispose actions. Normally such actions will involve freeing external resources: for example a class describing file descriptors may redefine *dispose* so that whenever a descriptor object is garbage-collected the corresponding file will be closed.

> This example is typical of proper uses of *dispose*. In a *dispose* procedure you should not include any instruction that could modify the Eiffel object structure, especially if some objects in that structure may themselves have become unreachable: these instructions could conflict with the garbage collector's operations and cause catastrophic behavior. The legitimate use of *dispose* redefinitions is for disposing of non-Eiffel resources.

Other features of *MEMORY* provide direct control over the operation of the garbage collector. You can in particular stop garbage collection through a call to *collection_off*, and restart it through a call to *collection_on*. By default, garbage collection is always on (a testimony to its authors' trust in its efficiency).

Garbage collection is normally incremental, so as not to disrupt the application in a perceptible way. To start a complete garbage collection mechanism – reclaiming all unused objects – call procedure *full_collect*.

The remaining features of *MEMORY* enable finer control of the collection mechanism and are useful in special cases only. You will even find a *free* procedure providing brave (and competent) developers with a mechanism for reclaiming individual objects manually.

Two complementary classes are included in flat-short form after *MEMORY*. *MEM_INFO*, the result type for query *memory_statistics* in *MEMORY*, describes objects containing information collected about memory usage. The features of *GC_INFO* provide statistics about the garbage collector's operation.

23.21, page 465 and 23.22, 466.

13.7.4 Command-line arguments

Writing, assembling and compiling a system yields an executable command. The system's users will call that command with arguments. These are normally provided in textual form on the command line, as in

your_system arg1 arg2 arg3

although one may conceive of other ways of entering the command arguments, such as tabular or graphical form-filling. In any case the software must be able to access the values passed as command arguments.

A language mechanism is available for that purpose: the Root Class rule indicates that the creation procedure of the root class may have a single argument (in the Eiffel sense of argument to a routine) of type *ARRAY [STRING]*. The corresponding array of strings will be initialized at the beginning of the system's execution with the values entered as arguments to that execution of the command.

See section 3.4 of "Eiffel: The Language".

Although this facility suffices in many cases, it is not always convenient if you suddenly need to access the command arguments in a class that is far-away from the root. An alternative mechanism, class *ARGUMENTS*, is available. Once again, this is a class from which you should inherit if you need its facilities. It has just two exported features:

Class interface in 23.23, page 467.

- *argument_count*, a non-negative integer, is the number of command arguments.
- *argument (i)*, a string, is the *i*-th command argument. Here *i* must be between 0 and *argument_count*; the convention is that for *i* = 0 the result is the name of the command itself.

13.7.5 Internal object structures

Class *INTERNAL* provides low-level access to internal object structures. It, too, is meant to be used as ancestor by classes needing its features.

Class interface in 23.24, page 468.

Here are some of the most useful calls and what they yield, *obj* being an entity attached to an object O and *i* an integer:

- *class_name (obj)*: the name of the generator class for O.
- *dynamic_type (obj)*: the integer code for the type of O, where each type in a system is identified by a unique code.
- *field_count (obj)*: the number of fields in O.
- *physical_size (obj)*: the space occupied by O, in bytes.
- *field_xx (i, obj)* where *xx* is *name* or *offset*: name or offset of the *i*-th field of O.
- *field (i, obj)*: the value of the *i*-th field of O, if a reference; declared of type *ANY* in the class.
- *yy_field (i, obj)* where *yy* is *boolean, character, integer, real* or *double*: the value of the *i*-th field of O, if of the corresponding type; each declared of the appropriate type in the class.
- *is_special (obj)*, a boolean query which indicates whether O is a special object (the sequence of values representing the elements of an array or the characters of a string).

Only very special cases justify the use of this class. Unless you are writing the lowest level of an interface between an Eiffel application and external tools (such as a database management system), and this requires passing to those tools information about the internals of Eiffel objects, you almost certainly should not use *INTERNAL*.

Part C

Class reference

14

Classes for abstract container structures

14.1 OVERVIEW

An earlier chapter introduced the general taxonomy of data structures and explained the main deferred classes in the corresponding class graph, along the three main hierarchies: access, traversal, storage.

Chapter 4.

For ease of reference, the figure on the next page reproduces the general inheritance structure given in the earlier discussion.

This is the same figure as on page 124.

Here now are the interfaces, in flat-short form, of all these classes. The order in which they are given corresponds roughly to a left-to-right in-order traversal of the figure, that is to say, it takes care of the root (*CONTAINER*) and then recursively explores each subgraph. The order is:

CONTAINER, BOX, FINITE, BOUNDED, FIXED, RESIZABLE, UNBOUNDED, INFINITE, COLLECTION, BAG, TABLE, INDEXABLE, ACTIVE, CURSOR_STRUCTURE, DISPENSER, TRAVERSABLE, HIERARCHICAL, LINEAR

An important note about this chapter: because the classes described here serve mostly classification purposes, they each tend to have few new (introduced or redeclared) features, especially when compared to some of the classes in the following chapters. So the flat-short forms in this chapter are uncharacteristically short, since in most cases the interface given for a class does not retain the inherited features. But of course this does not detract from the importance of the classes.

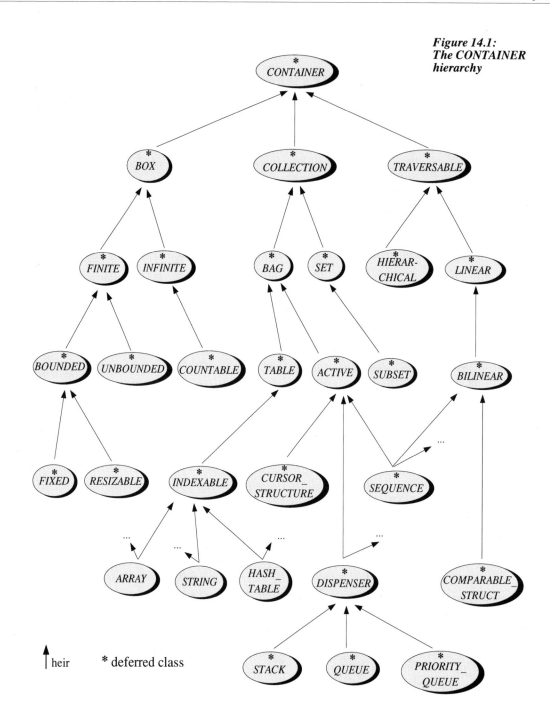

Figure 14.1:
The CONTAINER
hierarchy

14.2 CLASS *CONTAINER*

indexing

> *description*: "*Data structures of the most general kind, used
>   to hold zero or more items.*"
> *names*: *access*
> *access*: *membership*
> *contents*: *generic*

deferred class interface

> CONTAINER [G]

feature -- Access

> *has* (*v*: *G*): *BOOLEAN*
>> -- Does structure include *v*?
>> -- (Reference or object equality,
>> -- based on *object_comparison*.)
>> **ensure**
>>> *not_found_in_empty*: *Result* **implies not** *empty*

feature -- Status report

> *changeable_comparison_criterion*: *BOOLEAN*
>> -- May *object_comparison* be changed?
>> -- (Answer: yes by default.)

> *empty*: *BOOLEAN*
>> -- Is there no element?

> *object_comparison*: *BOOLEAN*
>> -- Must search operations use *equal* rather than =
>> -- for comparing references? (Default: no, use =.)

feature -- Status setting

> *compare_objects*
>> -- Ensure that future search operations will use *equal*
>> -- rather than = for comparing references.
>> **require**
>>> *changeable_comparison_criterion*
>> **ensure**
>>> *object_comparison*

> *compare_references*
>> -- Ensure that future search operations will use =
>> -- rather than *equal* for comparing references.
>> **require**
>>> *changeable_comparison_criterion*
>> **ensure**
>>> *reference_comparison*: **not** *object_comparison*

feature -- Conversion

> *linear_representation*: *LINEAR* [G]
>> -- Representation as a linear structure

end

14.3 CLASS *BOX*

BOX is an heir of *CONTAINER* and retains all its exported features. This interface only shows the feature introduced in class *BOX*.

indexing

    description: *"Data structures of the most general kind,*
      having the potential ability to become full, and
      characterized by their implementation properties."
    names: *storage*

deferred class interface

    BOX [*G*]

feature -- Status report

    full: *BOOLEAN*
        -- Is structure filled to capacity?

end

14.4 **CLASS** *FINITE*

FINITE is an heir of *BOX* and retains all its exported features including those coming from *CONTAINER*. This interface only shows the features introduced or redeclared in class *FINITE*.

indexing

    description: *"Structures with a finite item count"*
    names: *finite, storage*

deferred class interface

    FINITE [*G*]

feature -- Measurement

    count: *INTEGER*
        -- Number of items

feature -- Status report

    empty: *BOOLEAN*
        -- Is structure empty?

invariant

    empty_definition: *empty* = (*count* = 0);
    non_negative_count: *count* >= 0

end

14.5 CLASS *BOUNDED*

BOUNDED is an heir of *FINITE* and retains all its exported features including those coming from *BOX* and *CONTAINER*. This interface only shows the features introduced or redeclared in *BOUNDED*.

indexing

> *description*: *"Bounded data structures, with a notion of*
>   *capacity."*
> *names*: *bounded, storage*

deferred class interface

> *BOUNDED* [*G*]

feature -- Measurement

> *capacity*: *INTEGER*
>   -- Number of items that may be stored

feature -- Status report

> *full*: *BOOLEAN*
>   -- Is structure full?

> *resizable*: *BOOLEAN*
>   -- May *capacity* be changed?

end

14.6 CLASS *FIXED*

FIXED is an heir of *BOUNDED* and retains all its exported features including those coming from *FINITE*, *BOX* and *CONTAINER*. This interface only shows the feature redeclared in *BOUNDED*.

indexing

    description: "*Finite structures whose item count cannot be*
      changed"
    names: *fixed, storage*
    size: *fixed*

deferred class interface

    FIXED [G]

feature -- Status report

    resizable: *BOOLEAN* **is false**
        -- May *capacity* be changed? (Answer: no.)

invariant

    not_resizable: **not** *resizable*

end

14.7 CLASS *RESIZABLE*

For convenience, since this class is of relatively frequent use, the interface that appears here retains the features from *BOUNDED* and *FINITE*. It excludes those coming unchanged from *CONTAINER*.

indexing

  description: *"Finite structures whose item count is subject to change"*
  names: *storage*
  size: *resizable*

deferred class interface

  RESIZABLE [*G*]

feature -- Measurement

  additional_space: *INTEGER*
      -- Proposed number of additional items
    ensure
      at_least_one: *Result* >= *1*

  capacity: *INTEGER*
      -- Number of items that may be stored
      -- (From *BOUNDED*.)

  count: *INTEGER*
      -- Number of items
      -- (From *FINITE*.)

  Growth_percentage: *INTEGER* **is** *50*
      -- Percentage by which structure will grow automatically

  Minimal_increase: *INTEGER* **is** *5*
      -- Minimal number of additional items

feature -- Status report

  empty: *BOOLEAN*
      -- Is structure empty?
      -- (From *FINITE*.)

  full: *BOOLEAN*
      -- Is structure full?
      -- (From *BOUNDED*.)

  resizable: *BOOLEAN*
      -- May *capacity* be changed? (Answer: yes.)

feature -- Resizing

  automatic_grow
      -- Change the capacity to accommodate at least
      -- *Growth_percentage* more items.
    ensure
      increased_capacity: *capacity* >= **old** *capacity* + **old**
        capacity * *growth_percentage* // *100* + *1*

  grow (*i*: *INTEGER*)
      -- Ensure that capacity is at least *i*.
    ensure
      new_capacity: *capacity* >= *i*

invariant

  increase_by_at_least_one: *minimal_increase* >= *1*;
  valid_count: *count* <= *capacity*;
  full_definition: *full* = (*count* = *capacity*);
  empty_definition: *empty* = (*count* = *0*);
  non_negative_count: *count* >= *0*

end

14.8 CLASS *INFINITE*

INFINITE is an heir of *BOX* and retains all its exported features including those coming from *CONTAINER*. This interface only shows the features introduced or redeclared in *INFINITE*.

indexing

    description: *"Infinite containers."*
    names: *infinite, storage*

deferred class interface

    INFINITE [*G*]

feature -- Status report

    empty: *BOOLEAN is false*
        -- Is structure empty? (Answer: no.)

    full: *BOOLEAN is true*
        -- The structure is complete

invariant

    never_empty: *not empty*;
    always_full: *full*

end

14.9 CLASS *COLLECTION*

For convenience, since *COLLECTION* is more often used to build directly useful classes than *CONTAINER* just by itself, this is the complete interface, showing the features inherited from *CONTAINER* as well as those introduced or redeclared in *COLLECTION*.

indexing

> *description*: "*General container data structures,*
> *characterized by the membership properties of their*
> *items.*"
> *names*: *collection, access*
> *access*: *membership*
> *contents*: *generic*

deferred class interface

> *COLLECTION* [*G*]

feature -- Access

> *has* (*v*: *G*): *BOOLEAN*
> -- Does structure include *v*?
> -- (Reference or object equality,
> -- based on *object_comparison*.)
> -- (From *CONTAINER*.)
> **ensure**
> *not_found_in_empty*: *Result* **implies not** *empty*

feature -- Status report

> *changeable_comparison_criterion*: *BOOLEAN*
> -- May *object_comparison* be changed?
> -- (Answer: yes by default.)
> -- (From *CONTAINER*.)

> *empty*: *BOOLEAN*
> -- Is there no element?
> -- (From *CONTAINER*.)

> *extendible*: *BOOLEAN*
> -- May new items be added?

> *object_comparison*: *BOOLEAN*
> -- Must search operations use *equal* rather than =
> -- for comparing references? (Default: no, use =.)
> -- (From *CONTAINER*.)

> *prunable*: *BOOLEAN*
> -- May items be removed?

feature -- Status setting

> *compare_objects*
> -- Ensure that future search operations will use *equal*
> -- rather than = for comparing references.
> -- (From *CONTAINER*.)
> **require**
> *changeable_comparison_criterion*
> **ensure**
> *object_comparison*

> *compare_references*
> -- Ensure that future search operations will use =
> -- rather than *equal* for comparing references.
> -- (From *CONTAINER*.)
> **require**
> *changeable_comparison_criterion*
> **ensure**
> *reference_comparison*: **not** *object_comparison*

feature -- Element change

> *extend* (*v*: *G*)
> -- Ensure that structure includes *v*.
> **require**
> *extendible*:: *extendible*
> **ensure**
> *item_inserted*: *has* (*v*)

> *fill* (*other*: *CONTAINER* [*G*])
> -- Fill with as many items of *other* as possible.
> -- The representations of *other* and current structure
> -- need not be the same.
> **require**
> *other_not_void*: *other* /= *Void*;
> *extendible* : *extendible*

> *put* (*v*: *G*)
> -- Ensure that structure includes *v*.
> **require**
> *extendible* : *extendible*
> **ensure**
> *item_inserted*: *has* (*v*)

feature -- Removal

   prune (*v*: *G*)
         -- Remove one occurrence of *v* if any.
         -- (Reference or object equality,
         -- based on *object_comparison*.)
      require
         prunable: *prunable*

   prune_all (*v*: *G*)
         -- Remove all occurrences of *v*.
         -- (Reference or object equality,
         -- based on *object_comparison*.)
      require
         prunable
      ensure
         no_more_occurrences: **not** *has* (*v*)

   wipe_out
         -- Remove all items.
      require
         prunable
      ensure
         wiped_out: *empty*

feature -- Conversion

   linear_representation: *LINEAR* [*G*]
         -- Representation as a linear structure
         -- (From *CONTAINER*.)

end

14.10 CLASS *BAG*

BAG is an heir of *COLLECTION* and retains all its exported features including those coming from *CONTAINER*. This interface only shows the features introduced or redeclared in *BAG*.

indexing

> description: "Collections of items, where each item may
>   occur zero or more times, and the number of occurrences is
>   meaningful."
> names: bag, access
> access: membership
> contents: generic

deferred class interface

> *BAG* [G]

feature -- Measurement

> occurrences (v: G): INTEGER
>   -- Number of times v appears in structure
>   -- (Reference or object equality,
>   -- based on object_comparison.)
>   **ensure**
>   non_negative_occurrences: Result >= 0

feature -- Element change

> extend (v: G)
>   -- Add a new occurrence of v.
>   **require**
>   extendible: extendible
>   **ensure**
>   one_more_occurrence: occurrences (v) = **old**
>   (occurrences (v)) + 1

end

14.11 CLASS *TABLE*

For convenience, since *TABLE* is often used as parent to build directly useful classes, this interface shows all the features, including inherited ones.

indexing

description: "Containers whose items are accessible through keys"
names: table, access
access: key, membership
contents: generic

deferred class interface

TABLE [G, H]

feature -- Access

has (v: G): BOOLEAN
-- Does structure include v?
-- (Reference or object equality,
-- based on object_comparison.)
-- (From *CONTAINER*.)
ensure
not_found_in_empty: Result **implies not** empty

item (k: H): G
-- Entry of key k.
require
valid_key: valid_key (k)

infix "@" (k: H): G
-- Entry of key k.
require
valid_key: valid_key (k)

feature -- Measurement

occurrences (v: G): INTEGER
-- Number of times v appears in structure
-- (Reference or object equality,
-- based on object_comparison.)
-- (From *BAG*.)
ensure
non_negative_occurrences: Result >= 0

feature -- Status report

changeable_comparison_criterion: BOOLEAN
-- May object_comparison be changed?
-- (Answer: yes by default.)
-- (From *CONTAINER*.)

empty: BOOLEAN
-- Is there no element?
-- (From *CONTAINER*.)

extendible: BOOLEAN
-- May new items be added?
-- (From *COLLECTION*.)

object_comparison: BOOLEAN
-- Must search operations use *equal* rather than =
-- for comparing references? (Default: no, use =.)
-- (From *CONTAINER*.)

prunable: BOOLEAN
-- May items be removed?
-- (From *COLLECTION*.)

valid_key (k: H): BOOLEAN
-- Is k a valid key?

feature -- Status setting

compare_objects
-- Ensure that future search operations will use *equal*
-- rather than = for comparing references.
-- (From *CONTAINER*.)
require
changeable_comparison_criterion
ensure
object_comparison

compare_references
-- Ensure that future search operations will use =
-- rather than *equal* for comparing references.
-- (From *CONTAINER*.)
require
changeable_comparison_criterion
ensure
reference_comparison: **not** object_comparison

feature -- Element change

extend (v: G)
-- Add a new occurrence of v.
-- (From *BAG*.)
require
extendible: extendible
ensure
one_more_occurrence: occurrences (v) = **old**
(occurrences (v)) + 1
ensure then
item_inserted: has (v)

fill (*other*: *CONTAINER* [*G*])
> -- Fill with as many items of *other* as possible.
> -- The representations of *other* and current structure
> -- need not be the same.
> -- (From *COLLECTION*.)
>
> **require**
> > *other_not_void*: *other* /= *Void*;
> > *extendible*: *extendible*

put (*v*: *G*; *k*: *H*)
> -- Associate value *v* with key *k*.
>
> **require**
> > *valid_key*: *valid_key* (*k*)

feature -- Removal

prune (*v*: *G*)
> -- Remove one occurrence of *v* if any.
> -- (Reference or object equality,
> -- based on *object_comparison*.)
> -- (From *COLLECTION*.)
>
> **require**
> > *prunable*: *prunable*

prune_all (*v*: *G*)
> -- Remove all occurrences of *v*.
> -- (Reference or object equality,
> -- based on *object_comparison*.)
> -- (From *COLLECTION*.)
>
> **require**
> > *prunable*
>
> **ensure**
> > *no_more_occurrences*: **not** *has* (*v*)

wipe_out
> -- Remove all items.
> -- (From *COLLECTION*.)
>
> **require**
> > *prunable*
>
> **ensure**
> > *wiped_out*: *empty*

feature -- Conversion

linear_representation: *LINEAR* [*G*]
> -- Representation as a linear structure
> -- (From *CONTAINER*.)

end

14.12 CLASS *INDEXABLE*

INDEXABLE is an heir of *TABLE* and retains all its exported features including those coming from ancestors. This interface only shows the features introduced, renamed or redeclared in *INDEXABLE*. Note that the generic parameter *H* representing the key type must now be *INTEGER* or a conforming type; for *TABLE* it is arbitrary.

indexing

> *description*: *"Tables whose keys are integers or equivalent"*
> *names*: *indexable, access*
> *access*: *index, membership*
> *contents*: *generic*

deferred class interface

> *INDEXABLE* [*G, H –> INTEGER*]

feature -- Access

> *infix "@"* (*k*: *H*): *G*
> > -- Entry of key *k*.
> > -- (From *TABLE*.)
> > *require*
> > *valid_key*: *valid_index* (*k*)

feature -- Element change

> *put* (*v*: *G*; *k*: *H*)
> > -- Associate value *v* with key *k*.
> > *require*
> > *valid_key*: *valid_index* (*k*)

end

14.13 CLASS *ACTIVE*

ACTIVE is an heir of *BAG* and retains all its exported features including those coming from *COLLECTION* and *CONTAINER*. This interface only shows the features introduced or redeclared in *INDEXABLE*.

indexing

     description: "*"Active" data structures, which at every stage*
        have a possibly undefined "current item". Basic access
        and modification operations apply to the current item."
     names: *active, access*
     access: *membership*
     contents: *generic*

deferred class interface

     ACTIVE [*G*]

feature -- Access

     item: *G*
        -- Current item
       require
        readable

feature -- Status report

     readable: *BOOLEAN*
        -- Is there a current item that may be read?

     writable: *BOOLEAN*
        -- Is there a current item that may be modified?

feature -- Element change

     replace (*v*: *G*)
        -- Replace current item by *v*.
       require
        writable: *writable*
       ensure
        item_replaced: *item* = *v*

feature -- Removal

     remove
        -- Remove current item.
       require
        prunable;
        writable

invariant

     writable_constraint: *writable* **implies** *readable*

end

14.14 **CLASS** *CURSOR_STRUCTURE*

Since *CURSOR_STRUCTURE* may be used as parent to build directly useful features, this interface shows all the features of the class including those inherited from ancestors, with the exception of the general features coming unchanged from *CONTAINER*.

indexing

    description: "Active structures, which always have a current
      position accessible through a cursor."
    names: *cursor_structure, access*
    access: *cursor, membership*
    contents: *generic*

deferred class interface

    CURSOR_STRUCTURE [*G*]

feature -- Access

    cursor: *CURSOR*
        -- Current cursor position

    item: *G*
        -- Current item
        -- (From *ACTIVE*.)
      require
        readable

feature -- Measurement

    occurrences (*v*: *G*): *INTEGER*
        -- Number of times *v* appears in structure
        -- (Reference or object equality,
        -- based on *object_comparison*.)
        -- (From *BAG*.)
      ensure
        non_negative_occurrences: *Result* >= *0*

feature -- Status report

    extendible: *BOOLEAN*
        -- May new items be added?
        -- (From *COLLECTION*.)

    prunable: *BOOLEAN*
        -- May items be removed?
        -- (From *COLLECTION*.)

    readable: *BOOLEAN*
        -- Is there a current item that may be read?
        -- (From *ACTIVE*.)

    valid_cursor (*p*: *CURSOR*): *BOOLEAN*
        -- Can the cursor be moved to position *p*?

    writable: *BOOLEAN*
        -- Is there a current item that may be modified?
        -- (From *ACTIVE*.)

feature -- Cursor movement

    go_to (*p*: *CURSOR*)
        -- Move cursor to position *p*.
      require
        cursor_position_valid: *valid_cursor* (*p*)

feature -- Element change

    extend (*v*: *G*)
        -- Add a new occurrence of *v*.
        -- (From *BAG*.)
      require
        extendible: *extendible*
      ensure
        one_more_occurrence: *occurrences* (*v*) = **old**
          (*occurrences* (*v*)) + *1*
      ensure then

    fill (*other*: *CONTAINER* [*G*])
        -- Fill with as many items of *other* as possible.
        -- The representations of *other* and current structure
        -- need not be the same.
        -- (From *COLLECTION*.)
      require
        other_not_void: *other* /= *Void*;
        extendible: *extendible*

    put (*v*: *G*)
        -- Ensure that structure includes *v*.
        -- (From *COLLECTION*.)
      require
        extendible: *extendible*

    replace (*v*: *G*)
        -- Replace current item by *v*.
        -- (From *ACTIVE*.)
      require
        writable: *writable*
      ensure
        item_replaced: *item* = *v*

feature -- Removal

    prune (*v*: *G*)
        -- Remove one occurrence of *v* if any.
        -- (Reference or object equality,
        -- based on *object_comparison*.)
        -- (From *COLLECTION*.)
      require
        prunable: *prunable*

prune_all (*v*: *G*)
    -- Remove all occurrences of *v*.
    -- (Reference or object equality,
    -- based on *object_comparison*.)
    -- (From *COLLECTION*.)
  require
    prunable

remove
    -- Remove current item.
    -- (From *ACTIVE*.)
  require
    prunable;
    writable

wipe_out
    -- Remove all items.
    -- (From *COLLECTION*.)
  require
    prunable

invariant

  writable_constraint: *writable* **implies** *readable*

end

14.15 CLASS *DISPENSER*

Since *DISPENSER* may be used as parent to build directly useful features, this interface shows all the features of the class including those inherited from ancestors, with the exception of the general features coming unchanged from *CONTAINER*.

All the features shown here are retained by the more specific dispenser classes of a later chapter, describing stacks, queues and priority queues.

indexing

> *description*: "*Dispensers: containers for which clients have no say as to what item they can access at a given time. Examples include stacks and queues.*"
> *names*: dispenser, active
> *access*: fixed, membership
> *contents*: generic

deferred class interface

> DISPENSER [G]

feature -- Access

> *item*: G
> -- Current item
> -- (From *ACTIVE*.)
> **require**
> readable

feature -- Measurement

> *count*: INTEGER
> -- Number of items
> -- (From *FINITE*.)

> *occurrences* (v: G): INTEGER
> -- Number of times *v* appears in structure
> -- (Reference or object equality,
> -- based on *object_comparison*.)
> -- (From *BAG*.)
> **ensure**
> *non_negative_occurrences*: Result >= 0

feature -- Status report

> *empty*: BOOLEAN
> -- Is structure empty?
> -- (From *FINITE*.)

> *extendible*: BOOLEAN
> -- May new items be added?
> -- (From *COLLECTION*.)

> *full*: BOOLEAN
> -- Is structure filled to capacity?
> -- (From *BOX*.)

> *prunable*: BOOLEAN
> -- May items be removed?
> -- (From *COLLECTION*.)

> *readable*: BOOLEAN
> -- Is there a current item that may be read?

> *writable*: BOOLEAN
> -- Is there a current item that may be modified?

feature -- Element change

> *append* (s: SEQUENCE [G])
> -- Append a copy of *s*.
> -- (Synonym for *fill*)

> *extend* (v: **like** item)
> -- Add item *v*.
> **require**
> extendible: extendible
> **ensure**
> one_more_occurrence: occurrences (v) = **old**
> (occurrences (v)) + 1
> **ensure then**

> *fill* (other: CONTAINER [G])
> -- Fill with as many items of *other* as possible.
> -- The representations of *other* and current structure
> -- need not be the same.
> -- (From *COLLECTION*.)
> **require**
> other_not_void: other /= Void;
> extendible: extendible

> *force* (v: **like** item)
> -- Add item *v*.

> *put* (v: **like** item)
> -- Add item *v*.
> **require**
> extendible: extendible

> *replace* (v: G)
> -- Replace current item by *v*.
> -- (From *ACTIVE*.)
> **require**
> writable: writable
> **ensure**
> item_replaced: item = v

feature -- Removal

    prune (*v*: *G*)
        -- Remove one occurrence of *v* if any.
        -- (Reference or object equality,
        -- based on *object_comparison*.)
        -- (From *COLLECTION*.)
      require
        prunable: *prunable*

    prune_all (*v*: *G*)
        -- Remove all occurrences of *v*.
        -- (Reference or object equality,
        -- based on *object_comparison*.)
        -- (From *COLLECTION*.)
      require
        prunable

    remove
        -- Remove current item.
        -- (From *ACTIVE*.)
      require
        prunable;
        writable

    wipe_out
        -- Remove all items.
        -- (From *COLLECTION*.)
      require
        prunable
      ensure
        wiped_out: *empty*

invariant

    readable_definition: *readable* = **not** *empty*;
    writable_definition: *writable* = **not** *empty*;
    writable_constraint: *writable* **implies** *readable*;
    empty_constraint: *empty* **implies** (**not** *readable*) **and** (**not**
      writable);
    empty_definition: *empty* = (*count* = *0*);
    non_negative_count: *count* >= *0*

end

14.16 CLASS *TRAVERSABLE*

TRAVERSABLE is an heir of *CONTAINER* and retains all its exported features. This interface only shows the features introduced or redeclared in *TRAVERSABLE*.

indexing

  description: "*Structures for which there exists a traversal*
     policy that will visit every element exactly once."
  names: *traversable, traversing*
  access: *cursor*
  contents: *generic*

deferred class interface

  TRAVERSABLE [*G*]

feature -- Access

  item: *G*
       -- Item at current position
     require
       not_off: **not** *off*

feature -- Status report

  off: *BOOLEAN*
       -- Is there no current item?

feature -- Cursor movement

  start
       -- Move to first position if any.

end

14.17 CLASS *HIERARCHICAL*

HIERARCHICAL is an heir of *TRAVERSABLE*. and retains all its exported features. This interface shows the features introduced or redeclared in *HIERARCHICAL* and *TRAVERSABLE*, but not those coming unchanged from any other ancestor.

indexing

> *description*: "*Hierarchical structures in which each item has*
> *zero or one immediate predecessor, and zero or more*
> *successors.*"
> *names*: *hierarchical, traversing*
> *access*: *cursor*
> *contents*: *generic*

deferred class interface

> *HIERARCHICAL* [*G*]

feature -- Access

> *item*: *G*
>> -- Item at current position
>> -- (From *TRAVERSABLE*.)
>> *require*
>> *not_off*: **not** *off*

> *successor_count*: *INTEGER*
>> -- Number of successors of current element
>> *require*
>> *not_off*: **not** *off*

feature -- Status report

> *off*: *BOOLEAN*
>> -- Is there no current item?
>> -- (From *TRAVERSABLE*.)

feature -- Cursor movement

> *down* (*i*: *INTEGER*)
>> -- Move to *i*-th successor.
>> *require*
>> *not_off*: **not** *off*;
>> *argument_within_bounds*: *i* >= *1* **and** *i* <= *successor_*
>> *count*

> *start*
>> -- Move to first position if any.
>> -- (From *TRAVERSABLE*.)

> *up*
>> -- Move to predecessor.
>> *require*
>> *not_off*: **not** *off*

invariant

> *non_negative_successor_count*: *successor_count* >= *0*

end

14.18 CLASS *LINEAR*

LINEAR is an heir of *TRAVERSABLE*. and etains all its exported features. This interface shows the features introduced or redeclared in *LINEAR* and *TRAVERSABLE*, but not those coming unchanged from any other ancestor.

indexing

   description: "Structures whose items may be accessed
      sequentially, one−way"
   names: sequential, traversing
   access: membership
   contents: generic

deferred class interface

   LINEAR [G]

feature -- Access

   has (v: **like** item): BOOLEAN
      -- Does structure include an occurrence of v?
      -- (Reference or object equality,
      -- based on object_comparison.)

   index: INTEGER
      -- Index of current position

   index_of (v: **like** item; i: INTEGER): INTEGER
      -- Index of i−th occurrence of v.
      -- 0 if none.
      -- (Reference or object equality,
      -- based on object_comparison.)
   require
      positive_occurrences: i > 0
   ensure
      non_negative_result: Result >= 0

   item: G
      -- Item at current position
      -- (From *TRAVERSABLE*.)
   require
      not_off: **not** off

   occurrences (v: G): INTEGER
      -- Number of times v appears.
      -- (Reference or object equality,
      -- based on object_comparison.)

   search (v: **like** item)
      -- Move to first position (at or after current
      -- position) where item and v are equal.
      -- (Reference or object equality,
      -- based on object_comparison.)
      -- If no such position ensure that exhausted will be true.

feature -- Status report

   after: BOOLEAN
      -- Is there no valid position to the right of current one?

   exhausted: BOOLEAN
      -- Has structure been completely explored?
   ensure
      exhausted_when_off: off **implies** Result

   off: BOOLEAN
      -- Is there no current item?

feature -- Cursor movement

   finish
      -- Move to last position.

   forth
      -- Move to next position; if no next position,
      -- ensure that exhausted will be true.
   require
      not_after: **not** after

   start
      -- Move to first position if any.
      -- (From *TRAVERSABLE*.)

feature -- Conversion

   linear_representation: LINEAR [G]
      -- Representation as a linear structure

invariant

   after_constraint: after **implies** off

end

15

Classes for mathematical properties

15.1 OVERVIEW

An earlier chapter introduced some mathematical properties that play an important role Chapter 5. in the Base libraries, and explained the corresponding classes.

Here now are the interfaces, in flat-short form, of all these classes.

The class interfaces appear in the order of the earlier discussion:

PART_COMPARABLE, COMPARABLE, NUMERIC, HASHABLE.

15.2 CLASS PART_COMPARABLE

indexing
> description: "Objects that may be compared according to a
> partial order relation"
> names: part_comparable, comparison

deferred class interface

PART_COMPARABLE

feature -- Comparison

infix "<" (other: like Current): BOOLEAN
> -- Is current object less than other?

infix "<=" (other: like Current): BOOLEAN
> -- Is current object less than or equal to other?

infix ">" (other: like Current): BOOLEAN
> -- Is current object greater than other?

infix ">=" (other: like Current): BOOLEAN
> -- Is current object greater than or equal to other?

end

15.3 CLASS *COMPARABLE*

indexing

   description: *"Objects that may be compared according to a
     total order relation"*
   names: *comparable*, *comparison*

deferred class interface

   COMPARABLE

feature -- Comparison

   infix "<" (*other*: **like** *Current*): *BOOLEAN*
      -- Is current object less than *other*?
    ensure
     smaller: *Result* **implies not** (*Current* >= *other*)

   infix "<=" (*other*: **like** *Current*): *BOOLEAN*
      -- Is current object less than or equal to *other*?
    ensure
     equals_smaller: *Result* **implies not** (*Current* > *other*)

   infix ">" (*other*: **like** *Current*): *BOOLEAN*
      -- Is current object greater than *other*?
    ensure
     larger: *Result* **implies not** (*Current* <= *other*)

   infix ">=" (*other*: **like** *Current*): *BOOLEAN*
      -- Is current object greater than or equal to *other*?
    ensure
     equals_larger: *Result* **implies not** (*Current* < *other*)

end

15.4 CLASS *NUMERIC*

indexing

  description: "*Objects to which numerical operations are applicable*"

deferred class interface

  NUMERIC

feature -- Basic operations

  infix "***" (*other*: *NUMERIC*): *NUMERIC*
        -- Product by *other*
    require
        other_exists: *other* /= *Void*

  prefix "+": *NUMERIC*
        -- Unary plus

  infix "+" (*other*: *NUMERIC*): *NUMERIC*
        -- Sum with *other*
    require
        other_exists: *other* /= *Void*

  prefix "−": *NUMERIC*
        -- Unary minus

  infix "−" (*other*: *NUMERIC*): *NUMERIC*
        -- Result of subtracting *other*
    require
        other_exists: *other* /= *Void*

  infix "/" (*other*: *NUMERIC*): *NUMERIC*
        -- Division by *other*
    require
        other_exists: *other* /= *Void*

  infix "^" (*other*: *NUMERIC*): *NUMERIC*
        -- Current object to the power *other*
    require
        other_exists: *other* /= *Void*

end

15.5 CLASS *HASHABLE*

indexing

> *description*: *"Values that may be hashed into an integer
> index"*

deferred class interface

> HASHABLE

feature -- Access

> *hash_code*: *INTEGER*
>> -- Hash code value
>> *require*
>> *is_hashable*
>> *ensure*
>> *valid_hash_value*: *Result* >= 0

feature -- Status report

> *is_hashable*: *BOOLEAN*
>> -- May current object be hashed?
>> -- (Answer: if and only if it is not the default value of
>> -- its type)
>> *ensure*
>> *Result* = (*Current* /= *default*)

end

16

Classes for linear structures

16.1 OVERVIEW

An earlier chapter introduced the notion of linear structure and explain the variants of this notion: bilinear structures, sequences, chains, lists, circular chains.

Chapter 6.

Here now are all the interfaces, in flat-short form, of all these classes except their common ancestor *LINEAR* whose specification has already been given.

The interface of LINEAR is in 14.18, page 285.

The corresponding inheritance hierarchy is repeated on the following page.

The figure appeared originally on page 140.

The order in which the class interfaces appear corresponds roughly to a preorder traversal of the inheritance graph (followed by the infinite structure *COUNTABLE_ SEQUENCE* and the two effective descendants of *CELL*, which are of auxiliary use only). The notation *C* / *D* means that the interfaces of classes *C* and *D*, being identical or almost identical, are given as a single flat-short form.

BILINEAR, SEQUENCE, CHAIN / LIST, LINKED_LIST / TWO_WAY_LIST, ARRAYED_LIST, MULTI_ARRAY_LIST, FIXED_LIST, PART_SORTED_ LIST, SORTED_LIST / TWO_WAY_SORTED_LIST, CIRCULAR, LINKED_CIRCULAR / TWO_WAY_CIRCULAR, ARRAYED_CIRCULAR, COMPARABLE_STRUCT, COUNTABLE_SEQUENCE, LINKABLE, BI_ LINKABLE

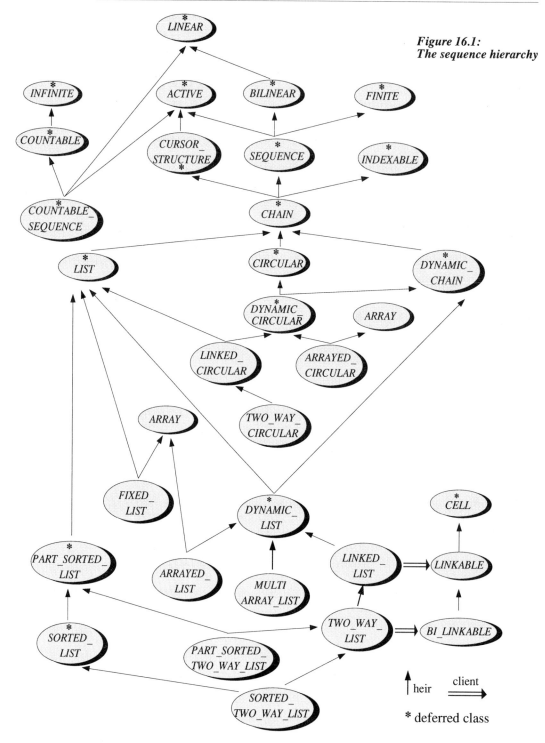

Figure 16.1:
The sequence hierarchy

16.2 CLASS *BILINEAR*

The classes of this chapter are descendants not just of *LINEAR* but also of its direct heir *BILINEAR*. The interface of *BILINEAR* as it appears below shows the features introduced or redeclared in the class itself and those coming from *LINEAR*, but not the features inherited unchanged from other ancestors.

indexing

> *description*: "*Structures that may be traversed forward and backward*"
> *names*: *bidirectional, traversing*
> *access*: *cursor, membership*
> *contents*: *generic*

deferred class interface

> *BILINEAR* [*G*]

feature -- Access

> *has* (*v*: **like** *item*): *BOOLEAN*
> > -- Does structure include an occurrence of *v*?
> > -- (Reference or object equality,
> > -- based on *object_comparison*.)
> > -- (From *LINEAR*.)
>
> *index*: *INTEGER*
> > -- Index of current position
> > -- (From *LINEAR*.)
>
> *index_of* (*v*: **like** *item*; *i*: *INTEGER*): *INTEGER*
> > -- Index of *i*-th occurrence of *v*.
> > -- 0 if none.
> > -- (Reference or object equality,
> > -- based on *object_comparison*.)
> > -- (From *LINEAR*.)
> > **require**
> > > *positive_occurrences*: *i* > 0
> > **ensure**
> > > *non_negative_result*: *Result* >= 0
>
> *occurrences* (*v*: *G*): *INTEGER*
> > -- Number of times *v* appears.
> > -- (Reference or object equality,
> > -- based on *object_comparison*.)
> > -- (From *LINEAR*.)
>
> *off*: *BOOLEAN*
> > -- Is there no current item?

feature -- Status report

> *after*: *BOOLEAN*
> > -- Is there no valid position to the right of current one?
> > -- (From *LINEAR*.)

> *exhausted*: *BOOLEAN*
> > -- Has structure been completely explored?
> > -- (From *LINEAR*.)
> > **ensure**
> > > *exhausted_when_off*: *off* **implies** *Result*

feature -- Cursor movement

> *back*
> > -- Move to previous position.
> > **require**
> > > *not_before*: **not** *before*
> > **ensure**
> > > *moved_back*: *index* = **old** *index* − 1
>
> *before*: *BOOLEAN*
> > -- Is there no valid position to the left of current one?
>
> *finish*
> > -- Move to last position.
> > -- (From *LINEAR*.)
>
> *forth*
> > -- Move to next position; if no next position,
> > -- ensure that *exhausted* will be true.
> > -- (From *LINEAR*.)
> > **require**
> > > *not_after*: **not** *after*
>
> *search* (*v*: **like** *item*)
> > -- Move to first position (at or after current
> > -- position) where *item* and *v* are equal.
> > -- If structure does not include *v* ensure that
> > -- *exhausted* will be true.
> > -- (Reference or object equality,
> > -- based on *object_comparison*.)

feature -- Conversion

> *linear_representation*: *LINEAR* [*G*]
> > -- Representation as a linear structure
> > -- (From *LINEAR*.)

invariant

> *not_both*: **not** (*after* **and** *before*);
> *empty_property*: *empty* **implies** (*after* **or** *before*;
> *before_constraint*: *before* **implies** *off*;
> *after_constraint*: *after* **implies** *off*;
> *empty_constraint*: *empty* **implies** *off*

end

16.3 CLASS *SEQUENCE*

The interface as it appears here only shows the features introduced or redeclared in the class itself.

indexing

description: *"Finite sequences: structures where existing*
items are arrangedand accessed sequentially, and new
ones can be added at the end."
names: *sequence*
access: *cursor*, *membership*
contents: *generic*

deferred class interface

SEQUENCE [*G*]

feature -- Status report

readable: *BOOLEAN*
-- Is there a current item that may be read?

writable: *BOOLEAN*
-- Is there a current item that may be modified?

feature -- Element change

append (*s*: *SEQUENCE* [*G*])
-- Append a copy of *s*.
require
argument_not_void: *s* /= *Void*

force (*v*: **like** *item*)
-- Add *v* to end.
require
extendible: *extendible*

put (*v*: **like** *item*)
-- Add *v* to end.
require
extendible: *extendible*

feature -- Removal

prune (*v*: **like** *item*)
-- Remove the first occurrence of *v* if any.
-- If no such occurrence go *off*.
require
prunable: *prunable*

prune_all (*v*: **like** *item*)
-- Remove all occurrences of *v*; go *off*.
require
prunable

invariant

writable_constraint: *writable* **implies** *readable*

end

16.4 CLASSES *CHAIN* **AND** *LIST*

The interfaces of *CHAIN* and *LIST* are almost the same. Since *CHAIN* is mostly of theoretical interest (as common ancestor to list and circular chains) the interface given here is that of *LIST*. For convenience it shows all exported features, including those inherited from ancestors.

indexing

    description: "*Sequential lists, without commitment to a*
      particular representation"
    names: *list, sequence*
    access: *index, cursor, membership*
    contents: *generic*

deferred class interface

LIST [*G*]

feature -- Access

    cursor: *CURSOR*
      -- Current cursor position
      -- (From *CURSOR_STRUCTURE*.)

    first: **like** *item*
      -- Item at first position
      -- (From *CHAIN*.)
      require
        not_empty: **not** *empty*

    has (*v*: **like** *item*): *BOOLEAN*
      -- Does chain include *v*?
      -- (Reference or object equality,
      -- based on *object_comparison*.)
      -- (From *CHAIN*.)
      ensure
        not_found_in_empty: *Result* **implies not** *empty*

    i_th (*i*: *INTEGER*): **like** *item*
      -- Item at *i*−th position
      -- (From *CHAIN*.)
      require
        valid_key: *valid_index* (*i*)

    index: *INTEGER*
      -- Current cursor index
      -- (From *CHAIN*.)

    index_of (*v*: **like** *item*; *i*: *INTEGER*): *INTEGER*
      -- Index of *i*−th occurrence of item identical to *v*.
      -- (Reference or object equality,
      -- based on *object_comparison*.)
      -- 0 if none.
      -- (From *CHAIN*.)
      require
        positive_occurrences: *i > 0*
      ensure
        non_negative_result: *Result >= 0*

    item: *G*
      -- Item at current position
      -- (From *TRAVERSABLE*.)
      require
        not_off: **not** *off*
      require else
        readable

    last: **like** *item*
      -- Item at last position
      -- (From *CHAIN*.)
      require
        not_empty: **not** *empty*

    occurrences (*v*: **like** *item*): *INTEGER*
      -- Number of times *v* appears.
      -- (Reference or object equality,
      -- based on *object_comparison*.)
      -- (From *CHAIN*.)
      ensure
        non_negative_occurrences: *Result >= 0*

    sequential_occurrences (*v*: *G*): *INTEGER*
      -- Number of times *v* appears.
      -- (Reference or object equality,
      -- based on *object_comparison*.)
      -- (From *LINEAR*.)
      ensure
        non_negative_occurrences: *Result >= 0*

    infix "*@*" (*i*: *INTEGER*): **like** *item*
      -- Item at *i*−th position
      -- (From *CHAIN*.)
      require
        valid_key: *valid_index* (*i*)

feature -- Measurement

    count: *INTEGER*
      -- Number of items
      -- (From *FINITE*.)

feature -- Status report

    after: *BOOLEAN*
      -- Is there no valid cursor position to the right of cursor?

    before: *BOOLEAN*
      -- Is there no valid cursor position to the left of cursor?

changeable_comparison_criterion: *BOOLEAN*
  -- May *object_comparison* be changed?
  -- (Answer: yes by default.)
  -- (From *CONTAINER*.)

empty: *BOOLEAN*
  -- Is structure empty?
  -- (From *FINITE*.)

exhausted: *BOOLEAN*
  -- Has structure been completely explored?
  -- (From *LINEAR*.)
 ensure
  exhausted_when_off: *off* **implies** *Result*

extendible: *BOOLEAN*
  -- May new items be added?
  -- (From *COLLECTION*.)

full: *BOOLEAN*
  -- Is structure filled to capacity?
  -- (From *BOX*.)

isfirst: *BOOLEAN*
  -- Is cursor at first position?
  -- (From *CHAIN*.)
 ensure
  valid_position: *Result* **implies not** *empty*

islast: *BOOLEAN*
  -- Is cursor at last position?
  -- (From *CHAIN*.)
 ensure
  valid_position: *Result* **implies not** *empty*

object_comparison: *BOOLEAN*
  -- Must search operations use *equal* rather than =
  -- for comparing references? (Default: no, use =.)
  -- (From *CONTAINER*.)

off: *BOOLEAN*
  -- Is there no current item?
  -- (From *CHAIN*.)

prunable: *BOOLEAN*
  -- May items be removed?
  -- (From *COLLECTION*.)

readable: *BOOLEAN*
  -- Is there a current item that may be read?
  -- (From *SEQUENCE*.)

valid_cursor (*p*: *CURSOR*): *BOOLEAN*
  -- Can the cursor be moved to position *p*?
  -- (From *CURSOR_STRUCTURE*.)

valid_cursor_index (*i*: *INTEGER*): *BOOLEAN*
  -- Is *i* correctly bounded for cursor movement?
  -- (From *CHAIN*.)
 ensure
  valid_cursor_index_definition: *Result* = (($i >= 0$) **and** ($i <= count + 1$))

valid_index (*i*: *INTEGER*): *BOOLEAN*
  -- Is *i* within allowable bounds?
  -- (From *CHAIN*.)
 ensure
  valid_index_definition: *Result* = ($i >= 1$) **and** ($i <= count$)

writable: *BOOLEAN*
  -- Is there a current item that may be modified?
  -- (From *SEQUENCE*.)

feature -- Status setting

compare_objects
  -- Ensure that future search operations will use *equal*
  -- rather than = for comparing references.
  -- (From *CONTAINER*.)
 require
  changeable_comparison_criterion
 ensure
  object_comparison

compare_references
  -- Ensure that future search operations will use =
  -- rather than *equal* for comparing references.
  -- (From *CONTAINER*.)
 require
  changeable_comparison_criterion
 ensure
  reference_comparison: **not** *object_comparison*

feature -- Cursor movement

back
  -- Move to previous position.
  -- (From *BILINEAR*.)
 require
  not_before: **not** *before*
 ensure
  moved_back: *index* = **old** *index* − *1*

finish
  -- Move cursor to last position.
  -- (No effect if empty)
  -- (From *CHAIN*.)
 ensure
  at_last: **not** *empty* **implies** *islast*

forth
 -- Move to next position; if no next position,
 -- ensure that *exhausted* will be true.
 require
 not_after: **not** *after*
 ensure
 moved_forth: *index* = **old** *index* + *1*

go_i_th (*i*: INTEGER)
 -- Move cursor to *i*–th position.
 -- (From *CHAIN*.)
 require
 valid_cursor_index: *valid_cursor_index* (*i*)
 ensure
 position_expected: *index* = *i*

go_to (*p*: CURSOR)
 -- Move cursor to position *p*.
 -- (From *CURSOR_STRUCTURE*.)
 require
 cursor_position_valid: *valid_cursor* (*p*)

move (*i*: INTEGER)
 -- Move cursor *i* positions. The cursor
 -- may end up *off* if the absolute value of *i*
 -- is too big.
 -- (From *CHAIN*.)
 ensure
 too_far_right: (**old** *index* + *i* > *count*) **implies** *exhausted*;
 too_far_left: (**old** *index* + *i* < *1*) **implies** *exhausted*;
 expected_index: (**not** *exhausted*) **implies** (*index* = **old** *index* + *i*)

search (*v*: **like** *item*)
 -- Move to first position (at or after current
 -- position) where *item* and *v* are equal.
 -- If structure does not include *v* ensure that
 -- *exhausted* will be true.
 -- (Reference or object equality,
 -- based on *object_comparison*.)
 -- (From *BILINEAR*.)
 ensure
 object_found: (**not** *exhausted* **and then** *object_comparison* **and then** *v* /= *Void* **and then** *item* /= *Void*) **implies** *v*.*is_equal* (*item*);
 item_found: (**not** *exhausted* **and not** *object_comparison*) **implies** *v* = *item*

start
 -- Move cursor to first position.
 -- (No effect if empty)
 -- (From *CHAIN*.)
 ensure
 at_first: **not** *empty* **implies** *isfirst*

feature -- Element change

append (*s*: SEQUENCE [*G*])
 -- Append a copy of *s*.
 -- (From *SEQUENCE*.)
 require
 argument_not_void: *s* /= *Void*
 ensure
 new_count: *count* >= **old** *count*

extend (*v*: *G*)
 -- Add a new occurrence of *v*.
 -- (From *BAG*.)
 require
 extendible: *extendible*
 ensure
 one_more_occurrence: *occurrences* (*v*) = **old** (*occurrences* (*v*)) + *1*
 ensure then
 item_inserted: *has* (*v*)

fill (*other*: CONTAINER [*G*])
 -- Fill with as many items of *other* as possible.
 -- The representations of *other* and current structure
 -- need not be the same.
 -- (From *COLLECTION*.)
 require
 other_not_void: *other* /= *Void*;
 extendible: *extendible*

force (*v*: **like** *item*)
 -- Add *v* to end.
 -- (From *SEQUENCE*.)
 require
 extendible: *extendible*
 ensure
 new_count: *count* = **old** *count* + *1*;
 item_inserted: *has* (*v*)

put (*v*: **like** *item*)
 -- Replace current item by *v*.
 -- (Synonym for *replace*)
 -- (From *CHAIN*.)
 require
 extendible: *extendible*
 ensure
 same_count: *count* = **old** *count*
 ensure then
 item_inserted: *has* (*v*)

put_i_th (*v*: **like** *item*; *i*: INTEGER)
 -- Put *v* at *i*–th position.
 -- (From *CHAIN*.)
 require
 valid_key: *valid_index* (*i*)
 ensure
 insertion_done: *i_th* (*i*) = *v*

replace (v: G)
-- Replace current item by v.
-- (From *ACTIVE*.)
require
writable: writable
ensure
item_replaced: item = v

feature -- Removal

prune (v: **like** item)
-- Remove the first occurrence of v if any.
-- If no such occurrence go *off*.
-- (From *SEQUENCE*.)
require
prunable: prunable

prune_all (v: **like** item)
-- Remove all occurrences of v; go *off*.
-- (From *SEQUENCE*.)
require
prunable
ensure
no_more_occurrences: **not** has (v)

wipe_out
-- Remove all items.
-- (From *COLLECTION*.)
require
prunable
ensure
wiped_out: empty

feature -- Transformation

swap (i: INTEGER)
-- Exchange item at i–th position with item
-- at cursor position.
-- (From *CHAIN*.)
require
not_off: **not** off;
valid_index: valid_index (i)
ensure
swapped_to_item: item = **old** i_th (i);
swapped_from_item: i_th (i) = **old** item

feature -- Conversion

linear_representation: LINEAR [G]
-- Representation as a linear structure
-- (From *LINEAR*.)

feature -- Duplication

duplicate (n: INTEGER): **like** Current
-- Copy of sub–chain beginning at current position
-- and having min (n, from_here) items,
-- where *from_here* is the number of items
-- at or to the right of current position.
-- (From *CHAIN*.)
require
not_off_unless_after: off **implies** after;
valid_subchain: n >= 0

invariant

before_definition: before = (index = 0);
after_definition: after = (index = count + 1);
non_negative_index: index >= 0;
index_small_enough: index <= count + 1;
off_definition: off = ((index = 0) **or** (index = count + 1));
isfirst_definition: isfirst = ((**not** empty) **and** (index = 1));
islast_definition: islast = ((**not** empty) **and** (index = count));
item_corresponds_to_index: (**not** off) **implies** (item = i_th (index));
writable_constraint: writable **implies** readable;
empty_constraint: empty **implies** (**not** readable) **and** (**not** writable);
not_both: **not** (after **and** before);
empty_property: empty **implies** (after **or** before);
before_constraint: before **implies** off;
after_constraint: after **implies** off;
empty_constraint: empty **implies** off;
empty_definition: empty = (count = 0);
non_negative_count: count >= 0

end

16.5 CLASSES *LINKED_LIST* AND *TWO_WAY_LIST*

The interface of *TWO_WAY_LIST* is the same as that of *LINKED_LIST*. *LINKED_LIST* uses less space, but is much slower if you need to traverse lists both ways.

The interface shown is the flat-short form of *LINKED_LIST*. For convenience, since these classes are of very common use, it includes all the exported features.

indexing

    description: "Sequential, one−way linked lists"
    names: *linked_list*, *sequence*
    representation: *linked*
    access: *index, cursor, membership*
    contents: *generic*

class interface

    LINKED_LIST [G]

creation
    make

feature -- Initialization

    make
        -- Create an empty list.
      ensure
        is_before: *before*

feature -- Access

    cursor: *CURSOR*
        -- Current cursor position

    first: **like** *item*
        -- Item at first position
      require
        not_empty: **not** *empty*

    has (*v*: **like** *item*): *BOOLEAN*
        -- Does chain include *v*?
        -- (Reference or object equality,
        -- based on *object_comparison*.)
        -- (From *CHAIN*.)
      ensure
        not_found_in_empty: *Result* **implies not** *empty*

    i_th (*i*: *INTEGER*): **like** *item*
        -- Item at *i*−th position
        -- (From *CHAIN*.)
      require
        valid_key: *valid_index* (*i*)

    index: *INTEGER*
        -- Index of current position

index_of (*v*: **like** *item*; *i*: *INTEGER*): *INTEGER*
    -- Index of *i*−th occurrence of item identical to *v*.
    -- (Reference or object equality,
    -- based on *object_comparison*.)
    -- 0 if none.
    -- (From *CHAIN*.)
  require
    positive_occurrences: *i* > 0
  ensure
    non_negative_result: *Result* >= 0

item: *G*
    -- Current item
  require
    readable
  require else
    not_off: **not** *off*

last: **like** *item*
    -- Item at last position
  require
    not_empty: **not** *empty*

occurrences (*v*: **like** *item*): *INTEGER*
    -- Number of times *v* appears.
    -- (Reference or object equality,
    -- based on *object_comparison*.)
    -- (From *CHAIN*.)
  ensure
    non_negative_occurrences: *Result* >= 0

sequential_occurrences (*v*: *G*): *INTEGER*
    -- Number of times *v* appears.
    -- (Reference or object equality,
    -- based on *object_comparison*.)
    -- (From *LINEAR*.)
  ensure
    non_negative_occurrences: *Result* >= 0

infix "@" (*i*: *INTEGER*): **like** *item*
    -- Item at *i*−th position
    -- (From *CHAIN*.)
  require
    valid_key: *valid_index* (*i*)

feature -- Measurement

   count: *INTEGER*
      -- Number of items

feature -- Status report

   after: *BOOLEAN*
      -- Is there no valid cursor position to the right of cursor?

   before: *BOOLEAN*
      -- Is there no valid cursor position to the left of cursor?

   changeable_comparison_criterion: *BOOLEAN*
      -- May *object_comparison* be changed?
      -- (Answer: yes by default.)
      -- (From *CONTAINER*.)

   empty: *BOOLEAN*
      -- Is structure empty?
      -- (From *FINITE*.)

   exhausted: *BOOLEAN*
      -- Has structure been completely explored?
      -- (From *LINEAR*.)
   ensure
      exhausted_when_off: *off* **implies** *Result*

   extendible: *BOOLEAN* **is true**
      -- May new items be added? (Answer: yes.)
      -- (From *DYNAMIC_CHAIN*.)

   full: *BOOLEAN* **is false**
      -- Is structured filled to capacity? (Answer: no.)

   isfirst: *BOOLEAN*
      -- Is cursor at first position?
   ensure
      valid_position: *Result* **implies not** *empty*

   islast: *BOOLEAN*
      -- Is cursor at last position?
   ensure
      valid_position: *Result* **implies not** *empty*

   object_comparison: *BOOLEAN*
      -- Must search operations use *equal* rather than =
      -- for comparing references? (Default: no, use =.)
      -- (From *CONTAINER*.)

   off: *BOOLEAN*
      -- Is there no current item?

   prunable: *BOOLEAN*
      -- May items be removed? (Answer: yes.)
      -- (From *DYNAMIC_CHAIN*.)

   readable: *BOOLEAN*
      -- Is there a current item that may be read?

   valid_cursor (*p*: *CURSOR*): *BOOLEAN*
      -- Can the cursor be moved to position *p*?

   valid_cursor_index (*i*: *INTEGER*): *BOOLEAN*
      -- Is *i* correctly bounded for cursor movement?
      -- (From *CHAIN*.)
   ensure
      valid_cursor_index_definition: *Result* = (($i >= 0$) **and** ($i <= count + 1$))

   valid_index (*i*: *INTEGER*): *BOOLEAN*
      -- Is *i* within allowable bounds?
      -- (From *CHAIN*.)
   ensure
      valid_index_definition: *Result* = ($i >= 1$) **and** ($i <= count$)

   writable: *BOOLEAN*
      -- Is there a current item that may be modified?
      -- (From *SEQUENCE*.)

feature -- Status setting

   compare_objects
      -- Ensure that future search operations will use *equal*
      -- rather than = for comparing references.
      -- (From *CONTAINER*.)
   require
      changeable_comparison_criterion
   ensure
      object_comparison

   compare_references
      -- Ensure that future search operations will use =
      -- rather than *equal* for comparing references.
      -- (From *CONTAINER*.)
   require
      changeable_comparison_criterion
   ensure
      reference_comparison: **not** *object_comparison*

feature -- Cursor movement

   back
      -- Move to previous item.
   require
      not_before: **not** *before*
   ensure
      moved_back: *index* = **old** *index* − *1*

   finish
      -- Move cursor to last position.
      -- (Go before if empty)
   ensure
      empty_convention: *empty* **implies** *before*
   ensure then
      at_last: **not** *empty* **implies** *islast*

forth
    -- Move cursor to next position.
    require
      not_after: **not** *after*
    ensure
      moved_forth: *index* = **old** *index* + *1*

go_i_th (*i*: *INTEGER*)
    -- Move cursor to *i*–th position.
    require
      valid_cursor_index: *valid_cursor_index* (*i*)
    ensure
      position_expected: *index* = *i*

go_to (*p*: *CURSOR*)
    -- Move cursor to position *p*.
    require
      cursor_position_valid: *valid_cursor* (*p*)

move (*i*: *INTEGER*)
    -- Move cursor *i* positions. The cursor
    -- may end up *off* if the offset is too big.
    ensure
      moved_if_inbounds: ((**old** *index* + *i*) >= *0* **and** (**old** *index*
        + *i*) <= (*count* + *1*)) **implies** *index* = (**old** *index* + *i*);
      before_set: (**old** *index* + *i*) <= *0* **implies** *before*;
      after_set: (**old** *index* + *i*) >= (*count* + *1*) **implies** *after*
    ensure then
      too_far_right: (**old** *index* + *i* > *count*) **implies** *exhausted*;
      too_far_left: (**old** *index* + *i* < *1*) **implies** *exhausted*;
      expected_index: (**not** *exhausted*) **implies** (*index* = **old**
        index + *i*)

search (*v*: **like** *item*)
    -- Move to first position (at or after current
    -- position) where *item* and *v* are equal.
    -- If structure does not include *v* ensure that
    -- *exhausted* will be true.
    -- (Reference or object equality,
    -- based on *object_comparison*.)
    -- (From *BILINEAR*.)
    ensure
      object_found: (**not** *exhausted* **and** **then** *object_*
        comparison **and** **then** *v* /= *Void* **and** **then** *item* /=
        Void) **implies** *v*. *is_equal* (*item*);
      item_found: (**not** *exhausted* **and not** *object_comparison*)
        implies *v* = *item*

start
    -- Move cursor to first position.
    ensure
      empty_convention: *empty* **implies** *after*
    ensure then
      at_first: **not** *empty* **implies** *isfirst*

feature -- Element change

append (*s*: *SEQUENCE* [*G*])
    -- Append a copy of *s*.
    -- (From *SEQUENCE*.)
    require
      argument_not_void: *s* /= *Void*
    ensure
      new_count: *count* >= **old** *count*

extend (*v*: **like** *item*)
    -- Add *v* to end.
    -- Do not move cursor.
    require
      extendible: *extendible*
    ensure
      one_more_occurrence: *occurrences* (*v*) = **old**
        (*occurrences* (*v*)) + *1*
    ensure then
      item_inserted: *has* (*v*)

fill (*other*: *CONTAINER* [*G*])
    -- Fill with as many items of *other* as possible.
    -- The representations of *other* and current structure
    -- need not be the same.
    -- (From *COLLECTION*.)
    require
      other_not_void: *other* /= *Void*;
      extendible: *extendible*

force (*v*: **like** *item*)
    -- Add *v* to end.
    -- (From *SEQUENCE*.)
    require
      extendible: *extendible*
    ensure
      new_count: *count* = **old** *count* + *1*;
      item_inserted: *has* (*v*)

merge_left (*other*: **like** *Current*)
    -- Merge *other* into current structure before cursor
    -- position. Do not move cursor. Empty *other*.
    require
      extendible: *extendible*;
      not_off: **not** *before*;
      other_exists: *other* /= *Void*
    ensure
      new_count: *count* = **old** *count* + **old** *other*. *count*;
      new_index: *index* = **old** *index* + **old** *other*. *count*;
      other_is_empty: *other*. *empty*

merge_right (*other*: **like** *Current*)
    -- Merge *other* into current structure after cursor
    -- position. Do not move cursor. Empty *other*.
  require
    extendible: *extendible*;
    not_off: **not** *after*;
    other_exists: *other* /= *Void*
  ensure
    new_count: *count* = **old** *count* + **old** *other.count*;
    same_index: *index* = **old** *index*;
    other_is_empty: *other.empty*

put (*v*: **like** *item*)
    -- Replace current item by *v*.
    -- (Synonym for *replace*)
    -- (From *CHAIN*.)
  require
    extendible: *extendible*
  ensure
    same_count: *count* = **old** *count*
  ensure then
    item_inserted: *has* (*v*)

put_front (*v*: **like** *item*)
    -- Add *v* to beginning.
    -- Do not move cursor.
  ensure
    new_count: *count* = **old** *count* + *1*;
    item_inserted: *first* = *v*

put_i_th (*v*: **like** *item*; *i*: *INTEGER*)
    -- Put *v* at *i*-th position.
    -- (From *CHAIN*.)
  require
    valid_key: *valid_index* (*i*)
  ensure
    insertion_done: *i_th* (*i*) = *v*

put_left (*v*: **like** *item*)
    -- Add *v* to the left of cursor position.
    -- Do not move cursor.
  require
    extendible: *extendible*;
    not_before: **not** *before*
  ensure
    new_count: *count* = **old** *count* + *1*;
    new_index: *index* = **old** *index* + *1*

put_right (*v*: **like** *item*)
    -- Add *v* to the right of cursor position.
    -- Do not move cursor.
  require
    extendible: *extendible*;
    not_after: **not** *after*
  ensure
    new_count: *count* = **old** *count* + *1*;
    same_index: *index* = **old** *index*

replace (*v*: **like** *item*)
    -- Replace current item by *v*.
  require
    writable: *writable*
  ensure
    item_replaced: *item* = *v*

feature -- Removal

prune (*v*: **like** *item*)
    -- Remove first occurrence of *v*, if any,
    -- after cursor position.
    -- If found, move cursor to right neighbor;
    -- if not, make structure *exhausted*.
    -- (From *DYNAMIC_CHAIN*.)
  require
    prunable: *prunable*

prune_all (*v*: **like** *item*)
    -- Remove all occurrences of *v*.
    -- (Reference or object equality,
    -- based on *object_comparison*.)
    -- Leave structure *exhausted*.
    -- (From *DYNAMIC_CHAIN*.)
  require
    prunable
  ensure
    is_exhausted: *exhausted*
  ensure then
    no_more_occurrences: **not** *has* (*v*)

remove
    -- Remove current item.
    -- Move cursor to right neighbor
    -- (or *after* if no right neighbor).
  require
    prunable;
    writable
  ensure
    after_when_empty: *empty* **implies** *after*

remove_left
    -- Remove item to the left of cursor position.
    -- Do not move cursor.
  require
    not_before: **not** *before*
  require else
    left_exists: *index* > *1*
  ensure
    new_count: *count* = **old** *count* − *1*;
    new_index: *index* = **old** *index* − *1*

remove_right
    -- Remove item to the right of cursor position.
    -- Do not move cursor.
  require
    right_exists: *index* < *count*
  ensure
    new_count: *count* = **old** *count* − *1*;
    same_index: *index* = **old** *index*

wipe_out
    -- Remove all items.
  require
    prunable
  ensure
    is_before: *before*
  ensure then
    wiped_out: *empty*

feature -- Transformation

swap (*i*: *INTEGER*)
    -- Exchange item at *i*–th position with item
    -- at cursor position.
    -- (From *CHAIN*.)
  require
    not_off: **not** *off*;
    valid_index: *valid_index* (*i*)
  ensure
    swapped_to_item: *item* = **old** *i_th* (*i*);
    swapped_from_item: *i_th* (*i*) = **old** *item*

feature -- Conversion

linear_representation: *LINEAR* [*G*]
    -- Representation as a linear structure
    -- (From *LINEAR*.)

feature -- Duplication

duplicate (*n*: *INTEGER*): **like** *Current*
    -- Copy of sub–chain beginning at current position
    -- and having min (*n*, *from_here*) items,
    -- where *from_here* is the number of items
    -- at or to the right of current position.
    -- (From *DYNAMIC_CHAIN*.)
  require
    not_off_unless_after: *off* **implies** *after*;
    valid_subchain: *n* >= *0*

invariant

  before_definition: *before* = (*index* = *0*);
  after_definition: *after* = (*index* = *count* + *1*);
  non_negative_index: *index* >= *0*;
  index_small_enough: *index* <= *count* + *1*;
  off_definition: *off* = ((*index* = *0*) **or** (*index* = *count* + *1*));
  isfirst_definition: *isfirst* = ((**not** *empty*) **and** (*index* = *1*));
  islast_definition: *islast* = ((**not** *empty*) **and** (*index* = *count*));
  item_corresponds_to_index: (**not** *off*) **implies** (*item* = *i_th*
    (*index*));

writable_constraint: *writable* **implies** *readable*;
empty_constraint: *empty* **implies** (**not** *readable*) **and** (**not**
  writable);
not_both: **not** (*after* **and** *before*);
empty_property: *empty* **implies** (*after* **or** *before*);
before_constraint: *before* **implies** *off*;
after_constraint: *after* **implies** *off*;
empty_constraint: *empty* **implies** *off*;
empty_definition: *empty* = (*count* = *0*);
non_negative_count: *count* >= *0*;
extendible: *extendible*;
prunable: *prunable*

end

16.6 CLASS *ARRAYED_LIST*

This interface only shows the features introduced or redeclared in the class itself, excluding any feature kept unchanged from the ancestors. *ARRAYED_LIST* keeps all the exported features of *LIST*; please refer to the interface of *LIST* for details.

The interface of LIST is in 16.4, page 295.

indexing

> *description*: "*Lists implemented by resizable arrays*"
> *names*: *sequence*
> *representation*: *array*
> *access*: *index*, *cursor*, *membership*
> *size*: *fixed*
> *contents*: *generic*

class interface

> *ARRAYED_LIST* [*G*]

creation
> *make*

feature -- Initialization

> *make* (*n*: *INTEGER*)
>   -- Allocate list with *n* items.
>   -- (*n* may be zero for empty list.)
>   **require**
>   *valid_number_of_items*: $n >= 0$

feature -- Access

> *cursor*: *CURSOR*
>   -- Current cursor position

> *first*: *G*
>   -- Item at first position
>   **require**
>   *not_empty*: **not** *empty*

> *index*: *INTEGER*
>   -- Index of *item*, if valid.

> *item*: **like** *first*
>   -- Current item
>   **require**
>   *index_is_valid*: *valid_index* (*index*)
>   **require else**
>   *readable*
>   **require else**
>   *not_off*: **not** *off*

> *last*: **like** *first*
>   -- Item at last position
>   **require**
>   *not_empty*: **not** *empty*

feature -- Measurement

> *count*: *INTEGER*
>   -- Number of items.

feature -- Status report

> *full*: *BOOLEAN*
>   -- Is structure filled to capacity? (Answer: no.)

> *prunable*: *BOOLEAN*
>   -- May items be removed? (Answer: yes.)

> *valid_cursor* (*p*: *CURSOR*): *BOOLEAN*
>   -- Can the cursor be moved to position *p*?

feature -- Cursor movement

> *back*
>   -- Move cursor one position backward.
>   **require**
>   *not_before*: **not** *before*
>   **ensure**
>   *moved_back*: *index* = **old** *index* − *1*

> *finish*
>   -- Move cursor to last position if any.

> *forth*
>   -- Move cursor one position forward.
>   **require**
>   *not_after*: **not** *after*
>   **ensure**
>   *moved_forth*: *index* = **old** *index* + *1*

> *go_i_th* (*i*: *INTEGER*)
>   -- Move cursor to *i*−th position.
>   **require**
>   *valid_cursor_index*: *valid_cursor_index* (*i*)
>   **ensure**
>   *position_expected*: *index* = *i*

> *go_to* (*p*: *CURSOR*)
>   -- Move cursor to position *p*.
>   **require**
>   *cursor_position_valid*: *valid_cursor* (*p*)

> *move* (*i*: *INTEGER*)
>   -- Move cursor *i* positions.

> *start*
>   -- Move cursor to first position if any.

feature -- Element change

extend (v: **like** item)
-- Add v to end.
-- Do not move cursor.
require
extendible : extendible

force (v: **like** item)
-- Add v to end.
-- Do not move cursor.
require
extendible : extendible
ensure
new_count: count = **old** count + 1;

merge_left (other: ARRAYED_LIST [G])
require
extendible: extendible;
not_off : **not** before;
other_exists: other /= Void
ensure
new_count: count = **old** count + **old** other.count;
new_index: index = **old** index + **old** other.count;

merge_right (other: ARRAYED_LIST [G])
require
extendible: extendible;
not_off : **not** after;
other_exists: other /= Void
ensure
new_count: count = **old** count + **old** other.count;
same_index: index = **old** index;

put_front (v: **like** item)
-- Add v to the beginning.
-- Do not move cursor.
ensure
new_count: count = **old** count + 1;
item_inserted: first = v

put_left (v: **like** item)
-- Add v to the left of current position.
-- Do not move cursor.
require
extendible: extendible;
not_before: **not** before
ensure
new_count: count = **old** count + 1;
new_index: index = **old** index + 1

put_right (v: **like** item)
-- Add v to the right of current position.
-- Do not move cursor.
require
extendible: extendible;
not_after: **not** after
ensure
new_count: count = **old** count + 1;
same_index: index = **old** index

replace (v: **like** first)
-- Replace current item by v.
require
writable: writable
ensure
item_replaced: item = v

feature -- Removal

prune (v: **like** item)
-- Remove first occurrence of v, if any,
-- after cursor position.
-- Move cursor to right neighbor
-- (or after if no right neighbor or v does not occur)
require
prunable: prunable

prune_all (v: **like** item)
-- Remove all occurrences of v.
-- (Reference or object equality,
-- based on object_comparison.)
-- Leave cursor after.
require
prunable

remove
-- Remove current item.
-- Move cursor to right neighbor
-- (or after if no right neighbor)
require
prunable;
writable

remove_left
-- Remove item to the left of cursor position.
-- Do not move cursor.
require
not_before: **not** before
require else
left_exists: index > 1
ensure
new_count: count = **old** count − 1;
new_index: index = **old** index − 1

remove_right
    -- Remove item to the right of cursor position
    -- Do not move cursor
  require
    right_exists: *index* < *count*
  ensure
    new_count: *count* = **old** *count* − *1*;
    same_index: *index* = **old** *index*

wipe_out
    -- Remove all items.
  require
    prunable

feature -- Transformation

swap (*i*: *INTEGER*)
    -- Exchange item at *i*–th position with item
    -- at cursor position.
  require
    not_off: **not** *off*;
    valid_index: *valid_index* (*i*)

feature -- Duplication

copy (*other*: **like** *Current*)

duplicate (*n*: *INTEGER*): **like** *Current*
    -- Copy of sub–list beginning at current position
    -- and having min (*n*, *count* − *index* + 1) items.
  require
    not_off_unless_after: *off* **implies** *after*;
    valid_subchain: *n* >= *0*

setup (*other*: **like** *Current*)
    -- Prepare current object so that *other*
    -- can be easily copied into it.
    -- It is not necessary to call *setup*
    -- (since *consistent* is always true)
    -- but it will make copying quicker.

invariant

  not_full: **not** *full*;
  prunable: *prunable*;
  non_negative_count: *count* >= *0*;
  non_negative_index: *index* >= *0*;
  index_small_enough: *index* <= *count* + *1*;
  extendible: *extendible*

end

16.7 CLASS *MULTI_ARRAY_LIST*

This interface only shows the features introduced or redeclared in the class itself, excluding any feature kept unchanged from the ancestors. *MULTI_ARRAY_LIST* keeps all the exported features of *LIST*; please refer to the interface of *LIST* for details.

The interface of LIST is in 16.4, page 295.

indexing

    description: *"Lists implemented as sequences of arrays, the last of which may be non–full. No limit on size (a new array is allocated if list outgrows its initial allocation)."*
    names: *list, sequence*
    representation: *array, linked*
    access: *index, cursor, membership*
    contents: *generic*

class interface

    MULTI_ARRAY_LIST [G]

creation
    make

feature -- Initialization

    make (*b*: *INTEGER*)
        -- Create an empty list, setting block_size to b

feature -- Access

    block_size: *INTEGER*

    cursor: *CURSOR*
        -- Current cursor position

    first: **like** *item*
        -- Item at first position
      require
        not_empty: **not** *empty*

    first_element: *BI_LINKABLE* [*ARRAYED_LIST* [G]]
        -- First array_sequence element of the list

    has (*v*: **like** *item*): *BOOLEAN*
        -- Does list include *v*?
        -- (Reference or object equality,
        -- based on *object_comparison*.)

    index: *INTEGER*
        -- Current cursor index

    item: *G*
        -- Item at cursor position
      require
        readable
      require else
        not_off: **not** *off*

    last: **like** *item*
        -- Item at last position
      require
        not_empty: **not** *empty*

    last_element: *BI_LINKABLE* [*ARRAYED_LIST* [G]]
        -- Last array_sequence element of the list

feature -- Measurement

    count: *INTEGER*
        -- Number of items

feature -- Status report

    full: *BOOLEAN*

    valid_cursor (*p*: *CURSOR*): *BOOLEAN*
        -- Can the cursor be moved to position *p*?

feature -- Cursor movement

    back
        -- Move cursor to previous position, if any.
      require
        not_before: **not** *before*
      ensure
        moved_back: *index* = **old** *index* − *1*

    finish
        -- Move cursor to last position.
        -- (No effect if empty)

    forth
        -- Move cursor to next position, if any.
      require
        not_after: **not** *after*
      ensure
        moved_forth: *index* = **old** *index* + *1*

    go_to (*p*: *CURSOR*)
        -- Move cursor to position *p*
      require
        cursor_position_valid: *valid_cursor* (*p*)

    move (*i*: *INTEGER*)
        -- Move cursor *i* positions. The cursor
        -- may end up *off* if the offset is too big.

    search (*v*: **like** *item*)
        -- Move cursor to first position (at or after current
        -- cursor position) where *item* and *v* are equal.
        -- (Reference or object equality,
        -- based on *object_comparison*.)

    start
        -- Move cursor to first position.
        -- (No effect if empty)

feature -- Element change

extend (*v*: **like** *item*)
-- Add *v* to end.
require
extendible: *extendible*
ensure
item_inserted: *has* (*v*)

put_front (*v*: **like** *item*)
-- Add *v* at the beginning.
-- Do not move cursor.
ensure
new_count: *count* = **old** *count* + *1*;
item_inserted: *first* = *v*

put_left (*v*: **like** *item*)
-- Add *v* to the left of current position.
-- Do not move cursor.
require
extendible: *extendible*;
not_before: **not** *before*
ensure
new_count: *count* = **old** *count* + *1*;
new_index: *index* = **old** *index* + *1*

put_right (*v*: **like** *item*)
-- Add *v* to the left of current position.
-- Do not move cursor.
require
extendible: *extendible*;
not_after: **not** *after*
ensure
new_count: *count* = **old** *count* + *1*;
same_index: *index* = **old** *index*

replace (*v*: **like** *item*)
-- Replace current item by *v*.
require
writable: *writable*
ensure
item_replaced: *item* = *v*

feature -- Removal

prune_all (*v*: **like** *item*)
require
prunable
ensure
no_more_occurrences: **not** *has* (*v*)
ensure then

remove
-- Remove current item
require
prunable;
writable

remove_left
require
not_before: **not** *before*
require else
left_exists: *index* > *1*
ensure
new_count: *count* = **old** *count* − *1*;
new_index: *index* = **old** *index* − *1*

remove_right
require
right_exists: *index* < *count*
ensure
new_count: *count* = **old** *count* − *1*;
same_index: *index* = **old** *index*

wipe_out
-- Remove all items.
require
prunable

feature -- Duplication

duplicate (*n*: *INTEGER*): **like** *Current*
-- Copy of sub−list beginning at cursor position
-- and having min (*n*, *count* − *index* + 1) items
require
not_off_unless_after: *off* **implies** *after*;
valid_subchain: *n* >= *0*

invariant

extendible_definition: *extendible*;
non_negative_index: *index* >= *0*;
index_small_enough: *index* <= *count* + *1*;
non_negative_count: *count* >= *0*;
extendible: *extendible*

end

16.8 CLASS *FIXED_LIST*

This interface shows the features introduced or redeclared in the class itself, and those coming from the class itself, but no feature obtained unchanged from any other ancestor.

indexing

    description: "*Lists with fixed numbers of items, implemented by arrays*"
    names: *fixed, sequence*
    representation: *array*
    access: *index, cursor, membership*
    contents: *generic*

class interface

    FIXED_LIST [*G*]

creation
    make

feature -- Initialization

    make (*n*: *INTEGER*)
      -- Create an empty list.

feature -- Access

    cursor: *CURSOR*
      -- Current cursor position

    first: *G*
      -- Item at first position
    require
      not_empty: **not** *empty*

    index: *INTEGER*
      -- Current position in the list

    item: *G*
      -- Current item
    require
      readable
    require else
      not_off: **not** *off*

    last: **like** *first*
      -- Item at last position
    require
      not_empty: **not** *empty*

feature -- Status report

    extendible: *BOOLEAN* **is false**

    valid_cursor (*p*: *CURSOR*): *BOOLEAN*
      -- Is *p* a valid cursor?

feature -- Cursor movement

    back
      -- Move cursor to previous position, if any.
    require
      not_before: **not** *before*
    ensure
      moved_back: *index* = **old** *index* − *1*

    finish
      -- Move cursor to last position.

    forth
      -- Move cursor to next position, if any.
    require
      not_after: **not** *after*
    ensure
      moved_forth: *index* = **old** *index* + *1*

    go_i_th (*i*: *INTEGER*)
      -- Move cursor to *i*−th position.
    require
      valid_cursor_index: *valid_cursor_index* (*i*)
    ensure
      position_expected: *index* = *i*

    go_to (*p*: *CURSOR*)
      -- Move cursor to element remembered in *p*.
    require
      cursor_position_valid: *valid_cursor* (*p*)

    move (*i*: *INTEGER*)
      -- Move cursor *i* positions.

    start
      -- Move cursor to first position.

feature -- Element change

    replace (*v*: **like** *first*)
      -- Replace current item by *v*.
    require
      writable: *writable*
    ensure
      item_replaced: *item* = *v*

feature -- Transformation

    swap (*i*: *INTEGER*)
      -- Exchange item at *i*−th position with item
      -- at cursor position.
    require
      not_off: **not** *off*;
      valid_index: *valid_index* (*i*)

feature -- Duplication

 duplicate (*n*: *INTEGER*): **like** *Current*
  -- Copy of sub–list beginning at cursor position
  -- and having min (*n*, *count* − *index* + 1) items
  require
   not_off_unless_after: *off* **implies** *after*;
   valid_subchain: *n* >= *0*

invariant

 non_negative_index: *index* >= *0*;
 not_resizable: **not** *resizable*

end

16.9 CLASS *PART_SORTED_LIST*

This interface only shows the features introduced or redeclared in the class itself, excluding any feature kept unchanged from the ancestors. *PART_SORTED_LIST* keeps all the exported features of *LIST*; please refer to the interface of *LIST* for details.

The interface of LIST is in 16.4, page 295.

indexing

> *description*: "Sequential lists whose items are sorted in
>   *ascending order according to the relational operators of*
>   *PART_COMPARABLE*"
> *names*: *sorted_list*, *sorted_struct*, *sequence*
> *access*: *index*, *cursor*, *membership*, *min*, *max*
> *contents*: *generic*

deferred class interface

> *PART_SORTED_LIST* [*G* –> *PART_COMPARABLE*]

feature -- Access

> *has* (*v*: *G*): *BOOLEAN*
>> -- Does structure include *v*?
>> -- (Reference or object equality,
>> -- based on *object_comparison*.)
>
> *search_after* (*v*: **like** *item*)
>> -- Go to first position with item greater
>> -- than or equal to *v*.
>
> *search_before* (*v*: **like** *item*)
>> -- Go to last position with item less
>> -- than or equal to *v*.

feature -- Status report

> *sorted*: *BOOLEAN*

feature -- Element change

> *extend* (*v*: **like** *item*)
>> -- Put *v* at proper position in list.
>> -- The cursor ends up on the newly inserted
>> -- item.
>
> **require**
>> *extendible*: *extendible*
>
> **ensure**
>> *remains_sorted*: (**old** *sorted*) **implies** *sorted*;
>
> **ensure then**
>> *item_inserted*: *has* (*v*)
>
> *merge* (*other*: *LINEAR* [*G*])
>> -- Add all items from *other* at their proper positions.
>
> **ensure**
>> *remains_sorted*: (**old** *sorted*) **implies** *sorted*

end

16.10 CLASSES *SORTED_LIST* AND *SORTED_TWO_WAY_LIST*

The interface of *SORTED_TWO_WAY_LIST* as it appears below only shows the features introduced or redeclared in the class itself, excluding any feature obtained unchanged from any ancestor. In addition, the *SORTED_TWO_WAY_LIST* exports all the features of *TWO_WAY_LIST*; please refer to the specification of that class for details.

The interface of TWO_ WAY_LIST is in 16.5, page 299.

This partial interface also serves for *SORTED_LIST*, excluding all features that this class inherits from its parent *LIST* and other ancestors. *SORTED_LIST*, which is deferred, retains all the exported features of *LIST*. Please refer to *LIST* for details.

The interface of LIST is in 16.4, page 295.

indexing

    description: "*Two−way lists, kept sorted.*"
    names: *sorted_two_way_list, sorted_struct, sequence*
    representation: *linked*
    access: *index, cursor, membership, min, max*
    contents: *generic*

class interface

    SORTED_TWO_WAY_LIST [*G −> COMPARABLE*]

creation
    make

feature -- Initialization

    make
        -- Create an empty list.
        -- (From *LINKED_LIST*.)
      ensure
        is_before: *before*

feature -- Access

    cursor: *CURSOR*
        -- Current cursor position
        -- (From *LINKED_LIST*.)

    first: **like** *item*
        -- Item at first position
        -- (From *LINKED_LIST*.)
      require
        not_empty: **not** *empty*

    first_element: *BI_LINKABLE* [*G*]
        -- Head of list
        -- (Anchor redefinition)
        -- (From *TWO_WAY_LIST*.)

    has (*v*: *G*): *BOOLEAN*
        -- Does structure include *v*?
        -- (Reference or object equality,
        -- based on *object_comparison*.)
        -- (From *PART_SORTED_LIST*.)
      ensure
        not_found_in_empty: *Result* **implies not** *empty*

    i_th (*i*: *INTEGER*): **like** *item*
        -- Item at *i*−th position
        -- (From *CHAIN*.)
      require
        valid_key: *valid_index* (*i*)

    index: *INTEGER*
        -- Index of current position
        -- (From *LINKED_LIST*.)

    index_of (*v*: **like** *item*; *i*: *INTEGER*): *INTEGER*
        -- Index of *i*−th occurrence of item identical to *v*.
        -- (Reference or object equality,
        -- based on *object_comparison*.)
        -- 0 if none.
        -- (From *CHAIN*.)
      require
        positive_occurrences: *i > 0*
      ensure
        non_negative_result: *Result >= 0*

    item: *G*
        -- Current item
        -- (From *LINKED_LIST*.)
      require
        readable
      require else
        not_off: **not** *off*

    last: **like** *item*
        -- Item at last position
        -- (From *LINKED_LIST*.)
      require
        not_empty: **not** *empty*

    last_element: **like** *first_element*
        -- Tail of the list
        -- (From *TWO_WAY_LIST*.)

occurrences (*v*: **like** *item*): *INTEGER*
    -- Number of times *v* appears.
    -- (Reference or object equality,
    -- based on *object_comparison*.)
    -- (From *CHAIN*.)
   ensure
    non_negative_occurrences: *Result* >= 0

search_after (*v*: **like** *item*)
    -- Go to first position with item greater
    -- than or equal to *v*.
    -- (From *PART_SORTED_LIST*.)
   ensure
    argument_less_than_item: (**not** *after*) **implies** (*v* <=
      item)

search_before (*v*: **like** *item*)
    -- Go to last position with item less
    -- than or equal to *v*.
    -- (From *PART_SORTED_LIST*.)

sequential_occurrences (*v*: *G*): *INTEGER*
    -- Number of times *v* appears.
    -- (Reference or object equality,
    -- based on *object_comparison*.)
    -- (From *LINEAR*.)
   ensure
    non_negative_occurrences: *Result* >= 0

sublist: **like** *Current*
    -- Result produced by last *split*
    -- (From *TWO_WAY_LIST*.)

infix *"@"* (*i*: *INTEGER*): **like** *item*
    -- Item at *i*-th position
    -- (From *CHAIN*.)
   require
    valid_key: *valid_index* (*i*)

feature -- Measurement

count: *INTEGER*
    -- Number of items
    -- (From *LINKED_LIST*.)

max: **like** *item*
    -- Maximum item
    -- (From *SORTED_LIST*.)
   ensure
    max_is_last: *Result* = *last*
    -- *largest*: For every item *it*, *it* <= *Result*

median: **like** *item*
    -- Median element
    -- (From *SORTED_LIST*.) **ensure**
    median_definition: *Result* = *i_th* ((*count* + 1) // 2)

min: **like** *item*
    -- Minimum item
    -- (From *SORTED_LIST*.)
   ensure
    min_is_first: *Result* = *first*
    -- *largest*: For every item *it*, *Result* <= *it*

feature -- Status report

after: *BOOLEAN*
    -- Is there no valid cursor position to the right of cursor?
    -- (From *LINKED_LIST*.)

before: *BOOLEAN*
    -- Is there no valid cursor position to the left of cursor?
    -- (From *LINKED_LIST*.)

changeable_comparison_criterion: *BOOLEAN*
    -- May *object_comparison* be changed?
    -- (Answer: yes by default.)
    -- (From *CONTAINER*.)

empty: *BOOLEAN*
    -- Is structure empty?
    -- (From *FINITE*.)

exhausted: *BOOLEAN*
    -- Has structure been completely explored?
    -- (From *LINEAR*.)
   ensure
    exhausted_when_off: *off* **implies** *Result*

extendible: *BOOLEAN* **is true**
    -- May new items be added? (Answer: yes.)
    -- (From *DYNAMIC_CHAIN*.)

full: *BOOLEAN* **is false**
    -- Is structured filled to capacity? (Answer: no.)
    -- (From *LINKED_LIST*.)

isfirst: *BOOLEAN*
    -- Is cursor at first position?
    -- (From *LINKED_LIST*.)
   ensure
    valid_position: *Result* **implies not** *empty*

islast: *BOOLEAN*
    -- Is cursor at last position?
    -- (From *TWO_WAY_LIST*.)
   ensure
    valid_position: *Result* **implies not** *empty*

object_comparison: *BOOLEAN*
    -- Must search operations use *equal* rather than =
    -- for comparing references? (Default: no, use =.)
    -- (From *CONTAINER*.)

off: *BOOLEAN*
    -- Is there no current item?
    -- (From *LINKED_LIST*.)

prunable: *BOOLEAN*
--- -- May items be removed? (Answer: yes.)
--- -- (From *DYNAMIC_CHAIN*.)

readable: *BOOLEAN*
--- -- Is there a current item that may be read?
--- -- (From *LINKED_LIST*.)

sorted: *BOOLEAN*
--- -- Is the structure sorted?

valid_cursor (*p*: *CURSOR*): *BOOLEAN*
--- -- Can the cursor be moved to position *p*?
--- -- (From *LINKED_LIST*.)

valid_cursor_index (*i*: *INTEGER*): *BOOLEAN*
--- -- Is *i* correctly bounded for cursor movement?
--- -- (From *CHAIN*.)
--- **ensure**
--- --- *valid_cursor_index_definition*: *Result* = ((*i* >= *0*) **and** (*i* <= *count* + *1*))

valid_index (*i*: *INTEGER*): *BOOLEAN*
--- -- Is *i* within allowable bounds?
--- -- (From *CHAIN*.)
--- **ensure**
--- --- *valid_index_definition*: *Result* = (*i* >= *1*) **and** (*i* <= *count*)

writable: *BOOLEAN*
--- -- Is there a current item that may be modified?
--- -- (From *SEQUENCE*.)

feature -- Status setting

compare_objects
--- -- Ensure that future search operations will use *equal*
--- -- rather than = for comparing references.
--- -- (From *CONTAINER*.)
--- **require**
--- --- *changeable_comparison_criterion*
--- **ensure**
--- --- *object_comparison*

compare_references
--- -- Ensure that future search operations will use =
--- -- rather than *equal* for comparing references.
--- -- (From *CONTAINER*.)
--- **require**
--- --- *changeable_comparison_criterion*
--- **ensure**
--- --- *reference_comparison*: **not** *object_comparison*

feature -- Cursor movement

back
--- -- Move cursor to previous position, if any.
--- -- (From *TWO_WAY_LIST*.)
--- **require**
--- --- *not_before*: **not** *before*
--- **ensure**
--- --- *moved_back*: *index* = **old** *index* − *1*

finish
--- -- Move cursor to last position.
--- -- (Go before if empty)
--- -- (From *TWO_WAY_LIST*.)
--- **ensure**
--- --- *not_after*: **not** *after*
--- **ensure then**
--- --- *empty_convention*: *empty* **implies** *before*
--- **ensure then**
--- --- *at_last*: **not** *empty* **implies** *islast*

forth
--- -- Move cursor to next position, if any.
--- -- (From *TWO_WAY_LIST*.)
--- **require**
--- --- *not_after*: **not** *after*
--- **ensure**
--- --- *moved_forth*: *index* = **old** *index* + *1*

go_i_th (*i*: *INTEGER*)
--- -- Move cursor to *i*–th position.
--- -- (From *LINKED_LIST*.)
--- **require**
--- --- *valid_cursor_index*: *valid_cursor_index* (*i*)
--- **ensure**
--- --- *position_expected*: *index* = *i*

go_to (*p*: *CURSOR*)
--- -- Move cursor to position *p*.
--- -- (From *LINKED_LIST*.)
--- **require**
--- --- *cursor_position_valid*: *valid_cursor* (*p*)

move (*i*: *INTEGER*)
--- -- Move cursor *i* positions. The cursor
--- -- may end up *off* if the offset is to big.
--- -- (From *TWO_WAY_LIST*.)
--- **ensure**
--- --- *moved_if_inbounds*: ((**old** *index* + *i*) >= *0* **and** (**old** *index* + *i*) <= (*count* + *1*)) **implies** *index* = (**old** *index* + *i*);
--- --- *before_set*: (**old** *index* + *i*) <= *0* **implies** *before*;
--- --- *after_set*: (**old** *index* + *i*) >= (*count* + *1*) **implies** *after*
--- **ensure then**
--- --- *too_far_right*: (**old** *index* + *i* > *count*) **implies** *exhausted*;
--- --- *too_far_left*: (**old** *index* + *i* < *1*) **implies** *exhausted*;
--- --- *expected_index*: (**not** *exhausted*) **implies** (*index* = **old** *index* + *i*)

search (*v*: **like** *item*)
    -- Move to first position (at or after current
    -- position) where *item* and *v* are equal.
    -- If structure does not include *v* ensure that
    -- *exhausted* will be true.
    -- (Reference or object equality,
    -- based on *object_comparison*.)
    -- (From *BILINEAR*.)
  ensure
    object_found: (**not** *exhausted* **and then** *object_*
      comparison **and then** *v* /= *Void* **and then** *item* /=
      Void) **implies** *v.is_equal* (*item*);
    item_found: (**not** *exhausted* **and not** *object_comparison*)
      implies *v* = *item*

start
    -- Move cursor to first position.
    -- (From *LINKED_LIST*.)
  ensure
    empty_convention: *empty* **implies** *after*
  ensure then
    at_first: **not** *empty* **implies** *isfirst*

feature -- Element change

append (*s*: *SEQUENCE* [*G*])
    -- Append a copy of *s*.
    -- (From *SEQUENCE*.)
  require
    argument_not_void: *s* /= *Void*
  ensure
    new_count: *count* >= **old** *count*

extend (*v*: **like** *item*)
    -- Put *v* at proper position in list.
    -- Move cursor to newly inserted item.
  require
    extendible: *extendible*
  ensure
    one_more_occurrence: *occurrences* (*v*) = **old**
      (*occurrences* (*v*)) + *1*
  ensure then
    item_inserted: *has* (*v*)
  ensure then
    remains_sorted: (**old** *sorted*) **implies** *sorted*;
    item_inserted: *item* = *v*

fill (*other*: *CONTAINER* [*G*])
    -- Fill with as many items of *other* as possible.
    -- The representations of *other* and current structure
    -- need not be the same.
    -- (From *COLLECTION*.)
  require
    other_not_void: *other* /= *Void*;
    extendible: *extendible*

force (*v*: **like** *item*)
    -- Add *v* to end.
    -- (From *SEQUENCE*.)
  require
    extendible: *extendible*
  ensure
    new_count: *count* = **old** *count* + *1*;
    item_inserted: *has* (*v*)

merge (*other*: *LINEAR* [*G*])
    -- Add all items from *other* at their proper positions.
    -- (From *PART_SORTED_LIST*.)
  ensure
    remains_sorted: (**old** *sorted*) **implies** *sorted*

merge_left (*other*: **like** *Current*)
    -- Merge *other* into current structure before cursor
    -- position. Do not move cursor. Empty *other*.
    -- (From *TWO_WAY_LIST*.)
  require
    extendible: *extendible*;
    not_off: **not** *before*;
    other_exists: *other* /= *Void*
  ensure
    new_count: *count* = **old** *count* + **old** *other.count*;
    new_index: *index* = **old** *index* + **old** *other.count*;
    other_is_empty: *other.empty*

merge_right (*other*: **like** *Current*)
    -- Merge *other* into current structure after cursor
    -- position. Do not move cursor. Empty *other*.
    -- (From *TWO_WAY_LIST*.)
  require
    extendible: *extendible*;
    not_off: **not** *after*;
    other_exists: *other* /= *Void*
  ensure
    new_count: *count* = **old** *count* + **old** *other.count*;
    same_index: *index* = **old** *index*;
    other_is_empty: *other.empty*

put (*v*: **like** *item*)
    -- Replace current item by *v*.
    -- (Synonym for *replace*)
    -- (From *CHAIN*.)
  require
    extendible: *extendible*
  ensure
    same_count: *count* = **old** *count*
  ensure then
    item_inserted: *has* (*v*)

put_front (*v*: **like** *item*)
    -- Add *v* to beginning.
    -- Do not move cursor.
    -- (From *TWO_WAY_LIST*.)
  ensure
    new_count: *count* = **old** *count* + *1*;
    item_inserted: *first* = *v*

put_i_th (*v*: **like** *item*; *i*: *INTEGER*)
    -- Put *v* at *i*–th position.
    -- (From *CHAIN*.)
  require
    valid_key: *valid_index* (*i*)
  ensure
    insertion_done: *i_th* (*i*) = *v*

put_left (*v*: **like** *item*)
    -- Add *v* to the left of cursor position.
    -- Do not move cursor.
    -- (From *TWO_WAY_LIST*.)
  require
    extendible: *extendible*;
    not_before: **not** *before*
  ensure
    new_count: *count* = **old** *count* + *1*;
    new_index: *index* = **old** *index* + *1*

put_right (*v*: **like** *item*)
    -- Add *v* to the right of cursor position.
    -- Do not move cursor.
    -- (From *TWO_WAY_LIST*.)
  require
    extendible: *extendible*;
    not_after: **not** *after*
  ensure
    new_count: *count* = **old** *count* + *1*;
    same_index: *index* = **old** *index*

replace (*v*: **like** *item*)
    -- Replace current item by *v*.
    -- (From *LINKED_LIST*.)
  require
    writable: *writable*
  ensure
    item_replaced: *item* = *v*

feature -- Removal

prune (*v*: **like** *item*)
    -- Remove first occurrence of *v*, if any,
    -- after cursor position.
    -- If found, move cursor to right neighbor;
    -- if not, make structure *exhausted*.
    -- (From *DYNAMIC_CHAIN*.)
  require
    prunable: *prunable*

prune_all (*v*: **like** *item*)
    -- Remove all items identical to *v*.
    -- (Reference or object equality,
    -- based on *object_comparison*.)
    -- Leave cursor *off*.
  require
    prunable
  ensure
    no_more_occurrences: **not** *has* (*v*)
  ensure then
    is_exhausted: *exhausted*

remove
    -- Remove current item.
    -- Move cursor to right neighbor
    -- (or *after* if no right neighbor).
    -- (From *TWO_WAY_LIST*.)
  require
    prunable;
    writable
  ensure
    after_when_empty: *empty* **implies** *after*

remove_left
    -- Remove item to the left of cursor position.
    -- Do not move cursor.
    -- (From *TWO_WAY_LIST*.)
  require
    not_before: **not** *before*
  require else
    left_exists: *index* > *1*
  ensure
    new_count: *count* = **old** *count* − *1*;
    new_index: *index* = **old** *index* − *1*

remove_right
    -- Remove item to the right of cursor position.
    -- Do not move cursor.
    -- (From *TWO_WAY_LIST*.)
  require
    right_exists: *index* < *count*
  ensure
    new_count: *count* = **old** *count* − *1*;
    same_index: *index* = **old** *index*

remove_sublist
    -- (From *TWO_WAY_LIST*.)

split (n: INTEGER)
    -- Remove from current list
    -- min (n, count − index - 1) items
    -- starting at cursor position.
    -- Move cursor right one position.
    -- Make extracted sublist accessible
    -- through attribute *sublist*.
    -- (From *TWO_WAY_LIST*.)
  require
    not_off: **not** off;
    valid_sublist: $n >= 0$

wipe_out
    -- Remove all items.
    -- (From *TWO_WAY_LIST*.)
  require
    prunable
  ensure
    is_before: before
  ensure then
    wiped_out: empty

feature -- Transformation

sort
    -- Sort all items.
    -- Has O(count * log (count)) complexity.

swap (i: INTEGER)
    -- Exchange item at i−th position with item
    -- at cursor position.
    -- (From *CHAIN*.)
  require
    not_off: **not** off;
    valid_index: valid_index (i)
  ensure
    swapped_to_item: item = **old** i_th (i);
    swapped_from_item: i_th (i) = **old** item

feature -- Conversion

linear_representation: LINEAR [G]
    -- Representation as a linear structure
    -- (From *LINEAR*.)

feature -- Duplication

duplicate (n: INTEGER): **like** Current
    -- Copy of sub−chain beginning at current position
    -- and having min (n, from_here) items,
    -- where *from_here* is the number of items
    -- at or to the right of current position.
    -- (From *DYNAMIC_CHAIN*.)
  require
    not_off_unless_after: off **implies** after;
    valid_subchain: $n >= 0$

invariant

  before_definition: before = (index = 0);
  after_definition: after = (index = count + 1);
  non_negative_index: $index >= 0$;
  index_small_enough: $index <= count + 1$;
  off_definition: off = ((index = 0) **or** (index = count + 1));
  isfirst_definition: isfirst = ((**not** empty) **and** (index = 1));
  islast_definition: islast = ((**not** empty) **and** (index = count));
  item_corresponds_to_index: (**not** off) **implies** (item = i_th (index));
  writable_constraint: writable **implies** readable;
  empty_constraint: empty **implies** (**not** readable) **and** (**not** writable);
  not_both: **not** (after **and** before);
  empty_property: empty **implies** (after **or** before);
  before_constraint: before **implies** off;
  after_constraint: after **implies** off;
  empty_constraint: empty **implies** off;
  empty_definition: empty = (count = 0);
  non_negative_count: $count >= 0$;
  extendible: extendible

end

16.11 CLASS *CIRCULAR*

This interface shows all the exported features of *CIRCULAR*. It also applies to the implementation given by the effective classes in the next two sections.

indexing

    description: "Circular chains, without commitment to a
       particular representation"
    names: circular, ring, sequence
    access: index, cursor, membership
    contents: generic

deferred class interface

    CIRCULAR [G]

feature -- Access

    cursor: *CURSOR*
        -- Current cursor position
        -- (From *CURSOR_STRUCTURE*.)

    first: *G*
        -- Item at position currently defined as first
      require
        not_empty: **not** *empty*

    has (*v*: **like** *item*): *BOOLEAN*
        -- Does chain include *v*?
        -- (Reference or object equality,
        -- based on *object_comparison*.)
        -- (From *CHAIN*.)
      ensure
        not_found_in_empty: *Result* **implies not** *empty*

    i_th (*i*: *INTEGER*): **like** *item*
        -- Item at *i*-th position
        -- (From *CHAIN*.)
      require
        valid_key: *valid_index* (*i*)

    index: *INTEGER*
        -- Current cursor index, with respect to position
        -- currently defined as first

    index_of (*v*: **like** *item*; *i*: *INTEGER*): *INTEGER*
        -- Index of *i*-th occurrence of item identical to *v*.
        -- (Reference or object equality,
        -- based on *object_comparison*.)
        -- 0 if none.
        -- (From *CHAIN*.)
      require
        positive_occurrences: *i* > *0*
      ensure
        non_negative_result: *Result* >= *0*

item: *G*
    -- Item at current position
    -- (From *TRAVERSABLE*.)
  require
    not_off: **not** *off*
  require else
    readable

last: **like** *first*
    -- Item at position currently defined as last
  require
    not_empty: **not** *empty*

occurrences (*v*: **like** *item*): *INTEGER*
    -- Number of times *v* appears.
    -- (Reference or object equality,
    -- based on *object_comparison*.)
    -- (From *CHAIN*.)
  ensure
    non_negative_occurrences: *Result* >= *0*

sequential_occurrences (*v*: *G*): *INTEGER*
    -- Number of times *v* appears.
    -- (Reference or object equality,
    -- based on *object_comparison*.)
    -- (From *LINEAR*.)
  ensure
    non_negative_occurrences: *Result* >= *0*

infix "@" (*i*: *INTEGER*): **like** *item*
    -- Item at *i*-th position
    -- (From *CHAIN*.)
  require
    valid_key: *valid_index* (*i*)

feature -- Measurement

count: *INTEGER*
    -- Number of items
    -- (From *FINITE*.)

feature -- Status report

after: *BOOLEAN*
    -- Is there no valid cursor position to the right of cursor?

before: *BOOLEAN*
    -- Is there no valid cursor position to the right of cursor?

changeable_comparison_criterion: *BOOLEAN*
    -- May *object_comparison* be changed?
    -- (Answer: yes by default.)
    -- (From *CONTAINER*.)

empty: *BOOLEAN*
    -- Is structure empty?
    -- (From *FINITE*.)

exhausted: *BOOLEAN*
    -- Has structure been completely explored?
    ensure
      exhausted_when_off: *off* **implies** *Result*

extendible: *BOOLEAN*
    -- May new items be added?
    -- (From *COLLECTION*.)

full: *BOOLEAN*
    -- Is structure filled to capacity?
    -- (From *BOX*.)

isfirst: *BOOLEAN*
    -- Is cursor at first position?
    -- (From *CHAIN*.)
    ensure
      valid_position: *Result* **implies not** *empty*

islast: *BOOLEAN*
    -- Is cursor at last position?
    -- (From *CHAIN*.)
    ensure
      valid_position: *Result* **implies not** *empty*

object_comparison: *BOOLEAN*
    -- Must search operations use *equal* rather than =
    -- for comparing references? (Default: no, use =.)
    -- (From *CONTAINER*.)

off: *BOOLEAN*
    -- Is there no current item?
    ensure
      only_when_empty: *Result* = *empty*

prunable: *BOOLEAN*
    -- May items be removed?
    -- (From *COLLECTION*.)

readable: *BOOLEAN*
    -- Is there a current item that may be read?
    -- (From *SEQUENCE*.)

valid_cursor (*p*: *CURSOR*): *BOOLEAN*
    -- Can the cursor be moved to position *p*?
    -- (From *CURSOR_STRUCTURE*.)

valid_cursor_index (*i*: *INTEGER*): *BOOLEAN*
    -- Is *i* a possible cursor position?
    ensure
      valid_cursor_index_definition: *Result* = (($i >= 0$) **and** (i
        $<= count$))
    ensure then
      valid_cursor_index_definition: *Result* = (($i >= 0$) **and** (i
        $<= count + 1$))

valid_index (*i*: *INTEGER*): *BOOLEAN*
    -- Is *i* within allowable bounds?
    -- (From *CHAIN*.)
    ensure
      valid_index_definition: *Result* = ($i >= 1$) **and** ($i <=$
        count)

writable: *BOOLEAN*
    -- Is there a current item that may be modified?
    -- (From *SEQUENCE*.)

feature -- Status setting

compare_objects
    -- Ensure that future search operations will use *equal*
    -- rather than = for comparing references.
    -- (From *CONTAINER*.)
    require
      changeable_comparison_criterion
    ensure
      object_comparison

compare_references
    -- Ensure that future search operations will use =
    -- rather than *equal* for comparing references.
    -- (From *CONTAINER*.)
    require
      changeable_comparison_criterion
    ensure
      reference_comparison: **not** *object_comparison*

feature -- Cursor movement

back
    -- Move cursor to previous item, cyclically.
    require
      not_before: **not** *before*
    ensure
      moved_back: *index* = **old** *index* − *1*

finish
    -- Move cursor to last position.
    -- (No effect if empty)
    -- (From *CHAIN*.)
    ensure
      at_last: **not** *empty* **implies** *islast*

forth
    -- Move cursor to next item, cyclically.
    require
      not_after: **not** *after*
    ensure
      moved_forth_at_end: (**old** *index* = *count*) **implies** (*index*
        = *1*)

go_i_th (*i*: *INTEGER*)
    -- Move cursor to *i*–th position from current start,
        cyclically.
  require
    index_big_enough: *i* >= *1*;
    not_empty: **not** *empty*
  require else
    valid_cursor_index: *valid_cursor_index* (*i*)
  ensure
    position_expected: *index* = *i*

go_to (*p*: *CURSOR*)
    -- Move cursor to position *p*.
    -- (From *CURSOR_STRUCTURE*.)
  require
    cursor_position_valid: *valid_cursor* (*p*)

move (*i*: *INTEGER*)
    -- Move cursor to *i*–th item from current position,
    -- cyclically.
  ensure
    too_far_right: (**old** *index* + *i* > *count*) **implies** *exhausted*;
    too_far_left: (**old** *index* + *i* < *1*) **implies** *exhausted*;
    expected_index: (**not** *exhausted*) **implies** (*index* = **old**
      index + *i*)

search (*v*: **like** *item*)
    -- Move to first position (at or after current
    -- position) where *item* and *v* are equal.
    -- If structure does not include *v* ensure that
    -- *exhausted* will be true.
    -- (Reference or object equality,
    -- based on *object_comparison*.)
    -- (From *BILINEAR*.)
  ensure
    object_found: (**not** *exhausted* **and then** *object_
      comparison* **and then** *v* /= *Void* **and then** *item* /=
      Void) **implies** *v.is_equal* (*item*);
    item_found: (**not** *exhausted* **and not** *object_comparison*)
      implies *v* = *item*

set_start
    -- Define current position as the first.
  require
    not_empty: **not** *empty*

start
    -- Move cursor to first position.
    -- (No effect if empty)
    -- (From *CHAIN*.)
  ensure
    at_first: **not** *empty* **implies** *isfirst*

feature -- Element change

append (*s*: *SEQUENCE* [*G*])
    -- Append a copy of *s*.
    -- (From *SEQUENCE*.)
  require
    argument_not_void: *s* /= *Void*
  ensure
    new_count: *count* >= **old** *count*

extend (*v*: *G*)
    -- Add a new occurrence of *v*.
    -- (From *BAG*.)
  require
    extendible: *extendible*
  ensure
    one_more_occurrence: *occurrences* (*v*) = **old**
      (*occurrences* (*v*)) + *1*
  ensure then
    item_inserted: *has* (*v*)

fill (*other*: *CONTAINER* [*G*])
    -- Fill with as many items of *other* as possible.
    -- The representations of *other* and current structure
    -- need not be the same.
    -- (From *COLLECTION*.)
  require
    other_not_void: *other* /= *Void*;
    extendible: *extendible*

force (*v*: **like** *item*)
    -- Add *v* to end.
    -- (From *SEQUENCE*.)
  require
    extendible: *extendible*
  ensure
    new_count: *count* = **old** *count* + *1*;
    item_inserted: *has* (*v*)

put (*v*: **like** *item*)
    -- Replace current item by *v*.
    -- (Synonym for *replace*)
    -- (From *CHAIN*.)
  require
    extendible: *extendible*
  ensure
    same_count: *count* = **old** *count*
  ensure then
    item_inserted: *has* (*v*)

put_i_th (*v*: **like** *item*; *i*: *INTEGER*)
    -- Put *v* at *i*–th position.
    -- (From *CHAIN*.)
  require
    valid_key: *valid_index* (*i*)
  ensure
    insertion_done: *i_th* (*i*) = *v*

replace (*v*: *G*)
    -- Replace current item by *v*.
    -- (From *ACTIVE*.)
  require
    writable: *writable*
  ensure
    item_replaced: *item* = *v*

feature -- Removal

prune (*v*: **like** *item*)
    -- Remove the first occurrence of *v* if any.
    -- If no such occurrence go *off*.
    -- (From *SEQUENCE*.)
  require
    prunable: *prunable*

prune_all (*v*: **like** *item*)
    -- Remove all occurrences of *v*; go *off*.
    -- (From *SEQUENCE*.)
  require
    prunable
  ensure
    no_more_occurrences: **not** *has* (*v*)

remove
    -- Remove item at cursor position.
    -- Move cursor to right neighbor (cyclically).
    -- If removed item was at current starting position,
    -- move starting position to right neighbor.
  require
    prunable;
    writable

wipe_out
    -- Remove all items.
    -- (From *COLLECTION*.)
  require
    prunable
  ensure
    wiped_out: *empty*

feature -- Transformation

swap (*i*: *INTEGER*)
    -- Exchange item at *i*–th position with item
    -- at cursor position.
    -- (From *CHAIN*.)
  require
    not_off: **not** *off*;
    valid_index: *valid_index* (*i*)
  ensure
    swapped_to_item: *item* = **old** *i_th* (*i*);
    swapped_from_item: *i_th* (*i*) = **old** *item*

feature -- Conversion

linear_representation: *LINEAR* [*G*]
    -- Representation as a linear structure
    -- (From *LINEAR*.)

feature -- Duplication

duplicate (*n*: *INTEGER*): **like** *Current*
    -- Copy of sub–chain beginning at current position
    -- and having min (*n*, *from_here*) items,
    -- where *from_here* is the number of items
    -- at or to the right of current position.
    -- (From *CHAIN*.)
  require
    not_off_unless_after: *off* **implies** *after*;
    valid_subchain: *n* >= 0

invariant

  not_before_unless_empty: *before* **implies** *empty*;
  not_after_unless_empty: *after* **implies** *empty*;
  not_off_unless_empty: *off* **implies** *empty*;
  non_negative_index: *index* >= *0*;
  index_small_enough: *index* <= *count* + *1*;
  off_definition: *off* = ((*index* = *0*) **or** (*index* = *count* + *1*));
  isfirst_definition: *isfirst* = ((**not** *empty*) **and** (*index* = *1*));
  islast_definition: *islast* = ((**not** *empty*) **and** (*index* = *count*));
  item_corresponds_to_index: (**not** *off*) **implies** (*item* = *i_th*
    (*index*));
  writable_constraint: *writable* **implies** *readable*;
  empty_constraint: *empty* **implies** (**not** *readable*) **and** (**not**
    writable);
  not_both: **not** (*after* **and** *before*);
  empty_property: *empty* **implies** (*after* **or** *before*);
  before_constraint: *before* **implies** *off*;
  after_constraint: *after* **implies** *off*;
  empty_constraint: *empty* **implies** *off*;
  empty_definition: *empty* = (*count* = *0*);
  non_negative_count: *count* >= *0*

end

16.12 CLASSES *LINKED_CIRCULAR* AND *TWO_WAY_CIRCULAR*

This interface for *LINKED_CIRCULAR*, which also applies to *TWO_WAY_CIRCULAR*, only includes the features introduced or redeclared in the class. In addition, these two classes retain all the features of *CIRCULAR*, as they appear in the previous section.

indexing

> *description*: "Circular chains implemented as linked lists"
> *names*: *linked_circular*, *ring*, *sequence*
> *representation*: *linked*
> *access*: *index*, *cursor*, *membership*
> *contents*: *generic*

class interface

> *LINKED_CIRCULAR* [G]

creation
> *make*

feature -- Initialization

> *make*
> > -- Create an empty list

feature -- Access

> *cursor*: *CURSOR*
> > -- Current cursor position

> *item*: G
> > -- Current item
> > **require**
> > *readable*
> > **require else**
> > *not_off*: **not** *off*

feature -- Measurement

> *count*: *INTEGER*
> > -- Number of items

feature -- Status report

> *full*: *BOOLEAN* **is false**
> > -- Is structured filled to capacity? (Answer: no.)

> *isfirst*: *BOOLEAN*
> > -- Is cursor on first item?

> *islast*: *BOOLEAN*
> > -- Is cursor on last item?

> *readable*: *BOOLEAN*
> > -- Is there a current item that may be read?

> *valid_cursor* (p: *CURSOR*): *BOOLEAN*
> > -- Can the cursor be moved to position *p*?

> *writable*: *BOOLEAN*
> > -- Is there a current item that may be written?

feature -- Cursor movement

> *go_to* (p: *CURSOR*)
> > -- Move cursor to position *p*.
> > **require**
> > *cursor_position_valid*: *valid_cursor* (p)

> *set_start*
> > -- Select current item as the first.
> > **require**
> > *not_empty*: **not** *empty*

> *start*
> > -- Move to position currently selected as first.

feature -- Element change

> *extend* (v: **like** *item*)
> > -- Add *v* to end.
> > -- Do not move cursor.
> > **require**
> > *extendible*: *extendible*

> *merge_left* (*other*: **like** *Current*)
> > -- Merge *other* into current structure before cursor
> > -- position. Do not move cursor. Empty *other*.
> > **require**
> > *extendible*: *extendible*;
> > *not_off*: **not** *before*;
> > *other_exists*: *other* /= *Void*
> > **ensure**
> > *new_count*: *count* = **old** *count* + **old** *other.count*;

> *merge_right* (*other*: **like** *Current*)
> > -- Merge *other* into current structure after cursor
> > -- position. Do not move cursor. Empty *other*.
> > **require**
> > *extendible*: *extendible*;
> > *not_off*: **not** *after*;
> > *other_exists*: *other* /= *Void*
> > **ensure**
> > *new_count*: *count* = **old** *count* + **old** *other.count*;

> *put_front* (v: **like** *item*)
> > -- Add *v* to beginning.
> > -- Do not move cursor.
> > **ensure**
> > *new_count*: *count* = **old** *count* + 1;

put_left (*v*: **like** *item*)
>   -- Add *v* to the left of cursor position.
>   -- Do not move cursor.
>
> **require**
>   *extendible*: *extendible*;
>   *not_before*: **not** *before*
> **ensure**
>   *new_count*: *count* = **old** *count* + *1*;

put_right (*v*: **like** *item*)
>   -- Add *v* to the right of cursor position.
>   -- Do not move cursor.
>
> **require**
>   *extendible*: *extendible*;
>   *not_after*: **not** *after*
> **ensure**
>   *new_count*: *count* = **old** *count* + *1*;

replace (*v*: *G*)
>   -- Replace current item by *v*.
>
> **require**
>   *writable*: *writable*
> **ensure**
>   *item_replaced*: *item* = *v*

feature -- Removal

remove_left
>   -- Remove item to the left of cursor position.
>   -- Do not move cursor.
>
> **require**
>   *count* > *1*
> **require else**
>   *left_exists*: *index* > *1*
> **ensure**
>   *new_count*: *count* = **old** *count* − *1*;

remove_right
>   -- Remove item to the right of cursor position.
>   -- Do not move cursor.
>
> **require**
>   *count* > *1*
> **require else**
>   *right_exists*: *index* < *count*
> **ensure**
>   *new_count*: *count* = **old** *count* − *1*;

invariant

> *writable_constraint*: *writable* **implies** *readable*;
> *non_negative_count*: *count* >= *0*;
> *extendible*: *extendible*

end

16.13 CLASS *ARRAYED_CIRCULAR*

This interface only includes the features introduced or redeclared in *ARRAYED_CIRCULAR*. In addition, this class retains all the features of *CIRCULAR*; please refer to the interface given in an earlier section.

The interface of CIRCULAR is in 16.11, page 318.

indexing
  description: "*Circular chains implemented by resizable arrays*"
  names: *arrayed_circular*, *ring*, *sequence*
  representation: *array*
  access: *index*, *cursor*, *membership*
  contents: *generic*

class interface

  ARRAYED_CIRCULAR [G]

creation
  make

feature -- Initialization

  make (n: *INTEGER*)
      -- Create a circular chain with *n* items.
    require
      at_least_one: n >= 1

feature -- Access

  cursor: *CURSOR*
      -- Current cursor position

  item: G
      -- Current item
    require
      readable
    require else
      not_off: **not** *off*

feature -- Measurement

  count: *INTEGER*
      -- Number of items

feature -- Status report

  full: *BOOLEAN*
      -- Is structure filled to capacity?

  isfirst: *BOOLEAN*
      -- Is cursor on first item?

  islast: *BOOLEAN*
      -- Is cursor on last item?

  readable: *BOOLEAN*
      -- Is there a current item that may be read?

  valid_cursor (p: *CURSOR*): *BOOLEAN*
      -- Can the cursor be moved to position *p*?

  writable: *BOOLEAN*
      -- Is there a current item that may be written?

feature -- Cursor movement

  go_to (p: *CURSOR*)
      -- Move cursor to position *p*.
    require
      cursor_position_valid: *valid_cursor* (p)

  set_start
      -- Select current item as the first.
    require
      not_empty: **not** *empty*

  start
      -- Move to position currently selected as first.

feature -- Element change

  extend (v: **like** *item*)
      -- Add *v* to end.
      -- Do not move cursor except when off.
    require
      extendible: *extendible*
    ensure
      new_count: *count* = **old** *count* + 1;

  merge_left (other: **like** *Current*)
      -- Merge *other* into current structure before cursor
      -- position. Do not move cursor. Empty *other*.
    require
      extendible: *extendible*;
      not_off: **not** *before*;
      other_exists: *other* /= *Void*
    ensure
      new_count: *count* = **old** *count* + **old** *other*.*count*;

  merge_right (other: **like** *Current*)
      -- Merge *other* into current structure after cursor
      -- position. Do not move cursor. Empty *other*.
    require
      extendible: *extendible*;
      not_off: **not** *after*;
      other_exists: *other* /= *Void*
    ensure
      new_count: *count* = **old** *count* + **old** *other*.*count*;

  put_front (v: **like** *item*)
      -- Add *v* to beginning.
      -- Do not move cursor.
    ensure
      new_count: *count* = **old** *count* + 1;

put_left (*v*: **like** *item*)
    -- Add *v* to the left of cursor position.
    -- Do not move cursor.
  require
    extendible: *extendible*;
    not_before: **not** *before*
  ensure
    new_count: *count* = **old** *count* + *1*;

put_right (*v*: **like** *item*)
    -- Add *v* to the right of cursor position.
    -- Do not move cursor.
  require
    extendible: *extendible*;
    not_after: **not** *after*
  ensure
    new_count: *count* = **old** *count* + *1*;

replace (*v*: *G*)
    -- Replace current item by *v*.
  require
    writable: *writable*
  ensure
    item_replaced: *item* = *v*

feature -- Removal

remove_left
    -- Remove item to the left of cursor position.
    -- Do not move cursor.
  require
    count > *1*
  require else
    left_exists: *index* > *1*
  ensure
    new_count: *count* = **old** *count* − *1*;

remove_right
    -- Remove item to the right of cursor position.
    -- Do not move cursor.
  require
    count > *1*
  require else
    right_exists: *index* < *count*
  ensure
    new_count: *count* = **old** *count* − *1*;

wipe_out
    -- Remove all items.
  require
    prunable

invariant

  non_negative_count: *count* >= *0*;
  writable_constraint: *writable* **implies** *readable*;
  non_negative_count: *count* >= *0*;
  extendible: *extendible*

end

16.14 CLASSES *SORTED_STRUCT* **AND** *COMPARABLE_STRUCT*

For brevity only the interface of *SORTED_STRUCT* appears below; it includes the features introduced in *COMPARABLE_STRUCT* but none of those inherited from the other parents. Of the features shown, only *min* and *max* are available in *COMPARABLE_STRUCT*.

indexing

> *description*: "*Structures whose items are sorted according to*
>   *a total order relation*"
> *names*: *sorted_struct, comparable_struct*
> *access*: *index, membership, min, max*
> *contents*: *generic*

deferred class interface

> *SORTED_STRUCT* [*G* –> *COMPARABLE*]

feature -- Measurement

> *max*: **like** *item*
>   -- Maximum item
>   **require**
>   *is_sorted*: *sorted*
>   **require else**
>   *min_max_available*
>   **ensure**
>   *maximum_present*: *has (Result)*
>   -- *largest*: For every item *it*, *it* <= *Result*

> *median*: **like** *item*
>   -- Median element
>   **ensure**
>   *median_present*: *has (Result)*

> *min*: **like** *item*
>   -- Minimum item
>   **require**
>   *is_sorted*: *sorted*
>   **require else**
>   *min_max_available*
>   **ensure**
>   *minimum_present*: *has (Result)*
>   -- *smallest*: For every item *it*, *Result* <= *it*

feature -- Status report

> *sorted*: *BOOLEAN*
>   -- Is structure sorted?

feature -- Transformation

> *sort*
>   -- Sort structure.
>   **ensure**
>   *is_sorted*: *sorted*

end

16.15 CLASS *COUNTABLE_SEQUENCE*

This interface includes all the features of *COUNTABLE_SEQUENCE* except for those inherited unchanged from *CONTAINER*.

indexing

  description: "Circular chains implemented by resizable
    arrays"
  names: *arrayed_circular*, *ring*, *sequence*
  representation: *array*
  access: *index*, *cursor*, *membership*
  contents: *generic*

class interface

  ARRAYED_CIRCULAR [G]

creation
  make

feature -- Initialization

  make (*n*: *INTEGER*)
      -- Create a circular chain with *n* items.
      require
        at_least_one: *n* >= *1*

feature -- Access

  cursor: *CURSOR*
      -- Current cursor position

  item: *G*
      -- Current item
      require
        readable
      require else
        not_off: *not* *off*

feature -- Measurement

  count: *INTEGER*
      -- Number of items

feature -- Status report

  full: *BOOLEAN*
      -- Is structure filled to capacity?

  isfirst: *BOOLEAN*
      -- Is cursor on first item?

  islast: *BOOLEAN*
      -- Is cursor on last item?

  readable: *BOOLEAN*
      -- Is there a current item that may be read?

  valid_cursor (*p*: *CURSOR*): *BOOLEAN*
      -- Can the cursor be moved to position *p*?

  writable: *BOOLEAN*
      -- Is there a current item that may be written?

feature -- Cursor movement

  go_to (*p*: *CURSOR*)
      -- Move cursor to position *p*.
      require
        cursor_position_valid: *valid_cursor* (*p*)

  set_start
      -- Select current item as the first.
      require
        not_empty: *not* *empty*

  start
      -- Move to position currently selected as first.

feature -- Element change

  extend (*v*: *like item*)
      -- Add *v* to end.
      -- Do not move cursor except when off.
      require
        extendible: *extendible*
      ensure
        new_count: *count* = *old* *count* + *1*;

  merge_left (*other*: *like Current*)
      -- Merge *other* into current structure before cursor
      -- position. Do not move cursor. Empty *other*.
      require
        extendible: *extendible*;
        not_off: *not* *before*;
        other_exists: *other* /= *Void*
      ensure
        new_count: *count* = *old* *count* + *old* *other.count*;

  merge_right (*other*: *like Current*)
      -- Merge *other* into current structure after cursor
      -- position. Do not move cursor. Empty *other*.
      require
        extendible: *extendible*;
        not_off: *not* *after*;
        other_exists: *other* /= *Void*
      ensure
        new_count: *count* = *old* *count* + *old* *other.count*;

  put_front (*v*: *like item*)
      -- Add *v* to beginning.
      -- Do not move cursor.
      ensure
        new_count: *count* = *old* *count* + *1*;

put_left (*v*: **like** *item*)
    -- Add *v* to the left of cursor position.
    -- Do not move cursor.
    require
        extendible: *extendible*;
        not_before: **not** *before*
    ensure
        new_count: *count* = **old** *count* + *1*;

put_right (*v*: **like** *item*)
    -- Add *v* to the right of cursor position.
    -- Do not move cursor.
    require
        extendible: *extendible*;
        not_after: **not** *after*
    ensure
        new_count: *count* = **old** *count* + *1*;

replace (*v*: *G*)
    -- Replace current item by *v*.
    require
        writable: *writable*
    ensure
        item_replaced: *item* = *v*

feature -- Removal

remove_left
    -- Remove item to the left of cursor position.
    -- Do not move cursor.
    require
        count > *1*
    require else
        left_exists: *index* > *1*
    ensure
        new_count: *count* = **old** *count* − *1*;

remove_right
    -- Remove item to the right of cursor position.
    -- Do not move cursor.
    require
        count > *1*
    require else
        right_exists: *index* < *count*
    ensure
        new_count: *count* = **old** *count* − *1*;

wipe_out
    -- Remove all items.
    require
        prunable

invariant

    non_negative_count: *count* >= *0*;
    writable_constraint: *writable* **implies** *readable*;
    non_negative_count: *count* >= *0*;
    extendible: *extendible*

end

16.16 CLASS *LINKABLE*

indexing

> *description*: "Linkable cells containing a reference to their
>   right neighbor"
> *names*: linkable, cell
> *representation*: linked
> *contents*: generic

class interface

> LINKABLE [G]

feature -- Access

> *right*: **like** Current
>   -- Right neighbor
>
> *item*: G
>   -- Content of cell.
>   -- (From *CELL*.)

feature -- Element change

> *replace* (*v*: **like** *item*)
>   -- Make *v* the cell's *item*.
>   -- (From *CELL*.)
>   **ensure**
>   *item_inserted*: item = v

end

16.17 CLASS *BI_LINKABLE*

indexing

> *description*: "*Linkable cells with a reference to the left and*
>   *right neighbors*"
> *names*: *bi_linkable*, *cell*
> *representation*: *linked*
> *contents*: *generic*

class interface

> BI_LINKABLE [G]

feature -- Access

> *left*: **like** *Current*
>   -- Left neighbor

> *right*: **like** *Current*
>   -- Right neighbor
>   -- (From *LINKABLE*.)

> *item*: *G*
>   -- Content of cell.
>   -- (From *CELL*.)

feature -- Element change

> *replace* (*v*: **like** *item*)
>   -- Make *v* the cell's *item*.
>   -- (From *CELL*.)
>   **ensure**
>   *item_inserted*: *item* = *v*

invariant

> *right_symmetry*: (*right* /= *Void*) **implies** (*right.left* =
>   *Current*);
> *left_symmetry*: (*left* /= *Void*) **implies** (*left.right* = *Current*)

end

17

Dispenser classes

17.1 OVERVIEW

An earlier chapter introduced the notion of dispenser and explained the main classes in the corresponding class graph, describing stacks, queues and priority queues.

Chapter 7.

Here now are the interfaces, in flat-short form, of all these classes. The corresponding inheritance hierarchy is repeated on the following page.

The figure appeared originally on page 160.

The class interfaces appear in the following order, corresponding roughly to a preorder traversal of the inheritance graph. The notation *C / D* means that the interfaces of classes *C* and *D*, being identical or almost identical, are given as a single flat-short form.

> *STACK, ARRAYED_STACK, BOUNDED_STACK, LINKED_STACK, QUEUE, ARRAYED_QUEUE, BOUNDED_QUEUE, LINKED_QUEUE, PRIORITY_QUEUE / LINKED_PRIORITY_QUEUE / HEAP_PRIORITY_ QUEUE.*

Also relevant to this discussion is the interface of class *DISPENSER* itself, which was given in an earlier chapter.

14.15, page 281.

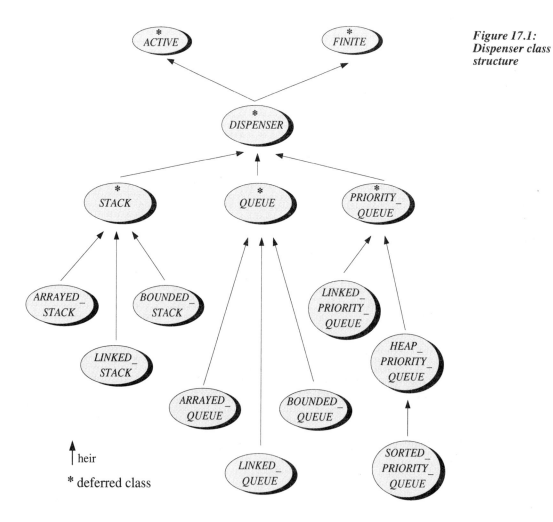

Figure 17.1:
Dispenser class
structure

17.2 CLASS *STACK*

As it appears here the interface shows all the features of class *STACK* including those inherited from ancestors. They also apply to the implementations given next (*ARRAYED_STACK*, *LINKED_STACK*, *BOUNDED_STACK*), whose interfaces are essentially the same except for the creation procedures and some extra assertions.

indexing

   description: "*Stacks (last−in, first-out dispensers), without commitment to a particular representation*"
   names: *stack*, *dispenser*
   access: *fixed*, *lifo*, *membership*
   contents: *generic*

deferred class interface

   STACK [G]

feature -- Access

   has (v: G): BOOLEAN
      -- Does structure include *v*?
      -- (Reference or object equality,
      -- based on *object_comparison*.)
      -- (From *CONTAINER*.)
     ensure
      not_found_in_empty: Result **implies not** empty

   item: G
      -- Current item
      -- (From *ACTIVE*.)
     require
      readable

feature -- Measurement

   count: INTEGER
      -- Number of items
      -- (From *FINITE*.)

   occurrences (v: G): INTEGER
      -- Number of times *v* appears in structure
      -- (Reference or object equality,
      -- based on *object_comparison*.)
      -- (From *BAG*.)
     ensure
      non_negative_occurrences: Result >= 0

feature -- Status report

   changeable_comparison_criterion: BOOLEAN
      -- May *object_comparison* be changed?
      -- (Answer: yes by default.)
      -- (From *CONTAINER*.)

   empty: BOOLEAN
      -- Is structure empty?
      -- (From *FINITE*.)

   extendible: BOOLEAN
      -- May new items be added?
      -- (From *COLLECTION*.)

   full: BOOLEAN
      -- Is structure filled to capacity?
      -- (From *BOX*.)

   object_comparison: BOOLEAN
      -- Must search operations use *equal* rather than =
      -- for comparing references? (Default: no, use =.)
      -- (From *CONTAINER*.)

   prunable: BOOLEAN
      -- May items be removed?
      -- (From *COLLECTION*.)

   readable: BOOLEAN
      -- Is there a current item that may be read?
      -- (From *DISPENSER*.)

   writable: BOOLEAN
      -- Is there a current item that may be modified?
      -- (From *DISPENSER*.)

feature -- Status setting

   compare_objects
      -- Ensure that future search operations will use *equal*
      -- rather than = for comparing references.
      -- (From *CONTAINER*.)
     require
      changeable_comparison_criterion
     ensure
      object_comparison

   compare_references
      -- Ensure that future search operations will use =
      -- rather than *equal* for comparing references.
      -- (From *CONTAINER*.)
     require
      changeable_comparison_criterion
     ensure
      reference_comparison: **not** *object_comparison*

feature -- Element change

   append (s: SEQUENCE [G])
      -- Append a copy of *s*.
      -- (Synonym for *fill*)
      -- (From *DISPENSER*.)

extend (*v*: **like** *item*)
    -- Push *v* onto top.
  require
    extendible: *extendible*
  ensure
    item_pushed: *item* = *v*
  ensure then
    one_more_occurrence: *occurrences* (*v*) = **old**
      (*occurrences* (*v*)) + *1*
  ensure then
    item_inserted: *has* (*v*)

fill (*other*: *LINEAR* [*G*])
    -- Fill with as many items of *other* as possible.
    -- Fill items with greatest index from *other* first.
    -- Items inserted with lowest index (from *other*) will
    -- always be on the top of stack.
    -- The representations of *other* and current structure
    -- need not be the same.
  require
    other_not_void: *other* /= *Void*;
    extendible: *extendible*

force (*v*: **like** *item*)
    -- Push *v* onto top.
  ensure
    item_pushed: *item* = *v*

put (*v*: **like** *item*)
    -- Push *v* onto top.
  require
    extendible: *extendible*
  ensure
    item_pushed: *item* = *v*
  ensure then
    item_inserted: *has* (*v*)

replace (*v*: **like** *item*)
    -- Replace top item by *v*.
  require
    writable: *writable*
  ensure
    item_replaced: *item* = *v*

feature -- Removal

remove
    -- Remove current item.
    -- (From *ACTIVE*.)
  require
    prunable;
    writable

wipe_out
    -- Remove all items.
    -- (From *COLLECTION*.)
  require
    prunable
  ensure
    wiped_out: *empty*

feature -- Conversion

linear_representation: *LINEAR* [*G*]
    -- Representation as a linear structure
    -- (From *CONTAINER*.)

invariant

  readable_definition: *readable* = **not** *empty*;
  writable_definition: *writable* = **not** *empty*;
  writable_constraint: *writable* **implies** *readable*;
  empty_constraint: *empty* **implies** (**not** *readable*) **and** (**not**
    writable);
  empty_definition: *empty* = (*count* = 0);
  non_negative_count: *count* >= 0

end

17.3 CLASS *ARRAYED_STACK*

Since *ARRAYED_STACK* is probably the most commonly used implementation of stacks the interface shown below includes for convenience all the features inherited from *STACK* and *DISPENSER*, but not those from any other ancestor unless the class redeclares them.

indexing

description: "Stacks implemented by resizable arrays"
names: dispenser, array
representation: array
access: fixed, lifo, membership
size: fixed
contents: generic

class interface

ARRAYED_STACK [G]

creation
make

feature -- Initialization

make (n: INTEGER)
-- Allocate list with n items.
-- (n may be zero for empty list.)
-- (From ARRAYED_LIST.)
require
valid_number_of_items: n >= 0

feature -- Access

item: **like** first
-- Current item
-- (From ARRAYED_LIST.)
require
readable

feature -- Measurement

count: INTEGER
-- Number of items.
-- (From ARRAYED_LIST.)

feature -- Status report

full: BOOLEAN
-- Is structure filled to capacity? (Answer: no.)
-- (From ARRAYED_LIST.)

prunable: BOOLEAN
-- May items be removed? (Answer: yes.)
-- (From ARRAYED_LIST.)

readable: BOOLEAN
-- Is there a current item that may be read?
-- (From DISPENSER.)

writable: BOOLEAN
-- Is there a current item that may be modified?
-- (From DISPENSER.)

feature -- Element change

append (s: SEQUENCE [G])
-- Append a copy of s.
-- (Synonym for fill)
-- (From DISPENSER.)
require
argument_not_void: s /= Void
ensure
new_count: count >= **old** count

extend (v: **like** item)
-- Push v on top.
require
extendible: extendible
ensure
item_pushed: item = v
ensure then
one_more_occurrence: occurrences (v) = **old**
(occurrences (v)) + 1
ensure then
item_inserted: has (v)

fill (other: LINEAR [G])
-- Fill with as many items of other as possible.
-- Fill items with greatest index from other first.
-- Items inserted with lowest index (from other) will
-- always be on the top of stack.
-- The representations of other and current structure
-- need not be the same.
-- (From STACK.)
require
other_not_void: other /= Void;
extendible: extendible

force (v: **like** item)
-- Push v on top.
require
extendible: extendible
ensure
item_pushed: item = v
ensure then
new_count: count = **old** count + 1;

put (*v*: **like** *item*)
    -- Push *v* on top.
   require
    extendible: *extendible*
   ensure
    item_pushed: *item* = *v*
   ensure then
    one_more_occurrence: *occurrences* (*v*) = **old**
      (*occurrences* (*v*)) + *1*

replace (*v*: **like** *first*)
    -- Replace current item by *v*.
    -- (From *ARRAYED_LIST*.)
   require
    writable: *writable*
   ensure
    item_replaced: *item* = *v*

feature -- Removal

remove
    -- Remove top item.
   require
    not_empty: *count* /= *0*
   require else
    prunable;
    writable

wipe_out
    -- Remove all items.
    -- (From *ARRAYED_LIST*.)
   require
    prunable

feature -- Conversion

linear_representation: *ARRAYED_LIST* [*G*]
    -- Representation as a linear structure
    -- (in the reverse order of original insertion)

feature -- Duplication

copy (*other*: **like** *Current*)
    -- (From *ARRAYED_LIST*.)

setup (*other*: **like** *Current*)
    -- Prepare current object so that *other*
    -- can be easily copied into it.
    -- It is not necessary to call *setup*
    -- (since *consistent* is always true)
    -- but it will make copying quicker.
    -- (From *ARRAYED_LIST*.)

invariant

    writable_constraint: *writable* **implies** *readable*;
    non_negative_count: *count* >= *0*;
    not_full: **not** *full*;
    prunable: *prunable*;
    extendible: *extendible*

end

17.4 CLASS *BOUNDED_STACK*

The interface of *BOUNDED_STACK* is very similar to that of *ARRAYED_STACK*. The
main difference is that *extendible*, the precondition of *put*, is not always true any more,
but has the value *not full*.

The interface as it appears here only shows the features introduced or redeclared in
the class, and those inherited from *BOUNDED*. In addition, *BOUNDED_STACK* has
all the exported features of *STACK*; please refer to the interface of *STACK* as it appears
at the beginning of this chapter.

*The interface of STACK is in
17.2, page 333.*

indexing

    description: "*Stacks with a bounded physical size,*
      implemented by arrays"
    names: *dispenser, array*
    representation: *array*
    access: *fixed, lifo, membership*
    size: *fixed*
    contents: *generic*

class interface

    BOUNDED_STACK [*G*]

creation
    make

feature -- Initialization

    make (*n*: *INTEGER*)
        -- Create a stack for at most *n* items.
      require
        non_negative_argument: *n* >= *0*
      ensure
        stack_allocated: *capacity* = *n*;
        empty_stack: *count* = *0*

feature -- Access

    has (*v*: *G*): *BOOLEAN*
        -- Does *v* appear in stack?
        -- (Reference or object equality,
        -- based on *object_comparison*.)
      ensure
        not_found_in_empty: *Result* **implies not** *empty*

    item: *G*
        -- Last item pushed (i.e. top)
      require
        not_empty: *count* > *0*
      require else
        readable

feature -- Measurement

    capacity: *INTEGER*

    count: *INTEGER*

    occurrences (*v*: *G*): *INTEGER*
      ensure
        non_negative_occurrences: *Result* >= *0*

feature -- Status report

    empty: *BOOLEAN*
        -- Is structure empty?
        -- (From *FINITE*.)

    extendible: *BOOLEAN*
      ensure
        Result = **not** *full*

    full: *BOOLEAN*
        -- Is structure full?
        -- (From *BOUNDED*.)

    prunable: *BOOLEAN* **is true**

    resizable: *BOOLEAN* **is true**

feature -- Element change

    extend (*v*: **like** *item*)
        -- Push *v* on top.
      require
        extendible : *extendible*
      ensure
        item_pushed: *item* = *v*
      ensure then
        one_more_occurrence: *occurrences* (*v*) = **old**
          (*occurrences* (*v*)) + *1*
      ensure then
        item_inserted: *has* (*v*)

    force (*v*: **like** *item*)
        -- Push *v* on top.
      ensure
        item_pushed: *item* = *v*

put (*v*: **like** *item*)
    -- Push *v* on top.
  require
    extendible: *extendible*
  ensure
    item_pushed: *item* = *v*
  ensure then
    one_more_occurrence: *occurrences* (*v*) = **old**
      (*occurrences* (*v*)) + *1*
  ensure then
    item_inserted: *has* (*v*)

replace (*v*: **like** *item*)
    -- Replace top item by *v*.
  require
    writable: *writable*
  ensure
    item_replaced: *item* = *v*

feature -- Removal

remove
    -- Remove top item.
  require
    not_empty: *count* /= 0
  require else
    prunable;
    writable

wipe_out
    -- Remove all items.
  require
    prunable
  ensure
    wiped_out: *empty*

feature -- Conversion

linear_representation: *ARRAYED_LIST* [*G*]
    -- Representation as a linear structure
    -- (in the reverse order of original insertion)

invariant

  count_small_enough: *count* <= *capacity*;
  extendible_definition: *extendible* = **not** *full*;
  empty_definition: *empty* = (*count* = 0);
  non_negative_count: *count* >= 0;
  valid_count: *count* <= *capacity*;
  full_definition: *full* = (*count* = *capacity*)

end

17.5 CLASS *LINKED_STACK*

The interface as it appears here only shows the exported features introduced or redeclared in the class. In addition, *LINKED_STACK* has all the features of *STACK*. Please refer to the interface of *STACK* as it appears at the beginning of this chapter.

The interface of STACK is in 17.2, page 333.

indexing

"*Unbounded stacks implemented as linked lists*"
names: *linked_stack, dispenser, linked_list*
representation: *linked*
access: *fixed, lifo, membership*
contents: *generic*

class interface

LINKED_STACK [G]

creation
make

feature -- Initialization

make
    -- Create an empty list.
    -- (From *LINKED_LIST*.)

feature -- Access

item: *G*
    -- Item at the first position
    require
      not *empty*
    require else
      readable

feature -- Element change

extend (*v*: **like** *item*)
    -- Push *v* onto top.
    require
      extendible: *extendible*
    ensure
      item_pushed: *item* = *v*

force (*v*: **like** *item*)
    -- Push *v* onto top.
    require
      extendible: *extendible*
    ensure
      item_pushed: *item* = *v*
    ensure then

put (*v*: **like** *item*)
    require
      extendible: *extendible*
    ensure
      item_pushed: *item* = *v*
    ensure then

feature -- Conversion

linear_representation: *ARRAYED_LIST* [*G*]
    -- Representation as a linear structure
    -- (order is reverse of original order of insertion)

feature -- Duplication

duplicate (*n*: *INTEGER*): **like** *Current*
    -- New stack containing the *n* latest items inserted
    -- in current stack.
    -- If *n* is greater than *count*, identical to current stack.
    require
      positive_argument: $n > 0$
    require else
      valid_subchain: $n >= 0$

invariant

    extendible: *extendible*

end

17.6 CLASS *QUEUE*

The interface of *QUEUE* is almost identical to that of *STACK*; the only difference is in the assertions, since the last-in-first-out properties of stacks (see for example the postcondition of *put* in the interface of *STACK*) do not apply to queues.

As with *STACK*, the interface shown here for *QUEUE* includes all the features of the class including those inherited from ancestors. They also apply to the implementations given next (*ARRAYED_QUEUE*, *LINKED_QUEUE*, *BOUNDED_QUEUE*), whose interfaces are essentially the same except for the creation procedures and some extra assertions.

indexing

   description: "Queues (first–in, first-out dispensers), without
      commitment to a particular representation"
   names: queue, dispenser
   access: fixed, fifo, membership
   contents: generic

deferred class interface

   QUEUE [G]

feature -- Access

   has (v: G): BOOLEAN
         -- Does structure include *v*?
         -- (Reference or object equality,
         -- based on *object_comparison*.)
         -- (From *CONTAINER*.)
      ensure
         not_found_in_empty: Result **implies not** empty

   item: G
         -- Current item
         -- (From *ACTIVE*.)
      require
         readable

feature -- Measurement

   count: INTEGER
         -- Number of items
         -- (From *FINITE*.)

   occurrences (v: G): INTEGER
         -- Number of times *v* appears in structure
         -- (Reference or object equality,
         -- based on *object_comparison*.)
         -- (From *BAG*.)
      ensure
         non_negative_occurrences: Result >= 0

feature -- Status report

   changeable_comparison_criterion: BOOLEAN
         -- May *object_comparison* be changed?
         -- (Answer: yes by default.)
         -- (From *CONTAINER*.)

   empty: BOOLEAN
         -- Is structure empty?
         -- (From *FINITE*.)

   extendible: BOOLEAN
         -- May new items be added?
         -- (From *COLLECTION*.)

   full: BOOLEAN
         -- Is structure filled to capacity?
         -- (From *BOX*.)

   object_comparison: BOOLEAN
         -- Must search operations use *equal* rather than =
         -- for comparing references? (Default: no, use =.)
         -- (From *CONTAINER*.)

   prunable: BOOLEAN
         -- May items be removed?
         -- (From *COLLECTION*.)

   readable: BOOLEAN
         -- Is there a current item that may be read?
         -- (From *DISPENSER*.)

   writable: BOOLEAN
         -- Is there a current item that may be modified?
         -- (From *DISPENSER*.)

feature -- Status setting

   compare_objects
         -- Ensure that future search operations will use *equal*
         -- rather than = for comparing references.
         -- (From *CONTAINER*.)
      require
         changeable_comparison_criterion
      ensure
         object_comparison

compare_references
>   -- Ensure that future search operations will use =
>   -- rather than *equal* for comparing references.
>   -- (From *CONTAINER*.)
>   **require**
>   *changeable_comparison_criterion*
>   **ensure**
>   *reference_comparison*: **not** *object_comparison*

feature -- Element change

append (*s*: *SEQUENCE* [*G*])
>   -- Append a copy of *s*.
>   -- (Synonym for *fill*)
>   -- (From *DISPENSER*.)

extend (*v*: **like** *item*)
>   -- Add item *v*.
>   -- (From *DISPENSER*.)
>   **require**
>   *extendible*: *extendible*
>   **ensure**
>   *one_more_occurrence*: *occurrences* (*v*) = **old**
>   (*occurrences* (*v*)) + *1*
>   **ensure then**
>   *item_inserted*: *has* (*v*)

fill (*other*: *CONTAINER* [*G*])
>   -- Fill with as many items of *other* as possible.
>   -- The representations of *other* and current structure
>   -- need not be the same.
>   -- (From *COLLECTION*.)
>   **require**
>   *other_not_void*: *other* /= *Void*;
>   *extendible*: *extendible*

force (*v*: **like** *item*)
>   -- Add *v* as newest item.

put (*v*: **like** *item*)
>   -- Add item *v*.
>   -- (From *DISPENSER*.)
>   **require**
>   *extendible*: *extendible*
>   **ensure**
>   *item_inserted*: *has* (*v*)

replace (*v*: *G*)
>   -- Replace current item by *v*.
>   -- (From *ACTIVE*.)
>   **require**
>   *writable*: *writable*
>   **ensure**
>   *item_replaced*: *item* = *v*

feature -- Removal

remove
>   -- Remove current item.
>   -- (From *ACTIVE*.)
>   **require**
>   *prunable*;
>   *writable*

wipe_out
>   -- Remove all items.
>   -- (From *COLLECTION*.)
>   **require**
>   *prunable*
>   **ensure**
>   *wiped_out*: *empty*

feature -- Conversion

linear_representation: *LINEAR* [*G*]
>   -- Representation as a linear structure
>   -- (From *CONTAINER*.)

invariant

>   *readable_definition*: *readable* = **not** *empty*;
>   *writable_definition*: *writable* = **not** *empty*;
>   *writable_constraint*: *writable* **implies** *readable*;
>   *empty_constraint*: *empty* **implies** (**not** *readable*) **and** (**not**
>   *writable*);
>   *empty_definition*: *empty* = (*count* = 0);
>   *non_negative_count*: *count* >= *0*

end

17.7 CLASS *ARRAYED_QUEUE*

The interface shown below includes for convenience all the features inherited from
QUEUE and *DISPENSER*, but not those from any other ancestor unless the class
redeclares them.

indexing

    description: "*Unbounded queues, implemented by resizable
      arrays*"
    names: *dispenser, array*
    representation: *array*
    access: *fixed, fifo, membership*
    size: *fixed*
    contents: *generic*

class interface

    ARRAYED_QUEUE [G]

creation
    make

feature -- Initialization

    make (*n*: *INTEGER*)
        -- Create queue for at most *n* items.
      require
        non_negative_argument: *n* >= 0

feature -- Access

    has (*v*: **like** *item*): *BOOLEAN*
        -- Does queue include *v*?
        -- (Reference or object equality,
        -- based on *object_comparison*.)
      ensure
        not_found_in_empty: *Result* **implies not** *empty*

    item: *G*
        -- Oldest item.
      require
        readable

feature -- Measurement

    count: *INTEGER*
        -- Number of items.

feature -- Status report

    empty: *BOOLEAN*
        -- Is the structure empty?

    extendible: *BOOLEAN*
        -- May items be added? (Answer: yes.)

    full: *BOOLEAN*
        -- Is structure filled to capacity?
        -- (Answer: no.)

    off: *BOOLEAN*
        -- Is the structure empty?

    prunable: *BOOLEAN*
        -- May items be removed? (Answer: yes.)

    readable: *BOOLEAN*
        -- Is there a current item that may be read?
        -- (From *DISPENSER*.)

    writable: *BOOLEAN*
        -- Is there a current item that may be modified?
        -- (From *DISPENSER*.)

feature -- Element change

    append (*s*: *SEQUENCE* [G])
        -- Append a copy of *s*.
        -- (Synonym for *fill*)
        -- (From *DISPENSER*.)

    extend (*v*: *G*)
        -- Add *v* as newest item.
      require
        extendible: *extendible*
      ensure
        item_inserted: *has* (*v*)

    force (*v*: *G*)
        -- Add *v* as newest item.

    put (*v*: *G*)
        -- Add *v* as newest item.
      require
        extendible: *extendible*
      ensure
        item_inserted: *has* (*v*)

    replace (*v*: **like** *item*)
        -- Replace oldest item by *v*.
      require
        writable: *writable*
      ensure
        item_replaced: *item* = *v*

feature -- Removal

    remove
        -- Remove oldest item.
      require
        prunable;
        writable

wipe_out
      -- Remove all items.
   require
      prunable
   ensure
      wiped_out: *empty*

feature -- Conversion

   linear_representation: *ARRAYED_LIST* [*G*]
      -- Representation as a linear structure
      -- (in the original insertion order)

invariant

   not_full: **not** *full*;
   extendible: *extendible*;
   prunable: *prunable*;
   readable_definition: *readable* = **not** *empty*;
   writable_definition: *writable* = **not** *empty*;
   writable_constraint: *writable* **implies** *readable*;
   empty_constraint: *empty* **implies** (**not** *readable*) **and** (**not**
      writable);
   empty_definition: *empty* = (*count* = *0*);
   non_negative_count: *count* >= *0*

end

17.8 CLASS *BOUNDED_QUEUE*

The interface of *BOUNDED_QUEUE* is very similar to that of *ARRAYED_QUEUE*. The main difference is that *extendible*, the precondition of *put*, is not always true any more, but has the value *not full*.

The interface as it appears here only shows the features introduced or redeclared in the class, and those inherited from *BOUNDED*. In addition, *BOUNDED_QUEUE* has all the exported features of *QUEUE*; please refer to the interface of *QUEUE* as it appears earlier in this chapter.

The interface of QUEUE is in 17.6, page 340.

indexing

    description: "*Queues with a bounded physical size, implemented by arrays*"
    names: *dispenser, array*
    representation: *array*
    access: *fixed, fifo, membership*
    size: *fixed*
    contents: *generic*

class interface

    BOUNDED_QUEUE [G]

creation
    make

feature -- Initialization

    make (*n*: *INTEGER*)
        -- Create queue for at most *n* items.
      require
        non_negative_argument: *n* >= *0*
      ensure
        capacity_expected: *capacity* = *n*

feature -- Access

    has (*v*: **like** *item*): *BOOLEAN*
        -- Does queue include *v*?
        -- (Reference or object equality,
        -- based on *object_comparison*.)

    item: *G*
        -- Oldest item.
      require
        readable

feature -- Measurement

    capacity: *INTEGER*
        -- Number of items that may be kept.

    count: *INTEGER*
        -- Number of items.

    occurrences (*v*: *G*): *INTEGER*
      ensure
        non_negative_occurrences: *Result* >= *0*

feature -- Status report

    extendible: *BOOLEAN*

    full: *BOOLEAN*
        -- Is structure full?
        -- (From *BOUNDED*.)

    off: *BOOLEAN*
        -- Is there no current item?

    prunable: *BOOLEAN* **is true**

    readable: *BOOLEAN*
        -- Is there a current item that may be read?
        -- (From *DISPENSER*.)

    resizable: *BOOLEAN* **is true**

    writable: *BOOLEAN*
        -- Is there a current item that may be modified?
        -- (From *DISPENSER*.)

feature -- Cursor movement

    finish
        -- Move cursor to last position.

    forth
        -- Move cursor to next position.

    start
        -- Move cursor to first position.

feature -- Element change

    append (*s*: *SEQUENCE* [G])
        -- Append a copy of *s*.
        -- (Synonym for *fill*)
        -- (From *DISPENSER*.)

    extend (*v*: *G*)
        -- Add *v* as newest item.
      require
        extendible: *extendible*
      ensure
        one_more_occurrence: *occurrences* (*v*) = **old**
          (*occurrences* (*v*)) + *1*
      ensure
        item_inserted: *has* (*v*)

force (*v*: *G*)
    -- Add *v* as newest item.

put (*v*: *G*)
    -- Add *v* as newest item.
  require
    extendible: *extendible*
  ensure
    item_inserted: *has* (*v*)

replace (*v*: **like** *item*)
    -- Replace oldest item by *v*.
  require
    writable: *writable*
  ensure
    item_replaced: *item* = *v*

feature -- Removal

prune (*v*: **like** *item*)
  require
    prunable: *prunable*

remove
    -- Remove oldest item.
  require
    prunable;
    writable

wipe_out
    -- Remove all items.
  require
    prunable

feature -- Conversion

linear_representation: *ARRAYED_LIST* [*G*]
    -- Representation as a linear structure
    -- (in the original insertion order)

invariant

  extendible_definition: *extendible* = **not** *full*;
  writable_constraint: *writable* **implies** *readable*;
  non_negative_count: *count* >= *0*;
  valid_count: *count* <= *capacity*;
  full_definition: *full* = (*count* = *capacity*)

end

17.9 CLASS *LINKED_QUEUE*

The interface as it appears here only shows the exported features introduced or redeclared in the class. In addition, *LINKED_QUEUE* has all the features of *QUEUE*. Please refer to the interface of *QUEUE* as it appears earlier in this chapter.

The interface of QUEUE is in 17.6, page 340.

indexing

   description: "*Unbounded queues implemented as linked lists*"
   names: *linked_queue, dispenser, linked_list*
   representation: *linked*
   access: *fixed, fifo, membership*
   contents: *generic*

class interface

   LINKED_QUEUE [G]

creation
   make

feature -- Initialization

   make

feature -- Access

   item: *G*
        -- Oldest item
      require
        not *empty*
      require else
        readable

feature -- Element change

   extend (*v*: *G*)
        -- Add *v* as newest item.
      require
        extendible: *extendible*

   force (*v*: *G*)
        -- Add *v* as newest item.
      require
        extendible: *extendible*

   put (*v*: *G*)
        -- Add *v* as newest item.
      require
        extendible: *extendible*

feature -- Conversion

   linear_representation: *ARRAYED_LIST* [G]
        -- Representation as a linear structure
        -- (order is same as original order of insertion)

feature -- Duplication

   duplicate (*n*: *INTEGER*): **like** *Current*
        -- New queue containing the *n* oldest items in current
           queue.
        -- If *n* is greater than *count*, identical to current queue.
      require
        positive_argument: $n > 0$
      require else
        valid_subchain: $n >= 0$

invariant

   extendible: *extendible*

end

17.10 CLASSES *HEAP_PRIORITY_QUEUE, LINKED_PRIORITY_QUEUE* AND *PRIORITY_QUEUE*

The deferred class *PRIORITY_QUEUE* and the two effective implementations provided have exactly the same interface, which is that of *DISPENSER*. The interface shown here is the flat-short form of *HEAP_PRIORITY_QUEUE*. For convenience it includes all the features coming from *DISPENSER*, but not those from other ancestors unless the class redeclares them.

indexing

   description: "Priority queues implemented as heaps"
   names: sorted_priority_queue, dispenser, heap
   representation: heap
   access: fixed, membership
   contents: generic

class interface

   HEAP_PRIORITY_QUEUE [G –> COMPARABLE]

creation
   make

feature -- Initialization

   make (n: INTEGER)
      -- Allocate heap space.

feature -- Access

   item: G
      -- Entry at top of heap.
   require
      readable

feature -- Measurement

   count: INTEGER

feature -- Status report

   extendible: BOOLEAN
      -- May items be added?

   full: BOOLEAN
      -- Is structure filled to capacity?

   prunable: BOOLEAN **is true**
      -- May items be removed? (Answer: yes.)

   readable: BOOLEAN
      -- Is there a current item that may be read?
      -- (From *DISPENSER*.)

   writable: BOOLEAN
      -- Is there a current item that may be modified?
      -- (From *DISPENSER*.)

feature -- Element change

   append (s: SEQUENCE [G])
      -- Append a copy of s.
      -- (Synonym for *fill*)
      -- (From *DISPENSER*.)

   force (v: **like** item)
      -- Insert item v at its proper position.

   put (v: **like** item)
      -- Insert item v at its proper position.
   require
      extendible: extendible

feature -- Removal

   remove
      -- Remove item of highest value.
   require
      prunable;
      writable

feature -- Conversion

   linear_representation: ARRAYED_LIST [G]
      -- Representation as a linear structure
      -- (Sorted according to decreasing priority)

feature -- Duplication

   duplicate (n: INTEGER): **like** Current
      -- New priority queue containing the n greatest items

invariant

   writable_constraint: writable **implies** readable;
   non_negative_count: count >= 0

end

18

Tree classes

18.1 OVERVIEW

An earlier chapter introduced the variants of the notion of tree and explained the corresponding classes. Here now are the interfaces, in flat-short form, of all these classes.

Chapter 8.

For ease of reference, the figure on the next page reproduces the general inheritance structure given in the earlier discussion.

This is the same figure as on page 164.

The class interfaces appears in the following order, where the notation *C / D* indicates that two classes with the same interface are given together:

> *TREE, LINKED_TREE / TWO_WAY_TREE, ARRAYED_TREE, FIXED_TREE, BINARY_TREE, BINARY_SEARCH_TREE, CURSOR_TREE, LINKED_CURSOR_TREE / TWO_WAY_CURSOR_TREE, COMPACT_CURSOR_TREE.*

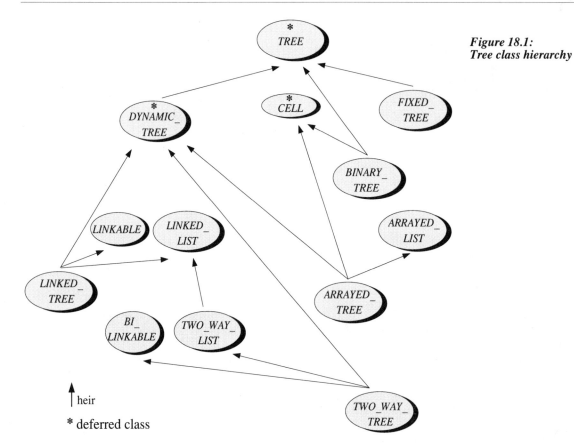

Figure 18.1:
Tree class hierarchy

↑ heir

* deferred class

18.2 CLASS *TREE*

This interface shows all the features of class *TREE* including the general features
inherited from *CONTAINER*.

indexing

  description: "Trees, without commitment to a particular
    representation"
  names: tree
  access: cursor, membership
  representation: recursive
  contents: generic

deferred class interface

  TREE [G]

feature -- Access

  child: **like** parent
      -- Current child node
    require
      readable: readable_child

  child_cursor: CURSOR
      -- Current cursor position

  child_index: INTEGER
      -- Index of current child
    ensure
      valid_index: Result >= 0 **and** Result <= arity + 1

child_item: **like** *item*
-- Item in current child node
require
readable: *child_readable*

first_child: **like** *parent*
-- Leftmost child
require
is_not_leaf: **not** *is_leaf*

has (*v*: *G*): *BOOLEAN*
-- Does subtree include *v*?
-- (Reference or object equality,
-- based on *object_comparison*.)
ensure
not_found_in_empty: *Result* **implies not** *empty*

is_sibling (*other*: **like** *parent*): *BOOLEAN*
-- Are current node and *other* siblings?
ensure
not_root: *Result* **implies not** *is_root*;
other_not_root: *Result* **implies not** *other*.*is_root*;
same_parent: *Result* = **not** *is_root* **and** *other*.*parent* =
parent

item: *G*
-- Item in current node

last_child: **like** *first_child*
-- Right most child
require
is_not_leaf: **not** *is_leaf*

left_sibling: **like** *parent*
-- Left neighbor (if any)
require
is_not_root: **not** *is_root*
ensure
is_sibling: *is_sibling* (*Result*);
right_is_current: (*Result* /= *Void*) **implies** (*Result*.*right_
sibling* = *Current*)

parent: *TREE* [*G*]
-- Parent of current node

right_sibling: **like** *parent*
-- Right neighbor (if any)
require
is_not_root: **not** *is_root*
ensure
is_sibling: *is_sibling* (*Result*);
left_is_current: (*Result* /= *Void*) **implies** (*Result*.*left_
sibling* = *Current*)

feature -- Measurement

arity: *INTEGER*
-- Number of children

count: *INTEGER*
-- Number of items

feature -- Status report

changeable_comparison_criterion: *BOOLEAN*
-- May *object_comparison* be changed?
-- (Answer: yes by default.)
-- (From *CONTAINER*.)

child_after: *BOOLEAN*
-- Is there no valid child position to the right of cursor?

child_before: *BOOLEAN*
-- Is there no valid child position to the left of cursor?

child_isfirst: *BOOLEAN*
-- Is cursor under first child?
ensure
not_is_leaf: *Result* **implies not** *is_leaf*

child_islast: *BOOLEAN*
-- Is cursor under last child?
ensure
not_is_leaf: *Result* **implies not** *is_leaf*

child_off: *BOOLEAN*
-- Is there no current child?

child_readable: *BOOLEAN*
-- Is there a current *child_item* to be read?

child_writable: *BOOLEAN*
-- Is there a current *child_item* that may be modified?

empty: *BOOLEAN*
-- Is structure empty of items?

is_leaf: *BOOLEAN*
-- Are there no children?

is_root: *BOOLEAN*
-- Is there no parent?

object_comparison: *BOOLEAN*
-- Must search operations use *equal* rather than =
-- for comparing references? (Default: no, use =.)
-- (From *CONTAINER*.)

readable: *BOOLEAN* **is true**

readable_child: *BOOLEAN*
-- Is there a current child to be read?

valid_cursor_index (*i*: *INTEGER*): *BOOLEAN*
-- Is *i* correctly bounded for cursor movement?
ensure
valid_cursor_index_definition: *Result* = (*i* >= *0*) **and** (*i*
<= *arity* + *1*)

writable: *BOOLEAN* **is true**
-- Is there a current item that may be modified?

writable_child: *BOOLEAN*
-- Is there a current child that may be modified?

feature -- Status setting

compare_objects
-- Ensure that future search operations will use *equal*
-- rather than = for comparing references.
-- (From *CONTAINER*.)
require
changeable_comparison_criterion
ensure
object_comparison

compare_references
-- Ensure that future search operations will use =
-- rather than *equal* for comparing references.
-- (From *CONTAINER*.)
require
changeable_comparison_criterion
ensure
reference_comparison: **not** *object_comparison*

feature -- Cursor movement

child_back
-- Move cursor to next child.

child_finish
-- Move cursor to last child.
ensure
is_last_child: **not** *is_leaf* **implies** *child_islast*

child_forth
-- Move cursor to next child.

child_go_i_th (*i*: *INTEGER*)
-- Move cursor to *i*–th child.
require
valid_cursor_index: *valid_cursor_index* (*i*)
ensure
position: *child_index* = *i*;
is_before: (*i* = 0) **implies** *child_before*;
is_after: (*i* = *arity* + *1*) **implies** *child_after*

child_go_to (*p*: *CURSOR*)
-- Move cursor to position *p*.

child_start
-- Move cursor to first child.
ensure
is_first_child: **not** *is_leaf* **implies** *child_isfirst*

feature -- Element change

child_put (*v*: **like** *item*)
-- Put *v* at current child position.
require
child_writable: *child_writable*
ensure
item_inserted: *child_item* = *v*

child_replace (*v*: **like** *item*)
-- Put *v* at current child position.
require
child_writable: *child_writable*
ensure
item_inserted: *child_item* = *v*

fill (*other*: *TREE* [*G*])
-- Fill with as many items of *other* as possible.
-- The representations of *other* and current node
-- need not be the same.

prune (*n*: **like** *parent*)
-- Remove *n* from the children
require
is_child: *n*.*parent* = *Current*
ensure
n_is_root: *n*.*is_root*

put (*v*: **like** *item*)
-- Replace element at cursor position by *v*.
require
is_writable: *writable*
ensure
item_inserted: *item* = *v*

replace (*v*: **like** *item*)
-- Replace element at cursor position by *v*.
require
is_writable: *writable*
ensure
item_inserted: *item* = *v*

replace_child (*n*: **like** *parent*)
-- Put *n* at current child position.
require
writable_child: *writable_child*;
was_root: *n*.*is_root*
ensure
child_replaced: *child* = *n*

sprout
-- Make current node a root.

feature -- Conversion

  binary_representation: *BINARY_TREE* [*G*]
        -- Convert to binary tree representation:
        -- first child becomes left child,
        -- right sibling becomes right child.
    ensure
        result_is_root: *Result.is_root*;
        result_has_no_right_child: **not** *Result.has_right*

  linear_representation: *LINEAR* [*G*]
        -- Representation as a linear structure

feature -- Duplication

  duplicate (*n*: *INTEGER*): **like** *Current*
        -- Copy of sub-tree beginning at cursor position and
        -- having min (*n*, *arity* − *child_index* + 1)
        -- children.
    require
        not_child_off: **not** *child_off*;
        valid_sublist: $n >= 0$

invariant

  leaf_definition: *is_leaf* = (*arity* = 0);
  child_off_definition: *child_off* = *child_before* **or** *child_after*;
  child_before_definition: *child_before* = (*child_index* = 0);
  child_isfirst_definition: *child_isfirst* = (**not** *is_leaf* **and** *child_
    index* = 1);
  child_islast_definition: *child_islast* = (**not** *is_leaf* **and** *child_
    index* = *arity*);
  child_after_definition: *child_after* = (*child_index* >= *arity* +
    1);
  child_consistency: *child_readable* **implies** *child.parent* =
    Current

end

18.3 CLASSES *LINKED_TREE* AND *TWO_WAY_TREE*

LINKED_TREE and *TWO_WAY_TREE* have the same interface, shown below for *TWO_WAY_TREE*.

For convenience, since this class is commonly used by systems that need a simple and complete tree implementation, the interface retains all the features of the class except those inherited unchanged from *CONTAINER*.

ARRAYED_TREE has almost the same interface; the only difference is the creation procedure; see the next section.

indexing

> *description*: "*Trees implemented using a two way linked list representation*"
> *names*: *two_way_tree*, *tree*, *two_way_list*
> *representation*: *recursive*, *linked*
> *access*: *cursor*, *membership*
> *contents*: *generic*

class interface

> *TWO_WAY_TREE* [G]

creation
> *make*

feature -- Initialization

> *make* (*v*: **like** *item*)
>   -- Create single node with item *v*.

feature -- Access

> *child_cursor*: *CURSOR*
>   -- Current cursor position
>   -- (From *LINKED_LIST*.)

> *child_index*: *INTEGER*
>   -- Index of current position
>   -- (From *LINKED_LIST*.)
>   **ensure**
>   *valid_index*: *Result* >= *0* **and** *Result* <= *arity* + *1*

> *child_item*: *G*
>   -- Current item
>   -- (From *LINKED_LIST*.)
>   **require**
>   *readable*: *child_readable*
>   **require else**
>   *child_readable*
>   **require else**
>   *not_off*: **not** *child_off*

> *first_child*: **like** *parent*
>   -- Leftmost child

has (*v*: *G*): *BOOLEAN*
>   -- Does subtree include *v*?
>   -- (Reference or object equality,
>   -- based on *object_comparison*.)
>   -- (From *TREE*.)
>   **ensure**
>   *not_found_in_empty*: *Result* **implies not** *is_leaf*

i_th (*i*: *INTEGER*): **like** *child_item*
>   -- Item at *i*-th position
>   -- (From *CHAIN*.)
>   **require**
>   *valid_key*: *valid_index* (*i*)

index_of (*v*: **like** *child_item*; *i*: *INTEGER*): *INTEGER*
>   -- Index of *i*-th occurrence of item identical to *v*.
>   -- (Reference or object equality,
>   -- based on *object_comparison*.)
>   -- 0 if none.
>   -- (From *CHAIN*.)
>   **require**
>   *positive_occurrences*: *i* > *0*
>   **ensure**
>   *non_negative_result*: *Result* >= *0*

is_sibling (*other*: **like** *parent*): *BOOLEAN*
>   -- Are current node and *other* siblings?
>   -- (From *TREE*.)
>   **ensure**
>   *not_root*: *Result* **implies not** *is_root*;
>   *other_not_root*: *Result* **implies not** *other*.*is_root*;
>   *same_parent*: *Result* = **not** *is_root* **and** *other*.*parent* = *parent*

item: *G*
>   -- Content of cell.
>   -- (From *CELL*.)

last_child: **like** *parent*

left_sibling: **like** *Current*
>   -- Left neighbor
>   -- (From *BI_LINKABLE*.)

occurrences (*v*: **like** *child_item*): *INTEGER*
    -- Number of times *v* appears.
    -- (Reference or object equality,
    -- based on *object_comparison*.)
    -- (From *CHAIN*.)
  ensure
    non_negative_occurrences: *Result* >= *0*

parent: *TWO_WAY_TREE* [*G*]
    -- Parent node

right_sibling: **like** *Current*
    -- Right neighbor
    -- (From *LINKABLE*.)

sequential_occurrences (*v*: *G*): *INTEGER*
    -- Number of times *v* appears.
    -- (Reference or object equality,
    -- based on *object_comparison*.)
    -- (From *LINEAR*.)
  ensure
    non_negative_occurrences: *Result* >= *0*

sublist: **like** *Current*
    -- Result produced by last *split*
    -- (From *TWO_WAY_LIST*.)

infix *"@"* (*i*: *INTEGER*): **like** *child_item*
    -- Item at *i*–th position
    -- (From *CHAIN*.)
  require
    valid_key: *valid_index* (*i*)

feature -- Measurement

arity: *INTEGER*
    -- Number of items
    -- (From *LINKED_LIST*.)

count: *INTEGER*
    -- Number of items
    -- (From *TREE*.)

feature -- Status report

child_after: *BOOLEAN*
    -- Is there no valid cursor position to the right of cursor?
    -- (From *LINKED_LIST*.)

child_before: *BOOLEAN*
    -- Is there no valid cursor position to the left of cursor?
    -- (From *LINKED_LIST*.)

child_extendible: *BOOLEAN* **is true**
    -- May new items be added? (Answer: yes.)
    -- (From *DYNAMIC_CHAIN*.)

child_isfirst: *BOOLEAN*
    -- Is cursor under first child?
    -- (From *TREE*.)
  ensure
    not_is_leaf: *Result* **implies not** *is_leaf*
  ensure then
    valid_position: *Result* **implies not** *is_leaf*

child_islast: *BOOLEAN*
    -- Is cursor under last child?
    -- (From *TREE*.)
  ensure
    not_is_leaf: *Result* **implies not** *is_leaf*
  ensure then
    valid_position: *Result* **implies not** *is_leaf*

child_off: *BOOLEAN*
    -- Is there no current item?
    -- (From *LINKED_LIST*.)

child_readable: *BOOLEAN*
    -- Is there a current *child_item* to be read?
    -- (From *TREE*.)

child_writable: *BOOLEAN*
    -- Is there a current *child_item* that may be modified?
    -- (From *TREE*.)

empty: *BOOLEAN*
    -- Is structure empty of items?
    -- (From *TREE*.)

exhausted: *BOOLEAN*
    -- Has structure been completely explored?
    -- (From *LINEAR*.)
  ensure
    exhausted_when_off: *child_off* **implies** *Result*

extendible: *BOOLEAN* **is true**
    -- May new items be added?
    -- (From *DYNAMIC_TREE*.)

is_leaf: *BOOLEAN*
    -- Are there no children?
    -- (From *TREE*.)

is_root: *BOOLEAN*
    -- Is there no parent?
    -- (From *TREE*.)

prunable: *BOOLEAN*
    -- May items be removed? (Answer: yes.)
    -- (From *DYNAMIC_CHAIN*.)

readable: *BOOLEAN* **is true**
    -- (From *TREE*.)

readable_child: *BOOLEAN*
    -- Is there a current child to be read?
    -- (From *TREE*.)

valid_cursor_index (*i*: *INTEGER*): *BOOLEAN*
    -- Is *i* correctly bounded for cursor movement?
    -- (From *TREE*.)
  ensure
    valid_cursor_index_definition: *Result* = (*i* >= *0*) **and** (*i*
      <= *arity* + *1*)
  ensure then
    valid_cursor_index_definition: *Result* = ((*i* >= *0*) **and** (*i*
      <= *arity* + *1*))

valid_index (*i*: *INTEGER*): *BOOLEAN*
    -- Is *i* within allowable bounds?
    -- (From *CHAIN*.)
  ensure
    valid_index_definition: *Result* = (*i* >= *1*) **and** (*i* <= *arity*)

writable: *BOOLEAN* **is true**
    -- Is there a current item that may be modified?
    -- (From *TREE*.)

writable_child: *BOOLEAN*
    -- Is there a current child that may be modified?
    -- (From *TREE*.)

feature -- Cursor movement

child_back
    -- Move cursor to previous position, if any.
    -- (From *TWO_WAY_LIST*.)
  require
    not_before: **not** *child_before*
  ensure
    moved_back: *child_index* = **old** *child_index* − *1*

child_finish
    -- Move cursor to last position.
    -- (Go before if empty)
    -- (From *TWO_WAY_LIST*.)
  ensure
    not_after: **not** *child_after*
  ensure then
    is_last_child: **not** *is_leaf* **implies** *child_islast*
  ensure then
    empty_convention: *is_leaf* **implies** *child_before*
  ensure then
    at_last: **not** *is_leaf* **implies** *child_islast*

child_forth
    -- Move cursor to next position, if any.
    -- (From *TWO_WAY_LIST*.)
  require
    not_after: **not** *child_after*
  ensure
    moved_forth: *child_index* = **old** *child_index* + *1*

child_go_i_th (*i*: *INTEGER*)
    -- Move cursor to *i*–th position.
    -- (From *LINKED_LIST*.)
  require
    valid_cursor_index: *valid_cursor_index* (*i*)
  require else
    valid_cursor_index: *valid_cursor_index* (*i*)
  ensure
    position: *child_index* = *i*;
    is_before: (*i* = *0*) **implies** *child_before*;
    is_after: (*i* = *arity* + *1*) **implies** *child_after*
  ensure then
    position_expected: *child_index* = *i*

child_go_to (*p*: *CURSOR*)
    -- Move cursor to position *p*.
    -- (From *LINKED_LIST*.)
  require
    cursor_position_valid: *valid_cursor* (*p*)

child_start
    -- Move cursor to first position.
    -- (From *LINKED_LIST*.)
  ensure
    empty_convention: *is_leaf* **implies** *child_after*
  ensure then
    is_first_child: **not** *is_leaf* **implies** *child_isfirst*
  ensure then
    at_first: **not** *is_leaf* **implies** *child_isfirst*

move (*i*: *INTEGER*)
    -- Move cursor *i* positions. The cursor
    -- may end up *off* if the offset is to big.
    -- (From *TWO_WAY_LIST*.)
  ensure
    moved_if_inbounds: ((**old** *child_index* + *i*) >= *0* **and** (**old**
      child_index + *i*) <= (*arity* + *1*)) **implies** *child_index* =
      (**old** *child_index* + *i*);
    before_set: (**old** *child_index* + *i*) <= *0* **implies** *child_*
      before;
    after_set: (**old** *child_index* + *i*) >= (*arity* + *1*) **implies**
      child_after
  ensure then
    too_far_right: (**old** *child_index* + *i* > *arity*) **implies**
      exhausted;
    too_far_left: (**old** *child_index* + *i* < *1*) **implies**
      exhausted;
    expected_index: (**not** *exhausted*) **implies** (*child_index* =
      old *child_index* + *i*)

search_child (*v*: **like** *child_item*)
    -- Move to first position (at or after current
    -- position) where *item* and *v* are equal.
    -- If structure does not include *v* ensure that
    -- *exhausted* will be true.
    -- (Reference or object equality,
    -- based on *object_comparison*.)
    -- (From *BILINEAR*.)

feature -- Element change

child_extend (*v*: **like** *child_item*)
    -- Add *v* to end.
    -- Do not move cursor.
    -- (From *TWO_WAY_LIST*.)
  require
    child_extendible
  ensure
    one_more_occurrence: *occurrences* (*v*) = **old**
      (*occurrences* (*v*)) + *1*
  ensure then
    item_inserted: *has* (*v*)

child_put (*v*: **like** *child_item*)
    -- Replace current item by *v*.
    -- (Synonym for *replace*)
    -- (From *CHAIN*.)
  require
    child_writable: *child_writable*
  require else
    child_extendible
  ensure
    same_count: *arity* = **old** *arity*
  ensure then
    item_inserted: *child_item* = *v*
  ensure then
    item_inserted: *has* (*v*)

child_put_left (*v*: **like** *child_item*)
    -- Add *v* to the left of cursor position.
    -- Do not move cursor.
    -- (From *TWO_WAY_LIST*.)
  require
    not_child_before: **not** *child_before*
  require else
    extendible: *child_extendible*;
    not_before: **not** *child_before*
  ensure
    new_count: *arity* = **old** *arity* + *1*;
    new_index: *child_index* = **old** *child_index* + *1*

child_put_right (*v*: **like** *child_item*)
    -- Add *v* to the right of cursor position.
    -- Do not move cursor.
    -- (From *TWO_WAY_LIST*.)
  require
    not_child_after: **not** *child_after*
  require else
    extendible: *child_extendible*;
    not_after: **not** *child_after*
  ensure
    item_inserted_before: **old** *child_before* **implies**
      child. *item* = *v*
  ensure then
    new_count: *arity* = **old** *arity* + *1*;
    same_index: *child_index* = **old** *child_index*

child_replace (*v*: **like** *child_item*)
    -- Replace current item by *v*.
    -- (From *LINKED_LIST*.)
  require
    child_writable: *child_writable*
  require else
    writable: *child_writable*
  ensure
    item_inserted: *child_item* = *v*
  ensure then
    item_replaced: *child_item* = *v*

extend (*v*: **like** *item*)
    -- Add *v* as new child.
    -- (From *DYNAMIC_TREE*.)

fill (*other*: *TREE* [*G*])
    -- Fill with as many items of *other* as possible.
    -- The representations of *other* and current node
    -- need not be the same.
    -- (From *TREE*.)

force (*v*: **like** *child_item*)
    -- Add *v* to end.
    -- (From *SEQUENCE*.)
  require
    extendible: *child_extendible*
  ensure
    new_count: *arity* = **old** *arity* + *1*;
    item_inserted: *has* (*v*)

merge_tree_after (*other*: **like** *first_child*)
    -- Merge children of *other* into current structure
    -- after cursor position. Do not move cursor.
    -- Make *other* a leaf.
  require
    not_child_off: **not** *child_off*;
    other_exists: (*other* /= *Void*)
  ensure
    other_is_leaf: *other*. *is_leaf*

merge_tree_before (*other*: **like** *first_child*)
    -- Merge children of *other* into current structure
    -- after cursor position. Do not move cursor.
    -- Make *other* a leaf.
  require
    not_child_off: **not** *child_off*;
    other_exists: (*other* |= *Void*)
  ensure
    other_is_leaf: *other.is_leaf*

prune (*n*: **like** *first_child*)
  require
    is_child: *n.parent* = *Current*
  ensure
    n_is_root: *n.is_root*

put (*v*: **like** *item*)
    -- Make *v* the cell's *item*.
    -- (From *CELL*.)
  require
    is_writable: *writable*
  ensure
    item_inserted: *item* = *v*
  ensure then
    item_inserted: *item* = *v*

put_child (*n*: **like** *parent*)
    -- Add *n* to the list of children.
    -- Do not move child cursor.
  require
    non_void_argument: *n* |= *Void*

put_child_left (*n*: **like** *parent*)
    -- Add *n* to the left of cursor position.
    -- Do not move cursor.
  require
    not_child_before: **not** *child_before*;
    non_void_argument: *n* |= *Void*

put_child_right (*n*: **like** *parent*)
    -- Add *n* to the right of cursor position.
    -- Do not move cursor.
  require
    not_child_after: **not** *child_after*;
    non_void_argument: *n* |= *Void*

put_front (*v*: **like** *child_item*)
    -- Add *v* to beginning.
    -- Do not move cursor.
    -- (From *TWO_WAY_LIST*.)
  ensure
    new_count: *arity* = **old** *arity* + *1*;
    item_inserted: *first* = *v*

put_i_th (*v*: **like** *child_item*; *i*: *INTEGER*)
    -- Put *v* at *i*–th position.
    -- (From *CHAIN*.)
  require
    valid_key: *valid_index* (*i*)
  ensure
    insertion_done: *i_th* (*i*) = *v*

replace (*v*: **like** *item*)
    -- Make *v* the cell's *item*.
    -- (From *CELL*.)
  require
    is_writable: *writable*
  ensure
    item_inserted: *item* = *v*
  ensure then
    item_inserted: *item* = *v*

replace_child (*n*: **like** *parent*)
    -- Replace current child by *n*.
  require
    writable_child: *writable_child*;
    was_root: *n.is_root*
  ensure
    child_replaced: *child* = *n*

sprout
    -- Make current node a root.
    -- (From *TREE*.)

twl_merge_left (*other*: **like** *Current*)
    -- Merge *other* into current structure before cursor
    -- position. Do not move cursor. Empty *other*.
    -- (From *TWO_WAY_LIST*.)
  require
    extendible: *child_extendible*;
    not_off: **not** *child_before*;
    other_exists: *other* |= *Void*
  ensure
    new_count: *arity* = **old** *arity* + **old** *other.arity*;
    new_index: *child_index* = **old** *child_index* + **old**
      other.arity;
    other_is_empty: *other.is_leaf*

twl_merge_right (*other*: **like** *Current*)
    -- Merge *other* into current structure after cursor
    -- position. Do not move cursor. Empty *other*.
    -- (From *TWO_WAY_LIST*.)
  require
    extendible: *child_extendible*;
    not_off: **not** *child_after*;
    other_exists: *other* |= *Void*
  ensure
    new_count: *arity* = **old** *arity* + **old** *other.arity*;
    same_index: *child_index* = **old** *child_index*;
    other_is_empty: *other.is_leaf*

feature -- Removal

   prune_all (*v*: **like** *child_item*)
         -- Remove all occurrences of *v*.
         -- (Reference or object equality,
         -- based on *object_comparison*.)
         -- Leave structure *exhausted*.
         -- (From *DYNAMIC_CHAIN*.)
      require
         prunable
      ensure
         is_exhausted: *exhausted*
      ensure then
         no_more_occurrences: **not** *has* (*v*)

   remove_child
         -- Remove current item.
         -- Move cursor to right neighbor
         -- (or *after* if no right neighbor).
         -- (From *TWO_WAY_LIST*.)
      require
         child_not_off: **not** *child_off*
      require else
         prunable;
         child_writable
      ensure
         new_arity: *arity* = **old** *arity* − *1*;
         new_child_index: *child_index* = **old** *child_index*
      ensure then
         after_when_empty: *is_leaf* **implies** *child_after*

   remove_left_child
         -- Remove item to the left of cursor position.
         -- Do not move cursor.
         -- (From *TWO_WAY_LIST*.)
      require
         is_not_first: **not** *child_isfirst*
      require else
         not_before: **not** *child_before*
      require else
         left_exists: *child_index* > *1*
      ensure
         new_arity: *arity* = **old** *arity* − *1*;
         new_child_index: *child_index* = **old** *child_index* − *1*
      ensure then
         new_count: *arity* = **old** *arity* − *1*;
         new_index: *child_index* = **old** *child_index* − *1*

   remove_right_child
         -- Remove item to the right of cursor position.
         -- Do not move cursor.
         -- (From *TWO_WAY_LIST*.)
      require
         is_not_last: **not** *child_islast*
      require else
         right_exists: *child_index* < *arity*
      ensure
         new_arity: *arity* = **old** *arity* − *1*;
         new_child_index: *child_index* = **old** *child_index*
      ensure then
         new_count: *arity* = **old** *arity* − *1*;
         same_index: *child_index* = **old** *child_index*

   remove_sublist
         -- (From *TWO_WAY_LIST*.)

   split (*n*: *INTEGER*)
         -- Remove from current list
         -- min (*n*, *count* − *index* - 1) items
         -- starting at cursor position.
         -- Move cursor right one position.
         -- Make extracted sublist accessible
         -- through attribute *sublist*.
         -- (From *TWO_WAY_LIST*.)
      require
         not_off: **not** *child_off*;
         valid_sublist: *n* >= *0*

   twl_prune (*v*: **like** *child_item*)
         -- Remove first occurrence of *v*, if any,
         -- after cursor position.
         -- If found, move cursor to right neighbor;
         -- if not, make structure *exhausted*.
         -- (From *DYNAMIC_CHAIN*.)
      require
         prunable: *prunable*

   wipe_out
         -- Remove all items.
         -- (From *TWO_WAY_LIST*.)
      require
         prunable
      ensure
         is_before: *child_before*
      ensure then
         wiped_out: *is_leaf*

feature -- Transformation

   swap (*i*: *INTEGER*)
      -- Exchange item at *i*–th position with item
      -- at cursor position.
      -- (From *CHAIN*.)
    require
      not_off: **not** *child_off*;
      valid_index: *valid_index* (*i*)
    ensure
      swapped_to_item: *child_item* = **old** *i_th* (*i*);
      swapped_from_item: *i_th* (*i*) = **old** *child_item*

feature -- Conversion

   binary_representation: *BINARY_TREE* [*G*]
      -- Convert to binary tree representation:
      -- first child becomes left child,
      -- right sibling becomes right child.
      -- (From *TREE*.)
    ensure
      result_is_root: *Result.is_root*;
      result_has_no_right_child: **not** *Result.has_right*

   fill_from_binary (*b*: *BINARY_TREE* [*G*])
      -- Fill from a binary tree representation.
      -- Left child becomes first child.
      -- Right child becomes right sibling.
      -- Any right child of *b* is ignored.
      -- (From *DYNAMIC_TREE*.)

   linear_representation: *LINEAR* [*G*]
      -- Representation as a linear structure
      -- (From *TREE*.)

feature -- Duplication

   duplicate (*n*: *INTEGER*): **like** *Current*
      -- Copy of sub–tree beginning at cursor position and
      -- having min (*n*, *arity* – *child_index* + 1)
      -- children
      -- (From *DYNAMIC_TREE*.)
    require
      not_child_off: **not** *child_off*;
      valid_sublist: *n* >= *0*

feature -- Implementation

   child: **like** *first_child*
      -- Element at cursor position
      -- (From *LINKED_LIST*.)

invariant

   off_constraint: (*child* = *Void*) **implies** *child_off*;
   extendible_definition: *extendible*;
   child_after_definition: *child_after* = (*child_index* = *arity* + *1*);
   leaf_definition: *is_leaf* = (*arity* = *0*);
   child_off_definition: *child_off* = *child_before* **or** *child_after*;
   child_before_definition: *child_before* = (*child_index* = *0*);

   child_isfirst_definition: *child_isfirst* = (**not** *is_leaf* **and** *child_index* = *1*);
   child_islast_definition: *child_islast* = (**not** *is_leaf* **and** *child_index* = *arity*);
   child_after_definition: *child_after* = (*child_index* >= *arity* + *1*);
   child_consistency: *child_readable* **implies** *child.parent* = *Current*;
   right_symmetry: (*right_sibling* /= *Void*) **implies** (*right_sibling.left_sibling* = *Current*);
   left_symmetry: (*left_sibling* /= *Void*) **implies** (*left_sibling.right_sibling* = *Current*);
   prunable: *prunable*;
   empty_constraint: *is_leaf* **implies** ((*first_child* = *Void*) **and** (*child* = *Void*));
   not_void_unless_empty: (*child* = *Void*) **implies** *is_leaf*;
   before_constraint: *child_before* **implies** (*child* = *first_child*);
   after_constraint: *child_after* **implies** (*child* = *last_child*);
   before_definition: *child_before* = (*child_index* = *0*);
   after_definition: *child_after* = (*child_index* = *arity* + *1*);
   non_negative_index: *child_index* >= *0*;
   index_small_enough: *child_index* <= *arity* + *1*;
   off_definition: *child_off* = ((*child_index* = *0*) **or** (*child_index* = *arity* + *1*));
   isfirst_definition: *child_isfirst* = ((**not** *is_leaf*) **and** (*child_index* = *1*));
   islast_definition: *child_islast* = ((**not** *is_leaf*) **and** (*child_index* = *arity*));
   item_corresponds_to_index: (**not** *child_off*) **implies** (*child_item* = *i_th* (*child_index*));
   writable_constraint: *child_writable* **implies** *child_readable*;
   empty_constraint: *is_leaf* **implies** (**not** *child_readable*) **and** (**not** *child_writable*);
   not_both: **not** (*child_after* **and** *child_before*);
   empty_property: *is_leaf* **implies** (*child_after* **or** *child_before*);
   before_constraint: *child_before* **implies** *child_off*;
   after_constraint: *child_after* **implies** *child_off*;
   empty_constraint: *is_leaf* **implies** *child_off*;
   empty_definition: *is_leaf* = (*arity* = *0*);
   non_negative_count: *arity* >= *0*;
   extendible: *child_extendible*

end

18.4 CLASS *ARRAYED_TREE*

Except for the creation procedure, *ARRAYED_TREE* offers essentially the same features as *LINKED_TREE* and *TWO_WAY_TREE*. The interface appearing here only shows the features introduced or redeclared in the class.

indexing

> *description*: "*Trees where the children of each node are kept in an array*"
> *names*: *tree*
> *representation*: *recursive, array*
> *access*: *cursor, membership*
> *contents*: *generic*

class interface

> *ARRAYED_TREE* [*G*]

creation
> *make*

feature -- Initialization

> *make* (*n*: *INTEGER*; *v*: *G*)
> -- Create node with item *v*.
> -- Allocate space for *n* children.
> **require**
> *valid_number_of_children*: *n* >= *0*

feature -- Access

> *left_sibling*: **like** *parent*
> -- Left neighbor if any
> **require**
> *is_not_root*: **not** *is_root*
> **ensure**
> *right_is_current*: (*Result* /= *Void*) **implies** (*Result. right_ sibling* = *Current*)

> *parent*: *ARRAYED_TREE* [*G*]
> -- Parent of current node

> *right_sibling*: **like** *parent*
> -- Right neighbor if any
> **require**
> *is_not_root*: **not** *is_root*
> **ensure**
> *left_is_current*: (*Result* /= *Void*) **implies** (*Result. left_ sibling* = *Current*)

feature -- Status report

> *extendible*: *BOOLEAN* **is true**
> -- May new items be added?
> -- (From *DYNAMIC_TREE*.)

> *readable*: *BOOLEAN* **is true**
> -- (From *TREE*.)

> *writable*: *BOOLEAN* **is true**
> -- Is there a current item that may be modified?
> -- (From *TREE*.)

feature -- Element change

> *child_extend* (*v*: **like** *item*)
> -- Add *v* at end.
> -- Do not move child cursor.

> *child_put* (*v*: **like** *item*)
> -- Replace current child item with *v*.
> **require**
> *child_writable*: *child_writable*

> *child_put_left* (*v*: **like** *item*)
> -- Add *v* to the left of cursor position.
> -- Do not move child cursor.
> **require**
> *not_child_before*: **not** *child_before*

> *child_put_right* (*v*: **like** *item*)
> -- Add *v* to the right of cursor position.
> -- Do not move child cursor.
> **require**
> *not_child_after*: **not** *child_after*

> *child_replace* (*v*: **like** *item*)
> -- Replace current child item with *v*.
> **require**
> *child_writable*: *child_writable*

> *merge_tree_after* (*other*: **like** *first_child*)
> -- Merge children of *other* into current structure
> -- after cursor position. Do not move cursor.
> -- Make *other* a leaf.
> **require**
> *not_child_off*: **not** *child_off*;
> *other_exists*: (*other* /= *Void*)

> *merge_tree_before* (*other*: **like** *first_child*)
> -- Merge children of *other* into current structure
> -- before cursor position. Do not move cursor.
> -- Make *other* a leaf.
> **require**
> *not_child_off*: **not** *child_off*;
> *other_exists*: (*other* /= *Void*)

put_child (*n*: **like** *parent*)
    -- Add *n* to the list of children.
    -- Do not move child cursor.
  require
    non_void_argument: *n* /= *Void*

put_child_left (*n*: **like** *parent*)
    -- Add *n* to the left of cursor position.
    -- Do not move cursor.
  require
    not_child_before: **not** *child_before*;
    non_void_argument: *n* /= *Void*

put_child_right (*n*: **like** *parent*)
    -- Add *n* to the right of the cursor position.
    -- Do not move cursor.
  require
    not_child_after: **not** *child_after*;
    non_void_argument: *n* /= *Void*

replace_child (*n*: **like** *parent*)
    -- Make *n* the node's current child.
  require
    writable_child: *writable_child*;
    was_root: *n. is_root*
  ensure
    child_replaced: *n. parent* = *Current*

feature -- Removal

remove_child
    -- Remove child at cursor position.
    -- Move cursor to the next sibling, or *after* if none.
  require
    child_not_off: **not** *child_off*

remove_left_child
    -- Remove item to the left of cursor position.
    -- Do not move cursor.
  require
    is_not_first: **not** *child_isfirst*

remove_right_child
    -- Remove item to the right of cursor position.
    -- Do not move cursor.
  require
    is_not_last: **not** *child_islast*

feature -- Duplication

duplicate (*n*: *INTEGER*): **like** *Current*
    -- Copy of sub–tree beginning at cursor position and
    -- having min (*n*, *arity* − *child_index* + 1)
    -- children.
  require
    not_child_off: **not** *child_off*;
    valid_sublist: *n* >= *0*

invariant

  extendible: *extendible*

end

18.5 CLASS *FIXED_TREE*

Class *FIXED_TREE* is useful for trees in which whenever you create a node you know the number of children of that node, and it will not change (or at least will not grow). If that is not the case, use the more dynamic structures whose interfaces appear in the previous sections.

FIXED_TREE retains all the features of *TREE* and adds little to that parent. For this reason the interface that appears below only shows the features introduced or redeclared in the class. For the other features please refer to the interface of *TREE*.

See the interface of TREE in 18.2, page 350.

indexing

  description: "*Trees where each node has a fixed number of children (The number of children is arbitrary but cannot be changed once the node has been created*"
  names: *fixed_tree, tree, fixed_list*
  representation: *recursive, array*
  access: *cursor, membership*
  contents: *generic*

class interface

  FIXED_TREE [G]

creation
  make

feature -- Initialization

  make (*n*: *INTEGER*; *v*: *G*)
      -- Create node with *n* void children and item *v*.
    require
      valid_number_of_children: *n* >= *0*

feature -- Access

  child_item: *like item*
      -- Item of active child
    require
      readable: *child_readable*

  first_child: *like parent*
      -- Leftmost child
    require
      is_not_leaf: *not is_leaf*
    require else
      not_empty: *not is_leaf*

  left_sibling: *like parent*
      -- Left neighbor, if any
    require
      is_not_root: *not is_root*
    ensure
      right_is_current: (*Result* /= *Void*) *implies* (*Result.right_sibling* = *Current*)

  parent: *FIXED_TREE* [G]
      -- Parent of current node

  right_sibling: *like parent*
      -- Right neighbor, if any
    require
      is_not_root: *not is_root*
    ensure
      left_is_current: (*Result* /= *Void*) *implies* (*Result.left_sibling* = *Current*)

feature -- Status report

  child_contractable: *BOOLEAN*
      -- May items be removed?

  full: *BOOLEAN is true*
      -- Is tree full?

  readable: *BOOLEAN is true*
      -- (From *TREE*.)

  writable: *BOOLEAN is true*
      -- Is there a current item that may be modified?
      -- (From *TREE*.)

feature -- Element change

  child_put (*v*: *like item*)
      -- Replace current child item with *v*
    require
      child_writable: *child_writable*
    ensure
      item_inserted: *child_item* = *v*

  child_replace (*v*: *like item*)
      -- Replace current child item with *v*
    require
      child_writable: *child_writable*
    ensure
      item_inserted: *child_item* = *v*

  put_child (*n*: *like parent*)
      -- Make *n* the node's child.
    ensure
      child_replaced: *n.parent* = *Current*

put_left (*v*: **like** *item*)
    -- Add *v* to the left of current node.
  require
    is_not_root: **not** *is_root*;
    has_left_sibling: *left_sibling* /= *Void*

put_left_sibling (*other*: **like** *parent*)
    -- Make *other* the left sibling of current node.
  require
    is_not_root: **not** *is_root*;
    has_left_sibling: *left_sibling* /= *Void*
  ensure
    left_sibling_replaced: *left_sibling* = *other*

put_right (*v*: **like** *item*)
    -- Add *v* to the right of current node.
  require
    is_not_root: **not** *is_root*;
    has_right_sibling: *right_sibling* /= *Void*

put_right_sibling (*other*: **like** *parent*)
    -- Make *other* the right sibling of current node.
  require
    is_not_root: **not** *is_root*;
    has_right_sibling: *right_sibling* /= *Void*
  ensure
    right_sibling_replaced: *right_sibling* = *other*

replace_child (*n*: **like** *parent*)
    -- Make *n* the node's child.
  require
    writable_child: *writable_child*;
    was_root: *n.is_root*
  ensure
    child_replaced: *n.parent* = *Current*
  ensure then

feature -- Removal

remove_child
    -- Remove active child.

feature -- Duplication

duplicate (*n*: *INTEGER*): **like** *Current*
    -- Copy of sub–tree beginning at cursor position and
    -- having min (*n*, *arity* − *child_index* + 1)
    -- children.
  require
    not_child_off: **not** *child_off*;
    valid_sublist: *n* >= *0*
  require else
    not_off_unless_after: *child_off* **implies** *child_after*;
    valid_subchain: *n* >= *0*

invariant

  not_resizable: **not** *resizable*

end

18.6 CLASS *BINARY_TREE*

indexing

> *description*: "Binary tree: each node may have a left child
>   and a right child"
> *names*: *binary_tree, tree, fixed_tree*
> *representation*: *recursive, array*
> *access*: *cursor, membership*
> *contents*: *generic*

class interface

> *BINARY_TREE* [G]

creation
> *make*

feature -- Initialization

> *make* (*v*: **like** *item*)
>   -- Create a root node with value v
>   **ensure**
>   *is_root*;
>   *is_leaf*

feature -- Access

> *child*: **like** *parent*
>   -- Child at cursor position
>   **require**
>   *readable*: *readable_child*

> *child_cursor*: *CURSOR*
>   -- Current cursor position

> *child_index*: *INTEGER*
>   -- Index of cursor position

> *child_item*: **like** *item*
>   -- Item in current child node
>   -- (From *TREE*.)
>   **require**
>   *readable*: *child_readable*

> *first_child*: **like** *parent*
>   -- Left child
>   **require**
>   *is_not_leaf*: **not** *is_leaf*

> *has* (*v*: *G*): *BOOLEAN*
>   -- Does subtree include *v*?
>   -- (Reference or object equality,
>   -- based on *object_comparison*.)
>   -- (From *TREE*.)
>   **ensure**
>   *not_found_in_empty*: *Result* **implies not** *empty*

> *is_sibling* (*other*: **like** *parent*): *BOOLEAN*
>   -- Are current node and *other* siblings?
>   -- (From *TREE*.)
>   **ensure**
>   *not_root*: *Result* **implies not** *is_root*;
>   *other_not_root*: *Result* **implies not** *other.is_root*;
>   *same_parent*: *Result* = **not** *is_root* **and** *other.parent* =
>   *parent*

> *last_child*: **like** *parent*
>   -- Right child
>   **require**
>   *is_not_leaf*: **not** *is_leaf*

> *left_child*: **like** *parent*
>   -- Left child, if any

> *left_item*: **like** *item*
>   -- Value of left child
>   **require**
>   *has_left*: *left_child* /= *Void*

> *left_sibling*: **like** *parent*
>   -- Left neighbor, if any
>   **require**
>   *is_not_root*: **not** *is_root*
>   **ensure**
>   *is_sibling*: *is_sibling* (*Result*);
>   *right_is_current*: (*Result* /= *Void*) **implies** (*Result.right_
>   sibling* = *Current*)

> *parent*: *BINARY_TREE* [G]
>   -- Parent of current node

> *right_child*: **like** *parent*
>   -- Right child, if any

> *right_item*: **like** *item*
>   -- Value of right child
>   **require**
>   *has_right*: *right_child* /= *Void*

> *right_sibling*: **like** *parent*
>   -- Right neighbor, if any
>   **require**
>   *is_not_root*: **not** *is_root*
>   **ensure**
>   *is_sibling*: *is_sibling* (*Result*);
>   *left_is_current*: (*Result* /= *Void*) **implies** (*Result.left_
>   sibling* = *Current*)

feature -- Measurement

    arity: *INTEGER*
      -- Number of children
    ensure
      valid_arity: *Result* <= 2

    count: *INTEGER*
      -- Number of items
      -- (From *TREE*.)

feature -- Status report

    child_after: *BOOLEAN*
      -- Is there no valid child position to the right of cursor?

    child_before: *BOOLEAN*
      -- Is there no valid child position to the left of cursor?
      -- (From *TREE*.)

    child_isfirst: *BOOLEAN*
      -- Is cursor under first child?
      -- (From *TREE*.)
    ensure
      not_is_leaf: *Result* **implies not** *is_leaf*

    child_islast: *BOOLEAN*
      -- Is cursor under last child?
      -- (From *TREE*.)
    ensure
      not_is_leaf: *Result* **implies not** *is_leaf*

    child_off: *BOOLEAN*
      -- Is there no current child?
      -- (From *TREE*.)

    child_readable: *BOOLEAN*
      -- Is there a current *child_item* to be read?
      -- (From *TREE*.)

    child_writable: *BOOLEAN*
      -- Is there a current *child_item* that may be modified?
      -- (From *TREE*.)

    empty: *BOOLEAN*
      -- Is structure empty of items?
      -- (From *TREE*.)

    has_both: *BOOLEAN*
      -- Has current node two children?
    ensure
      Result = (*has_left* **and** *has_right*)

    has_left: *BOOLEAN*
      -- Has current node a left child?
    ensure
      Result = (*left_child* /= *Void*)

    has_none: *BOOLEAN*
      -- Are there no children?

    has_right: *BOOLEAN*
      -- Has current node a right child?
    ensure
      Result = (*right_child* /= *Void*)

    is_leaf: *BOOLEAN*
      -- Are there no children?

    is_root: *BOOLEAN*
      -- Is there no parent?
      -- (From *TREE*.)

    readable: *BOOLEAN* **is true**
      -- (From *TREE*.)

    readable_child: *BOOLEAN*
      -- Is there a current child to be read?
      -- (From *TREE*.)

    valid_cursor_index (*i*: *INTEGER*): *BOOLEAN*
      -- Is *i* correctly bounded for cursor movement?
      -- (From *TREE*.)
    ensure
      valid_cursor_index_definition: *Result* = (*i* >= *0*) **and** (*i*
        <= *arity* + *1*)

    writable: *BOOLEAN* **is true**
      -- Is there a current item that may be modified?
      -- (From *TREE*.)

    writable_child: *BOOLEAN*
      -- Is there a current child that may be modified?
      -- (From *TREE*.)

feature -- Cursor movement

    child_back
      -- Move cursor to previous child.

    child_finish
      -- Move cursor to last child.
    ensure
      is_last_child: **not** *is_leaf* **implies** *child_islast*

    child_forth
      -- Move cursor to next child.

    child_go_i_th (*i*: *INTEGER*)
      -- Move cursor to *i*-th child.
    require
      valid_cursor_index: *valid_cursor_index* (*i*)
    ensure
      position: *child_index* = *i*;
      is_before: (*i* = *0*) **implies** *child_before*;
      is_after: (*i* = *arity* + *1*) **implies** *child_after*

    child_go_to (*p*: *CURSOR*)
      -- Move cursor to child remembered by *p*.

child_start
    -- Move to first child.
    ensure
      is_first_child: **not** *is_leaf* **implies** *child_isfirst*

feature -- Element change

child_put (*v*: **like** *item*)
    -- Put *v* at current child position.
    require
      child_writable: *child_writable*
    ensure
      · *item_inserted*: *child_item* = *v*

child_replace (*v*: **like** *item*)
    -- Put *v* at current child position.
    require
      child_writable: *child_writable*
    ensure
      item_inserted: *child_item* = *v*

fill (*other*: *TREE* [*G*])
    -- Fill with as many items of *other* as possible.
    -- The representations of *other* and current node
    -- need not be the same.
    -- (From *TREE*.)

put_child (*n*: **like** *parent*)
    -- Put *n* at current child position.

put_left_child (*n*: **like** *parent*)
    -- Set *left_child* to *n*.
    require
      no_parent: *n* = *Void* **or else** *n.is_root*

put_right_child (*n*: **like** *parent*)
    -- Set *right_child* to *n*.
    require
      no_parent: *n* = *Void* **or else** *n.is_root*

replace_child (*n*: **like** *parent*)
    -- Put *n* at current child position.
    require
      writable_child: *writable_child*;
      was_root: *n.is_root*
    ensure
      child_replaced: *child* = *n*

sprout
    -- Make current node a root.
    -- (From *TREE*.)

feature -- Removal

child_remove

prune (*n*: **like** *parent*)
    require
      is_child: *n.parent* = *Current*
    ensure
      n_is_root: *n.is_root*

remove_left_child

remove_right_child

feature -- Conversion

binary_representation: *BINARY_TREE* [*G*]
    -- Convert to binary tree representation:
    -- first child becomes left child,
    -- right sibling becomes right child.
    -- (From *TREE*.)
    ensure
      result_is_root: *Result.is_root*;
      result_has_no_right_child: **not** *Result.has_right*

linear_representation: *LINEAR* [*G*]
    -- Representation as a linear structure
    -- (From *TREE*.)

feature -- Duplication

duplicate (*n*: *INTEGER*): **like** *Current*
    -- Copy of sub-tree beginning at cursor position and
    -- having min (*n*, *arity* − *child_index* + 1)
    -- children.
    require
      not_child_off: **not** *child_off*;
      valid_sublist: *n* >= 0

duplicate_all: **like** *Current*

invariant

    leaf_definition: *is_leaf* = (*arity* = 0);
    child_off_definition: *child_off* = *child_before* **or** *child_after*;
    child_before_definition: *child_before* = (*child_index* = 0);
    child_isfirst_definition: *child_isfirst* = (**not** *is_leaf* **and** *child_index* = 1);
    child_islast_definition: *child_islast* = (**not** *is_leaf* **and** *child_index* = *arity*);
    child_after_definition: *child_after* = (*child_index* >= *arity* + 1);
    child_consistency: *child_readable* **implies** *child.parent* = *Current*

end

18.7 CLASS *BINARY_SEARCH_TREE*

This interface only shows the features introduced or redeclared in *BINARY_SEARCH_TREE*. In addition, the class retains all the features from *BINARY_TREE*, as documented in the previous section.

indexing

> *description*: "*Binary search trees; left child item is less than current item, right child item is greater*"
> *names*: *binary_search_tree*, *tree*
> *representation*: *recursive*, *array*
> *access*: *cursor*, *membership*
> *contents*: *generic*

class interface

> *BINARY_SEARCH_TREE* [*G* –> *COMPARABLE*]

creation
> *make*

feature -- Initialization

> *make* (*v*: *like item*)
> -- Create single node with item *v*.

feature -- Access

> *has* (*v*: *like item*): *BOOLEAN*
> -- Does tree contain a node whose item
> -- is equal to *v* (object comparison)?
> **require**
> *argument_not_void*: *v* /= *Void*
> **require else** -- CONTAINER
> *precursor*: *True*
>
> *parent*: *BINARY_SEARCH_TREE* [*G*]
> -- Parent of current node.

feature -- Measurement

> *max*: *like item*
> -- Maximum item in tree
> **ensure**
> *maximum_present*: *has (Result)*
> -- *largest*: For every item *it* in tree, *it* <= *Result*
>
> *min*: *like item*
> -- Minimum item in tree
> **ensure**
> *minimum_present*: *has (Result)*
> -- *smallest*: For every item *it* in tree, *Result* <= *it*

feature -- Status report

> *sorted*: *BOOLEAN*
> -- Is tree sorted?

feature -- Cursor movement

> *i_infix*
> -- Apply node_action to every node's item
> -- in tree, using infix order.
>
> *node_action* (*v*: *like item*)
> -- Operation on node item,
> -- to be defined by descendant classes.
> -- Here it is defined as an empty operation.
> -- Redefine this procedure in descendant classes if useful
> -- operations are to be performed during traversals.
>
> *postorder*
> -- Apply node_action to every node's item
> -- in tree, using post–order.
>
> *preorder*
> -- Apply *node_action* to every node's item
> -- in tree, using pre–order.

feature -- Element change

> *extend* (*v*: *like item*)
> -- Put *v* at proper position in tree
> -- (unless *v* exists already).
> -- (Reference or object equality,
> -- based on *object_comparison*.)
> **require**
> *new_item_exists*: *v* /= *Void*
> **ensure**
> *item_inserted*: *has (v)*
>
> *put* (*v*: *like item*)
> -- Put *v* at proper position in tree
> -- (unless *v* exists already).
> -- (Reference or object equality,
> -- based on *object_comparison*.)
> **require**
> *new_item_exists*: *v* /= *Void*
> **ensure**
> *item_inserted*: *has (v)*

feature -- Transformation

> *sort*
> -- Sort tree.
> **ensure**
> *is_sorted*: *sorted*

end

18.8 CLASS *CURSOR_TREE*

This interface shows the features introduced or redeclared in *CURSOR_TREE*, and those inherited from *CURSOR_STRUCTURE*, *HIERARCHICAL* and *TRAVERSABLE*, but not the features from the other ancestors (*ACTIVE*, *COLLECTION*, *CONTAINER* and *LINEAR*) unless the class renames them.

indexing

    description: *"Trees as active structures that may be traversed*
      using a cursor"
    names: *cursor_tree*, *tree*
    access: *cursor*, *membership*
    contents: *generic*

deferred class interface

    CURSOR_TREE [G]

feature -- Access

    arity: *INTEGER*
      -- Number of successors of current element
      -- (From *HIERARCHICAL*.)
      require
        not_off: **not** *off*

    child_item (*i*: *INTEGER*): *G*
      -- Item in *i*–th child
      require
        argument_within_bounds: $i >= 1$ **and then** $i <= arity$;
        not_off: **not** *off*

    cursor: *CURSOR*
      -- Current cursor position
      -- (From *CURSOR_STRUCTURE*.)

    item: *G*
      -- Item at current position
      -- (From *TRAVERSABLE*.)
      require
        not_off: **not** *off*
      require else
        readable

    parent_item: *G*
      -- Item in parent.
      require
        not_on_root: **not** *is_root*

feature -- Measurement

    breadth: *INTEGER*
      -- Breadth of current level

    depth: *INTEGER*
      -- Depth of the tree

    level: *INTEGER*
      -- Level of current node in tree
      -- (Root is on level 1)

feature -- Status report

    above: *BOOLEAN*
      -- Is there no valid cursor position above cursor?

    after: *BOOLEAN*
      -- Is there no valid cursor position to the right of cursor?

    before: *BOOLEAN*
      -- Is there no valid cursor position to the left of cursor?

    below: *BOOLEAN*
      -- Is there no valid cursor position below cursor?

    extendible: *BOOLEAN*
      -- May new items be added?

    is_leaf: *BOOLEAN*
      -- Is cursor on a leaf?

    is_root: *BOOLEAN*
      -- Is cursor on root?

    isfirst: *BOOLEAN*
      -- Is cursor on first sibling?

    islast: *BOOLEAN*
      -- Is cursor on last sibling?

    off: *BOOLEAN*
      -- Is there no current item?
      -- (True if *empty*)

    readable: *BOOLEAN*
      -- Is there a current item that may be read?

    valid_cursor (*p*: *CURSOR*): *BOOLEAN*
      -- Can the cursor be moved to position *p*?
      -- (From *CURSOR_STRUCTURE*.)

    valid_cursor_index (*i*: *INTEGER*): *BOOLEAN*
      -- Can cursor be moved to *i*–th child?
      -- 0 is before and *arity* + 1 is after.

    writable: *BOOLEAN*
      -- Is there a current item that may be modified?

feature -- Cursor movement

    back
      -- Move cursor one position backward.

breadth_forth
    -- Move cursor to next position in breadth–first order.
    -- If the active node is the last in
    -- breadth–first order, the cursor ends up *off.*
    require
        not_off: **not** *off*

down (*i*: *INTEGER*)
    -- Move cursor one level downward:
    -- to *i*–th child if there is one,
    -- or *after* if *i* = *arity* + 1,
    -- or *before* if *i* = 0.
    require
        not_before: **not** *before*;
        not_after: **not** *after*;
        not_below: **not** *below*;
        valid_cursor_index: (*above* **and** *i* = *0*) **or else** *valid_
            cursor_index* (*i*)
    require else
        not_off: **not** *off*;
        argument_within_bounds: *i* >= *1* **and** *i* <= *arity*
    ensure
        gone_before: (*i* = *0*) **implies** *before*

forth
    -- Move cursor one position forward.

go_last_child
    -- Go to the last child of current parent.
    -- No effect if below
    require
        not_above: **not** *above*

go_to (*p*: *CURSOR*)
    -- Move cursor to position *p*.
    -- (From *CURSOR_STRUCTURE*.)
    require
        cursor_position_valid: *valid_cursor* (*p*)

level_back
    -- Move cursor to previous position of current level.

level_forth
    -- Move cursor to next position of current level.

postorder_forth
    -- Move cursor to next position in postorder.
    -- If the active node is the last in
    -- postorder, the cursor ends up *off.*
    require
        not_off: **not** *off*

postorder_start
    -- Move cursor to first position in postorder.
    -- Leave cursor off if tree is empty.

preorder_forth
    -- Move cursor to next position in preorder.
    -- If the active node is the last in
    -- preorder, the cursor ends up *off.*
    require
        not_after: **not** *after*

start
    -- Move cursor to root.
    -- Leave cursor *off* if *empty.*

start_on_level (*l*: *INTEGER*)
    -- Move the cursor to the first position
    -- of the *l*–th level counting from root.
    require
        argument_within_bounds: *l* >= *1* **and then** *depth* >= *l*
    ensure
        level_expected: *level* = *l*;
        is_first: *isfirst*

up
    -- Move cursor one level upward to parent,
    -- or *above* if *is_root* holds.
    require
        not_above: **not** *above*
    require else
        not_off: **not** *off*
    ensure
        not_before: **not** *before*;
        not_after: **not** *after*;
        not_below: **not** *below*;
        above = (**old** *is_root*)

feature -- Element change

extend (*v*: *G*)
    -- Add *v* after last child.
    -- Make *v* the *first_child* if *below* and place
    -- cursor *before.*
    require
        only_one_root: (*level* = *1*) **implies** *empty*
    require else
        extendible: *extendible*

fill (*other*: *CURSOR_TREE* [*G*])
    -- Fill with as many items of *other*
    -- as possible.
    -- The representations of *other* and current structure
    -- need not be the same.
    require
        is_empty: *empty*

fill_from_active (*other*: *CURSOR_TREE* [*G*])
    -- Copy subtree of 'other''s active node
    -- onto active node of current tree.
    require
        cursor_on_leaf: *is_leaf*

merge_left (*other*: *CURSOR_TREE* [*G*])
    -- Merge the items of *other* into current structure to
    -- the left of cursor position.
   require
     other_exists: *other* /= *Void*;
     not_before: **not** *before*;
     not_above: **not** *above*;
     only_one_root: (*level* = 1) **implies** *empty*

merge_right (*other*: *CURSOR_TREE* [*G*])
    -- Merge the items of *other* into current structure to
    -- the right of cursor position.
   require
     other_exists: *other* /= *Void*;
     not_after: **not** *after*;
     not_above: **not** *above*;
     only_one_root: (*level* = 1) **implies** *empty*

put (*v*: *G*)
    -- Put *v* at cursor position.
    -- (Synonym for *replace*)
   require
     extendible: *extendible*

put_left (*v*: *G*)
    -- Add *v* to the left of cursor position.
   require
     not_before: **not** *before*;
     not_above: **not** *above*;
     only_one_root: (*level* = 1) **implies** *empty*

put_right (*v*: *G*)
    -- Add *v* to the right of cursor position.
   require
     not_after: **not** *after*;
     not_above: **not** *above*;
     only_one_root: (*level* = 1) **implies** *empty*

feature -- Duplication

child_tree (*i*: *INTEGER*): **like** *Current*
    -- Subtree rooted at *i*-th child
   require
     argument_within_bounds: *i* >= 1 **and** **then** *i* <= *arity*;
     not_off: **not** *off*

parent_tree: **like** *Current*
    -- Subtree rooted at parent
   require
     not_on_root: **not** *is_root*;
     not_off: **not** *off*

subtree: **like** *Current*
    -- Subtree rooted at current node
   require
     not_off: **not** *off*

invariant

   non_negative_depth: *depth* >= 0;

   non_negative_breadth: *breadth* >= 0;
   is_leaf_definition: **not** *off* **implies** *is_leaf* = (*arity* = 0);
   above_property: *above* **implies** (*arity* <= 1);
   on_tree: (*isfirst* **or** *islast* **or** *is_leaf* **or** *is_root*) **implies** **not** *off*;
   off_definition: *off* = *after* **or** *before* **or** *above* **or** *below*;
   below_constraint: *below* **implies** ((*after* **or** *before*) **and** **not** *above*);
   above_constraint: *above* **implies** **not** (*before* **or** *after* **or** *below*);
   after_constraint: *after* **implies** **not** (*before* **or** *above*);
   before_constaint: *before* **implies** **not** (*after* **or** *above*);
   non_negative_successor_count: *arity* >= 0;
   writable_constraint: *writable* **implies** *readable*;
   after_constraint: *after* **implies** *off*

end

18.9 CLASSES *LINKED_CURSOR_TREE* AND *TWO_WAY_CURSOR_ TREE*

Classes *LINKED_CURSOR_TREE* and *TWO_WAY_CURSOR_TREE* have the same interface, shown here for *TWO_WAY_CURSOR_TREE*. Since these are effective classes meant to be used directly, the interface shows all the features from *CURSOR_ TREE* and the intermediate ancestor *RECURSIVE_CURSOR_TREE* but not those from any other ancestor unless they are redeclared.

indexing

    description: "*Cursor trees implemented in two−way linked
      representation*"
    names: *two_way_cursor_tree*, *cursor_tree*
    access: *cursor*, *membership*
    representation: *recursive*, *linked*
    contents: *generic*

class interface

    TWO_WAY_CURSOR_TREE [*G*]

creation
    make

feature -- Initialization

    make
        -- Create an empty tree.
      ensure
        is_above: *above*;
        is_empty: *empty*

feature -- Access

    child_item (*i*: *INTEGER*): *G*
        -- Item in *i*−th child
        -- (From *CURSOR_TREE*.)
      require
        argument_within_bounds: *i* >= *1* **and then** *i* <= *arity*;
        not_off: **not** *off*

    cursor: *CURSOR*
        -- Current cursor position
        -- (From *RECURSIVE_CURSOR_TREE*.)

    item: *G*
        -- Item at cursor position
        -- (From *RECURSIVE_CURSOR_TREE*.)
      require
        not_off: **not** *off*
      require else
        readable

    parent_item: *G*
        -- Item in parent.
        -- (From *CURSOR_TREE*.)
      require
        not_on_root: **not** *is_root*

feature -- Measurement

    arity: *INTEGER*
        -- Number of children of active node; if cursor is *above*,
        -- 0 if tree is empty, 1 otherwise.
        -- (From *RECURSIVE_CURSOR_TREE*.)
      require
        not_off: **not** *off*

    breadth: *INTEGER*
        -- Breadth of current level
        -- (From *CURSOR_TREE*.)

    count: *INTEGER*
        -- Number of items in the tree
        -- (From *RECURSIVE_CURSOR_TREE*.)

    depth: *INTEGER*
        -- Depth of the tree
        -- (From *CURSOR_TREE*.)

    level: *INTEGER*
        -- Level of current node in tree
        -- (Root is on level 1)
        -- (From *CURSOR_TREE*.)

feature -- Status report

    above: *BOOLEAN*
        -- Is there no valid cursor position above cursor?
        -- (From *RECURSIVE_CURSOR_TREE*.)

    after: *BOOLEAN*
        -- Is there no valid cursor position to the right of cursor?
        -- (From *RECURSIVE_CURSOR_TREE*.)

    before: *BOOLEAN*
        -- Is there no valid cursor position to the left of cursor?
        -- (From *RECURSIVE_CURSOR_TREE*.)

    below: *BOOLEAN*
        -- Is there no valid cursor position below cursor?
        -- (From *CURSOR_TREE*.)

empty: *BOOLEAN*
    -- Is the tree empty?
    -- (From *RECURSIVE_CURSOR_TREE*.)

extendible: *BOOLEAN*
    -- May new items be added?
    -- (From *CURSOR_TREE*.)

full: *BOOLEAN* **is false**
    -- Is tree filled to capacity? (Answer: no.)

is_leaf: *BOOLEAN*
    -- Is cursor on a leaf?
    -- (From *CURSOR_TREE*.)

is_root: *BOOLEAN*
    -- Is cursor on tree root?
    -- (From *RECURSIVE_CURSOR_TREE*.)

isfirst: *BOOLEAN*
    -- Is cursor on first sibling?
    -- (From *RECURSIVE_CURSOR_TREE*.)

islast: *BOOLEAN*
    -- Is cursor on last sibling?
    -- (From *RECURSIVE_CURSOR_TREE*.)

off: *BOOLEAN*
    -- Is there no current item?
    -- (True if *empty*)
    -- (From *CURSOR_TREE*.)

prunable: *BOOLEAN* **is true**

readable: *BOOLEAN*
    -- Is there a current item that may be read?
    -- (From *CURSOR_TREE*.)

valid_cursor (*p*: *CURSOR*): *BOOLEAN*
    -- Can the cursor be moved to position *p*?
    -- (From *RECURSIVE_CURSOR_TREE*.)

valid_cursor_index (*i*: *INTEGER*): *BOOLEAN*
    -- Can cursor be moved to *i*-th child?
    -- 0 is before and *arity* + 1 is after.
    -- (From *CURSOR_TREE*.)

writable: *BOOLEAN*
    -- Is there a current item that may be modified?
    -- (From *CURSOR_TREE*.)

feature -- Cursor movement

back
    -- Move cursor one position backward.
    -- (From *RECURSIVE_CURSOR_TREE*.)

breadth_forth
    -- Move cursor to next position in breadth–first order.
    -- If the active node is the last in
    -- breadth–first order, the cursor ends up *off*.
    -- (From *CURSOR_TREE*.)
    require
        not_off: **not** *off*

down (*i*: *INTEGER*)
    -- Move cursor one level downward:
    -- to *i*-th child if there is one,
    -- or *after* if *i* = *arity* + 1,
    -- or *before* if *i* = 0.
    -- (From *RECURSIVE_CURSOR_TREE*.)
    require
        not_before: **not** *before*;
        not_after: **not** *after*;
        not_below: **not** *below*;
        valid_cursor_index: (*above* **and** *i* = *0*) **or else** *valid_*
            cursor_index (*i*)
    require else
        not_off: **not** *off*;
        argument_within_bounds: *i* >= *1* **and** *i* <= *arity*
    ensure
        gone_before: (*i* = *0*) **implies** *before*

forth
    -- Move cursor one position forward.
    -- (From *RECURSIVE_CURSOR_TREE*.)

go_last_child
    -- Go to the last child of current parent.
    -- No effect if below
    -- (From *CURSOR_TREE*.)
    require
        not_above: **not** *above*

go_to (*p*: *CURSOR*)
    -- Move cursor to position *p*.
    -- (From *RECURSIVE_CURSOR_TREE*.)
    require
        cursor_position_valid: *valid_cursor* (*p*)

level_back
    -- Move cursor to previous position of current level.
    -- (From *CURSOR_TREE*.)

level_forth
    -- Move cursor to next position of current level.
    -- (From *CURSOR_TREE*.)

postorder_forth
    -- Move cursor to next position in postorder.
    -- If the active node is the last in
    -- postorder, the cursor ends up *off*.
    -- (From *CURSOR_TREE*.)
    require
        not_off: **not** *off*

postorder_start
>   -- Move cursor to first position in postorder.
>   -- Leave cursor off if tree is empty.
>   -- (From *CURSOR_TREE*.)

preorder_forth
>   -- Move cursor to next position in preorder.
>   -- If the active node is the last in
>   -- preorder, the cursor ends up *off*.
>   -- (From *CURSOR_TREE*.)
>   **require**
>   > *not_after*: **not** *after*

start
>   -- Move cursor to root.
>   -- Leave cursor *off* if *empty*.
>   -- (From *CURSOR_TREE*.)
>   **ensure**
>   > *on_root_unless_empty*: **not** *empty* **implies** *is_root*

start_on_level (*l*: *INTEGER*)
>   -- Move the cursor to the first position
>   -- of the *l*–th level counting from root.
>   -- (From *CURSOR_TREE*.)
>   **require**
>   > *argument_within_bounds*: *l* >= *1* **and then** *depth* >= *l*
>   **ensure**
>   > *level_expected*: *level* = *l*;
>   > *is_first*: *isfirst*

up
>   -- Move cursor one level upward to parent,
>   -- or *above* if *is_root* holds.
>   -- (From *RECURSIVE_CURSOR_TREE*.)
>   **require**
>   > *not_above*: **not** *above*
>   **require else**
>   > *not_off*: **not** *off*
>   **ensure**
>   > *not_before*: **not** *before*;
>   > *not_after*: **not** *after*;
>   > *not_below*: **not** *below*;
>   > *above* = (**old** *is_root*)

feature -- Element change

extend (*v*: *G*)
>   -- Put *v* after last child.
>   -- Put *v* as *first_child* if *below* and place
>   -- cursor *before*.
>   -- (From *CURSOR_TREE*.)
>   **require**
>   > *only_one_root*: (*level* = *1*) **implies** *empty*
>   **require else**
>   > *extendible*: *extendible*

fill (*other*: *CURSOR_TREE* [*G*])
>   -- Fill with as many items of *other*
>   -- as possible.
>   -- The representations of *other* and current structure
>   -- need not be the same.
>   -- (From *CURSOR_TREE*.)
>   **require**
>   > *is_empty*: *empty*

fill_from_active (*other*: *CURSOR_TREE* [*G*])
>   -- Copy subtree of 'other''s active node
>   -- onto active node of current tree.
>   -- (From *CURSOR_TREE*.)
>   **require**
>   > *cursor_on_leaf*: *is_leaf*

merge_left (*other*: *CURSOR_TREE* [*G*])
>   -- Merge the items of *other* into current structure to
>   -- the left of cursor position.
>   -- (From *CURSOR_TREE*.)
>   **require**
>   > *other_exists*: *other* /= *Void*;
>   > *not_before*: **not** *before*;
>   > *not_above*: **not** *above*;
>   > *only_one_root*: (*level* = *1*) **implies** *empty*

merge_right (*other*: *CURSOR_TREE* [*G*])
>   -- Merge the items of *other* into current structure to
>   -- the right of cursor position.
>   -- (From *CURSOR_TREE*.)
>   **require**
>   > *other_exists*: *other* /= *Void*;
>   > *not_after*: **not** *after*;
>   > *not_above*: **not** *above*;
>   > *only_one_root*: (*level* = *1*) **implies** *empty*

put (*v*: *G*)
>   -- Put *v* at cursor position.
>   -- (Synonym for *replace*)
>   -- (From *CURSOR_TREE*.)
>   **require**
>   > *extendible*: *extendible*

put_left (*v*: *G*)
>   -- Put *v* to the left of cursor position.
>   -- (From *CURSOR_TREE*.)
>   **require**
>   > *not_before*: **not** *before*;
>   > *not_above*: **not** *above*;
>   > *only_one_root*: (*level* = *1*) **implies** *empty*

put_right (*v*: *G*)
>   -- Add *v* to the right of cursor position.
>   -- (From *CURSOR_TREE*.)
>   **require**
>   > *not_after*: **not** *after*;
>   > *not_above*: **not** *above*;
>   > *only_one_root*: (*level* = *1*) **implies** *empty*

replace (*v*: *G*)
    -- Replace current item by *v*.
    -- (From *RECURSIVE_CURSOR_TREE*.)
  require
    writable: *writable*
  ensure
    item_replaced: *item* = *v*

feature -- Removal

remove
    -- Remove node at cursor position
    -- (and consequently the corresponding
    -- subtree). Cursor moved up one level.
    -- (From *RECURSIVE_CURSOR_TREE*.)
  require
    prunable;
    writable
  ensure
    not_off_unless_empty: *empty* **or else not** *off*

wipe_out
    -- Remove all items.
    -- (From *RECURSIVE_CURSOR_TREE*.)
  require
    prunable
  ensure
    cursor_above: *above*
  ensure then
    wiped_out: *empty*

feature -- Duplication

child_tree (*i*: *INTEGER*): **like** *Current*
    -- Subtree rooted at *i*–th child
    -- (From *CURSOR_TREE*.)
  require
    argument_within_bounds: *i* >= *1* **and then** *i* <= *arity*;
    not_off: **not** *off*

parent_tree: **like** *Current*
    -- Subtree rooted at parent
    -- (From *CURSOR_TREE*.)
  require
    not_on_root: **not** *is_root*;
    not_off: **not** *off*

subtree: **like** *Current*
    -- Subtree rooted at current node
    -- (From *CURSOR_TREE*.)
  require
    not_off: **not** *off*

invariant

non_negative_depth: *depth* >= *0*;
non_negative_breadth: *breadth* >= *0*;
is_leaf_definition: **not** *off* **implies** *is_leaf* = (*arity* = *0*);
above_property: *above* **implies** (*arity* <= *1*);
on_tree: (*isfirst* **or** *islast* **or** *is_leaf* **or** *is_root*) **implies not** *off*;

off_definition: *off* = *after* **or** *before* **or** *above* **or** *below*;
below_constraint: *below* **implies** ((*after* **or** *before*) **and not** *above*);
above_constraint: *above* **implies not** (*before* **or** *after* **or** *below*);
after_constraint: *after* **implies not** (*before* **or** *above*);
before_constaint: *before* **implies not** (*after* **or** *above*);
empty_below_constraint: (*empty* **and** (*after* **or** *before*)) **implies** *below*;
non_negative_successor_count: *arity* >= *0*;
empty_constraint: *empty* **implies** *off*;
writable_constraint: *writable* **implies** *readable*;
empty_constraint: *empty* **implies** (**not** *readable*) **and** (**not** *writable*);
after_constraint: *after* **implies** *off*

end

18.10 CLASS *COMPACT_CURSOR_TREE*

For this experimental implementation of cursor trees the interface only shows the features introduced or redeclared in the class itself.

indexing

> *description*: "*Compact trees as active structures that may be traversed using a cursor*"
> *names*: *compact_cursor_tree*, *cursor_tree*
> *representation*: *array*
> *access*: *cursor*, *membership*
> *size*: *resizable*
> *contents*: *generic*

class interface

> *COMPACT_CURSOR_TREE* [*G*]

creation
> *make*

feature -- Initialization

make (*i*: *INTEGER*)
>   -- Create an empty tree.
>   -- *i* is an estimate of the number of nodes.
> **ensure**
>   *is_above*: *above*;
>   *is_empty*: *empty*

feature -- Access

cursor: *CURSOR*
>   -- Current cursor position

has (*v*: **like** *item*): *BOOLEAN*
>   -- Does structure include an occurrence of *v*?
>   -- (Reference or object equality,
>   -- based on *object_comparison*.)
> **ensure**
>   *not_found_in_empty*: *Result* **implies not** *empty*

item: *G*
>   -- Current item
> **require**
>   *not_off*: **not** *off*
> **require else**
>   *readable*

occurrences (*v*: *G*): *INTEGER*
>   -- Number of times *v* appears.
>   -- (Reference or object equality,
>   -- based on *object_comparison*.)
> **ensure**
>   *non_negative_occurrences*: *Result* >= 0

feature -- Measurement

arity: *INTEGER*
>   -- Number of children
> **require**
>   *not_off*: **not** *off*

count: *INTEGER*
>   -- Number of items in subtree

feature -- Status report

above: *BOOLEAN*
>   -- Is there no valid cursor position above the cursor?

after: *BOOLEAN*
>   -- Is there no valid cursor position to the right of cursor?

before: *BOOLEAN*
>   -- Is there no valid cursor position to the left of cursor?

empty: *BOOLEAN*

full: *BOOLEAN* **is false**
>   -- Is tree filled to capacity? (Answer: no.)

is_root: *BOOLEAN*
>   -- Is cursor on root?

isfirst: *BOOLEAN*
>   -- Is cursor on first sibling?

islast: *BOOLEAN*
>   -- Is cursor on last sibling?

prunable: *BOOLEAN*

valid_cursor (*p*: *CURSOR*): *BOOLEAN*
>   -- Can the cursor be moved to position *p*?

feature -- Cursor movement

back
>   -- Move cursor one position backward.

down (*i*: *INTEGER*)
    -- Move cursor one level downward:
    -- to *i*-th child if there is one,
    -- or *after* if *i* = *arity* + 1,
    -- or *before* if *i* = 0.
  require
    true
  require else
    not_before: **not** *before*;
    not_after: **not** *after*;
    not_below: **not** *below*;
    valid_cursor_index: (*above* **and** *i* = *0*) **or else** *valid_
      cursor_index* (*i*)
  require else
    not_off: **not** *off*;
    argument_within_bounds: *i* >= *1* **and** *i* <= *arity*
  ensure
    gone_before: (*i* = *0*) **implies** *before*

forth
    -- Move cursor one position forward.

go_to (*p*: *CURSOR*)
    -- Move cursor to position *p*.
  require
    cursor_position_valid: *valid_cursor* (*p*)

up
    -- Move cursor one level upward, to parent
    -- or *above* if *is_root* holds.
  require
    not_above: **not** *above*
  require else
    not_off: **not** *off*
  ensure
    not_before: **not** *before*;
    not_after: **not** *after*;
    above = (**old** *is_root*)

feature -- Element change

extend (*v*: *G*)
  require
    only_one_root: (*level* = *1*) **implies** *empty*
  require else
    extendible: *extendible*
  ensure
    one_more_occurrence: *occurrences* (*v*) = **old**
      (*occurrences* (*v*)) + *1*
  ensure then
    item_inserted: *has* (*v*)

put_front (*v*: *G*)
    -- Add a leaf *v* as first child.
    -- If *above* and *empty*, make *v* the root value

put_left (*v*: *G*)
    -- Add *v* to the left of current position.
  require
    not_above: **not** *above*
  require else
    not_before: **not** *before*;
    not_above: **not** *above*;
    only_one_root: (*level* = *1*) **implies** *empty*

put_parent (*v*: *G*)
    -- insert a new node, with value v, as parent of
    -- current node and
    -- with the same position
    -- if above or on root, add a new root
  require
    not *after*;
    not *before*

put_right (*v*: *G*)
    -- Add a leaf *v̇* to the right of cursor position.
  require
    not_after: **not** *after*;
    not_above: **not** *above*;
    only_one_root: (*level* = *1*) **implies** *empty*

replace (*v*: *G*)
    -- Replace current item by *v*
  require
    is_writable: *writable*
  require else
    writable: *writable*
  ensure
    item_replaced: *item* = *v*

feature -- Removal

remove
    -- Remove node at cursor position
    -- (and consequently the corresponding subtree).
    -- Move cursor to next sibling, or *after* if none.
  require
    prunable;
    writable
  ensure
    not_before: **not** *before*

remove_node
    -- Remove node at cursor position; insert children into
    -- parent's children at current position; move cursor up.
    -- If node is root, it must not have more than one child.
  require
    not_off: **not** *off*;
    is_root **implies** *arity* <= *1*

wipe_out
    -- Remove all items.
  require
    prunable
  ensure
    cursor_above: *above*
  ensure then
    wiped_out: *empty*

invariant

  above_property: *above* **implies** (*arity* <= *1*);
  after_constraint: *after* **implies not** (*before* **or** *above*);
  before_constaint: *before* **implies not** (*after* **or** *above*);
  non_negative_successor_count: *arity* >= *0*

end

19

Set and hash table classes

19.1 OVERVIEW

An earlier chapter introduced the notion of set and hash tables and explained the classes in the corresponding class graph. *Chapter 9.*

Here now are the interfaces, in flat-short form, of all these classes.

For ease of reference, the figure on the next page reproduces the general inheritance structure given in the earlier discussion. *The figure appeared originally on page 174.*

The class interfaces appear in the order in which they were discussed in the earlier chapter:

HASH_TABLE, SET, SUBSET, LINKED_SET, COMPARABLE_SET, PART_
SORTED_SET, TWO_WAY_SORTED_SET, BINARY_SEARCH_TREE_SET

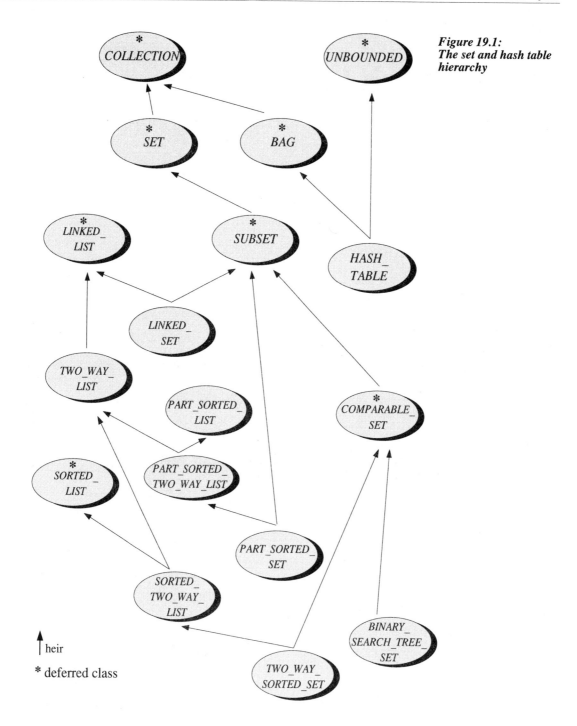

Figure 19.1:
The set and hash table
hierarchy

19.2 CLASS *HASH_TABLE*

For convenience this interface shows all features of *HASH_TABLE*, including those from ancestors *CONTAINER*, *COLLECTION* and *FINITE*.

indexing

>*description*: "*Hash tables, used to store items identified by hashable keys*"

class interface

>*HASH_TABLE* [*G, H* –> *HASHABLE*]

creation
>*make*

feature -- Initialization

>*make* (*n*: *INTEGER*)
>>-- Allocate hash table for at least *n* items.
>>-- The table will be resized automatically
>>-- if more than *n* items are inserted.

feature -- Access

>*current_keys*: *ARRAY* [*H*]
>>-- Array of actually used keys, from 1 to *count*
>>*ensure*
>>>*good_count*: *Result*. *count* = *count*

>*has* (*key*: *H*): *BOOLEAN*
>>-- Is there an item in the table with key *key*?

>*has_item* (*v*: *G*): *BOOLEAN*
>>-- Does structure include *v*?
>>-- (Reference or object equality,
>>-- based on *object_comparison*.)

>*item* (*key*: *H*): *G*
>>-- Item associated with *key*, if present;
>>-- otherwise default value of type *G*
>>*require*
>>>*valid_key*: *valid_key* (*key*)

>*item_for_iteration*: *G*
>>-- Element at current iteration position
>>*require*
>>>*not_off*: **not** *off*

>*key_at* (*n*: *INTEGER*): *H*
>>-- Key corresponding to entry *n*

>*key_for_iteration*: *H*
>>-- Key at current iteration position
>>*require*
>>>*not_off*: **not** *off*

>*position*: *INTEGER*
>>-- Hash table cursor, updated after each operation:
>>-- put, remove, has, replace, force, change_key...

infix "@" (*key*: *H*): *G*
>-- Item associated with *key*, if present;
>-- otherwise default value of type *G*
>*require*
>>*valid_key*: *valid_key* (*key*)

feature -- Measurement

>*capacity*: *INTEGER*
>>-- Number of items that may be stored.

>*count*: *INTEGER*
>>-- Number of items in table

feature -- Comparison

>*is_equal* (*other*: **like** *Current*): *BOOLEAN*
>>-- Does table contain the same information as *other*?

feature -- Status report

>*conflict*: *BOOLEAN*
>>-- Did last operation cause a conflict?

>*extendible*: *BOOLEAN* **is true**
>>-- May new items be added? (Answer: yes.)

>*found*: *BOOLEAN*
>>-- Did last operation find the item sought?

>*full*: *BOOLEAN* **is false**
>>-- Is structured filled to capacity? (Answer: no.)

>*inserted*: *BOOLEAN*
>>-- Did last operation insert an item?

>*off*: *BOOLEAN*
>>-- Is cursor past last item?

>*prunable*: *BOOLEAN*
>>-- May items be removed? (Answer: yes.)

>*removed*: *BOOLEAN*
>>-- Did last operation remove an item?

>*replaced*: *BOOLEAN*
>>-- Did last operation replace an item?

>*valid_key* (*k*: *H*): *BOOLEAN*
>>-- Is *k* a valid key?
>>-- Answer: yes if and only if *k* is not the default
>>-- value of type *H*.
>>*ensure*
>>>*Result* = (*k* /= *Void*) **and** **then** *k*. *is_hashable*

feature -- Cursor movement

  forth
          -- Advance cursor by one position.
     require
          not_off: **not** *off*

  start
          -- Bring cursor to first position.

feature -- Element change

  force (*new*: *G*; *key*: *H*)
          -- If *key* is present, replace corresponding item by *new*,
          -- if not, insert item *new* with key *key*.
          -- Make *inserted* true.
     require
          valid_key (*key*)
     ensure
          insertion_done: *item* (*key*) = *new*

  put (*new*: *G*; *key*: *H*)
          -- Insert *new* with *key* if there is no other item
          -- associated with the same key.
          -- Make *inserted* true if and only if an insertion has
          -- been made (i.e. *key* was not present).
     require
          valid_key: *valid_key* (*key*)

  replace (*new*: *G*; *key*: *H*)
          -- Replace item at *key*, if present,
          -- with *new*; do not change associated key.
          -- Make *replaced* true if and only if a replacement has
          -- been made (i.e. *key* was present).
     require
          valid_key (*key*)

  replace_key (*new_key*: *H*; *old_key*: *H*)
          -- If table contains an item at *old_key*,
          -- replace its key by *new_key*.
          -- Make *replaced* true if and only if a replacement has
          -- been made (i.e. *old_key* was present).
     require
          valid_keys: *valid_key* (*new_key*) **and** *valid_key* (*old_
          key*)

feature -- Removal

  clear_all
          -- Reset all items to default values.
     require
          prunable

  remove (*key*: *H*)
          -- Remove item associated with *key*, if present.
          -- Make *inserted* true if and only if an item has been
          -- removed (i.e. *key* was not present).
     require
          valid_key: *valid_key* (*key*)
     ensure
          removed: **not** *has* (*key*)

feature -- Conversion

  linear_representation: *ARRAYED_LIST* [*G*]
          -- Representation as a linear structure
          -- (order is same as original order of insertion)
     ensure
          result_exists: *Result* /= *Void*;
          good_count: *Result.count* = *count*

feature -- Duplication

  copy (*other*: **like** *Current*)
          -- Re−initialize from *other*.

invariant

  count_big_enough: *0* <= *count*;
  non_negative_count: *count* >= *0*

end

19.3 CLASS *SET*

This interface does not show the features inherited from the proper ancestors of *SET*, in particular *CONTAINER* and *COLLECTION*, except for those redeclared in the class.

indexing

> *description*: *"Collection, where each element must be unique."*
> *names*: *set*
> *access*: *membership*
> *contents*: *generic*

deferred class interface

> *SET* [*G*]

feature -- Access

> *has* (*v*: *G*): *BOOLEAN*
> > -- Does structure include *v*?
> > -- (Reference or object equality,
> > -- based on *object_comparison*.)
> > -- (From *CONTAINER*.)
> > *ensure*
> > > *not_found_in_empty*: *Result* **implies not** *empty*

feature -- Measurement

> *count*: *INTEGER*
> > -- Number of items

feature -- Status report

> *empty*: *BOOLEAN*
> > -- Is there no element?
> > -- (From *CONTAINER*.)
>
> *extendible*: *BOOLEAN*
> > -- May new items be added?
> > -- (From *COLLECTION*.)
>
> *object_comparison*: *BOOLEAN*
> > -- Must search operations use *equal* rather than =
> > -- for comparing references? (Default: no, use =.)
> > -- (From *CONTAINER*.)
>
> *prunable*: *BOOLEAN*
> > -- May items be removed?
> > -- (From *COLLECTION*.)

feature -- Status setting

> *compare_objects*
> > -- Ensure that future search operations will use *equal*
> > -- rather than = for comparing references.
> > -- (From *CONTAINER*.)
> > *require*
> > > *changeable_comparison_criterion*
> > *ensure*
> > > *object_comparison*

compare_references
> > -- Ensure that future search operations will use =
> > -- rather than *equal* for comparing references.
> > -- (From *CONTAINER*.)
> > *require*
> > > *changeable_comparison_criterion*
> > *ensure*
> > > *reference_comparison*: **not** *object_comparison*

feature -- Element change

> *extend* (*v*: *G*)
> > -- Ensure that set includes *v*.
> > *require*
> > > *extendible*: *extendible*
> > *ensure*
> > > *in_set_already*: **old** *has* (*v*) **implies** (*count* = **old** *count*);
> > > *added_to_set*: **not old** *has* (*v*) **implies** (*count* = **old** *count* + *1*)
> > *ensure then*
> > > *item_inserted*: *has* (*v*)
>
> *fill* (*other*: *CONTAINER* [*G*])
> > -- Fill with as many items of *other* as possible.
> > -- The representations of *other* and current structure
> > -- need not be the same.
> > -- (From *COLLECTION*.)
> > *require*
> > > *other_not_void*: *other* /= *Void*;
> > > *extendible*: *extendible*
>
> *put* (*v*: *G*)
> > -- Ensure that set includes *v*.
> > *require*
> > > *extendible*: *extendible*
> > *ensure*
> > > *in_set_already*: **old** *has* (*v*) **implies** (*count* = **old** *count*);
> > > *added_to_set*: **not old** *has* (*v*) **implies** (*count* = **old** *count* + *1*)
> > *ensure then*
> > > *item_inserted*: *has* (*v*)

feature -- Removal

> *changeable_comparison_criterion*: *BOOLEAN*
> > -- May *object_comparison* be changed?
> > -- (Answer: only if set empty; otherwise insertions might
> > -- introduce duplicates, destroying the set property.)
> > *ensure*
> > > *only_on_empty*: *Result* = *empty*

prune (*v*: *G*)
    -- Remove *v* if present.
  require
    prunable: *prunable*
  ensure
    removed_count_change: **old** *has* (*v*) **implies** (*count* = **old**
      count − *1*);
    not_removed_no_count_change: **not old** *has* (*v*) **implies**
      (*count* = **old** *count*);
    item_deleted: **not** *has* (*v*)

prune_all (*v*: *G*)
    -- Remove all occurrences of *v*.
    -- (Reference or object equality,
    -- based on *object_comparison*.)
    -- (From *COLLECTION*.)
  require
    prunable
  ensure
    no_more_occurrences: **not** *has* (*v*)

wipe_out
    -- Remove all items.
    -- (From *COLLECTION*.)
  require
    prunable
  ensure
    wiped_out: *empty*

feature -- Conversion

linear_representation: *LINEAR* [*G*]
    -- Representation as a linear structure
    -- (From *CONTAINER*.)

end

19.4 CLASS *SUBSET*

For brevity this interface does not show the features inherited from any of the ancestors of *SUBSET*, in particular *SET*. *SUBSET*, however, retains all the features of *SET* that it does not redeclare; you will find these features in the previous section.

For a complete description including both the set and subset features of *SUBSET* you may also refer to the following section, which provides a directly usable implementation. *SUBSET*, in contrast, is deferred.

indexing

    description: "Subsets with the associated operations, without
      commitment to a particular representation"
    names: subset, set
    access: membership
    contents: generic

deferred class interface

    SUBSET [G]

feature -- Comparison

    disjoint (*other*: **like** *Current*): *BOOLEAN*
        -- Do current set and *other* have no
        -- items in common?
      require
        set_exists: *other* /= *Void*;
        same_rule: *object_comparison* = *other.object_*
          comparison

    is_subset (*other*: **like** *Current*): *BOOLEAN*
        -- Is current set a subset of *other*?
      require
        set_exists: *other* /= *Void*;
        same_rule: *object_comparison* = *other.object_*
          comparison

    is_superset (*other*: **like** *Current*): *BOOLEAN*
        -- Is current set a superset of *other*?
      require
        set_exists: *other* /= *Void*;
        same_rule: *object_comparison* = *other.object_*
          comparison

feature -- Duplication

    duplicate (*n*: *INTEGER*): *SUBSET* [G]
        -- New structure containing min (*n*, *count*)
        -- items from current structure
      require
        non_negative: *n* >= *0*

feature -- Basic operations

    intersect (*other*: **like** *Current*)
        -- Remove all items not in *other*.
      require
        set_exists: *other* /= *Void*;
        same_rule: *object_comparison* = *other.object_*
          comparison
      ensure
        is_subset_other: *is_subset* (*other*)

    merge (*other*: **like** *Current*)
        -- Add all items of *other*.
      require
        set_exists: *other* /= *Void*;
        same_rule: *object_comparison* = *other.object_*
          comparison
      ensure
        is_superset: *is_superset* (*other*)

    subtract (*other*: **like** *Current*)
        -- Remove all items also in *other*.
      require
        set_exists: *other* /= *Void*;
        same_rule: *object_comparison* = *other.object_*
          comparison
      ensure
        is_disjoint: *disjoint* (*other*)

    symdif (*other*: **like** *Current*)
        -- Remove all items also in *other*, and add all
        -- items of *other* not already present.
      require
        set_exists: *other* /= *Void*;
        same_rule: *object_comparison* = *other.object_*
          comparison

end

19.5 CLASS *LINKED_SET*

Since this is an effective class meant to be used directly the interface as shown includes all of the commonly used features, coming from *SET* and *SUBSET*, but it excludes features from any other ancestor, except for those redeclared in the class.

indexing

> description: "Sets implemented by linked lists"
> names: linked_set, set, linked_list
> representation: linked
> access: membership
> contents: generic

class interface

> LINKED_SET [G]

creation
> make

feature -- Initialization

> make
> > -- Create an empty list.
> > -- (From *LINKED_LIST*.)

feature -- Comparison

> disjoint (other: **like** Current): BOOLEAN
> > -- Do current set and *other* have no
> > -- item in common?
> > -- (From *SUBSET*.)
> > **require**
> > > set_exists: other /= Void;
> > > same_rule: object_comparison = other.object_
> > >   comparison

> is_subset (other: **like** Current): BOOLEAN
> > -- Is current set a subset of *other*?
> > **require**
> > > set_exists: other /= Void;
> > > same_rule: object_comparison = other.object_
> > >   comparison

> is_superset (other: **like** Current): BOOLEAN
> > -- Is current set a superset of *other*?
> > -- (From *SUBSET*.)
> > **require**
> > > set_exists: other /= Void;
> > > same_rule: object_comparison = other.object_
> > >   comparison

feature -- Element change

> extend (v: G)
> > -- Ensure that set includes *v*.
> > **require**
> > > extendible: extendible

> merge (other: **like** Current)
> > -- Add all items of *other*.
> > **require**
> > > set_exists: other /= Void;
> > > same_rule: object_comparison = other.object_
> > >   comparison
> > **ensure**
> > > is_superset: is_superset (other)

> put (v: G)
> > -- Ensure that set includes *v*.
> > **require**
> > > extendible: extendible

feature -- Removal

> changeable_comparison_criterion: BOOLEAN
> > -- May *object_comparison* be changed?
> > -- (Answer: only if set empty; otherwise insertions might
> > -- introduce duplicates, destroying the set property.)
> > -- (From *SET*.)

> prune (v: **like** item)
> > -- Remove *v* if present.
> > **require**
> > > prunable: prunable

feature -- Basic operations

> intersect (other: **like** Current)
> > -- Remove all items not in *other*.
> > -- No effect if *other* is *empty*.
> > **require**
> > > set_exists: other /= Void;
> > > same_rule: object_comparison = other.object_
> > >   comparison
> > **ensure**
> > > is_subset_other: is_subset (other)

> subtract (other: **like** Current)
> > -- Remove all items also in *other*.
> > **require**
> > > set_exists: other /= Void;
> > > same_rule: object_comparison = other.object_
> > >   comparison
> > **ensure**
> > > is_disjoint: disjoint (other)

symdif (*other*: **like** *Current*)
        -- Remove all items also in *other*, and add all
        -- items of *other* not already present.
        -- (From *SUBSET*.)
    require
        set_exists: *other* /= *Void*;
        same_rule: *object_comparison* = *other*.*object_
            comparison*

invariant

    extendible: *extendible*

end

19.6 CLASS *COMPARABLE_SET*

COMPARABLE_SET is an heir of *SUBSET* and retains all of its features. This
interface only shows the features introduced in *COMPARABLE_SET*.

*See 19.4, page 385 for the
interface of SUBSET.*

indexing

> description: "Sets whose items may be compared according
>   to a total order relation"
> names: comparable_set, comparable_struct
> access: membership, min, max
> contents: generic

deferred class interface

> COMPARABLE_SET [G –> COMPARABLE]

feature -- Measurement

> max: G
>   -- Maximum item
>   **require**
>   not_empty: **not** empty
>   **ensure**
>   maximum_present: has (Result)
>   -- *largest*: For every item *it* in set, *it* <= Result
>
> min: G
>   -- Minimum item
>   **require**
>   not_empty: **not** empty
>   **ensure**
>   minimum_present: has (Result)
>   -- *smallest*: For every item *it* in set, Result <= it

end

19.7 CLASS *PART_SORTED_SET*

This interface shows the features introduced or redeclared in *PART_SORTED_SET* and the features inherited from *SUBSET*, and *SET*, but not those from any other ancestor.

indexing

> description: "Sets whose items may be compared according
> to a partial order relation; implemented as sorted
> two−way lists."
> names: sorted_set, set, two_way_list
> representation: linked
> access: membership, min, max
> contents: generic

class interface

> PART_SORTED_SET [G –> PART_COMPARABLE]

creation
> make

feature -- Comparison

> is_subset (other: **like** Current): BOOLEAN
> -- Is current set a subset of *other*?
> **require**
> set_exists: other /= Void;
> same_rule: object_comparison = other.object_
> comparison

> is_superset (other: **like** Current): BOOLEAN
> -- Is current set a superset of *other*?
> -- (From *SUBSET*.)
> **require**
> set_exists: other /= Void;
> same_rule: object_comparison = other.object_
> comparison

feature -- Status report

> extendible: BOOLEAN **is true**
> -- May new items be added? (Answer: yes.)
> -- (From *DYNAMIC_CHAIN*.)

feature -- Element change

> extend (v: G)
> -- Ensure that structure includes *v*.
> **require**
> extendible: extendible

> merge (other: **like** Current)
> -- Add all items of *other*.
> **require**
> set_exists: other /= Void;
> same_rule: object_comparison = other.object_
> comparison
> **ensure**
> is_superset: is_superset (other)

put (v: G)
> -- Ensure that structure includes *v*.
> **require**
> extendible: extendible

feature -- Removal

> prune (v: **like** item)
> -- Remove *v* if present.
> **require**
> prunable: prunable

feature -- Duplication

> duplicate (n: INTEGER): **like** Current
> -- Copy of sub−set beginning at cursor position
> -- and having min (*n*, *count* − *index* + 1) items
> **require**
> non_negative: n >= 0
> **require else**
> valid_subchain: n >= 0

feature -- Basic operations

> disjoint (other: **like** Current): BOOLEAN
> -- Do current set and *other* have no
> -- items in common?
> **require**
> set_exists: other /= Void;
> same_rule: object_comparison = other.object_
> comparison

> intersect (other: **like** Current)
> -- Remove all items not in *other*.
> **require**
> set_exists: other /= Void;
> same_rule: object_comparison = other.object_
> comparison
> **ensure**
> is_subset_other: is_subset (other)

> subtract (other: **like** Current)
> -- Remove all items also in *other*.
> **require**
> set_exists: other /= Void;
> same_rule: object_comparison = other.object_
> comparison
> **ensure**
> is_disjoint: disjoint (other)

symdif (*other*: **like** *Current*)
    -- Remove all items also in *other*, and add all
    -- items of *other* not already present.
  require
    set_exists: *other* /= *Void*;
    same_rule: *object_comparison* = *other*. *object_*
      comparison

invariant

  extendible: *extendible*

end

19.8 CLASSES *BINARY_SEARCH_TREE_SET* AND *TWO_WAY_SORTED_SET*

The classes *TWO_WAY_SORTED_SET* and *BINARY_SEARCH_TREE_SET* provide alternative implementations of *COMPARABLE_SET*. The interface of *TWO_WAY_SORTED_SET* as it appears below applies to both. It only shows set and subset features, excluding any features inherited from ancestors other than *SET* and *SUBSET*. except for those which are redeclared in the class.

indexing

> *description*: "*Sets whose items may be compared according to a total order relation; implemented as sorted two−way lists.*"
> *names*: *sorted_set, set, two_way_list*
> *representation*: *linked*
> *access*: *membership, min, max*
> *contents*: *generic*

class interface

> *TWO_WAY_SORTED_SET* [*G* –> *COMPARABLE*]

creation
> *make*

feature -- Comparison

> *disjoint* (*other*: *like Current*): *BOOLEAN*
> > -- Do current set and *other* have no
> > -- items in common?
> > *require*
> > > *set_exists*: *other* /= *Void*;
> > > *same_rule*: *object_comparison* = *other.object_comparison*

> *is_subset* (*other*: *like Current*): *BOOLEAN*
> > -- Is current set a subset of *other*?
> > *require*
> > > *set_exists*: *other* /= *Void*;
> > > *same_rule*: *object_comparison* = *other.object_comparison*

> *is_superset* (*other*: *like Current*): *BOOLEAN*
> > -- Is current set a superset of *other*?
> > -- (From *SUBSET*.)
> > *require*
> > > *set_exists*: *other* /= *Void*;
> > > *same_rule*: *object_comparison* = *other.object_comparison*

feature -- Element change

> *extend* (*v*: *G*)
> > -- Ensure that structure includes *v*.
> > *require*
> > > *extendible*: *extendible*

merge (*other*: *like Current*)
> -- Add all items of *other*.
> *require*
> > *set_exists*: *other* /= *Void*;
> > *same_rule*: *object_comparison* = *other.object_comparison*
> *ensure*
> > *is_superset*: *is_superset* (*other*)

put (*v*: *G*)
> -- Ensure that structure includes *v*.
> *require*
> > *extendible*: *extendible*

feature -- Removal

> *changeable_comparison_criterion*: *BOOLEAN*
> > -- May *object_comparison* be changed?
> > -- (Answer: only if set empty; otherwise insertions might
> > -- introduce duplicates, destroying the set property.)
> > -- (From *SET*.)

> *prune* (*v*: *like item*)
> > -- Remove *v* if present.
> > *require*
> > > *prunable*: *prunable*

feature -- Duplication

> *duplicate* (*n*: *INTEGER*): *like Current*
> > -- Copy of sub−set beginning at cursor position
> > -- and having min (*n, count − index* + 1) items
> > *require*
> > > *non_negative*: $n >= 0$
> > *require else*
> > > *valid_subchain*: $n >= 0$

feature -- Basic operations

> *intersect* (*other*: *like Current*)
> > -- Remove all items not in *other*.
> > *require*
> > > *set_exists*: *other* /= *Void*;
> > > *same_rule*: *object_comparison* = *other.object_comparison*
> > *ensure*
> > > *is_subset_other*: *is_subset* (*other*)

subtract (*other*: **like** *Current*)
    -- Remove all items also in *other*.
  require
    set_exists: *other* /= *Void*;
    same_rule: *object_comparison* = *other.object_*
      comparison
  ensure
    is_disjoint: *disjoint* (*other*)

symdif (*other*: **like** *Current*)
    -- Remove all items also in *other*, and add all
    -- items of *other* not already present.
  require
    set_exists: *other* /= *Void*;
    same_rule: *object_comparison* = *other.object_*
      comparison

invariant

  extendible: *extendible*

end

20

Iteration classes

20.1 OVERVIEW

An earlier chapter introduced the notion of iterator and explained the role of the corresponding classes.

Chapter 10.

Here now are the interfaces, in flat-short form, of all these classes.

For ease of reference, the figure on the next page reproduces the general inheritance structure given in the earlier discussion.

This is the same figure as on page 182.

The class interfaces appear in the following order:

> *ITERATOR,*
>
> *LINEAR_ITERATOR,*
>
> *TWO_WAY_CHAIN_ITERATOR,*
>
> *CURSOR_TREE_ITERATOR.*

20.2 CLASS *ITERATOR*

ITERATOR is the most general iteration class. All the other features in this chapter inherit its features.

The full class interface of *ITERATOR* follows.

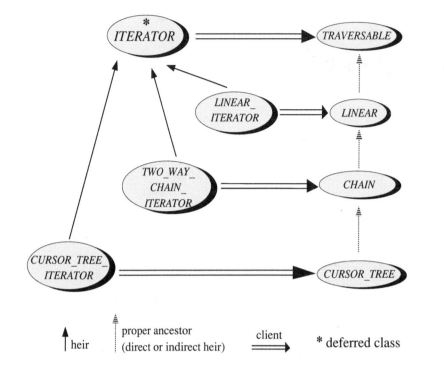

Figure 20.1:
Iteration class
hierarchy

↑ heir
⋮ proper ancestor
(direct or indirect heir)
⟹ client
* deferred class

indexing

    description: "*Objects that are able to iterate over traversable*
    structures, on which they can perform repeated actions and
    tests according to a number of predefined control
    structures such as "if", "until" and others."
    names: *iterators*, *iteration*

deferred class interface

    ITERATOR [*G*]

feature -- Status report

    invariant_value: *BOOLEAN*
        -- Is the invariant satisfied?
        -- (Redefinitions of this feature will usually involve
        -- *target*; if so, make sure that the result is defined
        -- when 'target = Void'.)
      require
        traversable_exists: *target* /= *Void*

    item_test (*v*: *G*): *BOOLEAN*
        -- Test to be applied to item *v*
        -- (default: false)

    target: *TRAVERSABLE* [*G*]
        -- The structure to which iteration features will apply

    test: *BOOLEAN*
        -- Test to be applied to item at current position in *target*
        -- (default: value of *item_test* on item)
      require
        traversable_exists: *target* /= *Void*;
        not_off: ***not*** *target.off*
      ensure
        not_off: ***not*** *target.off*

feature -- Status setting

    set (*s*: ***like*** *target*)
        -- Make *s* the new target of iterations.
      require
        s /= *Void*
      ensure
        target = *s*;
        target /= *Void*

feature -- Cursor movement

  do_all
    -- Apply *action* to every item of *target*.
    require
      traversable_exists: *target* /= *Void*

  do_if
    -- Apply *action* to every item of *target* satisfying *test*.
    require
      traversable_exists: *target* /= *Void*

  do_until
    -- Apply *action* to every item of *target* up to
    -- and including first one satisfying *test*.
    -- (Apply to full list if no item satisfies *test*).
    require
      traversable_exists: *target* /= *Void*

  do_while
    -- Apply *action* to every item of *target* up to
    -- and including first one not satisfying *test*.
    -- (Apply to full list if all items satisfy *test*).

  exists: *BOOLEAN*
    -- Is *test* true for at least one item of *target*?
    require
      traversable_exists: *target* /= *Void*

  forall: *BOOLEAN*
    -- Is *test* true for all items of *target*?
    require
      traversable_exists: *target* /= *Void*

  until_do
    -- Apply *action* to every item of *target* up to
    -- but excluding first one satisfying *test*.
    -- (Apply to full list if no items satisfy *test*.)
    require
      traversable_exists: *target* /= *Void*

  while_do
    -- Apply *action* to every item of *target* up to
    -- but excluding first one satisfying not *test*.
    -- (Apply to full list if all items satisfy *test*.)
    require
      traversable_exists: *target* /= *Void*

feature -- Element change

  action
    -- Action to be applied to item at current position
    -- in *target* (default: *item_action* on that item).
    -- For iterators to work properly, redefined versions of
    -- this feature should not change the traversable's
    -- structure.
    require
      traversable_exists: *target* /= *Void*;
      not_off: **not** *target.off*;
      invariant_satisfied: *invariant_value*
    ensure
      not_off: **not** *target.off*;
      invariant_satisfied: *invariant_value*

  item_action (*v*: *G*)
    -- Action to be applied to item *v*
    -- (Default: do nothing.)

end

20.3 CLASS *LINEAR_ITERATOR*

LINEAR_ITERATOR is the basic class for iterating over linear structures such as lists and circular chains. For convenience, the interface shows all the exported features of the class: those introduced in the class itself and those inherited from its parent *ITERATOR*.

indexing

    description: "*Objects that are able to iterate over linear structures*"
    names: *iterators, iteration, linear_iterators, linear_iteration*

class interface

    LINEAR_ITERATOR [*G*]

feature -- Status report

    invariant_value: *BOOLEAN*
        -- Is the invariant satisfied?
        -- (Redefinitions of this feature will usually involve
        -- *target*; if so, make sure that the result is defined
        -- when 'target = Void'.)
        -- (From *ITERATOR*.)
    require
        traversable_exists: *target* /= *Void*

    item_test (*v*: *G*): *BOOLEAN*
        -- Test to be applied to item *v*
        -- (default: false)
        -- (From *ITERATOR*.)

    test: *BOOLEAN*
        -- Test to be applied to item at current position in *target*
        -- (default: value of *item_test* on item)
        -- (From *ITERATOR*.)
    require
        traversable_exists: *target* /= *Void*;
        not_off: **not** *target.off*
    ensure
        not_off: **not** *target.off*

feature -- Status setting

    set (*s*: **like** *target*)
        -- Make *s* the new target of iterations.
        -- (From *ITERATOR*.)
    require
        s /= *Void*
    ensure
        target = *s*;
        target /= *Void*

feature -- Cursor movement

    continue_for (*n*, *k*: *INTEGER*)
        -- Apply *action* to every *k*–th item,
        -- *n* times if possible.
    require
        traversable_exists: *target* /= *Void*;
        valid_repetition: *n* >= *0*;
        valid_skip: *k* >= *1*

    continue_search (*b*: *BOOLEAN*)
        -- Search the first item of *target*
        -- satisfying: *test* equals to *b*
        -- (from the current position of *target*).
    require
        traversable_exists: *target* /= *Void*
    ensure
        found: **not** *exhausted* = (*b* = *test*)

    continue_until
        -- Apply *action* to every item of *target* up to
        -- and including first one satisfying *test*
        -- (from the current position of *target*).
    require
        traversable_exists: *target* /= *Void*;
        invariant_satisfied: *invariant_value*
    ensure
        achieved: **not** *exhausted* **implies** *test*

    continue_while
        -- Apply *action* to every item of *target* up to
        -- and including first one not satisfying *test*
        -- (from the current position of *target*).
    require
        traversable_exists: *target* /= *Void*;
        invariant_satisfied: *invariant_value*
    ensure
        finished: **not** *exhausted* **implies** **not** *test*

    do_all
        -- Apply *action* to every item of *target*.
        -- (from the *start* of *target*)
    require
        traversable_exists: *target* /= *Void*
    ensure
        exhausted

    do_for (*i*, *n*, *k*: *INTEGER*)
        -- Apply *action* to every *k*–th item,
        -- *n* times if possible, starting from *i*-th.
    require
        traversable_exists: *target* /= *Void*;
        valid_start: *i* >= *1*;
        valid_repetition: *n* >= *0*;
        valid_skip: *k* >= *1*

    do_if
        -- Apply *action* to every item of *target*
        -- satisfying *test*.
    require
        traversable_exists: *target* /= *Void*

do_until
>   -- Apply *action* to every item of *target* up to
>   -- and including first one satisfying *test*.
>   **require**
>   *traversable_exists*: *target* /= *Void*
>   **ensure**
>   *achieved*: **not** *exhausted* **implies** *test*

do_while
>   -- Apply *action* to every item of *target* up to
>   -- and including first one not satisfying *test*.
>   -- (from the *start* of *target*)
>   **ensure**
>   *finished*: **not** *exhausted* **implies not** *test*

exhausted: *BOOLEAN*
>   -- Is *target* exhausted?
>   **require**
>   *traversable_exists*: *target* /= *Void*

exists: *BOOLEAN*
>   -- Does *test* return true for
>   -- at least one item of *target*?
>   **require**
>   *traversable_exists*: *target* /= *Void*

forall: *BOOLEAN*
>   -- Does *test* return true for
>   -- all items of *target*?
>   **require**
>   *traversable_exists*: *target* /= *Void*

forth
>   -- Move to next position of *target*.
>   **require**
>   *traversable_exists*: *target* /= *Void*

off: *BOOLEAN*
>   -- Is position of *target* off?
>   **require**
>   *traversable_exists*: *target* /= *Void*

search (*b*: *BOOLEAN*)
>   -- Search the first item of *target* for which *test*
>   -- has the same value as *b* (both true or both false).
>   **require**
>   *traversable_exists*: *target* /= *Void*

start
>   -- Move to first position of *target*.
>   **require**
>   *traversable_exists*: *target* /= *Void*

target: *LINEAR* [*G*]
>   -- The structure to which iteration features will apply.

until_continue
>   -- Apply *action* to every item of *target* from current
>   -- position, up to but excluding first one satisfying *test*.
>   **require**
>   *traversable_exists*: *target* /= *Void*;
>   *invariant_satisfied*: *invariant_value*
>   **ensure**
>   *achieved*: *exhausted* **or else** *test*;
>   *invariant_satisfied*: *invariant_value*

until_do
>   -- Apply *action* to every item of *target* up to
>   -- but excluding first one satisfying *test*.
>   -- (Apply to full list if no item satisfies *test*.)
>   **require**
>   *traversable_exists*: *target* /= *Void*
>   **ensure**
>   *achieved*: **not** *exhausted* **implies** *test*

while_continue
>   -- Apply *action* to every item of *target* up to
>   -- but excluding first one not satisfying *test*.
>   **ensure**
>   *finished*: **not** *exhausted* **implies not** *test*

while_do
>   -- Apply *action* to every item of *target* up to
>   -- but excluding first one not satisfying *test*.
>   -- (Apply to full list if all items satisfy *test*.)
>   **require**
>   *traversable_exists*: *target* /= *Void*
>   **ensure**
>   *finished*: **not** *exhausted* **implies not** *test*

feature -- Element change

action
>   -- Action to be applied to item at current position
>   -- in *target* (default: *item_action* on that item).
>   -- For iterators to work properly, redefined versions of
>   -- this feature should not change the traversable's
>   -- structure.
>   -- (From *ITERATOR*.)
>   **require**
>   *traversable_exists*: *target* /= *Void*;
>   *not_off*: **not** *target*. *off*;
>   *invariant_satisfied*: *invariant_value*
>   **ensure**
>   *not_off*: **not** *target*. *off*;
>   *invariant_satisfied*: *invariant_value*

item_action (*v*: *G*)
>   -- Action to be applied to item *v*
>   -- (Default: do nothing.)
>   -- (From *ITERATOR*.)

end

20.4 CLASS *TWO_WAY_CHAIN_ITERATOR*

The interface does not show the features that *TWO_WAY_CHAIN_ITERATOR* inherits from its parent *LINEAR_ITERATOR* and its further ancestors, except for those that it renames or redeclares. Refer to the preceding section for the full interface of *LINEAR_ ITERATOR*.

indexing

   description: "*Objects that are able to iterate over two−way chains, on which they can perform repeated actions and tests according to a number of predefined control structures such as "if", "until" and others.*"
   names: *iterators, iteration, two_way_chain_iterators, two_ way_chain_iteration*
   traversal: *sequential*
   exploration: *forward, backward*

class interface

   TWO_WAY_CHAIN_ITERATOR [*G*]

feature -- Access

   target: *CHAIN* [*G*]

feature -- Cursor movement

   back
         -- Move cursor of *target* backward one position.
      require
         traversable_exists: *target* /= *Void*

   continue_for_back (*n*, *k*: *INTEGER*)
         -- Apply *action* to every *k*−th item,
         -- *n* times if possible.
         -- (From *LINEAR_ITERATOR*.)
      require
         traversable_exists: *target* /= *Void*;
         valid_repetition: *n* >= *0*;
         valid_skip: *k* >= *1*

   continue_search_back (*b*: *BOOLEAN*)
         -- Search the first item of *target*
         -- satisfying: *test* equals to *b*
         -- (from the current position of *target*).
         -- (From *LINEAR_ITERATOR*.)
      require
         traversable_exists: *target* /= *Void*

   continue_until_back
         -- Apply *action* to every item of *target* up to
         -- and including first one satisfying *test*
         -- (from the current position of *target*).
         -- (From *LINEAR_ITERATOR*.)
      require
         traversable_exists: *target* /= *Void*;
         invariant_satisfied: *invariant_value*

   continue_while_back
         -- Apply *action* to every item of *target* up to
         -- and including first one not satisfying *test*
         -- (from the current position of *target*).
         -- (From *LINEAR_ITERATOR*.)
      require
         traversable_exists: *target* /= *Void*;
         invariant_satisfied: *invariant_value*

   do_all_back
         -- Apply *action* to every item of *target*.
         -- (from the *finish* of *target*)
         -- (From *LINEAR_ITERATOR*.)
      require
         traversable_exists: *target* /= *Void*
      ensure
         exhausted

   do_for_back (*i*, *n*, *k*: *INTEGER*)
         -- Apply *action* to every *k*−th item,
         -- *n* times if possible, starting from *i*-th.
         -- (From *LINEAR_ITERATOR*.)
      require
         traversable_exists: *target* /= *Void*;
         valid_start: *i* >= *1*;
         valid_repetition: *n* >= *0*;
         valid_skip: *k* >= *1*

   do_if_back
         -- Apply *action* to every item of *target*
         -- satisfying *test*.
         -- (From *LINEAR_ITERATOR*.)
      require
         traversable_exists: *target* /= *Void*

   do_until_back
         -- Apply *action* to every item of *target* up to
         -- and including first one satisfying *test*.
         -- (From *LINEAR_ITERATOR*.)
      require
         traversable_exists: *target* /= *Void*

   do_while_back
         -- Apply *action* to every item of *target* up to
         -- and including first one not satisfying *test*.
         -- (from the *start* of *target*)
         -- (From *LINEAR_ITERATOR*.)

exists_back: *BOOLEAN*
    -- Does *test* return true for
    -- at least one item of *target*?
    -- (From *LINEAR_ITERATOR*.)
  require
    traversable_exists: *target* /= *Void*

finish
    -- Move cursor of *target* to last position.
  require
    traversable_exists: *target* /= *Void*

forall_back: *BOOLEAN*
    -- Does *test* return true for
    -- all items of *target*?
    -- (From *LINEAR_ITERATOR*.)
  require
    traversable_exists: *target* /= *Void*

search_back (*b*: *BOOLEAN*)
    -- Search the first item of *target* for which *test*
    -- has the same value as *b* (both true or both false).
    -- (From *LINEAR_ITERATOR*.)
  require
    traversable_exists: *target* /= *Void*

until_continue_back
    -- Apply *action* to every item of *target* from current
    -- position, up to but excluding first one satisfying *test*.
    -- (From *LINEAR_ITERATOR*.)
  require
    traversable_exists: *target* /= *Void*
    invariant_satisfied: *invariant_value*

until_do
    -- Apply *action* to every item of *target* up to
    -- but excluding first one satisfying *test*.
    -- (Apply to full list if no item satisfies *test*.)
    -- (From *LINEAR_ITERATOR*.)
  require
    traversable_exists: *target* /= *Void*

until_do_back
    -- Apply *action* to every item of *target* up to
    -- but excluding first one satisfying *test*.
    -- (Apply to full list if no item satisfies *test*.)
    -- (From *LINEAR_ITERATOR*.)
  require
    traversable_exists: *target* /= *Void*

while_continue_back
    -- Apply *action* to every item of *target* up to
    -- but excluding first one not satisfying *test*.
    -- (From *LINEAR_ITERATOR*.)

while_do_back
    -- Apply *action* to every item of *target* up to
    -- but excluding first one not satisfying *test*.
    -- (Apply to full list if all items satisfy *test*.)
    -- (From *LINEAR_ITERATOR*.)
  require
    traversable_exists: *target* /= *Void*

end

20.5 CLASS *CURSOR_TREE_ITERATOR*

The interface does not show the features that *CURSOR_TREE_ITERATOR* inherits from *ITERATOR* and *LINEAR_ITERATOR*, except for those that the class redeclares or renames (which actually is most of them except for the general iteration features *test*, *action*, *item_test*, *item_action*).

See 20.2, page 393 for ITERATOR and 20.3, page 396 for LINEAR_ITERATOR.

indexing

  description: "*Objects that are able to iterate over cursor trees, on which they can perform repeated actions and tests according to a number of predefined control structures such as "if", "until" and others.*"
  names: *iterators, iteration, cursor_tree_iterators, cursor_ tree_iteration, tree_iterators, tree_iteration*
  exploration: *depth_first, breadth_first*
  traversal: *preorder, postorder, inorder*

class interface

  CURSOR_TREE_ITERATOR [G]

feature -- Status report

  target: *CURSOR_TREE* [G]
        -- The structure to which iteration features will apply

feature -- Cursor movement

  breadth_continue_search (*b*: *BOOLEAN*)
        -- Search the first item of *target*
        -- satisfying: *test* equals to *b*
        -- (from the current position of *target*).
        -- (From *LINEAR_ITERATOR*.)
     require
        traversable_exists: *target* /= *Void*
     ensure
        found: **not** *exhausted* = (*b* = *test*)

  breadth_do_if
        -- Apply *action* to every item of *target*
        -- satisfying *test*.
        -- (From *LINEAR_ITERATOR*.)
     require
        traversable_exists: *target* /= *Void*

  breadth_do_until
        -- Apply *action* to every item of *target* up to
        -- and including first one satisfying *test*.
        -- (From *LINEAR_ITERATOR*.)
     require
        traversable_exists: *target* /= *Void*
     ensure
        achieved: **not** *exhausted* **implies** *test*

  breadth_do_while
        -- Apply *action* to every item of *target* up to
        -- and including first one not satisfying *test*.
        -- (from the *start* of *target*)
        -- (From *LINEAR_ITERATOR*.)
     ensure
        finished: **not** *exhausted* **implies** **not** *test*

  breadth_forth
        -- Move cursor of *target* to next position in breadth–first.
     require
        traversable_exists: *target* /= *Void*

  breadth_search (*b*: *BOOLEAN*)
        -- Search the first item of *target* for which *test*
        -- has the same value as *b* (both true or both false).
        -- (From *LINEAR_ITERATOR*.)
     require
        traversable_exists: *target* /= *Void*

  breadth_start
        -- Move cursor of *target* to root position
        -- (first position in preorder and breadth–first).

  breadth_until_do
        -- Apply *action* to every item of *target* up to
        -- but excluding first one satisfying *test*.
        -- (Apply to full list if no item satisfies *test*.)
        -- (From *LINEAR_ITERATOR*.)
     require
        traversable_exists: *target* /= *Void*
     ensure
        achieved: **not** *exhausted* **implies** *test*

  breadth_while_continue
        -- Apply *action* to every item of *target* up to
        -- but excluding first one not satisfying *test*.
        -- (From *LINEAR_ITERATOR*.)
     ensure
        finished: **not** *exhausted* **implies** **not** *test*

  breadth_while_do
        -- Apply *action* to every item of *target* up to
        -- but excluding first one not satisfying *test*.
        -- (Apply to full list if all items satisfy *test*.)
        -- (From *LINEAR_ITERATOR*.)
     require
        traversable_exists: *target* /= *Void*
     ensure
        finished: **not** *exhausted* **implies** **not** *test*

exhausted: *BOOLEAN*
    -- Is *target* exhausted?
    -- (From *LINEAR_ITERATOR*.)
  require
    traversable_exists: *target* /= *Void*

post_continue_for (*n*, *k*: *INTEGER*)
    -- Apply *action* to every *k*−th item,
    -- *n* times if possible.
    -- (From *LINEAR_ITERATOR*.)
  require
    traversable_exists: *target* /= *Void*;
    valid_repetition: *n* >= *0*;
    valid_skip: *k* >= *1*

post_continue_until
    -- Apply *action* to every item of *target* up to
    -- and including first one satisfying *test*
    -- (from the current position of *target*).
    -- (From *LINEAR_ITERATOR*.)
  require
    traversable_exists: *target* /= *Void*;
    invariant_satisfied: *invariant_value*
  ensure
    achieved: **not** *exhausted* **implies** *test*

post_continue_while
    -- Apply *action* to every item of *target* up to
    -- and including first one not satisfying *test*
    -- (from the current position of *target*).
    -- (From *LINEAR_ITERATOR*.)
  require
    traversable_exists: *target* /= *Void*;
    invariant_satisfied: *invariant_value*
  ensure
    finished: **not** *exhausted* **implies not** *test*

post_do_all
    -- Apply *action* to every item of *target*.
    -- (from the *start* of *target*)
    -- (From *LINEAR_ITERATOR*.)
  require
    traversable_exists: *target* /= *Void*
  ensure
    exhausted

post_do_for (*i*, *n*, *k*: *INTEGER*)
    -- Apply *action* to every *k*−th item,
    -- *n* times if possible, starting from *i*-th.
    -- (From *LINEAR_ITERATOR*.)
  require
    traversable_exists: *target* /= *Void*;
    valid_start: *i* >= *1*;
    valid_repetition: *n* >= *0*;
    valid_skip: *k* >= *1*

post_exists: *BOOLEAN*
    -- Does *test* return true for
    -- at least one item of *target*?
    -- (From *LINEAR_ITERATOR*.)
  require
    traversable_exists: *target* /= *Void*

post_forall: *BOOLEAN*
    -- Does *test* return true for
    -- all items of *target*?
    -- (From *LINEAR_ITERATOR*.)
  require
    traversable_exists: *target* /= *Void*

post_forth
    -- Move cursor of *target* to next position in postorder.
  require
    traversable_exists: *target* /= *Void*

post_start
    -- Move cursor of *target* to first position in postorder.
  require
    traversable_exists: *target* /= *Void*

pre_continue_for (*n*, *k*: *INTEGER*)
    -- Apply *action* to every *k*−th item,
    -- *n* times if possible.
    -- (From *LINEAR_ITERATOR*.)
  require
    traversable_exists: *target* /= *Void*;
    valid_repetition: *n* >= *0*;
    valid_skip: *k* >= *1*

pre_continue_search (*b*: *BOOLEAN*)
    -- Search the first item of *target*
    -- satisfying: *test* equals to *b*
    -- (from the current position of *target*).
    -- (From *LINEAR_ITERATOR*.)
  require
    traversable_exists: *target* /= *Void*
  ensure
    found: **not** *exhausted* = (*b* = *test*)

pre_continue_until
    -- Apply *action* to every item of *target* up to
    -- and including first one satisfying *test*
    -- (from the current position of *target*).
    -- (From *LINEAR_ITERATOR*.)
  require
    traversable_exists: *target* /= *Void*;
    invariant_satisfied: *invariant_value*
  ensure
    achieved: **not** *exhausted* **implies** *test*

pre_continue_while
    -- Apply *action* to every item of *target* up to
    -- and including first one not satisfying *test*
    -- (from the current position of *target*).
    -- (From *LINEAR_ITERATOR*.)
   require
    traversable_exists: *target* /= *Void*;
    invariant_satisfied: *invariant_value*
   ensure
    finished: **not** *exhausted* **implies not** *test*

pre_do_all
    -- Apply *action* to every item of *target*.
    -- (from the *start* of *target*)
    -- (From *LINEAR_ITERATOR*.)
   require
    traversable_exists: *target* /= *Void*
   ensure
    exhausted

pre_do_for (*i*, *n*, *k*: *INTEGER*)
    -- Apply *action* to every *k*-th item,
    -- *n* times if possible, starting from *i*-th.
    -- (From *LINEAR_ITERATOR*.)
   require
    traversable_exists: *target* /= *Void*;
    valid_start: $i >= 1$;
    valid_repetition: $n >= 0$
    valid_skip: $k >= 1$

pre_do_if
    -- Apply *action* to every item of *target*
    -- satisfying *test*.
    -- (From *LINEAR_ITERATOR*.)
   require
    traversable_exists: *target* /= *Void*

pre_do_until
    -- Apply *action* to every item of *target* up to
    -- and including first one satisfying *test*.
    -- (From *LINEAR_ITERATOR*.)
   require
    traversable_exists: *target* /= *Void*
   ensure
    achieved: **not** *exhausted* **implies** *test*

pre_do_while
    -- Apply *action* to every item of *target* up to
    -- and including first one not satisfying *test*.
    -- (from the *start* of *target*)
    -- (From *LINEAR_ITERATOR*.)
   ensure
    finished: **not** *exhausted* **implies not** *test*

pre_exists: *BOOLEAN*
    -- Does *test* return true for
    -- at least one item of *target*?
    -- (From *LINEAR_ITERATOR*.)
   require
    traversable_exists: *target* /= *Void*

pre_forall: *BOOLEAN*
    -- Does *test* return true for
    -- all items of *target*?
    -- (From *LINEAR_ITERATOR*.)
   require
    traversable_exists: *target* /= *Void*

pre_forth
    -- Move cursor of *target* to next position in preorder.
   require
    traversable_exists: *target* /= *Void*

pre_search (*b*: *BOOLEAN*)
    -- Search the first item of *target* for which *test*
    -- has the same value as *b* (both true or both false).
    -- (From *LINEAR_ITERATOR*.)
   require
    traversable_exists: *target* /= *Void*

pre_start
    -- Move cursor of *target* to root position
    -- (first position in preorder and breadth-first).

pre_until_do
    -- Apply *action* to every item of *target* up to
    -- but excluding first one satisfying *test*.
    -- (Apply to full list if no item satisfies *test*.)
    -- (From *LINEAR_ITERATOR*.)
   require
    traversable_exists: *target* /= *Void*
   ensure
    achieved: **not** *exhausted* **implies** *test*

pre_while_continue
    -- Apply *action* to every item of *target* up to
    -- but excluding first one not satisfying *test*.
    -- (From *LINEAR_ITERATOR*.)
   ensure
    finished: **not** *exhausted* **implies not** *test*

pre_while_do
    -- Apply *action* to every item of *target* up to
    -- but excluding first one not satisfying *test*.
    -- (Apply to full list if all items satisfy *test*.)
    -- (From *LINEAR_ITERATOR*.)
   require
    traversable_exists: *target* /= *Void*
   ensure
    finished: **not** *exhausted* **implies not** *test*
end

21

Lexical analysis classes

21.1 OVERVIEW

An earlier chapter introduced the Lex library and explained the corresponding classes.

Chapter 11.

Here now are the interfaces, in flat-short form, of all these classes.

For ease of reference, the figure on the next page reproduces the general inheritance structure given in the earlier discussion.

This is the same figure as on page 202.

The class interfaces appear in the following order, beginning with the three corresponding to the most frequent uses and continuing with those offering more advanced facilities:

> *SCANNING, LEXICAL, TOKEN, METALEX, LEX_BUILDER.*

21.2 CLASS *SCANNING*

Because *SCANNING* is meant to be easy to learn for simple uses, the interface only shows the features introduced or redeclared in the class itself. *SCANNING* is an heir of *METALEX* which in turn is a descendant of *LEX_BUILDER*; for more advanced features look at the specifications of *METALEX* and *LEX_BUILDER* later in this chapter.

*METALEX: 21.5, page 407;
LEX_BUILDER: 21.6, page 408.*

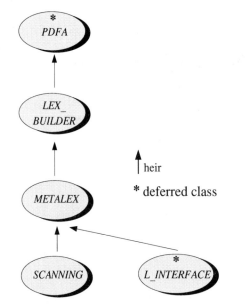

↑ heir

* deferred class

indexing

   description: "*Mechanisms for building and using lexical
      analyzers. This class may be used as ancestor by classes
      needing its facilities.*"

class interface

   SCANNING

creation
   make

feature -- Initialization

   build (*store_file_name, grammar_file_name*: *STRING*)
         -- Create a lexical analyzer.
         -- If *store_file_name* is the name of an existing file,
         -- use analyzer stored in that file.
         -- Otherwise read grammar from *grammar_file_name*,
         -- create an analyzer, and store it in *store_file_name*.
      require
         store_file_name /= *Void*
      ensure
         analyzer_exists: *analyzer* /= *Void*

   make
         -- (From *LEX_BUILDER*.)

feature -- Status setting

   analyze (*input_file_name*: *STRING*)
         -- Perform lexical analysis on file
         -- of name *input_file_name*.

feature -- Output

   begin_analysis
         -- Initialize lexical analysis
         -- This default version of the procedure
         -- simply prints header information.
         -- It may be redefined in descendants
         -- for specific processing.

   do_a_token (*read_token*: *TOKEN*)
         -- Handle *read_token*.
         -- This default version of the procedure
         -- simply prints information on *read_token*.
         -- It may be redefined in descendants
         -- for specific processing.
      require
         argument_not_void: *read_token* /= *Void*

   end_analysis
         -- Terminate lexical analysis.
         -- This default version of the procedure
         -- does nothing.
         -- It may be redefined in descendants
         -- for specific processing.

                              end

21.3 CLASS *LEXICAL*

indexing

   description: *"Lexical analyzers"*

class interface

   LEXICAL

creation
   make,
   make_new

feature -- Initialization

   make
      -- Set up lexical analyzer for retrieval.

   make_new
      -- Set up a new lexical analyzer

feature -- Access

   end_of_text: *BOOLEAN*
      -- Has end of input been reached?

   keyword_code (*word*: *STRING*): *INTEGER*
      -- Keyword code for *word*.
      -- −1 if not a keyword.

   keyword_string (*n*: *INTEGER*): *STRING*
      -- Keyword corresponding to keyword code *n*

   last_is_keyword: *BOOLEAN*
      -- Is the last read token a keyword?

   last_keyword_code: *INTEGER*
      -- Keyword code for last token.
      -- −1 if not a keyword.

   last_keyword_text: *STRING*
      -- Last read string if recognized as a keyword;
      -- void otherwise.

   last_string_read: *STRING*
      -- String value of last token read

   last_token: *TOKEN*
      -- Last token read

   No_token: *INTEGER* **is** *0*
      -- Token type for no token recognized.

   other_possible_tokens: *ARRAY* [*INTEGER*]
      -- Other candidate types for last recognized token

   token_column_number: *INTEGER*
      -- Column number of last token read
    ensure
      Result >= *1*

   token_line_number: *INTEGER*
      -- Line number of last token read
    ensure
      Result >= *1*

   token_type: *INTEGER*
      -- Type of last token read

feature -- Status setting

   set_separator_type (*type*: *INTEGER*)
      -- Set *type* to be the type of tokens
      -- used as separators.

feature -- Input

   get_any_token
      -- Try to read a new token.
      -- Recognize longest possible string.
    require
      not_end_of_text: **not** *end_of_text*;
      buffers_created: *buffer* /= *Void*

   get_fixed_token (*l*: *INTEGER*)
      -- Read new token that matches one of the
      -- lexical grammar's regular expressions.
      -- Recognize longest possible string with
      -- length less than or equal to *l*.
    require
      not_end_of_text: **not** *end_of_text*;
      buffers_created: *buffer* /= *Void*

   get_short_token
      -- Read shortest token that matches one of the
      -- lexical grammar's regular expressions.
    require
      not_end_of_text: **not** *end_of_text*;
      buffers_created: *buffer* /= *Void*

   get_token
      -- Read new token matching one of the regular
      -- expressions of the lexical grammar.
      -- Recognize longest possible string;
      -- ignore unrecognized tokens and separators.

feature -- Output

   trace
      -- Output information about the analyzer's
      -- current status.

end

21.4 CLASS *TOKEN*

indexing

   description: *"Individual elements of lexical analysis"*

class interface

   TOKEN

feature -- Access

   column_number: *INTEGER*
      -- Column number in the parsed text

   is_keyword (*i*: *INTEGER*): *BOOLEAN*
      -- If the token is a keyword,
      -- is *i* its identification number?

   keyword_code: *INTEGER*
      -- Identification number if the token is a keyword

   line_number: *INTEGER*
      -- Line number in the parsed text

   string_value: *STRING*
      -- The token's character string

   type: *INTEGER*
      -- Type of the token

feature -- Status setting

   set (*typ*, *lin*, *col*, *key*: *INTEGER*; *str*: *STRING*)
      -- Reset the contents of the token:
      -- type *type*, line number *lin*,
      -- column number *col*, keyword value *key*.

end

21.5 CLASS *METALEX*

This interface shows the features introduced or redeclared in *METALEX*'s parent
HIGH_BUILDER, but not those from for other parents, in particular *LEX_BUILDER*
which provides the more complete set of features. The interface of *LEX_BUILDER*
appears next.

indexing

    description: "*Mechanisms for building lexical analyzers from
      regular expressions.*"

class interface

    METALEX

creation

    make

feature -- Initialization

    make
        -- Set up analyzer.
        -- (From *LEX_BUILDER*.)

    make_analyzer
        -- Create analyzer (if Void) and initialize it.

feature -- Element change

    add_word (*s*: *STRING*; *n*: *INTEGER*)
        -- Record the word *s* and
      require
        s_not_void: *s* /= *Void*;

    build_dollar_any
        -- Build $., matching any character.
        -- (From *HIGH_BUILDER*.)

    build_dollar_b
        -- Build $B, matching any number of break characters:
        -- blank, new-line, tabulation, carriage-return.
        -- (From *HIGH_BUILDER*.)

    build_dollar_n
        -- Build $N, matching natural integer constants.
        -- +('0'..'9')
        -- (From *HIGH_BUILDER*.)

    build_dollar_p
        -- Build $P, matching any printable character.
        -- (From *HIGH_BUILDER*.)

    build_dollar_r
        -- Build $R, matching floating point constants.
        -- ['+' | '-'] +('0'..'9') '.' *('0'..'9') ['e' | 'E' ['+' | '-']
        -- +('0'..'9')]
        -- (From *HIGH_BUILDER*.)

    build_dollar_z
        -- Build $Z, matching possibly signed integer constants.
        -- ['+' | '-'] +('0'..'9')
        -- (From *HIGH_BUILDER*.)

    put_expression (*s*: *STRING*; *n*: *INTEGER*; *c*: *STRING*)
        -- Record the regular expression described by *s*
      require

    put_nameless_expression (*s*: *STRING*; *n*: *INTEGER*)
        -- Record the regular expression described
        -- (From *HIGH_BUILDER*.)
      require

feature -- Input

    No_token: *INTEGER* **is** *0*

    read_grammar (*token_file_name*: *STRING*)
        -- Create lexical analyzer for grammar in file of name
        -- *token_file_name*. File structure:
        -- One or more lines of the form
        -- *name regular_expression*
        -- then a line beginning with two dashes --
        -- then zero or more lines containing one keyword each.

end

21.6 CLASS *LEX_BUILDER*

For completeness this interface shows the features that *LEX_BUILDER* inherits from its ancestors *PDFA*, *NDFA* and *AUTOMATON*. These classes describe automata (partially deterministic, non-deterministic, general finite automata) and can actually be used for many applications outside of lexical analysis.

PDFA is itself an heir not just of *NDFA* (in turn an heir of *AUTOMATON*) but also of *ASCII* (for access to character constants) and *ARRAY*, but the features from these last two classes and their own ancestors are not shown.

indexing

    description: "*General mechanisms for building lexical analyzers*"

class interface

    LEX_BUILDER

creation

    make

feature -- Initialization

    initialize
        -- Set up attributes of *analyzer*.

    make
        -- Set up analyzer.

    pdfa_make (*n*, *i*: INTEGER)
        -- Make a PDFA with *n* states, and *i* + 1 inputs.
        -- (From *PDFA*.)

feature -- Access

    analyzer: LEXICAL
        -- The lexical analyzer built so far

    case_sensitive: BOOLEAN
        -- Will future tools be case-sensitive?

    categories_table: ARRAY [INTEGER]
        -- Table of category numbers for each input

    dfa: FIXED_DFA
        -- DFA built by routine construct_dfa,
        -- which recognizes the same language.
        -- (From *NDFA*.)

    error_list: ERROR_LIST
        -- List of error messages

    final_array: ARRAY [INTEGER]
        -- The *final* value for each state
        -- (regular expression, if any, for which it is final).
        -- (From *PDFA*.)

    greatest_input: INTEGER
        -- Greatest input used for the transitions from state
        -- to state (the smallest one is zero)
        -- (From *AUTOMATON*.)

    has_letters: BOOLEAN
        -- Are there any letters among the active transitions?
        -- (From *PDFA*.)

    input_array: ARRAY [FIXED_INTEGER_SET]
        -- For each input, set of the states which have
        -- a transition on this input to the following state
        -- (From *PDFA*.)

    keyword_h_table: HASH_TABLE [INTEGER, STRING]
        -- Keyword table

    keywords_case_sensitive: BOOLEAN
        -- Will future tools be case-sensitive for keywords?

    keywords_list: LINKED_LIST [STRING]
        -- Keywords associated with current automaton.
        -- (From *PDFA*.)

    last_created_tool: INTEGER
        -- Identification number of the last
        -- regular expression put in tool_list

    lexical_frozen: BOOLEAN
        -- Has the lexical grammar been finalized?
        -- | (in other words: has the DFA been built?)

    selected_tools: LINKED_LIST [INTEGER]
        -- Regular expressions included in the main one

    start_number: INTEGER
        -- Unique start state used for the beginning of
        -- the automaton's operation
        -- (From *AUTOMATON*.)

    token_type_list: LINKED_LIST [INTEGER]
        -- Token types of the selected tools.
        -- Indexed by tool numbers.

    tool_list: LINKED_LIST [PDFA]
        -- Regular expressions used as auxiliary tools

tool_names: *LINKED_LIST* [*STRING*]
-- Names of regular expressions in tool list

feature -- Measurement

nb_states: *INTEGER*
-- Number of states in the automaton
-- (From *AUTOMATON*.)

feature -- Status setting

distinguish_case
-- Make letter case significant in future tools.
-- Default is ignore case.
ensure
case_sensitive

ignore_case
-- Make letter case not significant in future tools.
-- This is the default.

keywords_distinguish_case
-- Make letter case not significant for keywords
-- in future tools.
-- Default is ignore case.
require
ensure
keywords_case_sensitive

keywords_ignore_case
-- Make letter case not significant for keywords
-- in future tools.
-- This is the default.
require

set_e_transition (*source*, *target*: *INTEGER*)
-- Set epsilon transition from *source* to *target*.
-- (From *PDFA*.)
require
source_in_automaton: *source* >= *1* **and** *source* <= *nb_
states*;
target_in_automaton: *target* >= *1* **and** *target* <= *nb_
states*

set_final (*s*, *r*: *INTEGER*)
-- Make *s* the final state of regular expression *r*.
-- (From *PDFA*.)

set_letters
-- Direct the active transitions to include letters.
-- (From *PDFA*.)

set_start (*n*: *INTEGER*)
-- Select state *n* as the starting state.
-- (From *AUTOMATON*.)
require
no_other_start: *start_number* = *0* **or** *start_number* = *n*;
is_in_automaton: *n* <= *nb_states* **and** *n* >= *1*

set_transition (*source*, *input_doc*, *target*: *INTEGER*)
-- Set transition from *source* to *target* on *input_doc*.
-- (From *PDFA*.)
require
source_in_automaton: *source* >= *1* **and** *source* <= *nb_
states*;
target_in_automaton: *target* >= *1* **and** *target* <= *nb_
states*;
possible_input_doc: *input_doc* >= *0* **and** *input_doc* <=
greatest_input;
good_successor: *target* = *source* + *1*

feature -- Element change

add_keyword (*word*: *STRING*)
-- Insert *word* in the keyword list.
-- (From *PDFA*.)

any_character
-- Create regular expression $. matching all characters.
require
not_frozen: **not** *lexical_frozen*

any_printable
-- Create regular expression $P matching all
-- printable characters.
require
not_frozen: **not** *lexical_frozen*

append (*p*, *s*: *INTEGER*)
-- Create regular expression *ps*:
-- *s* appended to *p*.
require
not_frozen: **not** *lexical_frozen*;
p_in_tool: *p* >= *1* **and** *p* <= *last_created_tool*;
s_in_tool: *s* >= *1* **and** *s* <= *last_created_tool*

append_optional (*p*, *s*: *INTEGER*)
-- Create regular expression *p*[*s*]:
-- *s* optionally appended to *p*.
require
not_frozen: **not** *lexical_frozen*;
p_in_tool: *p* >= *1* **and** *p* <= *last_created_tool*;
s_in_tool: *s* >= *1* **and** *s* <= *last_created_tool*

associate (*t*, *n*: *INTEGER*)
-- Associate the *t*-th tool with token type *n*.
-- If this routine is not used, the default value is *t*.
require
t_selected: *selected_tools.has* (*t*);
n_not_zero: *n* /= *0*;
n_not_minus_one: *n* /= – *1*

case_insensitive (*c*: *INTEGER*)
    -- Create regular expression ˜(*c*):
    -- like *c*, but case−insensitive.
  require
    not_frozen: **not** *lexical_frozen*;
    z_possible: *last_ascii* >= *lower_z*;
    c_in_tool: *c* >= *1* **and** *c* <= *last_created_tool*

difference (*r*: *INTEGER*; *c*: *CHARACTER*)
    -- Create regular expression representing
    -- the difference *r* − *c*.
    -- *r* must be a simple category, such as *a..z*,
    -- or a union of simple categories,
    -- such as *'a'..'z'* | *'0'..'9'*.
  require
    not_frozen: **not** *lexical_frozen*;
    r_exists: *r* >= *1* **and** *r* <= *last_created_tool*;
    r_simple_category: *tool_list.i_th* (*r*). *nb_states* = *2*

include (*fa*: *PDFA*; *shift*: *INTEGER*)
    -- Copy *fa* with state numbers shifted
    -- by *shift* positions in the transitions.
    -- Do not preserve the *final* values.
    -- (From *PDFA*.)
  require
    same_inputs: *greatest_input* = *fa.greatest_input*;
    nb_states_large_enough: *nb_states* >= *fa.nb_states* +
      shift

interval (*b*, *e*: *CHARACTER*)
    -- Create regular expression *b..e*, or *b* if *b* = *e*.
  require
    not_built: **not** *lexical_frozen*

iteration (*c*: *INTEGER*)
    -- Create regular expression *(*c*): zero or more
  require
    not_frozen: **not** *lexical_frozen*;
    c_in_tool: *c* >= *1* **and** *c* <= *last_created_tool*

iteration1 (*c*: *INTEGER*)
    -- Create regular expression +(*c*): one or more
  require
    not_frozen: **not** *lexical_frozen*;
    c_in_tool: *c* >= *1* **and** *c* <= *last_created_tool*

iteration_n (*n*, *c*: *INTEGER*)
    -- Create regular expression *n*(*c*):
  require
    not_frozen: **not** *lexical_frozen*;
    n_large_enough: *n* > *0*;
    c_in_tool: *c* >= *1* **and** *c* <= *last_created_tool*

optional (*c*: *INTEGER*)
    -- Create regular expression [*c*]:
    -- optional *c*.
  require
    not_frozen: **not** *lexical_frozen*;
    c_in_tool: *c* >= *1* **and** *c* <= *last_created_tool*

prepend_optional (*p*, *s*: *INTEGER*)
    -- Create regular expression [*p*]*s*:
    -- *s* appended to optional *p*.
  require
    not_frozen: **not** *lexical_frozen*;
    p_in_tool: *p* >= *1* **and** *p* <= *last_created_tool*;
    s_in_tool: *s* >= *1* **and** *s* <= *last_created_tool*

put_keyword (*s*: *STRING*; *exp*: *INTEGER*)
    -- Declare *s* as a keyword described by
    -- the regular expression of code *exp*.
  require
    not_frozen: **not** *lexical_frozen*;
    exp_selected: *token_type_list* /= *Void* **and then**
      token_type_list.has (*exp*)

recognize (*s*: *STRING*): *INTEGER*
    -- Token_type of *s*; 0 if not recognized

remove_case_sensitiveness
    -- Remove case sensitiveness.
    -- (From *PDFA*.)
  require
    z_possible: *greatest_input* >= *lower_z*

select_tool (*i*: *INTEGER*)
    -- Select the *i*_th tool for inclusion in the main
    -- regular expression.
  require
    not_frozen: **not** *lexical_frozen*;
    i_exist: *i* > *0* **and** *i* <= *last_created_tool*

set_word (*word*: *STRING*)
    -- Create regular expression for *word*:
    -- synonym for concatenation (*'w'* *'o'* *'r'* *'d'*).
  require

union (*a*, *b*: *INTEGER*)
    -- Create regular expression for the multiple union
    -- *a* | *a*+1 | .. | *b*: matches any occurrence of
    -- *a*, or *a*+1, .., or *b*.
  require
    not_frozen: **not** *lexical_frozen*;
    a_not_too_small: *a* >= *1*;
    b_not_too_large: *b* <= *last_created_tool*;
    a_smaller_than_b: *a* <= *b*

union2 (a, b: INTEGER)
-- Create regular expression *a | b*: union of
-- *a* and *b* (matches an occurrence of *a* or *b*)).
require
not_frozen: **not** *lexical_frozen*;
a_in_tool: *a >= 1* **and** *a <= last_created_tool*;
b_in_tool: *b >= 1* **and** *b <= last_created_tool*

up_to (word: STRING)
-- Create regular expression –>"*word*", which is a
-- set of any number of any characters ended by "*word*".
-- Example: "/* C comment */" matches (–>"*/").
-- The difference between (+$. ′*′ ′/′) and
-- (–>"*/") is that "*/..*/..*/" matches
-- the first but not the second.
-- The difference between
-- (((\$.–′*′) | (′*′(\$.-′/′))) +(′*′ ′/′))
-- and "(–>"*/")" is that "..**/" matches
-- the second but not the first.
require
not_frozen: **not** *lexical_frozen*

feature -- Removal

delete_transition (source, input_doc, target: INTEGER)
-- Delete transition from *source* to *target* on *input_doc*.
-- (From *PDFA*.)
require
source_in_automaton: *source >= 1* **and** *source <= nb_states*;
target_in_automaton: *target >= 1* **and** *target <= nb_states*;
possible_input_doc: *input_doc >= 0* **and** *input_doc <= greatest_input*;
good_successor: *target = source + 1*

remove
-- Remove the last regular expression
-- from the tool list.
require
not_frozen: **not** *lexical_frozen*;
at_least_one_regular: *last_created_tool >= 1*

feature -- Transformation

construct_dfa
-- Create an equivalent deterministic finite automaton.
-- (From *NDFA*.)
require
start_number_designated: *start_number > 0*

feature -- Input

retrieve_analyzer (file_name: STRING)
-- Retrieve *analyzer* from file named *file_name*.

feature -- Output

store_analyzer (file_name: STRING)
-- Store *analyzer* in file named *file_name*.

trace
-- Output an internal representation
-- of the current automaton.
-- (From *PDFA*.)

end

22

Parsing classes

22.1 OVERVIEW

An earlier chapter introduced the Parse library and explained the corresponding classes.

Chapter 12.

Here now are the interfaces, in flat-short form, of all these classes.

For ease of reference, the figure on the next page reproduces the general inheritance structure given in the earlier discussion.

This is the same figure as on page 220.

The class interfaces appear in the following order:

CONSTRUCT, AGGREGATE, CHOICE, REPETITION, TERMINAL, KEYWORD, L_INTERFACE, INPUT

22.2 CLASS *CONSTRUCT*

CONSTRUCT is an heir of *TWO_WAY_TREE*. Since practical uses of construct classes often require traversing the corresponding abstract syntax trees, the interface given here includes the features inherited from *TWO_WAY_TREE* and its own ancestors *DYNAMIC_TREE* and *TREE*, but not from any higher ancestor (such as *CONTAINER* or *LINKED_LIST*).

The full flat-short interface of TWO_WAY_TREE is in 18.3, page 354.

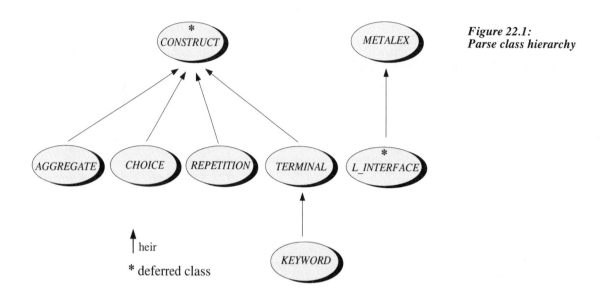

Figure 22.1:
Parse class hierarchy

heir

* deferred class

indexing

   description: *"The general notion of language construct,*
      characterized by a grammatical production and associated
      semantic actions"

deferred class interface

   CONSTRUCT

feature -- Initialization

   make
         -- Set up construct.

feature -- Access

   construct_name: *STRING*
         -- Name of the construct in the grammar

   document: *INPUT*
         -- The document to be parsed

   first_child: **like** *parent*
         -- Leftmost child
         -- (From *TWO_WAY_TREE*.)

   has (*v*: *CONSTRUCT*): *BOOLEAN*
         -- Does subtree include *v*?
         -- (Reference or object equality,
         -- based on *object_comparison*.)
         -- (From *TREE*.)
      ensure
         not_found_in_empty: *Result* **implies not** *is_leaf*

   is_sibling (*other*: **like** *parent*): *BOOLEAN*
         -- Are current node and *other* siblings?
         -- (From *TREE*.)
      ensure
         not_root: *Result* **implies not** *is_root*;
         other_not_root: *Result* **implies not** *other. is_root*

   last_child: **like** *parent*
         -- (From *TWO_WAY_TREE*.)

   production: *LINKED_LIST* [*CONSTRUCT*]
         -- Right–hand side of the production for the construct

feature -- Measurement

   count: *INTEGER*
         -- Number of items
         -- (From *TREE*.)

feature -- Status report

   child_isfirst: *BOOLEAN*
         -- Is cursor under first child?
         -- (From *TREE*.)
      ensure
         not_is_leaf: *Result* **implies not** *is_leaf*
      ensure then
         valid_position: *Result* **implies not** *is_leaf*

child_islast: *BOOLEAN*
    -- Is cursor under last child?
    -- (From *TREE*.)
  ensure
    not_is_leaf: *Result* **implies not** *is_leaf*
  ensure then
    valid_position: *Result* **implies not** *is_leaf*

child_readable: *BOOLEAN*
    -- Is there a current *child_item* to be read?
    -- (From *TREE*.)

child_writable: *BOOLEAN*
    -- Is there a current *child_item* that may be modified?
    -- (From *TREE*.)

committed: *BOOLEAN*
    -- Have enough productions been recognized to interpret
    -- failure of parsing as a syntax error in this construct?
    -- (Otherwise the parsing process will backtrack, trying
    -- other possible interpretations of the part already read.)

empty: *BOOLEAN*
    -- Is structure empty of items?
    -- (From *TREE*.)

extendible: *BOOLEAN* **is true**
    -- May new items be added?
    -- (From *DYNAMIC_TREE*.)

is_leaf: *BOOLEAN*
    -- Are there no children?
    -- (From *TREE*.)

is_optional: *BOOLEAN*
    -- Is construct optional?

is_root: *BOOLEAN*
    -- Is there no parent?
    -- (From *TREE*.)

left_recursion: *BOOLEAN*
    -- Is the construct's definition left−recursive?

parsed: *BOOLEAN*
    -- Has construct been successfully parsed?
    -- (True for optional components not present)

print_mode: *CELL* [*BOOLEAN*]
    -- Must the left−recursion test also print the production?
    -- (Default: no.)

readable: *BOOLEAN* **is true**
    -- (From *TREE*.)

readable_child: *BOOLEAN*
    -- Is there a current child to be read?
    -- (From *TREE*.)

valid_cursor_index (*i*: *INTEGER*): *BOOLEAN*
    -- Is *i* correctly bounded for cursor movement?
    -- (From *TREE*.)

writable: *BOOLEAN* **is true**
    -- Is there a current item that may be modified?
    -- (From *TREE*.)

writable_child: *BOOLEAN*
    -- Is there a current child that may be modified?
    -- (From *TREE*.)

feature -- Status setting

set_optional
    -- Define this construct as optional.
  ensure
    optional_construct: *is_optional*

feature -- Element change

extend (*v*: **like** *item*)
    -- Add *v* as new child.
    -- (From *DYNAMIC_TREE*.)

fill (*other*: *TREE* [*CONSTRUCT*])
    -- Fill with as many items of *other* as possible.
    -- The representations of *other* and current node
    -- need not be the same.
    -- (From *TREE*.)

merge_tree_after (*other*: **like** *first_child*)
    -- Merge children of *other* into current structure
    -- after cursor position. Do not move cursor.
    -- Make *other* a leaf.
    -- (From *TWO_WAY_TREE*.)
  require
    not_child_off: **not** *child_off*;
    other_exists: (*other* /= *Void*)
  ensure
    other_is_leaf: *other.is_leaf*

merge_tree_before (*other*: **like** *first_child*)
    -- Merge children of *other* into current structure
    -- after cursor position. Do not move cursor.
    -- Make *other* a leaf.
    -- (From *TWO_WAY_TREE*.)
  require
    not_child_off: **not** *child_off*;
    other_exists: (*other* /= *Void*)
  ensure
    other_is_leaf: *other.is_leaf*

prune (*n*: **like** *first_child*)
    -- (From *TWO_WAY_TREE*.)
  require
    is_child: *n.parent* = *Current*
  ensure
    n_is_root: *n.is_root*

put_child (*n*: **like** *parent*)
-- Add *n* to the list of children.
-- Do not move child cursor.
-- (From *TWO_WAY_TREE*.)
require
non_void_argument: *n* /= *Void*

put_child_left (*n*: **like** *parent*)
-- Add *n* to the left of cursor position.
-- Do not move cursor.
-- (From *TWO_WAY_TREE*.)
require
not_child_before: **not** *child_before*;
non_void_argument: *n* /= *Void*

put_child_right (*n*: **like** *parent*)
-- Add *n* to the right of cursor position.
-- Do not move cursor.
-- (From *TWO_WAY_TREE*.)
require
not_child_after: **not** *child_after*;
non_void_argument: *n* /= *Void*

replace_child (*n*: **like** *parent*)
-- Replace current child by *n*.
-- (From *TWO_WAY_TREE*.)
require
writable_child: *writable_child*;
was_root: *n.is_root*

sprout
-- Make current node a root.
-- (From *TREE*.)

feature -- Transformation

commit
-- If this construct is one among several possible ones,
-- discard the others.
-- By default this does nothing.

parse
-- Attempt to analyze incoming lexical
-- tokens according to current construct.
-- Set *parsed* to true if successful;
-- return to original position in input otherwise.

post_action
-- Semantic action executed after construct is parsed
-- (nothing by default; may be redefined in descendants).

pre_action
-- Semantic action executed before construct is parsed
-- (nothing by default; may be redefined in descendants).

process
-- Parse a specimen of the construct, then apply
-- semantic actions if parsing successful.

semantics
-- Apply semantic actions in order:
-- *pre_action, in_action, post_action*.

feature -- Conversion

binary_representation: *BINARY_TREE* [*CONSTRUCT*]
-- Convert to binary tree representation:
-- first child becomes left child,
-- right sibling becomes right child.
-- (From *TREE*.)
ensure
result_is_root: *Result.is_root;*
result_has_no_right_child: **not** *Result.has_right*

fill_from_binary (*b*: *BINARY_TREE* [*CONSTRUCT*])
-- Fill from a binary tree representation.
-- Left child becomes first child
-- Right child becomes right sibling.
-- Any right child of *b* is ignored.
-- (From *DYNAMIC_TREE*.)

linear_representation: *LINEAR* [*CONSTRUCT*]
-- Representation as a linear structure
-- (From *TREE*.)

feature -- Duplication

duplicate (*n*: *INTEGER*): **like** *Current*
-- Copy of sub-tree beginning at cursor position and
-- having min (*n*, *arity* − *child_index* + 1)
-- children
-- (From *DYNAMIC_TREE*.)
require
not_child_off: **not** *child_off*;
valid_sublist: *n* >= *0*

feature -- Output

print_name
-- Print the construct name on standard output.

invariant

extendible_definition: *extendible*;
writable_constraint: *child_writable* **implies** *child_readable*;
empty_constraint: *is_leaf* **implies** (**not** *child_readable*) **and**
(**not** *child_writable*);
extendible: *child_extendible*

end

22.3 CLASS *AGGREGATE*

For convenience the interface shows the features introduced or redeclared in *CONSTRUCT*. Those of *TWO_WAY_TREE* and other proper ancestors of *CONSTRUCT* have not been reproduced.

indexing

>   description: "*Constructs whose specimens are obtained by concatenating specimens of constructs of zero or more specified constructs*"

deferred class interface

>   AGGREGATE

feature -- Initialization

>   make
>   >   -- (From *CONSTRUCT*.)

feature -- Access

>   construct_name: STRING
>   >   -- Name of the construct in the grammar
>   >   -- (From *CONSTRUCT*.)

>   document: INPUT
>   >   -- The document to be parsed
>   >   -- (From *CONSTRUCT*.)

>   production: LINKED_LIST [CONSTRUCT]
>   >   -- Right–hand side of the production for the construct
>   >   -- (From *CONSTRUCT*.)

feature -- Status report

>   committed: BOOLEAN
>   >   -- Have enough productions been recognized to interpret
>   >   -- failure of parsing as a syntax error in this construct?
>   >   -- (Otherwise the parsing process will backtrack, trying
>   >   -- other possible interpretations of the part already read.)
>   >   -- (From *CONSTRUCT*.)

>   is_optional: BOOLEAN
>   >   -- Is construct optional?
>   >   -- (From *CONSTRUCT*.)

>   left_recursion: BOOLEAN
>   >   -- Is the construct's definition left–recursive?

>   parsed: BOOLEAN
>   >   -- Has construct been successfully parsed?
>   >   -- (True for optional components not present)
>   >   -- (From *CONSTRUCT*.)

>   print_mode: CELL [BOOLEAN]
>   >   -- Must the left–recursion test also print the production?
>   >   -- (Default: no.)
>   >   -- (From *CONSTRUCT*.)

feature -- Status setting

>   set_optional
>   >   -- Define this construct as optional.
>   >   -- (From *CONSTRUCT*.)
>   >   **ensure**
>   >   >   optional_construct: is_optional

feature -- Transformation

>   commit
>   >   -- If this construct is one among several possible ones,
>   >   -- discard the others.
>   >   **require**
>   >   >   only_commit_once: **not** has_commit

>   has_commit: BOOLEAN
>   >   -- Is current aggregate committed?

>   parse
>   >   -- Attempt to analyze incoming lexical
>   >   -- tokens according to current construct.
>   >   -- Set *parsed* to true if successful;
>   >   -- return to original position in input otherwise.
>   >   -- (From *CONSTRUCT*.)

>   post_action
>   >   -- Semantic action executed after construct is parsed
>   >   -- (nothing by default; may be redefined in descendants).
>   >   -- (From *CONSTRUCT*.)

>   pre_action
>   >   -- Semantic action executed before construct is parsed
>   >   -- (nothing by default; may be redefined in descendants).
>   >   -- (From *CONSTRUCT*.)

>   process
>   >   -- Parse a specimen of the construct, then apply
>   >   -- semantic actions if parsing successful.
>   >   -- (From *CONSTRUCT*.)

>   semantics
>   >   -- Apply semantic actions in order:
>   >   -- *pre_action, in_action, post_action.*
>   >   -- (From *CONSTRUCT*.)

feature -- Output

>   print_name
>   >   -- Print the construct name on standard output.
>   >   -- (From *CONSTRUCT*.)

end

22.4 CLASS *CHOICE*

For convenience the interface shows the features introduced or redeclared in *CONSTRUCT*. Those of *TWO_WAY_TREE* and other proper ancestors of *CONSTRUCT* have not been reproduced.

indexing

> *description*: "*Constructs whose specimens are specimens of constructs chosen among a specified list.*"

deferred class interface

> *CHOICE*

feature -- Initialization

> *make*
>> -- (From *CONSTRUCT*.)

feature -- Access

> *construct_name*: *STRING*
>> -- Name of the construct in the grammar
>> -- (From *CONSTRUCT*.)

> *document*: *INPUT*
>> -- The document to be parsed
>> -- (From *CONSTRUCT*.)

> *production*: *LINKED_LIST* [*CONSTRUCT*]
>> -- Right–hand side of the production for the construct
>> -- (From *CONSTRUCT*.)

> *retained*: *CONSTRUCT*
>> -- Child which matches the input document;
>> -- Void if none.

feature -- Status report

> *committed*: *BOOLEAN*
>> -- Have enough productions been recognized to interpret
>> -- failure of parsing as a syntax error in this construct?
>> -- (Otherwise the parsing process will backtrack, trying
>> -- other possible interpretations of the part already read.)
>> -- (From *CONSTRUCT*.)

> *is_optional*: *BOOLEAN*
>> -- Is construct optional?
>> -- (From *CONSTRUCT*.)

> *left_recursion*: *BOOLEAN*
>> -- Is the construct's definition left–recursive?

> *parsed*: *BOOLEAN*
>> -- Has construct been successfully parsed?
>> -- (True for optional components not present)
>> -- (From *CONSTRUCT*.)

> *print_mode*: *CELL* [*BOOLEAN*]
>> -- Must the left–recursion test also print the production?
>> -- (Default: no.)
>> -- (From *CONSTRUCT*.)

feature -- Status setting

> *set_optional*
>> -- Define this construct as optional.
>> -- (From *CONSTRUCT*.)
>> **ensure**
>>> *optional_construct*: *is_optional*

feature -- Transformation

> *commit*
>> -- If this construct is one among several possible ones,
>> -- discard the others.
>> -- By default this does nothing.
>> -- (From *CONSTRUCT*.)

> *parse*
>> -- Attempt to analyze incoming lexical
>> -- tokens according to current construct.
>> -- Set *parsed* to true if successful;
>> -- return to original position in input otherwise.
>> -- (From *CONSTRUCT*.)

> *post_action*
>> -- Semantic action executed after construct is parsed
>> -- (nothing by default; may be redefined in descendants).
>> -- (From *CONSTRUCT*.)

> *pre_action*
>> -- Semantic action executed before construct is parsed
>> -- (nothing by default; may be redefined in descendants).
>> -- (From *CONSTRUCT*.)

> *process*
>> -- Parse a specimen of the construct, then apply
>> -- semantic actions if parsing successful.
>> -- (From *CONSTRUCT*.)

> *semantics*
>> -- Apply semantic actions in order:
>> -- *pre_action*, *in_action*, *post_action*.
>> -- (From *CONSTRUCT*.)

feature -- Output

> *print_name*
>> -- Print the construct name on standard output.
>> -- (From *CONSTRUCT*.)

end

22.5 CLASS *REPETITION*

For convenience the interface shows the features introduced or redeclared in
CONSTRUCT. Those of *TWO_WAY_TREE* and other proper ancestors of *CONSTRUCT*
have not been reproduced.

indexing

> *description*: "*Constructs whose specimens are sequences of
> specimens of a specified base construct, delimited by a
> specified separator*"

deferred class interface

> REPETITION

feature -- Initialization

> *make*
> > -- (From *CONSTRUCT*.)

feature -- Access

> *construct_name*: *STRING*
> > -- Name of the construct in the grammar
> > -- (From *CONSTRUCT*.)
>
> *document*: *INPUT*
> > -- The document to be parsed
> > -- (From *CONSTRUCT*.)
>
> *production*: *LINKED_LIST* [*CONSTRUCT*]
> > -- Right–hand side of the production for the construct
> > -- (From *CONSTRUCT*.)

feature -- Status report

> *committed*: *BOOLEAN*
> > -- Have enough productions been recognized to interpret
> > -- failure of parsing as a syntax error in this construct?
> > -- (Otherwise the parsing process will backtrack, trying
> > -- other possible interpretations of the part already read.)
> > -- (From *CONSTRUCT*.)
>
> *is_optional*: *BOOLEAN*
> > -- Is construct optional?
> > -- (From *CONSTRUCT*.)
>
> *left_recursion*: *BOOLEAN*
> > -- Is the construct's definition left–recursive?
>
> *parsed*: *BOOLEAN*
> > -- Has construct been successfully parsed?
> > -- (True for optional components not present)
> > -- (From *CONSTRUCT*.)
>
> *print_mode*: *CELL* [*BOOLEAN*]
> > -- Must the left–recursion test also print the production?
> > -- (Default: no.)
> > -- (From *CONSTRUCT*.)

feature -- Status setting

> *set_optional*
> > -- Define this construct as optional.
> > -- (From *CONSTRUCT*.)
>
> *ensure*
> > *optional_construct*: *is_optional*

feature -- Transformation

> *commit*
> > -- If this construct is one among several possible ones,
> > -- discard the others.
> > -- By default this does nothing.
> > -- (From *CONSTRUCT*.)
>
> *parse*
> > -- Attempt to analyze incoming lexical
> > -- tokens according to current construct.
> > -- Set *parsed* to true if successful;
> > -- return to original position in input otherwise.
> > -- (From *CONSTRUCT*.)
>
> *post_action*
> > -- Semantic action executed after construct is parsed
> > -- (nothing by default; may be redefined in descendants).
> > -- (From *CONSTRUCT*.)
>
> *pre_action*
> > -- Semantic action executed before construct is parsed
> > -- (nothing by default; may be redefined in descendants).
> > -- (From *CONSTRUCT*.)
>
> *process*
> > -- Parse a specimen of the construct, then apply
> > -- semantic actions if parsing successful.
> > -- (From *CONSTRUCT*.)
>
> *semantics*
> > -- Apply semantic actions in order:
> > -- *pre_action*, *in_action*, *post_action*.
> > -- (From *CONSTRUCT*.)

feature -- Output

> *print_name*
> > -- Print the construct name on standard output.
> > -- (From *CONSTRUCT*.)

end

22.6 CLASS *TERMINAL*

TERMINAL is an heir of *CONSTRUCT*. The interface only shows the features
introduced or redeclared in *TERMINAL* itself, and does not include any feature inherited
directly or indirectly.

indexing

   description: "*Constructs to be parsed by lexical analysis
      classes*"

deferred class interface

   TERMINAL

feature -- Access

   token: *TOKEN*
         -- Token associated with terminal

feature -- Status report

   token_type: *INTEGER*
         -- Token code associated with terminal

invariant

   extendible_definition: *extendible*;
   extendible: *child_extendible*

end

22.7 CLASS *KEYWORD*

KEYWORD is an heir of *TERMINAL*. For convenience, the interface retains the features introduced in *KEYWORD*, but does not include any feature inherited in unchanged form from any proper ancestor of *TERMINAL*.

indexing

   description: *"Terminal constructs with just one specimen,*
      representing a language keyword or special symbol"

class interface

   KEYWORD

creation
   make

feature -- Initialization

   make (*s*: *STRING*)
      -- Set up terminal to represent *s*.

feature -- Access

   construct_name: *STRING*
         -- Name of the keyword

   lex_code: *INTEGER*
         -- Code of keyword in the lexical anayser

invariant

   extendible_definition: *extendible*;
   extendible: *child_extendible*

end

22.8 CLASS *L_INTERFACE*

For convenience the interface shows the features of *L_INTERFACE*'s two immediate ancestors, *METALEX* and *HIGH_BUILDER*. This suffices for most uses; to access finer lexical analysis facilities, you may have to rely on the features of other ancestors, in particular *LEX_BUILDER*.

The interface of LEX_BUILDER is in 21.6, page 408.

indexing

> *description*: "Interface with the Lexical Library classes"

deferred class interface

> *L_INTERFACE*

feature -- Initialization

> *build* (*doc*: *INPUT*)
>> -- Create lexical analyzer and set *doc*
>> -- to be the input document.
>> *require*
>>> *document_exists*: *doc* /= *Void*

> *make_analyzer*
>> -- Create analyzer (if Void) and initialize it.
>> -- (From *METALEX*.)
>> *ensure*
>>> *analyzer_created*: *analyzer* /= *Void*;
>>> *lexical_frozen*

> *obtain_analyzer*
>> -- Build lexical analyzer.
>> *ensure*
>>> *analyzer* /= *Void*

feature -- Element change

> *add_word* (*s*: *STRING*; *n*: *INTEGER*)
>> -- Record the word *s* and
>> -- associate it with token type *n*.
>> -- (From *METALEX*.)
>> *require*
>>> *s_not_void*: *s* /= *Void*;
>>> *s_not_empty*: *s*.*capacity* >= *1*

> *build_dollar_any*
>> -- Build $., matching any character.
>> -- (From *HIGH_BUILDER*.)

> *build_dollar_b*
>> -- Build $B, matching any number of break characters:
>> -- blank, new-line, tabulation, carriage-return.
>> -- (From *HIGH_BUILDER*.)

> *build_dollar_n*
>> -- Build $N, matching natural integer constants.
>> -- +('0'..'9')
>> -- (From *HIGH_BUILDER*.)

> *build_dollar_p*
>> -- Build $P, matching any printable character.
>> -- (From *HIGH_BUILDER*.)

> *build_dollar_r*
>> -- Build $R, matching floating point constants.
>> -- ['+' | '−'] +('0'..'9') '.' *('0'..'9') ['e' | 'E' ['+' | '−']
>> -- +('0'..'9')]
>> -- (From *HIGH_BUILDER*.)

> *build_dollar_z*
>> -- Build $Z, matching possibly signed integer constants.
>> -- ['+' | '−'] +('0'..'9')
>> -- (From *HIGH_BUILDER*.)

> *put_expression* (*s*: *STRING*; *n*: *INTEGER*; *c*: *STRING*)
>> -- Record the regular expression described by *s*
>> -- and associate it with token type *n* and name *c*.
>> -- (From *METALEX*.)
>> *require*
>>> *source_long_enough*: *s*.*capacity* > *0*

> *put_nameless_expression* (*s*: *STRING*; *n*: *INTEGER*)
>> -- Record the regular expression described
>> -- by *s*, and associate it with token type *n*.
>> -- (From *HIGH_BUILDER*.)
>> *require*
>>> *source_long_enough*: *s*.*count* > *0*

feature -- Input

> *No_token*: *INTEGER* **is** *0*
>> -- (From *METALEX*.)

> *read_grammar* (*token_file_name*: *STRING*)
>> -- Create lexical analyzer for grammar in file of name
>> -- *token_file_name*. File structure:
>> -- One or more lines of the form
>> -- *name regular_expression*
>> -- then a line beginning with two dashes --
>> -- then zero or more lines containing one keyword each.
>> -- (From *METALEX*.)
>> *ensure*
>>> *analyzer_exists*: *analyzer* /= *Void*

end

22.9 CLASS *INPUT*

INPUT is an heir of *LINKED_LIST* [*TOKEN*]. The interface only shows the features introduced or redeclared in *INPUT* itself, and does not include any feature inherited directly or indirectly. You may of course apply all the features of *LINKED_LIST* to an instance of *INPUT*.

For the interface of LINKED_LIST see 16.5, page 299.

indexing

    description: "*Handling of input documents through a lexical analyzer*"

class interface

    INPUT

creation
    make

feature -- Initialization

    make
        -- Create an empty list.
        -- (From *LINKED_LIST*.)

feature -- Access

    analyzer: *LEXICAL*
        -- Lexical analyzer used

    keyword_code (*s*: *STRING*): *INTEGER*
        -- Keyword code corresponding to *s*;
        -- -1 if no specimen of *s* is found.
      require
        lex_not_void: *analyzer* /= *Void*

    keyword_string (*code*: *INTEGER*): *STRING*
        -- Keyword string corresponding to *code*
      require
        lex_not_void: *analyzer* /= *Void*

    set_lexical (*lexical*: *LEXICAL*)
        -- Designate *lexical* as the *analyzer* to be used.
      require
        lex_not_void: *analyzer* /= *Void*

feature -- Status report

    end_of_document: *BOOLEAN*
        -- Has end of document been reached?

feature -- Status setting

    set_input_file (*filename*: *STRING*)
        -- Set the name of the input file to be read
        -- by the lexical analyzer.
      require
        lex_not_void: *analyzer* /= *Void*;
        name_not_void: *filename* /= *Void*

    set_input_string (*stringname*: *STRING*)
        -- Set the name of the input string to be read
        -- by the lexical analyzer.

feature -- Input

    get_token
        -- Make next token accessible with "token"

    retrieve_lex (*filename*: *STRING*)
        -- Retrieve *analyzer* from filename if exists.
      require
        name_not_void: *filename* /= *Void*

feature -- Output

    out_list
        -- Output tokens recognized so far.

    raise_error (*s*: *STRING*)
        -- Print error message *s*.

end

23

Kernel library classes

23.1 OVERVIEW

An earlier chapter introduced the Kernel library and explained the corresponding classes.

Chapter 13.

Here now are the interfaces, in flat-short form, of all these classes.

The class interfaces appear in the order in which they were presented in the earlier discussion, except for the basic types which have been moved to the end, *REAL* and *DOUBLE* being grouped under a single interface specification:

> *ANY, ARRAY, STRING, SPECIAL, BASIC_ROUTINES, DOUBLE_MATH / SINGLE_MATH, PRIMES, RANDOM, ASCII, STD_FILES, FILE, UNIX_ FILE, UNIX_STD, UNIX_FILE_INFO, DIRECTORY, STORABLE, EXCEPTIONS, UNIX_SIGNALS, MEMORY, MEM_INFO, GC_INFO, ARGUMENTS, INTERNAL, BOOLEAN, CHARACTER, INTEGER, DOUBLE / REAL.*

23.2 CLASSES *ANY*, *GENERAL* AND *PLATFORM*

As noted in the discussion of the universal classes, class *ANY* as delivered is empty. Its parent *PLATFORM* only introduces a few features describing platform dependencies; the fully universal features are inherited from *GENERAL*.

The interface given below is that of the default *ANY*, which shows the features from *GENERAL* and *PLATFORM*.

The values of the constant attributes from *PLATFORM*, such as *Integer_bits*, depend on the platform. The values given here characterize a 32-bit platform.

indexing

description: "Project−wide universal properties. This class is
an ancestor to all developer-written classes. ANY inherits
from PLATFORM, itself an heir of GENERAL, and may be
customized for individual projects or teams."

class interface

ANY

feature -- Access

Character_bits: INTEGER **is** 8
-- (From PLATFORM.)

conforms_to (other: **like** Current): BOOLEAN
-- Is dynamic type of current object a descendant of
-- dynamic type of other?
-- (From GENERAL.)
require
other_not_void: other /= Void

Double_bits: INTEGER **is** 64
-- (From PLATFORM.)

generator: STRING
-- Name of current object's generating class
-- (base class of the type of which it is a direct instance)
-- (From GENERAL.)

Integer_bits: INTEGER **is** 32
-- (From PLATFORM.)

Real_bits: INTEGER **is** 32
-- (From PLATFORM.)

feature -- Comparison

deep_equal (some: GENERAL; other: **like** some): BOOLEAN
-- Are some and other either both void
-- or attached to isomorphic object structures?
-- (From GENERAL.)

frozen equal (some: GENERAL; other: **like** some):
BOOLEAN
-- Are some and other either both void or attached
-- to field−by-field identical objects?
-- (From GENERAL.)
ensure
Result = (some = Void **and** other = Void) **or else** ((some
/= Void **and** other /= Void) **and then** some.is_equal
(other))

is_equal (other: **like** Current): BOOLEAN
-- Is other attached to an object field−by-field identical
-- to current object?
-- (From GENERAL.)
require
other_not_void: other /= Void

frozen standard_equal (some: GENERAL; other: **like** some):
BOOLEAN
-- Are some and other either both void or attached to
-- field−by-field identical objects?
-- Always uses default object comparison criterion.
-- (From GENERAL.)
ensure
Result = (some = Void **and** other = Void) **or else** ((some
/= Void **and** other /= Void) **and then** some.standard_
is_equal (other))

frozen standard_is_equal (other: **like** Current): BOOLEAN
-- Is other attached to an object field−by-field identical
-- to current object?
-- (From GENERAL.)
require
other_not_void: other /= Void

feature -- Status report

consistent (other: **like** Current): BOOLEAN
-- Is current object in a consistent state so that other
-- may be copied onto it? (Default answer: yes).
-- (From GENERAL.)

feature -- Duplication

frozen clone (other: GENERAL): **like** other
-- Void if other is void; otherwise new object
-- with contents copied from other.
--
-- For non-void other, clone calls copy;
-- to change copying/cloning semantics, redefine copy.
-- (From GENERAL.)
ensure
equal: equal (Result, other)

copy (other: **like** Current)
-- Copy the structure representing by other onto
-- that represented by current object.
-- (From GENERAL.)
require
other_not_void: other /= Void;
conformance: other.conforms_to (Current)
ensure
is_equal: is_equal (other)

frozen deep_clone (other: GENERAL): **like** other
-- Void if other is void: otherwise, new object structure
-- recursively duplicated from the one attached to other
-- (From GENERAL.)
ensure
deep_equal: deep_equal (other, Result)

frozen *deep_copy* (*other*: **like** *Current*)
    -- Effect equivalent to that of:
    --   *temp* := *deep_clone* (*other*);
    --   *copy* (*temp*)
    -- (From *GENERAL*.)
  require
    other_not_void: *other* /= *Void*
  ensure
    deep_equal: *deep_equal* (*Current*, *other*)

setup (*other*: **like** *Current*)
    -- Assuming current object has just been created,
      perform
    -- actions necessary to ensure that contents of *other*
    -- can be safely copied onto it.
    -- (From *GENERAL*.)
  ensure
    consistent (*other*)

frozen *standard_clone* (*other*: *GENERAL*): **like** *other*
    -- Void if *other* is void; otherwise new object
    -- field–by-field identical to *other*.
    -- Always uses default copying semantics.
    -- (From *GENERAL*.)
  ensure
    equal: *standard_equal* (*Result*, *other*)

frozen *standard_copy* (*other*: **like** *Current*)
    -- Copy every field of *other* onto corresponding field
    -- of current object.
    -- (From *GENERAL*.)
  require
    other_not_void: *other* /= *Void*;
    conformance: *other*. *conforms_to* (*Current*)
  ensure
    is_equal: *is_equal* (*other*)

feature -- Basic operations

frozen *default*: **like** *Current*
    -- Default value of object's type.
    -- (From *GENERAL*.)

die (*code*: *INTEGER*)
    -- Exit program with exit status *code*.
    -- (From *GENERAL*.)

frozen *do_nothing*
    -- Execute a null action.
    -- (From *GENERAL*.)

Void: *NONE*
    -- Void reference
    -- (From *GENERAL*.)

feature -- Output

io: *STD_FILES*
    -- Object providing access to standard files
    -- (input, output, error)
    -- (From *GENERAL*.)

out: *STRING*
    -- New string containing a terse, printable, field–by-field
    -- representation of current object.
    -- (From *GENERAL*.)

print (*some*: *GENERAL*)
    -- Write terse external representation of current object
    -- on standard output.
    -- (From *GENERAL*.)

frozen *tagged_out*: *STRING*
    -- New string containing a terse, printable, field–by-field
    -- representation of current object.
    -- (From *GENERAL*.)

end

23.3 CLASS *ARRAY*

The interface of *ARRAY* as it appears here omits the general features from *CONTAINER* and *COLLECTION*, but retains those from *FINITE* and *RESIZABLE*, which are essential for understanding arrays.

Class *SPECIAL*, whose interface appears later in this chapter, may be used for optimized array operations.

On array optimization see 13.4.3, page 249.

indexing

> description: "*Sequences of values, all of the same type or of a conforming one, accessible through integer indices in a contiguous interval*"

class interface

> *ARRAY* [G]

creation
> make

feature -- Initialization

> make (minindex, maxindex: INTEGER)
> -- Allocate array; set index interval to
> -- minindex .. maxindex
> -- (empty if minindex > maxindex).
> **ensure**
> no_capacity: (minindex > maxindex) **implies** (capacity = 0);
> capacity_constraint: (minindex <= maxindex) **implies** (capacity = maxindex − minindex + 1)

> setup (other: **like** Current)
> -- Perform actions on a freshly created object so that
> -- the contents of other can be safely copied onto it.

feature -- Access

> area: SPECIAL [G]
> -- Special data zone
> -- (From TO_SPECIAL.)

> has (v: G): BOOLEAN
> -- Does v appear in array?
> -- (Reference or object equality,
> -- based on object_comparison.)
> **ensure**
> not_found_in_empty: Result **implies not** empty

> item (i: INTEGER): G
> -- Entry at index i, if in index interval.
> **require**
> valid_key: valid_index (i)

> **infix** "@" (i: INTEGER): G
> -- Entry at index i, if in index interval.
> **require**
> valid_key: valid_index (i)

feature -- Measurement

> additional_space: INTEGER
> -- Proposed number of additional items
> -- (From RESIZABLE.)
> **ensure**
> at_least_one: Result >= 1

> capacity: INTEGER
> -- Available indices

> count: INTEGER
> -- Available indices

> Growth_percentage: INTEGER **is** 50
> -- Percentage by which structure will grow automatically
> -- (From RESIZABLE.)

> lower: INTEGER
> -- Minimum index

> Minimal_increase: INTEGER **is** 5
> -- Minimal number of additional items
> -- (From RESIZABLE.)

> occurrences (v: G): INTEGER
> -- Number of times v appears in structure
> **ensure**
> non_negative_occurrences: Result >= 0

> upper: INTEGER
> -- Maximum index

feature -- Comparison

> is_equal (other: **like** Current): BOOLEAN
> -- Is array made of the same items as other?

feature -- Status report

> all_cleared: BOOLEAN
> -- Are all items set to default values?

> consistent (other: **like** Current): BOOLEAN
> -- Is object in a consistent state so that other
> -- may be copied onto it? (Default answer: yes).

> empty: BOOLEAN
> -- Is structure empty?
> -- (From FINITE.)

extendible: *BOOLEAN*
> -- May items be added?
> -- (Answer: no, although array may be resized.)

full: *BOOLEAN*
> -- Is structure filled to capacity? (Answer: yes)

prunable: *BOOLEAN*
> -- May items be removed? (Answer: no.)

resizable: *BOOLEAN*
> -- May *capacity* be changed? (Answer: yes.)
> -- (From *RESIZABLE*.)

valid_index (*i*: *INTEGER*): *BOOLEAN*
> -- Is *i* a valid index?

feature -- Element change

force (*v*: **like** *item*; *i*: *INTEGER*)
> -- Assign item *v* to *i*-th entry.
> -- Always applicable: resize the array if *i* falls out of
> -- currently defined bounds; preserve existing items.
> **ensure**
> > *inserted*: *item* (*i*) = *v*;
> > *higher_capacity*: *capacity* >= **old** *capacity*

put (*v*: *G*; *i*: *INTEGER*)
> -- Replace *i*-th entry, if in index interval, by *v*.
> **require**
> > *valid_key*: *valid_index* (*i*)
> **ensure**
> > *insertion_done*: *item* (*i*) = *v*

feature -- Removal

clear_all
> -- Reset all items to default values.
> **ensure**
> > *all_cleared*: *all_cleared*

wipe_out
> -- Make array empty.
> **require**
> > *prunable*
> **ensure**
> > *wiped_out*: *empty*

feature -- Resizing

automatic_grow
> -- Change the capacity to accommodate at least
> -- *Growth_percentage* more items.
> -- (From *RESIZABLE*.)
> **ensure**
> > *increased_capacity*: *capacity* >= **old** *capacity* + **old**
> > *capacity* * *growth_percentage* // 100 + 1

grow (*i*: *INTEGER*)
> -- Change the capacity to at least *i*.
> **ensure**
> > *new_capacity*: *capacity* >= *i*

resize (*minindex*, *maxindex*: *INTEGER*)
> -- Rearrange array so that it can accommodate
> -- indices down to *minindex* and up to *maxindex*.
> -- Do not lose any previously entered item.
> **require**
> > *valid_indices*: *minindex* <= *maxindex*

feature -- Conversion

linear_representation: *LINEAR* [*G*]
> -- Representation as a linear structure

to_c: *ANY*
> -- Address of actual sequence of values,
> -- for passing to external (non-Eiffel) routines.

feature -- Duplication

copy (*other*: **like** *Current*)
> -- Reinitialize by copying all the items of *other*.
> -- (This is also used by *clone*.)
> **ensure**
> > *equal_areas*: *area*.*is_equal* (*other*.*area*)

invariant

> *consistent_size*: *capacity* = *upper* − *lower* + *1*;
> *non_negative_capacity*: *capacity* >= *0*;
> *increase_by_at_least_one*: *minimal_increase* >= *1*;
> *valid_count*: *count* <= *capacity*;
> *full_definition*: *full* = (*count* = *capacity*);
> *empty_definition*: *empty* = (*count* = *0*);
> *non_negative_count*: *count* >= *0*

end

23.4 CLASS *STRING*

The interface of *STRING* as it appears here omits the general features from *CONTAINER* and *COLLECTION*, but retains those from *BOUNDED*, *FINITE*, *COMPARABLE* and *RESIZABLE*.

indexing

>   description: "Sequences of characters, accessible through
>   integer indices in a contiguous range."

class interface

>   *STRING*

creation

>   make

feature -- Initialization

>   adapt (s: **like** Current): **like** Current
>   -- Object of a type conforming to the type of s,
>   -- initialized with attributes from s

>   from_c (c_string: ANY)
>   -- Reset contents of string from contents of c_string,
>   -- a string created by some external C function.
>   **require**
>   c_string /= Void

>   **frozen** make (n: INTEGER)
>   -- Allocate space for at least n characters.
>   **require**
>   non_negative_size: n >= 0
>   **ensure**
>   empty_string: count = 0;
>   area_allocated: capacity >= n

>   setup (other: **like** Current)
>   -- Perform actions on a freshly created object so that
>   -- the contents of other can be safely copied onto it.

feature -- Access

>   has (c: CHARACTER): BOOLEAN
>   -- Does string include c?
>   **ensure**
>   not_found_in_empty: Result **implies not** empty

>   hash_code: INTEGER
>   -- Hash code value.
>   **require**
>   is_hashable
>   **ensure**
>   valid_hash_value: Result >= 0

>   index_of (c: CHARACTER; start: INTEGER): INTEGER
>   -- Position of first occurrence of c at or after start;
>   -- 0 if none.

>   item (i: INTEGER): CHARACTER
>   -- Character at position i
>   **require**
>   valid_key: valid_index (i)

>   item_code (i: INTEGER): INTEGER
>   -- Numeric code of character at position i
>   **require**
>   index_small_enough: i <= count;
>   index_large_enough: i > 0

>   shared_with (other: **like** Current): BOOLEAN
>   -- Does string share the text of other?

>   substring_index (other: STRING; start: INTEGER):
>   INTEGER
>   -- Position of first occurrence of other at or after start;
>   -- 0 if none.

>   True_constant: STRING **is** "true"
>   -- Constant string "true"

>   **infix** "@" (i: INTEGER): CHARACTER
>   -- Character at position i
>   **require**
>   valid_key: valid_index (i)

feature -- Measurement

>   additional_space: INTEGER
>   -- Proposed number of additional items
>   -- (From RESIZABLE.)
>   **ensure**
>   at_least_one: Result >= 1

>   capacity: INTEGER
>   -- Allocated space

>   count: INTEGER
>   -- Actual number of characters making up the string

>   Growth_percentage: INTEGER **is** 50
>   -- Percentage by which structure will grow automatically
>   -- (From RESIZABLE.)

>   Minimal_increase: INTEGER **is** 5
>   -- Minimal number of additional items
>   -- (From RESIZABLE.)

>   occurrences (c: CHARACTER): INTEGER
>   -- Number of times c appears in the string
>   **ensure**
>   non_negative_occurrences: Result >= 0

feature -- Comparison

> *is_equal* (*other*: **like** *Current*): *BOOLEAN*
>> -- Is string made of same character sequence as *other*
>> -- (possibly with a different capacity)?

> *infix* "<" (*other*: *STRING*): *BOOLEAN*
>> -- Is string lexicographically lower than *other*?
>> -- (False if *other* is void)
>> *ensure*
>>> *smaller*: *Result* **implies not** (*Current* >= *other*)

> *infix* ">=" (*other*: **like** *Current*): *BOOLEAN*
>> -- Is current object greater than or equal to *other*?
>> -- (From *COMPARABLE*.)
>> *ensure*
>>> *equals_larger*: *Result* **implies not** (*Current* < *other*)

> *infix* ">" (*other*: **like** *Current*): *BOOLEAN*
>> -- Is current object greater than *other*?
>> -- (From *COMPARABLE*.)
>> *ensure*
>>> *larger*: *Result* **implies not** (*Current* <= *other*)

> *infix* "<=" (*other*: **like** *Current*): *BOOLEAN*
>> -- Is current object less than or equal to *other*?
>> -- (From *COMPARABLE*.)
>> *ensure*
>>> *equals_smaller*: *Result* **implies not** (*Current* > *other*)

feature -- Status report

> *changeable_comparison_criterion*: *BOOLEAN* **is false**

> *consistent* (*other*: **like** *Current*): *BOOLEAN*
>> -- Is object in a consistent state so that *other*
>> -- may be copied onto it? (Default answer: yes.)

> *empty*: *BOOLEAN*
>> -- Is structure empty?
>> -- (From *FINITE*.)

> *extendible*: *BOOLEAN* **is true**
>> -- May new items be added? (Answer: yes.)

> *full*: *BOOLEAN*
>> -- Is structure full?
>> -- (From *BOUNDED*.)

> *is_hashable*: *BOOLEAN*
>> -- May current object be hashed?
>> -- (Answer: if and only if it is not the default value of
>> -- its type)
>> -- (From *HASHABLE*.)
>> *ensure*
>>> *Result* = (*Current* /= *default*)

> *prunable*: *BOOLEAN*
>> -- May items be removed? (Answer: yes.)

> *resizable*: *BOOLEAN*
>> -- May *capacity* be changed? (Answer: yes.)
>> -- (From *RESIZABLE*.)

> *valid_index* (*i*: *INTEGER*): *BOOLEAN*
>> -- Is *i* correctly bounded?

feature -- Element change

> *append* (*s*: *STRING*)
>> -- Append a copy of *s* at end.
>> *ensure*
>>> *new_count*: *count* = **old** *count* + *s.count*
>>> -- *appended*: For every *i* in 1..*s.count*,
>>> --   *item* (**old** *count* + *i*) = *s.item* (*i*)

> *append_boolean* (*b*: *BOOLEAN*)
>> -- Append the string representation of *b* at end.

> *append_double* (*d*: *DOUBLE*)
>> -- Append the string representation of *d* at end.

> *append_integer* (*i*: *INTEGER*)
>> -- Append the string representation of *i* at end.

> *append_real* (*r*: *REAL*)
>> -- Append the string representation of *r* at end.

> *copy* (*other*: **like** *Current*)
>> -- Reinitialize by copying the characters of *other*.
>> -- (This is also used by *clone*.)
>> *ensure*
>>> *new_result_count*: *count* = *other.count*
>>> -- *same_characters*: For every *i* in 1..*count*,
>>> --   *item* (*i*) = *other.item* (*i*)

> *extend* (*c*: *CHARACTER*)
>> -- Append *c* at end.
>> *require*
>>> *extendible*: *extendible*
>> *ensure*
>>> *item_inserted*: *item* (*count*) = *c*
>> *ensure then*
>>> *one_more_occurrence*: *occurrences* (*c*) = **old**
>>>   (*occurrences* (*c*)) + *1*
>> *ensure then*
>>> *item_inserted*: *has* (*c*)

> *fill_blank*
>> -- Fill with blanks.
>> *ensure*
>>> -- *allblank*: For every *i* in 1..*count*, *item* (*i*) = *Blank*

> *head* (*n*: *INTEGER*)
>> -- Remove all characters except for the first *n*;
>> -- do nothing if *n* >= *count*.
>> *require*
>>> *non_negative_argument*: *n* >= *0*
>> *ensure*
>>> *new_count*: *count* = *min* (*n*, **old** *count*)
>>> -- *first_kept*: For every *i* in 1..*n*, *item* (*i*) = **old** *item* (*i*)

insert (*s*: **like** *Current*; *i*: *INTEGER*)
    -- Add *s* to the left of position *i* in current string.
  require
    string_exists: *s* /= *Void*;
    index_small_enough: *i* <= *count*;
    index_large_enough: *i* > *0*
  ensure
    new_count: *count* = **old** *count* + *s.count*

left_adjust
    -- Remove leading blanks.
  ensure
    new_count: (*count* /= *0*) **implies** (*item* (*1*) /= ' ')

precede (*c*: *CHARACTER*)
    -- Add *c* at front.
  ensure
    new_count: *count* = **old** *count* + *1*

prepend (*s*: *STRING*)
    -- Prepend a copy of *s* at front.
  require
    argument_not_void: *s* /= *Void*
  ensure
    new_count: *count* = **old** *count* + *s.count*

put (*c*: *CHARACTER*; *i*: *INTEGER*)
    -- Replace character at position *i* by *c*.
  require
    index_small_enough: *i* <= *count*;
    index_large_enough: *i* > *0*
  require else
    valid_key: *valid_index* (*i*)
  ensure
    insertion_done: *item* (*i*) = *c*

replace_substring (*s*: **like** *Current*; *start_pos*, *end_pos*:
INTEGER)
    -- Copy the characters of *s* to positions
    -- *start_pos* .. *end_pos*.
  require
    string_exists: *s* /= *Void*;
    index_small_enough: *end_pos* <= *count*;
    order_respected: *start_pos* <= *end_pos*;
    index_large_enough: *start_pos* > *0*
  ensure
    new_count: *count* = **old** *count* + *s.count* − *end_pos* +
      start_pos − *1*

right_adjust
    -- Remove trailing blanks.
  ensure
    new_count: (*count* /= *0*) **implies** (*item* (*count*) /= ' ')

set (*t*: **like** *Current*; *n1*, *n2*: *INTEGER*)
    -- Set current string to substring of *t* from indices *n1*
    -- to *n2*, or to empty string if no such substring.
  require
    argument_not_void: *t* /= *Void*
  ensure
    is_substring: *is_equal* (*t.substring* (*n1*, *n2*))

share (*other*: **like** *Current*)
    -- Make current string share the text of *other*.
    -- Subsequent changes to the characters of current string
    -- will also affect *other*, and conversely.
  require
    argument_not_void: *other* /= *Void*
  ensure
    shared_count: *other.count* = *count*
    -- *sharing*: For every *i* in 1..*count*,
    --   *Result.item* (*i*) = *item* (*i*)

tail (*n*: *INTEGER*)
    -- Remove all characters except for the last *n*;
    -- do nothing if *n* >= *count*.
  require
    non_negative_argument: *n* >= *0*

feature -- Removal

prune (*c*: *CHARACTER*)
    -- Remove first occurrence of *c*, if any.
  require
    true
  require else
    prunable: *prunable*

prune_all (*c*: *CHARACTER*)
    -- Remove all occurrences of *c*.
  require
    true
  require else
    prunable
  ensure
    changed_count: *count* = (**old** *count*) − (**old** *occurrences*
      (*c*))
    -- *removed*: For every *i* in 1..*count*, *item* (*i*) /= *c*
  ensure then
    no_more_occurrences: **not** *has* (*c*)

remove (*i*: *INTEGER*)
    -- Remove *i*–th character.
  require
    index_small_enough: *i* <= *count*;
    index_large_enough: *i* > *0*
  ensure
    new_count: *count* = **old** *count* − *1*

wipe_out
    -- Remove all characters.
    require
       prunable
    ensure
       empty_string: *count = 0;*
       empty_area: *capacity = 0*
    ensure then
       wiped_out: *empty*

feature -- Resizing

adapt_size
    -- Adapt the size to accommodate *count* characters.

automatic_grow
    -- Change the capacity to accommodate at least
    -- *Growth_percentage* more items.
    -- (From *RESIZABLE*.)
    ensure
       increased_capacity: *capacity >=* **old** *capacity +* **old**
          *capacity * growth_percentage // 100 + 1*

grow (*newsize*: *INTEGER*)
    -- Ensure that the capacity is at least *newsize*.
    require
       new_size_non_negative: *newsize >= 0*
    require else
       precursor: True
    ensure
       new_capacity: *capacity >= newsize*

resize (*newsize*: *INTEGER*)
    -- Reallocate space to accommodate
    -- *newsize* characters.
    -- May discard some characters if *newsize* is
    -- lower than the current number of characters.
    require
       new_size_non_negative: *newsize >= 0*

feature -- Conversion

linear_representation: *LINEAR* [*CHARACTER*]
    -- Representation as a linear structure

mirror
    -- Reverse the order of characters.
    -- "Hello world" –> "dlrow olleH".
    ensure
       same_count: *count =* **old** *count*
       -- *reversed*: For every *i* in 1..*count*,
       --   *item* (*i*) = **old** *item* (*count*+1–*i*)

mirrored: **like** *Current*
    -- Mirror image of string;
    -- result for "Hello world" is "dlrow olleH".
    ensure
       same_count: *Result.count = count*
       -- *reversed*: For every *i* in 1..*count*,
       --   *Result.item* (*i*) = *item* (*count*+1–*i*)

to_boolean: *BOOLEAN*
    -- Boolean value;
    -- "true" yields *true*, "false" yields *false*
    -- (case–insensitive)

to_c: *ANY*
    -- An integer which a C function may cast into a pointer
    -- to a *C* form of current string.
    -- Useful only for interfacing with C software.

to_double: *DOUBLE*
    -- "Double" value;
    -- for example, when applied to "123.0", will yield 123.0
       (double)

to_integer: *INTEGER*
    -- Integer value;
    -- for example, when applied to "123", will yield 123

to_lower
    -- Convert to lower case.

to_real: *REAL*
    -- Real value;
    -- for example, when applied to "123.0", will yield 123.0

to_upper
    -- Convert to upper case.

feature -- Duplication

substring (*n1*, *n2*: *INTEGER*): **like** *Current*
    -- Copy of substring containing all characters at indices
    -- between *n1* and *n2*
    require
       meaningful_origin: *1 <= n1*;
       meaningful_interval: *n1 <= n2*;
       meaningful_end: *n2 <= count*
    ensure
       new_result_count: *Result.count = n2 – n1 + 1*
       -- *original_characters*: For every *i* in 1..*n2–n1*,
       --   *Result.item* (*i*) = *item* (*n1+i*–1)

feature -- Output

out: **like** *Current*
    -- Printable representation

invariant

    extendible: *extendible*;
    increase_by_at_least_one: *minimal_increase >= 1*;
    valid_count: *count <= capacity*;
    full_definition: *full = (count = capacity)*;
    empty_definition: *empty = (count = 0)*;
    non_negative_count: *count >= 0*

end

23.5 CLASS *SPECIAL*

Although *SPECIAL* is used internally by *ARRAY* and *STRING*, most applications do not need to rely on it directly. It can be useful, however, as an optimization facility for large array computations. Its interface, given here in full, is a simpler version of the interface of *ARRAY*.

The optimization of array computations was discussed in 13.4.3, page 249.

indexing

  description: "*Special objects: homogeneous sequences of values, used to represent arrays and strings*"

class interface

  SPECIAL [*T*]

feature -- Access

  conforms_to (*other*: *SPECIAL* [*T*]): *BOOLEAN*
        -- Does special object conform to *other*?

  item (*i*: *INTEGER*): *T*
        -- Item at *i*–th position
        -- (indices begin at 0)
     require
     index_big_enough: *i* >= *0*;
     index_small_enough: *i* < *count*

feature -- Measurement

  count: *INTEGER*
        -- Count of the special area

feature -- Element change

  put (*v*: *T*; *i*: *INTEGER*)
        -- Replace *i*–th item by *v*.
        -- (Indices begin at 0.)
     require
     index_big_enough: *i* >= *0*;
     index_small_enough: *i* < *count*

end

23.6 CLASS *BASIC_ROUTINES*

indexing

   description: "*Some useful facilities on objects of basic types*"

class interface

   BASIC_ROUTINES

feature -- Conversion

   charcode (*c*: *CHARACTER*): *INTEGER*
      -- Integer ascii code corresponding to *c*

   charconv (*i*: *INTEGER*): *CHARACTER*
      -- Character corresponding to ascii code *i*

   double_to_integer (*d*: *DOUBLE*): *INTEGER*
      -- Integer conversion (truncation) of *d*

   double_to_real (*d*: *DOUBLE*): *REAL*
      -- Real conversion (truncation) of *d*

   real_to_integer (*r*: *REAL*): *INTEGER*
      -- Integer conversion (truncation) of *r*

feature -- Basic operations

   abs (*n*: *INTEGER*): *INTEGER*
      -- Absolute value of *n*
     ensure
      non_negative_result: *Result* >= *0*

   bottom_int_div (*n1*, *n2*: *INTEGER*): *INTEGER*
      -- Greatest lower bound of the integer division of *n1* by
        n2

   max (*n1*, *n2*: *INTEGER*): *INTEGER*
      -- Maximum of *n1* and *n2*
     ensure
      is_maximum: ($n2 >= n1$) = (*Result* = *n2*) **or else** ($n1 >$
       $n2$) = (*Result* = *n1*)

   min (*n1*, *n2*: *INTEGER*): *INTEGER*
      -- Minimum of *n1* and *n2*
     ensure
      is_minimum: ($n2 <= n1$) = (*Result* = *n2*) **or else** ($n1 <$
       $n2$) = (*Result* = *n1*)

   rmax (*r1*, *r2*: *REAL*): *REAL*
      -- Maximum of *r1* and *r2*
     ensure
      is_maximum: ($r2 >= r1$) = (*Result* = *r2*) **or else** ($r1 >$
       $r2$) = (*Result* = *r1*)

   rmin (*r1*, *r2*: *REAL*): *REAL*
      -- Minimum of *r1* and *r2*
     ensure
      is_minimum: ($r2 <= r1$) = (*Result* = *r2*) **or else** ($r1 < r2$)
       = (*Result* = *r1*)

   rsign (*r*: *REAL*): *INTEGER*
      -- Sign of *r*:
      -- -1 if $r < 0$
      -- 0 if $r = 0$
      -- +1 if $r > 0$
     ensure
      correct_negative: ($r < 0$) = (*Result* = − *1*);
      correct_zero: ($r = 0$) = (*Result* = *0*);
      correct_positive: ($r > 0$) = (*Result* = + *1*)

   sign (*n*: *INTEGER*): *INTEGER*
      -- Sign of *n*:
      -- -1 if $n < 0$
      -- 0 if $n = 0$
      -- +1 if $n > 0$
     ensure
      correct_negative: ($n < 0$) = (*Result* = − *1*);
      correct_zero: ($n = 0$) = (*Result* = *0*);
      correct_positive: ($n > 0$) = (*Result* = + *1*)

   up_int_div (*n1*, *n2*: *INTEGER*): *INTEGER*
      -- Least upper bound of the integer division
      -- of *n1* by *n2*

end

23.7 CLASSES *DOUBLE_MATH* AND *SINGLE_MATH*

Only the interface of *SINGLE_MATH* appears here. To obtain the interface of *DOUBLE_MATH* replace *REAL*, whenever used as the type of an argument or result, by *DOUBLE*.

indexing

　　description: "*Basic mathematical operations,*
　　　double−precision. This class may be used as ancestor by
　　　classes needing its facilities."

class interface

　　SINGLE_MATH

feature -- Access

　　arc_cosine (*v*: *REAL*): *REAL*
　　　　-- Trigonometric arccosine of *v*

　　arc_sine (*v*: *REAL*): *REAL*
　　　　-- Trigonometric arcsine of *v*

　　arc_tangent (*v*: *REAL*): *REAL*
　　　　-- Trigonometric arctangent of *v*

　　ceiling (*v*: *REAL*): *REAL*
　　　　-- Least integral value greater than or equal to *v*

　　cosine (*v*: *REAL*): *REAL*
　　　　-- Trigonometric cosine of radian *v* approximated
　　　　-- in the range [−pi/4, +pi/4]

　　floor (*v*: *REAL*): *REAL*
　　　　-- Greatest integral value less than or equal to *v*

　　log (*v*: *REAL*): *REAL*
　　　　-- Natural logarithm of *v*
　　　require
　　　　v > *0.0*

　　log10 (*v*: *REAL*): *REAL*
　　　　-- Base 10 logarithm of *v*
　　　require
　　　　v > *0.0*

　　log_2 (*v*: *REAL*): *REAL*
　　　　-- Base 2 logarithm of *v*
　　　require
　　　　v > *0.0*

　　sine (*v*: *REAL*): *REAL*
　　　　-- Trigonometric sine of radian *v* approximated
　　　　-- in range [−pi/4, +pi/4]

　　sqrt (*v*: *REAL*): *REAL*
　　　　-- Square root of *v*
　　　require
　　　　v >= *0.0*

　　tangent (*v*: *REAL*): *REAL*
　　　　-- Trigonometric tangent of radian *v* approximated
　　　　-- in range [−pi/4, +pi/4]

end

23.8 CLASS *PRIMES*

PRIMES is an heir of *COUNTABLE_SEQUENCE*. The interface does not show the general features inherited from *CONTAINER*, but does retain those from the other ancestors: *INFINITE*, *COUNTABLE* and *COUNTABLE_SEQUENCE*.

The interface of class *FIBONACCI* is similar to that of *PRIMES* but has not been included.

indexing

> *description*: "Prime number properties"
> *names*: *primes*

class interface

> PRIMES

feature -- Access

> *all_lower_primes* (*n*: *INTEGER*): *ARRAY* [*BOOLEAN*]
> > -- Array of *n* boolean values, where the
> > -- value at index *i* is true if and only if
> > -- *i* is prime.

> *higher_prime* (*n*: *INTEGER*): *INTEGER*
> > -- Lowest prime greater than or equal to *n*

> *i_th* (*i*: *INTEGER*): *INTEGER*
> > -- The *i*-th prime number
> > **require**
> > *positive_argument*: *i* > 0

> *index*: *INTEGER*
> > -- Index of current position
> > -- (From *COUNTABLE_SEQUENCE*.)

> *index_of* (*v*: **like** *item*; *i*: *INTEGER*): *INTEGER*
> > -- Index of *i*-th occurrence of *v*.
> > -- 0 if none.
> > -- (Reference or object equality,
> > -- based on *object_comparison*.)
> > -- (From *LINEAR*.)
> > **require**
> > *positive_occurrences*: *i* > 0
> > **ensure**
> > *non_negative_result*: *Result* >= 0

> *is_prime* (*n*: *INTEGER*): *BOOLEAN*
> > -- Is *n* a prime number?
> > **ensure**
> > *not_found_in_empty*: *Result* **implies not** *empty*

> *item*: *INTEGER*
> > -- Item at current position
> > -- (From *COUNTABLE_SEQUENCE*.)
> > **require**
> > *readable*
> > **require else**
> > *not_off*: **not** *off*

> *lower_prime* (*n*: *INTEGER*): *INTEGER*
> > -- Greatest prime lower than or equal to *n*
> > **require**
> > *argument_big_enough*: *n* >= *smallest_prime*

> *occurrences* (*v*: *INTEGER*): *INTEGER*
> > -- Number of times *v* appears.
> > -- (Reference or object equality,
> > -- based on *object_comparison*.)
> > -- (From *LINEAR*.)
> > **ensure**
> > *non_negative_occurrences*: *Result* >= 0

> *search* (*v*: **like** *item*)
> > -- Move to first position (at or after current
> > -- position) where *item* and *v* are equal.
> > -- (Reference or object equality,
> > -- based on *object_comparison*.)
> > -- If no such position ensure that *exhausted* will be true.
> > -- (From *LINEAR*.)

> *Smallest_odd_prime*: *INTEGER* **is** *3*

> *Smallest_prime*: *INTEGER* **is** *2*

feature -- Status report

> *after*: *BOOLEAN* **is false**
> > -- Is current position past last item? (Answer: no.)
> > -- (From *COUNTABLE_SEQUENCE*.)

> *empty*: *BOOLEAN* **is false**
> > -- Is structure empty? (Answer: no.)
> > -- (From *INFINITE*.)

> *exhausted*: *BOOLEAN*
> > -- Has structure been completely explored?
> > -- (From *LINEAR*.)
> > **ensure**
> > *exhausted_when_off*: *off* **implies** *Result*

extendible: *BOOLEAN* **is false**
    -- May items be added? (Answer: no.)
    -- (From *COUNTABLE_SEQUENCE*.)

full: *BOOLEAN* **is true**
    -- The structure is complete
    -- (From *INFINITE*.)

off: *BOOLEAN*
    -- Is there no current item?
    -- (From *LINEAR*.)

prunable: *BOOLEAN* **is false**
    -- May items be removed? (Answer: no.)
    -- (From *COUNTABLE_SEQUENCE*.)

readable: *BOOLEAN* **is true**
    -- Is there a current item that may be read?
    -- (Answer: yes.)
    -- (From *COUNTABLE_SEQUENCE*.)

writable: *BOOLEAN* **is false**
    -- Is there a current item that may be written?
    -- (Answer: no.)
    -- (From *COUNTABLE_SEQUENCE*.)

feature -- Cursor movement

forth
    -- Move to next position.
    -- (From *COUNTABLE_SEQUENCE*.)
  require
    not_after: **not** *after*

start
    -- Move to first position.
    -- (From *COUNTABLE_SEQUENCE*.)

invariant

  never_empty: **not** *empty*;
  always_full: *full*;
  writable_constraint: *writable* **implies** *readable*;
  empty_constraint: *empty* **implies** (**not** *readable*) **and** (**not**
    writable);
  after_constraint: *after* **implies** *off*;
  empty_constraint: *empty* **implies** *off*

end

23.9 CLASS *RANDOM*

RANDOM is an heir of *COUNTABLE_SEQUENCE*. The interface does not show the general features inherited from *CONTAINER*, but does retain those from the other ancestors: *INFINITE*, *COUNTABLE* and *COUNTABLE_SEQUENCE*.

indexing

> description: "Pseudo−random number sequence, linear
>   congruential method"
> names: random

class interface

> RANDOM

creation
> make,
> set_seed

feature -- Initialization

> make
>   -- Initialize structure using a default seed.
>   **ensure**
>   seed_set: seed = default_seed

> set_seed (s: INTEGER)
>   -- Initialize sequence using s as the seed.
>   **require**
>   non_negative: s >= 0
>   **ensure**
>   seed_set: seed = s

feature -- Access

> default_seed: INTEGER
>   -- Default value 123, 457;
>   -- may be redefined for a new generator.

> double_i_th (i: INTEGER): DOUBLE
>   -- The i−th random number as a double between 0 and 1

> double_item: DOUBLE
>   -- The current random number as a double between 0
>   and 1

> has (n: INTEGER): BOOLEAN
>   -- Will n be part of the random number sequence?
>   **ensure**
>   only_: Result = (n < modulus **and** n >= 0)
>   **ensure then**
>   not_found_in_empty: Result **implies not** empty

> i_th (i: INTEGER): INTEGER
>   -- The i−th random number
>   **require**
>   positive_argument: i > 0
>   **ensure**
>   in_range: (Result < modulus **and** (Result >= 0)

increment: INTEGER
>   -- Default value 0;
>   -- may be redefined for a new generator.

index: INTEGER
>   -- Index of current position
>   -- (From COUNTABLE_SEQUENCE.)

index_of (v: **like** item; i: INTEGER): INTEGER
>   -- Index of i−th occurrence of v.
>   -- 0 if none.
>   -- (Reference or object equality,
>   -- based on object_comparison.)
>   -- (From LINEAR.)
>   **require**
>   positive_occurrences: i > 0
>   **ensure**
>   non_negative_result: Result >= 0

item: INTEGER
>   -- Item at current position
>   -- (From COUNTABLE_SEQUENCE.)
>   **require**
>   readable
>   **require else**
>   not_off: **not** off

modulus: INTEGER
>   -- Default value 2^31 −1 = 2, 147, 483, 647;
>   -- may be redefined for a new generator.

multiplier: INTEGER
>   -- Default value 7^5 = 16, 807;
>   -- may be redefined for a new generator.

next_random (n: INTEGER): INTEGER
>   -- Next random number after n
>   -- in pseudo−random order
>   **require**
>   in_range: (n < modulus) **and** (n >= 0)
>   **ensure**
>   in_range: (Result < modulus) **and** (Result >= 0)

occurrences (v: INTEGER): INTEGER
>   -- Number of times v appears.
>   -- (Reference or object equality,
>   -- based on object_comparison.)
>   -- (From LINEAR.)
>   **ensure**
>   non_negative_occurrences: Result >= 0

real_i_th (*i*: *INTEGER*): *REAL*
  -- The *i*–th random number as a real between 0 and 1

real_item: *REAL*
  -- The current random number as a real between 0 and 1

search (*v*: **like** *item*)
  -- Move to first position (at or after current
  -- position) where *item* and *v* are equal.
  -- (Reference or object equality,
  -- based on *object_comparison*.)
  -- If no such position ensure that *exhausted* will be true.
  -- (From *LINEAR*.)

seed: *INTEGER*
  -- Seed for sequence.

feature -- Status report

after: *BOOLEAN* **is false**
  -- Is current position past last item? (Answer: no.)
  -- (From *COUNTABLE_SEQUENCE*.)

empty: *BOOLEAN* **is false**
  -- Is structure empty? (Answer: no.)
  -- (From *INFINITE*.)

exhausted: *BOOLEAN*
  -- Has structure been completely explored?
  -- (From *LINEAR*.)
  ensure
  exhausted_when_off: *off* **implies** *Result*

extendible: *BOOLEAN* **is false**
  -- May items be added? (Answer: no.)
  -- (From *COUNTABLE_SEQUENCE*.)

full: *BOOLEAN* **is true**
  -- The structure is complete
  -- (From *INFINITE*.)

off: *BOOLEAN*
  -- Is there no current item?
  -- (From *LINEAR*.)

prunable: *BOOLEAN* **is false**
  -- May items be removed? (Answer: no.)
  -- (From *COUNTABLE_SEQUENCE*.)

readable: *BOOLEAN* **is true**
  -- Is there a current item that may be read?
  -- (Answer: yes.)
  -- (From *COUNTABLE_SEQUENCE*.)

writable: *BOOLEAN* **is false**
  -- Is there a current item that may be written?
  -- (Answer: no.)
  -- (From *COUNTABLE_SEQUENCE*.)

feature -- Cursor movement

forth
  -- Move to next position.
  -- (From *COUNTABLE_SEQUENCE*.)
  require
  not_after: **not** *after*

start
  -- Move to first position.
  -- (From *COUNTABLE_SEQUENCE*.)

invariant

  non_negative_seed: *seed* >= *0*;
  non_negative_increment: *increment* >= *0*;
  positive_multiplier: *multiplier* > *0*;
  modulus_constraint: *modulus* > *1*;
  never_empty: **not** *empty*;
  always_full: *full*;
  writable_constraint: *writable* **implies** *readable*;
  empty_constraint: *empty* **implies** (**not** *readable*) **and** (**not**
    writable);
  after_constraint: *after* **implies** *off*;
  empty_constraint: *empty* **implies** *off*

end

23.10 CLASS *ASCII*

class interface

> *ASCII*

feature -- Access

> *Ack*: INTEGER *is* 6
>
> *Ampersand*: INTEGER *is* 38
>
> *Back_space*: INTEGER *is* 8
>
> *Backslash*: INTEGER *is* 92
>
> *Bar*: INTEGER *is* 124
>
> *Bel*: INTEGER *is* 7
>
> *Blank*: INTEGER *is* 32
>
> *Break*: INTEGER *is* −7
>
> *Bs*: INTEGER *is* 8
>
> *Buf_overflow*: INTEGER *is* −9
>
> *Can*: INTEGER *is* 24
>
> *Carriage_return*: INTEGER *is* 13
>
> *Case_diff*: INTEGER *is* 32
>   -- Lower_a – Upper_a
>
> *Character_set_size*: INTEGER *is* 128
>
> *Circumflex*: INTEGER *is* 94
>
> *Closing_brace*: INTEGER *is* 125
>
> *Colon*: INTEGER *is* 58
>
> *Comma*: INTEGER *is* 44
>
> *Commercial_at*: INTEGER *is* 64
>
> *Cr*: INTEGER *is* 13
>
> *Ctrl_a*: INTEGER *is* 1
>
> *Ctrl_b*: INTEGER *is* 2
>
> *Ctrl_backslash*: INTEGER *is* 28
>
> *Ctrl_c*: INTEGER *is* 3
>
> *Ctrl_circumflex*: INTEGER *is* 30
>
> *Ctrl_d*: INTEGER *is* 4
>
> *Ctrl_e*: INTEGER *is* 5
>
> *Ctrl_f*: INTEGER *is* 6

> *Ctrl_g*: INTEGER *is* 7
>
> *Ctrl_h*: INTEGER *is* 8
>
> *Ctrl_i*: INTEGER *is* 9
>
> *Ctrl_j*: INTEGER *is* 10
>
> *Ctrl_k*: INTEGER *is* 11
>
> *Ctrl_l*: INTEGER *is* 12
>
> *Ctrl_lbracket*: INTEGER *is* 27
>
> *Ctrl_m*: INTEGER *is* 13
>
> *Ctrl_n*: INTEGER *is* 14
>
> *Ctrl_o*: INTEGER *is* 15
>
> *Ctrl_p*: INTEGER *is* 16
>
> *Ctrl_q*: INTEGER *is* 17
>
> *Ctrl_questmark*: INTEGER *is* 127
>
> *Ctrl_r*: INTEGER *is* 18
>
> *Ctrl_rbracket*: INTEGER *is* 29
>
> *Ctrl_s*: INTEGER *is* 19
>
> *Ctrl_t*: INTEGER *is* 20
>
> *Ctrl_u*: INTEGER *is* 21
>
> *Ctrl_underlined*: INTEGER *is* 31
>
> *Ctrl_v*: INTEGER *is* 22
>
> *Ctrl_w*: INTEGER *is* 23
>
> *Ctrl_x*: INTEGER *is* 24
>
> *Ctrl_y*: INTEGER *is* 25
>
> *Ctrl_z*: INTEGER *is* 26
>
> *Dc1*: INTEGER *is* 17
>
> *Dc2*: INTEGER *is* 18
>
> *Dc3*: INTEGER *is* 19
>
> *Dc4*: INTEGER *is* 20
>
> *Del*: INTEGER *is* 127
>
> *Dle*: INTEGER *is* 16
>
> *Dollar*: INTEGER *is* 36
>
> *Dot*: INTEGER *is* 46
>
> *Doublequote*: INTEGER *is* 34
>
> *Down_arrow*: INTEGER *is* −3

Eight: *INTEGER* **is** *56*

Em: *INTEGER* **is** *25*

Enq: *INTEGER* **is** *5*

Eot: *INTEGER* **is** *4*

Equal_sign: *INTEGER* **is** *61*

Esc: *INTEGER* **is** *27*

Etb: *INTEGER* **is** *23*

Etx: *INTEGER* **is** *3*

Exclamation: *INTEGER* **is** *33*

First_printable: *INTEGER* **is** *32*

Five: *INTEGER* **is** *53*

Four: *INTEGER* **is** *52*

Fs: *INTEGER* **is** *28*

Grave_accent: *INTEGER* **is** *96*

Greaterthan: *INTEGER* **is** *62*

Gs: *INTEGER* **is** *29*

Home_arrow: *INTEGER* **is** *−6*

Ht: *INTEGER* **is** *9*

Last_ascii: *INTEGER* **is** *127*

Last_printable: *INTEGER* **is** *126*

Lbracket: *INTEGER* **is** *91*

Lcurly: *INTEGER* **is** *40*

Left_arrow: *INTEGER* **is** *−4*

Lessthan: *INTEGER* **is** *60*

Letter_layout: *INTEGER* **is** *70*

Line_feed: *INTEGER* **is** *10*

Lower_a: *INTEGER* **is** *97*

Lower_b: *INTEGER* **is** *98*

Lower_c: *INTEGER* **is** *99*

Lower_d: *INTEGER* **is** *100*

Lower_e: *INTEGER* **is** *101*

Lower_f: *INTEGER* **is** *102*

Lower_g: *INTEGER* **is** *103*

Lower_h: *INTEGER* **is** *104*

Lower_i: *INTEGER* **is** *105*

Lower_j: *INTEGER* **is** *106*

Lower_k: *INTEGER* **is** *107*

Lower_l: *INTEGER* **is** *108*

Lower_m: *INTEGER* **is** *109*

Lower_n: *INTEGER* **is** *110*

Lower_o: *INTEGER* **is** *111*

Lower_p: *INTEGER* **is** *112*

Lower_q: *INTEGER* **is** *113*

Lower_r: *INTEGER* **is** *114*

Lower_s: *INTEGER* **is** *115*

Lower_t: *INTEGER* **is** *116*

Lower_u: *INTEGER* **is** *117*

Lower_v: *INTEGER* **is** *118*

Lower_w: *INTEGER* **is** *119*

Lower_x: *INTEGER* **is** *120*

Lower_y: *INTEGER* **is** *121*

Lower_z: *INTEGER* **is** *122*

Minus: *INTEGER* **is** *45*

Nak: *INTEGER* **is** *21*

Nine: *INTEGER* **is** *57*

Nl: *INTEGER* **is** *10*

Np: *INTEGER* **is** *12*

Nul: *INTEGER* **is** *0*

Number_sign: *INTEGER* **is** *35*

One: *INTEGER* **is** *49*

Opening_brace: *INTEGER* **is** *123*

Overflow: *INTEGER* **is** *−8*

Percent: *INTEGER* **is** *37*

Plus: *INTEGER* **is** *43*

Questmark: *INTEGER* **is** *63*

Rbracket: *INTEGER* **is** *93*

Rcurly: *INTEGER* **is** *41*

Right_arrow: *INTEGER* **is** *−5*

Rs: *INTEGER* **is** *30*

Semicolon: *INTEGER* **is** *59*

Seven: *INTEGER* **is** *55*

Si: *INTEGER* **is** *15*

is_open_read: *BOOLEAN*
    -- Is file open for reading?

is_open_write: *BOOLEAN*
    -- Is file open for writing?

is_readable: *BOOLEAN*
    -- Is file readable?
  require
    file_descriptor_exists: *exists*

is_writable: *BOOLEAN*
    -- Is file writable?
  require
    file_descriptor_exists: *exists*

lastchar: *CHARACTER*
    -- Last character read

lastdouble: *DOUBLE*
    -- Last double read by *readdouble*

lastint: *INTEGER*
    -- Last integer read by *readint*

lastreal: *REAL*
    -- Last real read by *readreal*

laststring: *STRING*
    -- Last string read

readable: *BOOLEAN*
    -- Is there a current item that may be read?
    -- (From *SEQUENCE*.)

writable: *BOOLEAN*
    -- Is there a current item that may be modified?
    -- (From *SEQUENCE*.)

feature -- Status setting

close
    -- Close file.

open_append
    -- Open in append mode and create a file of name *name*
    -- if none exists.
  require
    is_closed: *is_closed*
  ensure
    opened_for_appending: *is_open_append*;
    file_exists: *exists*

open_read
    -- Open in read mode.
  require
    is_closed: *is_closed*
  ensure
    opened_for_reading: *is_open_read*

open_write
    -- Open in write mode and create a file of name *name*
    -- if none exists.
  require
    is_closed: *is_closed*
  ensure
    opened_for_writing: *is_open_write*;
    file_exists: *exists*

feature -- Cursor movement

back
    -- Move to previous position.
    -- (From *BILINEAR*.)
  require
    not_before: **not** *before*
  ensure
    moved_back: *index* = **old** *index* − *1*

before: *BOOLEAN*
    -- Is there no valid position to the left of current one?
    -- (From *BILINEAR*.)

finish
    -- Move to last position.
    -- (From *LINEAR*.)

forth
    -- Move to next position; if no next position,
    -- ensure that *exhausted* will be true.
    -- (From *LINEAR*.)
  require
    not_after: **not** *after*

search (*v*: **like** *item*)
    -- Move to first position (at or after current
    -- position) where *item* and *v* are equal.
    -- If structure does not include *v* ensure that
    -- *exhausted* will be true.
    -- (Reference or object equality,
    -- based on *object_comparison*.)
    -- (From *BILINEAR*.)

start
    -- Move to first position if any.
    -- (From *TRAVERSABLE*.)

feature -- Element change

append (*s*: *SEQUENCE* [*CHARACTER*])
    -- Append a copy of *s*.
    -- (From *SEQUENCE*.)
  require
    argument_not_void: *s* /= *Void*
  ensure
    new_count: *count* >= **old** *count*

extend (*v*: *CHARACTER*)
    -- Include *v* at end.
require
    extendible: *extendible*
ensure
    one_more_occurrence: *occurrences* (*v*) = **old**
    (*occurrences* (*v*)) + *1*
ensure then
    item_inserted: *has* (*v*)

force (*v*: **like** *item*)
    -- Add *v* to end.
    -- (From *SEQUENCE*.)
require
    extendible: *extendible*
ensure
    new_count: *count* = **old** *count* + *1*;
    item_inserted: *has* (*v*)

new_line
    -- Write a new line character at current position.
require
    extendible: *extendible*

put (*v*: **like** *item*)
    -- Add *v* to end.
    -- (From *SEQUENCE*.)
require
    extendible: *extendible*
ensure
    new_count: *count* = **old** *count* + *1*
ensure then
    item_inserted: *has* (*v*)

putbool (*b*: *BOOLEAN*)
    -- Write ASCII value of *b* at current position.
require
    extendible: *extendible*

putchar (*c*: *CHARACTER*)
    -- Write *c* at current position.
require
    extendible: *extendible*

putdouble (*d*: *DOUBLE*)
    -- Write ASCII value of *d* at current position.
require
    extendible: *extendible*

putint (*i*: *INTEGER*)
    -- Write ASCII value of *i* at current position.
require
    extendible: *extendible*

putreal (*r*: *REAL*)
    -- Write ASCII value of *r* at current position.
require
    extendible: *extendible*

putstring (*s*: *STRING*)
    -- Write *s* at current position.
require
    extendible: *extendible*

feature -- Removal

delete
    -- Remove link with physical file.
require
    file_exists: *exists*

prune_all (*v*: **like** *item*)
    -- Remove all occurrences of *v*; go *off*.
    -- (From *SEQUENCE*.)
ensure
    no_more_occurrences: **not** *has* (*v*)

reset (*fn*: *STRING*)
    -- Change file name to *fn* and reset
    -- all (internal) information.
require
    fn /= *Void*
ensure
    file_renamed: *name* = *fn*;
    file_closed: *is_closed*

feature -- Conversion

linear_representation: *LINEAR* [*CHARACTER*]
    -- Representation as a linear structure
    -- (From *LINEAR*.)

feature -- Input

readchar
    -- Read a new character.
    -- Make result available in *lastchar*.
require
    is_readable: *file_readable*

readdouble
    -- Read a new double.
    -- Make result available in *lastdouble*.
require
    is_readable: *file_readable*

readint
    -- Read a new integer.
    -- Make result available in *lastint*.
require
    is_readable: *file_readable*

readreal
    -- Read a new real.
    -- Make result available in *lastreal*.
require
    is_readable: *file_readable*

readstream (*nb_char*: *INTEGER*)
    -- Read a string of at most *nb_char* bound characters
    -- or until end of file is encountered.
    -- Make result available in *laststring*.
  require
    is_readable: *file_readable*

invariant

  non_negative_count: *count* >= *0*;
  writable_constraint: *writable* **implies** *readable*;
  not_both: **not** (*after* **and** *before*);
  before_constraint: *before* **implies** *off*;
  after_constraint: *after* **implies** *off*

end

23.12 CLASS *UNIX_FILE*

UNIX_FILE is an heir of *FILE*. The interface only shows the features introduced or redeclared in *UNIX_FILE* itself, and does not include any feature inherited directly or indirectly.

indexing

> description: "Objects describing files as seen by the
>   operating system"

class interface

> UNIX_FILE

creation

> make,
> make_open_read,
> make_open_write,
> make_open_append,
> make_open_read_write,
> make_create_read_write,
> make_open_read_append

feature -- Initialization

> make (fn: STRING)
>   -- Create file object with *fn* as file name.
>   **require**
>   string_exists: fn /= Void

> make_create_read_write (fn: STRING)
>   -- Create file object with *fn* as file name
>   -- and open file for both reading and writing;
>   -- create it if it does not exist.
>   **require**
>   string_exists: fn /= Void

> make_open_append (fn: STRING)
>   -- Create file object with *fn* as file name
>   -- and open file in append–only mode.
>   **require**
>   string_exists: fn /= Void

> make_open_read (fn: STRING)
>   -- Create file object with *fn* as file name
>   -- and open file in read mode.
>   **require**
>   string_exists: fn /= Void

> make_open_read_append (fn: STRING)
>   -- Create file object with *fn* as file name
>   -- and open file for reading anywhere
>   -- but writing at the end only.
>   -- Create file if it does not exist.
>   **require**
>   string_exists: fn /= Void

> make_open_read_write (fn: STRING)
>   -- Create file object with *fn* as file name
>   -- and open file for both reading and writing.
>   **require**
>   string_exists: fn /= Void

> make_open_write (fn: STRING)
>   -- Create file object with *fn* as file name
>   -- and open file for writing;
>   -- create it if it does not exist.
>   **require**
>   string_exists: fn /= Void

feature -- Access

>   -- Time stamp of last access made to the inode.
>   **require**
>   file_exists: exists

>   -- Time stamp (time of last modification)
>   **require**
>   file_exists: exists

> descriptor: INTEGER
>   -- File descriptor as used by the operating system.
>   **require**
>   file_opened: **not** is_closed

> file_info: UNIX_FILE_INFO
>   -- Collected information about the file.

> file_pointer: POINTER
>   -- File pointer as required in C

> group_id: INTEGER
>   -- Group identification of owner
>   **require**
>   file_exists: exists

> inode: INTEGER
>   -- I–node number
>   **require**
>   file_exists: exists

> links: INTEGER
>   -- Number of links on file
>   **require**
>   file_exists: exists

> owner_name: STRING
>   -- Name of owner
>   **require**
>   file_exists: exists

position: *INTEGER*
    -- Current cursor position.

protection: *INTEGER*
    -- Protection mode, in decimal value
  require
    file_exists: *exists*

separator: *CHARACTER*
    -- Ascii code of character following last word read

user_id: *INTEGER*
    -- User identification of owner
  require
    file_exists: *exists*

feature -- Measurement

count: *INTEGER*
    -- Size in bytes (0 if no associated physical file)

feature -- Status report

access_exists: *BOOLEAN*
    -- Does physical file exist?
    -- (Uses real UID.)

after: *BOOLEAN*
    -- Is there no valid cursor position to the right of cursor
    position?

before: *BOOLEAN*
    -- Is there no valid cursor position to the left of cursor
    position?

end_of_file: *BOOLEAN*
    -- Has an EOF been detected?
  require
    opened: **not** *is_closed*

exists: *BOOLEAN*
    -- Does physical file exist?
    -- (Uses effective UID.)

file_readable: *BOOLEAN*
    -- Is there a current item that may be read?

is_access_executable: *BOOLEAN*
    -- Is file executable by real UID?
  require
    file_exists: *exists*

is_access_owner: *BOOLEAN*
    -- Is file owned by real UID?
  require
    file_exists: *exists*

is_access_readable: *BOOLEAN*
    -- Is file readable by real UID?
  require
    file_exists: *exists*

is_access_writable: *BOOLEAN*
    -- Is file writable by real UID?
  require
    file_exists: *exists*

is_block: *BOOLEAN*
    -- Is file a block special file?
  require
    file_exists: *exists*

is_character: *BOOLEAN*
    -- Is file a character special file?
  require
    file_exists: *exists*

is_creatable: *BOOLEAN*
    -- Is file creatable in parent directory?
    -- (Uses effective UID to check that parent is writable
    -- and file does not exist.)

is_device: *BOOLEAN*
    -- Is file a device?
  require
    file_exists: *exists*

is_directory: *BOOLEAN*
    -- Is file a directory?
  require
    file_exists: *exists*

is_executable: *BOOLEAN*
    -- Is file executable?
    -- (Checks execute permission for effective UID.)
  require
    file_descriptor_exists: *exists*

is_fifo: *BOOLEAN*
    -- Is file a named pipe?
  require
    file_exists: *exists*

is_owner: *BOOLEAN*
    -- Is file owned by effective UID?
  require
    file_exists: *exists*

is_plain: *BOOLEAN*
    -- Is file a plain file?
  require
    file_exists: *exists*

is_readable: *BOOLEAN*
    -- Is file readable?
    -- (Checks permission for effective UID.)
  require
    file_descriptor_exists: *exists*

is_setgid: *BOOLEAN*
    -- Is file setgid?
  require
    file_exists: *exists*

is_setuid: *BOOLEAN*
    -- Is file setuid?
  require
    file_exists: *exists*

is_socket: *BOOLEAN*
    -- Is file a named socket?
  require
    file_exists: *exists*

is_sticky: *BOOLEAN*
    -- Is file sticky (for memory swaps)?
  require
    file_exists: *exists*

is_symlink: *BOOLEAN*
    -- Is file a symbolic link?
  require
    file_exists: *exists*

is_writable: *BOOLEAN*
    -- Is file writable?
    -- (Checks write permission for effective UID.)
  require
    file_descriptor_exists: *exists*

off: *BOOLEAN*
    -- Is there no item?

feature -- Status setting

close
    -- Close file.
  require
    is_open: ***not*** *is_closed*

create_read_write
    -- Open file in read and write mode;
    -- create it if it does not exist.

fd_open_append (*fd*: *INTEGER*)
    -- Open file of descriptor *fd* in append mode.

fd_open_read (*fd*: *INTEGER*)
    -- Open file of descriptor *fd* in read-only mode.

fd_open_read_append (*fd*: *INTEGER*)
    -- Open file of descriptor *fd*
    -- in read and write-at-end mode.

fd_open_read_write (*fd*: *INTEGER*)
    -- Open file of descriptor *fd* in read-write mode.

fd_open_write (*fd*: *INTEGER*)
    -- Open file of descriptor *fd* in write mode.

open_append
    -- Open file in append-only mode;
    -- create it if it does not exist.
  require
    is_closed: *is_closed*
  ensure
    file_exists: *exists*

open_read
    -- Open file in read-only mode.
  require
    is_closed: *is_closed*

open_read_append
    -- Open file in read and write-at-end mode;
    -- create it if it does not exist.

open_read_write
    -- Open file in read and write mode.

open_write
    -- Open file in write-only mode;
    -- create it if it does not exist.
  require
    is_closed: *is_closed*
  ensure
    file_exists: *exists*

recreate_read_write (*fname*: *STRING*)
    -- Reopen in read-write mode with file of name *fname*;
    -- create file if it does not exist.
  require
    is_open: ***not*** *is_closed*;
    valid_name: *fname* /= *Void*

reopen_append (*fname*: *STRING*)
    -- Reopen in append mode with file of name *fname*;
    -- create file if it does not exist.
  require
    is_open: ***not*** *is_closed*;
    valid_name: *fname* /= *Void*

reopen_read (*fname*: *STRING*)
    -- Reopen in read-only mode with file of name *fname*;
    -- create file if it does not exist.
  require
    is_open: ***not*** *is_closed*;
    valid_name: *fname* /= *Void*

reopen_read_append (*fname*: *STRING*)
    -- Reopen in read and write-at-end mode with file
    -- of name *fname*; create file if it does not exist.
  require
    is_open: ***not*** *is_closed*;
    valid_name: *fname* /= *Void*

reopen_read_write (*fname*: *STRING*)
     -- Reopen in read–write mode with file of name *fname*.
     require
          is_open: **not** *is_closed*;
          valid_name: *fname* /= *Void*

reopen_write (*fname*: *STRING*)
     -- Reopen in write–only mode with file of name *fname*;
     -- create file if it does not exist.
     require
          is_open: **not** *is_closed*;
          valid_name: *fname* /= *Void*

feature -- Cursor movement

back
     -- Go back one position.
     require
          not_before: **not** *before*
     ensure
          moved_back: *position* = **old** *position* − *1*

finish
     -- Go to last position.
     require
          file_opened: **not** *is_closed*

forth
     -- Go to next position.
     require
          file_opened: **not** *is_closed*
     require else
          not_after: **not** *after*

go (*abs_position*: *INTEGER*)
     -- Go to the absolute *position*.
     -- (New position may be beyond physical length.)
     require
          file_opened: **not** *is_closed*;
          non_negative_argument: *abs_position* >= *0*

move (*offset*: *INTEGER*)
     -- Advance by *offset* from current location.
     require
          file_opened: **not** *is_closed*

next_line
     -- Move to next input line.
     require
          is_readable: *file_readable*

recede (*abs_position*: *INTEGER*)
     -- Go to the absolute *position* backwards,
     -- starting from end of file.
     require
          file_opened: **not** *is_closed*;
          non_negative_argument: *abs_position* >= *0*

start
     -- Go to first position.
     require
          file_opened: **not** *is_closed*

feature -- Element change

add_permission (*who*, *what*: *STRING*)
     -- Add read, write, execute or setuid permission
     -- for *who* ('u', 'g' or 'o') to *what*.
     require
          who_is_not_void: *who* /= *Void*;
          what_is_not_void: *what* /= *Void*;
          file_descriptor_exists: *exists*

append (*f*: *UNIX_FILE*)
     -- Append a copy of the contents of *f*.
     require
          target_is_closed: *is_closed*;
          source_is_closed: *f*.*is_closed*
     require else
          argument_not_void: *f* /= *Void*
     ensure
          new_count: *count* = **old** *count* + *f*.*count*;
     ensure then
          new_count: *count* >= **old** *count*

     -- Time stamp of last change.
     require
          file_exists: *exists*

change_group (*new_group_id*: *INTEGER*)
     -- Change group of file to *new_group_id* found in
     -- system password file.
     require
          file_exists: *exists*

change_mode (*mask*: *INTEGER*)
     -- Replace mode by *mask*.
     require
          file_exists: *exists*

change_name (*new_name*: *STRING*)
     -- Change file name to *new_name*
     require
          not_new_name_void: *new_name* /= *Void*;
          file_exists: *exists*

change_owner (*new_owner_id*: *INTEGER*)
     -- Change owner of file to *new_owner_id* found in
     -- system password file. On some systems this
     -- requires super–user privileges.
     require
          file_exists: *exists*

flush
>   -- Flush buffered data to disk.
>   -- Note that there is no guarantee that the operating
>   -- system will physically write the data to the disk.
>   -- At least it will end up in the buffer cache,
>   -- making the data visible to other processes.
>   **require**
>   *is_open*: **not** *is_closed*

link (*fn*: *STRING*)
>   -- Link current file to *fn*.
>   -- *fn* must not already exist.
>   **require**
>   *file_exists*: *exists*

new_line
>   -- Write a new line character at current position.
>   **require**
>   *extendible*: *extendible*

putbool (*b*: *BOOLEAN*)
>   -- Write ASCII value of *b* at current position.
>   **require**
>   *extendible*: *extendible*

putchar (*c*: *CHARACTER*)
>   -- Write *c* at current position.
>   **require**
>   *extendible*: *extendible*

putdouble (*d*: *DOUBLE*)
>   -- Write ASCII value *d* at current position.
>   **require**
>   *extendible*: *extendible*

putint (*i*: *INTEGER*)
>   -- Write ASCII value of *i* at current position.
>   **require**
>   *extendible*: *extendible*

putreal (*r*: *REAL*)
>   -- Write ASCII value of *r* at current position.
>   **require**
>   *extendible*: *extendible*

putstring (*s*: *STRING*)
>   -- Write *s* at current position.
>   **require**
>   *extendible*: *extendible*

remove_permission (*who*, *what*: *STRING*)
>   -- Remove read, write, execute or setuid permission
>   -- for *who* ('u', 'g' or 'o') to *what*.
>   **require**
>   *who_is_not_void*: *who* /= *Void*;
>   *what_is_not_void*: *what* /= *Void*;
>   *file_descriptor_exists*: *exists*

set_access (*time*: *INTEGER*)
>   -- Stamp with *time* (access only).
>   **require**
>   *file_exists*: *exists*
>   **ensure**
>   *acess_date_updated*: *access_date* = *time*;
>   *date_unchanged*: *date* = **old** *date*

set_date (*time*: *INTEGER*)
>   -- Stamp with *time* (modification time only).
>   **require**
>   *file_exists*: *exists*
>   **ensure**
>   *access_date_unchanged*: *access_date* = **old** *access_date*;
>   *date_updated*: *date* = *time*

stamp (*time*: *INTEGER*)
>   -- Stamp with *time* (for both access and modification).
>   **require**
>   *file_exists*: *exists*
>   **ensure**
>   *date_updated*: *date* = *time*

touch
>   -- Update time stamp (for both access and modification).
>   **require**
>   *file_exists*: *exists*
>   **ensure**
>   *date_changed*: *date* /= **old** *date*

feature -- Removal

delete
>   -- Remove link with physical file.
>   -- File does not physically disappear from the disk
>   -- until no more processes reference it.
>   -- I/O operations on it are still possible.
>   -- A directory must be empty to be deleted.
>   **require**
>   *file_exists*: *exists*

reset (*fn*: *STRING*)
>   -- Change file name to *fn* and reset
>   -- file descriptor and all information.
>   **require**
>   *fn* /= *Void*

wipe_out
>   -- Remove all items.
>   **require**
>   *is_closed*: *is_closed*

feature -- Input

readchar
    -- Read a new character from file.
    -- Make result available in *lastchar*.
    require
        is_readable: *file_readable*

readdouble
    -- Read the ASCII representation of a new double
    -- from file. Make result available in *lastdouble*.
    require
        is_readable: *file_readable*

readint
    -- Read the ASCII representation of a new integer
    -- from file. Make result available in *lastint*.
    require
        is_readable: *file_readable*

readline
    -- Read a string until new line or end of file.
    -- Make result available in *laststring*.
    -- New line will be consumed but not part of *laststring*.
    require
        is_readable: *file_readable*

readreal
    -- Read the ASCII representation of a new real
    -- from file. Make result available in *lastreal*.
    require
        is_readable: *file_readable*

readstream (*nb_char*: *INTEGER*)
    -- Read a string of at most *nb_char* bound characters
    -- or until end of file.
    -- Make result available in *laststring*.
    require
        is_readable: *file_readable*

readword
    -- Read a string, excluding white space and stripping
    -- leading white space.
    -- Make result available in *laststring*.
    -- White space characters are: blank, new_line, tab,
    -- vertical tab, formfeed, end of file.
    require
        is_readable: *file_readable*

invariant

non_negative_count: *count* >= *0*;
not_both: **not** (*after* **and** *before*);
before_constraint: *before* **implies** *off*;
after_constraint: *after* **implies** *off*

end

23.13 CLASS *UNIX_FILE_INFO*

indexing

  description: *"Internal file information"*

class interface

  UNIX_FILE_INFO

creation
  make

feature -- Initialization

  make
        -- Creation procedure

feature -- Access

        -- Date of last access

        -- Date of last status change

        -- Last modification date

  device: *INTEGER*
        -- Device number on which inode resides

  device_type: *INTEGER*
        -- Device type on which inode resides

  file_name: *STRING*
        -- File name to which information applies.

  group_id: *INTEGER*
        -- GID of the file

  group_name: *STRING*
        -- Name of the file group, if available from /etc/group.
        -- Otherwise, the GID

  inode: *INTEGER*
        -- Inode number

  links: *INTEGER*
        -- Number of links

  owner_name: *STRING*
        -- Name of the file owner, if available from /etc/passwd.
        -- Otherwise, the UID

  protection: *INTEGER*
        -- Protection mode of file (12 lower bits)

  size: *INTEGER*
        -- File size, in bytes

  type: *INTEGER*
        -- File type (4 bits, 12 lowest bits zeroed)

  user_id: *INTEGER*
        -- UID of the file owner

feature -- Status report

  is_access_executable: *BOOLEAN*
        -- Is file executable by real UID?

  is_access_owner: *BOOLEAN*
        -- Is file owned by real UID?

  is_access_readable: *BOOLEAN*
        -- Is file readable by real UID?

  is_access_writable: *BOOLEAN*
        -- Is file writable by real UID?

  is_block: *BOOLEAN*
        -- Is file a device block special file?

  is_character: *BOOLEAN*
        -- Is file a character block special file?

  is_device: *BOOLEAN*
        -- Is file a device?

  is_directory: *BOOLEAN*
        -- Is file a directory?

  is_executable: *BOOLEAN*
        -- Is file executable by effective UID?

  is_fifo: *BOOLEAN*
        -- Is file a named pipe?

  is_owner: *BOOLEAN*
        -- Is file owned by effective UID?

  is_plain: *BOOLEAN*
        -- Is file a plain file?

  is_readable: *BOOLEAN*
        -- Is file readable by effective UID?

  is_setgid: *BOOLEAN*
        -- Is file setgid?

  is_setuid: *BOOLEAN*
        -- Is file setuid?

  is_socket: *BOOLEAN*
        -- Is file a named socket?

  is_sticky: *BOOLEAN*
        -- Is file sticky?

  is_symlink: *BOOLEAN*
        -- Is file a symbolic link?

  is_writable: *BOOLEAN*
        -- Is file writable by effective UID?

feature -- Element change

  update (*f_name*: *STRING*)
        -- Update information buffer: fill it in with information
        -- from the inode of *f_name*.

end

23.14 CLASS *UNIX_STD*

UNIX_STD inherits from *STD_FILES*. The interface only shows the features introduced in *UNIX_STD*, and does not include any feature inherited directly or indirectly.

For the interface of STD_FILES see 23.16, page 457.

indexing

  description: "*Commonly used Unix input and output
    mechanisms. This class may be used as ancestor by classes
    needing its facilities.*"

class interface

  UNIX_STD   .

creation
  make_open_stdin,
  make_open_stdout,
  make_open_stderr

feature -- Initialization

  make_open_stderr (fn: *STRING)*
      -- Create an unix standard error file.

  make_open_stdin (fn: *STRING)*
      -- Create an unix standard input file.
    require
      string_exists: *fn* /= *Void*

  make_open_stdout (fn: *STRING)*
      -- Create an unix standard output file.
    require
      string_exists: *fn* /= *Void*

end

23.15 CLASS *DIRECTORY*

indexing

> description: *"Directories, in the Unix sense, with creation*
> *and exploration features"*

class interface

> *DIRECTORY*

creation
> *make,*
> *make_open_read*

feature -- Initialization

create
> -- Create a physical directory.
> **require**
> *physical_not_exists*: **not** *exists*

make (*dn*: *STRING*)
> -- Create directory object for the directory
> -- of name *dn*.
> **require**
> *string_exists*: *dn* /= *Void*

make_open_read (*dn*: *STRING*)
> -- Create directory object for the directory
> -- of name *dn* and open it for reading.
> **require**
> *string_exists*: *dn* /= *Void*

feature -- Access

close
> -- Close directory.
> **require**
> *is_open*: **not** *is_closed*

has_entry (*entry_name*: *STRING*): *BOOLEAN*
> -- Has directory the entry *entry_name*?
> -- The use of *dir_temp* is required not
> -- to change the position in the current
> -- directory entries list.
> **require**
> *string_exists*: *entry_name* /= *Void*

name: *STRING*
> -- Directory name

open_read
> -- Open directory *name* for reading.

readentry
> -- Read next directory entry;
> -- make result available in *lastentry*.
> -- Make result void if all entries have been read.
> **require**
> *is_opened*: **not** *is_closed*

start
> -- Go to first entry of directory.
> **require**
> *is_opened*: **not** *is_closed*

feature -- Measurement

count: *INTEGER*
> -- Number of entries in directory.

feature -- Status report

exists: *BOOLEAN*
> -- Does the directory exist?

is_closed: *BOOLEAN*
> -- Is current directory closed?

lastentry: *STRING*
> -- Last entry read by *readentry*

feature -- Conversion

linear_representation: *ARRAYED_LIST* [*STRING*]
> -- The entries, in sequential format.

end

23.16 CLASS *STD_FILES*

indexing

> *description*: "*Commonly used input and output mechanisms. This class may be used as either ancestor or supplier by classes needing its facilities.*"

class interface

> STD_FILES

feature -- Access

> *default_output*: *UNIX_FILE*
> -- Default output.

> *error*: *UNIX_FILE*
> -- Standard error file

> *input*: *UNIX_FILE*
> -- Standard input file

> *output*: *UNIX_FILE*
> -- Standard output file

> *standard_default*: *UNIX_FILE*
> -- Return the *default_output* or *output*
> -- if *default_output* is Void.

feature -- Status report

> *lastchar*: *CHARACTER*
> -- Last character read by readchar

> *lastdouble*: *DOUBLE*

> *lastint*: *INTEGER*
> -- Last integer read by readint

> *lastreal*: *REAL*
> -- Last real read by readreal

> *laststring*: *STRING*
> -- Last string read by readline,
> -- readstream, or readword

feature -- Element change

> *new_line*
> -- Write line feed at end of default output.

> *putbool* (*b*: *BOOLEAN*)
> -- Write *b* at end of default output.

> *putchar* (*c*: *CHARACTER*)
> -- Write *c* at end of default output.

> *putdouble* (*d*: *DOUBLE*)
> -- Write *d* at end of default output.

> *putint* (*i*: *INTEGER*)
> -- Write *i* at end of default output.

> *putreal* (*r*: *REAL*)
> -- Write *r* at end of default output.

> *putstring* (*s*: *STRING*)
> -- Write *s* at end of default output.
> **require**
> *s* /= *Void*

> *set_error_default*
> -- Use standard error as default output.

> *set_output_default*
> -- Use standard output as default output.

feature -- Input

> *next_line*
> -- Move to next input line on standard input.

> *readchar*
> -- Read a new character from standard input.
> -- Make result available in *lastchar*.

> *readdouble*
> -- Read a new double from standard input.
> -- Make result available in *lastdouble*.

> *readint*
> -- Read a new integer from standard input.
> -- Make result available in *lastint*.

> *readline*
> -- Read a line from standard input.
> -- Make result available in *laststring*.

> *readreal*
> -- Read a new real from standard input.
> -- Make result available in *lastreal*.

> *readstream* (*nb_char*: *INTEGER*)
> -- Read a string of at most *nb_char* bound characters
> -- from standard input.
> -- Make result available in *laststring*.

> *readword*
> -- Read a new word from standard input.
> -- Make result available in *laststring*.

end

23.17 CLASS *STORABLE*

indexing

> *description*: "*Objects that may be stored and retrieved along with all their dependents. This class may be used as ancestor by classes needing its facilities.*"

class interface

> *STORABLE*

feature -- Access

> *retrieved* (*file*: *UNIX_FILE*): *STORABLE*
>> -- Retrieved object structure, from external
>> -- representation previously stored in *file*.
>> -- To access resulting object under correct type,
>> -- use assignment attempt.
>> -- Will raise an exception (code *Retrieve_exception*)
>> -- if file content is not a *STORABLE* structure.
>
>> *require*
>>> *file_not_void*: *file* /= *Void*;
>>> *file_exists*: *file.exists*;
>>> *file_is_open_read*: *file.is_open_read*
>
>> *ensure*
>>> *result_exists*: *Result* /= *Void*

feature -- Element change

> *basic_store* (*file*: *UNIX_FILE*)
>> -- Produce on *file* an external representation of the
>> -- entire object structure reachable from current object.
>> -- Retrievable within current system only.
>
>> *require*
>>> *file_not_void*: *file* /= *Void*;
>>> *file_exists*: *file.exists*;
>>> *file_is_open_write*: *file.is_open_write*

> *general_store* (*file*: *UNIX_FILE*)
>> -- Produce on *file* an external representation of the
>> -- entire object structure reachable from current object.
>> -- Retrievable from other systems for same platform
>> -- (machine architecture).
>
>> *require*
>>> *file_not_void*: *file* /= *Void*;
>>> *file_exists*: *file.exists*;
>>> *file_is_open_write*: *file.is_open_write*

end

23.18 CLASS *EXCEPTIONS*

EXCEPTIONS inherits from *EXCEP_CONST*, which defines the codes for common exceptions. The interface of *EXCEPTIONS* shows the features of both classes.

indexing

> *description*: *"Facilities for adapting the exception handling mechanism. This class may be used as ancestor by classes needing its facilities."*

class interface

EXCEPTIONS

feature -- Access

Check_instruction: *INTEGER* **is** *7*
    -- Exception code for violated check
    -- (From *EXCEP_CONST*.)

Class_invariant: *INTEGER* **is** *6*
    -- Exception code for violated class invariant
    -- (From *EXCEP_CONST*.)

Developer_exception: *INTEGER* **is** *24*
    -- Exception code for developer exception
    -- (From *EXCEP_CONST*.)

External_exception: *INTEGER* **is** *18*
    -- Exception code for operating system error
    -- which does not set the *errno* variable
    -- (Unix–specific)
    -- (From *EXCEP_CONST*.)

Floating_point_exception: *INTEGER* **is** *5*
    -- Exception code for floating point exception
    -- (From *EXCEP_CONST*.)

Incorrect_inspect_value: *INTEGER* **is** *9*
    -- Exception code for inspect value which is not one
    -- of the inspect constants, if there is no Else_part
    -- (From *EXCEP_CONST*.)

Io_exception: *INTEGER* **is** *21*
    -- Exception code for I/O error
    -- (From *EXCEP_CONST*.)

Loop_invariant: *INTEGER* **is** *11*
    -- Exception code for violated loop invariant
    -- (From *EXCEP_CONST*.)

Loop_variant: *INTEGER* **is** *10*
    -- Exception code for non–decreased loop variant
    -- (From *EXCEP_CONST*.)

No_more_memory: *INTEGER* **is** *2*
    -- Exception code for failed memory allocation
    -- (From *EXCEP_CONST*.)

Operating_system_exception: *INTEGER* **is** *22*
    -- Exception code for operating system error
    -- which sets the *errno* variable
    -- (Unix–specific)
    -- (From *EXCEP_CONST*.)

Postcondition: *INTEGER* **is** *4*
    -- Exception code for violated postcondition
    -- (From *EXCEP_CONST*.)

Precondition: *INTEGER* **is** *3*
    -- Exception code for violated precondition
    -- (From *EXCEP_CONST*.)

Rescue_exception: *INTEGER* **is** *14*
    -- Exception code for exception in rescue clause
    -- (From *EXCEP_CONST*.)

Retrieve_exception: *INTEGER* **is** *23*
    -- Exception code for retrieval error;
    -- may be raised by *retrieved* in *STORABLE*.
    -- (From *EXCEP_CONST*.)

Routine_failure: *INTEGER* **is** *8*
    -- Exception code for failed routine
    -- (From *EXCEP_CONST*.)

Signal_exception: *INTEGER* **is** *12*
    -- Exception code for operating system signal
    -- (From *EXCEP_CONST*.)

Void_assigned_to_expanded: *INTEGER* **is** *19*
    -- Exception code for assignment of void value
    -- to expanded entity
    -- (From *EXCEP_CONST*.)

Void_call_target: *INTEGER* **is** *1*
    -- Exception code for feature applied to void reference
    -- (From *EXCEP_CONST*.)

feature -- Status report

assertion_violation: *BOOLEAN*
    -- Is last exception originally due to a violated
    -- assertion or non–decreasing variant?

class_name: *STRING*
    -- Name of the class that includes the recipient
    -- of original form of last exception

developer_exception_name: *STRING*
    -- Name of last developer–raised exception

exception: *INTEGER*
    -- Code of last exception that occurred

is_developer_exception: *BOOLEAN*
    -- Is the last exception originally due to
    -- a developer exception?

is_developer_exception_of_name (*name*: *STRING*):
BOOLEAN
    -- Is the last exception originally due to a developer
    -- exception of name *name*?

is_signal: *BOOLEAN*
    -- Is last exception originally due to an external
    -- event (operating system signal)?

is_system_exception: *BOOLEAN*
    -- Is last exception originally due to an
    -- external event (operating system error)?

meaning (*except*: *INTEGER*): *STRING*
    -- A message in English describing what *except* is

original_class_name: *STRING*
    -- Name of the class that includes the recipient
    -- of original form of last exception

original_exception: *INTEGER*
    -- Original code of last exception that triggered
    -- current exception

original_recipient_name: *STRING*
    -- Name of the routine whose execution was
    -- interrupted by original form of last exception

original_tag_name: *STRING*
    -- Assertion tag for original form of last
    -- assertion violation.

recipient_name: *STRING*
    -- Name of the routine whose execution was
    -- interrupted by last exception

tag_name: *STRING*
    -- Tag of last violated asssertion clause

feature -- Status setting

catch (*code*: *INTEGER*)
    -- Make sure that any exception of code *code* will be
    -- caught. This is the default.

ignore (*code*: *INTEGER*)
    -- Make sure that any exception of code *code* will be
    -- ignored. This is not the default.

message_on_failure
    -- Print an exception history table
    -- in case of failure.
    -- This is the default.

no_message_on_failure
    -- Do not print an exception history table
    -- in case of failure.

raise (*name*: *STRING*)
    -- Raise a developer exception of name *name*.

end

23.19 CLASS *UNIX_SIGNALS*

indexing

> *description*: "Constants used for signal handling. This class
> may be used as ancestor by classes needing its facilities."

class interface

UNIX_SIGNALS

feature -- Access

is_defined (sig: INTEGER): BOOLEAN
-- Is *sig* a signal defined for this platform?

is_ignored (sig: INTEGER): BOOLEAN
-- Is *sig* currently set to be ignored?

meaning (sig: INTEGER): STRING
-- A message in English describing what *sig* is

Sigabrt: INTEGER
-- Code for "Abort" signal

Sigalrm: INTEGER
-- Code for "Alarm clock" signal

Sigbus: INTEGER
-- Code for "Bus error" signal

Sigchld: INTEGER
-- Code for "Death of a child" signal.
-- Signal ignored by default

Sigcld: INTEGER
-- Code for "Death of a child" signal.
-- Signal ignored by default

Sigcont: INTEGER
-- Code for "Continue after stop" signal.
-- Signal ignored by default

Sigemt: INTEGER
-- Code for "EMT instruction" signal

Sigfpe: INTEGER
-- Code for "Floating point exception" signal

Sighup: INTEGER
-- Code for "Hangup" signal

Sigill: INTEGER
-- Code for "Illegal instruction" signal

Sigint: INTEGER
-- Code for "Interrupt" signal

Sigio: INTEGER
-- Code for "Pending I/O on a descriptor" signal.
-- Signal ignored by default

Sigiot: INTEGER
-- Code for "IOT instruction" signal

Sigkill: INTEGER
-- Code for "Terminator" signal

Siglost: INTEGER
-- Code for "Resource lost" signal

Sigphone: INTEGER
-- Code for "Line status change" signal

Sigpipe: INTEGER
-- Code for "Broken pipe" signal

Sigpoll: INTEGER
-- Code for "Selectable event pending" signal

Sigprof: INTEGER
-- Code for "Profiling timer alarm" signal

Sigpwr: INTEGER
-- Code for "Power-fail" signal

Sigquit: INTEGER
-- Code for "Quit" signal

Sigsegv: INTEGER
-- Code for "Segmentation violation" signal

Sigstop: INTEGER
-- Code for "Stop" signal

Sigsys: INTEGER
-- Code for "Bad argument to system call" signal

Sigterm: INTEGER
-- Code for "Software termination" signal

Sigtrap: INTEGER
-- Code for "Trace trap" signal

Sigtstp: INTEGER
-- Code for "Stop from tty" signal

Sigttin: INTEGER
-- Code for "Tty input from background" signal.
-- Signal ignored by default

Sigttou: INTEGER
-- Code for "Tty output from background" signal.
-- Signal ignored by default

Sigurg: INTEGER
-- Code for "Urgent condition on socket" signal.
-- Signal ignored by default

Sigusr1: INTEGER
-- Code for "User-defined signal #1"

Sigusr2: *INTEGER*
-- Code for "User–defined signal #2"

Sigvtalarm: *INTEGER*
-- Code for "Virtual time alarm" signal

Sigwinch: *INTEGER*
-- Code for "Window size changed" signal.
-- Signal ignored by default

Sigwind: *INTEGER*
-- Code for "Window change" signal

Sigxcpu: *INTEGER*
-- Code for "Cpu time limit exceeded" signal

Sigxfsz: *INTEGER*
-- Code for "File size limit exceeded" signal

feature -- Status report

signal: *INTEGER*
-- Code of last signal

feature -- Status setting

catch (*sig*: *INTEGER*)
-- Make sure that future occurrences of *sig*
-- will be treated as exceptions.
-- (This is the default for all signals.)
-- No effect if signal not defined.

ignore (*sig*: *INTEGER*)
-- Make sure that future occurrences of *sig*
-- will be ignored. (This is not the default.)
-- No effect if signal not defined.

reset_all_default
-- Make sure that all exceptions will lead to their
-- default handling.

reset_default (*sig*: *INTEGER*)
-- Make sure that exception of code code will lead
-- to its default action.
    require
        is_defined (*sig*)

end

23.20 CLASS *MEMORY*

indexing

> *description*: *"Facilities for tuning up the garbage collection mechanism. This class may be used as ancestor by classes needing its facilities."*

class interface

> MEMORY

feature -- Access

> *C_memory*: *INTEGER* **is** *2*
>   -- Code for the C memory managed
>   -- by the garbage collector
>   -- (From *MEM_CONST*.)

> *Eiffel_memory*: *INTEGER* **is** *1*
>   -- Code for the Eiffel memory managed
>   -- by the garbage collector
>   -- (From *MEM_CONST*.)

> *Full_collector*: *INTEGER* **is** *0*
>   -- Statistics for full collections
>   -- (From *MEM_CONST*.)

> *Incremental_collector*: *INTEGER* **is** *1*
>   -- Statistics for incremental collections
>   -- (From *MEM_CONST*.)

> *Total_memory*: *INTEGER* **is** *0*
>   -- Code for all the memory managed
>   -- by the garbage collector
>   -- (From *MEM_CONST*.)

feature -- Measurement

> *gc_statistics* (*collector_type*: *INTEGER*): *GC_INFO*
>   -- Garbage collector information for *collector_type*.
>   **require**
>   *type_ok*: *collector_type* = *full_collector* **or** *collector_
>   type* = *incremental_collector*

> *memory_statistics* (*memory_type*: *INTEGER*): *MEM_INFO*
>   -- Memory usage information for *memory_type*
>   **require**
>   *type_ok*: *memory_type* = *total_memory* **or** *memory_type*
>   = *eiffel_memory* **or** *memory_type* = *c_memory*

feature -- Status report

> *collecting*: *BOOLEAN*
>   -- Is the garbage collector running?

> *collection_period*: *INTEGER*
>   -- Period of full collection.

> *largest_coalesced_block*: *INTEGER*
>   -- Size of largest coalesced block since last call to
>   -- *largest_coalesced*; 0 if none.

> *memory_threshold*: *INTEGER*
>   -- Minimum amount of bytes to be allocated before
>   -- starting an automatic garbage collection.

feature -- Status setting

> *allocate_compact*
>   -- Enter "memory" mode: will try to compact memory
>   -- before requesting more from the operating system.

> *allocate_fast*
>   -- Enter "speed" mode: will optimize speed of memory
>   -- allocation rather than memory usage.

> *allocate_tiny*
>   -- Enter "tiny" mode: will enter "memory" mode
>   -- after having freed as much memory as possible.

> *collection_off*
>   -- Disable the garbage collector.

> *collection_on*
>   -- Enable the garbage collector.

> *disable_time_accounting*
>   -- Disable GC time accounting (default).

> *enable_time_accounting*
>   -- Enable GC time accouting, accessible in *gc_statistics*.

> *set_collection_period* (*value*: *INTEGER*)
>   -- Set *collection_period*.
>   **require**
>   *positive_value*: *value* > *0*

> *set_memory_threshold* (*value*: *INTEGER*)
>   -- Set a new *memory_threshold*.
>   **require**
>   *positive_value*: *value* > *0*

feature -- Removal

> *collect*
>   -- Force a partial collection cycle if the garbage
>   -- collector is enabled; do nothing otherwise.

> *dispose*
>   -- Action to be executed just before the garbage collector
>   -- reclaims an object.
>   -- Default version does nothing; redefine in descendants
>   -- to perform specific dispose actions. Those actions
>   -- should only take care of freeing external resources;
>   -- they should not perform remote calls on other objects
>   -- since these may also be dead and reclaimed.

free (*object*: *ANY*)
> -- Free *object*, by−passing the garbage collector.
> -- Erratic behavior will result if the object is still
> -- referenced.

full_coalesce
> -- Coalesce the whole memory: merge adjacent free
> -- blocks to reduce fragmentation.

full_collect
> -- Force a full collection cycle if the garbage
> -- collector is enabled; do nothing otherwise.

mem_free (*addr*: *ANY*)
> -- Free memory of object at *addr*.
> -- (Preferred interface is *free*.)

end

23.21 CLASS *MEM_INFO*

indexing

   description: *"Properties of the memory management
      mechanism. This class may be used as ancestor by classes
      needing its facilities."*

class interface

   MEM_INFO

creation
   make

feature -- Initialization

   make (*memory*: *INTEGER*)
         -- Update Current for *memory* type.
      ensure
         type_updated: *type* = *memory*

   update (*memory*: *INTEGER*)
         -- Update Current for *memory* type.
      ensure
         type_updated: *type* = *memory*

feature -- Access

   C_memory: *INTEGER* **is** 2
         -- Code for the C memory managed
         -- by the garbage collector
         -- (From *MEM_CONST*.)

   Eiffel_memory: *INTEGER* **is** 1
         -- Code for the Eiffel memory managed
         -- by the garbage collector
         -- (From *MEM_CONST*.)

   Full_collector: *INTEGER* **is** 0
         -- Statistics for full collections
         -- (From *MEM_CONST*.)

   Incremental_collector: *INTEGER* **is** 1
         -- Statistics for incremental collections
         -- (From *MEM_CONST*.)

   Total_memory: *INTEGER* **is** 0
         -- Code for all the memory managed
         -- by the garbage collector
         -- (From *MEM_CONST*.)

   type: *INTEGER*
         -- Memory type (Total, Eiffel, C)

feature -- Measurement

   free: *INTEGER*
         -- Number of bytes still free for *type*
         -- before last call to *update*
      ensure
         computed: *Result* = *total* − *used* − *overhead*

   overhead: *INTEGER*
         -- Number of bytes used by memory management
         -- scheme for *type* before last call to *update*

   total: *INTEGER*
         -- Total number of bytes allocated for *type*
         -- before last call to *update*

   used: *INTEGER*
         -- Number of bytes used for *type*
         -- before last call to *update*

invariant

   consistent_memory: *total* = *free* + *used* + *overhead*

end

23.22 CLASS *GC_INFO*

indexing

   description: "*Garbage collector statistics.This class may be
   used as ancestor by classes needing its facilities.Time
   accounting is relevant only if 'enable_time_accounting'
   (from MEMORY) has been called.*"

class interface

   GC_INFO

creation
   make

feature -- Initialization

   make (*memory*: *INTEGER*)
      -- Fill in statistics for *memory* type

   update (*memory*: *INTEGER*)
      -- Fill in statistics for *memory* type

feature -- Access

   C_memory: *INTEGER* **is** 2
      -- Code for the C memory managed
      -- by the garbage collector
      -- (From *MEM_CONST.*)

   collected: *INTEGER*
      -- Number of bytes collected by the last cycle,
      -- for *type* before last call to *update*

   collected_average: *INTEGER*
      -- Average number of bytes collected by a cycle,
      -- for *type* before last call to *update*

   cpu_interval_time: *DOUBLE*
      -- Amount of CPU time elapsed since between last
      -- and penultimate cycles for *type* before
      -- last call to *update*

   cpu_interval_time_average: *DOUBLE*
      -- Average amount of CPU time between two cycles,
      -- for *type* before last call to *update*

   cpu_time: *DOUBLE*
      -- Amount of CPU time, in seconds, spent in cycle,
      -- for *type* before last call to *update*

   cpu_time_average: *DOUBLE*
      -- Average amount of CPU time spent in cycle,
      -- in seconds, for *type* before last call to *update*

   cycle_count: *INTEGER*
      -- Number of collection cycles for *type*
      -- before last call to *update*

   Eiffel_memory: *INTEGER* **is** 1
      -- Code for the Eiffel memory managed
      -- by the garbage collector
      -- (From *MEM_CONST.*)

   Full_collector: *INTEGER* **is** 0
      -- Statistics for full collections
      -- (From *MEM_CONST.*)

   Incremental_collector: *INTEGER* **is** 1
      -- Statistics for incremental collections
      -- (From *MEM_CONST.*)

   memory_used: *INTEGER*
      -- Total number of bytes used (counting overhead)
      -- after last cycle for *type* before last
      -- call to *update*

   real_interval_time: *INTEGER*
      -- Real interval time (as opposed to CPU time) between
      -- two automatically raised cycles, in centi−seconds,
      -- for *type* before last call to *update*

   real_interval_time_average: *INTEGER*
      -- Average real interval time between two automatic
      -- cycles, in centi−seconds,
      -- for *type* before last call to *update*

   real_time: *INTEGER*
      -- Real time in centi−seconds used by last cycle
      -- for *type*, before last call to *update*;
      -- this may not be accurate on systems which do not
      -- provide a sub−second accuracy clock (typically
      -- provided on BSD).

   real_time_average: *INTEGER*
      -- Average amount of real time, in centi−seconds,
      -- spent in collection cycle,
      -- for *type* before last call to *update*

   sys_interval_time: *DOUBLE*
      -- Amount of kernel time elapsed since between
      -- the last and the penultimate cycle,
      -- for *type* before last call to *update*

   sys_interval_time_average: *DOUBLE*
      -- Average amount of kernel time between two cycles,
      -- for *type* before last call to *update*

   sys_time: *DOUBLE*
      -- Amount of kernel time, in seconds, spent in cycle,
      -- for *type* before last call to *update*

   sys_time_average: *DOUBLE*
      -- Average amount of kernel time spent in cycle,
      -- for *type* before last call to *update*

   Total_memory: *INTEGER* **is** 0
      -- Code for all the memory managed
      -- by the garbage collector
      -- (From *MEM_CONST.*)

   type: *INTEGER*
      -- Collector type (Full, Collect),
      -- for *type* before last call to *update*

end

23.23 CLASS *ARGUMENTS*

indexing

　description: *"Access to command-line arguments."*

class interface

　ARGUMENTS

feature -- Access

　argument (*i*: *INTEGER*): *STRING*
　　　-- Command line argument number *i*
　　　-- (the command name if *i* = 0)
　　require
　　　0 <= *i*;
　　　i <= *argument_count*

　command_name: *STRING*
　　　-- Name of command that started application

feature -- Measurement

　argument_count: *INTEGER*
　　　-- Number of arguments on the command line
　　　-- (not including command name)

end

23.24 CLASS *INTERNAL*

indexing

> description: "*Access to internal object properties. This class may be used as ancestor by classes needing its facilities.*"

class interface

> *INTERNAL*

feature -- Access

> *Bit_type*: *INTEGER* **is** *8*
>
> *boolean_field* (*i*: *INTEGER*; *object*: *ANY*): *BOOLEAN*
> -- Boolean value of *i*–th field of *object*
> **require**
> *object_not_void*: *object* /= *Void*;
> *index_large_enough*: *i* >= *1*;
> *index_small_enough*: *i* <= *field_count* (*object*);
> *boolean_field*: *field_type* (*i*, *object*) = *boolean_type*
>
> *Boolean_type*: *INTEGER* **is** +
>
> *character_field* (*i*: *INTEGER*; *object*: *ANY*): *CHARACTER*
> -- Character value of *i*–th field of *object*
> **require**
> *object_not_void*: *object* /= *Void*;
> *index_large_enough*: *i* >= *1*;
> *index_small_enough*: *i* <= *field_count* (*object*);
> *character_field*: *field_type* (*i*, *object*) = *character_type*
>
> *Character_type*: *INTEGER* **is** *2*
>
> *class_name* (*object*: *ANY*): *STRING*
> -- Name of the class associated with *object*
> **require**
> *object_not_void*: *object* /= *Void*
>
> *double_field* (*i*: *INTEGER*; *object*: *ANY*): *DOUBLE*
> -- Double precision value of *i*–th field of *object*
> **require**
> *object_not_void*: *object* /= *Void*;
> *index_large_enough*: *i* >= *1*;
> *index_small_enough*: *i* <= *field_count* (*object*);
> *double_field*: *field_type* (*i*, *object*) = *double_type*
>
> *Double_type*: *INTEGER* **is** *6*
>
> *dynamic_type* (*object*: *ANY*): *INTEGER*
> -- Dynamic type of *object*
> **require**
> *object_not_void*: *object* /= *Void*

> *expanded_field_type* (*i*: *INTEGER*; *object*: *ANY*): *STRING*
> -- Class name associated with the *i*–th
> -- expanded field of *object*
> **require**
> *object_not_void*: *object* /= *Void*;
> *index_large_enough*: *i* >= *1*;
> *index_small_enough*: *i* <= *field_count* (*object*);
> *is_expanded*: *field_type* (*i*, *object*) = *expanded_type*
> **ensure**
> *result_exists*: *Result* /= *Void*
>
> *Expanded_type*: *INTEGER* **is** *7*
>
> *field* (*i*: *INTEGER*; *object*: *ANY*): *ANY*
> -- Object attached to the *i*–th field of *object*
> -- (directly or through a reference)
> **require**
> *object_not_void*: *object* /= *Void*;
> *index_large_enough*: *i* >= *1*;
> *index_small_enough*: *i* <= *field_count* (*object*);
> *not_special*: **not** *is_special* (*object*)
>
> *field_name* (*i*: *INTEGER*; *object*: *ANY*): *STRING*
> -- Name of *i*–th field of *object*
> **require**
> *object_not_void*: *object* /= *Void*;
> *index_large_enough*: *i* >= *1*;
> *index_small_enough*: *i* <= *field_count* (*object*);
> *not_special*: **not** *is_special* (*object*)
> **ensure**
> *result_exists*: *Result* /= *Void*
>
> *field_offset* (*i*: *INTEGER*; *object*: *ANY*): *INTEGER*
> -- Offset of *i*–th field of *object*
> **require**
> *object_not_void*: *object* /= *Void*;
> *index_large_enough*: *i* >= *1*;
> *index_small_enough*: *i* <= *field_count* (*object*);
> *not_special*: **not** *is_special* (*object*)
>
> *field_type* (*i*: *INTEGER*; *object*: *ANY*): *INTEGER*
> -- Type of *i*–th field of *object*
> **require**
> *object_not_void*: *object* /= *Void*;
> *index_large_enough*: *i* >= *1*;
> *index_small_enough*: *i* <= *field_count* (*object*)
>
> *integer_field* (*i*: *INTEGER*; *object*: *ANY*): *INTEGER*
> -- Integer value of *i*–th field of *object*
> **require**
> *object_not_void*: *object* /= *Void*;
> *index_large_enough*: *i* >= *1*;
> *index_small_enough*: *i* <= *field_count* (*object*);
> *integer_field*: *field_type* (*i*, *object*) = *integer_type*

Integer_type: *INTEGER* **is** *4*

is_special (*object*: *ANY*): *BOOLEAN*
    -- Is *object* a special object?
  require
    object_not_void: *object* /= *Void*

pointer_field (*i*: *INTEGER*; *object*: *ANY*): *POINTER*
    -- Pointer value of *i*–th field of *object*
  require
    object_not_void: *object* /= *Void*;
    index_large_enough: *i* >= *1*;
    index_small_enough: *i* <= *field_count* (*object*);
    pointer_field: *field_type* (*i*, *object*) = *pointer_type*

Pointer_type: *INTEGER* **is** *0*

real_field (*i*: *INTEGER*; *object*: *ANY*): *REAL*
    -- Real value of *i*–th field of *object*
  require
    object_not_void: *object* /= *Void*;
    index_large_enough: *i* >= *1*;
    index_small_enough: *i* <= *field_count* (*object*);
    real_field: *field_type* (*i*, *object*) = *real_type*

Real_type: *INTEGER* **is** *5*

Reference_type: *INTEGER* **is** *1*

feature -- Measurement

bit_size (*i*: *INTEGER*; *object*: *ANY*): *INTEGER*
    -- Size (in bit) of the *i*–th bit field of *object*
  require
    object_not_void: *object* /= *Void*;
    index_large_enough: *i* >= *1*;
    index_small_enough: *i* <= *field_count* (*object*);
    is_bit: *field_type* (*i*, *object*) = *bit_type*
  ensure
    positive_result: *Result* > *0*

field_count (*object*: *ANY*): *INTEGER*
    -- Number of logical fields in *object*
  require
    object_not_void: *object* /= *Void*

physical_size (*object*: *ANY*): *INTEGER*
    -- Space occupied by *object* in bytes
  require
    object_not_void: *object* /= *Void*

end

23.25 CLASS *BOOLEAN*

indexing

description: *"Truth values, with the boolean operations"*

expanded class interface

BOOLEAN

feature -- Basic operations

  infix *"and"* (*other*: *BOOLEAN*): *BOOLEAN*
    -- Boolean conjunction with *other*
  require
    other_exists: *other* /= *Void*

  infix *"and then"* (*other*: *BOOLEAN*): *BOOLEAN*
    -- Boolean semi−strict conjunction with *other*
  require
    other_exists: *other* /= *Void*

  infix *"implies"* (*other*: *BOOLEAN*): *BOOLEAN*
    -- Boolean implication of *other*
    -- (semi−strict)
  require
    other_exists: *other* /= *Void*

  prefix *"not"*: *BOOLEAN*
    -- Negation.

  infix *"or"* (*other*: *BOOLEAN*): *BOOLEAN*
    -- Boolean disjunction with *other*
  require
    other_exists: *other* /= *Void*

  infix *"or else"* (*other*: *BOOLEAN*): *BOOLEAN*
    -- Boolean semi−strict disjunction with *other*
  require
    other_exists: *other* /= *Void*

  infix *"xor"* (*other*: *BOOLEAN*): *BOOLEAN*
    -- Boolean exclusive or with *other*
  require
    other_exists: *other* /= *Void*

feature -- Output

  out: *STRING*
    -- Printable representation of boolean.
    -- (From *BOOLEAN_REF.*)

end

23.26 CLASS *CHARACTER*

indexing

> *description*: "*Characters, with comparison operations and an ASCII code*"

expanded class interface

> *CHARACTER*

feature -- Access

> *code*: *INTEGER*
> > -- Associated integer value

> *item*: *CHARACTER*
> > -- Character value
> > -- (From *CHARACTER_REF*.)

feature -- Comparison

> *infix* "<" (*other*: *CHARACTER*): *BOOLEAN*
> > -- Is *other* greater than current character?
> > *require*
> > *other_exists*: *other* /= *Void*
> > *ensure*
> > *smaller*: *Result* **implies not** (*Current* >= *other*)

> *infix* ">=" (*other*: **like** *Current*): *BOOLEAN*
> > -- Is current object greater than or equal to *other*?
> > -- (From *COMPARABLE*.)
> > *ensure*
> > *equals_larger*: *Result* **implies not** (*Current* < *other*)

> *infix* ">" (*other*: **like** *Current*): *BOOLEAN*
> > -- Is current object greater than *other*?
> > -- (From *COMPARABLE*.)
> > *ensure*
> > *larger*: *Result* **implies not** (*Current* <= *other*)

> *infix* "<=" (*other*: **like** *Current*): *BOOLEAN*
> > -- Is current object less than or equal to *other*?
> > -- (From *COMPARABLE*.)
> > *ensure*
> > *equals_smaller*: *Result* **implies not** (*Current* > *other*)

feature -- Output

> *out*: *STRING*
> > -- Printable representation of character.
> > -- (From *CHARACTER_REF*.)

end

23.27 CLASS *INTEGER*

indexing

　description: "Integer values"

expanded class interface

　INTEGER

feature -- Access

　hash_code: *INTEGER*
　　　-- Hash code value
　　　-- (From *INTEGER_REF*.)
　　require
　　　is_hashable
　　ensure
　　　valid_hash_value: *Result* >= *0*

feature -- Comparison

　infix "<" (*other*: *INTEGER*): *BOOLEAN*
　　　-- Is *other* greater than current integer?
　　require
　　　other_exists: *other* /= *Void*
　　ensure
　　　smaller: *Result* **implies not** (*Current* >= *other*)

　infix ">=" (*other*: **like** *Current*): *BOOLEAN*
　　　-- Is current object greater than or equal to *other*?
　　　-- (From *COMPARABLE*.)
　　ensure
　　　equals_larger: *Result* **implies not** (*Current* < *other*)

　infix ">" (*other*: **like** *Current*): *BOOLEAN*
　　　-- Is current object greater than *other*?
　　　-- (From *COMPARABLE*.)
　　ensure
　　　larger: *Result* **implies not** (*Current* <= *other*)

　infix "<=" (*other*: **like** *Current*): *BOOLEAN*
　　　-- Is current object less than or equal to *other*?
　　　-- (From *COMPARABLE*.)
　　ensure
　　　equals_smaller: *Result* **implies not** (*Current* > *other*)

feature -- Status report

　is_hashable: *BOOLEAN*
　　　-- May current object be hashed?
　　　-- (Answer: if and only if it is not the default value of
　　　-- its type)
　　　-- (From *HASHABLE*.)
　　ensure
　　　Result = (*Current* /= *default*)

feature -- Basic operations

　infix "*" (*other*: *INTEGER*): *INTEGER*
　　　-- Product by *other*
　　require
　　　other_exists: *other* /= *Void*

　prefix "+": *INTEGER*
　　　-- Unary plus

　infix "+" (*other*: *INTEGER*): *INTEGER*
　　　-- Sum with *other*
　　require
　　　other_exists: *other* /= *Void*

　prefix "-": *INTEGER*
　　　-- Unary minus

　infix "-" (*other*: *INTEGER*): *INTEGER*
　　　-- Result of subtractiing *other*
　　require
　　　other_exists: *other* /= *Void*

　infix "/" (*other*: *INTEGER*): *REAL*
　　　-- Division by *other*
　　require
　　　good_divisor: *other* /= *0*

　infix "//" (*other*: *INTEGER*): *INTEGER*
　　　-- Integer division of Current by *other*
　　require
　　　other_exists: *other* /= *Void*

　infix "\\" (*other*: *INTEGER*): *INTEGER*
　　　-- Remainder of the integer division of Current by *other*
　　require
　　　other_exists: *other* /= *Void*

　infix "^" (*other*: *INTEGER*): *INTEGER*
　　　-- Integer power of Current by *other*
　　require
　　　other_exists: *other* /= *Void*

feature -- Output

　out: *STRING*
　　　-- Printable representation of current object.
　　　-- (From *INTEGER_REF*.)

end

23.28 CLASSES *REAL* AND *DOUBLE*

Classes *REAL* and *DOUBLE* describe floating point numbers. Their interface is the same with the exception of some feature signatures, which involve arguments and results of type *REAL* in one case and *DOUBLE* in the other.

Only *REAL*'s interface appears here; to obtain the interface of *DOUBLE*, replace *REAL*, whenever used as the type of an argument or result, by *DOUBLE*. Remember that the balancing rule makes it possible to mix arguments of both types freely.

On the Balancing rule see 13.4.1, page 248, and chapter 23 of "Eiffel: The Language".

indexing

  description: "Real values"

expanded class interface

  REAL

feature -- Comparison

  infix "<" (other: REAL): BOOLEAN
    -- Is *other* greater than current real?
  require
    other_exists: other /= Void
  ensure
    smaller: Result **implies not** (Current >= other)

  infix ">=" (other: **like** Current): BOOLEAN
    -- Is current object greater than or equal to *other*?
    -- (From *COMPARABLE*.)
  ensure
    equals_larger: Result **implies not** (Current < other)

  infix ">" (other: **like** Current): BOOLEAN
    -- Is current object greater than *other*?
    -- (From *COMPARABLE*.)
  ensure
    larger: Result **implies not** (Current <= other)

  infix "<=" (other: **like** Current): BOOLEAN
    -- Is current object less than or equal to *other*?
    -- (From *COMPARABLE*.)
  ensure
    equals_smaller: Result **implies not** (Current > other)

feature -- Basic operations

  infix "*" (other: REAL): REAL
    -- Product by *other*
  require
    other_exists: other /= Void

  prefix "+": REAL
    -- Unary plus

  infix "+" (other: REAL): REAL
    -- Sum with *other*
  require
    other_exists: other /= Void

  prefix "−": REAL
    -- Unary minus

  infix "−" (other: REAL): REAL
    -- Result of subtracting *other*
  require
    other_exists: other /= Void

  infix "/" (other: REAL): REAL
    -- Division by *other*
  require
    good_divisor: other /= 0.0

  infix "^" (other: REAL): REAL
    -- Current real to the power *other*
  require
    other_exists: other /= Void

feature -- Output

  out: STRING
    -- Printable representation of real value.
    -- (From *REAL_REF*.)

end

Bibliography

A few reference books on data structures and algorithms (Knuth, Aho et al.) have been listed in addition to the references cited in the text.

The acronym TOOLS stands for "Technology of Object-Oriented Languages and Systems" – a regular conference series.

Alfred V. Aho, John E. Hopcroft and Jeffrey D. Ullman: *The Design and Analysis of Computer Algorithms*, Addison-Wesley, 1974.

Alfred V. Aho, John E. Hopcroft and Jeffrey D. Ullman: *Data Structures and Algorithms*, Addison-Wesley, 1983.

Jon Avotins and Christine Mingins: *Metrics for Object-Oriented Design*, in TOOLS 12 & 9, Prentice Hall, 1993, pages 127-141.

Richard Bielak and James McKim: *The Many Faces of a Class*: *Views and Contracts*, in TOOLS 11, Prentice Hall, 1992, pages 153-161.

Eduardo Casais: *Managing Class Evolution in Object-Oriented Systems*, in *Object Management*, ed. Dennis Tsichritzis, Université de Genève, Centre Universitaire d'Informatique, 1990, pages 133-195.

Bohdan Durnota and Christine Mingins: *Tree-based Coherence Metrics in Object-Oriented Design*, in TOOLS 12 & 9, Prentice Hall, 1993, pages 489-504.

Per Grape and Kim Waldén: *Automating the Development of Syntax Tree Generators for an Evolving Language*, in TOOLS 8, Prentice Hall, 1992, pages 185-195.

Interactive Software Engineering Inc.: *LDL User's Manual*, Report TR-AN-2/UM, version 1.5, 1992.

Ralph Johnson and Brian Foote: *Designing Reusable Classes*, Journal of Object-Oriented Programming, volume 1, number 2, pages 22-35, June-July 1988.

S.C. Johnson: *Yet Another Compiler-Compiler*, CSTR 32, Bell Laboratories, Murray Hill (N.J.), 1975. Usually included (often in revised form) in the documentation of Unix platforms.

Donald E. Knuth: *The Art of Computer Programming*; volume 1, *Fundamental algorithms*, second printing, 1969; volume 2, *Seminumerical algorithms*, second edition, 1981; volume 3, *Searching and sorting*, 1973; Addison-Wesley.

M. Douglas McIlroy: *Mass-produced Software Components*, in *Software Engineering Concepts and Techniques* (1968 NATO Conference on Software Engineering), eds. J. M. Buxton, P. Naur and B. Randell, Van Nostrand Reinhold, 1976, pages 88-98.

Bertrand Meyer: *Principles of Package Design*, Communications of the ACM, volume 25, number 7, July 1982, pages 419-428.

Bertrand Meyer: *The New Culture of Software Development: Reflections on the Practice of Object-Oriented Design*, in *Advances in Object-Oriented Software Engineering*, eds. D. Mandrioli and B. Meyer, Prentice Hall, 1992, pages 51-63.

Bertrand Meyer: *Eiffel*: *The Language*, Prentice Hall, 1992. (Second printing.)

Bertrand Meyer and Jean-Marc Nerson (eds.): *Object-Oriented Applications*, Prentice Hall, 1993.

Bertrand Meyer: *Object-Oriented Software Construction*, Prentice Hall, 1988. Second edition, 1994.

Bertrand Meyer: *An Object-Oriented Environment*: *Principles and Application*, Prentice Hall, 1994.

Christine Mingins, Bohdan Durnota and Glen Smith: *Collection and Analysis of Software Metrics from the Eiffel Class Hierarchy*, in TOOLS 11, Prentice Hall, 1993, pages 427-435.

Jean-Marc Nerson and Kim Waldén: *Seamless Object-Oriented Software Architectures*: *Analysis and Design of Reliable Systems*, Prentice Hall, 1994.

John Potter and Christine Mingins: *The Eiffel Method*, tutorial notes, TOOLS PACIFIC, Melbourne, December 1993.

Dennis Tsichritzis (ed.): *Object Management*, *Object-Oriented Development*, *Object Frameworks*, etc. (various titles): yearly publication of the Centre Universitaire d'Informatique, Université de Genève, Switzerland, since 1988.

Index

Together with terms from the discussions in parts A and B, this index lists all the classes whose official flat-short specifications make up part C, and their exported features as they appear in these specifications.

Following the standard Eiffel conventions, feature names appear in *lower-case italics* and class names, when making up index entries, in *UPPER-CASE ITALICS*. Operator functions appear under ***prefix*** and ***infix***; for example division appears under ***infix "/"***. This also applies to boolean operators, which appear under ***infix "and"***, ***infix "and then"*** and so on. References to elements of the text other than classes and features appear in standard (roman) font.

Each reference to a feature name is followed by the name of the classes in which it is available, each with the corresponding page. To avoid any confusion with occurrences of the class name in its other role – as an index entry pointing to the beginning of the class specification – the class name in this case appears in UPPER-CASE ROMAN.

When a class or feature is discussed in part A or B, these informal references are listed too; given the book's organization, the occurrence in the flat-short specification corresponds to the last page reference in such a class or feature entry.

Because the method developed in this book and systematically applied to the Base libraries promotes a systematic naming policy, some feature names – *item* is a typical one – appear in many classes to denote features with related semantics, and so have correspondingly long index entries.

The naming conventions are introduced in 3.8, page 92.

HOW TO OBTAIN

THE LIBRARIES DESCRIBED IN THIS BOOK

The Base libraries presented in this book are available as part of ISE Eiffel 3, an object-oriented development environment for the production of quality software. Besides Base the environment offers a number of tools and libraries:

- EiffelBench, the graphical development workbench ensuring fast turnaround thanks to the Melting Ice compiling technology, and supporting browsing and class documentation through "typed drag-and-drop" and flat-short forms.
- EiffelBuild,the graphical interface and application generator.
- EiffelVision, the GUI library.
- EiffelCase, the analysis and design workbench based on the BON method.
- EiffelStore, the general persistence library and uniform interface to Database Management Systems.
- And many more.

ISE Eiffel 3 is available on a great variety of platforms. Developed primarily for the needs of medium and large-scale industrial developments, it is also a good vehicle for teaching modern computing science and software engineering at all levels, from "Introduction to Programming" courses through Data Structures and Algorithms to advanced graduate seminars.

ISE Eiffel 3 is backed by an international network of distributors and by consulting services for both application and library development.

SEMINARS AND VIDEO COURSES

Bertrand Meyer's seminar *Library design: building reusable components*, based on the ideas of this book, is regularly offered in public sessions and can be taught in-house for groups of 10 or more attendees. Other available courses include: *Design by contract* (one day), *Object-Oriented Software Construction* (two or three days), *Building Graphical User Interface applications* (three days, hands-on) and many other technical presentations, as well as *Object Technology: A Management Overview* (one day), *Managing O-O projects* (one day) and other management-oriented sessions.

Also available is the 6-hour video course ***Object-Oriented Software Construction*** by Bertrand Meyer (NTSC, PAL or SECAM).

FOR MORE INFORMATION

Return the coupon below to: Interactive Software Engineering Inc., 270 Storke Road Suite 7, Goleta C A 93117 (USA), Telephone 805-685-1006, Fax 805-685-6869, E-mail <info@eiffel.com>. If more convenient, you may also contact SOL, 104 rue Castagnary, 75015 Paris (France), Telephone +33/1-45 32 58 80, Fax 45 32 58 81, E-mail <info@eiffel.fr>.

Please send me information about ISE Eiffel 3 and how to obtain the libraries presented in *Reusable Software: The Base Object-Oriented Libraries*.

I am particularly interested in the following ISE Eiffel products: _____

My possible hardware-operating system platforms are: _____

Name: _____ Company: _____

Department, Mail Stop etc.: _____

Address: _____

Please send: Seminar schedules in my area ❑   Information about the OOSC video ❑